A

SOUTHERN

READER

A SOUTHERN READER

BY WILLARD THORP

NEW YORK:

ALFRED · A · KNOPF

1955

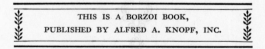

TO THE MEMORY

OF

Urban Joseph Peters Rushton

SOUTHERNER AND CITIZEN OF THE WORLD

PREFACE

Since it is my intention to let Southerners do most of the talking in this book, this preface will be brief. Still, I think I need to explain why an upstate New Yorker (a subspecies of Yankee) wished to compile *A Southern Reader*.

The story of this venture really begins many years ago in a village school in Delaware County, New York, a stronghold of rural Republicanism. In the eighth grade we were studying the Civil War with a teacher who was a black abolitionist. To her the Confederates had deliberately and treacherously provoked the war and richly deserved their defeat and the loss of their property in slaves. The war was the War of the Rebellion, and Jefferson Davis was a traitor who should not have escaped hanging. For some reason this seemed to me absurd. To the delight of my schoolmates I stood up for the Confederate cause, drawing my arguments from the files of *Harper's Magazine* and *Harper's Weekly* for the war years, which we happened to have at home. Not that these loyal Northern journals had defended states' rights and slavery, but they had reported the battles of the Civil War with a remarkable accuracy and vividness. Even a boy could gather from these accounts that the South had won many victories in spite of the iniquity of its cause. For my teacher it was a bad war; but I knew already that someday I must stand where men had died at Bull Run and Antietam and the Wilderness.

Thus it was that when I visited Washington at the age of sixteen, crossed the Potomac, and stood on Virginia soil for the first time, I felt that I had seen for a moment an enchanted land. (Meanwhile my imagination had been fed on Cooke's *Virginia Comedians*, Churchill's *The Crisis*, and *The Birth of a Nation*.) Ever since, in the many happy excursions I have made in the South, the old excitement has returned. Despite what I know about the sober realities of Southern life, the only "realities" of which many Americans are aware—racial intolerance and Negro slums, eroded hillsides and silt-choked rivers, demagogues and the one-party system—I still find the South the most exotic and exciting region in America. It is my hope that this book will convey to its readers the kind of pleasure I have known in exploring the byways of the South, reading its history, and listening to my Southern friends tell stories of their kin to the seventh degree of relationship.

Fortunately for the anthologist, Northern and European writers in successive generations have discovered the exoticism and excitement of Southern life and have left an extensive record of their impressions. Southerners themselves, increasingly on the defensive in ante-bellum days, explained their way of life in hundreds of articles, tracts, and novels. The Civil War was the first war to be covered minutely by correspondents and artists and to be written about by thousands who fought in it, from privates to generals. After Appomattox, readers in the North and in Europe, so it seems, were insatiable consumers of accounts of the South in defeat. In fact the written record of more than three centuries, from Jamestown to Norris Dam, surpasses in richness and color that possessed by any other region in the country. Nearly every selection in this book competed for its place with a half-dozen others quite as good.

Each selection is, I think, representative, accurate in what it reports, and interesting. The reader should find something to hold his attention wherever he opens the book. Nevertheless the book does have a plan. The selections are arranged topically under sixteen headings. These topics move from the land itself to the ways men have worked the land and then to the features of Southern life which are characteristic. This part of the book ends with the section on the Negro, which is long, as it needs to be. In it a group of Negroes speak for their people, and are followed by seven white men who represent the principal views of the Negro problem which white Southerners have entertained. It was inevitable that there should be sections on Politics and Religion since these have always been serious preoccupations in the South. It was also inevitable that there should be selections grouped under Cities and Towns and Business and Industry, since the old issues of rural versus urban life and industry versus agriculture have been long debated in the South and are still more intensely alive than in any other region. The concluding section on the Arts will, I hope, convince those who need to be convinced that the South has contributed more to American culture than Jelly Roll Morton and corn-pone.

Within the topical divisions the selections are arranged with some attention to chronology and to the patterns of life in particular sub-regions and states. Thus the reader who is partial to Virginia can, if he wishes, put together a Virginia reader out of selections dispersed under various topics. I should point out that some selections fit into more than one niche. Selections that might be grouped under Writing, for example, can be found in sections other than the one so designated. For the convenience of readers who wish to follow a particular subject through the book in this way, I am listing here the cross-references that can be made.

Preface

ix

VIOLENCE

Gander-Pulling (p. 229); Andrew Jackson Kills Charles Dickinson at Twenty-four Paces (p. 266).

POLITICS

"We would hunt him down and kill him" (p. 389); Fighting the Ku Klux Klan in the 1920's (p. 419).

RELIGION

The Fundamentalists and the Schools (p. 207); A "Sacred Harp" Convention (p. 609); Negro Spirituals (p. 627).

CITIES AND TOWNS

The Creoles of New Orleans (p. 90); Hail Rex! (p. 234); "Will you not be forced to submit?"—"Never!" (p. 289); William Johnson, Free Negro of Natchez (p. 331); Into a Strange New Land (p. 357).

BUSINESS AND INDUSTRY

Why the Tennessee (p. 61); Correspondent Reid Inspects the Defeated South (p. 119); Henry Clay Appeals to the South to Support His "American System" (p. 433); Andrew Jackson Vetoes the Bill for Rechartering the Bank of the United States (p. 437).

WRITING

In an anthology of Southern literature many selections that are used in this volume to illustrate aspects of Southern life might well be included as examples of Southern writing and oratory. The reader who wishes a broader acquaintance with Southern literature than that furnished by the section on Writing should look in the index for selections by the following authors: James Lane Allen, George W. Bagby, John Peale Bishop, Sterling Brown, William Byrd, John C. Calhoun, Hodding Carter, Henry Clay, Samuel L. Clemens, John Esten Cooke, Virginius Dabney, W. E. B. Du Bois, John Gould Fletcher, John Fox, Jr., Henry W. Grady, Andrew Jackson, Thomas Jefferson, William Alexander Percy, A. B. Longstreet, J. Saunders Redding, Irwin Russell, Lyle Saxon, John Taylor of Caroline, Robert Toombs, and Booker T. Washington.

WILLARD THORP

Princeton
September 1954

SOME WORDS OF THANKS

FROM the time I began work on *A Southern Reader* I have had advice from many Southerners about the plan of the book and selections that might be included. They have answered my questions over lunch or over bourbon and branch-water. They have passed me on to friends who were also unsparing of their time. The enthusiasm that these men and women showed for the venture encouraged me at the start and their suggestions were invaluable as the anthology took shape. If it had been possible to include all the selections they felt belonged in such a collection as this, it would have become a six-volume work.

In Richmond, I was privileged to talk over plans for the *Reader*, in its early stages, with the late Douglas Southall Freeman, the Reverend Clayton Torrence, secretary of the Virginia Historical Society, and Mr. Virginius Dabney, editor of the Richmond *Times-Dispatch*. In Durham, Professor Lewis Leary, then teaching at Duke, gave me advice and hospitality. I profited also from the extensive knowledge of Southern literature possessed by Professors Jay B. Hubbell and Clarence Gohdes. I wish I might have recorded, during my stay in Durham, one evening's "table-talk" of Mrs. Frances Gray Patton, but the memory of her Southern stories does not fade. Also in Durham I received many excellent suggestions from Mr. Charles A. Ray, director of the News Bureau of the North Carolina College, and from several of his colleagues.

At Chapel Hill, Professor A. P. Hudson took me in charge and saw to it that I had a chance to ask questions of most of the specialists in Southern history and sociology who have made the University of North Carolina outstanding in these fields. Professors Howard W. Odum, Rupert Vance, Archibald Henderson, Hugh Lefler, and James W. Patton gave me excellent leads. Dr. J. G. de Roulhac Hamilton offered me the use of materials from the great Southern Historical Collection which he has built up at the library of the university. Mr. Lambert Davis, director of the University of North Carolina Press, helped me work out the grouping of the sections of the book. An evening's conversation with Professor Hudson and Mr. Paul Green ranged all the way from the Lost Colony to frontier days in Mississippi.

At Columbia, South Carolina, the late W. Bedford Moore, Jr., and Mrs. Moore devoted two days to my problems. At their house I met for the first time Professor Francis B. Simkins, to whom I have turned repeatedly for help of various kinds. At the University of South Carolina, Professor R. L. Meriwether took a morning off, in the Christmas season, to show me some of the treasures of the South Caroliniana Library, of which he is director. I also sought advice from Mrs. Louise Jones DeBose, director of the University of South Carolina Press, and from Dr. J. H. Easterby, Archivist of the state.

At a later time, in New Orleans, I combined palate-pleasures with research. My friend and former student at Princeton, Mr. Bryan Bell, with the help of Robert and Peter Walmsley, opened many doors for me. Through them I met Mr. George Logan of the New Orleans Public Library, and Mrs. Robert L. Crager, each of whom has an extensive knowledge of the history of the city. Mrs. Crager in turn arranged a session with Father Edward Murphy of Xavier University and Mr. Robert Tallant, the novelist. Mr. Harnett T. Kane also generously gave me a morning of his time. At Baton Rouge, Professor Arlin Turner, who was then at Louisiana State University, saw to it that I met Professors T. Harry Williams and E. A. Davis. Later, in Birmingham, my friend Mr. William J. Rushton, president of the Protective Life Insurance Company, arranged a session with several leaders in Birmingham's civic affairs. Among them were Mr. James E. Mills, editor of the *Post-Herald*, Mr. Charles Fell, managing editor of the *News*, and Mr. M. H. Sterne, whose avocational interest in the past of the South would make the reputation of a professional historian. Mr. and Mrs. Joseph Forney Johnston were also hospitable and helpful.

In Atlanta, Professor Thomas H. English, a friend of many years, took me in charge. Through him I obtained sound advice from Professor Walter B. Posey, authority on Southern church history, and from Professor Richard Harwell, who is the curator of the Confederate Collection in the Emory University Library. Mr. Beverley M. DuBose, Sr., showed me important items in the library of the Atlanta Historical Society, of which he was for many years the president. Mr. Ralph McGill, editor of the *Atlanta Constitution*, talked to me about Georgia as it is today. Mr. Wilbur G. Kurtz, technical adviser to the production of *Gone with the Wind*, refought the Atlanta campaign for me, over the big maps rolled out on his living-room floor. At Howard University I benefited from excellent suggestions made by Professors Sterling A. Brown, E. Franklin Frazier, Rayford W. Logan, and John Hope Franklin.

This record of courtesy and of assistance given should be much longer, but I cannot bring it to a close without mentioning the names of the five friends of mine who have taught me most about the South: Mr. and Mrs. Allen Tate, Dr. and Mrs. Julian Boyd, and Professor Samuel H. Monk. And I wish to acknowledge my debt to the mem-

Some Words of Thanks

bers of my graduate seminar at the Rice Institute in the spring term of 1953. From them I learned as much about the South as I taught them.

In the preparation of the book I enjoyed during the summer of 1953 the invaluable help of Professor Lawrence Barrett of Kalamazoo College. Three undergraduate assistants helped me at various times: Messrs. Herbert Strauss, Howard MacAyeal, and Glenn Johnson. My thanks are also due to Dr. and Mrs. William S. Dix, Professor Samuel H. Monk, Dr. Otis Singletary, and Professor Albert Leland Jamison for reading many of the notes and saving me from errors that a Yankee would be likely to commit. I am greatly indebted to Mrs. Helen Wright for her continuous assistance in preparing the manuscript.

In the early stages of the book I enjoyed the counsel of Mr. Earl Schenck Miers, then with the firm of Alfred A. Knopf, Inc. Since then I have received help from various members of Mr. Knopf's staff: Mr. Harold Strauss, Mr. John T. Hawes, Mr. William Koshland, and especially from Thomas Bledsoe, as resourceful an editor and as loyal a Southerner as I know. I have also benefited from the suggestions made by Mr. Knopf, whose great interest in the regions of this country has been abundantly shown by the important books about America which he has published.

WILLARD THORP

CONTENTS

Contents

Contents

Contents

ILLUSTRATIONS

ILLUSTRATIONS

A
SOUTHERN
READER

I

PROLOGUE

Each in his own way, John Peale Bishop (1892–1944) and W. J. Cash (1901–41), who speak the prologue to this book, loved the South of their ancestors and their youth and wrote movingly and perceptively about it. Their views of the South are as divergent as the lives they led.

Bishop, on his mother's side, came of tidewater stock that had settled in Virginia in the late seventeenth century. His ancestors moved to the valley of Virginia at the close of the French and Indian wars. Bishop himself was born in Charles Town, West Virginia. Educated at Mercersburg Academy and Princeton, he belonged to the literary generation of Archibald MacLeish, Edmund Wilson, and Allen Tate, who were his closest friends. For seven years after the First World War, Bishop lived at the Château du Petit Tressancourt, a few kilometers northeast of Paris.

Bishop was not a prolific writer, but the poems, fiction, and essays he completed are distinguished. His collection of short stories, *Many Thousands Gone* (1931), and his novel, *Act of Darkness* (1935), are on Southern themes. They deserve to be better remembered than they are. Though Bishop was never a member of the group of Southern Agrarians who produced the symposium *I'll Take My Stand* in 1930, his attitude toward the past and present of the South coincided with theirs.

W. J. Cash was a man of a very different stamp. In ante-bellum days his people were "good upcountry farmers" in South Carolina, "never rich or aristocratic" but with the spirit of enterprise in their blood. His grandfather built one of the earliest cotton mills in the state and an uncle organized, with success, a half-dozen others. Cash was educated at Wofford College and at Wake Forest. He became a successful newspaperman in Charlotte, North Carolina, and as a free-lance writer contributed to the *American Mercury* in the H. L. Mencken days. As a young man, Cash once confessed, he was an intense sentimentalist toward the South—his favorite dream as a boy had been fighting the Civil War over again, "and myself leading the charge on the cannon's mouth with the Confederate battle flag." His Bourbon sympathies were abruptly altered when his newspaper sent him to cover a textile strike in the thirties. Cash's one book, *The Mind of the South* (1941), has already become a classic. However much professional historians may quibble over some of his bold generalizations, they quote him as an authority when it suits their purpose to do so. For readers generally his book has become a kind of touchstone of opinion about the South.

"The South and Tradition" (here slightly condensed) is reprinted from *The Collected Essays of John Peale Bishop*, edited by Edmund Wilson; copyright 1933, 1936, 1948 by Charles Scribner's Sons; used by permission of the publisher.

"Of an Ideal and Conflict" is reprinted from *The Mind of the South* by W. J. Cash, by permission of Alfred A. Knopf, Inc.; copyright 1941 by Alfred A. Knopf, Inc.

The South and Tradition

Iт is a certain temerity to approach the Southern tradition. And we do not think that many persons, except a few old ladies and Mr. Hergesheimer, are likely to lose themselves in moonlight on the lawns, lamenting the lost valor, or wandering among the neglected trees to let themselves assume romance under the vanished colonnes. On the contrary, we suspect the past. We do not want a history of the South that points up the gallant Confederates and forgets the Colonel's mulatto daughter. Ours is a generation that, having been through a later than the Civil War, likes to believe the worst of everybody. So that when we search old closets it is more often to come out with a skeleton than carrying the remnants of grandmother's wedding gown.

Yet when we really begin to think about the closet and its contents, we know that the skeleton was once a man and that grandmother's wedding dress, for all the quaint cut of the sleeves and the yellowing color of the satin, belonged to a woman. We see that bed to which she came as a bride: there she was to suffer childbirth, and when she was carried from it she went feet first. And grandfather, too, though he had his faults, was once alive. His economy may have been worse than his morals; he may, if he were a Virginian, have come to the conclusion about the time of his marriage, that is to say, somewhere around 1850, that the only way he could make both ends meet was to encourage the breeding of the blacks. Yet, when we have listened to the scholars who have lately been at the records and have examined the account-books, not passing the papers in the secret drawer or omitting to uproot the family tree—even when we have heard the full scandal of statistics relating to grandfather, we still know, not only that he was alive, but that he had arrived at a manner of living somewhat more amiable than any other that has ever been known on this continent.

This life continued the English social tradition, and was in many aspects as crude as country existence under Queen Anne. It had been adapted to the climate, which was warm and republican; but it kept a provincial look. The White Sulphur Springs may be made to do duty for Bath, but there was no city to take the place of London. The roads were bad. Yet there was ease, and, as in eighteenth-century England, a surprising policy. When in her carriage grandmother passed an acquaintance, she knew that her bow must be a bend of her whole

5

haughty back and not a mere nod of the head. And~~n her kitchen,~~
where so many concessions had to be made to the A... ~~an fondness~~
for grease, the hand-copied recipes were many, varied ... ~~elaborate.~~
For the South, whatever may be said, had at least passe... ~~ose two~~
tests which the French have devised for a civilization an... ~~which~~
they admit only themselves and the Chinese. It had devised ~~of~~
etiquette and created a native cookery.

There could have been neither, had grandfather been, as most
compatriots were, forever on the move. But he was attached t...
land, and from it and the remembered experience of the past he ...
arranged his living in quite another fashion than the industrial E...
and the wandering West. And he was quite aware of the difference.
So much so that, when circumstances pressed to war, he could, along
with General Lee, refer to the opposing Americans simply as "those
people." No phrase could show a greater alienation. However, his own
way satisfied him, and he was quite prepared to fight for it. Since
slavery was a part of his system, he could defend slavery. And so he
did, with what effort is known.

That is, of course, our fictional grandfather did. But to keep the
record straight and not run away from the unforgivable fact, I must
put it down that my own Virginian progenitor did not fight. He was,
in 1861, though still comparatively young, so far advanced in corpu-
lency that he could only with the greatest difficulty move from the
front porch. He saw a neighbor of his, quite as fat as he, drive off one
morning, whipping down the road, to join the cavalry in a one-horse
buggy. But he did not emulate him.

Yet, combatant or not, he held to his tradition. We are so accustomed
to take it for granted that this is what the Southerner would do, that
we forget how strange this was in America. For though for the country
as a whole there are traditions of a sort (as in our foreign policy, for
example) they are not there as aids to living. And this is the use of
customs, courteous manners, and inherited wisdom. While there is always much that a young man must, of necessity, face in complete
nakedness without so much as a tatter from the past, it is not a very
profitable way to go through life. It means an emotional impoverishment. To have to learn everything for one's self is, as Ben Jonson remarked, to have a fool for a master.

And yet nothing is more common for Americans. It is constantly
said that America is too young to have acquired traditions. But this
is not exactly true. It is because we are continually beginning the world
again, every ten or fifteen years, that we wear that desperate look of
youth. Ours is a mechanic's conviction that history is all bunk. There
was never before, I suppose, a generation sent out so thinly prepared
by its parents as that which went to make the Great War. The first

6

wind from a shell shook the last metaphysical rag from our backs. We had no tradition of bravery, none of endurance; we only said, "What anybody else can do, we can do." In consequence, having stomached the war as best we could, we were presently found glorifying cowardice. A little later, we were quite as ready to cover the Chicago bandits with glory because we had heard from the newspapers that they at least were brave. Ten years' experiment taught confusion. But there is no need to repeat that tale. Let us remember grandfather sitting on his front porch; or his brothers, spurred and slender in their sashes, riding off toward a battle, which may have been Bull Run and was ultimately Appomattox. They, at all events, had a tradition, which they carried with them and found as useful as a bodyservant. And yet they were, as Americans, far younger than those who tell us we are still too young.

For it is to be noted that the Confederacy, for all the brevity of its formal existence, achieved more surely the qualities of a nation than the enduring Republic has been able to do. There were more emotions shared; its soldiers knew how to speak to one another or without speaking to arrive at a common understanding. Their attitude toward life was alike, and when they faced death it was in the same way. This makes for integrity, as it certainly also makes for a sounder emotional life.

It is not simple to say why this was so. But for one thing, Jamestown was not settled by Pilgrim Fathers. Now, I know it has been recently discovered that very few gentlemen came to Virginia, and I dare say another scholar will soon say that almost none of those who made New England were Puritans. Already we are told that more came for cod than for conscience' sake. But it will not do to let our modern obsession with numbers construe the seventeenth century; nor, because our contemporary intellectuals are ineffectual, must we suppose that the early New England theologians were anything of the sort. It required only a few men of character to set whatever thought there was, just as in Virginia we may be sure that, small though the number of gentlemen was, it was they who determined the colony's complexion.

True, Puritanism in its fine strictness and rigor did not outlast a generation; it was too uncompromising a creed for respectability, and when Jonathan Edwards tried to revive it a century later, he was cast out as a social menace. But the trick had been done, and a cast given the mind; that conscience was not henceforth to be silenced. But in the place of the old dependence on the arbitrarians of God, the younger men had begun to devise a doctrine which was later to be called self-reliance. It was they who have determined America, and they were, no less than their uncompromising fathers before them, enemies of custom.

7

The Puritan set out to destroy tradition; how much he made away with in England is only beginning to be understood. And on the rocks of New England, where he had nothing but hardship to oppose him, he was relentless. On the other hand, there were not so many who came South who did not hope to live as well as their plantations would allow them. And with tobacco that was very well.

This is the significance of their loyalty to the Stuarts: it may well be that they thought no more about the Divine Right of Kings than the Cape Cod fishermen did of the Divine, *tout court;* but they did subscribe to an ancient and aristocratic ordering of society. Sailing from England, they had not, like the Puritans, consciously cut from the past. They imported customs when their pockets were empty; they made an effort after gentility, even when the wilderness decided for simplicity. And though later, using their intelligences, they, along with the other colonists, rejected the past politically, the best of them continued, as far as their purses would let them, to live traditionally, unbending in manners only so far as was necessary to fit the times. In short, they lived as well as their plantations would allow them.

So much would seem to be the fact of the Cavalier South. The myth is something else again; possibly it is more important. For when all is said and done, a myth is far more exciting to the mind than most discoveries of mere things. So long as Rome was a myth, a matter for the imagination, stirred only by a few battered columns and a dismantled Forum, Europe was able to produce an architecture from its forms, through three centuries incomparable for fecundity. But as soon as Pompeii and Herculaneum were unearthed, the facts of the Roman world uncovered, classical architecture died and in its place succeeded only the lifeless excellence of archaeology.

Just when Southerners first began to find ancestors among the adherents of the Stuarts I do not know. But I suspect that Sir Walter Scott put them on that trace. Scott was enormously read throughout the South, and he undoubtedly made more conscious a romantic disposition that was already there. For if the Cavaliers were not ancestors, they could at least be seen as antecedents. Call it a myth: grandfather's parentage was all Scotch-Irish and grandmother could name only a Jacobite great-grandfather who had come scurrying from the battle of Culloden. There still remains that assumption of charm, that very real desire to please, a high-heartedness with hope, a recklessness against odds; all of which qualities may be seen riding and fighting in Jeb Stuart's cavalry. One Stuart at least is ours authentically. No one can deny those young men their horses, their hard riding and hard drinking, and a strange and not very thoughtful capacity for despair. They were not, if you will, very much like the pretty nobles who rode with Prince Rupert, but neither were they like those clear-eyed, stern young men who came down from Massachusetts and wrote letters home full of moral observations on the inhabitants of the Peninsula. The type persists. It has been finely portrayed by Mr. Faulkner in his *Sartoris*. In the conclusion of his novel, meditating on his pilot of the last war, he suggests that his qualities are now anachronistic. Certainly, they seem to have small place in modern life. And yet it is to be wondered whether they ever made for anything more telling than admirable failure. Even at Roncevaux.

In the same way we may assume that there was in the South an aristocracy, that is to say a class which, having the wealth, also took on the power and the responsibility of rule. Everywhere—at least this is true of the past, and the past is all we know that is true—the rich, as Lorenzo de' Medici has said, must have the state. But what distinguishes an aristocracy is that the government is directed in the interests of a class which acts together and whose individuals do not, as plutocrats do, destroy one another—and eventually the state—in a mean competition for privileges. It is this which gives it stability. A government by businessmen, as we have seen, not only corrupts government, but, being a cut-throat affair, frequently ends by destroying business.

An aristocratic class arises from wealth; descent has nothing to do with it at the start, though later the qualities of breeding begin to count and in the long run an aristocracy serves powerfully to mitigate the pure influence of money. Mr. Jefferson could not find any particular information on his paternal ancestors back of his grandfather; he was, however, to the curve of his calves an aristocrat; no man ever lived in more civilized elegance than the doctrinaire of Monticello. Nor did he shirk the responsibilities of rule. Manners must be acquired young. But it is not necessary to inherit them from forbears who, like those of Orlando, came out of the mists of the North wearing coronets on their heads. A grandfather will do, if the servants are good.

What is necessary, if a tradition is to be carried on, is that it should be inculcated in children before they have acquired minds of their own. It is too late to teach a child morality at seven. And in modern America, where the parents have given up all hope of controlling their progeny and have thrust the moral task on the school—which, in the more modern classes, is now passing it on to the children themselves—we have not only a great number of unmannerly brats, but a constantly increasing host of youthful criminals. That was where, in the South, the Negroes came in. They have, as someone said of cats and children, an "ancient and complicated culture of their own." But what they taught the young put in their charge was not their own, but their masters' morality. Of that they had acquired quite enough for the purpose; profoundly conservative, and possessed even as Africans of an instinct for courtesy and great tact, they were no small factor in en-

9

riching the Southern tradition. What they had to impart was of value, since they had lived always under that society to which later their charges would belong. Whereas, there is nothing, or next to nothing, that an immigrant nursemaid can pass on to an American child; she herself has been displaced, and whatever she knew in Scandinavia or Ireland has already lost much of its meaning; to the child it will be of no use whatsoever.

Tradition is all the learning life which men receive from their fathers and which, having tried it in their own experience, they consent to pass on to their sons. What remains is, if you will, a technique. Like anything else that is living, a tradition is in constant change. Not only does each generation have to face and survive new conditions; but what is more significant, it must, in civilized societies, come to a new conception even of what is least changeable in human nature, its fears and appetites. Thus we find our ways of making love, eating and drinking, facing war and approaching death, subject to fashion. And in high civilizations there is a continuous succession of manners, which apply not only to the fine arts but, perhaps more essentially, to the arts of living. . . .

I have possibly, in insisting on the Southern tradition, represented it as being richer than it ever actually was. I have indeed meant to put it at its best; and though I have been accused of having elsewhere shown it as already in decline before the Civil War, I had rather accept that accusation than try to prove the contrary. What is true is that of the several social revolutions which America has undergone, the South escaped the effects of the first two. The separation of the colonies from England left her with the upper classes secure on their plantations. Jefferson seems to have affected his Virginia neighbors more by his example as a highly civilized country gentleman with a taste for architecture and gardening than by his writings as a democratic doctrinaire. Jackson and his followers certainly did attaint the tradition; but the full effects of the backwoods rebellion were not greatly evident before the divisions of armed conflict in the sixties revealed them. Of the Civil War and the Populist Revolt it is not necessary to speak. That they were disastrous to the traditional manner of living is tragically evident.

The South developed the virtues of an agrarian civilization. In some respects that civilization was poor. How account for that poverty, in literature let us say, as well as for a decline in the quality of Southern thought even where it had been most vigorous, in politics? It sprang, I should say, less from the exasperating presence of slavery in an age which could not well defend it, than from the South's rapid increase in size without a corresponding increase in means of communication. There were no cities to serve as centres of attraction. We cannot read the contemporary records of those marvelously talented Virginians who declared for independence and set the Republic on its foundations without being struck by the intense realism of their minds. They were critical as the statesmen of the Confederacy did not dare to be. And no small part of this vigor and alertness is to be traced to their conversations. They were, it appears, in constant contact with one another. Their wits were edged by talk, their idiosyncrasies corrected, their courage confirmed. In a word, they were worldly men, which is what statesmen ought to be. Williamsburg was a capital such as Richmond never was, and Alexandria heard more sound sense than has since been talked beside the Potomac.

So it is that we return to this tradition, not because it was romantic, but because it was, in so many ways, right. Grandfather as he sits on the front porch in the hazy heat of a summer afternoon is not an heroic figure. But he is a solid one and that not only in the sense of those too, too many pounds of flesh. He was clear as to his political position. And though there were many even then who saw him as out of his times, pathetic in the stubbornness of his eighteenth-century opinions, a late time has confounded his opponents. He saw that there must be a symmetry between agriculture and industry; that if you import labor for exploitation you must let it breed but not govern; while a Republic was doubtless the most propitious form of government for Americans, it would last and hold its integrity only so long as you did not let it become a real democracy. His opinions were sound; only one wishes he had not been so nervous about them. He mixed his juleps and pointed his country manners; he had, alas, only a realistic conception of justice, so that, unlike our present state, with its noble experiments and its perfectly moral laws, his jails were empty.

So it is, when we discover that without a past we are living not in the present, but in a vague and rather unsatisfactory future, we turn back to him. And suddenly even his fat becomes eloquent, for it speaks of imperfection. His day was simpler than ours. That is not to say it cannot instruct us. And we have this for our encouragement, that if there is anything profitable we can learn from him, it will have come from a man who had not only his social attachments but also his lonely being. That is a start, and a good one, in these days when everyone is ready to make a civilization in which nothing so fallible as grandfather will be left, but all will be ordered for the best in the best of dehumanized worlds.

Of an Ideal and Conflict

With all these characteristics established, we are in a position to turn to the examination of the South's claim to a superior culture. Or, more correctly, since everything we have seen falls within the meaning of culture in the wide sense, to that claim in so far as it relates to culture in the narrow sense—to intellectual and æsthetic attainments.

And in this respect, it may be said without ceremony that it was perhaps the least well founded of the many poorly founded claims which the Southerners so earnestly asserted to the world and to themselves and in which they so warmly believed.

I know the proofs commonly advanced by apologists—that at the outbreak of the war the section had more colleges and students in those colleges, in proportion to population, than the North; that many planters were ready and eager to quote you Cicero or Sallust; that Charleston had a public library before Boston, and its famous St. Cecilia Society from the earliest days; that these Charlestonians, and with them the older and wealthier residents of Richmond and Norfolk and New Orleans, regularly imported the latest books from London, and brought back from the grand tour the paintings and even the statuary of this or that fashionable artist of Europe; that, in the latest days, the richest among the new planters of the deep South began to imitate these practices; that in communities like those of the Scotch Highlanders in the Cape Fear country there were Shakespeare libraries and clubs; that Langdon Cheves of South Carolina is reported by Joseph LeConte to have discussed the idea of evolution in private conversation long before *The Origin of Species;* and so on *ad infinitum.*

But such proofs come to little. Often, as they are stated, they are calculated to give a false picture of the facts. Thus, the majority of the colleges were no more than academies. And of the whole number of them perhaps the University of Virginia alone was worthy to be named in the same breath with half a dozen Yankee universities and colleges, and as time went on, even it tended to sink into a hotbed of obscurantism and a sort of fashionable club, propagating dueling, drinking, and gambling.

Thus again, the general quoting of Latin, the flourish of "Shakespeare says," so far from indicating that there was some profound and esoteric sympathy with the humanities in the South, a deliberate preference for the Great Tradition coming down from the ancients, a wide and deep acquaintance with and understanding of the authors quoted, really means only this, it seems to me: that the great body of men in the land remained continuously under the influence of the simple man's almost superstitious awe for the classics, as representing an arcanum beyond the reach of the ordinary.

And over and behind these considerations lies the fact that the South far overran the American average for (white) illiteracy—that not only the great part of masses but a considerable number of planters never learned to read and write, and that a very great segment of the latter class kept no book in their houses save only the Bible.

But put this aside. Say that the South is entitled to be judged wholly by its highest and its best. The ultimate test of every culture is its productivity. What ideas did it generate? Who were its philosophers and artists? And—perhaps the most searching test of all—what was its attitude toward these philosophers and artists? Did it recognize and nurture them when they were still struggling and unknown? Did it salute them before the world generally learned to salute them?

One almost blushes to set down the score of the Old South here. If Charleston had its St. Cecilia and its public library, there is no record that it ever added a single idea of any notable importance to the sum total of man's stock. If it imported Mrs. Radcliffe, Scott, Byron, wet from the press, it left its only novelist, William Gilmore Simms, to find his reputation in England, and all his life snubbed him because he had no proper pedigree. If it fetched in the sleek trumpery of the schools of Van Dyck and Reynolds, of Ingres and Houdon and Flaxman, it drove its one able painter, Washington Allston (though he was born an aristocrat), to achieve his first recognition abroad and at last to settle in New England.

And Charleston is the peak. Leaving Mr. Jefferson aside, the whole South produced, not only no original philosopher but no derivative one to set beside Emerson and Thoreau; no novelist but poor Simms to measure against the Northern galaxy headed by Hawthorne and Melville and Cooper; no painter but Allston to stand in the company of Ryder and a dozen Yankees; no poet deserving the name save Poe— only half a Southerner. And Poe, for all his zeal for slavery, it despised in life as an inconsequential nobody; left him, and with him the *Southern Literary Messenger*, to starve, and claimed him at last only when his bones were whitening in Westminster churchyard.

Certainly there were men in the Old South of wide and sound learning, and with a genuine concern for ideas and, sometimes, even the arts. There were the old Jeffersons and Madisons, the Pinckneys and the Rutledges and the Henry Laurenses, and their somewhat shrunken but not always negligible descendants. Among both the scions of colonial aristocracy and the best of the newcomers, there were men for whom

Langdon Cheves might stand as the archetype and Matterhorn—though we must be careful not to assume, what the apologists are continually assuming, that Cheves might just as well have written *The Origin of Species* himself, if only he had got around to it. For Darwin, of course, did not launch the idea of evolution, nor yet of the struggle for existence and the survival of the fittest. What he did was laboriously to clarify and organize, to gather and present the first concrete and convincing proof for notions that, in more or less definite form, had been the common stock of men of superior education for fifty years and more. There is no evidence that Cheves had anything original to offer; there is only evidence that he was a man of first-rate education and considerable intellectual curiosity, who knew what was being thought and said by the first minds of Europe.

To be sure, there were such men in the South: men on the plantation, in politics, in the professions, in and about the better schools, who, in one degree or another, in one way or another, were of the same general stamp as Cheves. There were even men who made original and important contributions in their fields, like Joseph LeConte himself, one of the first of American geologists; like Matthew Fontaine Maury, author of *Physical Geography of the Sea*, and hailed by Humboldt as the founder of a new science; like Audubon, the naturalist. And beneath these were others: occasional planters, lawyers, doctors, country schoolmasters, parsons, who, on a more humble scale, sincerely cared for intellectual and æsthetic values and served them as well as they might.

But in the aggregate these were hardly more than the exceptions which prove the rule—too few, too unrepresentative, and, above all, as a body themselves too sterile of results very much to alter the verdict.

In general, the intellectual and æsthetic culture of the Old South was a superficial and jejune thing, borrowed from without and worn as a political armor and a badge of rank; and hence (I call the authority of old Matthew Arnold to bear me witness) not a true culture at all.

This is the fact. The reason for it is not too far to seek.

If we were dealing with the cotton South alone, one might be tempted to think, indeed, that it resides wholly in the question of time, in the consideration I have emphasized, that there were but seventy years between the invention of the cotton gin and the outbreak of the Civil War. But even here the answer is hardly adequate; in view of the wealth and leisure ultimately afforded the master class, in view of the fact that the second generation had largely grown up in this wealth and leisure, one might have expected, even though this cotton South had stood quite alone, to find a greater advance, something more than the blank in production we actually find.

But we are not dealing with the cotton South alone, of course. As we have sufficiently seen, it was the Virginians, too. Here was the completed South, the South in flower—a South that, rising out of the same fundamental conditions as the great South, exhibiting, with the obvious changes, the same basic pattern, and played upon in the first half of the nineteenth century by the same forces, had enjoyed riches, rank, and a leisure perhaps unmatched elsewhere in the world, for more than a hundred years at least; a South, therefore, which, by every normal rule, ought to have progressed to a complex and important intellectual culture, to have equaled certainly, probably to have outstripped, New England in production, and to have served as a beacon to draw the newer South rapidly along the same road. And if it did none of these things, why, then, we shall have to look beyond the factor of time for a satisfactory explanation, not only of its barrenness but, to a considerable extent, of that of the great South also.

In reality, the reason is immanent, I think, in the whole of Southern life and psychology. Complexity in man is invariably the child of complexity in environment. The desire for knowledge when it passes beyond the stage of being satisfied with the most obvious answer, thought properly so called, and, above all, æsthetic concern, arise only when the surrounding world becomes sufficiently complicated to make it difficult or impossible for human energies to escape on a purely physical plane, or, at any rate, on a plane of direct activity. Always they represent, among other things, a reaching out vicariously for satisfaction of the primitive urge to exercise of muscle and nerve, and achievement of the universal will to mastery. And always, too, they feed only upon variety and change. Whence it is, no doubt, that they have never reached any notable development save in towns, and usually in great towns.

But the Southern world, you will remember, was basically an extremely uncomplex, unvaried, and unchanging one. Here economic and political organization was reduced to its simplest elements. Here were no towns to rank as more than trading posts save New Orleans, Charleston, Richmond, and Norfolk; here, perhaps, were no true towns at all, for even these four (three of which were scarcely more than overgrown villages) were rather mere depots on the road to the markets of the world, mere adjuncts to the plantation, than living entities in their own right, after the fashion of Boston and New York and Philadelphia. Here was lacking even that tremendous ferment of immigration which was so important in lending variety to the rest of the American scene. And here everywhere were wide fields and blue woods and flooding yellow sunlight. A world, in fine, in which not a single factor operated to break up the old pattern of outdoor activity laid down on the frontier, in which, on the contrary, everything conspired to perpetuate it; a world in which even the Virginian could and inevitably did discharge his energies on the purely physical plane as fully as his earliest ancestor in the land; a world in which horses, dogs, guns, not books, and ideas and art, were his normal and absorbing interests.

And if this was not enough? If his energies and his ambition demanded a wider field of action? He went, in this world at battle, inescapably into politics. To be a captain in the struggle against the Yankee, to be a Calhoun or a Brooks in Congress, or, better still, to be a Yancey or a Rhett ramping through the land with a demand for the sword—this was to be at the very heart of one's time and place, was, for the plantation youth, full of hot blood, the only desirable career. Beside it the pursuit of knowledge, the writing of books, the painting of pictures, the life of the mind, seemed an anemic and despicable business, fit only for eunuchs. "Why," growled a friend of Philip Pendleton Cooke, Virginia aristocrat and author of the well-known lyric, *Florence Vane*, "Why do you waste your time on a damned thing like poetry? A man of your position could be a useful man"—and summed it up exactly.

But it was not only the consumption of available energy in direct action. The development of a considerable intellectual culture requires, in addition to complexity of environment, certain predisposing habits of mind on the part of a people. One of these is analysis. *"L'état de dissociation des lieux communs de la morale semble en corrélation assez étroite avec le degré de la civilization intellectuelle,"* says Remy de Gourmont—and says truly. Another is hospitality to new ideas. Still another is a firm grip on reality; and in this connection I am not forgetting the kind of art which is called romantic and the more fanciful varieties of poetry; in so far as they are good, in so far as they are truly art, they also must rise ultimately from the solid earth. And, finally, there is the capacity, at least, for detachment, without which no thinker, no artist, and no scholar can do his work.

But turn back now and examine the South in the light of this. Analysis is largely the outcome of two things: the need to understand a complex environment (a consideration already disposed of) and social dissatisfaction. But, as we are aware, satisfaction was the hallmark of Southern society; masters and masses alike were sunk in the deepest complacency; nowhere was there any palpable irritation, any discontent and conflict, and so nowhere was there any tendency to question. Again, being static and unchanging, the South was, of course, an inherently conservative society—one which, under any circumstances, would have naturally been cold to new ideas as something for which it had no need or use. As for the grip on reality, we know that story fully already. Imagination there was in plenty in this land with so much of the blood of the dreamy Celt and its warm sun, but it spent itself on puerilities, on cant and twisted logic, in rodomontade and the feckless vaporings of sentimentality. And as for detachment, the South, you will recall, was, before all else, personal, an attitude which is obviously the negation of detachment. Even its love of rhetoric required the immediate and directly observable satisfactions of speech rather than the more remote ones of writing.

There is still more here. As well as having nothing to give rise to a developed intellectual culture, as well as having much that was implicitly hostile, much that served as a negative barrier, the Old South also had much that was explicitly hostile and served as a quite positive barrier. The religious pattern will come to mind at once. Theologians have everywhere been the enemies of analysis and new ideas, and in whatever field they have appeared—feeling, quite correctly, that, once admitted, there is no setting limits to them. And in this country in which the evangelical ministers had already won to unusual sway, in which they had almost complete control of the schools, in which they had virtually no opposition, they established their iron wall with an effectiveness which went well beyond even its American average.

But the greatest force of all was the result of conflict with the Yankee. In Southern unity before the foe lay the final bulwark of every established commonplace. And the defense of slavery not only eventuated, as we have seen, in a taboo on criticism; in the same process it set up a ban on all analysis and inquiry, a terrified truculence toward every new idea, a disposition to reject every innovation out of hand and hug to the whole of the *status quo* with fanatical resolution. Detachment? In a world in which patriotism to the South was increasingly the first duty of men, in which coolness about slavery was accounted treason, it was next to impossible.

In sum, it was the total effect of Southern conditions, primary and secondary, to preserve—but let Henry Adams tell it, in the pages of the *Education*, from direct observation of Roony Lee, the son of Robert E. Lee, and other young Southerners he knew at Harvard between 1854 and 1858, who had behind them two hundred years of shaping in the pattern, and who are to be taken, as Adams infers, as the typical flower of the Old South at its highest and best:

"Tall, largely built, handsome, genial, with liberal Virginia openness toward all he liked, he [Lee] had also the Virginian habit of command. . . . For a year, at least . . . was the most popular and prominent man in his class, but then seemed slowly to drop into the background. The habit of command was not enough, and the Virginian had little else. He was simple beyond analysis; so simple that even the simple New England student could not realize him. No one knew enough to know how ignorant he was; how childlike; how helpless before the relative complexity of a school. As an animal the Southerner seemed to have every advantage, but even as an animal he steadily lost ground.

". . . Strictly, the Southerner had no mind; he had temperament. He was not a scholar; he had no intellectual training; he could not analyze an idea, and he could not even conceive of admitting two. . . ."

There it is, then. We return to the point with which we began. It was the total effect of Southern conditions, primary and secondary, to preserve the Southerner's original simplicity of character as it were in perpetual suspension. From first to last, and whether he was a Virginian or a *nouveau*, he did not (typically speaking) think; he felt; and discharging his feelings immediately, he developed no need or desire for intellectual culture in its own right—none, at least, powerful enough to drive him past his taboos to its actual achievement.

I I

THE LAND

SCHOOL CHILDREN in the Middle and North Atlantic states who dutifully learn such terms as *Coastal Plain, Piedmont, the Fall Line,* and *the Appalachian Plateau* can have little conception of what these evidently significant words mean. Where is New York's Coastal Plain? Where is the Fall Line in Pennsylvania? To Southerners living in the great crescent of states curving south and west from Virginia to Mississippi these features of the landscape are realities.

The Coastal Plain, on which the first settlers made their homes, is 250 miles wide in North Carolina. In Florida it occupies nearly the whole of the state. In Virginia the name for it is Tidewater; in South Carolina it is the Low Country. The rich soils of the Coastal Plain extend across the Gulf states into east Texas. Thus it was always easy, when one's acres were used up by a too intensive cultivation of tobacco or cotton, to move into the Black Belt, a zone of dark soil in Alabama and Mississippi, or even farther west into the "black waxy" land of eastern Texas.

In the seaboard and Gulf states a Southerner knows how to locate the fall line. He knows because on that line (in geologic times the shore line of the ocean) important cities have grown up: Richmond, Raleigh, Columbia, Augusta, and Montgomery. At the "falls" mill wheels were turned by the swiftly descending rivers, which, this duty done, were then deep and placid enough to carry inland cargoes down to the sea. In earlier times the soils of the Coastal Plain produced most of the wealth of the South. Today the Piedmont, where agriculture and industry are in balance, is the more prosperous region.

To the modern tourist the Southern spurs of the Appalachians, the Blue Ridge, the Great Smokies, the Cumberland Plateau, are pleasure grounds. To the early settlers they were difficult barriers to rich lands in Tennessee and Kentucky. Earliest known of the routes through these mountains was the Great Valley, which begins in Virginia (where

19

the Shenandoah is the first of its rivers) and continues as a trough between Appalachian ridges through all of Tennessee. For the emigrants
it provided a back door to the coastal states of North and South Carolina and Georgia. The Southern gate to the Bluegrass basin of Kentucky—the Cumberland Gap—was not used by white men until Dr.
Thomas Walker entered the region by this pass in 1750 and Daniel
Boone led advance parties of emigrants to Fort Boonesboro just before
the Revolution.

To the stranger who sees the South for the first time the variety of
the landscape is wonderfully impressive. Unless he is driving east or
west along the levels of the Gulf coast, the scenery changes by the
hour. Following the sun in a day's drive in Virginia, for instance, he
leaves the historic tidewater area within two hours, passes the fall line
at Richmond, climbs the Blue Ridge at Swift Run Gap (where in 1716
Governor Spotswood and his Knights of the Golden Horseshoe gazed
in wonder at the Shenandoah), crosses the Great Valley, and before
night falls has reached the western mountains, the day's journey ending
beside the Cow Pasture River, less than fifty miles from Hot Springs.

As the experienced European tourist has his favorite Italian hill town
to tell you about, its patron saint, its cathedral, and its *albergo* which
serves the best *lasagne* in Italy, so the enraptured tourist who knows
the by-ways of the South will talk you down with his description of
the view of the Central Basin of Tennessee as seen from the last Cumberland ridge at Sewanee; of the knob country of Kentucky, where no
road pursues a straight line for more than three hundred yards; of the
Big Cypress Swamp in the Florida Everglades; of the hyacinth-choked
bayous of the Cajun country of Louisiana; of the marshes of Glynn,
near Brunswick, Georgia, which—

> Green, and all of a height, and unflecked with a
>   light or a shade,
> Stretch leisurely off, in a pleasant plain,
> To the terminal blue of the main.

As one roves deeper into the South, the exotic succession of flowers
and trees hints of the approaching equatorial sun. The traveler notes
first the crape myrtle in the dooryards and the profusion of *Magnolia
grandiflora*. Shrubs and trees which are carefully nurtured through the
winter in the North—azaleas, mountain laurel, rhododendron, holly,
and redbud—now grow wild in the woods. New trees appear—the
sweet gum, chinaberry, ginkgo, yaupon, and tupelo. Finally come the
live oaks, green the winter through and hung with the ghostly Spanish
moss, the pecan trees, the palmettos, and—in Florida—the true palms.
The climate is now subtropical.

Those who have visited the South often during the past thirty years are gratified to see how the land has come back. Only that long ago the problem of erosion seemed hopeless. Rich soils that once made the slopes blossom like the land of Sharon were pouring down the gullies into the mud-choked rivers. Since then wonders have been accomplished by terracing and contour plowing and the tying down of the soil with brush mats and cover crops. The South has become again what nature intended it to be—"exceeding fertile and productive."

Bryant Tours the South

Although William Cullen Bryant (1794–1878), poet, critic, and editor for many years of the New York Evening Post, *was as early as 1826 an opponent of slavery and in 1855 one of the founders of the Republican Party, his ties of affection with the pre-war South were strong. His 1843 journey through the east-coast states from Virginia to Florida was instigated by his friend William Gilmore Simms, the Southern novelist. Bryant was prepared to enjoy what, to a New Englander, was novel and exotic about Southern scenery and the Southern way of life. With a romantic poet's careful eye he scanned and then recorded in his travel-letters the lay of the land, the—to him—new kinds of trees and plants, and the interesting folkways that he encountered. His descriptions of the cities he visited are more perfunctory and have therefore been omitted from these selections from his* Letters of a Traveller; or, Notes of Things Seen in Europe and America *(New York: George P. Putnam, 1850), pp. 77–111.*

CHARLESTON, *March 6, 1843.*

I LEFT Richmond, on the afternoon of a keen March day, in the railway train for Petersburg, where we arrived after dark, and, therefore, could form no judgment of the appearance of the town. Here we were transferred to another train of cars. . . .

About two o'clock in the morning, we reached Blakely on the Roanoke, where we were made to get out of the cars, and were marched in long procession for about a quarter of a mile down to the river. A negro walked before us to light our way, bearing a blazing pine torch, which scattered sparks like a steam-engine, and a crowd of negroes followed us, bearing our baggage. We went down a steep path to the Roanoke, where we found a little old steamboat ready for us, and in about fifteen minutes were struggling upward against the muddy and rapid current. In little more than an hour, we had proceeded two miles and a half up the river, and were landed at a place called Weldon. Here we took the cars for Wilmington, in North Carolina, and shabby vehicles they were, denoting our arrival in a milder climate, by being extremely uncomfortable for cold weather. As morning dawned, we saw ourselves in the midst of the pine forests of North Carolina. Vast tracts of level sand, overgrown with the long-leaved pine, a tall, stately tree, with sparse and thick twigs, ending in long brushes of leaves, murmuring in the strong cold wind, extended everywhere around us. At great distances from each other, we passed log-houses, and sometimes a dwelling of more pretensions, with a piazza, and here and there fields in which cotton or maize had been planted last year, or an orchard with a few small mossy trees. The pools beside the roads were covered with ice just formed, and the negroes, who like a good fire at almost any season of the year, and who find an abundant supply of the finest fuel in these forests, had made blazing fires of the resinous wood of the pine, wherever they were at work. The tracts of sandy soil, we perceived, were interspersed with marshes, crowded with cypress-trees, and verdant at their borders with a growth of evergreens, such as the swamp-bay, the gallberry, the holly, and various kinds of evergreen creepers, which are unknown to our northern climate, and which became more frequent as we proceeded.

We passed through extensive forests of pine, which had been *boxed*, as it is called, for the collection of turpentine. Every tree had been scored by the axe upon one of its sides, some of them as high as the arm could reach down to the roots, and the broad wound was covered with the turpentine, which seems to saturate every fibre of the long-leaved pine. Sometimes we saw large flakes or crusts of the turpentine, of a light-yellow color, which had fallen, and lay beside the tree on the ground. The collection of turpentine is a work of destruction; it strips acre after acre of these noble trees, and, if it goes on, the time is not far distant when the long-leaved pine will become nearly extinct in this region, which is so sterile as hardly to be fitted for producing any thing else. We saw large tracts covered with the standing trunks of trees already killed by it; and other tracts beside them had been freshly attacked by the spoiler. I am told that the tree which grows up when the long-leaved pine is destroyed, is the loblolly pine, or, as it is sometimes called, the short-leaved pine, a tree of very inferior quality and in little esteem.

About half-past two in the afternoon, we came to Wilmington, a little town built upon the white sands of Cape Fear, some of the houses standing where not a blade of grass or other plant can grow. A few evergreen oaks, in places pleasantly overhang the water. Here we took the steamer for Charleston. . . .

The next morning, at eight o'clock, we found ourselves entering Charleston harbor; Sullivan's Island, with Fort Moultrie, breathing recollections of the revolution, on our right; James Island on our left; in front, the stately dwellings of the town, and all around, on the land side, the horizon bounded by an apparent belt of evergreens—the live-oak, the water-oak, the palmetto, the pine, and, planted about the dwellings, the magnolia and the wild orange—giving to the scene a summer aspect. The city of Charleston strikes the visitor from the north most agreeably. He perceives at once that he is in a different climate. The spacious houses are surrounded with broad piazzas, often a piazza to each story, for the sake of shade and coolness, and each house generally stands by itself in a garden planted with trees and shrubs, many of which preserve their verdure through the winter. We saw early flowers already opening; the peach and plum-tree were in full bloom; and the wild orange, as they call the cherry-laurel, was just putting forth its blossoms. . . .

BARNWELL DISTRICT, South Carolina, *March 29, 1843.*

Since I last wrote, I have passed three weeks in the interior of South Carolina; visited Columbia, the capital of the state, a pretty town; roamed over a considerable part of Barnwell district, with some part of the neighboring one of Orangeburg; enjoyed the hospitality of the planters—very agreeable and intelligent men; been out in a racoon hunt; been present at a corn-shucking; listened to negro ballads, negro jokes, and the banjo; witnessed negro dances; seen two alligators at least, and eaten bushels of hominy.

Whoever comes out on the railroad to this district, a distance of seventy miles or more, if he were to judge only by what he sees in his passage, might naturally take South Carolina for a vast pine-forest, with here and there a clearing made by some enterprising settler, and would wonder where the cotton which clothes so many millions of the human race, is produced. The railway keeps on a tract of sterile sand, overgrown with pines; passing, here and there, along the edge of a morass, or crossing a stream of yellow water. A lonely log-house under these old trees, is a sight for sore eyes; and only two or three plantations, properly so called, meet the eye in the whole distance. The cultivated and more productive lands lie apart from this tract, near streams, and interspersed with more frequent ponds and marshes. Here you find plantations comprising several thousands of acres, a considerable part of which always lies in forest; cotton and corn fields of vast extent, and a negro village on every plantation, at a respectful distance from the habitation of the proprietor. Evergreen trees of the oak family and others, which I mentioned in my last letter, are generally planted about the mansions. Some of them are surrounded with dreary clearings, full of the standing trunks of dead pines; others are pleasantly situated in the edge of woods, intersected by winding paths. A ramble, or a ride—a ride on a hand-gallop it should be—in these pine woods, on a fine March day, when the weather has all the spirit of our March days without its severity, is one of the most delightful recreations in the world. The paths are upon a white sand, which, when not frequently travelled, is very firm under foot; on all sides you are surrounded by noble stems of trees, towering to an immense height, from whose summits, far above you, the wind is drawing deep and grand harmonies; and often your way is beside a marsh, verdant with magnolias, where the yellow jessamine, now in flower, fills the air with fragrance, and the bamboo-briar, an evergreen creeper, twines itself with various other plants, which never shed their leaves in winter. These woods abound in game, which, you will believe me when I say, I had rather start than shoot,—flocks of turtle-doves, rabbits rising and scudding before you; bevies of quails, partridges they call them here, chirping almost under your horse's feet; wild ducks swimming in the pools, and wild turkeys, which are frequently shot by the practiced sportsman.

But you must hear of the corn-shucking. The one at which I was present was given on purpose that I might witness the humors of the Carolina negroes. A huge fire of *light-wood* was made near the corn-house. Light-wood is the wood of the long-leaved pine, and is so called, not because it is light, for it is almost the heaviest wood in the world, but because it gives more light than any other fuel. In clearing land, the pines are girdled and suffered to stand; the outer portion of the wood decays and falls off; the inner part, which is saturated with turpentine, remains upright for years, and constitutes the planter's provision of fuel. When a supply is wanted, one of these dead trunks is felled by the axe. The abundance of light-wood is one of the boasts of South Carolina. Wherever you are, if you happen to be chilly, you may have a fire extempore; a bit of light-wood and a coal give you a bright blaze and a strong heat in an instant. The negroes make fires of it in the fields where they work; and, when the mornings are wet and chilly, in the pens where they are milking the cows. At a plantation, where I passed a frosty night, I saw fires in a small inclosure, and was told by the lady of the house that she had ordered them to be made to warm the cattle.

The light-wood fire was made, and the negroes dropped in from the neighboring plantations, singing as they came. The driver of the plantation, a colored man, brought out baskets of corn in the husks, and piled it in a heap; and the negroes began to strip the husks from the ears, singing with great glee as they worked, keeping time to the music, and now and then throwing in a joke and an extravagant burst of laughter. The songs were generally of a comic character; but one of them was set to a singularly wild and plaintive air, which some of our musicians would do well to reduce to notation. These are the words:

25

Johnny come down de hollow.
                    Oh hollow!
Johnny come down de hollow.
                    Oh hollow!
De nigger-trader got me.
                    Oh hollow!
De speculator bought me
                    Oh hollow!
I'm sold for silver dollars.
                    Oh hollow!
Boys, go catch de pony.
                    Oh hollow!
Bring him round de corner
                    Oh hollow!
I'm goin' away to Georgia.
                    Oh hollow!
Boys, good-by forever!
                    Oh hollow! . . .

PICOLATA, East Florida, *April 7, 1843.*

As I landed at this place, a few hours since, I stepped into the midst of summer. Yesterday morning when I left Savannah, people were complaining that the winter was not over. The temperature which, at this time of the year, is usually warm and genial, continued to be what they called chilly, though I found it agreeable enough, and the showy trees, called the *Pride of India,* which are planted all over the city, and are generally in bloom at this season, were still leafless. Here I find every thing green, fresh, and fragrant, trees and shrubs in full foliage, and wild roses in flower. The dark waters of the St. John's, one of the noblest streams of the country, in depth and width like the St. Lawrence, draining almost the whole extent of the peninsula, are flowing under my window. On the opposite shore are forests of tall trees, bright in the new verdure of the season. A hunter who has ranged them the whole day, has just arrived in a canoe, bringing with him a deer, which he has killed. I have this moment returned from a ramble with my host through a hammock, he looking for his cows, and I, unsuccessfully, for a thicket of orange-trees. He is something of a florist, and gathered for me, as we went, some of the forest plants, which were in bloom. "We have flowers here," said he, "every month in the year."

I have used the word hammock, which here, in Florida, has a peculiar meaning. A hammock is a spot covered with a growth of trees which require a richer soil than the pine, such as the oak, the mulberry, the gum-tree, the hickory, &c. The greater part of East Florida consists of pine barrens—a sandy level, producing the long leaved pine and the dwarf palmetto, a low plant, with fan-like leaves, and roots of a prodigious size. The hammock is a kind of oasis, a verdant and luxuriant island in the midst of these sterile sands, which make about nine-tenths of the soil of East Florida. In the hammocks grow the wild lime, the native orange, both sour and bittersweet, and the various vines and gigantic creepers of the country. The hammocks are chosen for plantations; here the cane is cultivated, and groves of the sweet orange planted. But I shall say more of Florida hereafter, when I have seen more of it. Meantime let me speak of my journey hither.

I left Charleston on the 30th of March, in one of the steamers which ply between that city and Savannah. These steamers are among the very best that float—quiet, commodious, clean, fresh as if just built, and furnished with civil and ready-handed waiters. We passed along the narrow and winding channels which divide the broad islands of South Carolina from the main-land—islands famed for the rice culture, and particularly for the excellent cotton with long fibres, named the sea-island cotton. Our fellow-passengers were mostly planters of these islands, and their families, persons of remarkably courteous, frank, and agreeable manners. The shores on either side had little of the picturesque to show us. Extensive marshes waving with coarse water-grass, sometimes a cane-brake, sometimes a pine grove or a clump of cabbage-leaved palmettoes; here and there a pleasant bank bordered with live-oaks streaming with moss, and at wide intervals the distant habitation of a planter—these were the elements of the scenery. The next morning early we were passing up the Savannah river, and the city was in sight, standing among its trees on a high bank of the stream. . . .

While in Savannah, I paid a visit to Bonaventure, formerly a county seat of Governor Tatnall, but now abandoned. A pleasant drive of a mile or two, through a budding forest, took us to the place, which is now itself almost grown up into forest. Cedars and other shrubs hide the old terraces of the garden, which is finely situated on the high bank of a river. Trees of various kinds have also nearly filled the space between the noble avenues of live-oaks which were planted around the mansion. But these oaks—I never saw finer trees—certainly I never saw so many majestic and venerable trees together. I looked far down the immense arches that overshadowed the broad passages, as high as the nave of a Gothic cathedral, apparently as old, and stretching to a greater distance. The huge boughs were clothed with gray moss, yards in length, which clung to them like mist, or hung in still festoons on

27

every side, and gave them the appearance of the vault of a vast vapory cavern. The cawing of the crow and the scream of the jay, however, reminded us that we were in the forest. Of the mansion there are no remains; but in the thicket of magnolias and other trees, among rose-bushes and creeping plants, we found a burial-place with monuments of some persons to whom the seat had belonged.

Savannah is more healthy of late years than it formerly was. An arrangement has been made with the owners of the plantations in the immediate vicinity, by which the culture of rice has been abandoned, and the lands are no longer allowed to be overflowed within a mile from the city. The place has since become much less subject to fevers than in former years.

I left, with a feeling of regret, the agreeable society of Savannah. The steamboat took us to St. Mary's, through passages between the sea-islands and the main-land, similar to those by which we had arrived at Savannah. In the course of the day, we passed a channel in which we saw several huge alligators basking on the bank. The grim creatures slid slowly into the water at our approach. We passed St. Mary's in the night, and in the morning we were in the main ocean, approaching the St. John's, where we saw a row of pelicans standing, like creatures who had nothing to do, on the sand. We entered the majestic river, the vast current of which is dark with the infusion of the swamp turf, from which it is drained. We passed Jacksonville, a little town of great activity, which has sprung up on the sandy bank within two or three years. Beyond, we swept by the mouth of the Black Creek, the water of which, probably from the color of the mud which forms the bed of its channel, has to the eye an ebony blackness, and reflects objects with all the distinctness of the kind of looking-glass called a black mirror. A few hours brought us to Picolata, lately a military station, but now a place with only two houses.

ST. AUGUSTINE, East Florida, *April 2, 1843.*

When we left Picolata, on the 8th of April, we found ourselves journeying through a vast forest. A road of eighteen miles in length, over the level sands, brings you to this place. Tall pines, a thin growth, stood wherever we turned our eyes, and the ground was covered with the dwarf palmetto, and the whortleberry, which is here an evergreen. Yet there were not wanting sights to interest us, even in this dreary and sterile region. As we passed a clearing, in which we saw a young white woman and a boy dropping corn, and some negroes covering it with their hoes, we beheld a large flock of white cranes which rose in the air, and hovered over the forest, and wheeled, and wheeled again, their spotless plumage glistening in the sun like new-fallen snow. We crossed the track of a recent hurricane, which had broken off the huge pines midway from the ground, and whirled the summits to a distance from their trunks. From time to time we forded little streams of a deep-red color, flowing from the swamps, tinged, as we were told, with the roots of the red bay, a species of magnolia. As the horses waded into the transparent crimson, we thought of the butcheries committed by the Indians, on that road, and could almost fancy that the water was still colored with the blood they had shed. . . .

At length we emerged upon a shrubby plain, and finally came in sight of this oldest city of the United States, seated among its trees on a sandy swell of land where it has stood for three hundred years. I was struck with its ancient and homely aspect, even at a distance, and could not help likening it to pictures which I had seen of Dutch towns, though it wanted a windmill or two, to make the resemblance perfect. We drove into a green square, in the midst of which was a monument erected to commemorate the Spanish constitution of 1812, and thence through the narrow streets of the city to our hotel. . . .

The other day I went out with a friend to a sugar plantation in the neighborhood of St. Augustine. As we rode into the inclosure we breathed the fragrance of young orange-trees in flower, the glossy leaves of which, green at all seasons, were trembling in the wind. A troop of negro children were at play at a little distance from the cabins, and one of them ran along with us to show us a grove of sour oranges which we were looking for. He pointed us to a copse in the middle of a field, to which we proceeded. The trees, which were of considerable size, were full of flowers, and the golden fruit was thick on the branches, and lay scattered on the ground below. I gathered a few of the oranges, and found them almost as acid as the lemon. We stopped to look at the buildings in which the sugar was manufactured. In one of them was the mill where the cane was crushed with iron rollers, in another stood the huge cauldrons, one after another, in which the juice was boiled down to the proper consistence; in another were barrels of sugar, of syrup—a favorite article of consumption in this city—of molasses, and a kind of spirits resembling Jamaica rum, distilled from the refuse of the molasses. The proprietor was absent, but three negroes, well-clad young men, of a very respectable appearance and intelligent physiognomy, one of whom was a distiller, were occupied about the buildings, and showed them to us. Near by in the open air lay a pile of sugar cane, of the ribbon variety, striped with red and white, which had been plucked up by the roots, and reserved for planting. The negroes of St. Augustine are a good-looking specimen of the race, and have the appearance of being very well treated. You rarely see a negro in ragged clothing, and the colored children, though

29

slaves, are often dressed with great neatness. In the colored people whom I saw in the Catholic church, I remarked a more agreeable, open, and gentle physiognomy than I have been accustomed to see in that class. The Spanish race blends more kindly with the African, than does the English, and produces handsomer men and women.

An Englishman Settles in Virginia in the 1870's

A. G. Bradley (1850–1943), a son of the Dean of Westminster Abbey, came out to North America early in the 1870's, shortly after he had finished his terms at Trinity College, Cambridge. He stayed for a while with relatives in Canada and then purchased a plantation in Virginia where he and his wife lived for nearly ten years. A good many Englishmen were buying land in Virginia after the Civil War because they thought they could find there "the prospects of a new country without the accompanying conditions of hardship and isolation" attendant on settlement in the West; so Bradley put it in his autobiography, Other Days, Recollections of Rural England and Old Virginia, 1860–1880 *(1913). Virginia, he said, was "the country of the moment for the educated Englishman, more particularly the married man." It had "a flavor of romance, due partly, I am sure, to the Christy Minstrel ballads, and to British upper-class sympathy for the South during the war"; land was cheap and, though it was known to be worked out, everyone was sure that it could be reclaimed. After his return to England, Bradley devoted himself to historical and topographical writing, drawing first on his American experience for articles in such periodicals as* Blackwood's *and* Macmillan's Magazine. *Eleven of these he gathered together in* Sketches from Old Virginia *(London: Macmillan and Co.; 1897). Among these eleven pieces is "On the Old Bethel Pike" from which the following excerpt is taken (pp. 102–9). It appeared first in the* Fortnightly Review *(August 1, 1896) as "An Old American Turnpike."*

EVER since the period following the war it has been my lot to traverse, at stated intervals, the same twenty miles or so of the old Bethel Pike.

And if I take as my text this particular line of road it is only because I know it best, and have been an eye-witness of its slow but sure decay, and have moreover the melancholy satisfaction as I ride along of peopling many of its deserted homesteads and abandoned fields with familiar names and well-remembered faces. For this, after all, is but a fraction of a large slice of Virginia which tells the same sad tale. Nor would it be a spectacle half so pathetic if the country, as here and there is actually the case, had been wholly abandoned to the forests of scrub, oak, and pine, that without intrinsic value of their own would, if unchecked, at least have thrown their kindly canopy over these dismal skeletons of the past. But life, as I have said, flickers feebly still upon these old estates. Heaven knows whom they now belong to. Most of them have changed hands, and that more than once, and always at declining prices, since I can first remember them. Many of them are now hardly worth paying taxes on, and taxes are low. Here and there a surviving scion of some old family may be found struggling with the briars, bearing but little likeness in appearance or education, and still less in the condition of his life, to his forbears. Sometimes the dilapidated acres are still owned by the family, who are scattered in trade or what not all over the United States, while some "poor white" or negro tenant undertakes to pay a rent which theoretically almost nominal is reduced in practice to microscopic proportions. Mortgagees own many through foreclosure, storekeepers, perhaps, or lawyers in the local towns, and if they get rent enough to pay the taxes and keep the buildings from actually falling, it is the utmost satisfaction, unless maybe a few days quail shooting in November, that they derive from the acquisition. In some places, indeed, the forests have reasserted themselves so freely that the very deer, after a banishment of a century, let us say, have found their way back to as great a solitude as that from which they were originally driven. But for the most part the landscape lies as open as of old, and the fields keep their former boundaries, marking them rather by the lusty growth of briars and saplings that have flourished especially along the fences than by the rotting rails they hide. And at the season of the year when, in happier days, the cheery shout of the negro, as he followed his plough or harrow over the red cornlands, and the busy stir of rural life filled the air, the blooms of the dog-wood and the wild cherry and the peach blow over wastes of broomsedge that are in themselves, perhaps, less depressing to look upon than the dismal efforts to fight against fate which break the desolation.

Here is a hillside on whose briery face the withered corn-stalks of two years ago are still standing, telling by their miserable attenuation a tale unmistakable. Here a few acres of wheat thin beyond belief upon the ground, and of a sickly colour, save where some old tobacco-barn or cabin has stood, and a bright, rank patch shows by contrast what wheat should be in April, and what it is not. There, again, a field of last year's corn has been followed in the ordinary local rotation by oats, which amid dead corn-stalks and a promising growth of weeds and bushes is making a desperate struggle for existence. If it achieves this last it may thresh out six bushels to the acre, a miserable output indeed, but one which the sickly wheat-field across the road will hardly run to. Fine horses, as everybody knows, once scampered and whinnied over these now tangled wastes, horses that were the pride of a sport-loving population, whose sires often had borne names of note upon Newmarket Heath and Epsom Downs, themselves distinguished upon Southern race-tracks, and not unfamiliar with the music of horn and hound. It is needless to remark that the Virginia horse, which still enjoys some reputation in America, does not find its model in the miserable drudges that, scarred by collar and trace-chain, toil in these unprofitable furrows, or drag the crazy, half-loaded waggons along the old rock road.

Following along the latter, it carries us every now and again with sharp descent and little ceremony into the waves of some rapid stream that brawls over its pebbly bed with a callous gaiety that seems somehow at variance with the scenes through which it is travelling. As our steed, after the fashion of all its kind in Virginia, stands in midstream and slakes an apparently unquenchable thirst, a pleasant vista unfolds itself to left and right of sunlit foam and gray rocks, and bowers of leaves that willow, alder, beech, and sycamore form with their spreading branches.

Here, too, are some remnants of fertility, and, indeed, all along the tortuous course of the little river strips of alluvial bottom land will be found hugging its banks, which in former days, on the greater estates, made up in some sort for the infertile uplands that spread on either hand. Still in those days such choice bits were treated with some forbearance. To protect them from washing floods at least was the planters' care, and to sow them from time to time in meadow grass or clover. Even such simple operations are beyond the scope of the hungry, shiftless occupier of modern days, whose reckless plough vies with the wayward stream in destroying those few spots where he can still hope to raise some apology for a crop.

But perhaps it is in the homesteads themselves that the contrast between the "then and now" is saddest. Many of them you would hardly notice from the turnpike, for though standing mostly upon hill-tops, those that have any past in a social sense are a long way back from the road, and often hidden by those stately groves of forest trees that throw their protecting arms around every well-constituted Virginia rooftree.

Here is one that, even after the war, remained for long a type of that simple, gracious, old-fashioned hospitality that distinguished the period before it. The track that wandered off the turnpike through the woods to the private entrance was easy enough to overlook even in those days, and now when the dead leaves lie upon it, undisturbed by passing wheel or hoof, it is difficult to trace up to the two rotting posts upon which once hung the ever-open and hospitable gate. The house itself in a score of years seems to have lived a lifetime, and to have hastened from cheerful and well-preserved middle age to decrepitude and decay, while the heavy portico over the door, resting, in the English fashion of the Georgian period, on lofty fluted columns, has shed the plaster from its ceiling in big cakes upon the rotting steps. The windows have mostly fallen out, and a battered shutter hangs here and there by a single hinge from the sash to emphasize the woe-begone aspect of the walls. And these again are scarred with ominous-looking cracks in the brick that no inmates whose interest in life was vigorous and circulation normal could contemplate without dismay. A family of "poor whites" occupy one wing of the decaying mansion and work their wild will on a portion of the surrounding acres. And the "poor white" of Eastern Virginia is both in appearance and ways of life the most unlovely sample of Anglo-Saxon, of rural Anglo-Saxon at any rate, that an inscrutable Providence has fashioned. To suppose too that a single window-pane would be replaced, a single nail driven into a loose plank, or a gate hung upon its hinges under the auspices of these gentry, would be not to know them. If anything were wanted to intensify the melancholy of this spectre of an old Virginia home the gaunt forms and yellow faces and vacant stare of its present occupants are well calculated to do so.

The Virginia squires troubled their heads little about landscape gardening. An acre or so of old turf shaded with forest trees and sprinkled with a few exotics filled, and upon the whole filled well, every requirement of dignity and comfort. But not even this relic of former days, however, has here escaped the aggressive inroad which nature abandoned to itself makes beneath these Southern suns. For the briars and weeds from the half-tilled fields without have leaped the broken palings of the lawn and are disputing every yard of ground with the old sod that seemed to have in it the resisting power of a century's growth and care.

In the vegetable garden, on which chiefly in olden days the care of the household, and above all of its ladies, used to be expended, the turf walks can still be traced, and the posts and trellis-work over which the grape-vines once clambered with such profusion are even yet partly standing. Out of a jungle of weeds waist-high old-fashioned herbs still push their heads up here and there for life and light, and the box-edgings of the beds have struggled up into rank bushes, stiff and straight amid the chaos.

And yet perhaps it is the inside of the house that awakens the saddest memories. Each chamber in its musty silence has some tale of its own to tell, and the tale told within these particular walls is not that of a single family, but of hundreds—the story of a whole race who once were powerful, were a leading factor in the life, not of a province, but of a nation, and who have within a period comparatively brief passed out of existence. The nails are still sticking in the walls from which used to hang those homely but none the less treasured paintings of gentlemen in wigs and swords, and ladies who danced with Braddock's fated officers at Williamsburg, and as sober matrons turned up no doubt their pretty noses (in secret) at Patrick Henry's rustic eloquence and Mr. Jefferson's dowdy clothes. It needs not the memory of these vanished symbols to remind us how Virginia in prosperity and political influence was once the foremost of American commonwealths, and had much more than her share in a numerical sense, considerable though this was, in guiding and shaping the early history of the United States.

Virginia, nowadays, as a state, is, upon the whole, by no means unprosperous. We have been looking at her moribund and historic part. That other portion which represents her increase and prosperity, which fattens cattle and grows corn with moderate success, which delves for coal and iron, rears blast furnaces and factories and summer hotels, though beautiful indeed by nature, belongs otherwise to the commonplace tale of modern progress, and has no connection with the point of view from which this chapter is written. But this pleasant and prosperous western half that hugs the foot-hills of the Blue Ridge and lies amid the shadow of the Alleghanies is not, to any appreciable extent, the Virginia of the days when her opinion was listened to by sister colonies and sister states with a deference that reads strangely now.

It is this older Virginia, this famous cradle of the English race beyond the sea, that now, so much of it lies an almost hopeless desert, or what, compared to any other agricultural country in the Anglo-Saxon world, is practically a desert—and seems likely to remain so.

The Delta

This selection is taken from Lanterns on the Levee, Recollections of a Planter's Son (*1941*), *the autobiography of William Alexander Percy (1885–1942). After graduating from the University of the South and the Harvard Law School, Percy nominally practiced law in Greenville, Mississippi. In actuality he was the quiet and effective champion of nearly every good cause of his place and time. In the great flood of 1927, for example, he found himself charged "with the rescuing, housing, and feeding of sixty thousand human beings and thirty thousand head of stock"—because, as a matter of course, the Mayor appointed him chairman of the Flood Relief Committee. This was typical. Someone was always asking Will Percy to take over. The extent of his private charities and encouragements will never be reckoned. No one knew the Delta country better than he and no author has written of it —its people, its problems, its potentialities, and the reaches of the "gaunt and terrible river" that flows through it—as lovingly as he did.*

This excerpt from Lanterns on the Levee (*pp. 3–7, 13–15*) *is reprinted with the permission of the publisher, Alfred A. Knopf.*

My country is the Mississippi Delta, the river country. It lies flat, like a badly drawn half oval, with Memphis at its northern and Vicksburg at its southern tip. Its western boundary is the Mississippi River, which coils and returns on itself in great loops and crescents, though from the map you would think it ran in a straight line north and south. Every few years it rises like a monster from its bed and pushes over its banks to vex and sweeten the land it has made. For our soil, very dark brown, creamy and sweet-smelling, without substrata of rock or shale, was built up slowly, century after century, by the sediment gathered by the river in its solemn task of cleansing the continent and deposited in annual layers of silt on what must once have been the vast depression between itself and the hills. This ancient depression, now filled in and level, is what we call the Delta. Some say it was the floor of the sea itself. Now it seems still to be a floor, being smooth from one end to the other, without rise or dip or hill, unless the mysterious scattered monuments of the mound-builders may be called hills. The land does not drain into the river as most riparian lands do, but tilts back from it towards the hills of the south and east. Across this wide flat alluvial stretch—north and south it measures one hundred and ninety-six miles, east and west at the widest point fifty miles—run slowly and circuitously other rivers and creeks, also high-banked, with names pleasant to remember—Rattlesnake Bayou, Quiver River, the Bogue Phalia, the Tallahatchie, the Sunflower—pouring their tawny waters finally into the Yazoo, which in turn loses itself just above Vicksburg in the river. With us when you speak of "the river," though there are many, you mean always the same one, the great river, the shifting unappeasable god of the country, feared and loved, the Mississippi.

In the old days this was a land of unbroken forests. All trees grew there except the pine and its kindred, and, strangely enough, the magnolia. The water-oak, the pecan, the cypress, and the sweet-gum were perhaps the most beautiful and home-loving, but there were ash and elm, walnut and maple, and many others besides. They grew to enormous heights, with vast trunks and limbs, and between them spread a chaos of vines and cane and brush, so that the deer and bear took it for their own and only by the Indians was it penetrable, and by them only on wraiths of trails. Wild flowers were few, the soil being too rich and warm and deep, and those, like the yellow-top of early spring, apt to be rank and weed-like. A still country it must have been then, ankle-deep in water, mostly in shadow, with mere flickers of sunshine, and they motey and yellow and thick like syrup. The wild swans loved it; tides of green parakeets from the south and of gray pigeons from the north melted into its tree-tops and gave them sound; ducks— mallard, canvas-back, teal, and wood-duck—and Canadian geese, their wedges high in the soft air of autumn like winter's first arrows, have still not deserted it.

Such was my country hardly more than a hundred years ago. It was about then that slavery became unprofitable in the older Southern states and slave-holders began to look for cheap fertile lands farther west that could feed the many black mouths dependent on them. So younger sons from Virginia, South Carolina, and Kentucky with their gear, live-stock, and chattels, human and otherwise, started a leisurely migration into the Delta. Forests were cleared, roads constructed (such dusty or muddy roads!), soil shaped into fields, homes built. They settled first on the banks and bends of the river, later on the banks and bends of the smaller streams, for those were high ground over which the then yearly inundations of the river, as yet uncurbed by levees, never quite reached. There is still a great curve of the shoreline called Kentucky Bend, and another, mostly sandbar now, called Carolina.

The roads they built were local affairs, connecting plantation with plantation or with hamlets which grew slowly and without booms into our present small towns. In wet weather, of which we have much, they were bottomless, and old-timers believed they could never be anything else.

The real highway was the river. All life, social and economic, centered there. The river steamers furnished transportation, relaxation, and information to the whole river people. In our town the *Pargo* landed regularly on Sunday, usually between eleven o'clock and noon. Everybody would be at church, but when she blew, the male members of the congregation to a man would rise and, in spite of indignant glares from their wives and giggles from the choir, make their exits, with a severe air of business just remembered. With the *Pargo* came the week's mail and gossip of the river-front from St. Louis to New Orleans and rumors from the very distant outside world. If the occasion was propitious a little round of poker might be started and a few toddies drunk. They were a fine fleet, those old sidewheelers which plied between St. Louis and New Orleans and stopped on signal at the various plantations and river settlements—the *White*, the *Pargo*, the *Natchez*, the *Robert E. Lee*. The last and least of them was the *Belle of the Bends*, which as a small boy I could never see steaming majestically through the sunset to the landing without a fine choky feeling. They had pleasant outside cabins opening on an enormous white dining-saloon, decorated in the most abandoned gingerbread style, which after supper became a ballroom. Almost as comfortable as our ocean liners of today, they were far easier and more sociable; anybody who was anybody knew everybody else, and each trip was rather like a grand house-party, with dancing and gambling and an abundance of Kentucky whisky and French champagne. The ladies (who never partook of these beverages—maybe a sip of champagne) were always going to New Orleans for Mardi Gras or to shop or to hear the opera (well established there before it was begun in New York) or to visit cousins and aunts in the Louisiana and Natchez territory; and as those were days of enormous families, cousins and aunts were plentiful. There never was a Southern family that was a Southern Family some member of which, incredibly beautiful and sparkling, had not opened the ball with Lafayette. For years apparently his sole occupation was opening balls in New Orleans, Charleston, Natchez, and St. Louis. After looking at a hundred or more badly painted portraits of these belles I am a firm believer in this tradition.

If the ladies loved going to New Orleans, the men-folks were never at a loss for reasons to take the same trip. Memphis was hardly more than a country town. The commission merchants (forerunners of the modern bank, co-operative association, Federal Land Bank, insurance company with funds to invest) had their offices in New Orleans and it was they who supplied the planters with the cash for their extensive and costly operations. Here was an ever ready reason to board the boat going south, and one that made unnecessary any reference to the lottery, the races, the masked balls, the fantastic poker games, the hundred and one amiable vices of that most European and sloe-eyed of American cities. . . .

And the river? It is changed and eternally the same. The early settlers soon began to rebuff its yearly caress, that impregnated and vitalized the soil, by building small dikes around their own individual plantations. This was a poor makeshift and in time, not without ruction and bitter debate, was abandoned in favor of levee districts which undertook to levee the river itself at the cost of the benefited landowners within the districts. After reconstruction no more vital problem perplexed Delta statesmen than how to convince the Federal government of the propriety of contributing to the cost of building levees. At first they failed, but later niggardly aid was doled out—a bit some years, others none. Only within the last fifteen years has the government accepted the view urged for half a century by our people that the river's waters are the nation's waters and fighting them is the nation's fight. The United States Engineers under the War Department are now in full charge of levee and revetment work from one end of the river to the other.

But this work has not changed the savage nature and austere beauty of the river itself. Man draws near to it, fights it, uses it, curses it, loves it, but it remains remote, unaffected. Between the fairy willows of the banks or the green slopes of the levees it moves unhurried and unpausing; building islands one year to eat them the next; gnawing the bank on one shore till the levee caves in and another must be built farther back, then veering wantonly and attacking with equal savagery the opposite bank; in spring, high and loud against the tops of the quaking levees; in summer, deep and silent in its own tawny bed; bearing eternally the waste and sewage of the continent to the cleansing wide-glittering Gulf. A gaunt and terrible stream, but more beautiful and dear to its children than Thames or Tiber, than mountain brook or limpid estuary. The gods on their thrones are shaken and changed, but it abides, aloof and unappeasable, with no heart except for its own task, under the unbroken and immense arch of the lighted sky where the sun, too, goes a lonely journey.

As a thing used by men it has changed: the change is not in itself, but in them. No longer the great white boats and their gallant companies ply to and fro on its waters. A certain glamour is gone forever. But the freighters and barge lines of today keep one reminder of the vanished elder packets—their deep-throated, long-drawn-out, giant voices. And still there is no sound in the world so filled with mystery and longing and unease as the sound at night of a river-boat blowing for the land-ing—one long, two shorts, one long, two shorts. Over the somber levels of the water pours that great voice, so long prolonged it is joined by echoes from the willowed shore, a chorus of ghosts, and, roused from sleep, wide-eyed and still, you are oppressed by vanished glories, the last trump, the calling of the ends of the earth, the current, ceaselessly moving out into the dark, of the eternal dying. Trains rushing at night under the widening pallor of their own smoke, bearing in wild haste their single freightage of wild light, over a receding curve of thunder, have their own glory. But they are gone too quickly, like a meteor, to become part of your deep own self. The sound of the river-boats hangs inside your heart like a star.

Arkansas: a Look round the Land

It is easy to explain why John Gould Fletcher's Arkansas, *from which this passage comes, is outstanding among the general books that have been written about the Southern states. Born in Little Rock in 1886, Fletcher could trace the Arkansas beginnings of his family back to 1825 on his father's side, to the 1840's on his mother's. Though he was Harvard educated and had lived abroad many years while his reputation as one of the "New Poets" grew, Fletcher never lost his affection for his native state. It was strengthened when he identified himself with the Southern Agrarians in their 1930 manifesto,* I'll Take My Stand, *and when he married in 1936 Charlie May Simon, a writer whose understanding of the Ozark people, among whom she lived, was extraordinary. With Fletcher it was the old story of the American who can come home again. When he died, in 1950, he had been living for many years in Little Rock and doing what he could for the arts and education in Arkansas.*

This passage is the first chapter of Fletcher's Arkansas *(Chapel Hill: University of North Carolina Press; 1947). It is reprinted here with the permission of the publishers.*

WHERE the Mississippi River cuts the southern border of Missouri lies the State of Arkansas. Except for an area roughly forty miles square between the Saint Francis and the Great River where Missouri bites a chunk off its northeast corner, the state stretches westward for over three hundred miles to the prairies of eastern Oklahoma. Most of those miles are in the Ozarks, the mountain region. From the north boundary, Arskansas runs southward for about two hundred and fifty miles to the northern edge of Louisiana. Here, thanks to another chunk of about the same size bitten off the southwest corner by Texas, and thanks, too, to the generally southwest trend of the Great River, the state is no more than a hundred and seventy miles across from east to west. Every foot of this is river-delta plain. Hence one may say that there are roughly two regions in Arkansas: the highlands, occupying the northwestern half, and the lowlands, occupying the southeastern half of the area. These two are distinct in types of population, in scenery, and in culture.

But to the native Arkansawyer, each of these two regions falls into at least two subdivisions. The lowland area, densely forested, when the first man entered it, with oak, elm, ash, sweetgum, hickory, and cypress, was broken, from the beginning, by a great prairie extending northward from the first settlement at Arkansas Post to the present city of Brinkley—a distance of at least seventy miles north and south and from fifteen to twenty miles east and west. This prairie, since the first road in Arkansas ran directly across it, afforded an early access to the interior; and except for a few smaller prairies along the western border, it is the chief treeless region in the state. It has its own peculiar history.

The upland region, too, is cut into irregular halves by two different types of mountain formation. North of the Arkansas River, which cuts diagonally through the center of the state, are the Ozarks proper, composed mainly of limestone rocks lying in flat strata, which have been worn down through ages on ages of rainfall into flat-topped plateaus. These are divided by steep winding hollows, through which the streams straggle irregularly like the branches of a vine. South of the river, in the Ouachitas, the rocks are more varied and uptilted in their strata; their ridges run more regularly east and west and the valleys are usually wider, with parallel east-west-running streams in them. Also, the southern mountain region and the northern are different in the appearance of their forests. The Ozarks, to the north and west, are clad for the most part in dense hardwoods: oak, hickory, ash, with occasional patches of dark cedar and the shortleaf pine. But south and west of Little Rock, a dense, unvaried shortleaf pine forest extends for miles, with patches of sweetgum, scrub-oaks, and, by the bed of rock-bordered, leaf-hidden streams, the wild holly sometimes growing in dense groves.

Each of these two mountain areas is distinct from the other; and both, in turn, vary greatly from the flat monotony of the lowlands, covered originally with trackless forest, broken only by immense swamps of cypress and cane and vine. Through the midst of this lowland area runs the Grand Prairie region already mentioned, so named by the earliest settlers, now the great rice field of the state and an important factor in its history.

These distinctions between Ozark and Ouachita, between rice and cotton lowland, and fruit-growing or forested upland are important; for, possibly more than in any other Southern state, the native of this region is dependent, not on industry, but on nature for his material well-being. Of the small number of manufactures in the state, over half are directly connected with the forests and with lumbering. Up to a period which may be set roughly as about fifty years ago, a considerable proportion of the population lived largely on fish caught in the rivers and wild game shot in the forest; and to this day, the state is known as a paradise for sportsmen. Except for the counties bordering directly on the Mississippi and those along the Arkansas River southeast of Little Rock, the plantation system, so important elsewhere in the South, never took firm hold. The typical Arkansawyer was far more likely to be a frontier settler in coonskin cap, blanket cape, and buckskin trousers—or its modern equivalent of blue denim jumper, checkered shirt, blue overalls, and greasy black hat—than a planter in broadcloth coat, satin vest, and ruffled shirt, drinking his mint julep on a pillared verandah while his Negro slave waved palm-leaf fans in his direction.

One thing, however, the sections of Arkansas all have in common— the climate. For the last sixty years, since temperature records were first kept, these records have shown a remarkable uniformity. For the northwestern third of the state, to a line beginning about Corning and running thence southwest to about Searcy, thence due west to Fort Smith, the average annual temperature has been between 56 and 60 degrees. South of this, to a region which begins about at DeQueen or Nashville on the west and ends at the site of Arkansas Post on the east, runs a belt which averages between 60 and 62. Still farther south, for the lower third of the state, the average is between 62 and 66. The average winter temperature, for the state as a whole, is about 42, the spring 61, the summer nearly 80, the fall 61. These seasons, too, are uniformly divided, spring running usually from March to June, summer from June to October, fall from October to the end of December, winter from Christmas to March. Summer, however, as any native son or daughter can testify, is actually longer than the other seasons; it often starts in May, and does not end till the middle of November. Its first part is usually humid, with tremendous thunderstorms; its last part is usually intensely scorching and dry. Indeed, as an early traveller wisely observed, "Throughout this territory, there are no grasses nor other vegetables of consequence in agriculture (except the cane) which retain their verdure beyond the close of September." And I myself have seen, as early as the middle of July, pavements thick with those yellow leaves which usually drift down in heaps by August.

It is probably this climate—capricious in winter, when December rains drench the bottomlands and sudden, hard February freezes sweep from Nebraska and Kansas down across the Ozarks, and also in spring, when violent April winds of tornado intensity come up from Texas and Oklahoma, while in summer all is an overpowering blaze of humid torpor under an eternal scorching sun—that has made Arkansas a Southern state. Southern and yet Southwestern. With Texas we share the distinction of being the only Southern state that lies altogether west of the Mississippi. But where Texas is overwhelmingly a plains state, Arkansas is a mixed mountain and lowland state. Yet the Ozarks, though having six peaks of over two thousand feet, will never be a successful summer resort. Nothing is more strange as an experience than to attempt a motor trip among them at the close of June, when windless stillness holds rigid the endless rows of scalloped-leaved oaks and pointed-leaved hickories at the roadside, and a heat of tropic intensity broods over the densely thicketed hollow and beyond to where another rugged ridge, showing no sign of human habitation, cuts the sky. Then one understands why the true Arkansawyer, from June to September, moves slowly, if he moves at all.

The inhabitant of the Ozarks, though much has been written about him to prove his culture unique, is, in fact, extremely like any other Southern mountaineer. In the lowlands bordering on the Mississippi or on the lower Arkansas there are great cotton plantations, akin to those elsewhere in the South, staffed by armies of tenant sharecroppers—at first almost altogether Negro but now becoming increasingly white. But in the Ozarks it is only with difficulty that the forests are cleared and a few stony acres kept plowed to receive the seeds of cotton or of corn. There are far fewer people; and these are invariably white. The five hundred thousand Negroes of the state have, for the most part, never seen, let alone known, the quality of life of the mountain region.

This region is unique in yet another way. Circumstances made of the inhabitant of the Ozarks—and the inhabitant of the Ouachitas differed in no way from him except that he lived in still greater isolation—not alone a mountaineer, but still more, a frontiersman facing the semi-civilized Indian Territory. Up to about fifty years ago, well within the lifetime of persons now living, the Ozarker was self-contained and self-dependent. He ground his own corn. His women spun their own thread, made their own clothes. He distilled his own whisky. Crude furniture was made by whittling, and chairs were seated with twisted withes of willow or untanned oxhides. Houses were built by unskilled labor; and I have seen and spent hours in a four-room log cabin—with two massive stone chimneys—built by unskilled mountaineers as late as 1932. Bedspread coverlets there were elaborately made out of patchwork pieces, or woven; and many days in the year were spent in the woods near by, recruiting the scanty larder with squirrels, rabbits, deer, or possums. The life of the Ozarks was wild and primitive, but not without its savor. The proximity of the Indian Territory—it must be remembered that the Cherokee Strip was not opened to settlers before 1889—and the scarcity of all settlements served not only to preserve old mountaineer traditions brought from Tennessee or the Carolinas, but to intensify the frontier type. It is not too much to say that the Ozarker was, if not himself an outlaw, at least in sympathy with the outlaw breed. His favorite heroes had all a strong touch of Jesse James about them and were good men with a gun.

All this is different enough from the life of the lowlands, where, from the eighteen-thirties on, the plantation system, resting on its basis of Negro slavery, crept westward and northward from Alabama, Mississippi, Tennessee, Louisiana, to shape much of the state's political life previous to the Civil War and to resume its control after: for the plantation system held the predominant economic power up to the threshold of the twentieth century. One can see the plantation system still in full flower along any of the highways between Little Rock and Memphis. Here, in a land as flat as any table, are the endless rows of cotton, plowed in March, seeded in April. Here, bordering the "turn row," are lines of two-roomed cabins of unpainted lumber, sometimes whitewashed and sometimes not, looking intensely hot and shadeless and comfortless, as indeed they are. Here are the houses of the "riding bosses" and overseers, made of better lumber, neatly painted, with small flower gardens and shade trees. Here, occasionally, is the two-story house of an owner, usually on higher ground. Here is where cotton grows up to the front doors, and to the back doors as well—and here are rows of Negroes swinging their hoes in May, June, July, under the blazing sun: creeping with long sacks at their shoulders through the fields from September to past Thanksgiving, picking. Here is the corrugated iron gin house—ugly, yet useful. Here is the commissary store, with its advertisements of chill-remedy and of snuff—which are seen frequently, too, in the highlands—and the usual group of listless sharecroppers in their high boots, sitting on its porch. And here, finally, is the dense cypress swamp, with its lightly plumed arms, green in summer, brown in winter, blocking the flat horizon.

It is all very different from those lonely unpainted cabins with a "dog-run" between two rooms, resting on their rickety unmortared stone foundations, half-disengaged from the surrounding forest, which surprise the traveller at a sudden turning on a narrow solitary road in the Ozarks. There, not infrequently, the towheaded native children still run to the doors to stare at the uncommon spectacle of a passing car; and Negroes are unknown. In fact, in spite of the similarity of climate, the mountain region and the plantation region of this state might well belong to two different continents, to two different worlds.

Out of the interactions of highland upon lowland, of lowland upon highland; out of the significant historic fact that slavery existed here from the beginning of the state's existence as a territory, and that southwest lay Texas, and west the region designed for the Indians as early as Jefferson's day; out of all these has emerged a history both tragic and comic—with its deep, legendary roots going far back into the remote, prehistoric past.

III

RIVERS

T HE first settlers in the South carved out their plantations on the Coastal Plain or along the Gulf. In consequence they found their highways already made for them—in the many navigable rivers that flow wide and deep eastward into the Atlantic or southward into the Gulf of Mexico. In frontier times no other section of the country was able to use water transportation as the South did. If possible a plantation had to have a river frontage and wharves along it where ships from Europe could dock and exchange the luxuries of the Old World for cargoes of tobacco and cotton and rice. The plantation-owner and members of his family took to the river when they went visiting, traveling by barge—which could mean anything from a canoe hollowed out of a cypress log to a boat rowed by slaves and capable of carrying fifty passengers.

Early travelers in the South complained constantly about the bad roads. Plantation-owners saw no reason to spend money on them since the rivers served well enough. In the early nineteenth century when the turnpike fever was spreading in the North, the coastal gentry of South Carolina blocked a road-building program in that state, contending that two thirds of all market products in South Carolina were "raised within five miles of a navigable stream." Plantation-owners who opposed the Whig leader, Henry Clay of Kentucky, disliked chiefly his program of internal improvements. What need was there for a great system of roads and canals—to be paid for by the Federal government (thus strengthening its power)—when the Savannah and the Tombigbee and the Rappahannock freighted one's products to the sea?

Now that river traffic in the inland South has all but ceased, except on the Tennessee and the Mississippi and a few other streams, it is difficult to imagine how deep into the states this traffic once could penetrate. In Virginia, the Potomac, the Rappahannock, the York, and the

James were navigable to the fall line. North Carolina's Cape Fear River carried ships from the port of Wilmington one hundred and fifteen miles to Fayetteville. Most remarkable of all were the river routes in Georgia and Alabama. Milledgeville and Macon, towns in the center of Georgia, could ship their cotton to Darien on the coast and thence to Savannah by using the Oconee, the Ocmulgee, and the Altamaha rivers. In Alabama, flatboats using the Coosa and Alabama rivers at high water could float cargoes all the way from the northeastern corner of the state to the port of Mobile. In 1702 Mobile Bay had been chosen as the site of the first French colony in the region because of the easy access to the interior which the Alabama and its tributaries provided. In the 1850's, when steamboat transportation in Alabama reached its peak, Selma, one hundred and sixty miles from Mobile, was an important river town. When the Civil War began, Selma became, because of its strategic location on the Alabama, one of the chief supply depots for the Confederate States.

The glory of the river towns has departed. The boatmen—the "Snag," the "Snapping Turtle," and the "Salt River Roarer" (one squint of whose eye would blister a bull's heel)—no longer swarm in the dives at Natchez-under-the-Hill. Indeed, nothing is left of that hell-hole except one silent and respectable street. But the wealth of the new South flows through the old ports, Norfolk, Charleston, Mobile, New Orleans, inbound and outward bound. And the old rivers serve in new ways. At Baton Rouge the Mississippi brings ore boats to the plants that have made this once dormant state capital an industrial city, happily troubled with smog, traffic problems, and labor unions. In Houston local enterprise and Federal funds have transformed Buffalo Bayou, which once produced nothing but floods and alligators, into a fifty-mile ship channel. It brings freighters into the center of the city and makes Houston, so they tell you there, the second port in the United States. Its rival, Dallas, three hundred miles from the Gulf, is dreaming about what it can make the Trinity River do.

Robert Beverley Notes How the First Virginians
Used Their Rivers

When Robert Beverley (?1673–1722) published his History and Present State of Virginia *in London in 1705, he proudly announced on the title-page that it was the work of "a Native and Inhabitant of the Place." Though he was a member of the inner circle of the planters who ruled the colony—William Byrd of Westover was his brother-in-law—Beverley differed from many of his friends in his pride in being a Virginian. He did not look back wistfully to England, as did his brother-in-law, who tried to be an English gentleman while resident in the barbarous New World. Beverley's important* History *was written to correct errors in the section about Virginia prepared for John Old-mixon's* The British Empire in America, *which had been shown him in manuscript. His own account is valued by historians for its accuracy and the first-hand information it contains. Beverley wished the* History *to be widely read (as it was), for he wrote it in a plain but engaging style. As he says in his Preface: "I am an Indian, and don't pretend to be exact in my Language: But I hope the Plainness of my Dress, will give [the reader] the kinder Impressions of my Honesty, which is what I pretend to. Truth desires only to be understood, and never affects the Reputation of being finely equipped. It depends upon its own intrinsick Value, and, like Beauty, is rather conceal'd, than set off, by Ornament."*

The passage printed here is to be found on pages 4–5 of Book II in the 1705 edition.

THE Largeness of the Bay of *Chesapeak* I have mention'd already. From one End of it to the other, there's good Anchorage, and so little Danger of a Wreck, that many Masters, who have never been there before, venture up to the Head of the Bay, upon the slender Knowledge of a common Sailor. But the Experience of one Voyage teaches any Master to go up afterwards, without a Pilot.

Besides this Bay, the Country is water'd with Four great Rivers, *viz.* *James, York, Rappahannock,* and *Patowmeck* Rivers; all which are full of convenient and safe Harbours. There are also abundance of lesser Rivers, many of which are capable of receiving the biggest Merchant-Ships, *viz. Elizabeth* River, *Nansamond, Chickahomony, Pocoson, Pamunky, Mattapony*, (which Two last are the Two upper Branches of *York* River) *North* River, *Eastermost* River, *Corotoman, Wiccocomoco, Pocomoke, Chissenessick, Pungotegue*, and many others: But because they are so well describ'd in the large Maps of *Virginia*, I shall forbear any farther Description of them.

These Rivers are of such Convenience, that, for almost every Half Dozen Miles of their Extent, there's a commodious and safe Road for a whole Fleet; which gives Opportunity to the Masters of Ships, to lie up and down straggling, according as they have made their Acquaintance, riding before that Gentleman's Door where they find the best Reception, or where 'tis most suitable to their Business.

These Rivers are made up, by the Conflux of an infinite Number of Chrystal Springs of cool and pleasant Water, issuing every-where out of the Banks, and Sides of the Valleys. These Springs flow so plentifully, that they make the River Water fresh Fifty, Threescore, and sometimes an Hundred Miles below the Flux and Reflux of the Tides; And sometimes within 30, or 40 Miles of the Bay itself. The Conveniencies of these Springs are so many, they are not to be number'd: I shall therefore content myself to mention that one of supplying the Country every-where, except in the low Lands, with as many Mills as they can find Work for: And some of these send forth such a Glut a Water, that in less than Half a Mile below the Fountain-head, they afford a Stream sufficient to supply a Grist-Mill; of which there are several Instances.

The Flatboat War at Vicksburg

H. S. Fulkerson, the author of Random Recollections of Early Days in Mississippi *(1885), was a Kentuckian who went to Mississippi in 1836 at about the age of twenty and lived in such river towns as Rodney, Port Gibson, Natchez, and Vicksburg. With an amused but affectionate eye he watched the brawling life around him—the riots at Natchez-under-the-Hill, the hangings of gamblers, and the flatboat wars. The*

river life he knew and recorded was a law unto itself, full of the spirit of robust violence which was a part of the frontier South.

After the canoes of the Indians and the early fur-traders, the flat-boats were the first means of transportation on the river. They were nothing more than unwieldy barges loaded with produce from the hinterlands, drifting on the current toward the cities of the South. A long oar was placed on the roof on each side, near the bow. Because of the appearance the oars gave these flatboats, they were commonly called broadhorns. Once at his destination, the flatboatman sold his goods, broke up his boat and sold it for lumber, and then made his way northward, on foot or by horse, to bring another load south the next season.

The flatboats were followed, though not superseded, by the keel-boats—long and slender, so that they would offer little resistance to the current, and sharp fore and aft. They could be propelled by setting-poles and the cordelle or long rope. Steamboat travel on the river began in 1811 with the voyage of the New Orleans *from her building yards in Pittsburgh down the Ohio and Mississippi to New Orleans.*

The following passage is quoted from H. S. Fulkerson: Random Recollections of Early Days in Mississippi (*Vicksburg, Miss.: Vicksburg Printing and Publishing Company; 1885), pp. 97–9.*

At that day, the flatboatman was an important factor in the business of the place as well as its social status. The later comers to our city will be surprised to learn that in those earlier times it was no uncommon thing to see in the Winter months as many as four or five hundred "broad horns" as the flatboats were called, tied up at our landing. They averaged about four men to the boat, giving a transient population of some fifteen hundred to two thousand souls, of this class alone. These flatboats were in active competition with the regular dealers in the city, and no good feeling at the time existed between them.

In the Winter of 1838, when McGinty was Mayor, and Schofney was Chief of Police, this hostility came near culminating in a bloody war between the flatboatmen and citizens. The City Council had levied a tax of $1 per month on all flatboats, which was promptly paid. Subsequently the tax, or wharfage, was raised to $2.00 per day, which was also promptly paid. But this heavy tax failed to run the flatboats off, and at a later meeting of the Council an ordinance was adopted raising the tax to $50.00 per day. At this the flatboatmen rebelled and determined upon resistance by force, if necessary, if enforcement of collection were attempted before adjudication in court could be had.

To this end they armed themselves with the one or more rifles or shot-guns on each boat, and with heavy bludgeons cut from a boat load of hickory hoop-poles lying at the landing. There were four hundred boats at the landing, and in two hours time the sum of $2000 was raised to test the matter in court. But before the proceedings could be instituted the day for enforcement of the new ordinance arrived, when two companies of military, in full uniform, with muskets and fixed bayonets, and a piece of ordnance in front—perhaps the four pounder piece with which Captain Miller "brought to" the suspected boat twenty years afterwards—the whole preceded by the Mayor and Chief of Police, took up the line of march for the levee. A breastwork of cotton bales had been made opposite the wharfboat owned by Hall and Eddie, who were in the rebellion and who had a cannon loaded for the expected conflict. The flatboatmen assembled at the landing with their clubs—the guns being near at hand—mingled freely and fearlessly with the soldiers, and it is said, spiked their cannon. After much quarreling and threatening, and some feeble attempts at casting off the lines of some boats, disgust at the situation suddenly seized the citizens and soldiers, and they "marched up the hill again," concluding it was best to let the courts decide the question. Finally the Circuit Court decided against the city, and my informant, an intelligent gentleman who was an active party on the side of the resisters, says, taxed Guion and Prentiss, the owners of the landing, and for whose benefits the suits were instituted, with the costs. The distinguished lawyer, Joseph Holt, who in later years acquired a national reputation, was attorney for the flatboatmen. And this ended what at one time threatened to be a bloody conflict. The story is related more to illustrate the character of the times and of the people than for any intrinsic merit in it.

An English Scientist Travels by Steamboat
on the Alabama River

Sir Charles Lyell (1797–1875), the foremost English geologist of the nineteenth century, stated in his Life: *"We must preach up travelling as the first, second, and third requisites for a modern geologist." Sir Charles practiced what he "preached up." He was always trying out*

some new mountain or glacier or river. He made two extensive tours in North America, enjoyed himself heartily, and wrote accounts of his travels. The first of these books, Travels in North America *(1845), is less interesting than* A Second Visit to the United States of North America *(2 vols.; London: John Murray; 1849), chiefly because on his second tour Sir Charles spent as much time in talking to all kinds of people and observing their customs as he did in geologizing. On the second trip he also travelled deeper into the South, whose human as well as natural features fascinated him. He was much concerned about the Negro problem. Though he detested slavery and later sided with the North in 1861, he was careful not to be taken in by the lurid tales of abolitionists. As a travel-writer Lyell tells us what later generations always wish to know—what the land looked like, how people lived, talked, made their journeys, brought up their children, and conducted their business affairs.*

The excerpts given here from A Second Visit to the United States *are reprinted from Volume II, pages 45–58.*

Wednesday, Jan. 28. 1846—The steamer Amaranth was lying at the bluff at Montgomery on the Alabama river, and was advertised to sail for Mobile, a navigation of more than 300 miles, at ten o'clock in the morning. From information obtained here, I had determined to follow up my geological inquiries by going next to Tuscaloosa, on the Black Warrior river, about 100 miles distant by land, in a north-westerly direction. Every one agreed, however, that it was better for me to go 800 miles by water, half of it against the stream, instead of taking the direct road; so I determined to go first to Mobile, due south, and then up the Tombecbee to the capital of Alabama, being assured that I should gain, both in time and money, by this great detour. Should I attempt the straight road at this season, no one could ensure my making two miles an hour, so tenaciously does the marlite of the cretaceous formation, when it is wet, hold the carriage wheels which sink into it. . . .

At length we went on board, and, having engaged a good private cabin, made up our minds to read and write there, and consider it as our inn. It was the first of these magnificent southern river boats we had seen, fitted for the two-fold purpose of carrying as many bales of cotton as can be heaped upon them without their sinking, and taking in as many passengers as can enjoy the luxuries which southern manners and a hot climate require, especially spacious cabins, abundance of fresh air, and protection from the heat of the sun. We afterwards saw many larger steam-vessels, and some of them fitted up in finer style, but none which made such an impression on our minds as the Amaranth. A vessel of such dimensions makes a grand appearance in a river so narrow as the Alabama at Montgomery; whereas, if she were a third longer, she would be comparatively insignificant on the Mississippi. The principal cabins run the whole length of the ship on a deck above that on which the machinery is placed, and where the cotton is piled up. This upper deck is chiefly occupied with a handsome saloon, about 200 feet long, the ladies' cabin at one end, opening into it with folding doors. Sofas, rocking-chairs, tables, and a stove are placed in this room, which is lighted by windows from above. On each side of it is a row of sleeping apartments, each communicating by one door with the saloon, while the other leads out to the guard, as they call it, a long balcony or gallery, covered with a shade or verandah, which passes round the whole boat. The second class, or deck passengers, sleep where they can on the lower floor, where, besides the engine and the cotton, there are prodigious heaps of wood, which are devoured with marvelous rapidity by the furnace, and are as often restored at the different landings, a set of negroes being purposely hired for that work.

These steamers, notwithstanding their size, draw very little water, for they are constructed for rivers which rise and fall very rapidly. They cannot quite realise the boast of a western captain, "that he could sail wherever it was damp"; but I was assured that some of them could float in two-foot water. The high-pressure steam escapes into the air, by a succession of explosions alternately from the pipes of the two engines. It is a most unearthly sound, like that of some huge monster gasping for breath; and when they clear the boilers of the sediment collected from the river-water, it is done by a loud and protracted discharge of steam, which reminded us of the frightful noise made by the steam gun exhibited at the Adelaide Gallery in London. Were it not for the power derived from the high-pressure principle, of blowing out from the boilers the deposit collected in them, the muddiness of the American rivers would soon clog the machinery. Every stranger who has heard of fatal accidents by the bursting of boilers believes, the first time he hears this tremendous noise, that it is all over with him, and is surprised to see that his companions evince no alarm. Habit soon reconciled us to the sound; and I was amused afterwards to observe that the wild birds perched on the trees which overhung the river, looked on with indifference while the paddle-wheels were splashing in the water, and the steam-pipes puffing and gasping loud enough to be heard many miles off. . . .

The pilot put into my hands a list of the landings on the Alabama river from Wetumpka to Mobile, no less than 200 of them in a distance of 434 miles. A small part only of these consisted of bluffs, or those points where the high land comes up to the river's edge—in other words, where there is no alluvial plain between the great stream and the higher country. These spots, being the only ones not liable to inundation, and which can therefore serve as inland ports when the river is full, or when the largest boats can sail up and down, are of great importance in the inland navigation of the country. A proprietor whose farm is thus advantageously situated, usually builds a warehouse, not only for storing up for embarkation the produce of his own land, but large enough to take in the cotton of his neighbours. A long and steeply-inclined plane is cut in the high bank, down which one heavy bale after another is made to slide. The negroes show great dexterity in guiding these heavy packages; but occasionally they turn over and over before reaching the deck of the boat, and sometimes, though rarely, run off the course and plunge into the river, where they float till recovered. . . .

When it was growing dusk, and nearly all had retired to their cabins, and some to their beds, we were startled by a loud crash, as if parts of the woodwork of the steamer were giving way over our heads. At the same moment a shower of broken glass came rattling down on the floor of the cabin. As I expected to land in the course of the night at Claiborne, I had not taken off my clothes, so I rushed immediately on deck, and learnt from the captain that there was no danger. I then went down to tell the passengers, especially the women, who were naturally in no small alarm, that all was safe. I found them, in great consternation, crowded together at the door of the ladies' cabin, several mothers with children in their arms. When I returned to see what had happened, a most singular and novel scene presented itself. Crash after crash of broken spars and the ringing of shattered window-glasses were still heard, and the confusion and noise were indescribable. "Don't be alarmed; we have only got among the trees," said the captain. This, I found, was no uncommon occurrence when these enormous vessels are sweeping down at full speed in the flood season. Strange as it may seem, the higher the waters rise the narrower is the river channel. It is true that the adjoining swamps and low lands are inundated far and wide; but the steamers must all pass between two rows of tall trees which adorn the opposite banks, and as the branches of these noble trees stretch half way over the stream, the boat, when the river has risen forty or sixty feet, must steer between them. In the dark, when they are going at the rate of sixteen miles an hour or more, and the bends are numerous, a slight miscalculation carries the woodwork of the great cabin in among the heads of the trees. In this predicament I found the Amaranth when I got on deck. Many a strong bough had pierced right through the cabin-windows on one side, throwing down the lights, and smashing the wooden balustrade and the roof of the long gallery, and tearing the canvas awning from the verandah. The engine had been backed, or its motion reversed, but the steamer, held fast by the trees, was swinging round with the force of the current. A large body of men were plying their axes freely, not only cutting off boughs, but treating with no respect the framework of the cabin itself. I could not help feeling thankful that no branch had obtruded itself into our berths. At length we got off, and the carpenters and glaziers set to work immediately to make repairs.

The evening before this adventure we had been sitting for some hours enjoying the privacy of our own state-room, from the windows of which we had a good view of the river's bank, when at length my wife had thought it polite to visit the ladies' cabin as they might otherwise think her unsociable. She found there a young Irish milliner who had come out from the county of Monaghan, and was settled at Selma, one of the towns on this river, where she said she was getting on extremely well. There was also a cracker family, consisting of a squalling child and its two parents, who were "moving to the Washita river in Louisiana." The young mother was smoking a pipe, which her husband, a rough-looking backwoodsman, had politely lighted for her. As this practice was against the regulations, my wife joined the other ladies in remonstrating, and she immediately went out to smoke in the open air on the guard. I had been before amused by seeing a girl, about nine years old, employed, by way of imitating her elders, in smoking a paper cigar on the deck, and a mother, after suckling an infant of two years, give it some tobacco to chew. . . .

In a Southern steamer abundant opportunities are afforded of witnessing the inconveniences arising out of the singular relation subsisting between the negroes, whether free or slave, and the white race. The succession of breakfasts, dinners, and suppers entailed by it appears endless. In a Northern boat, after the passengers and officers of the ship have dined, the few servants who waited on them have their meal; but here we had five distinct repasts set out, one after the other. First, the cabin passengers dine; then come the white nurses, children, and officers of the ship; thirdly, the deck passengers, being white, answering to our steerage; fourthly, the white waiters, waited upon by coloured men; fifthly, coloured passengers, free or slave, and coloured waiters. It sometimes happens that a free negro who has made a good deal of money is on board; he must wait till all the white aristocracy, including the waiters, are served, and then take his turn with the lowest of the blacks. . . .

In the course of the night we were informed that the Amaranth had reached Claiborne. Here we found a flight of wooden steps, like a ladder, leading up the nearly perpendicular bluff, which was 150 feet high. By the side of these steps was a framework of wood, forming the inclined plane down which the cotton bales were lowered by ropes. Captain Bragdon politely gave his arm to my wife, and two negroes preceded us with blazing torches of pine-wood, throwing their light on the bright shining leaves of several splendid magnolias which covered the steep. We were followed by a long train of negroes, each carrying some article of our baggage. . . .

Sam Clemens Completes His Education
on the Mississippi

Around the Mississippi, its majesty and caprice, the legends of those who explored it, settled near it, poled or sailed their boats upon it, has grown one of the most powerful of American myths. Even the names of the river towns—Hannibal, St. Louis, Cape Girardeau, Cairo, Memphis, Vicksburg, Natchez, Baton Rouge, New Orleans—ring magically in our ears. The poets have helped to elaborate the myth. Hart Crane's Mississippi—

> *Poised wholly on its dream, a mustard glow*
> *Tortured with history, its one will—flow!*

—was felt by T. S. Eliot, in his St. Louis boyhood; its rhythm,

> *present in the nursery bedroom,*
> *In the rank ailanthus of the April dooryard,*
> *In the smell of grapes on the autumn table,*
> *And the evening circle in the winter gaslight.*

But the work that has fixed for succeeding generations the excitement and prodigality of the ante-bellum days on the river is Samuel L. Clemens's Life on the Mississippi, *published in book form in 1883. What Melville did in* Moby-Dick *for the era of whaling, Clemens did for the "flush times of steamboating."*

Young Sam Clemens was in New Orleans in the spring of 1857 when he decided to fulfill the "one permanent ambition" of his childhood comrades in Hannibal: he would become a river pilot. The man who agreed to teach him, for five hundred dollars, was Horace Bixby, pilot of the Paul Jones. *After eighteen months of exacting apprenticeship*

Sam received his license—in September 1858. Not quite twenty-three years old, he was on top of the world. He knew every snag and bank and dead tree and reef in the endless miles between New Orleans and St. Louis. He was a member of one of the most exclusive clubs in America, for the pilots were the princes of the river, more powerful than the steamboat captains, and they commanded princely salaries.

What the great river was like in those halcyon days, Clemens got round to telling in a series of articles, "Old Times on the Mississippi," published in the Atlantic Monthly *in 1875. Seven years later he revisited the river. The old scenes delighted him. He swapped stories in the pilothouse with the new generation of steamboatmen and even took a turn at the wheel. In New Orleans he met his former master, Bixby, now captain of the* City of Baton Rouge. *But his journey into the past was not all pleasure. The old days were going or were gone. The railroads were taking traffic from the river and decay had begun to erode many of the once-thriving river towns.*

From his magazine articles of 1875 and the recorded impressions of his return to the river, Clemens made Life on the Mississippi, *adding prefatory matter on the early history of the river and four new chapters on his experiences as a pilot. The chapter printed here is the tenth: "Completing My Education." The text is that of the first edition (Boston: James R. Osgood & Company; 1883).*

WHOSOEVER has done me the courtesy to read my chapters which have preceded this may possibly wonder that I deal so minutely with piloting as a science. It was the prime purpose of those chapters; and I am not quite done yet. I wish to show, in the most patient and painstaking way, what a wonderful science it is. Ship channels are buoyed and lighted, and therefore it is a comparatively easy undertaking to learn to run them; clear-water rivers, with gravel bottoms, change their channels very gradually, and therefore one needs to learn them but once; but piloting becomes another matter when you apply it to vast streams like the Mississippi and the Missouri, whose alluvial banks cave and change constantly, whose snags are always hunting up new quarters, whose sand-bars are never at rest, whose channels are forever dodging and shirking, and whose obstructions must be confronted in all nights and all weathers without the aid of a single light-house or a single buoy; for there is neither light nor buoy to be found anywhere in all this three or four thousand miles of villainous river.[1] I feel justified in enlarging upon this great science for the reason that I feel sure

---

[1] True at the time referred to; not true now (1882).

no one has ever yet written a paragraph about it who had piloted a steamboat himself, and so had a practical knowledge of the subject. If the theme were hackneyed, I should be obliged to deal gently with the reader; but since it is wholly new, I have felt at liberty to take up a considerable degree of room with it.

When I had learned the name and position of every visible feature of the river; when I had so mastered its shape that I could shut my eyes and trace it from St. Louis to New Orleans; when I had learned to read the face of the water as one would cull the news from the morning paper; and finally, when I had trained my dull memory to treasure up an endless array of soundings and crossing-marks, and keep fast hold of them, I judged that my education was complete; so I got to tilting my cap to the side of my head, and wearing a toothpick in my mouth at the wheel. Mr. Bixby had his eye on these airs. One day he said,—

"What is the height of that bank yonder, at Burgess's?"

"How can I tell, sir? It is three quarters of a mile away."

"Very poor eye—very poor. Take the glass."

I took the glass and presently said,—

"I can't tell. I suppose that that bank is about a foot and a half high."

"Foot and a half! That's a six-foot bank. How high was the bank along here last trip?"

"I don't know; I never noticed."

"You didn't? Well, you must always do it hereafter."

"Why?"

"Because you'll have to know a good many things that it tells you. For one thing, it tells you the stage of the river—tells you whether there's more water or less in the river along here than there was last trip."

"The leads tell me that." I rather thought I had the advantage of him there.

"Yes, but suppose the leads lie? The bank would tell you so, and then you would stir those leadsmen up a bit. There was a ten-foot bank here last trip, and there is only a six-foot bank now. What does that signify?"

"That the river is four feet higher than it was last trip."

"Very good. Is the river rising or falling?"

"Rising."

"No it ain't."

"I guess I am right, sir. Yonder is some driftwood floating down the stream."

"A rise *starts* the driftwood, but then it keeps on floating awhile after the river is done rising. Now the bank will tell you about this. Wait till you come to a place where it shelves a little. Now here; do you see this narrow belt of fine sediment? That was deposited while the water was higher. You see the drift-wood begins to strand, too. The bank helps in other ways. Do you see that stump on the false point?"

"Ay, ay, sir."

"Well, the water is just up to the roots of it. You must make a note of that."

"Why?"

"Because that means that there's seven feet in the chute of 103."

"But 103 is a long way up the river yet."

"That's where the benefit of the bank comes in. There is water enough in 103 *now*, yet there may not be by the time we get there; but the bank will keep us posted all along. You don't run close chutes on a falling river, up-stream, and there are precious few of them that you are allowed to run at all down-stream. There's a law of the United States against it. The river may be rising by the time we get to 103, and in that case we'll run it. We are drawing—how much?"

"Six feet aft,—six and a half forward."

"Well, you do seem to know something."

"But what I particularly want to know is, if I have got to keep up an everlasting measuring of the banks of this river, twelve hundred miles, month in and month out?"

"Of course!"

My emotions were too deep for words for a while. Presently I said,—

"And how about these chutes? Are there many of them?"

"I should say so! I fancy we sha'n't run any of the river this trip as you've ever seen it run before—so to speak. If the river begins to rise again, we'll go up behind bars that you've always seen standing out of the river, high and dry like a roof of a house; we'll cut across low places that you've never noticed at all, right through the middle of bars that cover three hundred acres of river; we'll creep through cracks where you've always thought was solid land; we'll dart through the woods and leave twenty-five miles of river off to one side; we'll see the hind-side of every island between New Orleans and Cairo."

"Then I've got to go to work and learn just as much more river as I already know."

"Just about twice as much more, as near as you can come at it."

"Well, one lives to find out. I think I was a fool when I went into this business."

"Yes, that is true. And you are yet. But you'll not be when you've learned it."

"Ah, I never can learn it!"

"I will see that you *do*."

By and by I ventured again:—

"Have I got to learn all this thing just as I know the rest of the river —shapes and all—and so I can run it at night?"

"Yes. And you've got to have good fair marks from one end of the river to the other, that will help the bank tell you when there is water enough in each of these countless places—like that stump, you know. When the river first begins to rise, you can run half a dozen of the deepest of them; when it rises a foot more you can run another dozen; the next foot will add a couple of dozen, and so on: so you see you have to know your banks and marks to a dead moral certainty, and never get them mixed; for when you start through one of those cracks, there's no backing out again, as there is in the big river; you've got to go through, or stay there six months if you get caught on a falling river. There are about fifty of these cracks which you can't run at all except when the river is brimful and over the banks."

"This new lesson is a cheerful prospect."

"Cheerful enough. And mind what I've just told you; when you start into one of those places you've got to go through. They are too narrow to turn around in, too crooked to back out of, and the shoal water is always *up at the head;* never elsewhere. And the head of them is always likely to be filling up, little by little, so that the marks you reckon their depth by, this season, may not answer for next."

"Learn a new set, then, every year?"

"Exactly. Cramp her up to the bar! What are you standing up through the middle of the river for?"

The next few months showed me strange things. On the same day that we held the conversation above narrated, we met a great rise coming down the river. The whole vast face of the stream was black with drifting dead logs, broken boughs, and great trees that had caved in and been washed away. It required the nicest steering to pick one's way through this rushing raft, even in the day-time, when crossing from point to point; and at night the difficulty was mightily increased; every now and then a huge log, lying deep in the water, would suddenly appear right under our bows, coming head-on; no use to try to avoid it then; we could only stop the engines, and one wheel would walk over that log from one end to the other, keeping up a thundering racket and careening the boat in a way that was very uncomfortable to passengers. Now and then we would hit one of these sunken logs a rattling bang, dead in the centre, with a full head of steam, and it would stun the boat as if she had hit a continent. Sometimes this log would lodge, and stay right across our nose, and back the Mississippi up before it; we would have to do a little crawfishing, then, to get away from the obstruction. We often hit *white* logs, in the dark, for we could not see them until we were right on them, but a black log is a pretty distinct object at night. A white snag is an ugly customer when the daylight is gone.

Of course, on the great rise, down came a swarm of prodigious timber-rafts from the head waters of the Mississippi, coal barges from Pittsburgh, little trading scows from everywhere, and broadhorns from "Posey County," Indiana, freighted with "fruit and furniture" —the usual term for describing it, though in plain English the freight thus aggrandized was hoop-poles and pumpkins. Pilots bore a mortal hatred to these craft; and it was returned with usury. The law required all such helpless traders to keep a light burning, but it was a law that was often broken. All of a sudden, on a murky night, a light would hop up, right under our bows, almost, and an agonized voice, with the backwoods "whang" to it, would wail out:—

"Whar'n the —— you goin' to! Cain't you see nothin', you dash-dashed aig-suckin', sheep-stealin', one-eyed son of a stuffed monkey!"

Then for an instant, as we whistled by, the red glare from our furnaces would reveal the scow and the form of the gesticulating orator, as if under a lightning-flash, and in that instant our firemen and deck-hands would send and receive a tempest of missiles and profanity, one of our wheels would walk off with the crashing fragments of a steering-oar, and down the dead blackness would shut again. And that flat-boatman would be sure to go into New Orleans and sue our boat, swearing stoutly that he had a light burning all the time, when in truth his gang had the lantern down below to sing and lie and drink and gamble by, and no watch on deck. Once, at night, in one of those forest-bordered crevices (behind an island) which steamboatmen intensely describe with the phrase "as dark as the inside of a cow," we should have eaten up a Posey County family, fruit, furniture, and all, but that they happened to be fiddling down below and we just caught the sound of the music in time to sheer off, doing no serious damage, unfortunately, but coming so near it that we had good hopes for a moment. These people brought up their lantern, then, of course; and as we backed and filled to get away, the precious family stood in the light of it—both sexes and various ages—and cursed us till everything turned blue. Once a coal-boatman sent a bullet through our pilot-house when we borrowed a steering-oar of him in a very narrow place.

Why the Tennessee

The following account of how the Tennessee Valley Authority came into existence and the purposes for which it was established is Chapter iii (slightly condensed) of R. L. Duffus's The Valley and its People, A Portrait of TVA *(New York, 1946). The selection is reprinted with the permission of Alfred A. Knopf, Inc.*

WHY the Tennessee? Why not some other river?

In looking for answers to these two questions we come to an interesting fact. There has been controversy as to how and by whom the Tennessee should be developed. There has been no controversy worth mentioning as to whether it ought to be developed. Just to look at the Tennessee made an engineer's fingers tingle. It was there, so handy, falling from such heights, moving so fast and so far, that something had to be done about it.

The Tennessee had been linked with people's lives long before the white man showed up on its banks. It had determined the course of Indian trails and the location of Indian villages. It drew to itself the first white man's trading routes, the early white towns. Traders coming down the mountain valleys from eastern Pennsylvania and across the tall ridges from the Carolinas were bound to hit and follow the Tennessee. It is easier to float downstream with a raft or canoe than to carry a pack through the woods, as every camper knows. We hear a good deal about the famous Wilderness Road, which cut through the mountains just north of the present Tennessee state line. Throngs of people followed that hard route to get into Kentucky or to hit the Cumberland or the Ohio River. Rivers were in their minds, even when they topped the pass and gazed silently westward over the untenanted forest. But some went down the Clinch or another tributary into the Tennessee and up the Ohio or the Cumberland, singing with the current, grunting and swearing when they had to work against it.

The first use of the river, therefore, was as a thoroughfare. The pioneer settlements were often way stations on the rivers: Knoxville, founded in 1786 as White's Fort; Nashville, on the Cumberland, near a French trading post established in the 1690's; Fort Loudoun, on the

Little Tennessee, near the Big Tennessee, first stockaded in 1757; the settlements on the Watauga and Nolichucky rivers, up in the north-eastern hills, just before the Revolution; Memphis, where John Overton set up his trading post in 1794; Chattanooga, junction of trade routes and war trails in Indian times, settled by white people in 1835.

It was the same with smaller towns. They were strung like beads along the watercourses, because it was convenient to be there and often, too, the best land was there. Roads cut across from one river town to another—say, from Knoxville to Nashville, over the Cumberland Plateau. The off-river towns were where such roads crossed or divided, or, later, on the railroad lines. And some of the earliest settlers never got out of the mountains. Maybe their wagons broke down. Maybe they just liked it there.

But the rivers, big and little, pulled hard. They pulled people to their banks. They fascinated them and made them wonder. So much energy going by—what could you do with it?

There were more and more folks around to ask this question. The state of Tennessee alone had 35,691 inhabitants in 1790, at the time of the first census; 105,602 in 1800; 422,823 in 1820; 829,210 in 1840; passed the million mark in 1850, the two million mark in 1900, the three million mark, probably, as these words were being written.

And more and more of these inhabitants and those in adjoining states kept looking at the Tennessee River and thinking about it. The Muscle Shoals stretch of thirty-seven miles, with a drop of one hundred and thirty-four feet, both attracted and annoyed them. It was an obstacle to navigation, and it was more than that. Secretary of War John C. Calhoun recommended in 1824 that a survey be made for a canal around the Shoals. The state of Alabama built the canal, with seventeen locks, and opened it in 1834. It was later enlarged by the Federal Government, under an act passed in 1871.

Congress kept coming back to the Valley. Between 1852 and 1918 it authorized seventeen surveys or projects on the main Tennessee, ten on the tributaries. The river became well known to engineers. It was almost classic in the variety of problems it offered. Down to 1915 nearly ten million dollars (once this was quite a lot of money) had been spent in studying and improving the channel. Mostly this money was wasted. As the Army Corps of Engineers reported in 1916: "It has been impracticable to establish reliable through navigation or even an uninterrupted local navigation extending over any of the reaches."

The Shoals remained, with white water in them when the river was high. The river was high whenever it had rained hard upstream, especially when the mountain snows were also melting. The water went down the Valley, sometimes doing serious harm, swelling the floods of the Ohio and the Mississippi to do more harm below. It came down yellow with mud, with soil that would never raise any more crops in the Tennessee Valley.

Yet this unruly, cantankerous stream drew the eyes of anyone who looked at a map of the eastern United States. Its valley was a link between the industrial North and the agricultural South. It had a strategic relationship with the Southern industrial outposts around Birmingham and Atlanta, just over the divide. It dipped into cotton country in the West. It delivered itself into a highly industrialized river, the Ohio—and the Ohio was in some respects an example of how not to control and use a river.

Electric power came into the picture to make it more complicated. In 1899 a company obtained a charter to build a dam and powerhouse at Muscle Shoals. The charter lapsed. In 1905 President Theodore Roosevelt vetoed a bill to give a similar privilege to another company because it seemed to him that it would benefit "private individuals of the vicinage" at the expense of the taxpayers. He had not arrived at the point where he wished the Government to make the whole investment and reap corresponding benefits, but he did think the river ought to pay its own way. In 1905 private interests made a somewhat more generous offer and were permitted to build a dam and powerhouse at Hales Bar, not far below Chattanooga. This dam had a lock, in case a bargeload of stone or something came along.

This kind of development was not satisfactory. The Tennessee, viewed as an engineering prospect, was small enough, if boldly attacked, to be handled as a whole. It was too big to be taken over as a whole by any private organization. And people were realizing that the piecemeal attack wouldn't do. The National Waterways Commission of 1907 laid it down that "with the increasing unity of our national life and the growing necessity of securing for human needs the maximum beneficial use of the waters of every stream it will become increasingly necessary to treat every stream with all its tributaries as a unit."

The possible uses of the Tennessee River system obviously included the old one of navigation and the new one of electric power. But other elements were getting recognition. The channels kept silting up. Where did the silt come from? Off the land, of course. It came off because mountain slopes were being deforested and because farms were being injudiciously cultivated. The soils of the Tennessee Valley, like those of many other parts of the South, were becoming less productive. Fertilizers, as used, were not enough. Different methods of cultivation, rotation of crops, a change from the old one-crop system —all were indicated.

These problems of land and water, of river and farms, were interrelated. Try to solve one set of them and you ran into another set.

And back of them all was the problem of people—good people somehow falling behind in the struggle for a satisfactory life.

In Europe in 1914 a war began, and it became more and more probable that the United States would be forced to take a hand. Modern war required large quantities of nitrates for explosives just as soil demanded nitrates to remain productive. Chile had a supply of natural nitrates, but in time of war it might not be easy to bring them to the United States. In 1916, therefore, Congress appropriated money to build at Muscle Shoals a dam, a hydraulic powerhouse, some steam-power equipment, and two plants to derive nitrogen from the air by an electrical process already successfully used in Europe. The surveys made during so many years were bearing fruit. The engineers got them out.

Muscle Shoals did not win the war. One of the nitrate plants was a failure from the start. The other was capable of output, but it was obsolescent almost as soon as it was completed. What is now the Wilson Dam, begun in 1917, was not actually ready for operation until 1925. But it had its effect. It kept attention focused on the Tennessee.

From 1921 till 1933 the installations at the Shoals were an object of repeated inquiries, discussions, and negotiations. In 1921 Henry Ford made an offer to buy the nitrate plants, to use them for the manufacture of fertilizer, to complete the Wilson Dam and build another upstream for the Government at Government expense, and to pay off the bills over a course of one hundred years. There was something pathetic in the eagerness with which many American farmers reacted to this proposal. Their wartime prosperity had disappeared. Maybe cheap fertilizers—and they had a naïve faith that Mr. Ford's would be both cheap and good—would bring it back.

But the Ford offer, analyzed in cold blood, did not strike Congress as good enough. Senator George W. Norris of Nebraska, chairman of the Committee on Agriculture and Forestry, had much to do with killing this and similar offers for private operation of the Shoals properties. This was Senator Norris's campaign as much as it was any man's. But he couldn't have won it all by himself. It was not that the tide of opinion in Washington during the presidencies of Harding, Coolidge, and Hoover was running against private enterprise. President Coolidge in 1928 gave a pocket veto to a bill providing for a Government corporation to make fertilizer and sell surplus power at the Shoals. In 1931 President Hoover vetoed a bill to lease the nitrate plants but let the Government produce and sell the electric power. Mr. Hoover said that this step would be "the negation of the ideals upon which our civilization had been based."

Yet President Coolidge's own Muscle Shoals Commission had stated the issue with painful candor:

It is with great reluctance that we turn toward Government operation, being well advised of all the infirmities inherent in such an undertaking. The great investment of the Government at Muscle Shoals, however, the importance of its continued maintenance as a part of our national defense, the crying need of agriculture for more and cheaper fertilizer, and the favorable opportunity for meeting the need, all compel us to disregard our prejudices, for we are convinced that to longer permit this great investment to stand idle when it can be of such great service to our people would be little less than a public calamity.

Senator Norris's committee, reporting in the last year of President Hoover's administration, was even more explicit:

In every bid which has been made it has always been discovered that the proposition had somewhere, very beautifully concealed within itself, a joker which, when exposed, clearly showed that the object of the lease was to get possession of the power facilities at Muscle Shoals, and that the lessee was using the fertilizer proposition only as a blind to gain possession for private profit of the enormous power facilities which exist at Muscle Shoals.

The voice here may have been that of Senator Norris himself. It was not his voice alone. The basic idea of TVA was coming into existence as the result of logical processes which some very conservative men would have avoided if they could—but they couldn't. TVA was to bloom under the New Deal, but it was planted under the Old Deal.

It was no political and partisan invention. It was an American invention. It was an American way of dealing with a problem for which no other suitable solution presented itself. It was as American as an old-fashioned barn-raising.

The Federal Government had intervened in the Tennessee Valley when it built the Wilson Dam and the nitrate plants. There was no other way in which to be sure of getting the desired results. The inexorable force of circumstances required it to intervene again. Three years of depression had added to the sorrows of the South, as of other sections. The intervention had to come in 1933. The particular form it took was determined by the new Roosevelt administration, but in some form it was inevitable. In those years of loss and bewilderment the Tennessee couldn't have been allowed to go undeveloped while idle men looking for work lived along its banks. It would have been like hungry people fenced off from food in a land of plenty.

The Valley had resources. It needed help if it were to benefit by them. TVA's first chairman, Dr. Arthur E. Morgan, testified:

In the fall of 1933 there were counties in the southern highlands with more than fifty per cent of the families on relief. One county had eighty-seven per cent of their families on relief. There are many prosperous communities in that region, but there is also a considerable part of that population that is on the verge of starvation. . . . This is a very desperate economic situation.

The very land was wasting. Seven million out of twenty-six million acres in the Valley were suffering from erosion. In Jefferson County, in east Tennessee, "thirty-five per cent of the land had lost more than one-half of its topsoil, 42.4 per cent had lost two-thirds or more of its topsoil and 2.9 per cent had substantially been destroyed." There was dangerous reliance on one-crop farming of corn, tobacco, or cotton, with the land left exposed between seasons. Floods were causing an average annual loss of $1,780,000. Ninety-eight farms out of a hundred were still without electricity. Taxes were high in proportion to incomes, yet there was not enough money to support good schools, public health services, hospitals, or highways.

Power and fertility going to waste down the rivers, the most ambitious and energetic of the younger generation drifting away from the Valley—that was the picture.

The Valley wasn't sunk in hopeless gloom, to be sure. It was no hell on earth at the end of 1932 any more than it is heaven on earth now. It was lovable and loved. Farming practices had improved. Industries had come in, though some of them paid wages too low for decent living. But there was a restlessness, a sense of loss, a doubt of the future. As Stuart Chase brilliantly demonstrated regarding one Southern county, the region was in danger of insolvency: more was going out than was coming in.

One observer who visited the Valley just before TVA began operations thought there was then a stir of hope mixed with apprehension. People were waiting, they hardly knew what for. They had waited a long time. At the Wilson Dam two generators out of eight installed, out of at least sixteen for which there was room and power, were running. Not all the time, either. A single power company was buying the output. It didn't need it all the time. The Valley in early 1933 was like that.

What Senator Norris called a "twelve years' struggle waged on behalf of the common people against the combined forces of monopoly and human greed" ended suddenly. On April 10, 1933 President Roosevelt suggested to Congress the creation of "a Tennessee Valley Authority—a corporation clothed with the power of government but possessed of the flexibility and initiative of a private enterprise." By May 17 the two Houses had agreed on a bill, and on May 18 the President signed it. . . .

On May 26 the President appointed Dr. Arthur E. Morgan, President of Antioch College, to be chairman of TVA. Besides being an outstanding figure in the educational world, Dr. Morgan had planned and built seventy-five water-control projects, notable among them those of the Miami Conservancy District and the Pueblo Conservancy District, both designed to prevent floods. On June 3 Mr. Roosevelt appointed as the other two members Dr. Harcourt A. Morgan, President of the University of Tennessee, an agricultural specialist with an intimate knowledge of Southern people and problems; and David E. Lilienthal, who had practiced law in Chicago and then become a member of the Wisconsin Public Service Commission.

Flood-control; the land and its uses; the law and practice of public utilities: it looked as though the TVA board had them all under its three hats.

The new directors met and organized on June 16, 1933. Then they went to work.

I V

SOUTHERNERS AT HOME

J UST as the landscape changes constantly in the South, so do the
ways people live. In each state there are variations in folkways
which are directly related to the main geographical regions. In Virginia, for example, the people of tidewater cherish and live by traditions different from those possessed by the Valley people. In South
Carolina the traditional differences between life in the Low Country
and in the upcountry persist. But there are finer distinctions still. In
Mississippi, which suggests to the casual observer three cultural variations, the "human geographer" can discern eight subcultures in which
life descends from the plenty (and even opulence) of the Delta region to the poverty that clings to the worn-out red soil of the Central Hills.

Besides these often minute and always fascinating regional differences in the way life is lived, one encounters nearly everywhere in the
South the endless differences between the ways of the Negroes and of
the white folks. The white Southerner knows less than he thinks he
does about life across the tracks in "darkey-town." For one thing, he
seldom goes there. But his Negro cook or the graduate of Talladega
College who is working as a yard-boy knows the white man's ways.
In days past the Negro had to know even the white man's whims, if
he wished to live in peace.

Though industry is rapidly transforming the face of the South, the
agrarian tradition is strong and will continue to be, in spite of Alcoa
in Baton Rouge and U.S. Rubber in Hogansville, Georgia. There are
other manifestations of this tradition than the pastel colors of the cotton blossoms and the green rice fields of east Texas: the slow mule
teams that raise the blood-pressure of the speeding tourist; the un-
fenced cattle that wander with legal immunity on the highways; the
farm families that shop and visit round in the towns on Saturday night.

To be noticed, also, is the significant fact that the North Carolinian who is transplanted to the city must continue to have his turnip salad cooked with pork. He will send home from far places for a supply of white corn meal ground by the old-fashioned water mill.

In many regions of the South the past is a living force in the present. What Douglas Freeman said of Virginia in this respect applies to all of the older regions, and to some that are acquiring a patina which age has not given them:

> There is a deliberate cult of the past along with typically American business activity. All eastern Virginians are Shintoists under the skin. Genealogy makes history personal in terms of family. Kinship to the eighth degree is usually recognized.

Among Southern "Shintoists" conversation sooner or later gets round to the Confederate War, and Shiloh and Antietam are refought during the rest of the evening. (The Northern guest must remember to apologize for the depravity of the Union troops who carried off millions of silver spoons.) Yet in the "Yankee South," where the gigantic new mills are obliterating the landscape, the sacred names of Lee and Longstreet are as seldom heard as in Bemidji, Minnesota.

There are other reminders of the potency of the past. Southerners have always been churchgoing people and so they are today. If you are a guest in a Southern house you must expect to mend your lax habits and turn out for church on Sunday morning. There seems to be a church on every corner, and it is evident that years ago its congregation worked and saved to make its solid Ruskinian Gothic pile as magnificent as possible. On country roads when you think you have at last spotted the directional sign you need, it is more likely to be an arrow pointing to Mt. Pisgah (Methodist) or Bethel (Baptist) in a grove up the steep hillside.

In no other section of the country can one so quickly move back into the past simply by turning into a particular road or valley. This is why folklorists swarm in the Kentucky mountains and on Ocracoke Island, listening for ballads and weather saws and remnants of seventeenth-century English speech. Often the new or sophisticated has the frontier in its back yard. In the flat pine woods of Florida you will find motel-proprietors who revert to the ways of their ancestors, of Appalachian stock, as soon as the last cars of the season have departed. Within a few minutes' walk of the University of the South (at Sewanee, Tennessee), where the young gentlemen wear Oxford gowns to class in their senior year, you can find mountain cabins whose owners resist the introduction of the privy as an unnecessary luxury.

Partly because of his agrarian past and partly because he can be out of doors so much of the year, the Southerner lives closer to the soil than the Northerner or Westerner does. He likes hunting and fishing and he finds the leisure to indulge in these pastimes. He also has leisure to swap stories or just sit. Throughout the day the squatters on the courthouse steps follow the shade round the building from west to east. Some energy goes into mitigating the hot weather, though not much is required to make a mint julep, and electricity turns the ceiling fan. Eventually the Southerner may be lured indoors from his gallery and garden, for even lower-priced houses in the deep South are now being built with air-conditioning units.

Southern hospitality is a fact. Your host is not the only one who feels obligated to give you a good time. His friends rally to his assistance and you soon find yourself moving in a round of parties, each of which seems to have been planned to do you honor. The spirit of Southern hospitality has never been better expressed than by the Tennessee farmer who, after hearing President Van Buren speak, came up to shake his hand and invited him to "come out and r'ar round with the boys."

The Inhabitants of Lubberland

North Carolinians have not yet forgiven William Byrd (1674–1744) for the witty but undoubtedly exaggerated descriptions of their slovenly ancestors whom he encountered while helping to fix the boundary between the two colonies in 1728 and subsequently wrote about in his History of the Dividing Line. *It is not to be wondered at that Byrd should have been amused by and sometimes contemptuous of the pork-eating settlers on the Line. In his lifetime he increased his landholdings from 26,231 acres to 179,440. He inherited and rebuilt Westover, on the James, the most beautiful of Virginia baronial mansions. His private library is said to have been the largest in the colonies. From 1708 until his death he was a member of Virginia's all-powerful Council of State. Aristocrat though he was, Byrd was a hard worker, as farsighted in his own affairs as he was in the public concerns of his beloved Virginia.*

The dividing line between the two colonies had been the subject of dispute from 1663, when the northern boundary of Carolina was set forth in its charter. As the land under dispute filled up with pioneers, the controversy grew sharper. In 1710 a survey was made which settled nothing. In 1727 the Privy Council gave its sanction to another. Byrd was one of the commissioners appointed for Virginia.

Much to the annoyance of their sobersided colleagues from North Carolina, the Virginia commissioners prepared to carry out their duties in a spirit of gay adventure. From the time the two groups began their work at Currituck Inlet on March 5, 1728 until the job was completed, on the present borders of Stokes County, North Carolina, there was constant dissension. This culminated in the North Carolinians returning home before the survey was carried through the Roanoke region.

Byrd wrote two accounts of the survey: The History of the Dividing Line betwixt Virginia and North Carolina run in the Year of our Lord 1728 *and the more outspoken* The Secret History of the Line. *He published neither account, though it is believed that the first-named was intended for circulation among interested persons.*

The text of these selections from the History *is a modernized version of that printed in* History of the Dividing Line and other Tracts. *From the* Papers of William Byrd, of Westover, in Virginia Esquire *(Richmond, 1866).*

10 MARCH. The Sabbath happened very opportunely to give some ease to our jaded people, who rested religiously from every work, but that of cooking the kettle. We observed very few cornfields in our walks, and those very small, which seemed the stranger to us, because we could see no other tokens of husbandry or improvement. But, upon further inquiry, we were given to understand people only made corn for themselves and not for their stocks, which know very well how to get their own living.

Both cattle and hogs ramble into the neighboring marshes and swamps, where they maintain themselves the whole winter long, and are not fetched home till the spring. Thus these indolent wretches, during one half of the year, lose the advantage of the milk of their cattle, as well as their dung, and many of the poor creatures perish in the mire, into the bargain, by this ill management.

Some, who pique themselves more upon industry than their neighbors, will, now and then, in compliment to their cattle, cut down a tree whose limbs are loaden with the moss aforementioned. The trouble would be too great to climb the tree in order to gather this provender, but the shortest way (which in this country is always counted the best) is to fell it, just like the lazy Indians, who do the same by such trees as bear fruit, and so make one harvest for all. By this bad husbandry milk is so scarce, in the winter season, that were a big-bellied woman to long for it, she would lose her longing. And, in truth, I believe this is often the case, and at the same time a very good reason why so many people in this province are marked with a custard complexion.

The only business here is raising of hogs, which is managed with the least trouble, and affords the diet they are most fond of. The truth of it is, the inhabitants of North Carolina devour so much swine's flesh, that it fills them full of gross humors. For want too of a constant supply of salt, they are commonly obliged to eat it fresh, and that begets the highest taint of scurvy. Thus, whenever a severe cold happens to constitutions thus vitiated, tis apt to improve into the yaws, called there very justly the country-distemper. This has all the symptoms of the pox,[1] with this aggravation, that no preparation of mercury will touch it. First it seizes the throat, next the palate, and lastly shows its spite to the poor nose, of which tis apt in a small time treacherously to undermine the foundation.

This calamity is so common and familiar here, that it ceases to be a scandal, and in the disputes that happen about beauty, the noses have in some companies much ado to carry it. Nay, tis said that once, after three good pork years, a motion had like to have been made in the house of burgesses, that a man with a nose should be incapable of hold-

[1] Syphilis.

ing any place of profit in the province; which extraordinary motion could never have been intended without some hopes of a majority.

11 March. . . . We had encamped so early, that we found time in the evening to walk near half a mile into the woods. There we came upon a family of mulattoes that called themselves free, though by the shyness of the master of the house, who took care to keep least in sight, their freedom seemed a little doubtful. It is certain many slaves shelter themselves in this obscure part of the world, nor will any of their righteous neighbors discover them. On the contrary, they find their account in settling such fugitives on some out-of-the-way corner of their land, to raise stocks for a mean and inconsiderable share, well knowing their condition makes it necessary for them to submit to any terms.

Nor were these worthy borderers content to shelter runaway slaves, but debtors and criminals have often met with the like indulgence. But if the government of North Carolina has encouraged this un-neighborly policy in order to increase their people, it is no more than what ancient Rome did before them, which was made a city of refuge for all debtors and fugitives, and from that wretched beginning grew up in time to be mistress of a great part of the world. And, considering how fortune delights in bringing great things out of small, who knows but Carolina may, one time or other, come to be the seat of some other great empire?

12 March. Everything had been so soaked with the rain, that we were obliged to lie by a good part of the morning and dry them. However, that time was not lost, because it gave the surveyors an opportunity of platting off their work and taking the course of the river. It likewise helped to recruit the spirits of the men, who had been a little harassed with yesterday's march. Notwithstanding all this, we crossed the river before noon, and advanced our line three miles. It was not possible to make more of it, by reason good part of the way was either marsh or pocoson.[2] The line cut two or three plantations, leaving part of them in Virginia, and part of them in Carolina. This was a case that happened frequently, to the great inconvenience of the owners, who were therefore obliged to take out two patents and pay for a new survey in each government.

In the evening we took up our quarters in Mr. Ballance's pasture, a little above the bridge built over Northwest river. There we discharged the two periaugas, which in truth had been very serviceable in transporting us over the many waters in that dirty and difficult part of our business.

Our landlord had a tolerable good house and clean furniture, and yet we could not be tempted to lodge in it. We chose rather to lie

[2] An Algonquian word meaning a tract of swampy ground.

in the open field, for fear of growing too tender. A clear sky, spangled with stars, was our canopy, which being the last thing we saw before we fell asleep, gave us magnificent dreams. The truth of it is, we took so much pleasure in that natural kind of lodging, that I think at the foot of the account mankind are great losers by the luxury of feather beds and warm apartments.

15 March. While the surveyors were thus painfully employed, the commissioners discharged the long score they had with Mr. Wilson, for the men and horses which had been quartered upon him during our expedition to Coratuck. From thence we marched in good order along the east side of the Dismal, and passed the long bridge that lies over the south branch of Elizabeth river. At the end of 18 miles we reached Timothy Ivy's plantation, where we pitched our tent for the first time, and were furnished with everything the place afforded.

We perceived the happy effects of industry in this family, in which every one looked tidy and clean, and carried in their countenances the cheerful marks of plenty. We saw no drones there, which are but too common, alas, in that part of the world. Though, in truth, the distemper of laziness seizes the men oftener much than the women. These last spin, weave and knit, all with their own hands, while their husbands, depending on the bounty of the climate, are slothful in everything but getting of children, and in that only instance make themselves useful members of an infant colony.

There is but little wool in that province, though cotton grows very kindly, and, so far south, is seldom nipped by the frost. The good women mix this with their wool for their outer garments; though, for want of fulling, that kind of manufacture is open and sleazy. Flax likewise thrives there extremely, being perhaps as fine as any in the world, and I question not might, with a little care and pains, be brought to rival that of Egypt; and yet the men are here so intolerable lazy, they seldom take the trouble to propagate it.

16 March. . . . In our journey we remarked that the north side of this great swamp lies higher than either the east or the west, nor were the approaches to it so full of sunken grounds. We passed by no less than two Quaker meeting houses, one of which had an awkward ornament on the west end of it, that seemed to ape a steeple. I must own I expected no such piece of foppery from a sect of so much outside simplicity.

That persuasion prevails much in the lower end of Nansemond county, for want of ministers to pilot the people a decenter way to heaven.

The ill reputation of tobacco planted in those lower parishes makes the clergy unwilling to accept of them, unless it be such whose abil-

74

ities are as mean as their pay.[3] Thus, whether the churches be quite void or but indifferently filled, the Quakers will have an opportunity of gaining proselytes. Tis a wonder no Popish missionaries are sent from Maryland to labor in this neglected vineyard, who we know have zeal enough to traverse sea and land on the meritorious errand of making converts.

Nor is it less strange that some wolf in sheep's clothing arrives not from New England to lead astray a flock that has no shepherd. People uninstructed in any religion are ready to embrace the first that offers. Tis natural for helpless man to adore his Maker in some form or other, and were there any exception to this rule, I should suspect it to be among the Hottentots of the cape of Good Hope and of North Carolina.

17 March. . . . We ordered several men to patrol on the edge of the Dismal, both towards the north and towards the south, and to fire guns at proper distances. This they performed very punctually, but could hear nothing in return, nor gain any sort of intelligence. In the meantime whole flocks of women and children flew hither to stare at us, with as much curiosity as if we had lately landed from Bantam or Morocco.

Some borderers, too, had a great mind to know where the line would come out, being for the most part apprehensive lest their lands should be taken into Virginia. In that case they must have submitted to some sort of order and government; whereas, in North Carolina, every one does what seems best in his own eyes. There were some good women that brought their children to be baptized, but brought no capons along with them to make the solemnity cheerful. In the meantime it was strange that none came to be married in such a multitude, if it had only been for the novelty of having their hands joined by one in holy orders. Yet so it was, that though our chaplain christened above an hundred, he did not marry so much as one couple during the whole expedition. But marriage is reckoned a lay contract in Carolina, as I said before, and a country justice can tie the fatal knot there, as fast as an archbishop.

25 March. . . . In the meantime, we who stayed behind had nothing to do, but to make the best observations we could upon that part of the country. The soil of our landlord's plantation, though none of the best, seemed more fertile than any thereabouts, where the ground is near as sandy as the deserts of Africa, and consequently barren. The road leading from thence to Edenton, being in distance about twenty-seven miles, lies upon a ridge called Sandy ridge, which is so wretchedly poor that it will not bring potatoes.

[3] In the tidewater region ministerial salaries were paid in tobacco.

The pines in this part of the country are of a different species from those that grow in Virginia: their bearded leaves are much longer and their cones much larger. Each cell contains a seed of the size and figure of a black-ey'd pea, which, shedding in November, is very good mast for hogs, and fattens them in a short time.

The smallest of these pines are full of cones, which are eight or nine inches long, and each affords commonly sixty or seventy seeds. This kind of mast has the advantage of all other, by being more constant, and less liable to be nipped by the frost, or eaten by the caterpillars. The trees also abound more with turpentine, and consequently yield more tar, than either the yellow or the white pine; and for the same reason make more durable timber for building. The inhabitants hereabouts pick up knots of lightwood in abundance, which they burn into tar, and then carry it to Norfolk or Nansemond for a market. The tar made in this method is the less valuable, because it is said to burn the cordage, though it is full as good for all other uses, as that made in Sweden and Muscovy.

Surely there is no place in the world where the inhabitants live with less labor than in North Carolina. It approaches nearer to the description of Lubberland than any other, by the great felicity of the climate, the easiness of raising provisions, and the slothfulness of the people.

Indian corn is of so great increase, that a little pains will subsist a very large family with bread, and then they may have meat without any pains at all, by the help of the low grounds, and the great variety of mast that grows on the high land. The men, for their parts, just like the Indians, impose all the work upon the poor women. They make their wives rise out of their beds early in the morning, at the same time that they lie and snore, till the sun has risen one third of his course, and dispersed all the unwholesome damps. Then, after stretching and yawning for half an hour, they light their pipes, and, under the protection of a cloud of smoke, venture out into the open air; though, if it happens to be never so little cold, they quickly return shivering into the chimney corner. When the weather is mild, they stand leaning with both their arms upon the cornfield fence, and gravely consider whether they had best go and take a small heat at the hoe: but generally find reasons to put it off till another time.

Thus they loiter away their lives, like Solomon's sluggard, with their arms across, and at the winding up of the year scarcely have bread to eat.

To speak the truth, 'tis a thorough aversion to labor that makes people file off to North Carolina, where plenty and a warm sun confirm them in their disposition to laziness for their whole lives.

26 March. Since we were like to be confined to this place, till the people returned out of the Dismal, 'twas agreed that our chaplain might

safely take a turn to Edenton, to preach the Gospel to the infidels there, and christen their children. He was accompanied thither by Mr. Little, one of the Carolina commissioners, who, to show his regard for the church, offered to treat him on the road with a fricassee of rum. They fried half a dozen rashers of very fat bacon in a pint of rum, both which being dished up together, served the company at once both for meat and drink.

Most of the rum they get in this country comes from New England, and is so bad and unwholesome, that it is not improperly called "Kill-Devil." It is distilled there from foreign molasses, which, if skillfully managed, yields near gallon for gallon. Their molasses comes from the same country, and has the name of "long sugar" in Carolina, I suppose from the ropiness of it, and serves all the purposes of sugar, both in their eating and drinking.

When they entertain their friends bountifully, they fail not to set before them a capacious bowl of Bombo, so called from the admiral of that name. This is a compound of rum and water in equal parts, made palatable with the said long sugar. As good humor begins to flow, and the bowl to ebb, they take care to replenish it with sheer rum, of which there always is a reserve under the table. But such generous doings happen only when that balsam of life is plenty; for they have often such melancholy times, that neither landgraves nor cassiques can procure one drop for their wives, when they lie in, or are troubled with the colic or vapors. Very few in this country have the industry to plant orchards, which, in a dearth of rum, might supply them with much better liquor.

The truth is, there is one inconvenience that easily discourages lazy people from making this improvement: very often, in autumn, when the apples begin to ripen, they are visited with numerous flights of paroqueets, that bite all the fruit to pieces in a moment, for the sake of the kernels. The havoc they make is sometimes so great, that whole orchards are laid waste in spite of all the noises that can be made, or mawkins that can be dressed up, to fright them away. These ravenous birds visit North Carolina only during the warm season, and so soon as the cold begins to come on, retire back towards the sun. They rarely venture so far north as Virginia, except in a very hot summer, when they visit the most southern parts of it. They are very beautiful; but like some other pretty creatures, are apt to be loud and mischievous.

27 March. Betwixt this and Edenton there are many thuckleberry slashes, which afford a convenient harbor for wolves and foxes. The first of these wild beasts is not so large and fierce as they are in other countries more northerly. He will not attack a man in the keenest of his hunger, but run away from him, as from an animal more mischievous than himself.

The foxes are much bolder, and will sometimes not only make a stand, but likewise assault any one that would balk them of their prey. The inhabitants hereabouts take the trouble to dig abundance of wolf-pits, so deep and perpendicular, that when a wolf is once tempted into them, he can no more scramble out again, than a husband who has taken the leap can scramble out of matrimony.

Most of the houses in this part of the country are log-houses, covered with pine or cypress shingles, three feet long, and one broad. They are hung upon laths with pegs, and their doors too turn upon wooden hinges, and have wooden locks to secure them, so that the building is finished without nails or other iron work. They also set up their pales without any nails at all, and indeed more securely than those that are nailed. There are three rails mortised into the posts, the lowest of which serves as a sill with a groove in the middle, big enough to receive the end of the pales: the middle part of the pale rests against the inside of the next rail, and the top of it is brought forward to the outside of the uppermost. Such wreathing of the pales in and out makes them stand firm, and much harder to unfix than when nailed in the ordinary way.

Within three or four miles of Edenton, the soil appears to be a little more fertile, though it is much cut with slashes, which seem all to have a tendency towards the Dismal.

This town is situated on the north side of Albemarle Sound, which is thereabout five miles over. A dirty slash runs all along the back of it, which in the summer is a foul annoyance, and furnishes abundance of that Carolina plague, mosquitoes. There may be forty or fifty houses, most of them small and built without expense. A citizen here is counted extravagant, if he has ambition enough to aspire to a brick chimney. Justice herself is but indifferently lodged, the courthouse having much of the air of a common tobacco-house. I believe this is the only metropolis in the Christian or Mahometan world, where there is neither church, chapel, mosque, synagogue, or any other place of public worship of any sect or religion whatsoever.

What little devotion there may happen to be is much more private than their vices. The people seem easy without a minister, as long as they are exempted from paying him. Sometimes the Society for propagating the Gospel has had the charity to send over missionaries to this country; but unfortunately the priest has been too lewd for the people, or, which oftener happens, they too lewd for the priest. For these reasons these reverend gentlemen have always left their flocks as arrant heathen as they found them. Thus much however may be said for the inhabitants of Edenton, that not a soul has the least taint of hypocrisy, or superstition, acting very frankly and above-board in all their excesses.

Provisions here are extremely cheap, and extremely good, so that people may live plentifully at trifling expense. Nothing is dear but law, physic, and strong drink, which are all bad in their kind, and the last they get with so much difficulty, that they are never guilty of the sin of suffering it to sour upon their hands. Their vanity generally lies not so much in having a handsome dining room, as a handsome house or office: in this kind of structure they are really extravagant.

They are rarely guilty of flattering or making any court to their governors, but treat them with all the excesses of freedom and familiarity. They are of opinion their rulers would be apt to grow insolent, if they grew rich, and for that reason take care to keep them poorer, and more dependent, if possible, than the saints in New England used to do their governors. They have very little coin, so they are forced to carry on their home traffic with paper money. This is the only cash that will tarry in the country, and for that reason the discount goes on increasing between that and real money, and will do so to the end of the chapter.

15 November. About three miles from our camp we passed Great Creek, and then, after traversing very barren grounds for five miles together, we crossed the Trading Path, and soon after had the pleasure of reaching the uppermost inhabitant. This was a plantation belonging to colonel Mumford, where our men almost burst themselves with potatoes and milk. Yet as great a curiosity as a house was to us foresters, still we chose to lie in the tent, as being much the cleanlier and sweeter lodging.

A Plantation Tutor at Nomini Hall

Philip Vickers Fithian (1747–76) was graduated from the College of New Jersey at Princeton in September 1772 and began to prepare himself for the Presbyterian ministry. In the fall of 1773, on the recommendation of the president of the college, Dr. John Witherspoon, he accepted an appointment as tutor to the children of Mr. Robert Carter III, of Nomini Hall in Virginia. Carter was a grandson of "King" Carter, the richest and most powerful landowner on the Northern Neck. He was himself a man of charm and cultivation as well as an able planter and public servant. Tobacco was the chief product of his

79

*seventy thousand acres, but he had mills and mines and subsidiary plan-
tations producing supplies for Nomini Hall. He was a member of the
Governor's Council and the General Court at Williamsburg, a colonel
of militia, and a vestryman and warden of his church in Cople Parish.
Fithian became much attached to him and to his lovely and intelligent
wife as well as to the boys and girls, eight in all, whom he taught from
October 1773 to October 1774. The ample life of the Virginia planter's
family, so different from that in which he had been brought up in New
Jersey, interested the young man greatly. Most of it pleased him,
though there were points on which he had his reservations: part of the
social life seemed to him frivolous and he was often distressed by
glimpses of the cruelties of slavery. His daily observations during his
year in Virginia Fithian set down in a frank and lively diary from
which the following excerpts are taken. At the end of his year Fithian
left Nomini Hall with regret. He was licensed to preach by the Presbytery of Philadelphia in December 1774, married the following year,
enlisted in 1776 as a chaplain in the Revolutionary forces, and died as
the result of exposure in camp shortly after the Battle of White Plains.*

Colonial Williamsburg, Incorporated, issued the Journal & Letters of
Philip Vickers Fithian, 1773–1774: A Plantation Tutor of the Old
Dominion *in 1943, ably edited by Hunter Dickinson Farish. The ex-
cerpts given here are printed with the kind permission of Colonial
Williamsburg, Incorporated. The notes to the text are those of Mr.
Farish.*

Monday 13 [December 1773]

MR. CARTER is preparing for a Voyage in his Schooner, the Hariot,[1]
to the Eastern Shore in Maryland, for Oysters: there are of the party,
Mr. *Carter*, Captain *Walker* Colonel *Richd Lee*, & Mr. *Lancelot Lee*.
With Sailors to work the vessel—I observe it is a general custom on
Sundays here, with Gentlemen to invite one another home to dine,
after Church; and to consult about, determine their common business,
either before or after Service—It is not the Custom for Gentlemen to
go into Church til Service is beginning, when they enter in a Body,
in the same manner as they come out; I have known the Clerk to come
out and call them in to prayers.—They stay also after the Service is
over, usually as long, sometimes longer, than the Parson was preaching
—Almost every Lady wears a red Cloak; and when they ride out

[1] This schooner had been named for Carter's daughter, Hariot Lucy.

they tye a white handkerchief over their Head and face, so that when I first came into Virginia, I was distress'd whenever I saw a Lady, for I thought She had the Tooth-Ach!—The People are extremely hospitable, and very polite both of which are most certainly universal Characteristics of the Gentlemen in Virginia—some swear bitterly, but the practise seems to be generally disapproved—I have heard that this Country is notorious for Gaming, however this be, I have not seen a Pack of *Cards*, nor a *Die*, since I left home, nor gaming nor Betting of any kind except at the Richmond-Race. Almost every Gentleman of Condition, keeps a Chariot and *Four;* many drive with six horses—I observe that all the Merchants & shopkeepers in the Sphere of my acquaintance and I am told it is the Case through the Province, are young Scotch-Men; Several of whom I know, as *Cunningham, Jennings, Hamilton, Blain;*—And it has been the custom heretofore to have all their Tutors, and Schoolmasters from Scotland, tho' they begin to be willing to employ their own Countrymen—Evening Ben Carter and myself had a long dispute on the practice of fighting—He thinks it best for two persons who have any dispute to go out in good humour & fight manfully, & says they will be sooner and longer friends than to brook and harbour malice—Mr. *Carter* is practising this Evening on the *Guittar* He begins with the *Trumpet Minuet.* He has a good Ear for Music; a vastly delicate Taste: and keeps good Instruments, he has here at Home a *Harpsichord, Forte-Piano, Harmonica,*[2] *Guittar, Violin,* & *German Flutes,* & at Williamsburg, has a good *Organ,* he himself also is indefatigable in the Practice.

Tuesday 18 [*January 1774*]

Mrs. *Carter,* & the young Ladies came Home last Night from the Ball, & brought with them Mrs. *Lane,* they tell us there were upwards of Seventy at the Ball; forty one Ladies; that the company was genteel; & that Colonel *Harry Lee,*[3] from *Dumfries,* & his Son *Harrey* who was with me at College, were also there; Mrs. Carter made this an argument, and it was a strong one indeed, that to-day I must dress & go with her to the Ball—She added also that She Desired my Company in the Evening when she should come Home as it would be late—After considering a while I consented to go, & was dressed—we set away from Mr. Carters at two; Mrs. *Carter* & the young Ladies in the

[2] Carter described the harmonica as "the musical glasses without water, framed into a complete instrument capable of through bass and never out of tune." Quoted in Williams, ed., *Fithian,* p. 59 fn. 1.

[3] Colonel Henry Lee of "Leesylvania."

Chariot, Mrs. Lane in a Chair, & myself on Horsback—As soon as I had handed the Ladies out, I was saluted by Parson *Smith;* I was introduced into a small Room where a number of Gentlemen were playing Cards, (the first game I have seen since I left Home) to lay off my Boots Riding-Coat &c—Next I was directed into the Dining-Room to see Young Mr. *Lee;* He introduced me to his Father—With them I conversed til Dinner, which came in at half after four. The Ladies dined first, when some Good order was preserved; when they rose, each nimblest Fellow dined first—The Dinner was as elegant as could be well expected when so great an Assembly were to be kept for so long a time.—For Drink, there was several sorts of Wine, good Lemon Punch, Toddy, Cyder, Porter &c.—About Seven the Ladies & Gentlemen begun to dance in the Ball-Room—First Minuets one Round; Second Giggs; third Reels; And last of All Country-Dances; tho' they struck several Marches occasionally—The Music was a French-Horn and two Violins—The Ladies were Dressed Gay, and splendid, & when dancing, their Silks & Brocades rustled and trailed behind them!—But all did not join in the Dance for there were parties in Rooms made up, some at Cards; some drinking for Pleasure; some toasting the Sons of america; some singing "Liberty Songs" as they call'd them, in which six, eight, ten or more would put their Heads near together and roar, & for the most part as unharmonious as an affronted—Among the first of these Vociferators was a young Scotch-Man, Mr. *Jack Cunningham;* he was nimis bibendo appotus; noisy, droll, waggish, yet civil in his way & wholly inoffensive—I was solicited to dance by several, Captain Chelton, Colonel Lee, Harry Lee, and others; But George Lee,[4] with great Rudeness as tho' half drunk, asked me why I would come to the Ball & neither dance nor play Cards? I answered him shortly, (for his Impudence moved my resentment) that my Invitation to the Ball would Justify my Presence; & that he was ill qualified to direct my Behaviour who made so indifferent a Figure himself—Parson Smiths, & Parson Gibberns Wives danced, but I saw neither of the Clergymen either dance or game—[5] At Eleven Mrs. Carter call'd upon me to go, I listned with gladness to the summons & with Mrs. Lane in the Chariot we rode Home, the Evening sharp and cold!—I handed the Ladies out, waited on them to a warm Fire, then ran over to my own Room, which was warm and had a good Fire; oh how welcome! Better this than to be at the Ball in some corner nodding, and awaked now & then with a midnight Yell!—In my Room by half after twelve; & exceeding happy that I could break away with Reputation.—

[4] Apparently George Fairfax Lee of "Mount Pleasant."

[5] Parson Giberne was not so fortunate in escaping criticism on other occasions. Fithian, himself, notes his gambling several times, and the Reverend Jonathan Boucher, Landon Carter and Robert Wormeley Carter all comment upon it in their journals.

Fryday 24 [June 1774]

Last night we had a Gust of Rain & Thunder; very acceptable—To Day in course Mr. Christians Dance happens here—He came before Breakfast—Miss *Jenny Washington* came also, & Miss *Priscilla Hale* while we were at Breakfast—Miss Washington is about seventeen; She has not a handsome Face, but is neat in her Dress, of an agreeable Size & well proportioned, & has an easy winning Behaviour; She is not forward to begin a conversation, yet when spoken to She is extremely affable, without assuming any Girlish affectation, or pretending to be overcharg'd with Wit; She has but lately had oppertunity of Instruction in Dancing, yet She moves with propriety when she dances a *Minuet* & without any *Flirts* or vulgar *Capers*, when She dances a *Reel* or *Country-Dance:* She plays well on the Harpsichord, & Spinet; understands the principles of Musick, & therefore performs her Tunes in perfect time, a Neglect of which always makes music intolerable, but it is a fault almost universal among young Ladies in the practice; She sings likewise to her instrument, has a strong, full voice, & a well-judging Ear; but most of the Virginia-Girls think it labour quite sufficient to thump the Keys of a Harpsichord into the air of a tune mechanically, & think it would be Slavery to submit to the Drudgery of acquiring Vocal Music; Her Dress is rich & well-chosen, but not tawdry, nor yet too plain; She appears to Day in a Chintz cotton Gown with an elegant blue Stamp, a Sky-Blue silk Quilt, spotted Apron; Her Hair is a light Brown, it was crap'd up, with two Rolls at each Side, & on the top a small cap of beautiful Gauze and rich Lace, with an artificial Flower interwoven—Her person & carriage at a small distance resembles not a little my much respected *Laura.* But on close examination her Features are something masculine, those of *Laura* are mild and delicate: Mr. *Christien* very politely requested me to open the Dance by stepping a Minuet with this amiable Girl, but I excused myself by assuring Him that I never was taught to Dance.—Miss Hale is about fourteen; a slim, puny silent Virgin; She has black Eyes, & black Hair, a good sett of Eye-Brows, which are esteem'd in Virginia essential to Beauty; She looks innocent of every human Failing, does not speak five Words in a Week, & I dare say from her Carriage that her Modesty is invincible; She is drest in a white Holland Gown, cotton Diaper quilt very fine, a Lawn apron, has her Hair crap'd up, & on it a small Tuft of Ribbon for a Cap She is but just innitiated into the School. and only hobbles yet Once I saw her standing; I rose immeditely and begg'd her to accept my Chair; She answered most kindly, "Sir I thank you." that was all I could extract from this Wonder of the Sex for the two Days she stay'd, & I seemed to have an equal Share too in the Favours of her Conversation; so that I cannot be any way

83

particular in describing the mental faculties of Miss *Hale*. it is sufficient to say that I think She is far removed from most of the foibles of Women—Some time after these came Colonel Lee's [6] Chariot with five young Misses—These five, with Miss Washington & Miss Hale & Miss Nancy Carter, & Bob are Mr. Christiens Compliment of Scholars in this School except Miss Turburville who is just now up the country with an Uncle, where She is to Stay some time together with Miss Corbin. Miss Betsy Lee [7] is about thirteen; a tall slim genteel Girl; She is very far from Miss Hale's taciturnity, yet is by no means disagreeably forward; She dances extremely well, & is just beginning to play the Spinet—She is drest in a neat shell Callico Gown has very light Hair done up with a Feather, & her whole carriage is easy inoffensive, & graceful—The other Miss Lee's are small Towards evening came in George Lee, & Mr. *Grubb*, an English Gentleman; the Company danced after candle-light a Minuet round, three Country Dances, several Reels, when we were Rung to Supper after Supper we Set til twelve drinking loyal Toasts—

Thursday 7 [*July 1774*]

Yes Fanny may sit down to Breakfast—Where's Ben—The Weather is hot & Ben for enjoyment had stript himself naked—Of every thing but his shirt & Trowsers—Where's Ben—He is not very well, Madam,— This Day says the Colonel after having Prefac'd our Breakfast with a —"God bless us in what we are to receive"—is our Rye yonder to be mown down; mown down thinks I, do they mow their Grain in Virginia—Yes two Negroes take naked Sythes & mow down the Grain; others are imploy'd in raking it into heaps, but much of it is left—Shall I help you, Mr. Fithian, to a Dish of Coffee?—I choose a deep Plate, if you please, Ma'am, & Milk—Our Corn, Madam, in Jersey is inferior to yours in this Province—Or your Cooks, Sir, are less Skilful in managing it—Well, Nancy, I have tuned your Guitar; you are to practice to Day with Priscilla, who is to play the Harpsichord, till twelve o Clock; you can repeat the Verses of the Funeral Hymn?—I can Sir— What, Harry, do you hesitate at that Plain Sum in Arithmetical Progression?—*Bob*, attend to your Business—When I am bedizen'd with these clamorous children, sometimes I silently exclaim—Once I was told, now I know I feel how irksome the Pedagoging Scheme is— Fanny—I say, Fanny, dont you hear me, Fanny, and Betsy, sit down —pray, Sir, must I multiply here by 32—Yes, thick-Scull—But Mr.

[6] Colonel Richard Henry Lee of "Chantilly."
[7] This Betsey Lee was perhaps Elizabeth, the daughter of John Lee of Essex County, a nephew of President Thomas Lee.

Fithian, I dont know how to divide by 5½—Look, Sir, do you see what Mouth's *Harry Willis* is making?—I can say my Lesson—Buz, Buz—To divide by 5½ you must double both your Dividend & divide —Half after two we were rung to Dinner; poor *Tasker*, his Fever has continued high since yesterday afternoon, he lies quiet, and asks for nothing—If his Disorder does not abate to night, I shall give him in the morning a dose of "James's Powder"—Will you lend me Jack, he meant my Horse, says Mr. Randolph, to ride tomorrow to Captain Cheltons; Yes Mr. Randolph, I will oblige Jenny so far.

Tuesday 2 [August 1774]

Ben & I drest ourselves pretty early with an intention to Breakfast with Colonel *Tayloe,* but the Servant who went with us was so slow in preparing that we breakfasted before we set out—We arrived at Colonel Tayloe's however by half after nine—The young Ladies we found in the Hall playing the Harpsichord—The morning cool with a fine Breeze from the North for I forgot to mention that about Midnight last Night a violent Gust of Blackness, Rain, & Thunder came on & gave us present Relief from the Scorching Sun; there was no Dust & the riding was pleasant—The Colonel, his Lady, Miss Polly, Miss Kitty, Miss Sally, rode in their Great Coach to the Ferry—Distance about 4 miles—Ben & I on Horseback—From Colonel Tayloe's to this Ferry opposite to Hobbs's Hole the Land is levil & extremely good; Corn here looks very rank is set thick with Ears, & they are high & large, three commonly on a Stalk—Here I saw about an Acre & a half of Flax, which the people were just pulling, exceedingly out of Season —This is the only Flax I have seen since I have been in the Colony; I am told they raise much in the upper Counties—Here too is a great Marsh covered with thick high Reed—The Face of this part of the Country looks fertile, but I apprehend it is far from being healthy— We came to the Bank of the Rappahannock; it is here about 2 Miles over the Shipping on the other Side near the Town lying at Anchor look fine; no large Vessels can haul along the Wharves on account of shoal Water—There were six Ships riding in the Harbour, and a number of Schooners & Smaller Vessels—Indeed, says Mrs. *Tayloe,* Captain Dobby has forgot us. here we have been waiting for a full half hour, shall we take the Ferry Boat Colonel & cross over, & not stand any longer in the burning heat?—I was pleased not a little with the proposal tho' at the same time, I laughed with myself at Mrs. Tayloe's truely Womanish impatience!—At last they are coming—The long-Boat came, well furnished with a large Awning, and rowed with four Oars—We entered the Ship about half after twelve where we were

received by Captain Dobby, with every possible token of welcome—
Since I have been in Virginia, my inclination, & my fixed purpose
before I left home, both of which were very much assisted by a strict
Attention to the instructing my little Charge, these have kept me
pretty constantly, almost wholly, indeed out of that kind of Company
where dissipation & Pleasure have no restraint—This entertainment of
Captain Dobby's elegant indeed, & exceeding agreeable, I consider as
one among a prodigeous throng of more powerful similar Causes, of
the fevers & other Disorders which are common in this Colony, & generally attributed to the Climate which is thought to be noxious & un-
healthy. The Weather here indeed is remarkably variable But taking
away & changing the usual & necessary Time of Rest; Violent Exercise
of the Body & Spirits; with drinking great quanities of variety of
Liquors, these bring on Virginia Fevers—The Beaufort is a Stately
Ship; Captain Dobby had an awning from the Stern over the Quarter
quite to the Mizen-Mast, which made great Room, kept off the Sun, &
yet was open on each Side to give the Air a free passage. At three we
had on Board about 45 Ladies, and about 60 Gentlemen besides the
Ships Crew, & Waiters Servants &c. We are not throng'd at all, & dined
all at twice—I was not able to inform myself, because it seemed improper to interrupt the General pleasure, with making circumstantial
inquiries concerning Individuals, & saying pray, Sir, what young Lady
is that yonder in a Lute-String Gown? She seems genteel; where does
her Father live? Is she a Girl of Family & Breeding? Has She any
Suitors? This when one could not be out of the Inspection of the
Company, would have seemed impertinent so that I did not much enlarge my Acquaintance with the Ladies, which commonly seems pleasing & desirable to me; But I took Notice of Several, & shall record my
remarks—

The Boats were to Start, to use the Language of Jockeys, immediately
after Dinner; A Boat was anchored down the River at a Mile Distance
—Captain *Dobby* and Captain *Benson* steer'd the Boats in the Race—
Captain Benson had 5 Oarsmen; Captain *Dobby* had 6—It was *Ebb-
Tide*—The Betts were small—& chiefly given to the Negroes who
rowed—Captain Benson won the first Race—Captain Purchace offered
to bett ten Dollars that with the same Boat & same Hands, only having
Liberty to put a small Weight in the Stern, he would beat Captain
Benson—He was taken, & came out best only half the Boats Length—
About Sunset we left the Ship, & went all to Hobbs's Hole, where a
Ball was agreed on—This is a small Village, with only a few Stores,
& Shops, it is on a beautiful River, & has I am told commonly six,
eight, & ten Ships loading before it the Crews of which enliven the
Town—Mr. Ritche [8] Merchant; he has great influence over the Peo-

[8] Archibald Ritchie was a prominent merchant of Hobb's Hole.

ple, he has great Wealth; which in these scurvy Times gives Sanction to Power; nay it seems to give countenance to Tyranny—The Ball Room—25 Ladies—40 Gentlemen The Room very long, well-finished, airy & cool, & well-seated—two Fidlers—Mr. *Ritche* stalk'd about the Room—He was Director, & appointed a sturdy two fisted Gentleman to open the Ball with Mrs. *Tayloe*—He danced midling tho'. There were about six or eight married Ladies—At last Miss *Ritche* danced a Minuet with —— She is a tall slim Girl, dances nimble & graceful—She was Ben Carters partner—Poor Girl She has had the third Day Ague for twelve months past, and has it yet She appeared in a blue Silk Gown; her Hair was done up neat without powder, it is very Black & Set her to good Advantage—Soon after her danced Miss *Dolly Edmundson* [9]—A Short pretty Stump of a Girl; She danced well, sung a Song with great applause, seemed to enter into the Spirit of the entertainment—A young Spark seemed to be fond of her; She seemed to be fond of him; they were both fond, & the Company saw it—He was Mr. Ritche's Clerk, a limber, well dress'd, pretty-handsome Chap he was—The insinuating Rogue waited on her home, in close Hugg too, the Moment he left the Ball-Room—Miss *Aphia Fantleroy* danced next, the best Dancer of the whole absolutely—And the finest Girl—Her head tho' was powdered white as Snow, & crap'd in the newest Taste—She is the Copy of the goddess of Modesty—Very handsome; she seemed to be loved by all her Acquaintances and admir'd by every Stranger, Miss *McCall*—Miss *Ford*—Miss *Brokenberry* [10]—*Ball*—Two of the younger Miss *Ritche's*—Miss *Wade*—They danced til half after two. Captain Ritche invited Ben & I, Colonel Tayloe & his Family with him—We got to Bed by three after a Day spent in constant Violent exercise, & drinking an unusual Quantity of Liquor; for my part with Fatigue, Heat, Liquor, Noise, Want of sleep, And the exertion of my Animal spirits, I was almost brought to believe several times that I felt a Fever fixing upon me, attended with every Symptom of the Fall Disorders—

[*The next passage, dated August 12, 1774, is from a detailed letter Fithian wrote his schoolfriend and Princeton classmate John Peck, who was to succeed him as tutor at Nomini Hall. Fithian cautions young Peck about many things. He must not be dismayed by the extravagance of life among the Virginia planters or be annoyed by the distinctions in rank which they observe. He must assert and maintain his proper*

[9] The Edmundsons were a prominent family in Essex County. Thomas Edmundson, whose will was proved in 1759, had a daughter named Dorothy Edmundson.

[10] The Brockenbrough family had been a well-known one in Richmond County since the beginning of the eighteenth century. William Brockenbrough (1715–c. 1778) had married Elizabeth Fauntleroy, whose sister Mary was the wife of Parson Giberne.

place in the family, at a "perfect equidistance between the father & the
eldest son." In his conduct he should be retired and modest and "ab-
stain totally from Women." As things turned out, Peck did very well
for himself in Fithian's post: he later married one of his pupils, Anne
Tasker Carter, and settled in Richmond County, Virginia.]

In this place I think it needful to caution you against hasty & ill
founded prejudices. When you enter among a people, & find that their
manner of living, their *Eating, Drinking, Diversions, Exercise* &c, are
in many respects different from anything you have been accustomed
to, you will be apt to fix your opinion in an instant, & (as some divines
deal with poor Sinners) you will condemn all before you without any
meaning or distinction what seems in your Judgment disagreeable at
first view, when you are smitten with the novelty. You will be making
ten thousand Comparisons. The face of the Country, The *Soil,* the
Buildings, the *Slaves,* the *Tobacco,* the method of spending *Sunday*
among Christians; *Ditto* among the Negroes; the three grand divisions
of time at the Church on Sundays, Viz. before Service giving & receiving letters of business, reading Advertisements, consulting about the
price of Tobacco, Grain &c, & settling either the lineage, Age, or qualities of favourite Horses 2. In the Church at Service, prayrs read
over in haste, a Sermon seldom under & never over twenty minutes,
but always made up of sound morality, or deep studied Metaphysicks.
3. After Service is over three quarters of an hour spent in strolling
round the Church among the Crowd, in which time you will be invited by several different Gentlemen home with them to dinner. The
Balls, the Fish-Feasts, the Dancing-Schools, the Christnings, the Cock
fights, the Horse-Races, the Chariots, the Ladies Masked, for it is a
custom among the Westmorland Ladies whenever they go from home,
to muffle up their heads, & Necks, leaving only a narrow passage for
the Eyes, in Cotton or silk handkerchiefs; I was in distress for them
when I first came into the Colony, for every Woman that I saw
abroad, I looked upon as ill either with the *Mumps* or Tooth-Ach!—I
say, you will be often observing & comparing these things which I
have enumerated, & many more that now escape me, with the manner
of spending Money time & credit at Cohansie: You are young, &, (you
will allow me the Expression) in the morning of Life. But I hope you
have plann'd off, and entered upon the work which is necessary to be
performed in the course of your Day; if not, I think it my duty to
acquaint you, that a combination of the amusements which I have just
now mentioned, being always before your Eyes, & inviting your Com-
pliance will have a strong tendency to keep you doubtful & unsetled,
in your notions of Morality & Religion, or else will fix you in a false &
dangerous habit of *thinking* & *acting,* which must terminate at length

in Sorrow & despair. You are therefore, if you count any thing upon the value of my advice, to fix the plan in which you would spend your life; let this be done with deliberation, Candour, & precission, looking to him for direction, by fervent Prayr, who is the "Wonderful Counsellor"; & when you have done this, let no importunity of whatever kind prevail over you, & cause you to transgress your own Limitations. I have already exceeded the usual bounds of an Epistle. But you will easily pardon a little prolixity, when I assure you it flows from a heart deeply impressed with a sense of the many difficulties which you must encounter, & the dangers which will surround you when you come first out from the peaceful recess of Contemplation, & enter, young and unexperienced, into the tumultuous undiscerning World. I submit these hints to your consideration, & have nothing more than sincere & ardent wishes for your present & perpetual Felicity.

Thursday 25 [August 1774]

Still stormy. The Gentlemen who are sailing up the Bay to the Congress have a disagreeable time—This is a true August Northeaster, as we call it in Cohansie—*Ben* is in a wonderful *Fluster* lest he shall have no company to-morrow at the Dance—But blow high, blow low, he need not be afraid; *Virginians* are of genuine Blood—They will dance or die!—I wrote some of my letter for Mr. *Peck*—The people here pronounce Shower "Sho-er"—And what in New Jersey we call a Vendue here they a "Sale"—All Taverns they call "Ordinary's"— When a Horse is frolicsome & brisk, they, say at once he is "gayly"— she is michievous, they call him, "vicious."—At five, with *Ben.* I rode out for exercise—After a while we arrived at *George-Lee's*—He gave us some excellent Peaches—He returned with us to Mr. Turberville's —We met here with Miss *Betsy Lee*, Mr. *Grubb, Lancelot Lee* & here we spent the evening—*Fish-Feasts*, & *Fillies*, Loud disputes concerning the Excellence of each others Colts—Concerning their Fathers, Mothers (for so they call the Dams) Brothers, Sisters, Uncles, Aunts, Nephews, Nieces, & Cousins to the fourth Degree!—All the Evening Toddy constantly circulating—Supper came in, & at Supper I had a full, broad, sattisfying View of Miss *Sally Panton*—I wanted to hear her converse, but poor Girl any thing She attempted to say was drowned in the more polite & useful Jargon about Dogs & Horses!— For my Part, as I was unwilling to be singular, if I attempted to push in a word, I was seldom heard, & never regarded, & yet they were constantly refering their Cases to me, as to a supposed honest fellow, I suppose because I wear a black Coat, & am generally silent; at Home I am thought to be noisy enough; here I am thought to be silent &

circumspect as a *Spy*—How different the Manners of the People! I try to be as cheerful as I can. & yet I am blamed for being stupid as a Nun—

Thursday 15 [September 1774]

Ben is much better; he has return'd to his Bed in my Room, but complains often of the pain in his Breast.—I put him to begin & read some select odes in Horace—He works arithmetic but is only in Reduction —He dispises Greek, & therefore makes little or no progress in that Language—He is reading in course the Eneid Lib 3—He has an unconquerable Love for Horses; he often tells me that he should have been a skilfull, & useful Groom; that he should be more fond & careful of a favourite Horse than of a *Wife*, or than his *victuals*, or than any thing whatever! I never saw a Person, in any Diversion, Recreation or amusement, who seemed so full of Pleasure & enjoyment as he is when on Horse back, or even in the company of a Horse! He seems to possess as warm a regard for them as Dr. *Swift* had for the Houyhnhnms —But I cannot discover that Ben has so cordial an enmity to Mankind as *Swift* had for the Yahoos.—*Bobs* passion for the same Animal is no less strong, but it is furious, & cruel, he rides excessive hard, & would ride always—*Harry's* Genius seems towards Cocks, & low Betts, much in company with the waiting Boys, &, against my strongest Remonstrances, & frequent severe corrections, he will curse, at times, horribly, & swear fearfully! he always, however, omits it when I am Present.—

The Creoles of New Orleans

One of the most fascinating books produced by the Federal Writers' Project is Gumbo Ya-Ya, A Collection of Louisiana Folk Tales *(1945), from which the following passage is taken. Although the book was a cooperative project to which many writers contributed their work anonymously, one can see throughout the literary skill of two excellent New Orleans novelists who helped to supervise the Louisiana Writers' Project—the late Lyle Saxon and Robert Tallant. The preface to* Gumbo Ya-Ya *notes that in the collecting of materials on Creole life*

much of the work was done by Madame Jeanne Arguedas, Madame Henriette Michinard, Monsieur Pierre Lelong, Caroline Durieux, and Hazel Breaux.

The origin of the proud name of "Creole" has been misunderstood by Americans. The French settlers of Louisiana had been in the region more than sixty years when the Spanish conquerors arrived in 1765. Though hated at first, the Spaniards soon intermarried with the French. They also gave the inhabitants a name to call themselves by. Criollo (corrupted to Criado) was the Spanish word for "children born in the colonies." The French took over the word, kept its signification, and soon changed it to Creole.

The selections from Saxon, Dreyer, and Tallant's Gumbo Ya-Ya are reprinted by permission of and arrangement with Houghton Mifflin Company, the authorized publishers.

"Gumbo Ya-Ya" is a Bayou Country phrase meaning "everybody talks at once."

CREOLES were predominantly French, though much Spanish blood had been absorbed. Some German and Irish settlers also intermarried in the early days, but all the national characteristics of these peoples seem to have completely vanished. They became "so Frenchified," says Gayarré, "that they appear to be of Gallic parentage." German family names were, in many instances, literally translated; Zweig, for instance, became La Branche. An Irish family of O'Briens pronounced their name Obreeong!

All Creole children received a French education. Often the boys were sent to Paris, and the girls were instructed in local convents guided by French nuns. French thought, literature and art impregnated them so deeply that they existed in a completely French culture, their ideas and manners as much imported as their household furnishings, wines, books, clothes and pictures.

No true Creole ever had colored blood. This erroneous belief, still common among Americans in other sections of the country, is probably due to the Creoles' own habit of calling their slaves "Creole slaves" and often simply "Creoles." Too, there are proud light-colored families in New Orleans today who are known as "Creoles" among themselves. But Creoles were always pure white. Any trace of *café au lait* in a family was reason for complete ostracism.

Among themselves Creoles divided into various castes or strata, both socially and financially, though no one seems ever to have agreed as to the category in which his family belonged. There were Creoles,

Chacks, Chacas, Catchoupines, Chacalatas, Bambaras and Bitacaux. The term "Chacalata," for instance, indicated much the same thing as does "Hoosier" or "countrified"; "Bambaras" (untidiness) perhaps hinted at uncleanliness. "Cachumas" were those whose ancestors had acquired a strain of *café noir*, and even today in the Barataria section this term is sometimes heard.

Everything they used or possessed received, like their slaves, the Creole appellation: their cooking, horses, chickens, vegetables and axe-handles. To become acclimated was to be "Creolized."

They were seven to one in the city in 1803, three to one in 1812, only two to one by 1830. But between 1812 and the Civil War they were wealthiest and their influence most dominant.

And this was not entirely confined to New Orleans. Many of the plantations lining both sides of the Mississippi River belonged to them. Far out in western Louisiana, in the land of the Attacapan Indians and the Cajuns, they founded a little town then known as Petit Paris. Here French noblemen, refugees from the Revolution and "Madame Guillotine," tried to recreate the courtly days just past, and Petit Paris was soon a tiny Versailles, the residence of such as Le Baron du Cloyal, Le Chevalier Louis de Blanc and Le Comte Louis de la Houssaye. Later Petit Paris became St. Martinville.

In New Orleans the Creoles were resentful and contemptuous of the American strangers, even considered them wicked. "They do not even attach importance to the Commandment of honoring their fathers and mothers," wrote one shocked Creole lady. "The sons marry to please themselves, and even the daughters do not ask their parents' permission!" For the Creole boy or girl who married one of these "foreigners" there was no forgiveness; they had stepped beyond the pale.

The Creoles refused to speak English. The Americans refused to speak French. Creole boys ran behind Americans in the streets singing this taunting song:

'Méricain coquin	*'Merican rogues*
Billé en naquin	*Dressed in nankeen*
Voleur di pain	*Stole loaves of bread*
Chez Miche D'Aquin!	*From Mr. D'Aquin!*

Monsieur D'Aquin was a well-known baker in the Vieux Carré.

Americans reacted by disliking the Creoles with equal enthusiasm. One wrote home to New England, "Smiles and bows are abundant and cheap and in these they are profuse and liberal, but there is little sterling, honest friendship in existence; and exhibition, outward show and pretensions are the ruling passions!"

Gradually New Orleans became not one city but two, Canal Street splitting them apart, dividing the old Creole city from the "uptown" section, where the Americans were rapidly settling. To cross Canal Street in either direction was to enter another world. Even today these differences are noticeable.

Among themselves, Creoles were warm, affectionate, extremely loyal. *La famille* was the very core of their life, and, like the humbler Cajuns, this extended to the utmost limits of relationship. Cable wrote: "One thing I never knew a Creole to do; he will not utterly go back on the ties of blood, no matter what sort of knots those ties may be. For one reason he is ashamed of his or his father's sins; for another he will tell you he is *all heart*."

Creole gentlemen could only enter certain professions and occupations. Most of them were planters, bankers, brokers in rice, sugar or cotton, occasionally clerks in establishments of these types. Sometimes they ventured into politics. They were barred from entering trade or working in a store or shop. Because of these rigid limitations in their caste system, ambition was often stunted, opportunity ignored. No Creole could do anything that would cause him to work with his hands or to remove his coat. A gentleman never appeared in public without coat, cravat and gloves.

Most family heads had a few *fainéants*—loafers—in their homes who could not—or would not—work. These relatives or old friends must be supported, and usually without complaint. Occasionally a male *fainéant* might be jokingly accused of having *les côtes en long*—vertical ribs; this was the extent of the criticism. Of course there was no way in which any Creole woman could earn money, so spinster *tantes* —aunts—and *cousines* must be "carried on." Many of these more than earned their maintenance, however, in helping to raise the children. Aged relatives and orphans could never be placed in an institution. No Creole was ever guilty of such a thought.

Within the Creole world the father was absolute head of his household and his word was final in all matters. Merely to upset any of his convictions required tremendous skill and subtlety on the part of his wife, combined with every *tante* and *cousine* in *la famille*. But this Creole father was always generous, devoted, kind to a fault, unless some member of his household transgressed one of the rules set down to keep the family free of *scandale;* then his wrath was terrible, sometimes without forgiveness; otherwise he would lavish all he possessed or could earn on his numerous children and perhaps a half-dozen *fainéants*.

The Creole mother, though she might have been a beauty in her day, was nearly always of generous proportions. Creole ladies did not diet, and meals were always sumptuous. She was an excellent housekeeper— economical, hospitable and a devoted mother. Usually she possessed an equal number of social assets, was a skilled dancer, a charming conversationalist, a perfect hostess, and accomplished in all the graces and manners of her world. Deeply religious, she prodded her men toward the Church and saw that the children were trained in all its teachings. She was loyal to her husband until death. Even if she knew he maintained a beautiful quadroon in a separate establishment, no word of the matter ever passed her lips. At her husband's death she invariably manifested great grief, rarely remarried, and always observed strictest mourning in dress and deportment for the required period of several years. . . .

The Creole girl was never left alone with her young man, even after the engagement was announced. Often the entire family remained in the parlor throughout the evening. And when they went out, the future husband must expect plenty of company. It was perfectly proper that as many members of the family accompany them as felt so inclined.

After the formal announcement of the betrothal there was the *déjeuner de fiançailles*—engagement breakfast—which all members of both families attended. The ring, presented to the girl at this event, was not the usual solitaire of today, but a large ruby surrounded by diamonds, in a flat, yellow gold setting.

As the wedding day approached, the future groom presented his bride-to-be with the *corbeille de noce*—wedding basket. This contained several articles of lace—a handkerchief, veil and fan—a Cashmere shawl, gloves and bits of jewelry. None of the jewelry was ever worn before the wedding day, nor could she leave home for three days before the marriage.

Monday and Tuesday were fashionable days for weddings, Saturday and Sunday being considered "common" and Friday "Hangman's Day." The latter was the day for all local executions.

For many years the old Saint Louis Cathedral had a detail of Swiss Guards, who met all wedding and funeral processions and preceded them up the aisle. Behind them, at the wedding, would walk the bride, accompanied by her father. Then came the groom, escorting the bride's mother. Next would be the groom's mother and father, the best man escorting a sister or some other relative of the bride, followed by every brother, sister, aunt, uncle and cousin either of the pair possessed.

The bride's gown was usually of tulle or silk muslin, trimmed with pearls and lace handed down through generations in *la famille*. She wore a short veil, orange blossoms in her hair, carried a bouquet. There were no ring bearers, no matron or maid of honor, nor any floral decorations in the church. The ceremony was always in the evening, as Creoles would have considered it embarrassing to have the couple around all day after a morning marriage. Thus, as the Catholic Church does not permit the celebration of Mass after noon, Creoles were never married at Nuptial Mass. Not until 1910, when the Archbishop issued a decree forbidding Catholics to marry in church after twelve o'clock noon, did marriages at Mass become popular in New Orleans.

The wedding ring, called the alliance ring, was a double ring of gold, which when opened became two interlocking bands revealing the initials of the bride and groom and the date of the wedding. Both parties wore alliance rings. These can still be purchased in New Orleans.

After the ceremony all the relatives signed the register, sometimes as many as fifty. Rice was never thrown, nor did the bride toss her bouquet; it was sent to the church, the cemetery or to the convent where she had been educated.

A great reception always followed. Champagne and a supper were served. The bride and groom mingled for an hour or so, then it was considered decent that they retire. The bride cut her cake, every girl present receiving a piece. This was placed under the pillow at night along with the names of three eligible young men of her acquaintance. The one she dreamed of would be her husband—and she always retired determined to dream.

The Creole newlyweds went on no honeymoon. Usually they remained in the bride's home. After the hour at the reception, the bride was escorted to her room by her mother. Here she was assisted in disrobing and carefully dressed in the hand-embroidered nightgown and négligée made for this great occasion. Her flowing hair was tied back with a ribbon or perhaps adorned with an elaborate boudoir cap. Then she was propped against the pillows in the heavy four-posted bed and left to await her new husband. The Creole bride, often sixteen years old, and unbelievably sheltered until now, must lie there, trembling and frightened at the unknown, gazing up at the pale blue bridal tester above her until the groom appeared. Apparently young Creole grooms were not without their own qualms. One cautiously carried an immense umbrella into the bridal chamber and undressed behind it! . . .

Young Creole men, though also bound by the restrictions of caste, lived in a much broader world than their sisters. Theirs was the privilege of attending the famous quadroon balls, to dance and flirt with beautiful young women, so lightly touched with *café au lait* that a stranger would never have suspected their mixed blood, and eventually to select one as a mistress.

In 1790, New Orleans, a city of eight thousand, had fifteen hundred unmarried women of color. The fairest of these were trained and educated by their mothers and presented each year at the quadroon balls.

These balls were always conducted with great dignity and elegance, and attendance there risked no social stigma. The affairs were gay and lavish, but never vulgar, the young women being quite as well trained and as ladylike as the white belles of the era. Many of them were so fair that they boasted blonde hair and blue eyes.

When a young Creole took a fancy to a particular girl, he approached her mother, gave satisfactory proof of his ability to support her, and a small home was established in the quadroon section of the Vieux Carré. Many a father willingly footed his son's bills for the upkeep of his mistress, for the custom was practically universal. The arrangement usually terminated at the young man's marriage, a financial settlement being made, the girl afterward marrying another quadroon or going into the rooming-house business. Some, however, seem to have continued for life, a genuine attachment having arisen between the Creole and his quadroon sweetheart. Children born of these unions were well cared for, often splendidly educated. The girls often followed in their mother's footsteps. . . .

The Civil War marked the beginning of the end for this Creole world. Very slowly the structure of their culture crumbled.

From the beginning of the coming of the Americans the Creoles were doomed. These Anglo-Saxons were too aggressive, too practical. Everywhere they rose to ascendancy, in politics, in business and in trade. Every year the leading places in commerce, banking, planting and the professions were taken over by the newcomers. Unlike the Creoles, they were not ashamed to soil their hands. They did not have the Creole's secret contempt for hard work. They almost made a fetish of it.

Even the French language began to lose popularity. For a long time generations were bilingual, speaking one tongue at home, another outside. In the new public schools Creole children were Americanized, eventually refused even to speak French because the others taunted them with the appellation of "Kis-kee-dee!" when they did so.

Through the years Creole jealousy of the Americans continued to be bitter. They held themselves aloof, refusing to mix with the strangers. But as the American city grew larger, swiftly passed the old town in size, it became very evident that these "foreigners" were faring quite well without their aid. They saw it was a choice between acquiescence or complete commercial domination. In one matter, however, the Creoles remained the masters for many years; they set the standard for and exercised control over everything related to social life.

As long ago as 1892 a certain Creole gentleman, famous for his impeccable attire, his erect carriage, his monocle, his evening strolls along Esplanade Avenue, bemoaned the passing of the old ways of life. Each sunset he would appear on the Esplanade, bowing to ladies of his acquaintance with a lordly flourish, tipping his top hat to men. He constantly regaled friends with nostalgic tales of the *bon vieux temps*, as compared to what he considered the vulgar and *parvenu* customs and manners of this later period. He told of days when a gentleman never crossed his legs in a drawing-room; when a lady had no legs at all, but floated mysteriously on the hems of her skirts, wore steel corsets and a daring décolleté; when a gentleman did not ask a lady's permission to smoke—no lady could refuse, and the odor of tobacco was obnoxious to all females!—and would have died before he did so in her presence; when cocktails were unknown; when gentlemen supported their dancing partners with the lightest touch of the back of their white-gloved hands at their waists; when to appear at a social affair in an intoxicated condition meant certain and permanent ostracism, and when the telling of a risqué joke in the presence of a woman was equivalent to inviting one's self to a duel. He particularly deplored the passing of dueling, which custom, he averred firmly, "held down murders, preserved good manners, upheld the sanctity of woman and safeguarded the sacredness of the home!"

But little by little the majority of the Creoles became poorer. Their fine homes had to go. Family records were lost or destroyed, heirlooms, precious and treasured for generations, were sold as desperation drove these gentle people, scarcely capable of earning their livelihoods, to antique dealers and the Americans. The past began to be a thin memory in the minds of very old people.

Striving to maintain their independent culture, the Creoles organized a Creole Association as late as 1886. Bitterly attacked by outsiders as an exclusive organization, Charles A. Villeré, himself of a distinguished Creole family, vigorously denied this, saying their aim was to aid the state as a whole, to assist in the spread of education and the growth of the culture of all its peoples. In his speech at the first meeting of the Association he said, in part, "We are battling for our rights; we are scoffed at, ridiculed, blackened, tortured, deformed, caricatured. . . . This is our soil."

But the life of the Creole Association was short. Internal differences ensued, and it quickly passed out of existence.

Most of the old ways are gone now, though tangible evidences of the splendid past are not difficult to find. There are the old houses in the Vieux Carré, with balconies of wrought iron like fine lace and winding stairs and tinkling crystal chandeliers and dreamy patios. There still remains the Saint Louis Cathedral where Creoles knelt in prayer, with its rear garden where rapiers flashed in moonlight and in sunlight, until the flow of Creole blood appeased the tempestuous heat of Creole anger. And the convent in Orleans Street, where the warm laughter and gay music of the past has been displaced by the mystic silence of the *religieuse*. These things remain.

A Southern Lady Endures the Shock of War

Of the many diaries kept (and later published) by Southern ladies during the Civil War, that of Mrs. Judith Brockenbrough McGuire stands out by virtue of its being so completely in character. As Douglas Southall Freeman said of it in The South to Posterity, *it "was not one of those spuriously confidential documents written with an eye to subsequent publication. In its naturalness and informality, it is a perfect picture of the mind of the high-bred, religious Southern woman of middle life. The gentility it displays without a single self-conscious touch, the faith it exemplifies, and the light it throws on the hopes and fears of the South make it as interesting psychologically as it is historically."*

Mrs. McGuire was forty-eight when the Federal invaders moved on Alexandria, where her husband was principal of the Episcopal High School. Forced to flee at once, she moved down through Virginia and settled finally in Richmond, where she watched with extraordinary keenness all the events in the war capital from the inauguration of Jefferson Davis to the capture of the city and the fire that destroyed much of it.

The Diary of a Southern Refugee during the War, by a Lady of Virginia *was published in New York (E. J. Hale & Son) in 1867.*

February 23, 1862

Notwithstanding the violence of the rain yesterday, the Capitol Square, the streets around it, and the adjacent houses, were crowded. The President stood at the base of that noble equestrian statue of Washington, and took the oath which was taken by the "Father of his Country" more than seventy years ago—just after the "great rebellion," in the success of which we all, from Massachusetts to Georgia, so heartily gloried. No wonder that he spoke as if he were inspired. Was it not enough to inspire him to have the drawn sword of Washington, unsheathed in defence of his invaded country, immediately over his head, while the other hand of his great prototype points encouragingly to the South? Had he not the life-like representations of Jefferson, George Mason, and, above all, of Patrick Henry, by his side? The latter with his scroll in his outstretched hand, his countenance beaming, his lips almost parted, and seeming on the point of bursting into one blaze of eloquence in defence of his native South. How could Southern tongues remain quiet, or Southern hearts but burn within us, when we beheld our heroes, living and dead, surrounding and holding up the hands of our great chief? By him stood his cabinet, composed of the talent and the patriotism of the land; then was heard the voice of our beloved Assistant Bishop, in tones of fervid eloquence, beseeching the blessings of Heaven on our great undertaking. I would that every young man, from the Potomac to the Rio Grande, could have witnessed the scene.

Last night was the first levee. The rooms were crowded. The president looked weary and grave, but was all suavity and cordiality, and Mrs. Davis won all hearts by her usual unpretending kindness. I feel proud to have those dear old rooms, arousing as they do so many associations of my childhood and youth, filled with the great, the noble, the *fair* of our land, every heart beating in unison, with one great object in view, and no wish beyond its accomplishment, as far as this world is concerned. But to-day is Saturday, and I must go to the hospital to take care of our sick—particularly to nurse our little soldier-boy. Poor child, he is very ill!

June 14, 1862

While quietly sitting on the porch yesterday evening, I saw a young man rapidly approaching the house, on foot; at first we took it for granted that he was a Yankee, but soon found from his dress that he was one of our soldiers, and from his excited manner that there was something unusual the matter. He was Lieutenant Latané, of Stuart's Brigade. They had been fighting on the road from Hanover Court-House to the Old Church, and his brother, the captain of the Essex Troop, had been killed about two miles from W. The mill-cart from W. soon after passed along, and he put his brother's body into it, and brought it to W. There he found a Yankee picket stationed. C. immediately took the dead soldier into her care, promising to bury him as tenderly as if he were her brother; and having no horse left on the place, (the enemy had taken them all,) sent him here, by a private way, to elude the vigilance of the picket, to get M's only remaining horse—for the poor fellow had given up his to a soldier whose horse had been killed. The horse was soon ready, and as soon as we saw him safely off, we went over to W. to assist in preparing the body for the burial. Oh, what a sad office! This dear young soldier, so precious to many hearts, now in the hands of sorrowing, sympathizing friends, yet, personally, strangers to him! He looked so young—not more than twenty years of age. He was shot in four places; one ball had entered the region of his heart and passed out at the back. We cut a large lock of his hair, as the only thing we could do for his mother. We have sent for Mr. Carraway to perform the funeral services, and shall bury him by our dear Willie Phelps, another victim to this unholy war.

June 15, 1862

Yesterday was the only day for three weeks that we have been free from the hated presence of Yankees. Aaron, whom we sent for Mr. C., was not allowed to pass the picket-post, so we took the body of our poor young captain and buried it ourselves in the S. H. grave-yard, with no one to interrupt us. The girls covered his honoured grave with flowers. He and our precious W. lie side by side, martyrs to a holy cause.

July 4, 1862

A beautiful, glorious day, and one which the Yankees expected confidently to spend triumphantly in Richmond. Last Fourth of July old General Scott expected to be there, to tread in triumph the fallen fortunes of his quondam friends, and to-day McClellan has been obliged to yield his visions of glory. "Man proposes, but God disposes." Many of their companions in arms are there, in the Libby and other prisons, wounded in the hospitals, and dead in the swamps and marshes, or buried on the battle-fields while the "Grand Army" and the "Young Napoleon" are struggling desperately to get out of the bogs of the Chickahominy to his gunboats on James River. I sent the carriage to Richmond a day or two ago for Mr. N., but he writes that he is sending it backwards and forwards to the battlefields for the wounded. It is a season of wide-spread distress; parties are going by constantly to seek their husbands, brothers, sons, about whose fate they are uncertain. Some old gentlemen passed yesterday, *walking* all the way from Lancaster County. All the boats and bridges have been destroyed on the rivers, and conveyances can't be put across. Ladies are sent from river to river by those persons who have conveyances and horses left to them. Oh, I trust that blood enough has been spilled now! Dr. S. has just arrived; he has been twenty miles below Richmond. He says the Yankee dead still lie unburied in many places—our men are too much worn out to undertake to bury them. The Yankee hospitals, as well as our own, are all along the roads; their hospital flag is red; ours is orange. They have their own surgeons, and, of course, many delicacies that our men can't have. The Northern papers speak of this retreat of McClellan's as a "strategic movement." The bloody fights of eight days, the retreat of thirty miles, attended by immense loss of life, thousands of prisoners, many guns, stores of all kinds, etc., a "strategic movement!" But our loss is heavy—so many valuable lives, and such suffering among the wounded. O God! interpose and stop this cruel war!

March 5, 1863

Again I have applied for an office, which seems necessary to the support of the family. If I fail, I shall try to think that it is not right for me to have it. Mr. —'s salary is not much more than is necessary to pay our share of the expenses of the mess. Several of us are engaged in making soap, and selling it, to buy things which seem essential to our wardrobes. A lady who has been perfectly independent in her circumstances, finding it necessary to do something of the kind for her support, has been very successful in making pickles and catsups for the restaurants. Another, like Mrs. Primrose, rejoices in her success in making gooseberry wine, which sparkles like champagne, and is the best domestic wine I ever drank; this is designed for the highest bidder. The exercise of this kind of industry works two ways: it supplies our wants, and gives comfort to the public. Almost every girl plaits her own hat, and that of her father, brother, and lover, if she has the bad taste to have a lover out of the army, which no girl of spirit would do unless he is incapacitated by sickness or wounds. But these hats are beautifully plaited of rye straw, and the ladies' hats are shaped so becomingly, that though a Parisian milliner might pronounce them old-fashioned, and laugh them to scorn, yet our Confederate girls look fresh and lovely in them, with their gentle countenances and bright enthusiastic eyes; and what do we care for Parisian style, particularly as it would have to come to us through Yankeeland? The blockade has taught our people their own resources; but I often think that when the great veil is removed, and reveals us to the world, we will, in some respects, be a precious set of antiques. . . . A gentleman, lately from

101

Columbia, tells me that the South Carolina girls pride themselves on their palmetto hats; and the belle of large fortune, who used to think no bonnet presentable but one made by the first New York or Parisian milliner, now glories in her palmetto. The balmoral, too, the product of our own spinning-wheel and loom, would show well with the prettiest imported ones. I have seen several, which the young wearers told me were "dyed in the wool, spun, and woven by the *poor* of our own neighbourhood. The dye-stuffs were from our own woods." These are little things, but, proving the independence of our people, I rejoice in them. The croakers are now indulging themselves with fears of famine; they elongate their gloomy visages, and tell us, in sad accents, that butter was $3.50 per pound in market this morning, and other things in proportion. I am sorry to say that it is true, and that it is evident we must have scarcity, particularly of such things as butter, for the cattle must go to feed the army. The soldiers must be fed; our gardens will give us vegetables; God will give us the fruits of the earth abundantly, as in days past, and if we are reduced, which I do not anticipate, to bread and water, we will bear it cheerfully, thank God, and take courage:

> "Brought safely by his hand thus far,
> Why should we now give place to fear?"

The *poor*, being well supplied with Government work, are better off than usual.

April 3, 1865

Yesterday morning (it seems a week ago) we went, as usual, to St. James's Church, hoping for a day of peace and quietness, as well as of religious improvement and enjoyment. How shortsighted we are, and how little do we know of what is coming, either of judgment or mercy! The sermon being over, as it was the first Sunday in the month, the sacrament of the Lord's Supper was administered. The day was bright, beautiful, and peaceful, and a general quietness and repose seemed to rest upon the congregation, undisturbed by rumours and apprehensions. While the sacred elements were being administered, the sexton came in with a note to General Cooper, which was handed him as he walked from the chancel, and he immediately left the church. It made me anxious; but such things are not uncommon, and caused no excitement in the congregation. The services being over, we left the church, and as the congregations from the various churches were being mingled on Grace Street, our children, who had been at St. Paul's, joined us, on their way to the usual family gathering in our room on Sunday. After the salutations of the morning, J. remarked, in an agitated voice, to his father, that he had just returned from the War Department, and that there was sad news—General Lee's lines had been broken, and the city would probably be evacuated within twenty-four hours. Not until then did I observe that every countenance was wild with excitement. The inquiry, "What is the matter?" ran from lip to lip. Nobody seemed to hear or to answer. An old friend ran across the street, pale with excitement, repeating what J. had just told us, that unless we heard better news from General Lee the city would be evacuated. We could do nothing; no one suggested any thing to be done. We reached home with a strange, unrealizing feeling. In an hour J. (who is now Professor of Mathematics in the Naval School) received orders to accompany Captain Parker to the South with the Corps of Midshipmen. Then we began to understand that the Government was moving, and that the evacuation was indeed going on. The office-holders were now making arrangements to get off. Every car was ordered to be ready to take them south. Baggage-wagons, carts, drays, and ambulances were driving about the streets; every one was going off that could go, and now there were all the indications of alarm and excitement of every kind which could attend such an awful scene. The people were rushing up and down the streets, vehicles of all kinds were flying along, bearing goods of all sorts and people of all ages and classes who could go beyond the corporation lines. We tried to keep ourselves quiet. We could not go south, nor could we leave the city at all in this hurried way. J. and his wife had gone. The "Colonel," with B., intended going in the northern train this morning—he to his home in Hanover County, and she to her father's house in Clarke County, as soon as she could get there. Last night, when we went out to hire a servant to go to Camp Jackson for our sister, we for the first time realized that our money was worthless here, and that we are in fact penniless. About midnight she walked in, escorted by two of the convalescent soldiers. Poor fellows! all the soldiers will go who can, but the sick and wounded must be captured. We collected in one room, and tried to comfort one another; we made large pockets and filled them with as many of our valuables as we could suspend from our waists. The gentlemen walked down to the War Office in the night to see what was going on. Alas! every sight and sound was grievous and heavy.

A telegram just received from General Lee hastened the evacuation. The public offices were all forsaken. They said that by three o'clock in the morning the work must be completed, and the city ready for the enemy to take possession. Oh, who shall tell the horror of the past night! Hope seemed to fade; none but despairing words were heard, except from a few brave hearts. Union men began to show themselves;

treason walked abroad. A gloomy pall seemed to hang over us, but I do not think that any of us felt keenly, or have yet realized our overwhelming calamity. The suddenness and extent of it is too great for us to feel its poignancy at once. About two o'clock in the morning we were startled by a loud sound like thunder; the house shook and the windows rattled; it seemed like an earthquake in our midst. We knew not what it was, nor did we care. It was soon understood to be the blowing up of a magazine below the city. In a few hours another exploded on the outskirts of the city, much louder than the first, and shivering innumerable plate-glass windows all over Shockoe Hill. It was then daylight, and we were standing out upon the pavement. The Colonel and B. had just gone. Shall we ever meet again? Many ladies were now upon the streets. The lower part of the city was burning. About seven o'clock I set off to go to the central depot to see if the cars would go out. As I went from Franklin to Broad Street, and on Broad, the pavements were covered with broken glass; women, both white and coloured, were walking in multitudes from the Commissary offices and burning stores with bags of flour, meal, coffee, sugar, rolls of cotton cloth, etc.; coloured men were rolling wheelbarrows filled in the same way. I went on and on towards the depot, and as I proceeded shouts and screams became louder. The rabble rushed by me in one stream. At last I exclaimed, "Who are those shouting? What is the matter?" I seemed to be answered by a hundred voices, "The Yankees have come." I turned to come home, but what was my horror, when I reached Ninth Street, to see a regiment of Yankee cavalry come dashing up, yelling, shouting, hallooing, screaming! All Bedlam let loose could not have vied with them in diabolical roarings. I stood riveted to the spot; I could not move nor speak. Then I saw the iron gates of our time-honoured and beautiful Capitol Square, on the walks and greensward of which no hoof had been allowed to tread, thrown open and the cavalry dash in. I could see no more; I must go on with a mighty effort, or faint where I stood. I came home amid what I thought was the firing of cannon. I thought that they were thundering forth a salute that they had reached the goal of their ardent desires; but I afterwards found that the Armory was on fire, and that the flames having reached the shells deposited there for our army, they were exploding. These explosions were kept up until a late hour this evening; I am rejoiced they are gone; they, at least, can never be turned against us. I found the family collected around the breakfast-table, and was glad to see Captain M's family with them. The captain has gone, and the ladies have left their home on "Union Hill" to stay here among friends, Colonel P. having kindly given them rooms. An hour or two after breakfast we all retired to our rooms exhausted. No one had slept; no one had sought repose or thought of their own comfort. The Federal

soldiers were roaming about the streets; either whiskey or the excess of
joy had given some of them the appearance of being beside themselves.
We had hoped that very little whiskey would be found in the city, as,
by order of the Mayor, casks were emptied yesterday evening in the
streets, and it flowed like water through the gutters; but the rabble had
managed to find it secreted in the burning shops, and bore it away in
pitchers and buckets. It soon became evident that protection would be
necessary for the residences, and at the request of Colonel P. I went to
the Provost Marshal's office to ask for it. Mrs. P. was unfortunately in
the country, and only ladies were allowed to apply for guards. Of
course this was a very unpleasant duty, but I must undertake it. Mrs.
D. agreed to accompany me, and we proceeded to the City Hall—the
City Hall, which from my childhood I had regarded with respect and
reverence, as the place where my father had for years held his courts,
and in which our lawyers, whose names stand among the highest in the
Temple of Fame, for fifty years expounded the Constitution and the
laws, which must now be trodden under foot. We reached it. After
passing through crowds of negro soldiers there, we found on the steps
some of the elderly gentlemen of the city seeking admittance, which
was denied them. I stopped to speak to Mr. ——, in whose commission
house I was two days ago, and saw him surrounded by all the stores
which usually make up the establishment of such a merchant; it was
now a mass of blackened ruins. He had come to ask protection for his
residence, but was not allowed to enter. We passed the sentinel, and an
officer escorted us to the room in which we were to ask our country's
foe to allow us to remain undisturbed in our own houses. Mrs. D. leant
on me tremblingly; she shrank from the humiliating duty. For my own
part, though my heart beat loudly and my blood boiled, I never felt
more high-spirited or lofty than at that moment. A large table was surrounded by officials, writing or talking to the ladies, who came on the
same mission that brought us. I approached the officer who sat at the
head of the table, and asked him politely if he was the Provost Marshal.
"I am the Commandant, madam," was the respectful reply. "Then to
whom am I to apply for protection for our residence?" "You need
none, madam; our troops are perfectly disciplined, and dare not enter
your premises." "I am sorry to be obliged to undeceive you, sir, but
when I left home seven of your soldiers were in the yard of the residence opposite to us, and one has already been into our kitchen." He
looked surprised, and said, "Then, madam, you are entitled to a guard.
Captain, write a protection for the residence on the corner of First and
Franklin Streets, and give these ladies a guard." This was quickly done,
and as I turned to go out, I saw standing near me our old friend, Mrs.
——. Oh! how my heart sank when I looked into her calm, sad face,
and remembered that she and her venerable and highly esteemed hus-

105

band must ask leave to remain in peace in their home of many years. The next person who attracted my attention was that sweet young girl, S. W. Having no mother, she of course must go and ask that her father's beautiful mansion may be allowed to stand uninjured. Tears rolled down her cheeks as she pressed my hand in passing. Other friends were there; we did not speak, we could not; we sadly looked at each other and passed on. Mrs. D. and myself came out, accompanied by our guard. The fire was progressing rapidly, and the crashing sound of falling timbers was distinctly heard. Dr. Read's church was blazing. Yankees, citizens, and negroes were attempting to arrest the flames. The War Department was falling in; burning papers were being wafted about the streets. The Commissary Department, with our desks and papers, was consumed already. Warwick & Barksdale's mill was sending its flames to the sky. Cary and Main Streets seemed doomed throughout; Bank Street was beginning to burn, and now it had reached Franklin. At any other moment it would have distracted me, but I had ceased to feel anything. We brought our guard to Colonel P., who posted him; about three o'clock he came to tell me that the guard was drunk, and threatening to shoot the servants in the yard. Again I went to the City Hall to procure another. I approached the Commandant and told him why I came. He immediately ordered another guard, and a corporal to be sent for the arrest of the drunken man. The flames had decreased, but the business part of the city was in ruins. The second guard was soon posted, and the first carried off by the collar. Almost every house is guarded; and the streets are now (ten o'clock) perfectly quiet. The moon is shining brightly on our captivity. God guide and watch over us!

The Pinch of Necessity

Although Paul Barringer was a small boy of four when the Civil War came, he remembered vividly the "pinch of necessity" which it inflicted on families like his, in western North Carolina, and what older folks recalled, later on, of those stringent days.

Miss Anna Barringer found it difficult to persuade her father, distinguished medical professor at the University of Virginia, "that his life could contain any element of interest to anyone." It is fortunate that

she did prevail on him to write The Natural Bent, the Memoirs of Dr.
Paul B. Barringer. *Otherwise we should have lost his recollections of
life in North Carolina and Virginia after the war. The* Memoirs *were
published at Chapel Hill* (*University of North Carolina Press*) *in 1949,
eight years after Dr. Barringer's death. This selection from them is
Chapter vii. It is reprinted with the permission of the publisher.*

❁

ALMOST at once we began to feel the pinch of war. White sugar disappeared immediately; not only were there no more lumps for gun-shy
horses, but there was no sugar for the table. There was, however, an
unlimited quantity of sorghum syrup, and around the barrels of
sorghum a thick crust of brown sugar often formed. This was carefully scraped off to be served with coffee and berries, the fluid product
going to the servants. They called it "long sweet'nin'" and the other
"short sweet'nin'." To provide a constant supply new cane was
planted every year. It was noted even then that the crystalizing power
of some sorghums was much greater than that of others. I remember
hearing this difference discussed.

The imperative demand for sweets soon brought the omnipresent
"bee-gum" to every yard and orchard, for that was what we called our
homemade beehive. Made from a hollow black gum tree, which was
often eighteen inches or two feet in diameter, this hollow log required
very little chiseling out. It was simply cut in two foot lengths, a board
nailed on top and a hole bored near the bottom, and it was ready for
the spring swarm. Our wild bee, as is well known, was the European
bee brought here about 1720 by the Palatine Germans who settled
above Fredericksburg, Virginia. Every swarm in the spring was
greeted with the beating of tin pans, the blowing of horns, and every
other noise-making device that could be thought of. Superstition dies
hard. We had the idea we could not secure the swarm unless we made
so much noise that the workers would be unable to hear the call of the
queen bee, but all that noise was useless, as the queen is found to be
practically a deaf mute.

In a very short time I noticed that matches had disappeared, and I
have learned that at the outbreak of the war there was not one match
factory in the South. However, flint and steel had passed out of use so
recently that many of these old relics, which were sticking around in
closets and hidden recesses in attics, were taken out and returned to
use. During the first year of the war I must have seen fifty "old-timers"
using these, as we now use lighters and with far more certainty of results than the average lighter will render. They held the "spark," a

fungus called punk which grew on oak trees, for lighting pipes and the already rare cigars. The cigarette of that day, wrapped in a corn shuck, was still a mere fad; it could not be lighted easily from punk. I learned later that the punk was usually soaked in a much diluted solution of saltpeter which everybody kept as standard equipment for hog-killing time.

Not every family had preserved the flint and steel, and even if they had, the fire on the hearth was husbanded as meticulously as ever it was in the old Vestal days. Although there was no curfew (cover-fire) sounded, the rite was enacted at a convenient hour in every household. Someone drew the andirons forward and turned the back log to face against the white brick. He covered the log with embers, shoveled ashes on top, and went to bed confident of starting a new fire in the morning. Sometimes the Vestal fires failed, or perhaps the morning spark had not been nursed with sufficient care by the boy whose duty it was to tend it. When that happened the boy would be soundly flailed and sent posthaste with a flowerpot to borrow fire from a more fortunate neighbor, a simple errand in town but out in the country the neighbor might be a mile or several miles away. They used to place a piece of slate in the bottom of an earthen flowerpot to regulate the size of the hole, fill the pot with burning embers covered with ashes, and carry it suspended from a green pawpaw twist. Sometimes they had paperbark flowerpots woven in the shape of a pear for convenience in carrying and soaked in water for safety, or covered inside with a layer of wet red clay.

At Cottage Home we would send a negro on a mule to Judge Shipp's or to the Reverend Doctor Thornley's but if these sources failed the man would have to go to some of our much despised "fox-hunting, whiskey-drinking" neighbors. I often wondered how it was that the ungodly seemed to keep fire better than the pure in heart.

Long before the war was over matches came back, but they were not the boxed kind that we were accustomed to use. The new matches came in blocks of wood, sawn nearly through with an old cotton-gin saw, and you broke your sulphur match from the block. Aside from the smell, which would disinfect a ballroom, and the fact that they got your fingers full of splinters, they were not bad matches.

Soap was another imperative necessity. In every family the fats were conserved, but soap cannot be made without alkalies, so for home and plantation use the ash hoppers were extended. When new ground was cleared for agricultural purposes the ash hopper was carried to the forest. A pine log some six or eight feet long was channeled on the upper side to within a foot of one end, and in this channel were laid, at an angle of forty-five degrees, clapboards some four feet long. Ashes from the burning of the logs were shoveled into this ash hopper, and the rains of heaven leached out the potash which, running down the inclined channel, was delivered into a stone tub, or some other receiving vessel made by hewing out a log at least two feet by four in dimensions. The ash hopper near the house usually drained into a pre-war cast-iron ham boiler, and in the South many were the children who perished from drinking lye from these tempting reservoirs of peril.

As the blockade grew tighter, whale oil became very scarce. Our beef tallow was saved for greasing cartridges, and fat was needed for soap making, so we were unable to make good candles. The de luxe candles of those days were called candlettes, and they were made by dipping a long strand of cotton into a mixture of beeswax, mutton suet, and lard until it became as thick as a lead pencil, when it was coiled into a roll. When lit, it gave a flickering smoky flame that was very hard on the eyes.

It seemed to me that an infinite number of little things were missing, such as toothpowder, for which we found a substitute in ground sassafras bark and chalk. We made a unique shoe polish by mixing lamp black with the ripe cortical pulp of the abundant chinaberry, and we made good ink from oak balls and burnt copperas.

Soon no more tea and coffee was brought through the blockade, and everybody was forced to use substitutes. We had tea made of sassafras roots, cleaned and dried, and we jokingly called our product "Grub Hyson," after a famous tea which was much in vogue before the war. For coffee we parched rye and wheat and browned sweet potatoes, making a mixture which was cut into quarter inch cubes before drying. Aunt Maria Barringer, when the blockade closed in, was fortunate in having a full bag of Mocha and half a bag of Java, but before long half of that was gone, and to preserve the precious remainder she also was obliged to use "ersatz." However, when she entertained a lieutenant, she had the cook add three grains of mixed Mocha and Java to the usual brew; a captain got five grains; a major, ten; a colonel, fifteen; and a rare brigadier general was given twenty of the precious grains.

Other shortages threatened of which I, as a child, saw only the signs and could not realize the seriousness. Paper was getting so scarce that my elders feared that even the dreaded deathlists might cease to come. Then it was discovered that wall paper could be used, and if properly removed from the walls and bleached, it could be printed on both sides. At the last, they used wall paper that could not be bleached, printing on one side only. I still have one of these old journals. Framed under glass it shows pink flowers on one side, while the bloody harvest of war is recorded on the other.

There was little opportunity to replenish such supplies of writing paper as were on hand when the war began. As the years passed my father wrote us letters on torn scraps of office paper and sometimes on the letter head of his division, but even that paper was of very poor grade.

Anxiety for the men at the front was ever present; many of them came home wounded, and there were many funerals. As the years passed, nearly all the women, mourning for some member of the family, dressed in black. All the young and strong men had long since joined the army, only old men and cripples remained at home, and the plantations were run by Negro men and boys of twelve or fourteen. All bronze church bells were taken down to be melted and made into howitzers or gun caps, and the sabbaths were silent. We—patriarchs, black-robed women, and children—went unbidden to church, where even in the hymns there was a note of sorrow, and the Negroes in the gallery became solemn under the universal strain. Things were surely serious when the Negroes looked solemn.

However, I cannot recall feeling depressed, nor do I remember that any of the other children were. Our conduct was normal and lively as usual.

As the war progressed the stringency deepened. Food portions were small and there was enough to eat, but the best went to the soldiers in the field. We had plenty of cotton as long as there were hands to work it, and we had wool from our sheep, so the looms, the spinning wheels, and cards were never idle. At Cottage Home all the looms were kept going day and night throughout the four years of war. They even rigged up an old, discarded loom and used that steadily.

Everyone worked at Cottage Home, white and black, young and old. We children could scrape lint, the forerunner of absorbent cotton, desperately needed in the hospitals. I worked at that nearly every morning, and in the afternoon I went out with the other children and gathered sweet gum balsam. The benzoic acid in these oleoresins was the most suitable material known for treating wounds before the coming of asepsis.

The Federal Government declared all drugs contraband of war, and almost no morphine or quinine came through the blockade. As a substitute for the latter, as I have already stated, we used boneset tea, which helped but did not cure malaria. To supply opiate we grew our own poppies, making incisions into the sides of the ovaries of these plants and with the flat of a case knife scraping up the exuded gum. The knife was then scraped off on the edge of a glass jar, and thus we found that we could raise gum opium that was 10 or 12 per cent morphine.

There was a poppy bed in every garden planted for this purpose, and when I was seven years old I worked daily for the soldiers, scraping the inspissated juice of the poppy from the bulbar ovaries which had been punctured a few days before, and, like everyone else, I worked under the eternal mandate, "Don't taste it!" On some fifty poppy heads it was a morning's work to get a mass about as big as a small peanut.

The time came when no more Chilean nitre could run the blockade, and the South must depend on its own resources for this essential element of explosives. It was then that the urine cart began to make its rounds, collecting the night's urine and hauling it to the boiling vats, where the urea and other nitrogenous constituents were extracted and shipped to Augusta, Georgia, for the manufacture of gunpowder. That plant was never more than a few days ahead of the needs of the firing line.

Later on the need became so great that many old cabins which stood up on four corner posts were raised by levers, so that men could crawl under them to scrape the ground for the thin layer of nitrogen charged clay at the top. As wondering children, we saw men crawling under old barns to scrape up the dry dust, and we saw old plaster taken from the walls and leached in the ash hopper. We heard that in Virginia and Kentucky searching parties invaded the caves where bats roosted to scrape the bat manure from the floor. All such gleanings were likewise sent to the plant in Augusta.

Looking back at it now, I can see the reason for that persistent and unceasing call to save and extend every natural resource in every section of the South. The need was desperate and the toil in the homes, the fields, and the improvised factories was unceasing.

In North Carolina, Wilmington was our sole open port, but it gave us little relief. The blockade runners brought in munitions and such light things as papers, magazines, and books. Uncle Victor subscribed to the *London Times,* and he literally wore out every copy, so hungry was he for European news. He also bought an ornately bound and illuminated copy of Johnson's *Rasselas,* and as that came early in February, 1865, in time for my eighth birthday, he and my aunt gave it to me as a birthday present. They wrote my name in it and made much of it. I was pleased until I was informed that I must learn enough of it by heart to get Johnson's peculiar style!

"They go about in their black masks"

Fortunately many Southern women who endured the anxieties and hardships of the Civil War kept diaries or wrote their memoirs. Of these, the diary of Mary Boykin Chesnut is the most famous, and justly so. The anthologist is tempted to pillage from it a variety of passages, so keen are her insights: passages on her father-in-law, an intransigent planter and slaveowner whose mentality fascinated her; intimate sketches of Confederate leaders and their kin; descriptions of the harrowing last days of the war.

But none of the diarists wrote so openly of the fear of slave defection and revolt which was much of the time in the consciousness of Southern women. It is for this reason that the selections from the diary printed here deal with this anxiety about what was going on in the minds of the Negroes as they went about "in their black masks."

Mary Boykin Miller (1823–86) married James Chesnut, Jr., in 1840. Her husband, a Princeton graduate, was a member of the United States Senate when war broke out. He accepted a place on General Beauregard's staff, but was soon on the staff of President Davis, who relied heavily on Chesnut's judgment. In effect he was a liaison officer between the Confederacy and South Carolina. Mrs. Chesnut already had many friends in the South, but as she moved from place to place with her husband, her circle of friends and acquaintances was further enlarged. One of the most delightful features of the diary is her easy, even gossipy reference to scores of civil and military leaders. She knew what was in their minds and put it all down for posterity. As she said to a friend, "I write current rumors. I do not vouch for anything."

The diary was first published in 1905, but this edition printed less than half of the manuscript. A new edition of A Diary from Dixie, *prefaced by Ben Ames Williams, was issued in 1949. Though still not complete, this edition restores passages elided by the first editors "either because they might offend persons then living, or because they shocked the editors, or because they presented a picture of conditions under slavery which the editors hoped might be forgotten." The selections from Ben Ames Williams's* A Diary from Dixie, *by Mary Boykin Chesnut, are reprinted by permission of and arrangement with Houghton Mifflin Company, the authorized publishers.*

MRS. CHESNUT: *"They Go About in Their Black Masks"*

March 14, 1861

I WONDER if it be a sin to think slavery a curse to any land. Men and women are punished when their masters and mistresses are brutes, not when they do wrong. Under slavery, we live surrounded by prostitutes, yet an abandoned woman is sent out of any decent house. Who thinks any worse of a Negro or mulatto woman for being a thing we can't name? God forgive us, but ours is a monstrous system, a wrong and an iniquity! Like the patriarchs of old, our men live all in one house with their wives and their concubines; and the mulattoes one sees in every family partly resemble the white children. Any lady is ready to tell you who is the father of all the mulatto children in everybody's household but her own. Those, she seems to think, drop from the clouds. My disgust sometimes is boiling over. Thank God for my country women, but alas for the men! They are probably no worse than men everywhere, but the lower their mistresses, the more degraded they must be.

June 22, 1861

Yesterday, some of the Negro men on the plantation were found with pistols. I have never seen aught about any Negro to show that they knew we had a war on hand, in which they have an interest.

September 21, 1861 and October 7, 1861

Last night when the mail came in, I was seated near the lamp. Mr. Chesnut, lying on a sofa at a little distance, called out to me: "Look at my letters and tell me whom they are from?" I began to read one of them aloud. It was from Mary Witherspoon, and I broke down; horror and amazement was too much for me. Poor cousin Betsey Witherspoon was murdered! She did not die peacefully in her bed, as we supposed, but was murdered by her own people, her Negroes. I remember when Dr. Keith was murdered by his Negroes, Mr. Miles met me and told me the dreadful story. "Very awkward indeed, this sort of thing. There goes Keith in the House always declaiming about the 'Beneficent Institution'—How now?" Horrible beyond words! Her household Negroes were so insolent, so pampered, and insubordinate. She lived alone. She knew, she said, that none of her children would have the patience she had with these people who had been indulged and spoiled by her until they were like spoiled children, simply intolerable. Mr. Chesnut and David Williams have gone over at once. . . .

And now comes back on us that bloody story that haunts me night and day, Mrs. Witherspoon's murder. The man William, who was the master spirit of the gang, once ran away and was brought back from somewhere west; and then his master and himself had a reconciliation and the master henceforth made a pet of him. The night preceding the murder, John Witherspoon went over to his mother's to tell her of some of William's and Rhody's misdeeds. While their mistress was away from home, they had given a ball fifteen miles away from Society Hill. To that place they had taken their mistress's china, silver, house linen, etc. After his conversation with his mother, as he rode out of the gate, he shook his whip at William and said: "Tomorrow I mean to come here and give every one of you a thrashing." That night Mrs. Witherspoon was talking it all over with her grandson, a half-grown boy who lived with her and slept indeed in a room opening into hers. "I do not intend John to punish these Negroes. It is too late to begin discipline now. I have indulged them past bearing. They all say I ought to have tried to control them, that it is all my fault." Mrs. Edwards, who was a sister of Mrs. Witherspoon, sometime ago was found dead in her bed. It is thought this suggested their plan of action to the Negroes. What more likely than she should die as her sister had done! When John went off, William said: "Listen to me and there will be no punishment here tomorrow." They made their plan, and then all of them went to sleep, William remaining awake to stir up the others at the proper hour.

What first attracted the attention of the family to the truth about her death was the appearance of black and blue spots about the face and neck of the body of their mother. Then someone, in moving the candle from the table at her bedside, found blood upon their fingers. Looking at the candlestick, they saw the print of a bloody hand which had held it. There was an empty bed in the entry, temporarily there for some purpose, and as they were preparing to lay her out, someone took up the counterpane from this bed to throw over her. On the under side of it, again, bloody fingers. Now they were fairly aroused. Rhody was helping Mary Witherspoon, a little apart from the rest. Mary cried: "I wish they would not say such horrid things. Poor soul, she died in peace with all the world. It is bad enough to find her dead, but nobody ever touched a hair of her head. To think any mortal could murder her. Never! I will not believe it!" To Mary's amazement Rhody drew near her and looking strangely in her eyes, she said: "Miss Mary, you stick to dat! You stick to dat!" Mary thrilled all over with suspicion and dread.

There was a trunk in Mrs. Witherspoon's closet where she kept money and a complete outfit ready for travelling at any moment; among other things, some new and very fine night gowns. One of her daughters noticed that her mother must have opened that trunk, for she was wearing one of those night gowns. They then looked into the closet and found the trunk unlocked and all the gold gone. The daughters knew the number of gold pieces she always kept under lock and key in that trunk. Now they began to scent mischief and foul play in earnest, and they sent for the detective.

The detective dropped in from the skies quite unexpectedly. He saw that one of the young understrappers of the gang looked frightened and uncomfortable. This one he fastened upon, and got up quite an intimacy with him; and finally, he told this boy that he knew all about it, that William had confessed privately to him to save himself and hang the others. But he said he had taken a fancy to this boy, and if he would confess everything, he would take him as State's evidence instead of William. The young man fell in the trap laid for him and told every particular from beginning to end. Then they were all put in jail, the youth who had confessed among them, as he did not wish them to know of his treachery to them.

This was his story. After John went away that night, Rhody and William made a great fuss. They were furious at Mars' John threatening them after all these years. William said: "Mars' John more than apt to do what he say he will do, but you all follow what I say and he'll have something else to think of beside stealing and breaking glass and china. If ole Marster was alive now, what would he say to talk of whipping us!" Rhody always kept the key to the house to let herself in every morning, so they arranged to go in at twelve, and then William watched and the others slept the sleep of the righteous. Before that, however, they had a "real fine supper and a heap of laughing at the way dey'd all look tomorrow." They smothered her with a counterpane from a bed in the entry. They had no trouble the first time, because they found her asleep and "done it all fore she waked." But after Rhody took her keys and went into the trunk and got a clean night gown—for they had spoiled the one she had on—and fixed everything, candle, medicine and all, she came to! Then she begged them hard for life. She asked them what she had ever done that they should want to kill her? She promised them before God never to tell on them. Nobody should ever know! But Rhody stopped her mouth with the counterpane, and William held her head and hands down, and the other sat on her legs. Rhody had a thrifty mind and wished to save the sheets and night gown so she did not destroy them. They were found behind her mantelpiece. There the money was also, all in a hole made among the bricks behind the wooden mantelpiece. A grandson of Rhody's slept in her house. Him she locked up in his room. She did not want him to know anything of this fearful night.

That innocent old lady and her gray hair moved them not a jot.

Fancy how we feel. I am sure I will never sleep again without this nightmare of horror haunting me.

November 12, 1861

That telegram to Mr. Chesnut was a grand secret, surely. Judge Withers knew it, so I heard in the street. I will not write it, even, for everybody reads my journal as it lies on the table in my room. I went to the turn-out at Mulberry for Mr. Chesnut. Minnie F. says they are hanging Negroes in Louisiana and Mississippi like birds in the trees, for an attempted insurrection; but out there they say the same thing of South Carolina, and we know it is as quiet as the grave here and as peaceful. We have no reason to suppose a Negro knows there is a war. I do not speak of the war to them; on that subject, they do not believe a word you say. A genuine slave owner, born and bred, will not be afraid of Negroes. Here we are mild as the moonbeams, and as serene; nothing but Negroes around us, white men all gone to the army. Mrs. Reynolds and Mrs. Withers, two of the very kindest and most considerate of slave owners, aver that the joy of their Negroes at the fall of Port Royal is loud and open; but there is no change of any kind whatever with ours. . . .

Mrs. Reynolds's conversation with her jet-black butler, Ammon. "Missis, at Beaufort they are burning the cotton and killing the Negroes. They do not mean the Yankees to have cotton or Negroes." She tried to make him understand, in vain: "Would I kill you, or let anybody else kill you? You know nobody kills Negroes here. Why will you believe they do it there?" "We know you won't own up to anything against your side. You never tell us anything that you can help." Ammon has been that nuisance, a pampered menial, for twenty years. The summer after we were married, when Mr. Chesnut was a candidate for the Legislature, he had to risk his election to defend Ammon, who was brought before a magistrate for insulting some gentleman of the town; and Mr. Chesnut got him off scatheless—to the regret of most people. His insolence has always been intolerable. The Chesnut Negroes are spoiled to a degree; but then they have such good manners, they are so polite you forget everything else. And they make you so comfortable, if you can afford ten to do the work of one servant.

December 6, 1861

Mr. Team was here today. He is a stalwart creature, a handsome old man, perhaps the finest black eyes I ever saw. He has been an overseer all his life. Most people detest overseers, but Mr. Team is an exception. He has the good will and respect of all the world; of our small world, I mean. How those magnificent eyes blazed today. . . . He said today: "In all my life I have only met one or two womenfolk who were not abolitionists in their hearts, and hot ones too. Mrs. Chesnut is the worst. They have known that of her here for years." We told him Uncle Tom's story, as invented or imagined by Mrs. Stowe. He said he had not seen many of that sort. If there were any, "money couldn't buy 'em." We said: "Daddy Abram was so good." "I never knew a Negro to be murdered or burnt. But, if the Marsters are bad or drunken, look out. Slavery is a thing too unjust, too unfair to last. Let us take the bull by the horns, set 'em free, let 'em help us fight to pay for their freedom."

Old Mr. Chesnut did not hear, and I noticed no voice was raised to enable him to hear. He is a Prince of Slaveholders, and so he will die. His forefathers paid their money for them, and they are his by that right divine—he thinks. Our votes are not counted. We are women, alas!

Team said: "Slavery does not make good masters." Then he told a tale of a woman so lazy she tied her child to her back and jumped in the river. She said she did not mean to work, nor should her child after her! He had had us crying over his stories, but now we laughed, so that we might not cry.

March 17, 1862

Mary P. was giving Wade Manning's story of his Aunt Camilla's Bed of Justice. The lady is of the stoutest, with a fiery red face and straggling grey hair. Her room opens on a stairway up and down which all the world goes, and is obliged to go, for it is the only staircase in the house. With her door wide open, she sat in bed with a bundle of switches; and every Monday morning, everybody in the yard was there to give an account of their deeds or misdeeds for the past week. They were mustered in a row and waited. She solemnly rehearsed their misdemeanors. Some were adroit enough to avert their fate. Those whom she condemned stepped up to the bedside and received their punishment screaming, howling and yelling to the utmost of their ability to soften her heart. She belabored them with her night cap flying, and her gown in horrid disarray from the exercise of her arm. Wade found her dreadful to think of as he fled from the sight and sound. Peace once restored and everybody once more at the daily avocations, they were as jolly as larks, with perspiration streaming. Wade moaned: "It shocks and makes me miserable, but they don't seem to mind a switching,

117

Cousin Mary, not ten seconds after it is over! And this is the place my father sends me to be educated!"

Mary C. said to Mr. Venable: "I would like that story of Wade's to be *bestowed*. What would she think of it or make of it?" "Mrs. Stowe would feel exactly as we do; but then she would take an extraordinary freak of nature as a specimen of a class, a common type." "Wade says everybody at breakfast was as jolly, as pleasant, as smiling as if there had been no human tornado raging a few minutes before." "The beswitched and all?" "Yes the howlers and all." "Don't take on so," said Mr. Venable. "A fat old thing like her can't hurt much."

They asked me if I had ever heard of this Devil's Matins before. "Yes, but I heard it was a daily service." "Oh, no, no," said Wade. "Once a week is as much as mortal could bear, of a row such as that in any house."

It is only on Mondays. One woman knows how to escape the switches; she says she gathers up all the scandals of the town. "Missus is too keen to hear the news to trouble me. I brings her plenty 'bout everybody, specially them she don't like."

March 18, 1862

Mr. Chesnut's Negroes offered to fight for him if he would arm them. He pretended to believe them. He says one man cannot do it. The whole country must agree to it. He would trust such as he would select, and he would give so many acres of land and his freedom to each one as he enlisted.

August 2, 1862 to October 27, 1863[1]

Seeing Dick, the butler here, reminds me that when we were children, our nurses gave us our tea out in the open on little pine tables, scrubbed white as milk pails. As Dick passed us, with his slow and consequential step, we called: "Do, Dick, come and wait on us." "No, little Missus. I never wait on pine tables. Wait till you git big enough to put your legs under your pa's mahogany."

I taught him to read as soon as I could read myself, perched on his knife board; but he won't look at me now. He looks over my head, he scents freedom in the air. He was always very ambitious. I do not think he ever troubled with books much, but then my father always said that Dick, standing in front of his sideboard, had heard all subjects of earth or Heaven discussed, and by the best heads in our world.

[1] There is a hiatus in the *Diary* here. In October 1863 Mrs. Chesnut wrote her memories of the intervening months.

He is proud, too, in his way. Hetty, his wife, complained that the other men servants were too fine in their livery. "Nonsense, old woman! A butler never demeans himself to wear livery. He is always in plain clothes." Somewhere he had picked up that.

He is the first Negro that I have felt a change in. They go about in their black masks, not a ripple or an emotion showing; and yet on all other subjects except the War they are the most excitable of all races. Now Dick might make a very respectable Egyptian Sphynx, so inscrutably silent is he. He did deign to inquire about General Richard Anderson. "He was my young Master once. I always will like him better than anybody else."

July 4, 1865

Saturday I was ill in bed with one of my worst headaches, but I came down when callers arrived. They talked of Negroes who flocked to the Yankees and showed them where the silver and valuables were hid by the white people; lady's maids dressing themselves in their mistress's gowns before their very faces and walking off. Before this, everyone has told me how kind and faithful and considerate the Negroes had been. I am sure, after hearing these tales, the fidelity of my own servants shines out brilliantly. I had taken it too much as a matter of course.

Yesterday there was a mass meeting of Negroes. Thousands of them were in town, eating, drinking, dancing, speechifying. Preaching and prayers were also a popular amusement. They have no greater idea of amusement than wild prayers, unless it be getting married and going to a funeral. But our people were all at home, quiet, orderly, respectful, and at their usual work. There was nothing to show that any one of them had ever seen a Yankee or knew that there was one in existence.

Correspondent Reid Inspects the Defeated South

Whitelaw Reid (1837–1912) was so able and ambitious a young journalist that at the age of thirty-five, following the death of Greeley, he became the editor of the most influential American newspaper of the

day, the New York Tribune. *He came to that post by way of successes on various Ohio papers, including the* Cincinnati Gazette, *for which he did brilliant war-reporting during the Civil War. His ability to grasp the complexities of battle maneuvers amazed generals. He soon made friends with Northern political leaders and thus was able to give historical depth to his war-reporting.*

Immediately after the fall of Richmond, Reid was invited to accompany a small official party that was to tour the South from Virginia to New Orleans and the Mississippi region and report to President Johnson on the extent of the disorganization of Southern life. Chief Justice Chase was head of the group. The tour lasted two months. Reid was soon off on another Southern expedition, this time on his own. His sharp observations on the devastation of the war, the state of mind of the defeated Southerners, the behavior of Northern troops, the attempts at recovery being made in such centers as Atlanta, were first sent in as newspaper reports. In 1866 Reid gathered them into a book, After the War, *which appeared in England as well as America.*

Reid was so much impressed with the opportunities which the South then afforded ambitious men who were willing to work hard that he unwisely attempted to become a cotton-planter in Louisiana. His dreams of making a fortune in a year quickly vanished, though after the Louisiana venture failed, he tried again in Alabama. He just managed to close out his holdings without loss.

Page references to the 1866 American edition (Moore, Wilstach & Baldwin of Cincinnati) of After the War; a Southern Tour *are given at the end of each excerpt printed here.*

GENERAL ASPECTS OF THE SOUTH AT THE CLOSE OF THE WAR

The months of May and June were the chaotic period of the returning Rebel States. All men were overwhelmed and prostrated under the sudden stroke of a calamity which the fewest number had anticipated. Many had believed the war hopeless, but nearly all had thought their armies strong enough, and their statesmen skillful enough, to extort from the North terms that would soften away, if not conceal, the rugged features of utter defeat. They expected the necessity of a return to the Union, but they hoped to march back with flying colors, with concessions granted and inducements offered that would give them the semblance of a victory. Studious encouragement had been given from the Rebel Capital to such hopes; and outside of Virginia there were scarcely a dozen men in a State who comprehended the

straits to which the Confederacy was reduced in the winter of 1864–
65, or were prepared for the instantaneous collapse of the spring.

The first feelings were those of baffled rage. Men who had fought
four years for an idea, smarted with actual anguish under the stroke
which showed their utter failure. Then followed a sense of bewilderment and helplessness. Where they were, what rights they had left,
what position they occupied before the law, what claim they had to
their property, what hope they had for an improvement of their condition in the future—all these were subjects of complete uncertainty.

Here was the opportunity for a statesman to grasp. I speak advisedly,
and after a careful review of our whole experiences through the
months of May and June, in all the leading centers of Southern influence, when I say that the National Government could at that time
have prescribed no conditions for the return of the Rebel States which
they would not have promptly accepted. They expected nothing; were
prepared for the worst; would have been thankful for anything.

In North and South Carolina, Georgia, and Florida, we found this
state of feeling universally prevalent. The people wanted civil government and a settlement. They asked no terms, made no conditions. They
were defeated and helpless—they submitted. Would the victors be
pleased to tell them what was to be done? Point out any way for a return to an established order of things, and they would walk in it. They
made no hypocritical professions of new-born Unionism. They had
honestly believed in the right of secession. The hatred of Yankees,
which had originally aided the conspirators in starting the movement,
had grown and strengthened with the war. Neither the constitutional
theory nor the personal hate of their lives could be changed in a day,
but both were alike impotent; and having been forced to abandon the
war, they longed for the blessings which any peace on any terms might
be expected to bring in its train. With unchanged faith in the constitutionality of their secession, they were ready to abandon or ignore it, at
the requirement of the victors. Fully believing the debts of their Rebel
Government legal and just, they were prepared to repudiate them at a
hint from Washington. Filled with the hatred to the negroes, nearly always inspired in any ruling class by the loss of accustomed power over
inferiors, they nevertheless yielded to the Freedmen's Bureau, and
acquiesced in the necessity for according civil rights to their slaves.
They were stung by the disgrace of being guarded by negro soldiers;
but they made no complaints, for they felt that they had forfeited their
right of complaint. They were shocked at the suggestion of negro suffrage; but if the Government required it, they were ready to submit.

The whole body politic was as wax. It needed but a firm hand to apply the seal. Whatever device were chosen, the community would at

once be molded to its impress. But if the plastic moment were suffered to pass—!

SAVANNAH

In the evening a stroll through the streets gave some other phases of the city life. As has been said, the place was full of returning rebel soldiers. At every corner their friends, and particularly their female acquaintances, were greeting them with a warmth that seemed in nowise tempered by contempt for their lack of success. Many a stalwart fellow, in coarse gray, was fairly surrounded on the sidewalk by a bevy of his fair friends; and if without an arm or a leg, so much the better— the compliments would rain upon him till the blushes would show upon his embrowned cheeks, and he was fairly convinced that he had taken the most gallant and manly course in the world.

Very pretty it was, nevertheless, if one could only forget what these men had been doing, to see the warmth of their welcome home; to watch little children clinging to the knees of papas they had almost forgotten; to observe wives promenading proudly with husbands they had not seen for years; to notice the delighted gathering of family groups around some chair in the piazza, long vacant, but filled again by a crippled soldier, home from the wars, with only his wounds and his glory for his pay.

The bearing of the rebel soldiers was unexceptionable. My companion was a staff officer, in undress uniform, and without arms. At times, for squares, there would be no sentry in sight; so that it was not the mere vulgar fear of immediate arrest that made them respectful. Occasionally I observed them look curiously and rather admiringly at the elegant texture and easy fit of the uniform, so unlike their own; often they straightened up to a thorough soldierly bearing, and even sometimes respectfully saluted as they passed.

Indeed, nothing was more touching, in all that I saw in Savannah, than the almost painful effort of the rebels, from Generals down to privates, to conduct themselves so as to evince respect for our soldiers, and to bring no severer punishment upon the city than it had already received. There was a brutal scene at the hotel, where a drunken sergeant, with a pair of tailors' shears, insisted on cutting the buttons from the uniform of an elegant gray-headed old Brigadier, who had just come in from Johnston's army; but he bore himself modestly and very handsomely through it. His staff was composed of fine-looking, stalwart fellows, evidently gentlemen, who appeared intensely mortified at such treatment—wholly unmerited, by the way, since they had no clothes save their Rebel uniforms, and had, as yet, had no time to procure others—but they avoided disturbance, and submitted to what they might, with some propriety, and with the general approval of our officers, have resented. What these men may become, under a lax rein, can not be said; but, supposing themselves under a tight rein, they are now behaving, in the main with very marked propriety.

THE INTERIOR OF VIRGINIA

Of course, the desolation of Virginia, even in the regions most exposed to the ravages of the war had been overrated. I do not think the white people were starving, or likely to starve, anywhere from Alexandria to Gordonsville, Richmond, Fredericksburg, or Lynchburg; and within these points Virginia had suffered more than in all the rest of the State. A little corn had been grown in the summer, and that little had been husbanded in a style at which a Western farmer would stare in amazement. Every blade had been stripped from the stalks, every top had been cut, and in the center of every little inclosure a stack of blades, thatched with tops, supplemented the lack of hay and other forage for the cattle, while the abundant ears furnished the great staple of diet for the classes most likely to suffer. A few little patches of cotton whitened inclosures near the houses, at rare intervals; but the yield was light, and the cultivation had evidently been bad. Between Richmond and Gordonsville scarcely a dozen wheat-fields were seen. Great surface drains had been furrowed out all over the fields, as if the owners were afraid they had too much wheat in, and wanted a considerable portion of it washed away. Beyond Gordonsville, they became plentier, and the crops had been put in in better style.

But in the main, between Richmond and Gordonsville, as between Fredricksburg and Richmond, abandoned fields alternated with pine forests, destroyed depots, and ruined dwellings. Imaginative writers have described the droves of wild beasts which they represent as having taken possession of these desolated regions; but the sportsman is likely to find nothing more formidable than abundant coveys of quails. Our train brought up from Richmond, and left at different points along the road, numbers of the decayed Virginia gentry, equipped with dogs and fowling pieces and eager for this result of the war, if not for others of more consequence.

Hanover Junction presented little but standing chimneys and the debris of destroyed buildings. Along the road a pile of smoky brick and mortar seemed a regularly recognized sign of what had once been a depot, and the train was sure to stop. Not a platform or water-tank had been left, and the rude contrivances hastily thrown up to get the road in running order were, in many cases, for miles and miles the only improvements visible. Young pines covered the old wheat-fields and corn-fields. Traces of breast-works wound off through the country in all directions. A coterie of young officers were constantly exclaiming, "Here we whipped the rebs." "There's a place where the rebs got after us mighty sharp." Gray-coated, heavy-bearded, ragged-looking fellows listened in scowling silence, or occasionally beguiled the way by reminding each other how "Here the Yanks caught hell."

At one or two points, where once had been considerable towns, the train was besieged by an outgrowth of the peculiar institution. A score or two of negro women, bearing trays on which were rudely arrayed what they called "snacks," surrounded us, loudly announcing the merits of their various preparations. "Sad" biscuit and fried chicken; "sad" biscuit and fried bacon; "sad" pie-crust, covering wild grapes, constituted the main attractions; and, as a grey-coated passenger sullenly remarked, "played the devil" with the hen-roosts of the surrounding country. Doubtless this petty traffic kept the wolf from many a negro's door through the winter.

The railroads had been supplied with rolling stock brought mainly from the supplies of our United States military railroads, or from Northern shops. One or two cars, however, of the best among all the trains we met, bore the marks of a Richmond firm. The tracks were comparatively solid; but the rails were in the worst possible condition. Looking from the rear platform, one saw every few yards a rail bent outward till he wondered why it did not throw us off; while half of them were crushed at the ends or worn off the face till scarcely half an inch remained for the wheel to touch. The roads hardly pretended to make over twelve miles per hour, and even that was in many places a very unsafe rate of speed. The conductors were, of course, ex-Rebels, so were the engineers and brakemen, and any complaint as to the running of trains was very effectually silenced by a suggestion of the improvement "since six months ago." Gangs of hands are at work on the roads, at distances of very few miles. Negroes and Rebel soldiers worked harmoniously side by side. "I tell you, sir," said a Yankee to a Virginian who didn't approve of this social equality, "a white man has got just the same right a nigger has—to starve if he won't work!"

ATLANTA

From Knoxville I went direct to Atlanta, Georgia, the key of the great campaigns in the West, the memorable surrender of which re-elected President Lincoln, and proved the beginning of the end.

The city was adapting itself, with remarkable rapidity, to the new order of things. "Sherman, his mark," was still written too plainly to be soon effaced, in gaping windows and roofless houses, heaps of ruins on the principal corners and traces of unsparing destruction everywhere. The burnt district of Richmond was hardly more thoroughly destroyed than the central part of Atlanta; yet, with all the advantages of proximity to the North, abundant capital, and an influx of business and money from above the Potomac, Richmond was not half so far rebuilt as Atlanta. What is more remarkable, the men who were bringing a city out of this desert of shattered brick—raising warehouses from ruins, and hastily establishing stores in houses half finished and unroofed—were not Yankees, but pure Southerners. These people were taking lessons from Chicago, and deserved to have, as they then seemed likely to have, the foremost of the interior cities of the Gulf States.

Not less than four thousand mechanics were at work; and at least as many more would have been employed, if it had been possible to secure building material enough to supply the enormous demand. A hundred and fifty or two hundred stores were already opened; and others found themselves unable to rent rooms for their goods. The streets were blockaded with drays and wagons. The four railroads were taxed to their utmost capacity, without beginning to supply all the demands upon them. The trade of the city was a third greater than it had ever been, in its most prosperous days before the war.

But the faces one saw on the street or behind the counters were not the faces of men with whom you would choose to do business. "I have spent five days here," exclaimed a simple-hearted scientific man, as he greeted me; "I have spent years among the Black Feet, and have been pretty much over the world, but I never saw such demoralized faces. The war has destroyed their moral character. There isn't one man in a score here I would trust with my carpet-bag." The geologist was too severe, but the traces of the bad passions and disregard of moral obligations which the war has taught, are written almost as plainly on the faces as are Sherman's marks on the houses of Atlanta. More tangible evidence of the war's demoralization was to be found in the alarming insecurity of property and even of life. Passing about the dark, crooked streets of Atlanta after night, unaccompanied and unarmed, was worse than attempting a similar exploration of the Five Points, in New York, ten years ago. Murders were of frequent occurrence; and so common a thing as garroting attracted very little attention.

The soil of the country, for many miles in all directions, is poor, but prices of land in the immediate vicinity were run up to fabulous rates. The people were infected with the mania of city building; and landholders gravely explained to you how well their plantations, miles distant, would cut up into corner lots.

125

COTTON LANDS FOR SALE

All the trains on which I had traveled for some days had contained numbers of Northerners going down to look at the cotton lands. Many went prepared to buy; all went either to buy or lease, if they found the prospects as encouraging as they hoped. To all these, the central belt of Alabama seemed a promising field. Its lands are the richest east of Louisiana and west of the South Carolina and Georgia Sea Islands; and the country is entirely healthy, which is more than can be said of either of the other regions. A bale to the acre could be made on the first-class lands, and the Alabama bale means a hundred pounds more than that of Louisiana or the west. Nearly all the lands could, with careful culture, be made to average half a bale. Then, within easy railroad connection, is Mobile on the south, while on the north, a twelve hours' ride carries the debilitated planter to the bracing breezes of the mountains.

In September and October these lands were selling at five dollars an acre. In November I imagine that the average was very nearly ten, and it was constantly rising. The papers were full of advertisements of plantations for rent or sale. The great rush was from men of small means at the North, who wanted from four hundred to a thousand acres; but a few were looking for heavier investments. Here are a couple of specimens of the kind of lands offering:

"For Sale or Rent.—A plantation on the Alabama River, containing fourteen hundred acres, one thousand of which are cleared, under good fence and in fine order for a crop. It has a three-story brick gin-house, a large brick stable and corn-crib, a new, well-finished dwelling with four rooms on the floor, all covered with tin roofs and built in the most substantial manner; nine double tenement framed negro houses, with piazzas in front; a large kitchen and smokehouse, a good blacksmith-shop, two never-failing wells of excellent water, some seven or eight miles of Osage-orange hedge. No plantation on the Alabama River lies better or is probably more healthy. The quality of land about the average of Alabama River. I think I risk nothing in saying it is the best improved plantation in the State of Alabama."

"For Sale or Rent.—My plantation, one mile above Montgomery, immediately on the river, containing about 2,000 acres, 1,300 in cultivation. There is a steam grist-mill, which propels two gins, on the place, and every other improvement which constitutes a complete plantation. I will rent for a share in the crop. This is well known as one of the very best cotton farms in the State."

126

"We begin now to realize the ruin to property
which the war has entailed upon us."

*The diary of Henry William Ravenel (1814–87) could be used to il-
lustrate many phases of Southern life before and after the Civil War,
but few of the entries are more revealing than those which tell, without
complaint, how he struggled and sacrificed to maintain his family after
the War had ruined him. As the excerpts printed here show, he sold his
valuable scientific library, book by book, as well as his extraordinary
botanical collections. He turned his scientific knowledge to account by
writing for newspapers and magazines and by raising seed for sale.
Tree by tree he despoiled the timber on his plantation and sold it to the
railroad. Even then it was necessary—as often with families so circum-
stanced—for his daughters to teach school and for his wife to take in
boarders.*

*Ravenel was a scion of the distinguished South Carolina Huguenot
family of that name. He showed remarkable aptitude in the sciences at
South Carolina College and wished to study medicine. Since his frail
health prevented this, his father established him on a plantation and
gave him slaves to run it. But like many other Southerners with scientific proclivities (whose important work has now been pretty well forgotten) he kept on with his studies while running his plantation. His
five-volume* The Fungi Caroliniani Exsicatti *(1853–60), published in an
edition of thirty copies, is an important landmark in cryptogamic
botany. His name was given to many plants which he first botanized.*

The Private Journal of Henry William Ravenel, *1859–1887, has been
carefully edited by Professor Arney Robinson Childs (Columbia: University of South Carolina Press; 1947). The extracts from it which are
printed here are published with the kind permission of the University
of South Carolina Press. The notes to the text are Professor Childs's.*

1865

May 22 We begin now to realize the ruin to property which the war
has entailed upon us. All classes & conditions of men will suffer who
had property, except the small farmers who owned no negroes. Con-

federate securities, I consider a total loss. Bank stock, confederation & private bonds, are all more or less dependent for their availability upon Confed securities, & upon the value of negro property; both of which are lost. The Rail road companies are nearly all ruined by the destruction of their roads & the heavy debt they must incur to rebuild. The only money now in possession of our people is coin in small quantities which had been hoarded through the war, & some bills of the local banks. There will be but little means of increasing this amount for some time to come, as provisions are scarce, & the cotton has been mostly burnt, captured or sold. The financial prospect is a gloomy one, & there will be much distress before our conditions can improve. My own loss (exclusive of the value of my property, & the losses from the Yankees in St. Johns, & Wheelers men up here) is as follows—$11,600 Confed. 8 per ct bonds—$6,500 Conf 8 per ct. stock—$2000 non taxable 6 per cts.—$1200 in 7.30 Treasury notes, $300 in 4 per ct scrip—$2400 in currency = $24,000 in Confed securities. I have also bonds from Charley & Peter Snowden amounting to $7770 for negroes purchased. If the negroes are emancipated I will return these bonds to them as their means of paying will be lost, & I would not wish to embarrass them with such a debt. I have 32 shares Charleston bank (par $100)—24 shares State Bank—& 90 shares Peoples bank (25)—all doubtful. $1060 in City of Charleston 6 per cts—$1050 in State of So. Ca. 6 per cts, $1500 in 6 per ct Bonds of Charleston & Savannah R. R. Co. The above with my farm (& 32 negro slaves?) is the total amount of my property. . . .

June 14 Our young men are going to work in earnest for a living. Every one sees the necessity of exertion—& as soon as business can be resumed & money begins to circulate, we hope to have more prosperous times. Parker Ravenel & Coffin have established a line of wagons, from this place to Orangeburg, from this place to Columbia, & from the latter place to Orangeburg. . . . This arrangement will go on until the Railroad is completed. The negroes are very foolishly leaving their former masters. Nearly every family in Aiken has lost some, many all their servants. The novelty of the situation tempts them to make use of it. Many who are well treated, & much better off than they can be by their own exertions, are going away. They all want to go to the cities, either Charleston or Augusta. The fields have no attractions. Mine are all still with me, that have been living here. Lander who was at GraniteVille has lost his place there & gone to look out for work,—& some of the other boys are working in the neighborhood. They have all professed a desire to remain with me—There are more than I need for servants or farm hands & [they] will have to provide for themselves. . . .

July 3 My Peach crop is a very abundant one this year, but we have no market. I am trying Augusta again, but that place is soon over-stocked. There are no distilleries in reach of my farm, & great quantities of peaches are falling from the trees & rotting on the ground. We cut up 12 to 15 baskets every day for drying. My crop of Peaches if we had New York market would be worth to me about $5000. . . .

July 6 . . . I have taken a contract to supply 200 cords wood to the R. Road at $2.50 per cord, which I hope will bring us in a little ready money. That with my Peach & Grape crop are the only sources of income that I can see at present. . . .

October 4 . . . I am now expecting to get some kind of employment & may sell out my farm & move away. This may be the beginning of a disruption & scattering of my happy family. I have spent eleven years of my life very happily at this place—& the thought of its being brought to a close, causes sadness. . . .

October 20 . . . The great Problem now before the country is that of securing profitable Labour for the wants of agriculture. The negroes seem indisposed to work in the country, & are flocking to the towns & cities. Where they have been under contract during the past season, they have in most cases disregarded their contracts,—& have made but little provision for the coming year. The planters are without means to engage them & furnish subsistance for the year. This is the almost universal case throughout the low country. Unless some means are devised of aiding the owners of land by an advance of funds or rations, hypothecated on the coming crop,—or the lands are sold to capitalists who can furnish this advance, they must remain idle. There must also be stringent laws to control the negroes, & require them to fulfill their contracts of labour on the farms. . . .

December 3 I went over to Augusta yesterday to collect my monthly amount for wood. This woodcutting is a God-send in reality to me at this time, when I am getting nothing from any other source. I get about $40 per month clear of cost of cutting &c. Without this source of profit since the war closed, I would not have been able to provide food & clothing for my family without sacrificing some articles of silver or furniture. I took over with me an advertisement offering my farm for sale which ought to appear in the Constitutionalist tomorrow.

December 22 . . . Received a letter from Peter Gaillard to whom I had written to consult as to the practicability of getting into business in Charleston. He gives a melancholy view of the condition of affairs. A large number of men who formerly did business in the city are thrown out of employment.—every one more or less ruined in money affairs & but little business as there is but little produce to be sold. It is a struggle for life—& those who are most active & prepared by previous habits & training will secure the places—others must do what they can for a living. I have had no application yet for my farm. . . .

December 26 I replied to Mr Walters letter yesterday, stating that I asked $15,000 for my farm—of which I would require a portion (⅓) in cash—the balance in bonds or other securities I might approve of. I have considered the propriety of selling my farm before I have a certainty of getting business—& have decided that it will be best to sell if the opportunity offers, & take the chances afterwards of finding employment.

My reasons are these—The sources from which I derived an annual income by which I supported my family are all lost—the present wood cutting business cannot last very long from scarcity of timber—my farm yields nothing except fruit & should the seasons be unfavourable, that resource is cut off, & I will be left without any means of support. . . .

December 28 . . . I wrote today to Prof P. A Chadbourne to offer him my set of Mougeot & Nestlers "Stirpes Cryptogamae Vogeso—Rhenanae," 12 vols at $100 in specie or $124 in currency—also "Grevilles Cryptogamic Flora" at $40—also De Candoles "Prodromus" 12 vols & "Kunths Enumeratio Plantarum" 5 vols for $50.[1]

1866

March 2 This day year Gen. Potters army passed through Pooshee & encamped there for the night, he making his headquarters at the house. It was during the night of the 1st that we had the visit from the gang of black troops who stole my horses, & all the meats and supplies we had outside of the house. They were at their devilish work until after 1 A M of the 2nd.

April 11 The negroes are busy preparing & planting their crops. My farm was in such bad condition that I told them if they repaired the fences they could plant whatever land they wanted. They have been for near two months past using their spare time from woodcutting in splitting rails & making fences. Yesterday they all came &

[1] Jean Baptiste Mougeot's and C. Nestler's *Stirpes Cryptogamae Vogesorum praefecturis collegerunt.* Bruyerii Voges. 1810–1843. Fascicles 13–15, published 1850–1861, had not been received by HWR, apparently; fascicle 16, published 1890, completed the set.

Robert Kaye Greville's *Scottish Cryptogamic Flora* . . . 6 vols. in 3, Edinburgh, 1823–1827.

Augustin Pyramus de Candolle's *Prodromus Systematis Naturalis Regni Vegetabilis* . . . Paris, 1824–1873. The set is composed of 17 volumes, but by the outbreak of hostilities HWR had apparently received only 12.

Karl Sigmund Kunth's *Enumeratio Plantarum Omnium Cogitarum* . . . 5 vols. in 6, Stuttgart, 1833–1850.

planted my crop of potatoes (about 30 rows). I wish my land was better, so they might get a better return for their labour. They have all behaved well, & seem to wish to get along. I believe after a while when a more settled state of affairs exist & the demand for labour is properly adjusted, that a good feeling generally will prevail towards the negroes. They surely have done nothing to cause any ill blood towards them. I feel nothing but sympathy for them as a poor, homeless & unprotected, proscribed race. That the low & ignorant classes of our white population should feel vindictively inclined towards them, may be expected. They will taunt & maltreat the negro, simply because he belongs to the proscribed race, & was once a slave. Even if we felt inclined to indulge a revengeful feeling at the loss of property in their emancipation, we should recollect that it was through no act of theirs, that emancipation was effected. It was simply the result of the chances of war, on which we had staked our cause & all that we had. Let us have the magnanimity to be just, if we have not the Christian principles of forgiveness.

June 9 We are under further obligations to the Ladies of Baltimore for provisions received yesterday, about 1 bush flour, 2 bushels meal & ½ of a side of bacon. These things were sent on here for distribution to certain persons who were named & to others whom the committee might think proper to give. I am indebted to some kind friend who presented my name & I have received more than I had any right to expect. . . .

June 27 Heard from Lyd yesterday—all well in Pinopolis. She & Atty are both keeping school, & getting a few pay scholars. . . . Heard also from Dr Engleman. I have been out today to collect Juncus setaceus which he wishes to have. Saw Burckhalter the supervisor of this division of the road this morning. He says they will want no more wood for two months. I must therefore try & provide other means of living if it is possible.

July 12 . . . I have been thinking of a project by which I might possibly find occupation that would give me a support—viz to make collections of plants, seeds &c for sale—to have agencies in Paris & London, through whom orders could be received & the transactions effected, to advertise my intentions & refer to the leading botanists of this country for my qualifications. I have written to Tuckerman & to Frank Porcher on the subject to ask their opinion. I hope something may come out of it.

July 22 This morning at breakfast table the subject of early struggling in life was discussed, & I endeavoured to impress upon my children the great advantages of self exertion & of early habits of training in making one's way through life. I have been thinking of it since, & record for their benefit my thoughts on the subject. After graduating at College, where I idled the first 18 months of my course, & made some amends in the last year, studying pretty hard and taking one of the high appointments, I came home intending to study medicine, & did really begin to read a work on Physiology. My father who had practised in the country & had to give it up on account of ill health dissuaded me from it, as too arduous a work for my constitution, thinking only of a hard country practice, & not estimating the advantages which I might have acquired from a knowledge of Anatomy, Physiology & Therapeutics. He offered me a plantation & negroes to begin life with. Of course the temptation to ease was strong, & I yielded. I have ever since regretted that I had not persevered in the study of medicine. It suited my previous inclination & my turn of mind. I had paid much attention to Chemistry & Natural Philosophy in College & was pleased with this glimpse I got of the world of Nature. . . .

I wish it impressed upon them that my error in the beginning was in taking to planting, a life of ease & non-exertion, instead of studying a profession by which I could have gained a livelihood through my own exertions. I would now have had that profession as a means of support. We cannot violate that primaeval law of our nature "In the sweat of thy brow shalt thou eat bread" without paying the penalty in after life. . . .

July 24 Wrote to Mr Walter in reference to the purchase of my farm by Capt Barkman. I have offered it at $10,000. . . .

September 1 Heard from Mr Dwight last night in reply to my letter of inquiry about locations around Summerville suitable for a market garden & Nursery. He writes from Winnsboro—thinks the soil & situation in the vicinity of Summerville well adapted for my purpose —& speaks of the health of the village in high terms. My plans however will depend upon my ability to sell my farm. If I cannot sell, I must of necessity remain here & do what I can! . . .

September 15 . . . Received by mail today a letter from Charles Bailey of Manchester England, who having seen my advertisement in Gardeners Chronicle, writes to inquire if I can supply him with about 250 species of our Phaenogams & Ferns—& on what terms.—Also one from Dr Engelman in reply to my last. The specimens of Juncus sent him in my letter prove to be, that from Wilkinsons mill pond, J. Canadensis var.—& that from my farm J. candatus, *Chapman,* both very desirable. . . .

November 6 I sent down today my Certificate for $1060 in City of Charleston Stock to James Wilson for sale. I hope by what I may realize from its sale to be able to commence my nursery business & make the necessary repairs on my farm. . . .

November 24 Received last night a letter from James Wilson inclosing my two certificates of Stock which he was unable to sell—also a letter from Meehan giving directions about the Evergreens. Today Mrs. Gregg sent me a large [quantity] of Rose trimmings which I have commenced cutting up for "cuttings."

1867

January 1 . . . Received last night a letter from Dr Curtis inclosing one to him from Prof Gray, to whom he had written at my request on the subject of making collections of plants for sale. Dr Gray writes in a very friendly manner, & although he cannot hold out expectations that the plan will pay well, offers to aid me in every way & to bring the matter to attention of botanists abroad. I think it likely I shall abandon the scheme, as one which will require too much of my time without a prospect of compensation, which I cannot now afford to devote to it. I have other employment for my time in the editing of our paper here, & in writing for Hills Magazine. . . .

1868

April 20 . . . Received a letter from Gen Hill, accepting an article on *Scuppernong Grape* for his magazine—& also one from Denslow. He has sold two sets of my plants one for $18 & one for $12.—the third he is to send to Judge Clinton for Buffalo Society. . . .

August 9 . . . Received yesterday evening a letter from Horace Mann with check for $49. in part payment for plants—& also a letter from Dr J. W. Bates Paris Texas inquiring for seeds of Lespedeza striata & enclosing 25 cts. . . .

1870

February 2 . . . I have put my farm in Woods' hands for sale. He does not think I can get over $8000 for it. . . .

December 20 Received last night a letter from the Librarian of University of S.C. on the subject of the purchase of my old newspapers. The Trustees had not yet held a meeting & no decision had been made. I offered the Newspapers 1865 at $200, & the old acts of Assembly &c at $25 & the old book at $25. . . .

1871

December 16 We have decided to make a change in our household arrangements. We have had Peggy cooking for us at $1.50 per week

& Leah washing at $1.30 per week. We find it necessary to curtail these expenses, & tomorrow we will begin to do our own cooking in the house, & Leah, Rony & Peggy will each give us a days washing every week for house rent. I will hire Ben to do work about the house, bringing water & wood &c. . . .

December 20 . . . I wrote to Prof Gray yesterday to offer my entire Collection of Cryptogams for $1000 as follows Fungi—3000 species (& all the duplicates, enough to be used in exchange to add another 1000); Musci about 624; Hepaticae about 85; Lichens about 750; Algae about 300—total about 4760. . . .

1875

June 17 I have written today to Wheatly to accept his proposal to take back Hampton Hill for the debt yet due, over $6000.—an unfortunate termenation [*sic*] to the business. I have had $2500 paid on it viz $2000 on principal & 500. as interest. With that I have paid off for the purchase of my Aiken lot $1800, leaving still $600 due. I am thus cut off from what I expected would be a source of annual income by investment of the proceeds of sale. . . .

June 18 . . . This morning after breakfast I walked out to Hampton Hill to take a look at property which again was to come into my possession after 18 months' alienation. The house has been improved perhaps to the value of about $500. A stair way leading downwards & the basement rooms excavated & inclosed. The fences have been brought in so as to enclose about 35 acres around the buildings. The vegetable garden is in a neglected & ruinous condition, nothing planted there— The fruit garden grown up in weeds & grass, & needing cultivation to keep things alive—the Asparagus field mostly lost from neglect,—the outbuildings, particularly Jimmys & Stephens houses very much delapidated [*sic*] & out of repair. No improvements whatever except in the house & no crop of any kind planted. . . .

June 21 . . . I have arranged with Jimmy to move out with his family to Hampton to stay there & take care of the place, when it is delivered up to me. He went out today & began making up the fences so as to plant a crop of Peas. . . .

1876

March 27 . . . Mary has taken Henry Smiths house, and is fitting it up for boarders. The rent is $60 the first month & $40 after. . . .

April 1 Mary made an arrangement yesterday evening with Mr

Chetfield to take two of the rooms for lodgers at $1.50 a room, & will probably take all she has furnished. A party of four ladies have taken two of the rooms, only as lodgers at $3 a day for the two rooms. . . .

April 3 Two more rooms taken by lodgers this morning—. . . .

April 10 . . . I have arranged with Henry Smith to take back the house on payment of $30. for half month. We have lost upwards of $30. by the 2 weeks operations. Enough for that speculation. . . .

April 20 Miss Blackman & Miss Beardsley came this morning to board at $15 each per week, having separate rooms. We have given up our chamber & fitted up the parlor for a bedroom. . . .

1879

December 1 . . . Received from James Wilson yesterday a Postal card announcing the sale of my two $500. S.C.R.R. Bonds at 24½ = $245.00 This is one of the last fragments of my property from the wreck of 15 years ago—I still have one $500. bond of Sav. & Ch. R R. which is unsalable & perhaps never will be worth any thing—& I have my Hampton Hill farm & this house & lot in Aiken. The Hampton Hill property is deteriorating yearly & I have offered it for 2 years past at $4500 but cannot get a purchaser. I find it rather hard to get on with my family of 8, with the little income I can muster. . . .

1881

April 29 . . . Mary looks thin after her close confinement & hard work with the boarders. The last of them left on Monday. . . .

1882

March 6 . . . I offered Hampton Hill for sale today at public auction, but could not sell. . . .

1885

February 9 . . . Received today from Col. Butler $200 for my services during the past summer in attending to the botanical collections from our State to New Orleans Exposition. . . .

Three Tenant Families

In the summer of 1936 James Agee, poet, novelist, and critic, and Walker Evans, distinguished photographer, investigated in a new way the lives of cotton tenant farmers in the deep South. As the Preface to their book says, they were trying to deal with their subject, "not as journalists, sociologists, politicians, entertainers, humanitarians, priests, or artists, but seriously." To do this they lived with one tenant family, meanwhile observing the lives of two other families as intimately and constantly as they could. They intended their record and analysis to be exhaustive, "with no detail, however trivial it may seem, left untouched, no relevancy avoided, which lies within the power of remembrance to maintain, of the intelligence to perceive, and of the spirit to persist in."

The book that records their experience, Let Us Now Praise Famous Men *(Three Tenant Families)* (1941), *is appalling in its revelation of the lower depths of farm tenantry in the years of the Depression, yet warm and human without being sentimental. Nothing escaped the eye and the ear of the poet and the lens of the photographer.*

The two selections from James Agee and Walker Evan's Let Us Now Praise Famous Men *(pages 115–21 and 209–10) are reprinted by permission of and arrangement with Houghton Mifflin Company, the authorized publishers.*

MONEY

Woods and Ricketts work for Michael and T. Hudson Margraves, two brothers, in partnership, who live in Cookstown. Gudger worked for the Margraves for three years; he now (1936) works for Chester Boles, who lives two miles south of Cookstown.

On their business arrangements, and working histories, and on their money, I wrote a chapter too long for inclusion in this volume without sacrifice of too much else. I will put in its place here as extreme a précis as I can manage.

Gudger has no home, no land, no mule; none of the more important farming implements. He must get all these of his landlord. Boles, for his share of the corn and cotton, also advances him rations money during four months of the year, March through June, and his fertilizer.

Gudger pays him back with his labor and with the labor of his family.

At the end of the season he pays him back further: with half his corn; with half his cotton; with half his cottonseed. Out of his own half of these crops he also pays him back the rations money, plus interest, and his share of the fertilizer, plus interest, and such other debts, plus interest, as he may have incurred.

What is left, once doctors' bills and other debts have been deducted, is his year's earnings.

Gudger is a straight half-cropper, or sharecropper.

Woods and Ricketts own no home and no land, but Woods owns one mule and Ricketts owns two, and they own their farming implements. Since they do not have to rent these tools and animals, they work under a slightly different arrangement. They give over to the landlord only a third of their cotton and a fourth of their corn. Out of their own parts of the crop, however, they owe him the price of two thirds of their cotton fertilizer and three fourths of their corn fertilizer, plus interest; and, plus interest, the same debts on rations money.

Woods and Ricketts are tenants: they work on third and fourth.

A very few tenants pay cash rent: but these two types of arrangement, with local variants (company stores; food instead of rations money; slightly different divisions of the crops) are basic to cotton tenantry all over the South.

From March through June, while the cotton is being cultivated, they live on the rations money.

From July through to late August, while the cotton is making, they live however they can.

From late August through October or into November, during the picking and ginning season, they live on the money from their share of the cottonseed.

From then on until March, they live on whatever they have earned in the year; or however they can.

During six to seven months of each year, then—that is, during exactly such time as their labor with the cotton is of absolute necessity to the landlord—they can be sure of whatever living is possible in rations advances and in cottonseed money.

During five to six months of the year, of which three are the hardest months of any year, with the worst of weather, the least adequacy of shelter, the worst and least of food, the worst of health, quite normal and inevitable, they can count on nothing except that they may hope least of all for any help from their landlords.

Gudger—a family of six—lives on ten dollars a month rations money during four months of the year. He has lived on eight, and on six. Woods—a family of six—until this year was unable to get better than eight a month during the same period; this year he managed to get it up to ten. Ricketts—a family of nine—lives on ten dollars a month during this spring and early summer period.

This debt is paid back in the fall at eight per cent interest. Eight per cent is charged also on the fertilizer and on all other debts which tenants incur in this vicinity.

At the normal price, a half-sharing tenant gets about six dollars a bale from his share of the cottonseed. A one-mule, half-sharing tenant makes on the average three bales. This half-cropper, then, Gudger, can count on eighteen dollars, more or less, to live on during the picking and ginning: though he gets nothing until his first bale is ginned.

Working on third and fourth, a tenant gets the money from two thirds of the cottonseed of each bale: nine dollars to the bale. Woods, with one mule, makes three bales, and gets twenty-seven dollars. Ricketts, with two mules, makes and gets twice that, to live on during the late summer and fall.

What is earned at the end of a given year is never to be depended on and, even late in a season, is never predictable. It can be enough to tide through the dead months of the winter, sometimes even better: it can be enough, spread very thin, to take through two months, and a sickness, or six weeks, or a month: it can be little enough to be completely meaningless: it can be nothing: it can be enough less than nothing to insure a tenant only of an equally hopeless lack of money at the end of his next year's work: and whatever one year may bring in the way of good luck, there is never any reason to hope that that luck will be repeated in the next year or the year after that.

The best that Woods has ever cleared was $1300 during a war year. During the teens and twenties he fairly often cleared as much as $300; he fairly often cleared $50 and less; two or three times he ended the year in debt. During the depression years he has more often cleared $50 and less; last year he cleared $150, but serious illness during the winter ate it up rapidly.

The best that Gudger has ever cleared is $125. That was in the plow-under year. He felt exceedingly hopeful and bought a mule: but when his landlord warned him of how he was coming out the next year, he sold it. Most years he has not made more than $25 to $30; and about one year in three he has ended in debt. Year before last he wound up $80 in debt; last year, $12; of Boles, his new landlord, the first thing he had to do was borrow $15 to get through the winter until rations advances should begin.

Years ago the Ricketts were, relatively speaking, almost prosperous. Besides their cotton farming they had ten cows and sold the milk, and they lived near a good stream and had all the fish they wanted. Ricketts went $400 into debt on a fine young pair of mules. One of the mules died before it had made its first crop; the other died the year after; against his fear, amounting to full horror, of sinking to the half-crop level where nothing is owned, Ricketts went into debt for other, inferior mules; his cows went one by one into debts and desperate exchanges and by sickness; he got congestive chills; his wife got pellagra; a number of his children died; he got appendicitis and lay for days on end under the ice cap; his wife's pellagra got into her brain; for ten consecutive years now, though they have lived on so little rations money, and have turned nearly all their cottonseed money toward their debts, they have not cleared or had any hope of clearing a cent at the end of the year.

It is not often, then, at the end of the season, that a tenant clears enough money to tide him through the winter, or even an appreciable part of it. More generally he can count on it that, during most of the four months between settlement time in the fall and the beginning of work and resumption of rations advances in the early spring, he will have no money and can expect none, nor any help, from his landlord: and of having no money during the six midsummer weeks of laying by, he can be still more sure. Four to six months of each year, in other words, he is much more likely than not to have nothing whatever, and during these months he must take care for himself: he is no responsibility of the landlord's. All he can hope to do is find work. This is hard, because there are a good many chronically unemployed in the towns, and they are more convenient to most openings for work and can at all times be counted on if they are needed; also there is no increase, during these two dead farming seasons, of other kinds of work to do. And so, with no more jobs open than at any other time of year, and with plenty of men already convenient to take them, the whole tenant population, hundreds and thousands in any locality, are desperately in need of work.

A landlord saves up certain odd jobs for these times of year: they go, at less than he would have to pay others, to those of his tenants who happen to live nearest or to those he thinks best of; and even at best they don't amount to much.

When there is wooded land on the farm, a landlord ordinarily per-

IV   *Southerners at Home*

mits a tenant to cut and sell firewood for what he can get. About the best a tenant gets of this is a dollar a load, but more often (for the market is glutted, so many are trying to sell wood) he can get no better than half that and less, and often enough, at the end of a hard day's peddling, miles from home, he will let it go for a quarter or fifteen cents rather than haul it all the way home again: so it doesn't amount to much. Then, too, by no means everyone has wood to cut and sell: in the whole southern half of the county we were working mainly in, there was so little wood that the negroes, during the hard winter of 1935–36, were burning parts of their fences, outbuildings, furniture and houses, and were dying off in great and not seriously counted numbers, of pneumonia and other afflictions of the lungs.

WPA work is available to very few tenants: they are, technically, employed, and thus have no right to it: and if by chance they manage to get it, landlords are more likely than not to intervene. They feel it spoils a tenant to be paid wages, even for a little while. A tenant who so much as tries to get such work is under disapproval.

There is not enough direct relief even for the widows and the old of the county.

Gudger and Ricketts, during this year, were exceedingly lucky. After they, and Woods, had been turned away from government work, they found work in a sawmill. They were given the work on condition that they stay with it until the mill was moved, and subject strictly to their landlord's permission: and their employer wouldn't so much as hint how long the work might last. Their landlords quite grudgingly gave them permission, on condition that they pay for whatever help was needed in their absence during the picking season. Gudger hired a hand, at eight dollars a month and board. Ricketts did not need to: his family is large enough. They got a dollar and a quarter a day five days a week and seventy-five cents on Saturday, seven dollars a week, ten hours' work a day. Woods did not even try for this work: he was too old and too sick.

GENERAL HABITABILITY

It is very easy, by mention of, for instance, a fireplace, to make a home or room seem more or less well-appointed than it actually is: also, in my enthusiasm for certain aspects, I have neglected others. I want here briefly to review the houses in terms of their function as shelter.

Even when a wall or roof passes the "daylight" test, i.e., if, in a darkened room, no light leaks through seams, it is a very poor protection indeed against the weather, particularly the wind wet and coldness of winter: for it is only one thin thickness of wood, surrounding a space which cannot be properly heated. Moreover, a tenant house is open to the weather from all six sides, for the floor is raised, and there are seldom protection boards between floor and earth; and ceilings are not at all common. Holes and broken windows are stopped as well as may be with rags, papers, ropes, raw cotton, and cardboard, but none of this is more than a fraction effective. Only the Ricketts have double walls and, in their bedroom, a big enough fireplace to heat the room. The others are large enough only to heat their immediate vicinity; their chimneys are badly made and do not draw well; the fires cannot be kept going at night; the bedding is ragged and inadequate; the uncarpeted floors are very cold. The warmest and best-protected room at the Gudgers' is the kitchen. It is too warm in summer. The worst room at the Woods' is the kitchen. It is too cold in winter. The Ricketts' kitchen is too large for comfort in winter. The only screen on all three farms is one at Gudger's. Aside from this, windows and doors are shut tight at night, in winter against cold, in summer by custom, and against "the night air," and against fever mosquitoes. As I have pointed out, two of Gudger's four rooms are so badly made as to be uninhabitable. There is no possibility of privacy at any time for any purpose. The water facilities are such as to hold laundering and personal cleanliness at or beneath its traditional minimum; to virtual nullity during the cold months of the year, and, in the case of the Ricketts and Woods, the water is very probably unhealthful. The beds, the bedding, and the vermin are such a crime against sex and the need of rest as no sadistic genius could much improve on. The furniture in general and the eating implements are all at or very near the bottom of their scale: broken, insecure, uncomfortable, ill-smelling, all that a man without money must constantly accept, when he can get it, and be glad of, or make do. Since I have talked of "esthetics" the least I can do is to add a note on it in their terms: they live in a steady shame and insult of discomforts, insecurities, and inferiorities, piecing these together into whatever semblance of comfortable living they can, and the whole of it is a stark nakedness of makeshifts and the lack of means: yet they are also, of course, profoundly anesthetized. The only direct opinion I got on the houses as such was from Mrs. Gudger, and it was, with the tears coming to her eyes, "Oh, I do *hate* this house *so bad!* Seems like they ain't nothing in the whole world I can do to make it pretty." As for the anesthesia: it seems to me a little more unfortunate, if possible, to be unconscious of an ill than to be conscious of it; though the deepest and most honest and incontrovertible rationalization of the middle-class southerner is that they are "used" to it.

Georgians at Home

The following passage is reprinted from Georgia, A Guide to its Towns and Countryside, *issued by the University of Georgia Press in 1940. This is one of the state guides compiled by the Federal Writers' Project.*

THE average Georgian votes the Democratic ticket, attends the Baptist or Methodist church, goes home to midday dinner, relies greatly on high cotton prices, and is so good a family man that he flings wide his doors to even the most distant of his wife's cousins' cousins. But these facts, significant as they are, should not be taken as all-revealing. In this, the largest of the southeastern states, there is no one characteristic type, even though the racial texture is relatively simple. The lethargic Georgia cracker of popular legend, with his drawl, his tattered overalls, and his corncob pipe, is no more typical than several other figures. The term "cracker," which originated in connection with the cracking whips of the early tobacco rollers, has evolved into a term of double meaning. Since it may designate any Georgia citizen or the most slovenly of the poor-white class, the visitor would be wiser not to thank his hostess for her delightful cracker hospitality.

Even in politics it is unsafe to make predictions. The average Georgian, close to the land and to family life, is inclined to be the protector of things as they are and the enemy of violent change. Often he is far more ready to acknowledge the presence of bad conditions than he is to suggest remedies, for he has the conservative feeling that the cure may be worse than the disease. Nevertheless, his political traditions sometimes compel his tacit support of a disturbingly liberal program merely because he cannot bring himself to change his party. In ante bellum and Reconstruction times the Georgian was hot with conviction as he hurried to the ballot box; in the twentieth century a crucial issue is needed to bring out a large poll. Although many citizens of the more populous centers, particularly businessmen, have broken wholly away from the political tradition of the Solid South, many a farmer and small-town merchant preserves a rather bewildered allegiance to his party merely because he finds any other course unthinkable.

142

This respect for ancestral usage, however, does not impel the Georgian to conceal himself from the modern world. Often he is boldly and genuinely liberal; almost always he responds to innovations that make his life more comfortable and efficient. Perhaps his attitude toward old ways is less one of respect than of an indulgent but unblinking affection. Old houses in Georgia have not been well preserved unless they were also agreeable to live in, and it is only in recent years that organizations in the state have begun to commemorate its historic spots. In most ways the Georgian does not linger long in the shadow of his forbears.

Nor is this condition entirely of modern times. With certain mutations, it is a normal evolution from Colonial days, when the settlers, despite the financial aid extended to them by the trustees, had to rely largely upon their own energy for economic survival. The Georgia colony, created partly as a protective rampart between South Carolina and the hostile Spaniards of Florida, was regarded as a stepsister of South Carolina, peopled by adventurers. Various visiting chroniclers of the early nineteenth century made allusion both favorable and unfavorable to the Georgian's shrewdness, his readiness to bargain keenly, and his energy in the pursuit of prosperity. Similar comments came from within. The state's own commentators seemed content to see their ideal embodied in the canny but honest country gentleman of Augustus Baldwin Longstreet's *Georgia Scenes*.

The modern prototype of that gentleman, equally robust, is found less frequently on the farm than in the small town. Other types may be more numerous, but none is more important or more characteristic of sectional culture. In this state the big man in a small town is so powerful that in certain communities he has the prerogatives of a patriarch and a dictator. Usually his despotism is benevolent, but it is seldom questioned. In a remote hamlet of south Georgia a stranger who wished to go hunting was informed that he must secure not only a hunting license but also the permission of the town's leading citizen. This gentleman not only granted that permission but offered free bed and board, and enthusiastically joined the visitor in the hunt. But without this royal consent the reception would not have been so pleasant. Far from resenting his highhanded ways, the autocrat's friends usually chuckle, "Well, you know how Mr. Ed is."

Although this Main Street monarch no longer lives on a farm, he usually owns one and is never very far away from it in spirit. If any generalization could be patterned to fit Georgians, it would be that even the most urbane ones have seldom traveled far from plowed fields and country lanes. About two thirds of the state population is actually engaged in agriculture, and the remaining third—although some do not realize it—is powerfully affected by the cotton crop. Rare indeed is the citizen with more than two generations of city life behind him. Even the most hard-driven city banker holds fast to his father's farm; even the most fashionable urban society takes pleasure in the rural amusements of barbecues, fish fries, and possum hunts. For all its industrial wealth, its factories, and its capital city of bright eastern smartness, Georgia is still an agricultural state.

The wagon-rutted red-clay roads of Georgia are not only farm-to-market but farm-to-courthouse highways; for the rural voter, stoutly fortified by the county-unit electoral system, is a powerful force in state politics. The norm is found neither in the lackadaisical poor-white sharecropper nor in the keen young graduate of a modern agricultural college, but somewhere between these two—in a rangy, slow-speaking man, red with sunburn and a little stiff from outdoor work in all sorts of weather. He gathers with his own kind at the cross-roads store, which is often the real seat of legislative decisions. To a stranger asking a direction he is as polite as he is loquacious, very ready to answer with "ma'am" or "sir," but in argument he is no easier to overcome than his own mule. Riding to town in his rumbling wagon or well-worn Ford, he is quietly aware that his place in the community is an important one. Although many of his kindred and friends have left the farm in poverty, he still keeps it the center of power.

Although the family has felt shattering forces here as elsewhere, there still persists the fierce and tenacious clan loyalty that was so mighty a cohesive force in Colonial society. This quality explains many common phenomena: the interminable "little visits" among brothers and sisters, the tolerance for crabbed uncles and crotchety aunts, the care for old family servants, the vigilance for favors from cousins in high places, the long and intricate tribal conferences whenever a daughter marries or a son changes his job.

Even in Atlanta, least typically southern of southern cities, a host will heartily urge his guests to stay even though he whisper to his wife that night in the bedroom, "How long do you reckon Cousin Annie Mae means to visit us?" Accepting all "kinfolks" as inevitable, he invites them to his daughter's wedding, which is likely to be a lavish affair with lovely bridesmaids in pastel dresses, and several rooms set aside for the sparkling display of wedding gifts. In their turn, the guests feel bound to send gifts, no matter how slight the actual intimacy. Georgia's tradition of social obligation seems unlikely to be lost, for it has survived almost intact through the War between the States and the bitter years of poverty that went on even into the new century.

Although Georgians are not "still fighting the Civil War," they mean that conflict and nothing later when they refer to "the war."

Margaret Mitchell's *Gone with the Wind* did not arouse, but merely confirmed, the sectional feeling of the old people who remember General Sherman's march to the sea, and even readers who did not like Scarlett O'Hara or Rhett Butler acclaimed the book for its picture of Georgia plantation life. The fire of sectional resentment no longer flames fiercely, but the invaders are not wholly forgotten. Although Georgia is only beginning to be well adorned with historic markers, the Union invasion has left towering monuments in the minds of its oldest citizens and of their children reared in the years of famine. With each generation the fire burns lower, but it still smoulders enough to make the War between the States a rather dubious topic to be introduced by the northern visitor. Only the most modern young Georgians can discuss impersonally the reasons for the destructive march to the sea.

Georgia's young people, more widely traveled than their parents, have lost much of their sectional individuality as they have acquired closer resemblance to young people throughout the nation. They have learned to accept many conditions formerly rejected in their state. Their attitude toward the educated Negro, for instance, may be different from that of their elders who still prefer the old-fashioned unlettered kind. The college-bred Negro is likely to be lonely except in Atlanta, the world's largest center of Negro education, where he finds many of his own kind. The older Georgian generally meets this type with civility but with aloofness, feeling a half-conscious distrust because he has not grown accustomed to the educated Negro's new and precise enunciation. The rich slurring tones of his old nurse are to him more natural.

But, however cool he may be toward the cause of Negro education, the Georgian is usually kind to his own servants and not a little apprehensive of hurting their feelings. Although many Georgia women do their own housework, many others still employ a general servant who is usually referred to as "the cook." Likewise, the gardener is called "the yard man." If these servants have been long with the families which they serve, they are loquacious, assured, and quite capable of showing strong preferences among their masters' friends. Only very old servants will go so far as to invite their favorites to dinner without first consulting higher authority, but few southern women would be heedless of the warning tone in which a cook mutters, "It's time you wuz havin' Miss Grace to supper."

In Georgia the past and the present sometimes are blended harmoniously, sometimes are separated sharply. Although many parts of the state move slowly, they almost never have that museum stillness which some visitors apparently expect. Change may come very gradually, but it does come, even in decorous Savannah, the most aristocratic of Georgia's larger cities; and often the younger generation appears more jaunty than it is because of the contrasting quiet background. Even in the villages of the north Georgia mountains is seen the sleek, tightly waved hair of native daughters who have visited the traveling "beautician." In many ways Georgia has become very much like other states.

Where, then, can a tourist expect to catch the characteristic flavor and experience the real "feel" of Georgia? He will not always find it in Atlanta, sprawling and rich; or in sedate and beautiful Savannah; or in Augusta, where the past is thrown into sharper relief by the smartness of wealthy tourists. Perhaps he will come nearest to finding it in rolling hills of red clay, brown cornfields, white patches of cotton, and green fields of watermelons. He will find it on many a quiet farm, where the plow has left long undulating furrows over the hills, and where, each Saturday, the children sweep the yard very clean and bare. He will find it after church on Sunday, when the young married couples join their parents about a table loaded with fried chicken, ham, hot biscuits, jelly, preserves, and all the vegetables from the garden. Afterward the men smoke and sit on the worm fence, talking crops and politics, and the women gossip on the porch while they watch the children at play.

This characteristic atmosphere may also be caught in the typical Georgia town, where the wide streets are bordered by magnificent trees and a rather sparse planting of grass. Downtown, amid brick shops of the 1880's and 1890's, a Confederate soldier of granite or marble leans on his musket as he watches over the quiet courthouse square. Sometimes the passing automobiles are packed tightly with boys and girls in slacks, polo shirts, and sun-back dresses, looking like young people everywhere. Their faces may seem very young to a visitor, for a Georgia girl begins "going out" a year or two earlier than northern girls, so that her debut is less an introduction than a triumphant affirmation of popularity.

In these towns the center of sociability has shifted from the livery stable to the corner drug store, the garage, and the filling station. Spanish mission bungalows and scrollwork cottages have sprung up amid the columned ante bellum houses, and even some of these latter have been modified by additions of bandsaw banisters or screened porches. The porch is a real Georgia institution. Here throughout the summer evenings sit thousands of Georgians, neither rushing into the future nor running away from it, but waiting to accept it as it comes.

146

V

WORKING THE LAND

THE most striking symbol of the newest South is the oil derrick in the midst of acres of cotton blossoms. As an Oklahoma farmer said, "It's hard to keep your mind on the plow when oil is coming up from down under." The changes taking place in the traditionally rural South are evident in other ways. The casual visitor to Memphis or Macon, watching the smoke from industrial plants of many kinds, will not imagine that these cities once flourished solely because they supplied the needs of cotton farmers. They are still "cotton towns," but their earlier function has been obscured. Nevertheless, in the South today Jefferson's famous words are still gospel: "Those who labour in the earth are the chosen people of God."

The first crops were those which pioneers everywhere in early America planted to feed their families—chiefly corn and pumpkins, which the Indians, North and South, taught them how to grow and use. In the South they also taught their white conquerors the pleasures of tobacco, the first of several agricultural products that were to become the South's own. In 1612 John Rolfe made it certain that Virginia's staple would be tobacco when he found a way to cure the native product so that it would lose its bitter taste and thus could supplant Spanish tobacco in the English market. Spanish missionaries brought oranges, lemons, figs, and sugar-cane to Florida. According to legend, rice imported from Madagascar in 1694 started that still important Southern crop on its way in the swamplands of South Carolina. Indigo, a difficult and nasty crop to cultivate, gave a brief prosperity to growers in South Carolina and Louisiana. The peak year for this now vanished crop was 1775. Cotton-growing did not become a major Southern occupation until after the invention of the cotton gin by a Yankee in 1793.

Why cotton was "king" in the Old South is easily explained. In the first place, there was a steady demand for it in the textile towns of New and Old England. It became, therefore, the great "cash crop" of the South. As it was easy to grow, even the least skilled and intelligent slaves could be trusted with it. Once the South achieved a virtual monopoly in the trade, the belief became fixed that the region's prosperity was based solely on cotton. During the early years of the Civil War many Southern leaders were certain that England would have to furnish aid to the South in order that it might keep its jennies and looms in operation.

Many of the ills of modern Southern agriculture can be traced to evils inherent in the plantation system as it developed in the great cotton belt that extends from Virginia to Texas. In the days of slavery the plantation-owner and his family lived well even though his cotton-factor might hold an expanding mortgage on his acres. The plantation provided subsistence crops for the master's family and his slaves. But the yearly pressure to produce as many bales of cotton as possible rapidly exhausted the land. There were two things one could do: use chemical fertilizer (which does not rebuild soil) or buy new plantations. The land-hungry planters were necessarily land-speculators.

When the Civil War shattered the plantation system, its inherent self-destructiveness came into play and impeded a diversified Southern agriculture until the 1930's. Tenancy and sharecropping, still the greatest ills of Southern rural life, were inevitable. The impoverished plantation-owners, deprived of slave labor, must either pay wages or rent their land for cash, which few white men and almost no Negroes had, or resort to sharecropping. Consequently the destructive overcultivation of the land was accelerated until, in this century, the red gashes in the eroded hillsides and the vast stretches of worn-out land covered with scrub oak and pine convinced the traveler from Illinois or Wisconsin that the South must indeed be the nation's number-one economic problem.

But the land, or much of it, has come back—with the help of state departments of agriculture, the county agents, the agricultural schools, TVA, and subsidies from the Federal government. And, of course, the gradually increasing wealth of the South, flowing from factories as well as farms, has in many regions made it possible to break the vicious circle of the one-crop system.

One can travel many miles in the South today and see agricultural prosperity—orchards, herds of beef and dairy cattle, new farm equipment, paint on the barns and houses—where once there was only hopeless poverty. This does not mean that the agricultural millennium has arrived. In 1945 over half of the *cotton* farmers were still tenants or sharecroppers. And the value of farm acreage in several Southern states is only about half what it is in the states in the North and West which have comparable amounts of land under cultivation.

The Northerner who persists in believing that the South is still the land of cotton, tobacco, and sugar-cane will be surprised to learn that the leading sweet-potato county in the United States is St. Landry, Louisiana; that Polk County, Florida, leads in fruits and nuts; Spartan-burg, South Carolina, in peaches; Dougherty, Georgia, in pecans; Hildago, Texas, in vegetables. He is probably also unaware of the fact that the westward movement of Southern agriculture, which began in colonial days, has culminated in the amazing productivity of Texas. Of the eighteen Southern counties that led nationally in the growing of particular crops at the time of the 1950 census, eight are in Texas, and of these, five border the Rio Grande. Texas may belong to the West rather than the South, as some argue, but it now stands in the forefront of the states that produce the traditionally Southern crops.

Jefferson on "Those who labour in the earth"

This famous passage from Jefferson's Notes on the State of Virginia *(first edition, 1785) is the most eloquent as well as the most extreme statement he ever made on the virtues of an agricultural economy. In part, it was motivated by sentiment: Jefferson was an excellent planter and loved the ten thousand acres he cultivated with farsighted skill. But there was also logic in the position he takes here. Earlier in this section (Query XIX—"The present state of manufactures, commerce, interior and exterior trade") he makes the point that in Europe the people must resort to manufactures and trade to support themselves, since the land is pre-empted. In America, for a long time to come, there will be "an immensity of land courting the industry of the husbandman."*

This, then, was Jefferson's personal attitude, partly moral and sentimental and partly political and theoretical. He became, it is true, the leader of the agrarian party in America, whose strength was largely in the South. Yet while he was President of the United States he made no effort to favor agriculture at the expense of industry or commerce, the "handmaid of agriculture."

This passage is reprinted from pages 274–5 of the first English edition of the Notes on the State of Virginia *(London, 1787).*

THOSE who labour in the earth are the chosen people of God, if ever he had a chosen people, whose breasts he has made his peculiar deposit for substantial and genuine virtue. It is the focus in which he keeps alive that sacred fire, which otherwise might escape from the face of the earth. Corruption of morals in the mass of cultivators is a phaenomenon of which no age nor nation has furnished an example. It is the mark set on those, who, not looking up to heaven, to their own soil and industry, as does the husbandman, for their subsistance, depend for it on casualties and caprice of customers. Dependance begets subservience and venality, suffocates the germ of virtue, and prepares fit tools for the designs of ambition. This, the natural progress and consequence of the arts, has sometimes perhaps been retarded by accidental circumstances: but, generally speaking, the proportion which the aggregate of the other classes of citizens bears in any state to that of its husbandmen, is the proportion of its unsound to its healthy parts, and is a good-enough barometer whereby to measure its degree of corruption. While we have land to labour then, let us never wish to see our citizens occupied at a workbench, or twirling a distaff. Carpenters, masons, smiths, are wanting in husbandry: but, for the general operations of manufacture, let our work-shops remain in Europe. It is better to carry provisions and materials to workmen there, than bring them to the provisions and materials, and with them their manners and principles. The loss by the transportation of commodities across the Atlantic will be made up in happiness and permanence of government. The mobs of great cities add just so much to the support of pure government, as sores do to the strength of the human body. It is the manners and spirit of a people which preserve a republic in vigour. A degeneracy in these is a canker which soon eats to the heart of its laws and constitution.

Blue Smoke

Who should speak, in this book, for the generations of Southerners who for more than three hundred years have put their hopes for a good life and the security of their families in tobacco, that most unpredictable of crops, tricky to grow and perpetually subject to the whims of buyers, manufacturers, and smokers and chewers the world over? An early Virginia parson who received his salary in sixteen thousand pounds of Sweet-Scented or Oronoko? Robert Carter of Nomini Hall, who in 1752 consigned more than one hundred hogsheads of tobacco, at a peak price, to the firm of Charles Goore of Liverpool? James B. ("Buck") Duke, who in 1890 formed the American Tobacco Company, the giant corporation that embraced practically the entire industry? One of the "night riders" in the war that raged between growers and buyers in the dark tobacco country of Kentucky between 1907 and 1909?

The election lights on Sherwood Anderson (1876–1941). After 1921 he lived much of the time in the South. Troutdale, in the hill country of southwest Virginia, was home. In these later years, as his powers as a writer of fiction waned, Anderson wrote many perceptive essays about Southern mineworkers, mill-hands, and the small farmers who, like the men and women in "Blue Smoke," were struggling during the

❁

You begin with the ground—Ground lugs—Bright lugs—Yellow red
—Long red—Short red and tips.

The big tobacco warehouse and sales-room is at the edge of a town
over the Virginia line in Tennessee. There are these big tobacco warehouses and sales-rooms in a dozen towns within a morning's truck-
driving distance of the town from which I write, and there are tobacco
farmers in town from over in Virginia, from North Carolina, from
Kentucky, and even from South Carolina.

A learned man at the post office in one of these towns told me that
this Southern Appalachian country is one of the oldest in the world.
He says he got it out of a book. He says that is the reason why the
hills are so soft and round. The towns are tucked away in the valleys
in the hills. From the hilltops there are little white towns with many
church spires.

A man from within ten miles of this town may take his tobacco to a
Virginia or South Carolina town, and a man from far over in Kentucky
may try his luck here. The towns scream on billboards along the high-
ways. The towns shout, "TAKE YOUR TOBACCO TO GREEN-
VILLE." "TRY ABINGDON." "ASHEVILLE, THE BEST TO-
BACCO MARKET IN THE SOUTH."

The towns want the market. The merchants hunger for it. In Asheville, two years ago, a merchant explained to me. That year the banks
began cracking up down there. "If we hadn't got a pretty good tobacco market we'd have been done for," he said. The market may be
important to the merchant, eager for the farmer's money, but it's ten
times as important to the little tobacco raisers. They come into town
filled with what the economists call "income expectancy."

What happens to them here, at this market, is the turning point of
the year.

To many of them it means a year's income, all they will get. The
kids need shoes and maybe a new suit or dress. And there is the "old
woman," the tobacco farmer's wife. Just because she is called the "old
woman" doesn't mean she is old. She is usually long and lean as is her
"old man." This is still the hill country, little farms tucked away in
little valleys in the hills—"hollers," they call them.

"Where's your place, Luther?"

I am not going to try to write in the dialect of the country.

"Why, I'm a Scott County man. It's in Scratchgravel Holler." He's a Virginian, that one. He has come over here into Tennessee, to try his luck in this Tennessee market. The native Virginian never locates himself by a town. He doesn't say, "I'm from over near Lynchburg, or Charlottesville," as a Middle-Western man would. He says, "I'm from Grayson, or Scott, or Albemarle," naming his county. I remember a Virginia Floyd County woman who had married into Augusta County. "How are you, Mrs. Greer?" I asked. "I'm just common," she said, "except I'm honing for Floyd." It's good. It's a land, not a town attachment.

The men stand wistfully in the road before the tobacco market. Some of them have come to the market alone, others have brought their families. The tobacco farmer rarely has a truck of his own to bring his tobacco to market. "I'm too small a feller for that," he explains. He may own a Model T Ford. You can't haul much tobacco in that.

So he goes in with half a dozen neighbors and they hire a truck to do the hauling—John's tobacco, Jim's, Luther's, Fred's. "A little feller like I am can't put out much, maybe one acre, or two, or three."

"It's really a woman's crop," John says. "You've got to mess and mess with it, all year long." He stands before the warehouse, where the selling is going on. Luther and Jim and Fred stand with him. Fred has had a few shots of moon. You can smell it on him. He keeps slapping Jim on the back and laughing, rather foolishly. He says two of his kids, little fellers, put out half an acre for themselves. He helped them. They are both boys, and one of them wants a bicycle and the other some red-top boots. A man named Love comes up. "Hello, Love," Fred says, and I am a bit startled. "Is that really your name?" I want to ask. Love is built like another Abraham Lincoln. He has a long, scrawny neck, and there are bright red spots on his cheeks. "Look out or tuberculosis will get you," I think. He stands and spits on the ground. He is suspicious of me.

"You ain't a government man, are you?"

Formerly, in these hills, among these hill men, to admit you were a government man, that you had anything to do with government—to say the least, it was somewhat dangerous.

But times have changed. They have changed fast in the last year. There is a curious, wistful looking toward government now. Government becomes, to these little men, grubbing in the earth in these little valleys, curiously the Almost God.

Personified in Mr. Roosevelt. They are nice about it, but it has its connotations. These little farmers have been stripped naked by the money-changers time and again. I suspect that these men could be made into brown or black or silver shirts easily enough. They hunger for leadership, and are looking to government and to Franklin D. Roosevelt with a curious boyish faith. "We can't do it by ourselves," they keep saying. They feel dimly that the big tobacco and cigarette companies are the common enemy. "We can't handle 'em. Government's got to help us or we're lost." Government at Washington is something far away and outside local county and state government, "the law."

"Look out. Here comes the law." A short fat man, a deputy sheriff, walks past us.

The men keep speaking of Roosevelt. "Ain't going to blame him for nothing he can't do." As though to say—"don't expect too much." There is this curious sweetness, humility, in these common men. A man going about among them, as I am doing just now, keeps asking himself, "Why does any one want to cheat them or hurt them?"

Most of the tobacco in this country is raised in small patches, one or two or three or at the most five acres. It is Burley tobacco. It's an exacting crop. You work at it all through the year. Now the tobacco is going to market and the farmer who has just sold his crop will go home from here to burn over his seed bed for next year's crop.

For the seed bed he'll try to find a little patch of new rich ground, usually at the edge of the woods. The ground for the seed bed needs to be rich, so he selects the new ground, and if it isn't rich enough, he piles on the manure or the fertilizer.

Then he burns it over, puts on some dry litter and burns it off. The seed goes in and he takes a trip to town and buys strips of cheese-cloth to spread over the patch. Soon now you will see the little white patches over these hills.

Hoeing and cultivating and working all through the year. In the spring the fields blossom with a mass of lovely white bloom, a sight to see. You leave a few blossoms for next year's seed plants, but all the rest of the blossoms you take off. Fred says he nips his out with his fingers, but Luther says he uses a knife.

Then there is the harvest. It's a ticklish matter getting this crop in. When it comes to the sales warehouse, the sale floor, everything counts for you or against you. What you want, to get the price, is the great wide thin bright yellow tobacco leaves. Leaves can be so easily spotted and spoiled. They can dry too fast or too slow. If they are seasoned just right they will be soft, like soft silk.

But to get them that way is a job. It takes the skill and the know-how. As I have already said, it begins at the ground. You break off the lower leaves, bind them together into a "hand." That's your "ground lugs." You won't get so much for your ground lugs. The rains have washed up onto the leaves. They are discolored where they have touched the ground. They will be coarse and spotty. Then come your "bright lugs," your "yellow red," your "long red." Here's your money tobacco, if it's cured right. Your "tips," at the very top of the plant are likely to be small, broken and spotty. They will go off at a low price. They will make snuff or cheap smoking tobacco.

When you have cut your tobacco you build racks in the field and let it hang out to dry. That is to get your fine yellow color.

Then into the barn. You want a barn the rain can't get into but that lets in plenty of air.

Now comes the grading, time to have an eye in your head, to have feel in your fingers. Fred says, "Can't one man in ten grade tobacco. It's like picking a new dress for a woman."

Now the tobacco goes into the sales warehouse. It is carefully piled, each grade in a separate basket, and now come the buyers, the auctioneer and the pin hookers.

The pin hookers are a special breed. Some of them do nothing else but this all through the year. They work two months and rest ten. The big rush in the tobacco market lasts through January and February. The pin hooker is a man who knows his tobacco. He lives and bets on his knowledge. He is a man often who never raised a stalk of tobacco in his life, but he is a trader, and a sharp one. He knows his tobacco, and he knows his Fred, his Luther, Jim, and Tom. Life is a poker game for him.

The tobacco market is a kind of fair. Every one comes. The great, roomy warehouse is out at the edge of town near the railroad.

The patent medicine man has come, and the horse trader is here. There are long lines of trucks waiting for their turn to get tobacco on to the floor. The warehouse is owned by a private company. It takes off a percentage for every pound of tobacco sold. When there is a big market a farmer may be two or three days getting his crop on to the sales floor. He has brought a basket of food from home, and often at night he and the old woman and the kids sleep on the tobacco in the truck.

Then, during the daytime you walk about and watch the sale. Hope. Hope. Hope. There are only four or five big tobacco companies in America, and each has its buyer here. The buyers are young, shrewd, fast-thinking, clever.

The men go to the sales floor and come back. The tobacco is stacked in long rows. Now they are selling Tom Whistler's baskets. How indifferent the buyers appear! Can they know what this means to Tom? You have been in a hospital and have seen a surgeon cut a man's arm off. It's like that. Each buyer puts his arm into the basket and jerks out a hand of the tobacco. He holds it up to the light, feels the leaves, throws the hand back into the basket.

"Eight-fifty."

"Nine."

That is Tom Whistler standing over there with his wife and kids. This sale is to decide everything for him. This is his year's income. Will the wife get a new dress, the kids new shoes? Will he have money to pay his taxes? I saw a tall man sitting on top of his basket after the buyers had passed. He put his face down in his hands and cried. Love pointed him out to me.

"Fred got four cents for his crop last year," Love says to me. "Did Fred cry? No! Fred went out and got a bottle of moon and that night he got pie-eyed."

The tobacco industry is a big, regulated, controlled industry. But the little farmers feel it isn't controlled for them. Some of them talk about it as they stand in the warehouse and in the street, waiting.

The pin hooker moves about among them. He goes to a farmer whose crop has not yet been sold. He tempts the farmer. Some few of the farmers, the smart ones, those who know how to cure and grade their tobacco, know as much as the pin hooker. Others are unfortunate. "A lot of us are pretty dumb," Fred says. The pin hooker makes a flat offer. If he sees a basket he thinks is badly graded, he will go to the farmer, buy it and regrade it. There are the pin hookers who work outside and the floor pin hookers. I stood on the floor on a day when tobacco took a sharp jump upward. A pin hooker wearing a fancy vest and with a big cigar in his mouth came and spoke to me. "I shaved off eight hundred bucks today," he said. By a little sharp trading he had managed to make more in a few hours that morning than Fred or Luther or Love had made by a month of work in the field.

The tobacco raisers, standing about in the warehouse and in the street outside, keep talking about government. Men are going through the country now signing them up. The crop is to be cut sharply next year. Government is going to try taking a hand at control in their favor. "It has to begin at the ground, like raising tobacco," Love says. You can't tell these men that prices paid on the floor—in spite of the auctioneer, each company is represented by its own buyer—you can't convince them that the big companies don't fix the price.

Luther, who is more skillful than the others and gets a better price for his tobacco, has a radio and he tells the others what he hears coming through the air at night when he is at home. He speaks about individualism, explaining to the others. "It means something what they call the New Deal. It means that people have got to be made to quit cutting each other's throats. Individualism means that—the devil take the hindermost. We're the hindermost," he says and grins.

On the floor of the great warehouses the sales go on. Men with hand trucks are wheeling away the sold baskets. In another warehouse across the street men are at work packing the tobacco into great hogsheads. A long train of tobacco-loaded cars will leave here tonight. This to-bacco, now being sold, may not get to the user for years. It will be handled and rehandled, cured and recured, sorted, graded, tested, treated.

There is a constant hubbub, the cry of the auctioneer, the quick bark of the buyers. The shrewd-eyed pin hookers move from group to group. In the street the patent medicine man keeps talking. "You got hookworms, I tell you."

And now look, it is Fred's turn. The auctioneer and the buyers have come to his baskets. We all go into the warehouse to stand watching, and Fred draws a little away. His old woman, a thin-cheeked one of thirty, already with six kids—they get married young in the moun-tains—the kids are clinging to her skirts. There is fear in her eyes, in Fred's eyes, and even in the eyes of the children. "You get out of here," Fred says gruffly, and she takes the smallest of the children into her arms and, followed by the others, goes reluctantly away. Fred has spoken gruffly to her, but there is something else back of the gruffness in his voice. He has already had two or three drinks of moon. "You take now your eighteen- or your twenty-cent tobacco—a man can live," Jim says, "but your five- or your six-cent stuff—it's starvation."

Fred walks a little away and I see him standing by the wall. He takes a bottle from his hip pocket and has himself another shot. His best tobacco, his bright lugs, bring nine cents, but all the rest of it, two-thirds of his crop, goes for two and three cents.

Jim, Luther, and Tom do not look at Fred. Luther spits on the floor. Jim steps over and pulls a hand of tobacco out of a nearby basket. "This is pretty good," he says to me. He spreads one of the yellow leaves out over his big hand. "You see, it has been cured right. See how thin it is. Like silk, ain't it?"

The men stand looking at me, and I am suddenly ashamed of my city clothes. Jim, Luther, and Tom all wear patched clothes. Their overalls are patched, and all have long, thin, sun-tanned, wind-bitten faces. "You ain't a government man, are you?" Love asks me again. "Because if you are, you had better tell government they got to keep on helping us what they can."

"We've got pretty puny, trying to help ourselves," Jim says, and they all turn and walk away out of the warehouse and into the street.

Eight-cent Cotton and Forty-cent Meat

*Though he has been a journalist (and a good one) since he was gradu-
ated in 1926 from the School of Journalism of the University of Missouri, Ben Robertson knows cotton and loves the red hills of South
Carolina, where his kinfolks have cultivated it for generations. In the
book from which this selection is taken he says of his parents and of the
way they brought him up: "They wanted to instruct me in the rural
beauties, to ground me in the Southern fields, to give me an anchor that
no storm could ever loose, to give me an attitude, a philosophy, a purpose. . . . I was to know one special life and to know all that could be
known about it. I was to understand cotton farming and how to live
with tenant farmers and colored people on a cotton farm."*

*Parental discipline did not make a cotton farmer of Ben Robertson,
but in his* Red Hills and Cotton *he is able to tell why many of his kin
are still faithful to the crop that has supported them for over a hundred
years. He remembers how it once felt to stand "between the swerving
handles of the plow, to hold the handles lightly, and to walk barefooted in the fresh earth." The reward is worth the effort. Cotton is a
cash crop. "So all summer long we plow in the cotton fields and sing
and tell the mule what we intend to do when we have the cash in hand
from our cotton."*

This passage from Red Hills and Cotton *(New York, 1942), pp.
157–64, is reprinted by permission of Alfred A. Knopf, Inc.*

Our wagon was hitched to cotton's star, where it had been hitched
for a hundred years and where it still is hitched. We have been growing cotton in Twelve Mile Valley since the time of the grandfather of
our grandfather's father. Cotton is a state of mind with us, a philosophy, and we continue to plant it in spite of the fact that we have not
made money on cotton more than once in about every ten years. We
were prosperous once—in the early 1900's—and once we became temporarily rich—shortly after the first World War when cotton went to
forty cents a pound. We went wild when cotton went to forty cents.
We bought big cars and traveled to California on the train and bought
twenty-five-dollar silk shirts and paid twenty dollars for shoes. We

burned the wind with our sudden wealth, we enjoyed ourselves, and we have never had a regret—we would have lost the money in banks if we had not spent it, and we had rather throw money out the window than lose it in a bank.

Thirty years ago our Great-Aunt Narcissa began telling us the cotton kingdom was doomed—the world market was slipping irrevocably from us, we should begin substituting other crops. For at least fifteen years all of us have been fully aware that our reckoning day for cotton would inevitably come to hand, but even under these circumstances we have not turned away from cotton. We have gone right on plowing and planting. It is never easy for a people to give up a hundred-year-old tradition—our lives and our fathers' fathers' lives have been built around cotton. We have bought our clothes with a bale of cotton; we have built our houses with cotton money; we have sold a bale of cotton to pay our way through school. We have even campaigned in politics atop a cotton bale. And even our Great-Aunt Narcissa stated once in public that she did not care what anybody in Washington or anywhere else in the world said about cotton, it still was the greatest crop that heaven ever gave to any country.

The truth is we like to grow cotton. It is a beautiful crop to cultivate and gather. It has been fearfully hard on our hills and fields, but it has made life easy for us in our country, and up to this very day we have hoped against hope that something would turn up—that somewhere somehow the magic of science would find a new use for cotton fiber and we would be enabled to keep on depending for our living on cotton. Even now my cousin Stephen John says he cannot really believe the cotton market is about to slip from us. He says ever since he can remember he has been hearing tales about the doom that was about to overtake us, but that we have managed to pull through. He remembers hearing years ago how West Texas was going to grow two bales to the acre without an ounce of fertilizer. But somehow the West Texas menace never materialized. Then there was the boll-weevil scare —every year it got closer and a little closer and everybody said we would have to go out of the cotton business for sure when the boll weevil hit us. But what happened—we learned to plant earlier, to rush and dust the crop, and the boll weevil did not knock us out; it just made us the more determined.

Stephen John feels about the cotton crop as Mary does about the mechanical cotton-picker. One morning Mary came in to inquire if it was true that a cotton-picker was on its way to South Carolina from Mississippi. She said Aunt Nan and Aunt Neat had told her such a story and that they had said when the picker reached Carolina it was going to put all of the colored people out of work.

"What did you say to that?" I asked.

"I told them," said Mary, "I have had so much trouble in my life that I wasn't worrying about any cotton-picker until it was right here on us."

Cotton is an easy crop to grow. We can plant it in April, plow it and hoe it, work hard in the fields until August, and then lay the crop by and go off to camp meetings and all-day singings and fish fries. We need work but six months in a year in a cotton culture. Diversified agriculture calls for a twelve-month working season, and it would do us good to work twelve months—we admit that. Still, it would interfere with a lot of hunting and fishing and going to church. We have turned down dairying in our country, principally because a man is never free from a cow. Cotton gives you freedom. It does not perish, either, like melons or like an acre of lettuce. You can pile cotton bales in a shed and sit back and enjoy the sight of it for two years if you choose to. Once my Uncle Philip kept a crop of cotton for ten years in a barn. He did not sell it because he did not need the money, and he said he had rather have cotton in bales than cash in banks. It is a fine feeling to see your own cotton in your own barn—it gives you a sense of security that few know any more anywhere. Hard times and bankers cannot undermine a man so long as there is cotton in the shed. We have a song about that—about cotton in the shed, boys, sugar in the gourd.

Cotton, with us, is almost human. Cotton is like some member of the family that the folks have had a lot of trouble with, but in whom they still believe. My cousin Stephen says in spite of all that cotton has cost us we would be poorer today if we had to exist without it. Mary says she had rather chop cotton than cook, and Jim says that of all the work he has ever done—cutting wood, mowing lawns, growing cotton, railroading, working around racehorses—cotton-growing is best. The white man in the South likes to grow cotton; the black man is a cotton man. Jim says even our mules like to work in a big field of cotton. Jim says when the Secretary of Agriculture ordered every third cotton row plowed up he had great difficulty with his mule—his mule knew he had no business walking on the boss's cotton. Sometimes I think a Southerner's idea of heaven is a fine cotton-growing country with the price of cotton pegged at ten cents a pound—I will amend that: heaven is a fine cotton-growing country with the price of cotton pegged at twenty cents a pound.

Speaking one time at the Courthouse, my Grandfather Bowen said he understood our feeling for cotton—cotton was the symbol of our existence, nevertheless, he said we would be obliged to turn to diversification, we must of necessity raise more feed, keep more cows, raise more chickens. We must live at home—it was our only hope of fighting off the machine civilization, our one chance of resisting the compli-

160

cated insecurity of an industrial world. He realized diversification would interfere with fishing, but he asked how many fish were left to fish for; he said there were two colored men and one white man sitting on the banks of Twelve Mile for every fish in the river.

"We must work harder," said my earnest grandfather. "Forty per cent of our land is so acid that it will produce no crop from which we can realize an adequate standard of living; another forty per cent will produce only cotton, corn, and tobacco, leaving only twenty per cent suitable for diversified agriculture. But this problem, big as it is, offers us great hope, for all these soils can be limed—a relatively cheap process—and can be brought back into use. Our soils could support us all in abundance if we would make intelligent use of them."

South Carolina, said my grandfather, maintained for many years the highest corn yield per acre in the United States and at the same time ranked at the foot of the list in the general average yield. "That fact alone," he said, "shows our waste of opportunity." He said we had a high rate of infant mortality; we had hookworm; we had pellagra.

"We must work," he said, and he began to talk about the 1890's. "Back in those days," he added, "the folks in South Carolina didn't expect to make money. They didn't care much what kind of clothes they wore, but they did expect to have plenty to eat. It didn't make much difference then what the price of cotton was; we sure had the rations. We lived at home in those days, and sometimes at camp-meeting time we would have thirty people at our house and it didn't cost us any money for victuals—we just cut down a ham in the smoke-house, and picked more beans from the garden, and rounded up enough chickens out of the yard. Today, if thirty people came to some of your houses and stayed for more than a meal or two, you would have to borrow money from the bank—you would try to borrow it, anyhow."

There was piercing laughter. Women in their best taffeta dresses fanned themselves with palmettos, red-faced outdoor men wiped little rivers of sweat from their foreheads.

"Cotton," said a tenant farmer, rising awkwardly from the audience, "used to be eight cents when we didn't know what it was to want an automobile, and now that we have paved roads and have to have automobiles and radios and electric lights, cotton is still eight cents."

"The reason cotton hasn't kept in line with other things," said my grandfather quietly, "is that we have to sell it on the world market—we have to grow it on a protected market but we have to sell it in an unprotected one."

"I understand that," said the tenant frowning, "I understand why cotton is still eight cents, but what puzzles me is the price of ham." He waved his long lean arms. "In the old days when cotton was eight cents, ham at the store was eight cents. Hogs in those days sold for eight and ten cents. Hogs sell now for seven cents, yet ham is anywhere from twenty-five to forty cents. It used to be eight-cent cotton and eight-cent meat—now, I be doggone if it isn't eight-cent cotton and forty meat." He raised his homely loud voice: "It's eight-cent cotton and forty-cent meat, and how in the world can the poor man eat?"

How? Indeed, how?

Olmsted Visits a Louisiana Sugar Plantation
in 1853

When Frederick Law Olmsted began the first of three journeys through the South, leaving Washington on December 11, 1852, he embarked on an enterprise that would make him famous in this country and abroad. Already an agriculturalist of distinction at the age of thirty and the author of the recently published Walks and Talks of an American Farmer in England *(1852), young Olmsted was ideally equipped to observe and describe Southern life, particularly Southern agriculture and the economics of slavery. He enjoyed travel, even when the country was raw and undeveloped and the accommodations wretched. He got on easily with all sorts of people, knew what questions to ask, understood what he saw, and had the ability to write simply and graphically*

Olmsted was on his way through the seaboard slave states because he wanted to be able to answer, from first-hand experience, some of the contentions of his red-hot abolitionist friends. Though not a defender of slavery, he was a gradualist on the issue of emancipation. His expedition was also motivated by his disgust with the "deluge of spoony fancy pictures" of the South which the presses were then spouting. He was determined to see how the plain people lived and to examine as many sides of Southern life as possible.

Olmsted's first journey lasted three months. The travel-letters which, by arrangement with the editor, he sent back to the New York Times *were well received. There were many favorable comments in Southern periodicals, the* Southern Literary Messenger *saying, for example: "this is exactly what we wish all well-disposed and well-behaved Northern people, who desire to know something of the South, would do."*

Olmsted made two other journeys through the South; the second being to Texas by way of Kentucky, Tennessee, and New Orleans; the third in what Olmsted called the Back Country, that is, the central region of Mississippi, and the highlands of Alabama, Tennessee, Georgia, North Carolina, and Virginia.

From the experiences of these journeys, covering fourteen months, Olmsted made three books, expanded from his newspaper articles. He gave his trilogy the general title of Our Slave States. *The individual works were called, respectively,* A Journey in the Seaboard Slave States *(1856),* A Journey through Texas *(1857), and* A Journey in the Back Country *(1860). At the instigation of his English publishers Olmsted compiled from the three books* The Cotton Kingdom: a Traveller's Observations on Cotton and Slavery in the American Slave States *(1861). A reprint of this work was issued by Alfred A. Knopf in 1953.*

As Olmsted's description of the activities on Mr. R.'s plantation says little about the beginnings of sugar-growing in the South, a brief historical note is needed here. Jesuit priests from Santo Domingo brought sugar-cane to Louisiana. After the slave revolts in that island (1791–5) many Creole sugar-planters sought refuge in the lower Mississippi region. At first only cane syrup was produced there. In 1795 Étienne Boré discovered how to granulate sugar from the cane juice and thus made large profits possible. The great sugar plantations of the Southwest came to be as opulent as those of the rice-planters in South Carolina. Development was rapid. In 1802 the sugar plantations of the area numbered 81; thirty years later there were 691.

But, as Olmsted points out, the Louisiana planters encountered special difficulties. Even a slight frost could destroy a whole crop, and the cane had to be replanted at least once in three years, whereas in the West Indies the same stock could be used from eight to twelve years. Efforts, generally unsuccessful, were made to grow sugar in other parts of the South. Shortly before the Civil War sugar culture flourished in Texas on the lower Brazos River and accounted for the prosperity of Old Brazoria, once a rival of Houston, but now a ghost town.

Of necessity sugar cultivation had to be a protected industry if the planters were to compete with the more favorable growing-conditions in the West Indies. At the time of the Civil War the ad valorem protection was thirty per cent. As a result of their concern over the tariff question, many of the sugar-planters were Whigs. Today the sugar-growers still enjoy high tariff protection, though the cane-sugar interests have to compete with beet sugar, which is grown in the Midwest

163

*and far West, often on irrigated lands, and with the sugar crop of
Cuba, Puerto Rico, Hawaii, and the Philippines. It should be noted,
however, that the United States consumes about four times as much
sugar as it produces.*

The passage from Olmsted is condensed from pages 656–73 of his
Journey in the Seaboard Slave States, with Remarks on Their Economy (*New York: Dix & Edwards; 1856*).

❁

I CAME to Mr. R.'s plantation by a steam-boat, late at night. As the
boat approached the shore, near his house, her big bell having been
rung some ten minutes previously, a negro came out with a lantern
to meet her. The boat's bow was run boldly against the bank; I leaped
ashore, the clerk threw out a newspaper and a package, saying to the
negro, "That's for your master, and that's for so and so, tell your
master, and ask him to give it to him." The boat bounded off by her
own elasticity, the starboard wheel was backed for a turn or two, and
the next minute the great edifice was driving up the stream again—not
a rope having been lifted, nor any other movement having been made
on board, except by the pilot and engineer. . . .

The plantation contained about nine hundred acres of tillage land,
and a large tract of "swamp," or woodland, was attached to it. The
tillage land was inclosed all in one field by a strong cypress post and
rail fence, and was drained by two canals, five feet deep, running about
twenty feet apart, and parallel—the earth from both being thrown together, so as to make a high, dry road between them, straight through
the middle of the plantation.

Fronting upon the river, and but six or eight rods from the public
road, which everywhere runs close along the shore inside the levee,
was the mansion of the proprietor: an old Creole house, the lower
story of brick and the second of wood, with a broad gallery, shaded
by the extended roof, runing all around it; the roof steep, and shedding
water on four sides, with ornaments of turned wood where lines met,
and broken by several small dormer windows. The gallery was supported by round brick columns, and arches. The parlors, library and
sleeping rooms of the white family were all on the second floor. Between the house and the street was a yard, planted formally with
orange-trees and other evergreens. A little on one side of the house
stood a large two-story, square dove-cot, which is a universal ap-
pendage of a sugar-planter's house. In the rear of the house was another
large yard, in which, irregularly placed, were houses for the family
servants, a kitchen, stable, carriage-house, smoke-house, etc. Behind

this rear-yard there was a vegetable garden, of an acre or more, in the charge of a negro gardener; a line of fig-trees were planted along the fence, but all the ground inclosed was intended to be cropped with vegetables for the family, and for the supply of "the people." I was pleased to notice, however, that the negro-gardener had, of his own accord, planted some violets and other flowering plants. From a corner of the court a road ran to the sugar-works and the negro settlement, which were five or six hundred yards from the house.

The negro houses were exactly like those I described on the Georgia Rice Plantation, except that they were provided with broad galleries in front. They were as neat and well-made externally as the cottages usually provided by large manufacturing companies in New-England, to be rented to their workmen. The clothing furnished the negroes, and the rations of bacon and meal, were the same as on other good plantations. During the grinding season extra rations of flour were served, and hot coffee was kept constantly in the sugar-house, and the hands on duty were allowed to drink it almost *ad libitum*. They were also allowed to drink freely of the hot *sirop*, of which they were extremely fond. A generous allowance of *sirop*, or molasses, was also given out to them, with their other rations, every week during the winter and early summer. In extremely hot weather it was thought to be unfavorable to health, and was discontinued. Rations of tobacco were also served. At Christmas, a sum of money, equal to one dollar for each hogshead of sugar made on the plantation, was divided among the negroes. The last year this had amounted to over two dollars a head. It was usually given to the heads of families. If any had been particularly careless or lazy, it was remembered at this Christmas dole. Of course, the effect of this arrangement, small as was the amount received by each person, was to give the laborers a direct interest in the economical direction of their labor: the advantage of it was said to be very evident.

Mr. R. had purchased the plantation but three years before of a Creole, and afterwards had somewhat increased its area by buying out several poor people, who had owned small farms adjoining. He had greatly extended and improved the drainage, and had nearly doubled the force of negroes employed upon it, adding to the number that he purchased with the land, nearly as many more whom he had inherited, and whom he transferred to it from an old cotton plantation that he had formerly lived upon.

He had considerably more than doubled the stock of mules and oxen; had built entirely new cabins for all the negroes, and new sugar-works and stables. His whole capital, he said, when he first bought the plantation, would not have paid half the price of it and of the cost of stocking it as he had done. Most men when they buy a plantation, he informed me, go very heavily in debt; frequently the purchase is made three quarters on credit.

"Buying a plantation," were his words, "whether a sugar or cotton plantation in this country, is usually essentially a gambling operation. The capital invested in a sugar plantation of the size of mine ought not to be less than $150,000. The purchaser pays down what he can, and usually gives security for the payment of the balance in six annual installments, with interest (10 per cent. per annum) from the date of the purchase. Success in sugar as well as cotton planting, is dependent on so many circumstances, that it is as much trusting to luck as betting on a throw of dice. If his first crop proves a bad one, he must borrow money of the Jews in New Orleans to pay his first note; they will sell him this on the best terms they can, and often at not less than 25 per cent. per annum. If three or four bad crops follow one another, he is ruined. But this is seldom the case, and he lives on, one year gaining a little on his debts, but almost as often enlarging them. Three or four years ago there was hardly a planter in Louisiana or Mississippi that was not in very embarrassed circumstances, nearly every one having his crops pledged to his creditors long before they were secured. The good prices and good crops of the last few years have set them all on their legs again; and this year all the jewelers' shops, and stores of rich furniture and dry-goods, in New Orleans, were cleared out by the middle of the season, and everybody feels strong and cheerful. I have myself been particularly fortunate; I have made three good crops in succession. Last year I made six hundred and fifty hogsheads of sugar, and twelve hundred barrels of molasses. The molasses alone brought me a sum sufficient to pay all my plantation expenses; and the sugar yields me a clear profit of twenty-five per cent. on my whole investment. If I make another crop this year as good as that, I shall be able to discount my outstanding notes, and shall be clear of debt at the end of four years, instead of six, which was the best I had hoped for." . . .

SUGAR CANE IN LOUISIANA

The Sugar-cane is a perennial-rooted plant, and the stalk does not attain its full size, under favorable circumstances, in less growing time than twelve months; and seed does not usually form upon it until the thirteenth or fourteenth month. This function (termed *arrowing*) it only performs in a very hot and steadily hot climate, somewhat rarely even in the West Indies. The plant is, at all stages, extremely susceptible to cold, a moderate frost not only suspending its growth, but disorganizing it so that the chemical qualities of its sap are changed, and it is rendered valueless for sugar-making.

As frosts of considerable severity are common in all parts of Louisiana, during three months of the year, of course the sugar cane is there never permitted to attain its full growth. To so much greater perfection does it arrive in the West Indies, that the cane produced on one acre will yield from 3,000 to 6,000 lbs. of sugar, while in Louisiana 1,000 is considered the average obtained. "I could make sugar in the climate of Cuba," said a Louisiana planter to me, "for half the price that, under the most favorable circumstances, it must cost here." In addition to the natural uncongeniality of the climate, the ground on which it grows in Louisiana, being lower than the surface of the river, is much of the time made cold by the infiltration of moisture. It is, therefore, only by reason of the extreme fertility of this alluvial deposit, assisted by a careful method of cultivation, that the cane is forced to a state of maturity which enables it to yield an amount of sugar which, with the assistance of a governmental protection against foreign competition, will be remunerative to the planter. . . .

CANE CULTURE

Planting commences immediately after the sugar-manufacturing season is concluded—usually in January. New or fallow land is prepared by plowing the whole surface: on this plantation the plow used was made in Kentucky, and was of a very good model, plowing seven to nine inches deep, with a single pair of mules. The ground being then harrowed, drills are opened with a double mould-board plow, seven feet apart. Cuttings of cane for seed are to be planted in them. These are reserved from the crop in the autumn, when some of the best cane on the plantation is selected for this purpose, while still standing. This is cut off at the roots, and laid up in heaps or stacks, in such a manner that the leaves and tops protect the stalks from frost. The heaps are called mattresses; they are two or three feet high, and as many yards across. At the planting season they are opened, and the cane comes out moist and green, and sweet, with the buds or eyes, which protrude at the joints, swelling. The immature top parts of the stalk are cut off, and they are loaded into carts, and carried to the ground prepared for planting. The carts used are large, with high sideboards, and are drawn by three mules—one large one being in the shafts, and two lighter ones abreast, before her. The drivers are boys, who use the whip a great deal, and drive rapidly.

In the field I found the laborers working in three divisions—the first, consisting of light hands, brought the cane by armsfull from the cart, and laid it by the side of the furrows; the second planted it, and the third covered it. Planting is done by laying the cuttings at the bottom of the furrow, in such a way that there shall be three always together, with the eyes of each a little removed from those of the others—that is, all "breaking joints." They are thinly covered with earth, drawn over them with hoes. The other tools were so well selected on this plantation, that I expressed surprise at the clumsiness of the hoes, particularly as the soil was light, and entirely free from stones. "Such hoes as you use at the North would not last a negro a day," said the planter.

Cane will grow for several years from the roots of the old plants, and, when it is allowed to do so, a very considerable part of the expense is avoided; but the vigor of the plant is less when growing from this source than when starting from cuttings, and the crop, when thus obtained, is annually less and less productive, until, after a number of years, depending upon the rigor of the seasons, fresh shoots cease to spring from the stubble. This sprouting of cane from the stools of the last crop is termed "ratooning." In the West India plantations the cane is frequently allowed to ratoon for eight successive crops. In Louisiana it is usual to plant once in three years, trusting to the ratooning for two crops only, and this was the practice on Mr. R.'s plantation. The cost of sugar growing would be very greatly increased if the crop needed planting every year; for all the cane grown upon an acre will not furnish seed for more than four acres—consequently one-twelfth of the whole of each crop has to be reserved for the planting of the following crop, even when two-thirds of this is to be of ratoon cane.

Planting is finished in a favorable season—early in March. Tillage is commenced immediately afterwards, by plowing *from* the rows of young cane, and subsequently continued very much after the usual plan of tillage for potatoes, when planted in drills, with us. By or before the first of July, the crop is all well earthed up, the rows of cane growing from the crest of a rounded bed, seven feet wide, with deep water-furrows between each. The cane is at this time five or six feet high; and that growing from each bed forms arches with that of the next, so as to completely shade the ground. The furrows between the beds are carefully cleaned out; so that in the most drenching torrents of rain, the water is rapidly carried off into the drains, and thence to the swamp; and the crop then requires no further labor upon it until frost is apprehended, or the season for grinding arrives.

The nearly three months' interval, commencing at the intensest heat of summer, corresponds in the allotment of labor to the period of winter in Northern agriculture, because the winter itself, on the sugar-plantations is the planting-season. The negroes are employed in cutting and carting wood for boiling the cane-juice, in making necessary repairs or additions to the sugar-house, and otherwise preparing for the grinding-season.

THE GRINDING SEASON

The grinding-season is the harvest of the sugar-planter; it commences in October, and continues for two or three months, during which time, the greatest possible activity and the utmost labor of which the hands are capable, are required to secure the product of the previous labor of the year. Mr. R. assured me that during the last grinding-season nearly every man, woman, and child on his plantation, including his overseer and himself, were at work fully eighteen hours a day. From the moment grinding first commences, until the end of the season, it is never discontinued; the fires under the boiler never go out, and the negroes rest only for six hours in the twenty-four, by relays—three-quarters of them being constantly at work. . . .

The business of manufacturing sugar is everywhere carried on in connection with the planting of the cane. The shortness of the season during which the cane can be used, is the reason assigned for this: the proprietors would not be willing to trust to custom-mills to manufacture their produce with the necessary rapidity. If cane should be cultivated in connection with other crops—that is, on small farms, instead of great "sugar only" plantations—neighborhood custom-mills would probably be employed. The profit of a sugar-plantation is now large, much in proportion to its size (if it be proportionally stocked); because only a very large supply of cane will warrant the proprietor in providing the most economical manufacturing apparatus. In 1849 there were 1,474 sugar estates in Louisiana, producing 236,547 hhds. of sugar; but it is thought that half of this quantity was produced on less than 200 estates—that is, that one-eighth of the plantations produced one-half the sugar. The sugar-works on some of the large estates cost over $100,000, and many of them manufacture over 1,000,000 lbs. per annum. The profits of these, in a favorable season, are immense.

The apparatus used upon the better class of plantations is very admirable, and improvements are yearly being made, which indicate high scientific acquirements, and much mechanical ingenuity on the part of the inventors. The whole process of sugar manufacturing, although chemical analysis proves that a large amount of saccharine is still wasted, has been within a few years greatly improved, principally by reason of the experiments and discoveries of the French chemists, whose labors have been directed by the purpose to lessen the cost of beet-sugar. Apparatus for various processes in manufacture, which they have invented or recommended, has been improved, and brought into practical operation on a large scale on some of the Louisiana plantations, the owners of which are among the most intelligent, enterprising, and wealthy men of business in the United States. Forty-three plantations in the State are now furnished with apparatus constructed in accordance with the best scientific knowledge on the subject; and 914 are driven by steam-engines—leaving but 560 to be worked by horse-power. Mr. R.'s sugar-house, for making brown sugar, was furnished with the best kind of apparatus, at a cost of $20,000. Preparations were making for the addition of works for the manufacture of white loaf sugar, which would cost $20,000 more. I visited one plantation on which the sugar works were said to have cost over $100,000.

SUGAR MANUFACTURING

The first operation in the manufacture of sugar from cane is, to express the saccharine juice it contains; this is done by passing it twice between rollers, on the same plan that apples are crushed in our best cider-mills. A great deal of ingenuity has been applied to the construction of the mills for this purpose, and they have been, from time to time, improved, but are yet far from satisfactory in their operation, as it is known that the crushed cane still retains nearly one-third of its original moisture, with a large share of the saccharine principle which belonged to it before it was passed between the rollers. No plan has yet been devised by which this can be economically secured.

The expressed juice is strained into a vessel, in which it is heated to a temperature of about 140° F., when it is clarified by the application of lime, the chemical action of which is not, I believe, perfectly understood; the effect is, to cause a precipitate of impurities, and to give a yellow color to the juice. In addition to this, the juice is sometimes further clarified by filtration. The next operation is the reduction of the cane-juice—by the evaporation of the greater part of its constituent water—to syrup. This is effected by the action of heat, which is applied in different ways, according to the apparatus used. There are seven different forms of this, in general use in Louisiana. In the simplest and rudest, the juice is boiled in open kettles; in the most improved, it is boiled in vacuo, on the principle that liquids boil at lower temperature, as the pressure of the atmosphere is removed. The sugar made by the latter process is much superior to that made by the former, which is always much burnt, and less pure, and it is also obtained at a much less expenditure for fuel.

The syrup having reached the proper degree of concentration, is next drawn off into vessels, in which it remains until granulation takes place. To separate the uncrystallizable syrup from the granulated sugar, in the more usual method, the mass of saccharine matter is placed in hogsheads, in the bottoms of which are holes, in which are inserted pieces of cane, which reach above the contents. As the granulation proceeds, a contraction takes place, which leaves an opening about the canes, by which the remaining liquid drains to the bottom, and, the canes being loosely inserted, it flows through the holes, out of the hogshead, leaving the comparatively dry sugar now completely granulated. The hogsheads are set upon a staging, or loose floor, over a large vat, in which the drainage is collected. This drainage is molasses. It is afterwards pumped out of the tanks into barrels, for market; commonly the purchaser buys it in the tank and provides barrels for its removal. Seventy gallons of molasses for each hogshead of sugar is considered a large estimate. The sugar is now in the condition known as "Muscovado," or raw brown sugar. Its color and quality depend on the caution and skill that have been used in the manufacture, and the excellence of the apparatus employed. The best Louisiana sugar is not inferior to any other plantation sugar of the world.

The raw sugar is further improved by filtering it (in the state of syrup), through animal black, or charcoal, made from bones, in the same way that liquors are "fined." This is done on several plantations. But the business of refining sugars is mainly carried on in well-known establishments, in all our large cities, and I need not describe it. In New York, alone, one thousand hogsheads a day are refined, and one house alone supplies to commerce as much as the whole manufacture of France. The difference between raw or brown sugar, and refined or white sugar, is simply one of cleanliness and purity.

Modern improvements have so greatly reduced the cost of refining sugar, that the consumption of the pure article, proportionately to that of the raw, has very rapidly increased; and it is probable that in a few years the use of the latter will be almost entirely discontinued for general purposes. Refined, or cleaned sugar is, doubtless, more wholesome, and can only be thought less palatable from habit or association. Pure sugar is now generally considered, by the best authorities, to be a very digestible and nutritious article of diet to most persons—even to infants —and the old idea that it injures the teeth, except mechanically, is considered a fallacy. But this is true only, I believe, of sugar in a pure crystallized or grained state; when cooked in the form of confectionery, or in combination with fatty substances, it seems to be very unwholesome.

John Taylor of Caroline and His *Arator*

Almost any American who knows anything about the state of agriculture in the Old South has heard that the growing of tobacco for quick profits rapidly depleted the land of the upper South and that the one-crop system in the days when "cotton was king" tied the lower South to disastrous fluctuations in the price of this staple. The later consequences of soil erosion in the South were finally made known to most Americans during the time of the New Deal.

What is still not at all well known is that many planters in the Old South were scientific farmers who not only strove to prevent the wastage of their acres, but also experimented with new crops, introduced new breeds of livestock, and practiced diversified farming. In Maryland, Virginia, and Georgia, in particular, agricultural reformers in the years just before the Civil War did much to rescue Southern agriculture "from the control of illiterate and routine-ridden overseers and made farming a serious profession, worthy of study for gentlemen" (Clement Eaton: A History of the Old South, *p. 237*).

In these reforms several names stand out: Edmund Ruffin of Virginia, whose Essay on Calcareous Manures (*1833*) *made him famous through the lower South; David Dickson, the leading spirit in the influential Planter's Club of Hancock County, Georgia, in the 1840's; and Thomas Spalding, owner of Sapelo Island, Georgia, and Dr. Martin W. Phillips of Mississippi, both of whom preached and practiced the diversification of crops.*

Of these agricultural reformers the pioneer was John Taylor (1753–1824) of Caroline County, Virginia. After fighting in the Revolution, Taylor returned to Virginia, where he soon became a rich man through the practice of law, his marriage to a wealthy cousin, and his success as a planter. In 1803 he began publishing a series of newspaper articles setting forth his ideas on agricultural reform and the place of agriculture in the national economy. These were collected and issued as Arator *in 1813, one of the most original books produced by an antebellum Southerner. "Arator" advocated the rotation of crops, deep plowing, and "inclosing" (the use of cover crops in manuring).*

But Taylor was not content with proposing ways in which farmers might use their land more effectually. He was of necessity a political economist as well, seeing clearly that the condition of Southern agriculture was dependent on many factors, national and international, beyond the control of individual planters. Fearing the growing dominance of the Federal government, he was one of the early advocates of states' rights, and of a Southern Confederacy. He believed that Hamiltonian capitalism was a threat to agriculture, particularly because it was producing a "paper aristocracy" whose power was derived from the manipulation of credit. Of Taylor's An Inquiry into the Principles and Policy of the Government of the United States (*1814*), Charles *Beard remarked: "Whatever its shortcomings in prolixity of style, it deserves to rank among the two or three really historic contributions to political science which have been produced in the United States."*

The text of these two essays from Arator *is that of the third edition, Baltimore (printed by J. Robinson, for John M. Carter), 1817.*

NUMBER 2
THE PRESENT STATE OF AGRICULTURE, CONTINUED

A PATIENT must know that he is sick, before he will take physick. A collection of a few facts, to ascertain the ill health of agriculture, is necessary to invigorate our efforts towards a cure. One, apparent to the most superficial observer, is, that our land has diminished in fertility.—Arts improve the work of nature—when they injure it, they are not arts, but barbarous customs. It is the office of agriculture, as an art, not to impoverish, but to fertilize the soil, and make it more useful than in its natural state. Such is the effect of every species of agriculture, which can aspire to the character of an art.—Its object being to furnish man with articles of the first necessity, whatever defeats that object, is a crime of the first magnitude. Had men a power to obscure or brighten the light of the sun, by obscuring it, they would imitate the morality of diminishing the fertility of the earth. Is not one as criminal as the other? Yet it is a fact, that lands in their natural state, are more valuable, than those which have undergone our habit of agriculture, of which emigrations are complete proofs.

The decay of a multitude of small towns, so situated as to depend for support on unalterable districts, is another proof of the impoverishment of the soil. It is true, that a few large towns have grown up, but this is owing, not to an increased product, but to an increased pasture; whereas, in every case, where the pasture is limited, or isolated by local circumstances, small towns have sprung up, whilst the lands were fresh, and decayed, as they were worn out. I have no facts to ascertain certainly the products of agriculture at different periods relatively to the number of people; such would furnish a demonstration of its state. But

I have understood, that sixty-thousand hogsheads of tobacco were exported from Virginia, when it contained about one-fourth of its present population. If so, had the fertility of the country remained undiminished, Virginia ought now to export two hundred and forty thousand hogsheads, or an equivalent. In this estimate, every species of export except tobacco, is excluded at one epoch, and exports of every kind included at the other; yet the latter would fall far short of exhibiting the equivalent necessary to bring itself on a footing, as to agriculture, with the former. Two hundred and forty thousand hogsheads of tobacco, which, or an equivalent, Virginia would now export, if the state of agriculture had been as flourishing as it was sixty or seventy years past, at the present value, by which all our exports are rated, would be worth above seventeen millions of dollars; and supposing Virginia to furnish one seventh part of the native agricultural exports of the United States, these ought now to amount to one hundred and twenty millions of dollars, had the products of agriculture kept pace with the increase of population. If this statement is not exactly correct, enough of it certainly is so, to demonstrate a rapid impoverishment of the soil of the United States.

The decay of the culture of tobacco is testimony to this unwelcome fact. It is deserted because the lands are exhausted. To conceal from ourselves a disagreeable truth, we resort to the delusion, that tobacco requires new or fresh land; whereas every one acquainted with the plant knows, that its quantity and quality, as is the case with most or all plants, are both greatly improved by manured land, or land, the fertility of which has been artificially increased. Whole counties, comprising large districts of country, which once grew tobacco in great quantities, are now too sterile to grow any of moment; and the wheat crops substituted for tobacco, have already sunk to an average below profit.

From the mass of facts, to prove that the fertility of our country has been long declining, and that our agriculture is in a miserable state, I shall only select one more. The average of our native exports, is about forty millions of dollars annually. Some portion of this amount consists of manufactures, the materials for which are not furnished by agriculture; another, as is extensively the fact in the case of flour, has passed through the hands of the manufacturer. Of the first portion he receives the whole price, of the second a proportion. And a third portion of our products is obtained from the sea: Of the forty millions exported, agriculture, therefore, receives about thirty five. The taxes of every kind, state and federal, may be estimated at twenty millions of dollars, of which agriculture pays at least fifteen, leaving twenty millions of her exports for her own use. Counting all the slaves, who ought to be counted both as sources of product and expense, in estimating the state of agriculture, the people of the United States may probably amount to about seven millions, and it may be fairly assumed, that the interest or occupation of six millions of these seven, is agricultural. Of the whole surplus product of agriculture exported, after deducting the taxes it pays, there remains for each individual a few cents above three dollars. Out of this mass of profit, he is to pay for the manufactures, luxuries and necessaries he consumes, not raised by himself; and the only remaining article to be carried to the credit of agriculture, is the small gain it derives from its domestick sales, not to itself, or from sales by one of its members to another, for that does not enrich it, but to other classes, such as manufacturers and soldiers. Against the former, agriculture is to be debited with the bounties she is made by law to pay them; against the latter, she has been already debited by deducting her taxes from her exports. Neither can be a source of much wealth or profit to her, because in one case she furnishes the money by taxation, and in the other by bounties, with which her products are purchased. It is, therefore, nearly true, that the income of agriculture is only three dollars per poll, and that this income is her whole fund for supplying her wants and extending her improvements. This estimate is infinitely more correct, than one drawn from individual wealth or poverty. To infer from the first, that every body might become rich, as a defence of our agricultural regimen, would be a conclusion as fallacious, as to infer from the second, that every body must become poor, as a proof of its badness. Extraordinary talents or industry will produce extraordinary effects. Instances of happiness or wealth under a despotism, do not prove that its regimen is calculated for general wealth or happiness. A system, commercial, political or agricultural, so wretched as not to exhibit cases of individual prosperity, has never appeared, because an universal scourge would be universally abhorred. It is not from partial, but general facts, that we can draw a correct knowledge of our agriculture. Even a personal view of the country, might deceive the thoughtless, because neither the shortness of life, nor the gradual impoverishment of land, are calculated to establish a visible standard of comparison. A man must be old and possess a turn for observation from his youth, to be able to judge correctly from this source. I have known many farms for above forty years, and though I think that all of them have been greatly impoverished, yet I rely more upon the general facts I have stated, for agreeing with Strickland in opinion, "that the agriculture of the United States affords only a bare subsistence—that the fertility of our lands is gradually declining—and that the agriculture of Virginia has arrived to the lowest state of degradation."

NUMBER 60
THE RIGHTS OF AGRICULTURE

It is lamentable to confess, that this, to be a true, must be almost a negative number.—This most useful and virtuous interest, enjoys no rights, except in the United States; and there it enjoys no exclusive rights, whilst the few in which it shares are daily contracted by the various arts of ambition and avarice. Every where else, agriculture is a slave; here she is only a dupe. Abroad she is condemned by avowed force to feed voluptuousness, avarice and ambition; here, she is deluded by flattery and craft, during fits of joy or of fury, to squander her property, to mortgage her labourers, and to shackle her freedom. Abroad, she suffers contempt, and is sensible of her degradation; here, she is a blind Quixote, mounted on a wooden horse, and persuaded by the acclamations of her foes, that she is soaring to the stars, whilst she is ready to tumble into the dust.

Privileges are rearing by laws all around at her expense, and whilst she is taught to believe that they will only take from her a few inconsiderable slips, they will at length draw a spacious circumvallation, within which will gradually grow up a power, beyond her control. Tricks, as well as inventions, are daily fortified with legal bulwarks, called charters, to transfer her wealth, and to secure frauds against her efforts. Capital in every form, save that of agriculture, is fed by taxes and by bounties, which she must pay; whilst not a single bounty is paid to her by capital in any form; and instead of being favoured with some prizes in the lottery of society, she pays most, and is rewarded herself by the blanks of underwriting the projects of statesmen, and bearing the burdens of government.

The use of society, is to secure the fruits of his own industry and talents to each associator. Its abuse consists in artifice or force, for transferring those fruits from some partners to others. Of this abuse, that interest covering the majority of partners is the victim. And the difficulty of discriminating laws, transferring such fruits for the benefit of society, from those having in view the gratification of avarice and ambition, produces a sympathy and combination between these distinct kinds of law. As the members of the government, and members of legal frauds, both extract power and income from the majority, they are apt to coalesce; and each party to favour the designs of its ally, in their operations upon the common enemy. Hence governments love to create exclusive rights, and exclusive rights cling to governments. The ligament of parent and child, binds them together, and the power creating these abuses, must make them props for its support, or instruments for its subversion. Its election between these alternatives is certain, and society is thus unavoidably thrown into two divisions. One containing all those who pay, and the other those who receive contributions, required either for publick use, or to foster private avarice or ambition. Good government is graduated by this latter kind of contribution thus unfortunately allied to the former. The highest amount constitutes the worst, and the lowest, the best possible species of government. But as both are drawn from the majority of every society, whenever the agricultural interest covers that majority, this interest is the victim of the coalition; and as it almost universally does cover this majority, the agricultural interest is almost universally its slaves.

The consequences to agriculture will be demonstrated by converting this coalition between government and its creatures, or of all who receive tolls given by law, into a political pope, and placing in his mouth an address to agriculture, in a parody of Ernulphus's form of excommunication.

"May you be taxed in your land, your slaves, your houses, your carriages, your horses, your clothing, your liquors, your coffee, your tea, and your salt. May you be taxed by banks, by protecting duties, by embargoes, and by charters of a thousand different forms. May the exemption of your exports from taxation be removed, and may you then be taxed through your wheat, your corn, your tobacco, your cotton, your rice, your indigo, your sugar, your hemp, your live stock, your beef, your pork, your tar, pitch and turpentine, your onions, your cheese, and your potatoes. May you be taxed for the support of government, or to enrich exclusive or chartered interests, through every article you import, and through every article you export, by duties called protecting, but intended to take away your constitutional protection against taxation for the benefit of capitalists. May you be taxed through every article produced by your labour or necessary to your subsistence, comfort and pleasure, by excises. And whilst every species of your products, and of your consumptions are thus taxed, may your capital, being visible, be moreover taxed in various modes. May all these taxes whether plain or intricate, (after deducting the small sum necessary to produce the genuine end of society) be employed in enriching capitalists, and buying soldiers, placemen and contractors, to make you submissive to usurpations, and as quiet under your burthens, as a martyr tied to the stake, under the flames. After you have been taxed as far as you can pay, may you by the bounty of God Almighty be moreover mortgaged up to your value or credit, for the benefit of the said coalition of capitalists. And finally, may none of this good and useful coalition, to whom is given the wealth of this world, as the kingdom of heaven is to the pope and his clergy, be taxed in their stock or principal held under any law or charter whatsoever; nor in their capital employed in any manufacture or speculation, nor in any profit drawn from such principal stock or capital; nor thro' any of their sinecures, salaries, contracts or incomes; but on the contrary, may such stock, principal, capital, profits, salaries, contracts, and sinecures, be constantly fostered by bounties in various injurious forms, to be paid by you, you damned dirty working, productive bitch, agriculture." Throughout the world, agriculture, like one of Ernulphus's contrite excommunicants, responds, amen, to this pious invocation.

Throughout the world, agriculture has enjoyed, and in England, continues to enjoy, one of the rights in which she has a share in the United States; that of a voice in elections.—And throughout the world, this right has been unable to shield her against an anathema, which prescribes for her as perfect a hell, as the formula of Ernulphus prescribes for his heretick. Let the agricultural interest of the United States, pause here and look around. Is a blind confidence in a right so universally ineffectual, a sufficient safeguard for its freedom and happiness? To me it seems, that an interest can never be long free, which blindly confides in a coalition, whose object it is to draw from that interest, power and wealth. That the major interest must be as cunning, as wise and as watchful, as the minor, or that the minor interest will enslave it. And that agriculture must as attentively keep her eyes upon the coalition, to avoid its operations upon her, as the coalition does upon agriculture, for the purpose of transfering to its members portions of her power and wealth, whenever she slumbers.

Hence have arisen the political suggestions to be found in these essays. I cannot discern much good in an improvement of agriculture, to get luxury, voluptuousness and tyranny for a few, and wretchedness for a multitude.—The best cultivated country in the world, abounds most in paupers and thieves. Agriculture must be a politician to avoid this fate; and those who ridicule her pretensions to knowledge in this science, intend by persuading her to repose in a blind confidence, built upon the frail right of election, to expose her to it. How can she even judiciously elect, if she cannot or will not judge of publick measures, by the light of her own interest?

The moral consequence of this supineness or ignorance, is, that social happiness gradually becomes the dependant of a minority, and of course it is provided for, by continually subtracting from the happiness of a majority. The visible immorality of this, demonstrates the virtue, as well as wisdom of suggestions designed to obstruct it.

The remaining right in which agriculture participates, in common with all other interests, having any thing to export, is bestowed by the constitutional prohibition of duties upon exports. This right originated in state jealousies, and not from a disposition to favour agriculture, but yet it is her best security, for the preservation of that portion of our government, which will longest be sensible of her elective influence; and its relinquishment will be the most fatal wound which can be inflicted on her. The coalition I have described will try every art in her most unguarded moments, to snatch it from her, and it will be the last relinquishment it will need. To determine whether her elective influence can bear further wounds, let agriculture re-survey the legislation of our whole term of independence, and compare the catalogues she may select, of laws for creating or fostering privileges and exclusive interests, with those for fostering herself; and let this comparison form the criterion for ascertaining her legislative influence. Thus only can she judiciously increase this influence, if it has settled too low, or diminish it, if it has raised too high. There is no fair mode of judging, except by these legislative acts. To infer, that the agricultural interest influences legislatures, because it chiefly elects them, would be like inferring, that the French nation influences the tribunate, because they wholly elect it. Let agriculture therefore hold fast the solitary security she enjoys in common with her industrious associates, against the ambitions of usurpers, and the avarice of capitalists, nor be deluded into the absurd notion, that it is wise to relinquish the only peculium of industry, for the sake of some temporary operation upon foreign nations, inevitably resulting upon herself in the form of retaliation, whilst the protection of exports against taxation, will be gone forever.

Duties of the Plantation Overseer

The overseer "stood at the actual centre of the plantation and made it go." Yet he has received little attention from either historians or novelists. For this reason Professor John Spencer Bassett's The Southern Plantation Overseer, as Revealed in His Letters, *from which this selection comes, is a valuable study of plantation life in the Old South, seen from one important point of view. Since the overseers were often semi-illiterate or in any case were not much given to setting down their observations in letters or diaries, Professor Bassett had to dig hard for the record of their lives.*

The overseer had a fixed and solitary place in the hierarchy of plantation society. "He was patronised by the benign planters and condemned by the heedless." To the Negroes he was "Buckra," a word "expressing scorn for a man of no standing." And to them, of course, he was the ever-present symbol of slavery.

The virtues required of the overseer were courage, industry, and common sense. His vices, often enough, were slovenliness, drunkenness, and cruelty. The overseer who was intelligent and ambitious might hope in time to own a small plantation and a few slaves. Or he might join the trek westward and try the life of the pioneer. The majority of overseers lacked ambition. They moved from plantation to plantation, but seldom bettered their lot.

This selection contains most of Chapter ii of The Plantation Overseer *(Northampton, printed for Smith College, 1925). It is reprinted here with the kind permission of Professor Bassett's heirs.*

THE first duty of the overseer, or manager, as he was frequently called, was to take care of the slaves and the stock. Next he was to see that enough food was produced for use on the place. By food was meant corn, bacon, potatoes, and vegetables for the slaves and corn, fodder, hay, and oats for the stock. These two duties done, he was to raise as much cotton, or rice in the rice region, as possible without overworking the slaves. Placing the production of supplies before the raising of a money crop was sound judgment. Now and again came a devastating drought and frequently some calamity tended to reduce the yield of food. It did not pay to run too close to the margin of safety in such a respect. A wise planter sought to insure against such inconvenience by having more supplies than he needed rather than not enough.

The routine of the overseer was as follows: An hour before dawn he rang the bell or blew the horn that called the hands from their beds. On some places they prepared their breakfasts in their cabins, on others they had breakfast brought to them in the fields after they had begun to work. It was always desired that they be assembled in the yards by the time it was broad daylight, and when the sun appeared above the horizon it was expected that they should be at their tasks. They worked in groups, each with a leader, or driver, who was one of the slaves. Throughout the day the overseer went from one to the other group to see that the labor was performed properly. At noon dinner was brought to the fields, if the gangs were working at a distance from the cabins, or eaten in their cabins if the cabins were close at hand.

The overseer was to inspect the food and see that is was wholesome. He gave the signal for leaving the fields when the sun had set. He looked after the feeding of the stock, the closing of the barns and stables, which must be locked and the keys taken by him and kept safely. One of the bad habits of the slaves was to take out horses or mules during the night and ride to remote places, and the overseer was expected to see that no such thing happened. At half past nine he rang a curfew bell and then went the rounds of the cabins to see that the occupants were abed. He was also expected to visit the houses unexpectedly during the night lest some of the people had slipped away after his inspection. If he did all these things continually he was a very busy man. No slave on the place served as long hours as the overseer was expected to serve. From an hour before dawn to ten at night was seventeen or eighteen hours. And if he got up to make inspections during the night he had little sleep. It is not likely that the details as here outlined were carried out with exactness.

The overseer was instructed to take the best possible moral care of his charges and to afford them fair opportunity, as far as he could, for getting religious instruction. "I want all my people," wrote one planter to his manager, "encouraged to cultivate religious feeling and morality and punished for inhumanity to their children or stock, for profanity, lying and stealing. . . . When ever the services of a suitable person can be secured have them instructed in religion. In view of the fanaticism of the age, it behooves the master or overseer to be present on all such occasions. They should be instructed on Sundays in day time if practicable; if not, then on Sunday night."

Judging by the overseer letters that have come into my hands the writers of them were not men of sufficient enlightenment to qualify as censors of preaching, to determine whether it was incendiary or not. They were probably safe enough to say that an open incitement to insurrection was objectionable. But such an incitement was not likely to be made by any man permitted to preach to the slaves. On utterances less open and direct the overseers were not safe judges. To make them censors of the sermons delivered to the slaves was ridiculous.

In all the preaching to slaves there was, in fact, something incongruous. In the first place the slave was not to be taught to read—this after the initiation of the active antislavery propaganda in 1831 by William Lloyd Garrison. If a slave could not read the Bible, the guide of his Christian life, how could he be expected to absorb the spirit of Christianity? He could not "search the scriptures" in which was eternal life. More than half of the Christian religion was diverted from him by condemning him to illiteracy.

Another incongruity was in the narrow range of the preaching that could be made to the slaves within the limits imposed by slavery. There must be no argument based on such texts as "The truth will make you free," and "The laborer is worthy of his hire." Doctrines that would make a man wish to raise himself to something better and higher were impossible; for they were sure to create dissatisfaction with slavery. The religious instructors of these people so unhappily placed had to recognize these facts and to preach a doctrine of contentment and humility. In an instinctive reaction against the hard lot of this world they dwelt at large upon the joys and beauties of a world to come.

Lunsford Lane, who was born in North Carolina, purchased his freedom and became an abolitionist lecturer in the North just before the civil war, gives the negro's views on this subject in the following words: "I often heard select portions of the Scriptures read in our social meetings and comments made upon them. On Sunday we always had one sermon prepared expressly for the colored people, which it was generally my privilege to hear. So great was the similarity of the texts that they were always fresh in my memory: 'Servants, be obedient to your masters'—'not with eye-service, as men-pleasers.' 'He that knoweth his master's will and doeth it not, shall be beaten with many stripes'; and some others of this class. Similar passages, with but few exceptions, formed the basis of most of these public instructions. . . . I will not do them the injustice to say that connected with these instructions there was not mingled much that was excellent. There was one very kindhearted clergyman whom I used often to hear; he was very popular with the colored people. But after he had preached a sermon to us in which he argued from the Bible that it was the will of Heaven from all eternity that we should be slaves, and our masters be our owners, many of us left him, considering, like the doubting disciple of old, 'This is a hard saying, who can hear it?' "

As the representative of the owner the overseer had the duty of sitting as judge over the wrongdoing of the slaves. He had wide authority, for evidence of guilt, procedure, and extenuating circumstances were within his discretion. In view of his slight degree of culture this fact placed the slave's case at the mercy of an unenlightened judge. On the other hand the thing needed was not a knowledge of law, but common sense; and it will be allowed that when a man had proved himself a successful manager of a plantation he had a fair store of that quality. Also, we must not forget that the negro did not make the same distinctions as men of higher degrees of progress in civilization. He recognized the propriety of discipline and quick and firm punishment when orders were violated. If now and then a man was punished too much, or when innocent, it nevertheless remained that most of those who were punished were not given more than was considered just, and most of those who were punished were believed to be guilty. By and large the slave did not feel very deeply any lapses the overseer may have made in awarding punishment unless it was done cruelly.

The decision once made the overseer saw that the execution of punishment was done in such a way as to make the victim respect the power that inflicted it. Some masters insisted that their slaves should be sent to a public official for the whipping. In most cases the overseer did the whipping himself. Sometimes he stood by while a driver, that is, a slave, applied the lash. In stubborn cases the victim was "salted." This process was very painful and it was dreaded by the slaves. It consisted in whipping the victim on the bare back until the thongs cut the flesh and then washing the back down with strong brine. In some cases this was repeated several times. In general, public opinion was against "salting" and other forms of extreme punishment. Humane masters did not resort to such means of breaking the resistance of a slave unless they thought the case an unusual one. If a slave had to be dealt with as severely as this they believed it was better to sell him to a trader.

Some planters believed that a plantation could be run without whipping. Few overseers agreed with the idea. For whipping the benevolent ones would substitute tact, patience, and a careful study of the peculiarities of the individual slaves. Not many masters and even fewer overseers had the address to carry out such ideas. It was the ordinary view that whipping was "the only thing that would do a negro any good." Probably most of the slaves would have accepted the view in an abstract way. The power to whip within his discretion was held to be a necessary thing for the overseer's success with the slaves under him. At the same time it placed an alarming power in the hands of men who were not always likely to use it with discretion.

In the absence of the master the overseer administered the regulations governing the marriage of slaves. It was a common rule that slaves should not marry slaves living off the plantation, since such marriages involved visiting and brought up the problem of disciplining such visitors when on the plantation of the wife's master. One master whose ideas we have in writing directed his overseer to permit separation when sufficient cause was shown on either side, the overseer, evidently, to be the judge of what was sufficient cause; but it was added, the offending party must be severely punished. If both were guilty both must be punished, and if after that they insisted on separation they must have a hundred lashes each. After such separation neither was to marry again for three years. For the first marriage a bounty of $5.00 was allowed to be invested in household articles. But if either had been married before the bounty was to be $2.50. A third marriage was not to be allowed.

It has been said that failure to breed was considered grounds for separation: the charge was denied by the masters as a class. Probably it was unusual for a separation to occur for this cause; but it was one of the peculiarities of slavery that great latitude was allowed to the owner, so that he might do as he chose about most things. Consequently things done by one master might not be done by another. Some were not ruled by feelings of humanity nor even by public opinion. If a man of this class decided that a young slave woman was not bearing children by the husband she had he probably made it as easy for her to separate and form another marriage as she desired. The law did not look on the union of slaves as legal marriage; and one of the first things to be done after emancipation was to take steps for remedying that defect.

It ought to be remembered that the negroes themselves did not esteem marriage as the white people esteemed it. In Africa a wife was considered property, and polygamy was practiced by many tribes. Divorce was easy and it was resorted to freely. The negro therefore arrived in America with ideas favorable to a loose marriage bond. Contact with the whites taught them to hold it in stricter esteem, but the old standards did not disappear suddenly. It is doubtful if the separations that occurred produced great distress in the minds of either party involved.

Dealing with runaways was one of the overseer's most difficult problems. Nearly every plantation had slaves who were accustomed to flee to the woods when they thought the discipline too severe. To get these persons back to their work was a thing that demanded address. Punishment for the liberty they had taken was a matter of course. It was expected by the runaway himself, and sometimes a form of negotiation seems to have been employed through the medium of some slaves who had not run off, by which it was agreed that the runaway would return provided his punishment did not go beyond a stipulated amount. The approach of cold weather could be counted on to bring many back. These conditions did not maintain in the parts of the South that permitted escape into the free states. In such sections the runaway was apt to turn his steps northward.

In the letters that follow are many allusions to runaways. None of them show such a group tendency to deal with the overseer in retaliation as the following incident related by a Georgia overseer and quoted by Professor Phillips: "I write you a few lines to let you know that six of your hands has left the plantation—every man but Jack. They displeased me with their worke and I give some of them a few lashes, Tom with the rest. On Wednesday morning they were missing. I think they are lying out until they can see you or your uncle Jack, as he is expected daily. They may be gone off, or they may be lying around in this neighborhood, but I don't know. I blame Tom for the whole. I don't think the rest of them would of left the plantation if Tom had not of persuaded them of for some design. I give Tom but a few licks, but if I ever get him in my power I will have satisfaction.

There was a part of them had no cause for leaving, only they thought that if they would all go it would injure me moore. They are as independent set for running as I have ever seen, and I think the cause is they have been treated too well. They want more whiping and no protector; but if our country is so that negroes can quit their homes and run off when they please without being taken they will have the advantage of us."

The tone of this letter indicates that the writer of it was not a man who should have been permitted to correct slaves. It shows that he lacked firmness and good judgment. Washington seems to have had a similar overseer, and he gives us a view of the man's character by writing: "Let Abram get his deserts when taken, but do not trust Crow to give it to him, for I have reason to believe he is swayed more by passion than by judgment in all his corrections."

Testimony shows that the overseer had more trouble with the slave women than with the men. Travelers in Africa have noticed that the women there have a marked ascendency over the men, that they keep them in awe of their sharp tongues and that they are in general of violent passions as compared with the men. These qualities appeared in the slaves in the South. As a result many plantations had women who kept the rest of the slaves in a state of unrest and thereby made it hard for the overseer to keep order.

Phillips mentions several slave women who stood out for one bad quality or another. The case of one, a certain Suckey, is so suggestive that I give it here in the words of the Virginia overseer who reported it to his employer. "I sent for hir to come in the morning," he wrote, "to hep Secoure the foder, but She sent me word that She would not come to worke that Day, and that you had ordered her to wash hir Cloaiths and goo to Any meeting She pleased any time in the weke without my leafe, and on Monday when I come to Reckon with her about it she said it was your orders and she would do it in Defiance of me. . . . I hope if Suckey is aloud that privilege more than the Rest, that she will be moved to some other place, and one Come in her Room."

In nothing was the master more concerned than in the increase of his slaves through the birth of children. He resented the charge that he was breeding slaves as other men bred horses. Nevertheless, he watched carefully the statistics of births and within the bounds of humanity he took pains to promote conditions that made for large families. He encouraged marriage because he thought they made for orderly living and a large number of children. In some states it was a common saying that a slave child was worth a hundred dollars as soon as it breathed.

In realization of this desire it devolved on the overseer to see that the women were taken care of that childbirth might be attended with no serious mishap. The ignorance of the women made it necessary to take many precautions. A large number of children died soon after being born. In many cases it was reported that the mothers lay on them in the night. How much this was due to sheer ignorance, how much to the alleged indifference of the slave women for their off-spring, and how much to a desire to bring no children into the world to live under slavery it is impossible to say. Perhaps each cause contributed to the result.

The instructions of the employers required the overseer to see that mothers did not nurse their children in hot weather for fifteen minutes after they had come from the fields, that they were not put to difficult labor when they were not physically able to perform it, that they had the proper food for nursing women, that they had time from their work to go to the houses to nurse their children, that a midwife was on the plantation, or nearby, and many other things pertaining to safe childbearing. I find no evidence that doctors were summoned in childbirth, and it seems to have been the custom to leave the case entirely to the midwife, who was invariably a slave. On the other hand it should be remembered that most of the early white settlers in this country followed the same practice.

Sir Charles Lyell Watches the Negroes Working at Hopeton Plantation

When Sir Charles Lyell, the English geologist, visited Hopeton in January 1856, he saw slavery in its best light. Situated on the Altamaha River, about eight miles by water from Darien, Georgia, Hopeton had been brought to such a high stage of cultivation by James Hamilton Couper that in 1825, twenty years after the land was cleared, it was already one of the show places of the South. Couper was a man of remarkable abilities, an amateur scientist of distinction, and an able planter and man of business.

Travelers from the North and from Europe frequently stopped at Hopeton, so famous had it become by the mid-century. When Fredrika Bremer visited there in 1851, she noted, rather naïvely, that she did not find Mr. Couper "a reformer, merely a disciplinarian, with great practical tact and also some benevolence in the treatment of Negroes." Miss Bremer should hardly have expected a planter who at one time had the supervision of fifteen hundred slaves to be a "reformer"—certainly not of the abolitionist variety.

The following passage is reprinted from Sir Charles Lyell's A Second Visit to the United States of North America (*London: John Murray; 1849*), *Vol. I, pp. 353–9. For a note on Lyell, see p. 50.*

❁

THERE are 500 negroes on the Hopeton estate, a great many of whom are children, and some old and superannuated. The latter class, who would be supported in a poor-house in England, enjoy here, to the end of their days, the society of their neighbours and kinsfolk, and live at large in separate houses assigned to them. The children have no regular work to do till they are ten or twelve years old. We see that some of them, at this season, are set to pick up dead leaves from the paths, others attend the babies. When the mothers are at work, the young children are looked after by an old negress, called Mom Diana. . . .

The out-door labourers have separate houses provided for them; even the domestic servants, except a few who are nurses to the white children, live apart from the great house—an arrangement not always convenient for the masters, as there is no one to answer a bell after a certain hour. But if we place ourselves in the condition of the majority of the population, that of servants, we see at once how many advantages we should enjoy over the white race in the same rank of life in Europe. In the first place all can marry; and if a mistress should lay on any young woman here the injunction so common in English newspaper advertisements for a maid of all-work "no followers allowed," it would be considered an extraordinary act of tyranny. The labourers begin work at six o'clock in the morning, have an hour's rest at nine for breakfast, and many have finished their assigned task by two o'clock, all of them by three o'clock. In summer they divide their work differently, going to bed in the middle of the day, then rising to finish their task, and afterwards spending a great part of the night in chatting, merry-making, preaching, and psalm-singing. At Christmas they claim a week's holidays, when they hold a kind of Saturnalia, and the owners can get no work done. Although there is scarcely any drinking, the master rejoices when this season is well over without mischief. The negro houses are as neat as the greater part of the cottages in Scotland (no flattering compliment it must be confessed), are provided always with a back door, and a hall, as they call it, in which is a chest, a table, two or three chairs, and a few shelves for crockery. On the door of the sleeping apartment they keep a large wooden padlock, to guard their valuables from their neighbours when they are at work in the field, for there is much pilfering among them. A little yard is often attached, in which are seen their chickens, and usually a yelping cur, kept for their amusement.

The winter, when the whites enjoy the best health, is the trying season for the negroes, who are rarely ill in the rice-grounds in summer, which are so fatal to the whites, that when the planters who have retreated to the sea-islands revisit their estates once a fortnight, they dare not sleep at home. Such is the indifference of the negroes to heat, that they are often found sleeping with their faces upwards in a broiling sun, instead of lying under the shade of a tree hard by. We visited the hospital at Hopeton, which consists of three separate wards, all perfectly clean and well-ventilated. One is for men, another for women, and a third for lying-in women. The latter are always allowed a month's rest after their confinement, an advantage rarely enjoyed by hard-working English peasants. Although they are better looked after, and kept more quiet, on these occasions in the hospital, the planters are usually baffled, for the women prefer their own houses, where they can gossip with their friends without restraint, and they usually contrive to be taken by surprise at home.

The negro mothers are often so ignorant or indolent, that they cannot be trusted to keep awake and administer medicine to their own children, so that the mistress has often to sit up all night with a sick negro child. In submitting to this, they are actuated by mixed motives —a feeling of kindness, and a fear of losing the services of the slave; but these attentions greatly attach the negroes to their owners. In general, they refuse to take medicine from any other hands but those of their master or mistress. The labourers are allowed Indian meal, rice, and milk; and occasionally pork and soup. As their rations are more than they can eat, they either return part of it to the overseer, who makes them an allowance of money for it at the end of the week, or they keep it to feed their fowls, which they usually sell, as well as their eggs, for cash, to buy molasses, tobacco, and other luxuries. When disposed to exert themselves, they get through the day's task in five hours, and then amuse themselves in fishing, and sell the fish they take; or some of them employ their spare time in making canoes out of large cypress trees, leave being readily granted them to remove such timber, as it aids the land owner to clear the swamps. They sell the canoes for about four dollars, for their own profit. . . .

One day, when walking alone, I came upon a "gang" of negroes, who were digging a trench. They were superintended by a black "driver," who held a whip in his hand. Some of the labourers were using spades, others cutting away the roots and stumps of trees which they had encountered in the line of the ditch. Their mode of proceeding in their task was somewhat leisurely, and eight hours a day of this work are exacted, though they can accomplish the same in five hours, if they undertake it by the task. The digging of a given number of feet in length, breadth, and depth is, in this case, assigned to each ditcher, and a deduction made when they fall in with a stump or root. The names of gangs and drivers are odious, and the sight of the whip was painful to me as a mark of degradation, reminding me that the lower orders of slaves are kept to their work by mere bodily fear, and that their treatment must depend on the individual character of the owner or overseer. That the whip is rarely used, and often held for weeks over them, merely in *terrorem*, is, I have no doubt, true on all well-governed estates; and it is not that formidable weapon which I have seen exhibited as formerly in use in the West Indies. It is a thong of leather, half an inch wide and a quarter of an inch thick. No ordinary driver is allowed to give more than six lashes for an offence, the head driver twelve, and the overseer twenty-four. When an estate is under superior management, the system is remarkably effective in preventing crime. The most severe punishment required in the last forty years for a body of 500 negroes at Hopeton was for the theft of one negro from another. In that period there has been no criminal act of the highest grade, for which a delinquent could be committed to the Penitentiary in Georgia, and there have been only six cases of assault and battery. As a race, the negroes are mild and forgiving, and by no means so prone to indulge in drinking as the white man or the Indian. There were more serious quarrels, and more broken heads, among the Irish in a few years, when they came to dig the Brunswick Canal, than had been known among the negroes in all the surrounding plantations for half a century. The murder of a husband by a black woman, whom he had beat violently, is the greatest crime remembered in this part of Georgia for a great length of time.

Under the white overseer, the principal charge here is given to "Old Tom," the head driver, a man of superior intelligence and higher cast of feature. He was the son of a prince of the Foulah tribe, and was taken prisoner, at the age of fourteen, near Timbuctoo. The accounts he gave of what he remembered of the plants and geography of Africa, have been taken down in writing by Mr. Couper, and confirm many of the narratives of modern travellers. He has remained a strict Mahometan, but his numerous progeny of jet-black children and grandchildren, all of them marked by countenances of a more European cast than those of ordinary negroes, have exchanged the Koran for the Bible.

V I

EDUCATION

I N THIS century the South has at last fully accepted the American system of free universal elementary education; [1] by 1850 it was established in the North. The course to Southern acceptance was long and difficult. The radical legislatures of Reconstruction days forced a nominal allegiance to the provision by writing it into the new state constitutions, but in many sections consent was lacking as well as means. Not until 1918 did Mississippi follow the lead of the other Southern states and pass a compulsory-school-attendance law. In 1900–1, when the national average spent per student was $21.14, in no Southern state was the amount half as much.

Yet proponents of the New South were as ardent in their advocacy of education as of industrialization. Indeed, they believed the two were inseparable. The new skilled workers must have at least a common school education, so the efforts of Northern philanthropists were welcome. As early as 1869 George Peabody, a Massachusetts banker, gave $3,500,000 which was used to establish model schools, found the Peabody Normal College at Nashville (1875), and propagandize for better elementary and secondary education. Thirty years later another Northerner, Robert C. Ogden of New York, financed a series of conferences on education in the South which had far-reaching effects. It was partly as a result of the "Ogden movement" that school revenues increased more than one hundred per cent between 1900 and 1910. But they were still inadequate even though some Southern states spent more proportionately on education than the North, for the birthrate in the South was high. There was also the problem of maintaining thousands of widely scattered rural schools, solved finally by the advent of the central school and its school bus. The heaviest drain, the

[1] What setback it may now receive, as a result of the Supreme Court's decision (May 1954) outlawing segregation in the public schools, remains to be seen.

segregated school system, increased year by year as the idea of "separate but equal" facilities for Negro education took hold.

The college and university picture is brighter. In ante-bellum days the sons of gentlemen could obtain an excellent classical education in the academies and in colleges like William and Mary, the University of Virginia, and Transylvania, and the South rightly claims to have invented the state university. Georgia chartered her university in 1785 but the University of North Carolina was the first to open its doors, on January 16, 1795. When Jefferson's admirable plans for the University of Virginia were fulfilled in 1825, its curriculum was the most advanced of any institution of higher study in America. He had based his university "on the illimitable freedom of the human mind. For here we are not afraid to follow the truth wherever it may lead or to tolerate any error so long as reason is left free to combat it."

The ante-bellum Southern universities ranked well in comparison with their Northern rivals but, as the war drew near, the more liberal professors were silenced or resigned. The pressure to conform, a pressure applied by legislatures, religious denominations, and public opinion, is still strong. A Harvard (with an endowment of $216,000,000) can set its own standards of academic freedom. A Southern denominational college, entirely dependent on its church and its alumni, finds it difficult to defend a professor whose social or religious views are even mildly unorthodox.

The chief weakness of the Southern university today is in its graduate and professional schools. Graduate education requires well-stocked libraries, scholars of distinction with time for research, and, for medicine at least, costly equipment. Too often in the past the best Southern students have gone north for their advanced training, and the professors who might have taught them at Vanderbilt or Louisiana State have been lured away by Northern salaries.

Yet the advances in the past thirty years have been impressive. The expanded campuses of Emory, Duke, the University of North Carolina, and the Rice Institute, to mention only a few, are indicative. Some universities have built a national reputation in particular fields— North Carolina, for example, in social science; Tulane in Middle American research; Texas in Latin American studies.

The great issue of the moment, in higher as in elementary and secondary education, is integration. Already most of the Southern graduate schools have made the breakthrough on the color front. In 1954 more than two thousand Negroes were attending classes in Southern state universities. Only four states—Mississippi, South Carolina, Georgia, and Alabama—were still barring Negroes. The implications of this rapid shift are tremendous, even though the number of students is small. Does it mean that integration will soon be achieved in all the private as well as the state-supported colleges and universities? If this does happen, and the odds are that it will, what becomes of the Negro colleges of the South, those of high standing like Fisk, Howard, and Atlanta University, and those that are now just able to survive? Already the enrollment in some of them has dropped as their potential students have gone to the state universities for professional study. What will happen to the faculty members? Will they go north? Will they be absorbed by the colleges that once were open only to white students?

In elementary and secondary education integration has become an immediate issue of the day, as a result of the Supreme Court's decision of May 1954. Some Southern governors and legislators have taken the position that the new law of the land which requires the abolition of segregation is as unenforceable as the Prohibition Amendment, that the South will never submit, that attempts to require her to submit will lead to bloodshed. Liberal opinion on the question was well expressed at the time of the decision by Professor Thomas Clark of the University of Kentucky, whose Southern background is unimpeachable (he was born in Mississippi and has lived in at least four other Southern states):

> It is the only decision the Supreme Court could make. Some of the Southern states may become emotional over it but there will be a gradual mixture of the two races and it will work out in the long run. The young Southerners are far ahead of their parents in thinking these things out.
>
> The decision will have a wholesome effect on the rest of the world where we are always hammered on the race question. The decision comes at a good time.

An Old Field School in Virginia

*John Davis was one of a group of by no means unimportant writers in
America who were overshadowed, in the early nineteenth century, by
the rising reputations of Irving, Bryant, and Cooper. He was born in
Salisbury, England, of parents who, having more books than money, endowed him with literary taste and the need to fend for himself. He
therefore became an itinerant teacher, a poet, a novelist, a critic, and a
publisher and seller of books. Apparently he was likewise endowed
with a wandering spirit, for he was on his way to Bombay before he
was fourteen, and by the time he was twenty-three he had visited the
chief countries of the Orient, sailed around Africa at least four times,
and seen something of Spain, France, and Germany. From 1798 to
1817, with the exception of a two-year period back in England, he was
in the United States, teaching school, cultivating the acquaintanceship
of people like Jefferson, writing, and trying his hand at publishing ventures. His* Captain Smith and the Princess Pocahontas (*Philadelphia,
1805*) *popularized the Pocahontas story. The book soon went into a
second edition, as did* The First Settlers of Virginia, An Historical
Novel (*New York, 1805*).*

*For a few months in 1802 Davis found himself teaching at Pohoke,
a plantation near New Market, Virginia. His account of his experiences
there clearly reflects the tutorial system, by which Southern landowners sought to put their children under the guidance of a cultured gentleman, preferably an Englishman. His school is typical of the local
"old field schools," privately founded and run, and open to almost
anyone in the neighborhood. Had schoolmaster Davis been somewhat
more conscientious, somewhat less enamored of Virginia Ball, and
somewhat less free in hanging other people's dogs, he might have
stayed to see his brick academy on the hill. That too would have been
typical, for out of old field schools of this kind many of the Southern
academies developed.*

The passage is condensed from John Davis: Travels of Four Years
and a Half in the United States (*London, 1803*), pp. 362–93.

THE following day every farmer came from the neighbourhood to the
house, who had any children to send to my Academy, for such they

did me the honour to term the log-hut in which I was to teach. Each man brought his son, or his daughter, and rejoiced that the day was arrived when their little ones could light their tapers at the torch of knowledge! I was confounded at the encomiums they heaped upon a man whom they had never seen before, and was at a loss what construction to put upon their speech. No price was too great for the services I was to render their children; and they all expressed an eagerness to exchange perishable coin for lasting knowledge. If I would continue with them seven years! only seven years! they would erect for me a brick seminary on a hill not far off; but for the present I was to occupy a log-house, which, however homely, would soon vie with the sublime College of *William and Mary*, and consign to oblivion the renowned Academy in the vicinity of *Fauquier Court-House*. I thought *Englishmen* sanguine; but these *Virginians* were infatuated.

I now opened what some called an Academy,[1] and others an Old Field School; and, however it may be thought that content was never felt within the walls of a seminary, I, for my part, experienced an exemption from care, and was not such a fool as to measure the happiness of my condition by what others thought of it.

It was pleasurable to behold my pupils enter the school over which I presided; for they were not composed only of truant boys, but some of the fairest damsels in the country. Two sisters generally rode on one horse to the school-door, and I was not so great a pedagogue as to refuse them my assistance to dismount from their steeds. A running-footman of the negro tribe, who followed with their food in a basket, took care of the beast; and after being saluted by the young ladies with the curtesies of the morning, I proceeded to instruct them, with gentle exhortations to diligence of study.

Common books were only designed for common minds. The unconnected Lessons of *Scot*, the tasteless Selections of *Bingham*, the florid Harangues of *Noah Webster*, and the somniferous Compilation of *Alexander*, were either thrown aside, or suffered to gather dust on the shelf; while the charming Essays of *Goldsmith*, and his not less

---

[1] It is worth the while to describe the *Academy* I occupied on Mr. *Ball's* plantation. It had one room and a half. It stood on blocks about two feet and a half above the ground, where there was free access to the hogs, the dogs, and the poultry. It had no ceiling; nor was the roof lathed or plastered; but covered with shingles. Hence, when it rained, like the nephew of old *Elwes*, I moved my bed (for I slept in my Academy) to the most comfortable corner. It had one window, but no glass, nor shutter. In the night to remedy this, the mulatto wench who waited on me, contrived very ingeniously to place a square board against the window with one hand, and fix the rail of a broken down fence against it with the other. In the morning, when I returned from breakfasting in the "great big-house," (my scholars being collected,) I gave the rail a forcible kick with my foot, and down tumbled the board with an awful roar. "Is not my window," said I to *Virginia*, "of a very curious construction?" "Indeed, indeed, Sir," replied my fair disciple, "I think it is a mighty noisy one."

delectable Novel, together with the impressive Work of *DeFoe*, and the mild productions of *Addison*, conspired to enchant the fancy, and kindle a love of reading. The thoughts of these writers became engrafted on the minds, and the combinations of their diction, on the language of the pupils.

Of the boys I cannot speak in very encomiastic terms; but they were perhaps like all other school-boys, that is, more disposed to play truant than enlighten their minds. The most important knowledge to an *American*, after that of himself, is the Geography of his country. I, therefore, put into the hands of my boys a proper book, and initiated them by an attentive reading of the Discoveries of the *Genoese;* I was even so minute as to impress on their minds the man who first descried land on board the ship of *Columbus*. That man was *Roderic Triana*, and on my exercising the memory of a boy by asking him the name, he very gravely made answer *Roderic Random*.

Among my male students was a *New Jersey* gentleman of thirty, whose object was to be initiated in the language of *Cicero* and *Virgil*. He had before studied the *Latin* grammar at an *Academy School* (I use his own words) in his native State; but the *Academy School* being burnt down, his grammar, alas! was lost in the conflagration, and he had neglected the pursuit of literature since the destruction of his book. When I asked him if he did not think it was some *Goth* who had set fire to his *Academy School*, he made answer, "So, it is like enough."

Mr. *Dye* did not study *Latin* to refine his taste, direct his judgment, or enlarge his imagination: but merely that he might be enabled to teach it when he opened school, which was his serious design. He had been bred a carpenter, but he panted for the honours of literature.

Optat ephippia bos; piger optat arare caballus.

Hor. . . .

Of my female students there was none equal in capacity to *Virginia*. The mind of this fair creature was susceptible of every culture; but it had been neglected, and I opened to her worlds of sentiment and knowledge. . . .

I had been three months invested in the first executive office of Pedagogue, when a cunning old fox of a *New Jersey* planter (a Mr. *Lee*) discovered that his eldest boy wrote a better hand than I. Fame is swift-footed; *vires acquirit eundo;* the discovery spread far and wide; and whithersoever I went, I was an object for the hand of scorn to point his slow unmoving finger at, as a school-master that could not write. *Virginia* gave me for the persecutions I underwent a world of sighs, her swelling heavens rose and with indignation at old *Lee* and his abettors. But the boys caught spirit from the discovery. I could perceive a mutiny breaking out among them; and had I not in time broke down a few branches from an apple tree before my door, it is

195

probable they would have displayed their gratitude for my instructions by throwing me out of my school-window. But by arguing with one over the shoulders, and another over the back, I maintained with dignity the first executive office of Pedagogue.

I revenged myself amply on old *Lee*. It was the custom of his son (a *lengthy* fellow of about twenty) to come to the *Academy* with a couple of huge mastiffs at his heels. Attached to their master (*par nobile fratrum*) they entered without ceremony *Pohoke* Academy, bringing with them myriads of fleas, wood-lice, and ticks. Nay, they would often annoy *Virginia*, by throwing themselves at her feet, and inflaming the choler of a little lap-dog, which I had bought because of his diminutive size, and which *Virginia* delighted to nurse for me. I could perceive the eye of *Virginia* rebuke me for suffering the dogs to annoy her; and there lay more peril in her eye than in the jaws of all the mastiffs in *Prince William County*.

"Mr. *Lee*," said I, "this is the third time I have told you not to convert the *Academy* into a kennel, and bring your dogs to school."—*Lee* was mending his pen "*judgmatically*." He made no reply, but smiled.

I knew old *Dick* the negro had a bitch, and that his bitch was proud. I walked down to *Dick's* log-house. *Dick* was beating flax.

"Dick," said I, "old Farmer *Lee* has done me much evil—(I don't like the old man myself, Master, said *Dick*)—and his son, repugnant to my express commands, has brought his father's two plantation dogs to the Academy. Revenge is sweet—

"Right, Master," said *Dick*. "I never felt so happy as when I bit off *Cuffey's* great toe and swallowed it—

"Do you, *Dick*," said I, "walk past the school-house with your bitch. Lee's dogs will come out after her. Go around with them to your log-house; and when you have once secured them, hang both of them up by the neck."

"Leave it to me, Master," said *Dick*. "I'll fix the business for you in a few minutes. I have a few fadoms of rope in my house—that will do it."

I returned to the *Academy*. The dogs were stretched at their ease on the floor. "Oh! I am glad you are come," exclaimed *Virginia;* "those great big dogs have quite scared me."

In a few minutes *Dick* passed the door with his slut. Quick from the floor rose Mr. *Lee's* two dogs, and followed the female. The rest may be supplied by the imagination of the reader. *Dick* hung up both the dogs to the branch of a pine-tree; old *Lee* lost the guards to his plantation; the negroes broke open his barn, pilfered his sacks of *Indian* corn, rode his horses in the night—and thus was I revenged on *Alexander the Copper Smith*.

Three months had now elapsed, and I was commanded officially to resign my sovereign authority to Mr. *Dye*, who was in every respect better qualified to discharge its sacred functions. He understood Tare and Tret, wrote a copper-plate hand, and, balancing himself upon one leg, could flourish angels and corkscrews. I, therefore, gave up the "Academy School" to Mr. *Dye*, to the joy of the boys, but the sorrow of *Virginia*.

Longstreet on Waddel's Academy

Augustus Baldwin Longstreet (1790–1870) was a Georgian, honored in his lifetime as a state legislator, judge, newspaper editor, and president first of Emory College and then of the University of South Carolina. Now he is remembered as well for his contributions to American literature, though he himself thought slightingly of his writing, considered it mere recreation, and published his most important book, Georgia Scenes (*1835*), *anonymously. The book is still a valuable historical source and its humorously realistic portrayal of provincial types made it the first in a literary tradition that eventually led to the characters of Bret Harte and to Huckleberry Finn.* Master William Mitten (*1864*) *is a novel about a young man whose misfortunes, attributed to bad luck, really go back to the indulgence of his mother, and it therefore contains suggestions of the modern psychological novel.*

There is no doubt that one of the strongest influences on Longstreet was Moses Waddel, whose famous academy in Willington, South Carolina, he attended from 1808 to 1810 and later portrayed in Master William Mitten *"just as it was," as he says in the introduction. Waddel's academy was famous not because it was unique in kind but because it achieved so well the ends at which all Southern academies aimed. These academies differed from the "old field" schools in that they did a far better job, enjoyed a wider reputation, and drew their students from much farther away. Usually holding state charters, they were more nearly public schools, for although founded by private interests, usually by clergymen, and supported by the tuition of their students rather than public funds, they served not the individual plantation-owner but the planter class.*

Waddel taught his students much the same subjects as did other academies of the kind, and working in an aristocratic tradition, he pre-

197

pared his students for leadership. He sent many of them to Harvard, Princeton, and Yale—Longstreet went to Yale from Waddel's school, as did John C. Calhoun—and not a few of his students, when they reached those universities, stepped immediately into the junior class. Eventually they became clergymen, senators, judges, and lawyers.

Many of these academies continued in full vigor through the nine-teenth century, and at the same time others were established in their pattern until, by the end of the century, more than five hundred such schools had been chartered in Tennessee alone. They were the an-cestors of the present Southern preparatory school. The Webb School at Bell Buckle, Tennessee, was one of them when it was founded in 1870 by W. R. (Sawney) Webb, "the father of preparatory school education in the South," and it is now one of the leading Southern boarding schools.

The passage below is from Augustus Baldwin Longstreet: Master William Mitten: or, A Youth of Brilliant Talents, Who was Ruined by Bad Luck (*Macon, Georgia: J. W. Burke and Co.; 1889), pp. 110–14 and 121–2.*

MONDAY morning came, and William moved sadly to the Academy. Soon the students of every size began to pour in from every quarter; and soon the whole school was in commotion. George Cary had got a thousand lines in Virgil! He was to leave his class, of course; for such a lesson had never been heard of before, even in Dr. Waddel's school, where the students seemed to take in Latin and Greek by absorption.[1] As his classmates came in, they compared notes, and not one of them had got more than three hundred lines.

"I didn't get but two hundred and ten," said one.

"I didn't get but two hundred," said another.

"Well, I'm at the foot of all," said a third, "I didn't get but a hundred and fifty; so I'm doubly distanced, and left, of course."

William heard these reports with overwhelming amazement. The largest lesson he had ever recited was thirty-five lines, and the largest he had ever heard of being recited was one hundred. He had been led to believe that his native village was the very focus of intellectual il-lumination and mental vigor, and that he himself was the centre-beam of the focus. He did not suppose that Latin and Greek were made for country folk at all, much less for poor folks; and, behold, there stood

[1] George McDuffie afterwards overtopped Cary, for he recited twelve hun-dred and twelve lines, in Horace, for a Monday morning's lesson.

before him homespun, [2] Gilbo-shod, potato-fed chaps, even smaller than himself, who had mastered one hundred and fifty lines in Virgil, acknowledging themselves the fag-end of their class, and "doubly distanced!" His mind was immediately made up to take the *selectæ* class, mortifying as it was to a gentleman of his calibre to have it known at home that he had retrograded; but could he keep up with this class? He had little hope of doing so; but so shocking was the idea of falling two classes below his home stand, that he resolved to try it at all events. He had one consolation, at least, and that was, that none of the schoolboys knew of his advancement before he came hither. Withal, he concluded that there must be a something about Dr. Waddel's school that made all the boys who came to it smart, and whatever that something might be he surely would catch it in a short time. The Doctor soon made his appearance, and William signified to him his choice of classes.

The school was summoned to prayer, and at the conclusion of this service the monitors bills were handed in, and the dancing room cleared. The Doctor read over to himself the bills, with an affected seriousness, while a deathlike silence reigned around him, his countenance, meantime, assuming all varieties of expressions. It was very easy for those well acquainted with him to collect from these indications the general character of the bills in hand; and the signs this morning were of things grave, novel, funny and common.

The reading finished, the Doctor began: "Pretty heavy bills! some things new even to me. Garrett Sandige, go and get the *change* to settle off these bills, and see that it is such as has the genuine *ring!*" To a correct understanding of the first case on the docket, it is necessary to premise a little. John Freeman had been exalted for the first time to the dignity of Monitor on the preceding week, and he had overacted his part a little; he was rather too vigilant and authoritative.

To economize time, while Garrett Sandige was collecting the change, the Doctor sounded the docket in a humorously emphatic and pompous style:

"*Austin B. Overstreet, for being idle repeatedly!* What say you, Austin?"

"I deny it, sir," said Overstreet.

"Monitors, speak!"

"Dr. Waddel, almost every day in the week he follows me all about

---

[2] We give this name as it was pronounced. We think it was spelled Guillebou. He was shoemaker-general for the school, and one of the best that ever lived. The soles of his shoes were about half an inch thick, and the heels three-quarters —the upper leather in exact proportion with the soles. In short, they were brogans, in all respects, of the stoutest sort. It took them about a month to show outward signs of an inward foot. Then they began to wrinkle down to something like foot-shape; with only a tolerable greasing, they were good for a year, certain.

with his Greek grammar in his hand and goes on in this way: *Tupto tupteis, tuptei,* (of all the monitors) *tupteton, tupteton,* (that I ever saw in my life) *tuptomen tuptete,* (John Freeman takes the lead) *tuptousi,* (rather rousy.) I told him I'd *spunk* him, (report him) if he didn't quit it, and he wouldn't, so I spunked him."

During these pleadings the Doctor's face put on all sorts of expressions; to maintain the dignity of the Monitor's character, it was of the first importance that he should hear him with the profoundest respect and gravity; and yet there was something so novel and farcical in this case, that he could with difficulty suppress open laughter. He drew his eyebrows to their closest, pressed his lips forcibly together for a moment, and then passed judgment:

"This is a new case—I confess it perplexes me not a little. It seems to be a case in which study and idleness are so equally and intimately blended that you can't hit *idleness* without at least grazing *study*, nor indulge *study* without indulging *idleness*. If, as soon as Overstreet began to make up his compound, you had informed me, Mr. Monitor, of his experiment, I could have given you a recipe that would have precipitated the feculent matter so entirely from the pure, that we might have dealt with it this morning without danger of disturbing the pure; but as it is, with no antecedent law to meet such a case, and under the maxim that it is best to err on the safe side—the side of mercy—if we err at all, I will let the matter pass for this time; but if you come up again, Austin, with such a mixture of Greek and English in the presence of a monitor, I'll teach you the first future tense of your Greek verb in such a style that you'll never think of mingling English with it again while you live, unless it be the true English."

Before this case was disposed of, Sandige had returned with about a half dozen hickories beautifully trimmed. The Doctor took one, drew it through his left hand, found it knotless, gave it an experimental flourish, liked the ring, and proceeded:

"Garry-Osko-Sapling, for being idle repeatedly!"

Garry stepped into the ring without defense.

The Doctor gave him one cut and paused—"Garry," said he, very good humoredly, "that doesn't sound right. My ear don't often deceive me." So saying he stooped down and raised up the pants of the left leg, pulled down the stocking, and discovered a tasteful and most artistic binding of the calf and its appurtenances, with long narrow strips of old shirt. The Doctor manifested not the least surprise at this, but very deliberately commenced unwinding. At about every yard detached, he would pause and look up to the school with an expression of countenance which seemed to say, "boys needn't try to fool me." Having unrolled about four yards and a half of swathing from this leg, he proceeded to the other, and did the like. During the whole process

200

the school was a roar of laughter, and few laughed more heartily than Garry himself. Having returned the stockings and pants to their places, "let us have fair play, Garry," said the Doctor! "Fair play is a jewel. Now stockings are fair, and pants are fair, thick or thin. If I can't get through them, why, that's my fault, not yours." So saying, he let Garry have the remaining six with a brilliancy that fully compensated for the lost pleiad. . . .

The morning's exercises were exceedingly interesting to Master Mitten, of course, and he was allowed half a day to muse upon them; for he was without the text book of his class, and could not be supplied until Doctor Waddel went home to his dinner. The forenoon of the day was employed chiefly in taking observations of the costumes, manners, and conduct of the boys; but part of the time was spent with young Hay and three of his classmates, with whom he studied during that day. They construed alternately a sentence aloud, and if the version of the reader was corrected by some one of the listeners, it was considered as properly rendered, and adopted by all. Occasionally, a dispute would arise between them as to the case of a noun, the mood and tense of a verb, or the application of some rule of syntax, and the dispute was invariably settled by an appeal to the grammar, which each one kept always by him in studying his lessons. Herein, he found one clue to a solution of the mystery which had astonished him so, at the opening of school—the prodigious lessons which the boys recited—and before the next day he discovered another which solved the mystery entirely; it was that the very idlest of the boys studied twice as much as any school-boys he had ever seen. In the afternoon his selectæ was furnished him, and he set in regularly with his class. He begged to be excused from reading in his turn, as the author was new to him. He was indulged; and thus he was virtually carried over his first lesson. One reading of it, to him, was enough to make him as perfect in it as any in the class, and consequently he recited it creditably. He had hardly concluded his first recitation, when the signal for evening prayer was given; the students were assembled, prayer was held, and they were dismissed for the night. Thus ended the most terrific day of William's pupilage. We have been particular in giving its history, not only for its effect upon Master Mitten, but that the reader might have a practical exhibition of Doctor Waddel's government. Terrific as the day was to William, it was the first of a long series of days pregnant with good luck.

College Life in the Old South

College life in the Old South differed little from college life in the Northern states. The curriculum, essentially "classical," was usually patterned after that of such already well-established Northern universities as Harvard, Yale, and Princeton. The organization and discipline of Southern colleges also followed the Northern pattern, as did such dominant institutions in student life as the debating clubs. Several of the founders of Franklin College, later to become the University of Georgia, were Yale men. In drawing up the charter for the new institution they had at hand the Yale charter. Though this did not prove to be of much assistance, since it had been granted in 1745 under an English King, in other respects the Yale influence was strong at Franklin College.

The president and faculty of any Northern college would have been no little distressed by the riotous conduct of the Southern student. Not that the conduct of the Southern student differed in kind from that of his Northern cousin; it differed only in degree. The rebelliousness that is apparently natural to a college student anywhere was intensified by the fierce independence bred into the Southerner from his boyhood. To the respect of all students for an honor code was added the Southern tradition of chivalry. And the student's natural delight in sheer animal roughness was intensified by the South's casual acceptance of violence.

In his College Life in the Old South *(New York, 1928), E. Merton Coulter, Professor of History at the University of Georgia, gives a full and colorful picture of what life was like when his university was Franklin College. The following passage, printed by his permission, is made up of selections from pages 77–132. It is a condensation of two of Professor Coulter's chapters: "Justice in the High Court of the Faculty" and "Between Lessons and Professors."*

HIGHER education was a new thing in the Lower South when the University of Georgia began its existence. Yale men brought the idea in, and Yale men made the machinery and set it in motion. As already noted, how Yale College did things was of much importance in Georgia. The inspiration for the laws governing the students was also of Yale origin and was Puritanical and puerile after the most approved fashion of the age. . . . The student's passport to classes was a set of the laws signed by the president; he was given ten days to digest them and thereafter he fell hard under their inexorable pains and penalties. His every action was guided by them. A law got him out of bed and put him back again. He ate by them, he studied by them, he recited by them—they were with him always. He kept them close at hand, hardly knowing until he should consult them what he could do next.

"If any scholar shall be guilty of prophaneness—of fighting or quarreling—if he shall break open the door of a fellow student—if he shall go more than two miles from Athens without leave from the President, a Professor or a Tutor,—if he shall disturb others by noisiness, loud talking or singing during the time of study—if he shall ring the Bell without order or permission—if he shall play at billiards, cards or any unlawful game—if he shall associate with vile, idle or dissolute persons, or shall admit them into his chamber,—if he shall instigate or advise any student to a refractory or stubborn behaviour—he shall for either of those offenses, be punished by fine, admonition, or rustication, as the nature and circumstances of the case may require." No student should "be allowed to keep any gun, pistol, Dagger, Dirk, sword cane or any other offensive weapon in his room in College or elsewhere," and it was made plain that *elsewhere* meant *anywhere* in the world. Furthermore, he should not keep "for his use or pleasure, any riding animal or dog."

There were crimes even much more serious than these, and students must never be guilty of them, to wit: "If any scholar shall be guilty of blasphemy, fornication, theft, robbery, forgery, or any other crime, for which an infamous punishment may be inflicted by the laws of the State, he shall be expelled." Gentlemen out in the state might fight a duel and evade the law against it, but expulsion awaited the student who should settle his differences in such a fashion. Naturally students were forbidden to fight among themselves, but for fear of a misunderstanding that the law went no further, it stated plainly that no student might "strike, or insult any person not being a member of the College." And even yet, fearing his fighting instincts might seek to find other and unusual outlets, the law solemnly said: "If any scholar shall assault, strike, or wound the President, a Professor, or a Tutor—or shall designedly break their doors or windows, he shall be expelled." Furthermore, admonition, suspension, or expulsion awaited anyone who should "lie, get drunk or be guilty of other gross immoralities.". . .

These were the rules on student conduct and this their process of enforcement—rules from Puritan New England for the untamed South. The Southern atmosphere proclaimed the doom of the whole system from the beginning, but the educational managers never admitted it or receded for almost three-quarters of a century. Young Georgians at Athens, young North Carolinians at Chapel Hill, young South Carolinians at Columbia, young Mississippians at Oxford—all objected to such a system and in much the same manner. The sons of planter aristocrats hated restrictions, for they knew that only slaves were made to be ordered around, and the sons of the aspiring gentry had grown up in communities which recognized few men's authority and cared little for the law. Robert Finley hesitated much on accepting the presidency of the Georgia university, of course, on account of the "high responsibility" of the position, but really because of "the insubordination of Southern youth." To do as one pleased was liberty, to be restrained was tyranny. And besides, a peculiar sense of honor was one of their most highly developed traits. A Georgia student asserted in 1855 that it was "mortifying to the feelings of the young men to have their words doubted, and must beget within them a sort of contempt and hatred for the Faculty. No graver insult could be offered to a gentleman than this." It is also a common human trait to delight in doing those things forbidden. . . .

The majority of students held firmly to the belief that the professors were the chief obstacle to their thorough enjoyment of life, and that, therefore, they were worthy objects of ridicule, scorn, and attacks. The professor was indeed a most colorless person who could not call forth a nickname from the students. Malthus Ward was always "Dr. Pegs" after the remark, "Words are only pegs on which to hang our ideas." James Jackson, the son of a former governor, was "the Major"; Professor William L. Broun was "Little Bruin"; President Waddel [1] was "Old Pewt"; and Professor Hull was "Old Cosine.". . .

The students were in their own estimation gentlemen and the sons of gentlemen, but often they forgot these things and dealt with their professors as their passions dictated. Thomas Beall was found "guilty of a most flagrant act of contumacy in wilfully disobeying and insulting an officer of the College" and was fined five dollars for it. A senior in 1860 having completed all work for his degree, made bold to express frankly his opinions of men and things and declared that there was only one gentleman on the whole faculty. This body at its regular weekly meeting being unable to agree on which one was the gentleman, expelled the senior and refused to grant him his degree. A junior, Perryman by name, was overheard one day engaging in the common pastime of cursing the faculty. When he learned that he had been expelled for it, he cursed them to their faces before he took his departure. . . .

[1] In 1819 the Reverend Moses Waddel left his famous academy at Willington, South Carolina, to become President of Franklin College. See "Longstreet on Waddel's Academy" (p. 197) for an account of this school.

Shooting pistols and carrying deadly weapons were practices which the professors long sought to suppress. President Waddel being a light sleeper was often awakened by shooting. On Christmas eve of 1824 he slept badly, being much "interrupted by bell and shooting." At one faculty court he "arraigned nine boys for shooting." In 1822 a ring of students were fined, some $5 and others $2.50, for "going full in the face of authority, by shooting during the late Xmas holidays." . . .

In 1836 two students armed with a pistol and a dirk in deadly and earnest fashion started about settling their argument. One was stabbed near the heart and dangerously wounded. Only by good luck did he recover. It was also in the dangerous 'thirties that a senior entered another student's room and "with violent gesticulations" attempted to stab him with a dirk. Other students rushed in and stopped his thrust. As he walked away he said, "The damned scoundrel:—I'll be the death of him before supper." In 1831 an argument developed the following results: One student said to the other, "If you will go down into the woods, I'll whip you like Hell." The other replied that "this is as good a place as any other," and the former agreeing stabbed him. Both were expelled, but both being experts at the art of petitioning and promising were able to get reinstated. . . .

Drinking whiskies and wines was, of course, a common practice among students, as it was, indeed, among people generally. Moses Waddel, who had a most exacting conscience, found wine and brandy necessary for his health. The Athens liquor shops and groceries displayed their "Malaga, Madeira, Teneriffe, Muscatelle, Cherry-Bounce, Shrub, Claret, and Porter"—all of which they sold "very low for cash." By 1858, the closing hours for the town liquor shops had been forced down to 11 P.M. Drinking could thus be carried on with such ease that drunkenness came second in frequency among all the crimes committed by the students—the indeterminate charge of disorderly conduct coming first. The faculty forbade student drunkenness and frowned on any drinking whatever, and the trustees expressed their concern more than once at too much student drinking. . . .

How should the faculty know when a student was drunk, or how even could a student know? This was an important question, as drinking was not necessarily punished unless it was done in a dormitory room or engaged in continuously. One Stanly in 1855 while visiting a young lady in town was accused by her of being drunk. He became indignant, and forgetting his chivalry, told her it was false. The case came before the faculty, and as the breach of Southern chivalry was not listed as a crime, he was tried for drunkenness. Stanly admitted drinking a third of a pint of champagne, but he convinced the faculty it did not make him drunk. Dawson, one of the friends of the lady, considering that justice had not been done, assaulted Stanly, and a fight followed costing Stanly $5 and Dawson $10 in the high court of the faculty. . . .

The ante-bellum college student was a rebellious, untamed spirit, who needed watching but who grew worse the more he was watched. Emerson said in 1837, "The Southerner asks concerning any man, 'How does he fight?' The Northerner asks, 'What can he do?'" There was a gentlemen's agreement among the colleges (or a sort of protective league) against admitting students expelled from another institution. . . .

An incomplete record for the forty-three years prior to 1873 shows the following dismissals—no regard being had for the almost countless lesser punishments: idleness and neglect, 16; drunkenness, 27; disorderly conduct, 50; gambling, 4; playing cards, 4; fighting, 18; stabbing and shooting, 7; disrespect to professors, 21; fighting chickens, 4; profanity, 1; cheating and lying, 1; indecency, 8; refusal to recite, 8; disturbing church, 3; and having firearms, 4.

Verily, the college student of the Old South was a happy creature; he had so many rules to disobey and did it so effectively. . . .

With all the hilarity that went with student life there was considerable seriousness. The books they studied were difficult and dry. They had no choices—every course was fixed and had to be taken. In 1825 a group of students pledged themselves "to one an other" to resist the faculty ruling that there should be two mathematics classes a day. Some of the rebels were expelled for this interference with the curriculum. Mathematics was considered especially difficult. The junior class in 1824 petitioned the faculty to excuse them from reciting "Cicero de Oratore" until they should have completed conic sections. The faculty refused. The students also disliked Greek, and hence they came up often with bad lessons. President Waddel noted in his diary, September 16, 1822, "bad Greek lesson"; the next day he recorded "bad Greek lesson again." In 1849 a student who had just stood an examination in Greek wrote, "missed the contemptible little word"—and he still was unable to write down what it was. What the students studied seemed far removed from the life around them and equally as far away from any they might ever expect to see or experience. Yet the training they received was valuable. They took on attitudes and characteristics that made of them the chief leaders of the state, and some of them, of the nation.

Student life at Franklin College had its pains and penalties, but with all of its rigors it afforded a rare experience to the sons of Georgia and of the surrounding states. Even while it was being lived it had a sort of daring wild charm about it, but in after years it took on a bewitchment irresistible. Indeed, distance lends enchantment to the view. The editor of the student magazine (the *Georgia University Magazine*) on taking up his duty in 1852 inquired what he should write about, and then immediately answered "We will tell you of ourselves, of our associates and of our beloved Institution, 'Old Franklin.'" And then the romance in and around "Old Franklin" flows through many of the pages of the G U M, as the magazine was familiarly called. Even so terrible a tyrant as the chapel bell called forth an ode:

> When Sol, from his couch in the East doth arise,
> Beams lightly on earth and mounts high in the skies—
> Loud peals of rich music his welcoming tell,
> All nature awakens with the "Old Chapel Bell."

The most hated and feared members of the faculty suddenly became likable and some of the suppers and entertainments they received at the homes of the president and professors were recalled. Alexander H. Stephens said the time he spent at Franklin College was "by far the happiest days of my life." Many another man who had one time been a Franklin College boy felt much the same way about it.

The Fundamentalists and the Schools

Even today in the South the schoolteacher, whether he watches over the sixth grade or is a professor in a college, must walk with care. Someone may report him to the authorities, sooner or later, if he belongs to the American Civil Liberties Union or fails to attend church regularly or advocates the admission of Negroes to his alma mater or doubts the historicity of Genesis or is known to enjoy an occasional cocktail among friends. For over a hundred years many of the more independent educators in the South have found it convenient to desert their region and seek posts in the North where their heterodoxies might be less conspicuous. One cannot deny that for this reason, among others, the South has been steadily drained of intellectual leadership.

But the obscurantists have not always been victorious. In the 1920's one of the most vigorous and prolonged assaults on the freedom of teaching was made by the Southern Fundamentalists—politicians and clergymen and their parishioners—who were determined to keep the diabolic ideas of Darwin out of the schools. Their efforts were epitomized, of course, in the celebrated trial of John T. Scopes, a high-

*school teacher of biology who deliberately and with the connivance of
his friends, who wanted to watch the fireworks, violated the Tennessee
anti-evolution law. Northern liberals and European observers, as soon
as they recovered from shock, took to the letters-column of the newspapers. Yet most of them failed to realize that there were also Southern
liberals who were as much perturbed as they and who were prepared
to fight it out with rural legislators and the powerful Southern Baptist
Convention.*

*The story of their fight is well told by Virginius Dabney in the fol-
lowing selections from the chapter on "Darwin and the New Demonol-
ogy" in his* Liberalism in the South. *For many years Dabney, editor
of the* Richmond Times-Dispatch, *has helped to carry on the liberal
fight in the South while others chose to run away. In his editorials and
his books—*Liberalism in the South (*1932*), Below the Potomac (*1942*),
and Dry Messiah: the Life of Bishop Cannon (*1949*)—*he has patiently
and with good humor explained the South to the North, and the rest
of the modern world to the South. Because he, and some others, have
stayed home and carried on in the tradition of Jefferson, Madison,
President Thomas Cooper (of South Carolina College), John Henry
Pleasants (another Richmond editor, of ante-bellum days), Howard
Odum, and Frank P. Graham, the South has become a more congenial
place for those who teach.*

These excerpts from Virginius Dabney's Liberalism in the South *are
reprinted with the permission of the publisher, the University of North
Carolina Press.*

❁

GEORGE WASHINGTON, who might reasonably be regarded as authoritative in his statements as to the origins of the republic, once placed his
imprimatur upon the dictum that "the government of the United
States is not in any sense founded upon the Christian religion." The
truth of this statement should be obvious to anyone who takes note of
the fact that so far from setting up Christianity as the country's official
creed, the founding fathers specifically provided in the First Amendment to the Constitution for the separation of church and state. Yet
for the past decade and more there have been frequent efforts below
Mason and Dixon's Line to accomplish a union of the religious and the
secular arms through the passage of legislation outlawing the teaching
of the evolutionary hypothesis. Not only so, but those efforts have
succeeded in Tennessee, Mississippi, and Arkansas.

Many Southerners had imagined that serious agitation over the au-
thenticity of Genesis had been terminated once and for all with the

heresy trials of the late nineteenth century, and that the scientist was free in this supposedly enlightened age to expound any theory as to the origin of the universe which seemed good to him. But they reckoned without the rampant Fundamentalists, who suddenly became vocal over a wide area about 1920. In the following year attempts to buttress the historicity of the Bible by legal formulæ were made in Kentucky and South Carolina. In the former state a bill outlawing the evolutionary theory came within one vote of passage in the lower branch of the legislature. In the latter, an anti-evolution rider on the general appropriation bill was stricken out in joint committee, after it had passed the Senate without opposition.

Encouraged by the strength they had exhibited in these two states, the Fundamentalists redoubled their efforts in 1923. They sponsored the introduction of legislation in Georgia, Florida, Alabama, Texas, Oklahoma, and West Virginia. In Florida they managed to get through a joint resolution condemning the teaching of Darwinism in tax-supported schools; in Texas they obtained the passage of an anti-evolution bill in the lower house by a better than two to one majority, but it died on the calendar of the upper house; and in Oklahoma the evolutionary hypothesis was definitely outlawed by a clause in the free textbook bill which passed both branches of the legislature.

The state of mind which led Oklahoma to take this step may be visualized in the pronunciamento of one of her statesmen who bellowed on the floor of the House while the anti-evolution bill was under discussion:

"I promised my people at home that if I had a chance to down this here hellish Darwin I would do it!"

This utterance compares favorably with that of Representative Hal Kimberly, a Fundamentalist member of the Georgia legislature, who proclaimed at the same period that the only books worth reading are the Bible, the hymnal, and the almanac.

"These are enough for anyone," he said. "Read the Bible. It teaches you how to act. Read the hymnbook. It contains the finest poetry ever written. Read the almanac. It shows you how to figure out what the weather will be. There isn't another book that is necessary for anyone to read, and therefore I am opposed to all libraries."

The anti-evolution issue was not clear-cut in Oklahoma in 1923, for the reason that the anti-evolution legislation was incorporated in the bill providing free textbooks in the public schools. Three years later the portion of the statute which related to Darwinism was repealed.

In 1925, two years after the Fundamentalist triumph in Oklahoma, a bill proscribing the theory that "man has descended from a lower order of animals" was introduced in Tennessee. The patron of the measure revealed the extent of his qualifications to deal with the problem by expressing the view that the Bible had been dictated by God in the English of the King James version. The bill passed by the astounding majorities of 71 to 5 in the House and 24 to 6 in the Senate, and was duly signed by Governor Austin Peay. A few months later Tennessee incurred the ridicule of the civilized world by bringing John T. Scopes to trial for teaching the doctrine of evolution in the high school at Dayton. To Europeans the news seemed almost incredible; it savored more of the sixteenth century than the twentieth. After a trial which was the journalistic event of the year and attracted correspondents from all parts of the country, Scopes was convicted and fined $100.

Having won so signal a victory, the Fundamentalists girded up their loins for a drive on other states. Early in 1926 they put an anti-evolution statute on the books of Mississippi. A leading lobbyist for the measure was the Rev. T. T. Martin of the Bible Crusaders of America, author of *Hell and the High Schools* and other works in opposition to the teaching of the evolutionary hypothesis. Only a year before he rendered such valiant service to the cause in Mississippi, he had submitted an essay in a prize contest on the theme: "Why Evolution Should be Taught in Our Schools Instead of the Book of Genesis." Seeking to win $50, he had signed a fictitious name and sent the paper in. Those in charge of the contest recognized his handwriting and forced him to acknowledge his duplicity. Yet the Rev. Mr. Martin was active thereafter in Mississippi and various other states on behalf of Fundamentalist legislation.

Alarmed by the trend of events in Tennessee, Mississippi, and elsewhere, the authorities of Louisiana State University declined to give a course on evolution, although many students requested it. Shortly afterward a measure outlawing the teaching of Darwinism was introduced in the Louisiana legislature. It passed one house but was killed by a parliamentary maneuver in the other.

The movement in opposition to Darwinian doctrine received tremendous impetus below the Potomac when the Southern Baptist Convention, representing the most numerous denomination in the South, formally adopted a statement in 1926 that "this convention accepts Genesis as teaching that man was a special creation of God, and rejects every theory, evolutionary or other, which teaches that man originated or came by way of lower animal ancestry." This affirmation of the Biblical cosmogony was adopted by the Southern Baptist Education Board a few months later, and by the Foreign Mission Board of the same church shortly thereafter. Southwestern Baptist Theological Seminary near Fort Worth hastened to announce that the convention's declaration "would be made a test of all officers and teachers of said seminary.". . .

The State of North Carolina became a special storm center of anti-evolutionist activity. An anti-evolution bill had been defeated there in 1925 after a bitter battle, thanks in large measure to the efforts of President Harry W. Chase of the state university and President William L. Poteat of Wake Forest College. When it was introduced, the all-important appropriation bill was still undisposed of, but Chase did not permit this fact to deter him. "If this university doesn't stand for anything but appropriations," he said, "I, for one, don't care to be connected with it." He appeared in open and uncompromising opposition to the Fundamentalist legislation and was an important factor in bringing about its defeat.

When the decision was reached to revive the anti-evolutionist crusade there, the Rev. T. T. Martin and other defenders of the faith began an intensive drive with a view to preparing the ground for the 1927 session of the legislature. Martin declared that North Carolina was "pivotal," and that if it could be won, the nation could be won. A "Committee of One Hundred" was formed to launch the movement, and the city of Charlotte, which boasts that it is the greatest "church-going town" in the world except Edinburgh, was selected as headquarters. The selection was a wise one, for bigotry flourishes there more abundantly, perhaps, than in any community of like size between the Potomac and the Rio Grande. The city enjoys an added advantage as the home of the Charlotte *Observer*, which has become in all probability the most reactionary newspaper of consequence in the South, now that Caldwell no longer directs its policies. But despite everything that the "Committee of One Hundred" could do, despite the *Observer's* efforts to pump life into the campaign, the anti-evolutionists failed to get their bill out of committee at the 1927 session. A factor in bringing about this result was a letter written from England by Professor Frank P. Graham of Chapel Hill and published widely. This failure of the Fundamentalists ended the agitation in North Carolina.

The same year witnessed the opening of a determined drive in Arkansas. That state was a fertile field for anti-evolutionist orators, for in 1924 its Baptist State Convention had adopted resolutions not only opposing all forms of evolution but providing at the same time that no Baptist board or institution in Arkansas could employ anyone, whether college president or janitor, who believed in Darwinism. The convention exempted janitors and other such minor employees the following year, but left the resolutions unchanged in other respects.

When the anti-evolution bill of 1927 was introduced in the state legislature, it passed the lower house by a narrow margin, but was tabled in the Senate. This result was due in large measure to Dr. Hay Watson Smith, Little Rock Presbyterian, who fearlessly opposed the bill. Dr. Smith published a pamphlet pointing out the absurdity of outlawing a theory to which every prominent living scientist subscribes. But if Arkansas successfully resisted the importunities of those who sought to ban modern scientific inquiry by legislative fiat, it entered the ranks of the "monkey states" in the popular referendum of the following year. In this, "the first anti-evolution initiative measure in history," the upholders of Genesis triumphed by the decisive majority of 45,000. Under the anti-evolution law thus adopted, it is illegal for any state-supported institution in Arkansas to make use of Webster's Dictionary, the *Encyclopædia Britannica,* or any other work which teaches that man is descended from a lower order of animals.

Since the capitulation of Arkansas in 1928, the Fundamentalists have not won any spectacular victories. They made unsuccessful attempts the following year to recapture Oklahoma and to bring Texas into the fold, but that was the extent of their efforts in the direction of state-wide anti-evolution bills. During the decade of the twenties a total of thirty-seven measures of various kinds designed to ban the teaching of evolutionary doctrine on a state-wide scale were introduced, the great majority of them in the South. In the border state of Oklahoma, as we have noted, a bill was passed and subsequently repealed, and in Missouri and West Virginia a fair amount of strength was mustered on behalf of the Old Testament story of the creation. But nowhere else, except in the South, was such legislation given serious consideration. . . .

Throughout the agitation against Darwinism in Dixie many brave spirits have stood out in opposition to the forces of ignorance and fanaticism which have threatened to engulf the entire region and drag it down to barbarism. Frequently they have done so at the risk of their jobs, and all too often they have suffered persecution and dismissal.

The individual who is generally credited with having brought about the discharge of the largest number of Southern professors because of their religious beliefs is the Rev. J. Frank Norris of Texas, who is said to have six such scalps in his belt. Norris, incidentally, has twice been indicted on criminal charges, once in 1912 for perjury and arson, when his outgrown church burned down, and again in 1926 for murder, when he shot to death an unarmed man who called on him in his study. Owing to the size of his following, this fire-eating Baptist has been able to keep the Lone Star State in turmoil over a good part of the past two decades. His handiwork may be seen in the ruling of the University of Texas in 1926 that it would not employ any "infidel, atheist or agnostic" or disbeliever "in God as the Supreme Being and Ruler of the Universe." In contrast to the course pursued by the authorities of this institution in the face of Fundamentalist threats was the splendid courage exhibited by the late Dr. S. P. Brooks, president of Baylor University, a Baptist seat of learning. Confronted with the anti-evolutionist manifesto of the Southern Baptist Convention at Houston, Dr. Brooks said: "I would die and rot in my grave before I would sign the Houston resolution.". . .

No story of the Fundamentalist attempt to seize the Southern legislatures and thus to control the educational processes of the Southern states would approach completeness without a reference to the magnificent fight waged by Dr. William Louis Poteat in North Carolina to save his state and his church from disgrace. Under fire for years because as a trained biologist he accepted the evolutionary hypothesis as a matter of course, Dr. Poteat refused to alter his position or to resign the presidency of Wake Forest College, a Baptist institution, although a numerous element in the Baptist church was demanding it. Not only so, but when the anti-evolutionist clamor was at its loudest, he proclaimed his faith in the forbidden theory firmly and emphatically. This audacious move brought down a storm of denunciation upon him, but he did not quail before it. Thanks to the loyal support of his faculty and alumni, he was never unhorsed. When at last he relinquished the presidency in 1927 because of his advanced age, after nearly a quarter of a century in office, North Carolina and the nation hailed him as a gallant and a dauntless spirit, liberal in his religious, educational and social attitudes, ever valiant in the search for truth.

Supreme Court Decision Outlawing Negro Segregation in the Public Schools

On May 17, 1954 the Supreme Court, in a unanimous decision, struck down the legal segregation of Negroes in the public schools of the country. The decision had been long awaited. Many expected that the Court would be divided on the issue and that it would find difficulty in resolving the constitutional problems involved. The Court took a bold line in deciding that legal precedents, including even the provisions of the Fourteenth Amendment, did not have as much bearing on the case as the immediate "sociological" question: "Does segregation of children in public schools solely on the basis of race, even though the physical facilities and other 'tangible' factors may be equal, deprive the

*children of the minority group of equal educational opportunities?"
The Court answered its question unequivocally: "We believe that it
does."*

*At the time this book went to press it was too early to predict what
the outcome in the South would be. Extremists among Southern politicians have declared their states will never submit. Plans for circum-
venting the Court's decision have varied all the way from the re-
districting of the school population, so that segregation would in effect
still be possible, to wild schemes for turning over a state's entire school
system to private interests. In the border states of the South, Delaware,
West Virginia, and Kentucky, it looks, at this writing, as if both the
letter and the spirit of the decision would be obeyed. In the great debate that arose as soon as the decision was made, one significant fact
was noticeable: the Southern politicians, in general, did most of the
shouting and denouncing. The school administrators talked more
softly. They had been anticipating the decision for many years and
evidently had some moderate plans in their pockets.*

*In reprinting the Court's decision here the footnotes have been
omitted.*

THESE cases come to us from the States of Kansas, South Carolina,
Virginia, and Delaware. They are premised on different facts and different local conditions, but a common legal question justifies their consideration together in this consolidated opinion.

In each of the cases, minors of the Negro race, through their legal
representatives, seek the aid of the courts in obtaining admission to the
public schools of their community on a nonsegregated basis. In each
instance, they had been denied admission to schools attended by white
children under laws requiring or permitting segregation according to
race.

This segregation was alleged to deprive the plaintiffs of the equal
protection of the laws under the Fourteenth Amendment. In each of
the cases other than the Delaware case, a three-judge Federal District
Court denied relief to the plaintiffs on the so-called "separate but
equal" doctrine announced by this court in Plessy v. Ferguson, 163
U.S. 537.

Under that doctrine, equality of treatment is accorded when the
races are provided substantially equal facilities, even though these facilities be separate. In the Delaware case, the Supreme Court of Delaware
adhered to that doctrine, but ordered that the plaintiffs be admitted to
the white schools because of their superiority to the Negro schools.

The plaintiffs contend that segregated public schools are not "equal" and cannot be made "equal," and that, hence, they are deprived of the equal protection of the laws. Because of the obvious importance of the question presented, the Court took jurisdiction. Argument was heard in the 1952 term, and reargument was heard this term on certain questions propounded by the Court.

Reargument was largely devoted to the circumstances surrounding the adoption of the Fourteenth Amendment in 1868. It covered, exhaustively, consideration of the Amendment in Congress, ratification by the states, then existing practices in racial segregation, and the views of proponents and opponents of the Amendment.

This discussion and our own investigation convince us that, although these sources cast some light, it is not enough to resolve the problem with which we are faced.

At best, they are inconclusive. The most avid proponents of the postwar Amendments undoubtedly intended them to remove all legal distinctions among "all persons born or naturalized in the United States."

Their opponents, just as certainly were antagonistic to both the letter and the spirit of the Amendments and wished them to have the most limited effect. What others in Congress and the State Legislatures had in mind cannot be determined with any degree or certainty.

An additional reason for the inconclusive nature of the Amendment's history, with respect to segregated schools, is the status of public education at that time. In the South, the movement toward free common schools, supported by general taxation, had not yet taken hold. Education of white children was largely in the hands of private groups. Education of Negroes was almost nonexistent, and practically all of the race were illiterate. In fact, any education of Negroes was forbidden by law in some states.

Today, in contrast, many Negroes have achieved outstanding success in the arts and sciences as well as in the business and professional world. It is true that public education had already advanced further in the North, but the effect of the Amendment on Northern States was generally ignored in the Congressional debates.

Even in the North, the conditions of public education did not approximate those existing today. The curriculum was usually rudimentary; ungraded schools were common in rural areas; the school term was but three months a year in many states; and compulsory school attendance was virtually unknown.

As a consequence, it is not surprising that there should be so little in the history of the Fourteenth Amendment relating to its intended effect on public education.

In the first cases in this court construing the Fourteenth Amendment, decided shortly after its adoption, the court interpreted it as proscribing all state-imposed discriminations against the Negro race.

215

The doctrine of "separate but equal" did not make its appearance in this court until 1896 in the case of Plessy v. Ferguson, supra, involving not education but transportation.

American courts have since labored with the doctrine for over half a century. In this court, there have been six cases involving the "separate but equal" doctrine in the field of public education.

In Cumming v. County Board of Education, 175 U.S. 528, and Gong Lum v. Rice, 275 U.S. 78, the validity of the doctrine itself was not challenged. In more recent cases, all on the graduate school level, inequality was found in that specific benefits enjoyed by white students were denied to Negro students of the same educational qualifications. Missouri ex rel. Gaines v. Canada, 305 U.S. 337; Sipuel v. Oklahoma, 332 U.S. 631; Sweatt v. Painter, 339 U.S. 629; McLaurin v. Oklahoma State Regents, 339 U.S. 637.

In none of these cases was it necessary to re-examine the doctrine to grant relief to the Negro plaintiff. And in Sweatt v. Painter, supra, the court expressly reserved decision on the question whether Plessy v. Ferguson should be held inapplicable to public education.

In the instant cases, that question is directly presented. Here, unlike Sweatt v. Painter, there are findings below that the Negro and white schools involved have been equalized, or are being equalized, with respect to buildings, curricula, qualifications and salaries of teachers, and other "tangible" factors.

Our decision, therefore, cannot turn on merely a comparison of these tangible factors in the Negro and white schools involved in each of the cases. We must look instead to the effect of segregation itself on public education.

In approaching this problem, we cannot turn the clock back to 1868, when the Amendment was adopted, or even to 1896, when Plessy v. Ferguson was written. We must consider public education in the light of its full development and its present place in American life throughout the nation. Only in this way can it be determined if segregation in public schools deprives these plaintiffs of the equal protection of the laws.

Today, education is perhaps the most important function of state and local governments. Compulsory school attendance laws and the great expenditures for education both demonstrate our recognition of the importance of education to our democratic society. It is required in the performance of our most basic public responsibilities, even service in the armed forces. It is the very foundation of good citizenship.

Today, it is a principal instrument in awakening the child to cultural values, in preparing him for later professional training, and in helping him to adjust normally to his environment.

In these days, it is doubtful that any child may reasonably be expected to succeed in life if he is denied the opportunity of an education. Such an opportunity, where the state has undertaken to provide it, is a right which must be made available to all on equal terms.

We come then to the question presented: Does segregation of children in public schools solely on the basis of race, even though the physical facilities and other "tangible" factors may be equal, deprive the children of the minority group of equal educational opportunities? We believe that it does.

In Sweatt v. Painter, supra, in finding that a segregated law school for Negroes could not provide them equal educational opportunities, this court relied in large part on "those qualities which are incapable of objective measurement but which make for greatness in a law school."

In McLaurin v. Oklahoma State Regents, supra, the court, in requiring that a Negro admitted to a white graduate school be treated like all other students, again resorted to intangible considerations: ". . . his ability to study, engage in discussions and exchange views with other students, and, in general, to learn his profession."

Such considerations apply with added force to children in grade and high schools. To separate them from others of similar age and qualifications solely because of their race generates a feeling of inferiority as to their status in the community that may affect their hearts and minds in a way unlikely ever to be undone.

The effect of this separation on their educational opportunities was well stated by a finding in the Kansas case by a court which nevertheless felt compelled to rule against the Negro plaintiffs:

"Segregation of white and colored children in public schools has a detrimental effect upon the colored children. The impact is greater when it has the sanction of the law; for the policy of separating the races is usually interpreted as denoting the inferiority of the Negro group.

"A sense of inferiority affects the motivation of a child to learn. Segregation with the sanction of law, therefore, has a tendency to retard the educational and mental development of Negro children and to deprive them of some of the benefits they would receive in a racially integrated school system."

Whatever may have been the extent of psychological knowledge at the time of Plessy v. Ferguson, this finding is amply supported by modern authority. Any language in Plessy v. Ferguson contrary to this finding is rejected.

We conclude that in the field of public education the doctrine of "separate but equal" has no place. Separate educational facilities are inherently unequal. Therefore, we hold that the plaintiffs and others similarly situated for whom the actions have been brought are, by reason of the segregation complained of, deprived of the equal protection

217

of the laws guaranteed by the Fourteenth Amendment. This disposition makes unnecessary any discussion whether such segregation also
violates the Due Process Clause of the Fourteenth Amendment.

Because these are class actions, because of the wide applicability of
this decision, and because of the great variety of local conditions, the
formulation of decrees in these cases presents problems of considerable
complexity. On reargument, the consideration of appropriate relief was
necessarily subordinated to the primary question—the constitutionality
of segregation in public education.

We have now announced that such segregation is a denial of the
equal protection of the laws. In order that we may have the full assistance of the parties in formulating decrees, the cases will be restored to
the docket, and the parties are requested to present further argument
on Questions 4 and 5 previously propounded by the court for the reargument this term.

The Attorney General of the United States is again invited to
participate. The Attorneys General of the states requiring or permitting segregation in public education will also be permitted to appear as
amici curiae upon request to do so by Sept. 15, 1954, and submission of
briefs by Oct. 1, 1954.

IT IS SO ORDERED.

VII

SPORTS AND PASTIMES

Despite the sobering influence of church and industry, Southerners today, like their ancestors, take their pleasures when and as often as they can, and do not apologize for enjoying life. In the swift, clear mountain streams of Tennessee brook and rainbow trout tease the fly-casters. In the slower waters of the Cumberland the small-mouth bass, jack salmon, drum, and catfish come to the hook compliantly. The supply of Florida game fish—the silver-scaled tarpon, sailfish, robalo or snook, pompano, and marlin—is never diminished. On the small lakes of Georgia more than thirty species of duck have been counted—and shot. These pleasures, and many more, the Southerner no longer keeps to himself. The chief industry of Florida is providing recreation for the rest of the country. But many another Southern pleasure-ground is held in affectionate regard by winter-bound Northerners. Such names as Myrtle Beach, Mobile, Biloxi, Pass Christian, Lake Pontchartrain, and Galveston call up memories of sun and leisure and venial sin away from home.

Since the Southerner can live out of doors most of the year, many of his recreations are rural. He hunts everything from doves and quail to alligators (in Louisiana), and the "Rooshian" wild hog (in Tennessee). The universal country sport is the possum hunt, which takes place on autumn nights. After the hounds tree the possum, the hunters flash their lights or torches in his eyes. He clings to his branch in fright and is either shaken down or bagged by a hunter who climbs after him.

Southerners spend much of their leisure time admiring the fine animals they raise on their farms. The Fat Stock Show in Fort Worth or Houston attracts thousands who come just to stand around and speculate about the new breeds of cattle, such as the Santa Gertrudis, which Texas has developed to thrive in fiercely hot weather, on meager pasture. In Marshall and Bedford counties, Tennessee, the Plantation

Walking Horse exhibits his three gaits—the walk, the running walk, and the canter—at shows and fairs. The thoroughbreds of Kentucky receive visitors in their sumptuous quarters the year round. In the field trials at Eufaula and Letohatchee, Alabama, one can watch the best bird dogs in the nation as they are matched for speed and skill. Even the mule, the "orneriest and workingest work-critter living," has his day, Mule Day—the first Monday in April—at Columbia, Tennessee.

The plantation-owner of the Old South might be a vestryman of the Established Church in Virginia or a Presbyterian elder in North Carolina, but he did not permit his religion to interfere with his pleasures any more than did the Catholic planter of Louisiana. The premier sport of the colonial gentry was fox-hunting. To provide acceptable quarry, the red fox was imported into the Old Dominion before 1700. Though an early Virginia court called horse-racing a "sport only for gentlemen," by the middle of the eighteenth century it was enjoyed by all classes. Many planters owned private racecourses, but any settlement that pretended to civilization maintained at least one public course.

Squires, overseers, and village hangers-on watched cockfights together in the days when champion cocks, like blooded horses, were known by name. Men who were men drank deep and gambled for high stakes. George Washington would not waste his time over small bets, but he must have been an accomplished card-player: in the careful record of gains and losses which he kept over a four-year period he noted a loss of only £6. The most exclusive gentlemen's club in the South, New Orleans' Boston Club, was named for a card game said to have been invented by French officers during the Revolution. Both poker and craps made their first American appearance, so it is believed, in New Orleans.

When the members of the planter's family unpacked their trunks and boxes at the St. Charles in New Orleans or the Planters' Hotel in Charleston, they were ready for a round of gaiety—balls, assemblies, concerts, theater parties, and race-meets. While the ladies were paying calls and inspecting the latest fashions, their gentlemen had business to attend to and some private pleasures, including, possibly, an engagement on the dueling grounds. The present gaiety of the more Catholic cities of the South is no new thing. The first Mardi Gras parade in New Orleans did not take place until 1835, but masked balls and street masking were features of this celebration in colonial times. In Mobile the Mardi Gras frolic was instituted in 1704 by the French Governor, Sieur de Bienville.

Many of the ancient sports and pastimes are gone. The horseplay and rough sports of Muster Day declined when the county militia system was abandoned. The ladies are no longer honored with jousts and tourneys, though it is reported that the Tryon (North Carolina) Riding and Hunt Club has tried to keep that elegant ceremony alive with its annual Laurel Tilting Tournament. But if anyone doubts the Southerner's ability to invent new and exotic sports and pastimes, let him get himself invited to the Alabama Deep Sea Fishing Rodeo on Dauphin Island or to the annual hunt sponsored by the Texas-Oklahoma Wolf Hunters' Association.

Taking the Springs Tour in Virginia

In the Old South any family in the coastal regions which could afford it journeyed to "the Springs" as soon as the malarial season or the yellow-fever season or just intolerable hot weather came around. The traveler today often encounters these old resorts, the outbuildings, for slaves and horses, long since decayed while the main house survives as a hotel or private school or tourist home. In the old springhouse the waters, smelling of sulphur or iron or iodine, may still bubble.

The most famous of these resorts were the Springs in the Virginia mountains, some of which have now grown to a magnificence undreamed of even in the ample times just before the Civil War. In the following passage Perceval Reniers describes the usual progress made by an ante-bellum family or roving bachelor from one of these Virginia resorts to the next. The selection is Chapter ii of his The Springs of Virginia: Life, Love, and Death at the Waters, 1775–1900 *(Chapel Hill: University of North Carolina Press; 1941). It is reprinted here with the permission of the publisher.*

By the 1830's, after more than half a century of trial and error, the Southerner had evolved his method of taking the waters: he took them in quantity and he took them seriatim. That is, he made the Springs Tour, visiting as many resorts in a season as time and money would allow. The phrase at home in the lowlands was, he was going "up to the Springs," always in the plural. He might own a cottage at the White Sulphur and expect to put in most of his time there, but he went to "the Springs" just the same; it was taken for granted that before he returned to the lowlands again he would sample the water and the company at anywhere from three to half a dozen other places, a few days here and a week there, if water and company agreed with him.

The region of the Virginia Springs straddled the continental divide, sprawling through the long valleys and over the equally long ridges of the Alleghenies. Anyone beginning at the Warm Springs, which was the northeasterly point of the region, and drawing a line around the principal watering places would have traced a lop-sided, diamond-shaped kite, a long kite pointing northeast and southwest, with Warm

Springs at the top and Gray Sulphur Springs at the bottom. The central axis running between them would be about seventy-five miles long and the transverse axis, running cross country from east to west between Rockbridge Alum on the east and Blue Sulphur on the west, would be approximately the same.

Outside the lines of this region there were numerous other Springs, some large and some small but most of them not destined to come into prominence until the Fifties. Now, in the Thirties, the shadow of the kite covered all that were of importance. Down through the center lay the inner group, the fountains most strongly impregnated with minerals, heat, fashion and fame—the Warm, the Hot, the White Sulphur, the Sweet, the Salt Sulphur and the Red Sulphur. For the most part they were connected by good turnpike roads, and in order to make the circuit of the lot one had to cut back and forth across the mountains, up out of one valley and down into another, travelling in all about a hundred and seventy miles.

Almost everybody went in at the Warm Springs and came out the same way. That was natural. The first turnpike that pierced the region was laid over the top of the Warm Springs Mountain, dipping swiftly down and skirting the edge of the wondrous bubbling pool as it ran westward. That is the way the Virginians first came with their Colonial spleens out of whack and their early-Republic joints creaking; thereafter everybody from the direction of Tidewater followed in the same tracks.

Standing on his high-pillared portico, Colonel John Fry, the happy landlord of the Warm, could see each stagecoach as it appeared in the gap of the mountain up on the sky line. It stopped there to rest the horses, pay toll at the gate, and let the passengers get the view. Then it tipped its weight toward the valley and with one wheel chain-locked raced down that dizzy, zig-zag mile until it pulled up at Colonel Fry's feet, every passenger dithering from fright.

The popular thing was, to alight at the Warm and then be off again with all possible speed. That would mean overnight and not more than over two nights. When we consider that Colonel Fry's hospitality was among the best at the Springs and that it was by all odds the most amusing, it seems a grateless thing for people to have flown from it as they were accustomed to fly from the cholera.

Their overnight stay was just long enough to see the Colonel cut his pigeonwing in the ballroom and to make a visit to Charley, the colored bartender, in the basement story, where the wine was cooled in a spring and stag horns bristled from the walls. It was just time to sink like a sigh into the soft warm liquid of the pool, just time to inquire what was the news from the White and to get it. It was always bad. The White was jammed, the crowding was disgraceful, the food was worse than last year, Major Anderson had grown more supercilious, people were sleeping two on a cot, there were not enough blankets and unless someone died or was murdered not another soul could get in. This long familiar story put them in a fever to get there with as little delay as possible. If there was a seat to be had in one of the morning coaches, they were away early. If there were no seats they hired a hack.

Colonel Fry was the kind of landlord who could see them spurning the delights that he and the Almighty had prepared for them and make a jest of it. He was on hand betimes to help them into the coach or hack and he sent them off with a joke, his own precious, perennial joke. Go, said he, and get well charged at the White Sulphur, well salted at the Salt, well sweetened at the Sweet, well boiled at the Hot and then let them return to him and he would Fry them. They would return, he knew, at least many of them would. A final stay at the Warm was the last move in the game they were at with the waters. "Here ends the course of the springs," noted Wheaton Bradish in his journal. But that was weeks or possibly months away. What concerned them now was to get off, to fly from this heavenly place and its host's delicious food.

If that brief landing at the Warm could be called a stop, then the White Sulphur was the second on the Springs Tour. The belles and beaux naturally presumed that fashion had laid out this course, but fashion originally had nothing to do with it; the fashionables were merely following on in the path beaten down long since by the invalids. When the doctors and the chemical analysts got around to charting the cure on scientific lines, they readily came to the conclusion that the invalids had by happy accident stumbled on a design of Nature's.

Nature herself had arranged the springs in order for their best action on the human system, and it was Nature's inscrutable purpose that the bowels of the ailing should have the White Sulphur purge first of all. These were the preparatory waters which so readjusted the component parts of the interior machinery, so sensitized and altered them ("altered" was the magic word) that the other springs could then get in their specialized whacks with incredible efficiency. The doctors, perceiving this, sensibly fell in with Nature's plan.

You should begin at the White Sulphur, said Dr. Horner, and stay there at least a fortnight, drinking. Dr. Huntt came to the same conclusion from experiments on himself, that being the exploratory method of hundreds of medicos in that day. Dr. Huntt tried starting at the Red Sulphur but, as he soon discovered and broadcast to the world in a pamphlet, he had started at the right end for phthisis but at the wrong end for dyspepsia. So he repaired quickly to the White Sulphur and subsequently had recourse to those waters for several years with startling results. He became marvelously improved, he testified, though as it turned out his colleagues were soon thereafter referring to him as "the late Dr. Huntt."

"That most valuable of all our watering places, the White Sulphur," said Dr. Burke, and it was most handsome of him too, considering that he was proprietor at the Red Sulphur. Peregrine Prolix, a Philadelphian, reported that it was the generally esteemed practice to prepare at the White, not alone for other stomachic waters but even for the baths at the Hot. "When the complaints are such as to require the powerful action of the bath at the Hot Springs, it is extremely beneficial, first, to drink the White Sulphur water three or four weeks, to improve the condition of the stomach." Nature was an all-wise physician and they were learning to take her bitter draughts in the order she meant them to be taken.

After the White there was no hard and fast rule; which Springs came next depended on many things and not the least of these was what the White Sulphur water had done to the working parts. The patient might now need the Sweet for the "tonic" which rehabilitated the over-purged, or he might need the Salt for its Glauber salt or its iodine. Dr. Horner, continuing his prescription, routed them first to the Salt, then on to the Red Sulphur, seventeen miles, then doubled them back through the Salt to the Sweet, recommending a week at each. By that time the animal economy, what was left of it, would be ready for the bathing at the Hot and Warm, thermal springs which Nature had so conveniently placed near the main exit from the region, just when one had done enough drinking and stood in need of a little steaming.

That was the tour that any invalid followed who wished to do a good job on himself. When it was all over he would have consumed six weeks and about twenty-six gallons of variegated mineral waters.

The beaux and the belles and the papas and mammas who rated as hearty, and all those whose anxiety lay not so much in their livers as in their wardrobe trunks and their hearts, when they took up the whirligig set going by the invalids followed no fixed course after the White either, but they kept going. Generally speaking, the turnpike over to the Sweet was the most crowded. There was an immutable law that required everybody in the fashion to converge on the Sweet for the last week in August and the first week in September, from whatever direction, whether from the White or the Salt or the Hot. There, after the unspeakable hilarity of crowding together for another fortnight, they separated, some striking straight South to Tennessee and the Carolinas, some going back east the Fincastle way, but most of them returning to the Warm for a last lingering farewell.

Mr. Featherstonhaugh, the geologist from England, had come crashing into the Virginia scene when the South, having found that Spring-going was a pastime agreeable to both its talents and its innards, was very busy enjoying it. The fact was, it was just now busier than it had ever been before. By the hundreds daily people were pouring through the mountain gaps into these long narrow valleys. Gigs and chaises, coaches, coachees and carioles, Berlins and an occasional calash, hacks and barouches and light Dearborn wagons with the baggage, some of them bright and new but most of them with a resurrected look, toiled up into this high promised land and then careered around from one healing water to another.

So many private carriages rolled into the White Sulphur that there was not enough space for them in the barns and they stood around everywhere under the trees. The guests complained that this was too much; after all, trees were not coach houses. That, somehow, was the kind of disorder that offended them.

Public stage lines were adding coaches and new routes; more "extras" were appearing from Charlottesville, even from as far east as Winchester; an extra cost double the fare of a regular coach. And the slaves in Staunton began hiring their masters' ancient hacks, leaky and loose in the joints, to such as had been too badly bruised in the cannonballs, as the fast stages were called, or who, while recuperating, had been left in the lurch.

Not everybody when the tour had been completed went out by way of the Warm. Those who were returning to the Deep South by steamboat departed in the opposite direction, westward toward the Ohio River, along with the Kentuckians. The Carolinians struck south from the Salt or the Red Sulphur or the Gray Sulphur, and the emigrant trains bound for Tennessee stood aside as the elegant coaches rolled heavily by. "Carolinians returning from the Springs!" said the pioneers to one another. It had a royal sound.

But most of the Springs folk wouldn't have missed the last days of parting at the Warm for anything. Colonel Fry awaited them, now that they had been charged, salted, sweetened and boiled at the other places; it was not in their hearts to disappoint him. The great scales on his portico awaited them too, those fine old scales with the seat under the beam where they had sat to weigh going in; now they must weigh going out and count the extra pounds.

During the final sad-happy week they exchanged their souvenirs and their mutual invitations for long visits; they gave each other sprigs of arbor-vitae, symbols of eternal friendship; they counted over the summer's gossip gathered from place to place and they soaked the accumulated minerals out of themselves in the delicious pool. For the last time that season they looked upon Colonel Fry and his fat wife and his fine ham and mutton and iced milk, and for the last time Charley mixed them an incomparable brandy julep downstairs. Then one September morning early Fry would help to boost them into their coaches and they would be off, toiling slowly up the steep road to the toll gate on the sky line. Until another year the Springs Tour was behind them.

Historian Ramsay on Deer-hunting in South Carolina

Although David Ramsay (1749–1815) was Pennsylvania-born and was educated at Princeton and, in medicine, at the College of Pennsylvania, he migrated to South Carolina in 1773 and was thereafter identified with that colony and state, as physician, legislator, and historian. His two-volume History of South-Carolina, from Its First Settlement in 1670, to the Year 1808 (*Charleston: David Longworth; 1809*), *relies too heavily on the first history of the region, Alexander Hewat's* Historical Account of the Rise and Progress of the Colonies of South Carolina and Georgia (1779), *but Ramsay's second volume contains a good deal of first-hand observation, much of it shrewd and amusing. In the section called "Miscellaneous History of South-Carolina" he discusses "Virtues, vices, customs, and diversions &c of the inhabitants," pauses to observe that men drink heavily in South Carolina because they worry too much about debts and "other embarrassments," has some words to say about duels, describes dress, complexion, the "female character" (which "appears to great advantage in Carolina"), and ends with a dissertation on "Fecundity, Population, and Longevity."*

The passage on the South Carolinians as hunters which is printed here comes from this section of Ramsay's History, Vol. II, pp. 404–7.

HUNTING, both as a business and a diversion, has always been useful and fashionable in Carolina. It contributed essentially to the support of the first settlers, and considerably to that of their successors in every period. It has also furnished the most valuable materials for the early commerce of the country, and has ever since added to the list of its exports. The same arts which were daily employed by the inhabitants in hunting, taught them to be expert, and always ready to defend themselves against enemies. The country, at its first settlement, was one continued forest abounding with wild beasts. To destroy them was both pleasant and profitable. This disposition has descended from father to son through the five or six generations which have intervened between the first and present settlers. To the inhabitants of cities it is matter of astonishment with what ease they who reside in the country can force their way at full speed through the thickest recesses of the forest. Impediments apparently insurmountable are readily got over. Dangers that seem to threaten life and limb—to tear riders from their horses, or horses from them, are escaped without injury. Hunting in some respects is war in miniature. The votaries of the one are in a good school of preparation for the other. This was amply experienced in the course of the american revolution. When Charlestown yielded to the conquerors in 1780, the contest was re-commenced by the huntsmen of the country under the auspices of their gallant leaders Sumpter and Marion. The same arts, arms, and equipments which had been used against wild beasts, were successfully employed against the invaders, and made all their movements in a woody country extremely dangerous. At present game affords the only trophies of hunters. In pursuing it they take great delight. Children are taught by their example, and early equipped for the chase with a dog, a gun, and a horse. Boys not more than ten years old can show with pride the deer they have killed. Exulting in their prowess they give an earnest of what they can do if their country should call for their services.

Hunting is a social diversion and is carried on by clubs. One of these exists in almost every district, especially in the low country. They meet once a month or fortnight, and the members by turns provide a dinner in a plain building erected for the purpose in some convenient central part, and called the club-house. They meet early in the day with their hounds, horses, and guns. Such as choose to take an active part in the sport, sally out in the rear of their dogs. As soon as a deer is discovered, the hounds in full cry commence the chase. The woods re-echo with sounds more exhilarating to the party than any musical instrument. The hunters pursue. From their knowledge of the country and the habits of the deer, they know the precise course that will be taken. They gallop through the woods with a swiftness sometimes exceeding that of the dogs and the deer. They take different stands, but all ahead of the game, and in the course which they know he will take. As soon as the deer appears within gun shot, he is levelled at by the hunters in succession; but most of them are such dexterous marksmen that he hardly ever escapes, and is often laid low by the first or second fire. Instances not unfrequently occur where the shot takes effect, though discharged when the shooter and the stricken deer are both in motion;

and the latter at full speed. The hunt seldom fails of success. When it is over, the parties return to the club-house with keen appetites and partake of the dinner provided for them in the woods. The remainder of the day is spent sociably. In the evening they divide the spoil and return home. The members will die, but the clubs are immortal; so far that a constant succession is kept up, and has been so for near half a century and bids fair to continue. The sons take the place of their fathers, and two or three generations in succession have hunted over the same ground. Any decent stranger coming to reside in the district, if he chooses, is proposed as a member and rarely rejected. Any such person being accidently in the neighborhood or even travelling by is invited to visit the club. If agreeable to him he is furnished with equipments and partakes of the sport as well as of the feast. Politeness and hospitality are incorporated with these social clubs. Good humor and good neighborhood are promoted by them, and they furnish excellent marksmen when wanted for the service of their country. The violence of the exercise is sometimes injurious. Disasters of a serious nature from accident or mistake occasionally take place. The cravings for food and drink, highly excited by the chase, are not always satisfied without subsequent irregularities; but such occurrences are rare.

Gander-Pulling

In the Old South gander-pulling was a kind of poor man's tournament or "riding at the ring." This account of the sport is taken from Thomas Henderson's Letter-Book, 1810–1811 (Manuscript in possession of the North Carolina Historical Commission). It has been printed in Professor Hugh T. Lefler's North Carolina History as Told by Contemporaries (Chapel Hill: University of North Carolina Press; 1948). The passage is reprinted here with the permission of the publishers.

ANOTHER of our games which is more especially worthy of attention than the rest is that of gander pulling. This consists in hanging an old tough gander by the heels, rubbing his neck well with grease and soap, then riding under him with speed, seizing him by the neck as you pass, and endeavouring to pull his head off. The amusement consists in the frequent failures of the rider to lay hold on the long necked animal, and the danger he is in of being pulled from his horse, while he endeavours to pull off the poor animal's head. I cannot help recommending this as a most delightful amusement to all lovers of fun. It is one of the games which are assigned to Easter. The arrival of this period is for some weeks anticipated with rapture, by all bruisers either at fist or grog, all heavy bottomed well balanced riders, all women who want a holiday, and who have a curosity to see the world, and particularly by all buxome young lasses, who wish to see the weight and prowess of their sweethearts tried in open field. In short all sporters, blackguards, mongrels and negroes take warning to collect their shillings and pence, that they may have wherewithal to buy whiskey, be generous to their companions, grow conspicuous by rattling their chink, or at least by showing that sort which is much of the colour and consistency of ground leaf tobacco. Then shall all overseers and enterprisers, have an opportunity to recount their exploits in beating up negro-quarters on a patrol night, in gouging a champion who was stout-hearted enough to attack them, or in shouting, quizzing, or chuckling at a gentleman traveller on a tobacco rolling. They shall then be able to prove their alertness in beating the earth with the body of a wrestler, by lifting & tossing him with a crotch lock or a cross buttock.

When the day has arrived and the company assembled, the whiskey is diligently plied in half broken tumblers, gourds and teacups. The ardour of joy springs up, and soon is lighted in every face. The target is fixed and many a bullet winged with invisible and unerring speed evinces the skill of the marksman, and sends his name on a shout of triumph to the skies. At length the rumour is abroad that the business of the day is prepared, and the hour of trial arrived, when champions, ponies and wagerers are to hold themselves in readiness, while all spectators, gentlemen, simpletons and raggamuffins are warned to enjoy the dodging, the gobbling and pulling of the great gander of the day. They flock in crowds to the appointed scene. On high you behold suspended by the heels from the flexile bough of some neighboring tree, or from some elastick pole, the grand object on which all eyes are fixed—A gander venerable for age, the sinews of whose neck hardened by years, are to contend in force with the sinews of many an arm that is the boast of its owner in the doughty field. In such a contest the chief hope of this prime emblem of all the geese and ganders on the plain above which he hangs, must be found in the armour of soap with which his limber neck is overlaid. On another side is raised to view the richly glittering hat which is to crown the head of him, who shall carry away the head of the father of goslings. The signal is given and the candi-

National Park Service, Blue Ridge Parkway

A Highland Farm from the Blue Ridge Parkway

ABOVE: Harvesting Cotton with a Mechanical Cotton-picker
BELOW: Harvesting Burley Tobacco

Lee after Appomattox—on the Porch of His Richmond House, with Major General George Washington Custis Lee and Colonel Walter Taylor. April 1865.

From *Chesapeake Bay and Tidewater*, by A. Aubrey Bodine

Cook Collection of the Valentine Museum, Richmond

ABOVE: The Christopher Wren Building of the College of William and Mary,
Williamsburg, Virginia
BELOW: A Virginia Negro School in the Nineties

Department of Conservation and Development of t[h]
Commonwealth of Virginia; photograph by Flourn[e]

Photograph by Brown Brothe[rs]

ABOVE: St. Luke's Episcopal Church, Isle of Wight County, Virginia, said to
have been built in 1632
BELOW: Methodist Church at Sharp's Station, Tennessee

Cotton Mill, Honea Path, South Carolina

Skyline, Houston, Texas

dates appear in the lists with their proud and prancing ponies. Away they fly in successive career to the destined prize, the high object of their aspiring hopes, while the hearts of the multitude whose due bills are at stake, but especially the hearts of those fond damsels whose muscular and sinewy lovers are to vindicate their prowess, beat high with expectation. A centinel is stationed to urge the lingering nag from the reeking victim. The rider rises forward in his might, to seize the squalling prize; the noble gander waves his easy neck, and laughs in triumph at the disappointed grasp. Another follows and is still succeeded till at length a resolute spirit determined on success lays hold with a vigorous gripe, and lies sprawling on the ground. His successor sees his fate, but still more firm to his purpose hangs dangling in the air. The air is rent with peals of applause, but it remains for one of greater power of muscles and weight of flesh and bone, to accomplish the glorious victory; he is found at last, and clinging to his beast with a force that almost stops him in mid career, he bears off in triumph and with the inmost exultation of his mistresses' heart the [gander's head].

The Hon. William Elliott Joins Judge P. and Doctor E. in a Wildcat Hunt

William Elliott (1788–1863) was an exceedingly busy man. Born into the planter class—the family had vast holdings near Beaufort, South Carolina—he was not content merely to manage his estate and enjoy the good living of pre-war Charleston. He served in the legislature of his state, though he resigned from the Senate because he could not follow the wishes of his constituents in voting for Nullification. Though a planter, he saw the dangers to the South in the one-crop system of agriculture and campaigned against it. He also disagreed with members of his class in advocating the promotion of industry. As the war drew near he opposed Secession.

As a relief from these arduous activities Elliott enjoyed all kinds of hunting and fishing. Relaxation, by means of sports, he held to "be a requirement of our mental as well as our physical constitution." He wrote engagingly about field sports, signing his pieces in a Charleston paper with the pseudonyms Piscator and Venator. These articles were collected in 1859 in a volume entitled Carolina Sports by Land and Water; including Incidents of Devil-Fishing, Wild-Cat, Deer and Bear Hunting, Etc. (*New York: Derby & Jackson*). *The selection printed here from "A Wild-Cat Hunt in Carolina" (pp. 163–8) is about one third of the chapter.*

❁

AND now we had nearly reached the extremity of the gall, and began to fear that we should start no other cat, when Rowser suddenly burst out into a fierce cry, as, emerging from the cover, he touched the open field. The hounds rush to the spot, second his alarm, and strike off at once for the margin near by. Hurra! they have struck a trail. Gather, huntsmen! Now we shall see sport! The ground was favorable for the sportsmen, for a road ran parallel with the direction of the cry, and thus the whole field got placed, and took a fair start with the dogs. "There they go! Look! for the hedge! Rowser leads—he leaps the hedge—ha! he has overrun the track. Black has caught it up—it is all right! There they go—look at them!—listen to them!—Huntsmen, is it not charming? Does it not make your pulse quicken? Is there not a thrill of pleasure shooting through your frame? Can you tell your name? Have you a wife? a child? *Have you a neck?*" If you can, at such a moment, answer questions such as these, you do not feel your position and are but half a sportsman!

The run was an uncommon one for a cat, as it lay for a mile on end, through an open field. Forewarned of his danger, by the din which the dogs had made in pursuit of the raccoon, he had made this push, in order to get out of their reach. Vain effort!—the scent lies too strong—the nose of his pursuers is too keen! And now, the sight was exhilarating in the extreme. The pack ran in a cluster; the scent breast high; the whole field keeping close in their rear, and animating them by their shouts. "Have a care! ride not too close! cross not the track! fair play for the hounds, and they will work it out. Now, rein in your horse along with me. Do you note the *tone* of the cry? It is not with such a tone they pursue a deer. I have blown off my hounds from a chase, on no better authority than the key on which they pitched their cry. This cry is not prompted by the instinct of hunger—it breathes hatred, antipathy! Look at Wormwood there, the rascal!—how his hair bristles on his back—what venom in his tones! and, let me tell you (take care of that stump), I have observed some packs, that run but upon two legs, eager, like this, to rend and destroy, who betrayed, by the tone of *their* cry, that their motive and their cue to action, was just as hound-like! But see, they push for the wood. He has tried a turn among the

232

saw palmettoes to perplex the scent. It won't do; they trail him out through the open field to the river-skirt! There we must have him!"

The ground on which the cat had sheltered himself, was a narrow thicket on the margin of the marsh. Briers and saw palmettoes covering the surface, made it very uncomfortable for the hounds to pursue; while an almost unbroken line of pine, oak, and bay-trees, intertwined with vines, made it impracticable for horsemen. There were narrow gaps, however, through which we expected to get an occasional glimpse of him—perhaps a shot. The hounds pressed eagerly on, through all this tangle, to the extremity of the skirt; and when we momently expected they would drive him out into the open land, behold! they had lost the track! We looked up at the trees, to see whether he had secreted himself among their dense branches. We tried, first this path, and then that; we beat the back track: all in vain—hunter and hound stood at complete fault. It was hard to say whose disappointment was the greater. But what is Rowser after? See, he is running down the old field to the extreme end of the thicket, where a fence crosses from the wood. What does he there? Shade of Watts, Duncan and Hedge! can he syllogize? Hark! hark! he has struck the trail—listen to his joyous cry, "ευρηκα!" He sound the alarm; how uproariously the whole pack second him. Sagacious animal, he has unmasked the stratagem of the cat—fairly countermined him!

While the hounds were running down the thicket, the cat, it would appear, unseen by hunter or hound, had executed a double, above their heads by leaping from tree to tree, until, having threaded out the thicket, he had again ventured on terra firma, to gain the shelter in the wood. We had hardly plunged into the wood, to follow the direction taken by the hounds, when a shot from the old field in the rear told us that the cat had again doubled, to regain the thicket. A neighboring planter, who had been called out by the unusual din of our sport, had stumbled on him while executing his retreat, and saluted him with a load of bird shot. Two terriers, which had followed him into the field, now fifed in, to the louder clamor of the hounds; the pointers, obedient to evil example, were no longer content to leave the sport to the regular practitioners, but chimed in likewise with their sharp and shrill notes; and the uproar was delicious!

Look at Dash! he is pushing for the margin as fast as spur can drive him—he reins in his horse and cracks away with duck-shot—"your distance is too great, that shot won't tell!" There is the cat, leaping from tree to tree, repeating the manœuvre by which he has already foiled us; but not unseen, as then. What! young cousin to a tiger, would you play the same game twice—on practised sportsmen, too? Dash starts to gain a nearer position. I reined up my horse, and took a hasty glance at the field. The movement of the cat was generally seen, and some were riding to get near, and some dismounting to get nearer; and many a gun was cocked, and many an eye fixed, and many a finger feeling for the trigger. This, then, is my chance, thought I; and off went one barrel charged with duck-shot, apparently without effect; for the cat, with huge leaps, clambered up a tree; and now he had reached the very pinnacle, and as he gathered himself up to take a flying leap for a neighboring tree, I caught up my gun, and let slip at him in mid-flight. The arrowy posture in which he made his pitch was suddenly changed, as the shot struck him to the heart; and doubling himself up, after one or two wild gyrations, into a heap, he fell dead, from a height of full fifty feet, into the very jaws of the dogs! It proved to be a female smaller than the first cat, but beautifully spotted.

We stopped not long to admire, for the sun had now passed his meridian full two hours, and we had more than five miles to ride to our dinner. Behold us, then, in full gallop on our return.

Hail Rex!

For the past hundred years the gayest and most widely known of Southern pastimes has been the New Orleans Mardi Gras celebration. The citizens of the city spend weeks working themselves into a fit state for the great day, and the rest of the year talking about past carnivals and the one to come next season. So do many other Americans, since more than one hundred thousand visitors storm New Orleans during Mardi Gras hoping to get an invitation to a ball. One can look at the parade for nothing, and the baubles thrown from the floats are largess.

There are hundreds of accounts of Mardi Gras. The anthologist's problem is merely to decide which one is most representative. Since the moment when a New Orleans boy first sees Rex on his throne is a great event in his life, it has seemed most suitable to present here the account that Lyle Saxon, the novelist, wrote of his first sight of the great parade. He had been entrusted to Robert, a Negro servant, who was admonished "never to let go of my hand for one instant in the crowds, and he was to see that I had a costume that I liked, and he was to see that I had something to eat at intervals."

Almost anything one writes about Mardi Gras is likely to be disputed, so fiercely are its inner mysteries guarded. Still, a few facts may be ventured as indisputable. Strictly, Mardi Gras, or Shrove Tuesday, denominates the last day before Lent. On this day in New Orleans the Mardi Gras carnival season reaches its climax, as the masked crowds in Canal Street await the arrival of Rex, Lord of Misrule, and his gorgeously attired court and retinue. But the celebrations have begun long before: officially on Twelfth Night, the date on which the krewes may begin to hold their balls. In the thirty or sixty days before Mardi Gras itself (the season is controlled by Pope Gregory's calendar) more than sixty balls are held.

Since there are now so many krewes that hold balls, almost any man who desires to, and has the necessary cash, may join one and thus make his wife and daughters happy. A ball may cost $2,000 to $35,000, and often even more. Conduct at the balls is fixed by custom. The men are almost invariably masked. The women, who are not masked, sit and wait until they receive a "call-out" to the dance floor. All the women want to know whose faces are behind the masks. At the after-midnight supper the masks come off and they know who their various partners were, if they haven't guessed before.

The day after Mardi Gras is Ash Wednesday. Good Catholics attend Mass, many of them well hung-over. The elaborate costumes have been laid away and the floats are stored in the secret dens to await the start of next year's parade.

"Hail Rex!" is a portion of chapter four of Lyle Saxon's Fabulous New Orleans *(New Orleans: Robert L. Crager & Company; 1950). The passage is reprinted here with the publisher's permission.*

❁

IT was nearly noon before we reached Canal Street again where the great street pageants were to take place; for Robert's return down Rampart Street was interrupted a hundred times. Rampart is the Broadway of New Orleans negroes and there are many shops, eating houses, and booths which sell those things so dear to the negro's heart, and to the negro's stomach.

After the Zulu King had passed Robert and I stood watching the stragglers who followed in his wake: masked yellow girls dressed as Spanish dancers, wearing high-heeled red shoes, spangled skirts, and black lace mantillas draped over their heads; negro men dressed as Indians with faces painted and feather head-dresses; men dressed in their everyday clothes, or even in overalls, but wearing grotesque masks; negro children of every shade from velvet black to the lightest *café au lait*, screaming and romping in the streets, enjoying the Carnival to the fullest degree. Robert was anxious to keep moving. He mumbled something under his mask to me—something about showing me things—and then ducked between the swinging doors of a negro saloon. It was a long, rather dingy room, with a bar, a watery mirror behind it; the bartender was a negro, and negro men were lined up drinking beer. While Robert quenched his thirst I drank a bottle of red pop which matched my costume, and sitting on a chair against the wall, looked about me. It was the first bar-room that I had ever seen at close quarters, except those aboard the Mississippi River steamboats, and I was interested in the signs and notices pasted on the walls. There was a notice that "The Poor Boys' Social Club" was entertaining with a "Monster Dance" and there was another notice that the "Hot Papa Café" was holding a contest that day for the funniest negro masker. I listened to the conversation, which went something like this:

"How yo' comin', Devil?"

"Po'ly, thank Gawd, an' yo'?"

"Oh, Ah can't complain, but Ah specks Ah'll feel mighty low an' broke down to-morrow. Me, Ah'm goin' tuh have me a *time* tuh-night!"

"What yuh doin tuh-night?"

"Ah'm goin' tuh de Boll Weevils' Ball. Plenty 'ooman, plenty gin."

"Dem wimmin ain't goin' tuh fool wid yo', ugly ole boy!"

"Mebbe not. But Ah sho goin' tuh trip 'em up, ef'n dey don't!"

This was considered very humorous and was greeted with a burst of guffaws. Robert, who had pushed up his mask to drink, looked funnier than ever, so very red and black he looked, and the woman's ruffled parasol which he carried closed in one hand gave an idiotic touch typical of the day.

When he had finished his beer and I my pop, we "took the street" again. There were strange things on display in the shops and in the show windows, and particularly in one drug store before which we paused while Robert examined the articles displayed there. He waited so long and looked so intently that I remember the things even now, but it was many years later that I realized their significance—and it is probable that I should have never realized it, had I not seen a similar shop window on Rampart Street a few years ago. Here was piled blue powder, yellow sulphur-like powder, black chicken feathers tied in neat bunches with bits of thread, black candles, small spirit lamps . . . many other seemingly unrelated things. But now I know why Robert stood spellbound contemplating them. These things were Voodoo accessories—the necessary ingredients for conjuring, the implements of devil-worship, the dark factors in a darker magic. I remember Robert's respectful interest, his rolling eyes, his intent scrutiny. And I remember that he vouchsafed no word of explanation to the small boy who stood by, awaiting his pleasure.

Finally, jerking himself away with an effort, Robert continued along Rampart Street toward Canal. It was not long before we caught up with the Zulu King again. His royal equipage stood abandoned in the street, and the royal court had entered a negro "barrel house" for refreshments. There was a burst of music from behind swinging doors, and within we could hear the shouts and guffaws of negro men and women. The saloon was crowded to its doors, and from somewhere in that dense-packed mass we could hear the sound of tinkling guitars and the shuffling of feet. Robert made one ineffectual effort to wedge his way in, but gave it up after a moment and returned to me, and hand in hand we threaded our way through the ever-thickening crowd.

Ahead of us lay Canal Street, now so tightly packed with people that it was impossible to move forward at more than a snail's pace. The wide street was filled with moving figures. About half of them were masked, the others dressed in everyday garb. High above the streets the balconies were massed with spectators, and in every window and even along the roofs of the buildings there were men and women. Flags fluttered everywhere.

If the street had seemed mildly insane before, it was bedlam now. A happy roar hung over the heads of the crowd, a hum of voices, punctuated with sharp cries, whistles, cat-calls. And everywhere the tinkling of tiny bells—an undercurrent of sound infinitely strange.

And color, color everywhere: red, purple, blue, arsenic green, and the glitter of metal head-dresses and spangles in the sunlight. There were clowns, of every size and of every color of costume; there were hundreds of ballet girls, often ten or more in a group, all dressed in black and white, exactly alike. There were animal disguises; men wearing purple elephants' heads of papier-mâché; huge donkeys' heads. Sometimes two men would combine in order to represent a comical horse or a violet-colored cow. A man passed by high on stilts, his pink and white striped coat tails blowing out in the breeze. Two men were dressed in black tights, painted with white to imitate skeletons; they were truly terrifying with their skull faces and macabre aspect. Accompanying the skeletons was a fat woman dressed in the uniform of a United States marine; she dragged a squalling child by one arm: "That's only your papa," she said, indicating the taller of the skeletons, but the child, unimpressed by this information, continued to squall.

There was a burst of music near us and a policeman rode by on horseback, clearing a narrow path through the crowd. Robert and I, crushed back against the curb, were almost under the feet of the marching men who came swinging by. It was one of the so-called "little parades" which amuse the crowds before the arrival of Rex, King of the Carnival. On a purple and gilt banner I could read the name of the organization: "The Jefferson City Buzzards"! And with a blare of cornets, they were upon us. First came twelve fat men dressed as little girls, all in white. Their huge stomachs were draped with the widest of baby-blue sashes, and they wore pale blue socks which ended half-way up their fat and hairy legs. All of them wore long flaxen curls surmounted with baby caps trimmed with blue rosettes. Nearly all of them were smoking cigars. They bowed right and left as they marched along and smiled widely, gold teeth glittering in the sunlight. Their "queen" was an unusually fat man who bulged out of a baby carriage, sucking a large stick of red and white striped candy. Another man—this one with a big mustache—was blacked up to represent a negro mammy, and pushed the carriage, perspiring copiously. The babies were followed by a group of men in white linen suits, each carrying an American flag. They strutted with the music and kept bowing and throwing kisses to the spectators. A negro band brought up the rear—a band which played the rowdiest and bawdiest jazz that I had ever heard.

The Jefferson City Buzzards had hardly passed before another marching club followed it. This time the marchers were in Oriental costumes—men of the desert and their houris. They carried a banner bearing the name of their organization. A few minutes later another club came by, the men dressed as negro minstrels.

Suddenly I became conscious of a swelling whisper which ran through the crowd. Necks were craned. Maskers stopped their antics and stood on tiptoe, all looking in the same direction. Robert, with his hand on my shoulder, tiptoed too, shading his devil mask with white gloved hand; and then he turned to me and said—his voice muffled behind his mask—"It's de parade!" And then, almost upon us, I saw twelve blue-coated policemen on horseback riding abreast. They came charging down upon the crowd and we moved back before them, falling over each other in our haste.

If the street had seemed tight-packed before, it was even worse now. Elbows came in contact with my forehead, feet smashed down upon mine; I was buffeted about, almost thrown down as the crowd became more congested around me. But Robert dragged me back to him with an effort, and in another moment I found myself seated with my legs around his neck, high over the heads of the others. And as I emerged from that undercurrent which had seemed to drag me down, I had the feeling of a swimmer rising upon the crest of a wave. And there before me, stretched out as far as I could see, was a mass of maskers, and beyond them a series of glittering mountains were moving toward me. . . . The Carnival King was coming.

First came the mounted policemen who cleared the way, and behind them were masked courtiers riding black horses; they wore gold plumes on their hats, and their purple velvet cloaks trailed out behind them over the flanks of the horses; they wore doublet and hose, and they carried gleaming swords in their hands. There were perhaps twelve of these outriders, gaily dressed except for the fact that they wore black masks which gave a sinister effect. Behind them came a brass band tooting lustily. Two negroes carried between them a large placard emblazoned with one word, "Rex."

And now the parade was actually upon us. The first float in the procession seemed to me the most wonderful thing that I had ever seen. It was a mass of blue sky and white clouds surmounted by a glittering rainbow, and under the rainbow's bridge were masked figures in fluttering silk, men and women who held uplifted golden goblets. It was the title car and upon its side was written the subject of the parade—a subject which I have wholly forgotten to-day, but which dealt with some phase of Greek mythology. The glittering float towered as high as the balconies which overhung the street from the second stories of the houses, and as this gay-colored mountain came gliding past me I was impressed with the fact that the car was swaying and that it seemed fragile for all its monumental size. It was almost as though the whole were on springs. The car was drawn by eight horses covered in white and with cowls over their heads.

A blaring band followed the title car, then more outriders, dressed this time in green and gold and wearing purple masks; and behind them came a car which was even larger than the first. It was like a gigantic frosted wedding cake and at the top on a golden throne was seated Rex, King of the Carnival. Such a perfect king he was, with his fat legs encased in white silk tights, a round fat stomach under shimmering satin, long golden hair and a magnificent curled yellow beard! His face was covered with a simpering wax mask, benign and jovial. On his head he wore the very grandest crown I had ever seen, all gold and jewels which sparkled in the sun; and he carried a diamond scepter in his hand which he waved good-naturedly at the cheering crowd. Behind him a gold-embroidered robe swept down behind the throne, cascaded over the sloping back of the float and trailed almost to the ground, its golden fringe shaking with the movement of the car. There was gauze and tinsel everywhere and thousands of spangles glittered in the sun. At the feet of the monarch two blonde pages stood, little boys no larger than I, with long golden curls and white silk tights, which were rather wrinkly at the knees. How I envied them!

Robert and I were both screaming with delight, and I clapped my hands. And then a preposterous thing happened—a magnificent thing. The blonde monarch, so high over my head and yet so near me, leaned out and with his scepter pointed directly to me as I sat perched upon the shoulder of the big red devil. He said something to one of the pages, something which I could not hear, and the page with a bored smile

239

tossed a string of green beads to me. It swirled through the air over the heads of the people between us and dropped almost into my out-stretched hands; but my clumsy fingers missed and it fell to the ground. Immediately there was a scramble. Robert stooped, I fell from his shoulders, and I found myself lying on the pavement as though swept under a stampede of cattle. Hands and feet were all around me, but somehow in the struggle I managed to retrieve those beads, and triumphant I scrambled up again and Robert put me back on his shoulder.

This had taken only a moment, but during that time the king's car had moved on and another car was in its place. I could see glittering serpents—monstrous golden pythons which twined around white columns, and there were nymphs with green hair who held up bunches of great purple grapes as large as oranges and which glimmered in the sunshine with their iridescent coloring. The float with the serpents and grapes seemed monstrously large to me, even larger than those two which had come before, and it came to a swaying halt directly before us. I had a good opportunity to examine the serpents at close range and was somewhat relieved to find that they did not move but remained twined about the fluted columns.

It was then that Robert pinched my leg to attract my attention. He was pointing toward the Carnival King, whose throne was now a short distance from us. The King's back was turned toward me now, but I could see that he was greeting some one upon a balcony opposite. I had not noticed this balcony before, oddly enough, but now as I looked I was conscious of tier after tier of seats rising from the second to the third floor of the building, the seats filled with men and women, not maskers but ordinary mortals dressed in their best. At the moment their hands were stretched out in greeting, and they were smiling. There in the first row of seats on the balcony was a beautiful girl wearing a big floppy pink hat. She stood with both hands outstretched toward Rex as he sat before her on his throne. They were separated by a distance of perhaps twenty feet, but his high throne was almost level with her, and both of them were far above the heads of the crowd in the street below. They were exchanging greetings. And then from somewhere came a man with a step-ladder which was set up in the street. Up the ladder a man ran nimbly, bearing a tray with a white napkin over it. He presented the tray to the King. Suddenly a bottle was opened with a loud pop, and I saw champagne poured out into a thin wine glass, champagne which spilled over the edge of the goblet and ran down into the street below. Rex, King of the Carnival, was toasting his queen. Years afterward, I heard the story of this, why it was done and how old the custom was, but then the small boy who looked upon it saw only another fantastic happening in that mad dream of Mardi Gras.

The ceremony was soon over, the step-ladder was whisked away again and Rex on his swaying throne was drawn slowly down the street. I could hear the cheers which greeted him as they grew fainter in the distance, drowned in the blare of bands. One by one the gorgeously decorated floats passed before us, each telling some mythological story. There were satyrs, fawns, mermaids, centaurs, the like of which I had never seen before. Here the whole of fairyland had become a reality before my eyes. I counted the glittering cars as they passed. There were twenty in all and almost as many bands of music. And always that strange, unreal quality, that gaudy, blatant thing which I could not define then and which I cannot define now, except that it gave to me the feeling of seeing a thousand circuses rolled into one.

VIII

THE IMAGE IN THE MIRROR

WHEN the wealthy ante-bellum planter looked into the mirror of Southern life, he saw an image of himself and his class which had increased in sharpness and color during the years from 1820 to 1860. Abolitionists in the North helped to substantiate this image by dividing Southerners into three classes: the slave-driving aristocrats, the poor whites, and the Negroes. But as the Southern quarrel with the North grew more and more intense in those forty years, white Southerners themselves defined and refined the image in thousands of articles, pamphlets, polemical works, orations, poems, and novels. The South, its propagandists maintained, had developed a distinctive way of life, a unique civilization in fact, which shone in contrast with the attitudes and pursuits of low-born, money-grubbing Yankees and the immigrants who were crowding into the slums of Northern seaports.

The dominant myth for these apologists was Southern aristocracy. The planter aristocrat exercised his power from the county or parish level, where he was magistrate and an officer in the militia, to the Governor's mansion and beyond—to Washington City. Slavery, therefore, was a beneficent institution since it enabled the planter to devote himself to the public weal and his family to enjoy the good life.

As the myth proliferated, the idea evolved that the blood of the planter families was a noble or at least a gentle blue. It was believed that New Englanders were descended from Roundhead, and thus plebeian, immigrants, while the Southerners traced their ancestry to the Cavaliers. These Cavalier forebears were soon raised in social rank from mere followers of the Stuart kings to noblemen or great gentlemen who had fought for Charles I or the Old Pretender. The knighting or ennobling of one's ancestors went even farther. As W. J. Cash says in *The Mind of the South*: "If [the Southern aristocrats] were of

English descent, then their forebears had infallibly ridden, not only with Rupert at Naseby, but also with William at Senlac; if Scotch or Scotch-Irish, they were invariably clansmen of the chieftain's family, and usually connections, often direct descendants, of the royal blood of the Bruce or Kenneth McAlpin; if plain Irish, they stemmed from Brian Boru."

Recent studies estimate that at least one half of all the white immigrants to the colonies south of New England were indentured servants. This fact their descendants chose not to remember. There were enough Southern families with squirearchical ancestors—Lees, Washingtons, and Randolphs—to furnish examples of what one wished the universal truth to be. That the progenitor of the Virginia Byrds was a London goldsmith and that the Carters could not find any ancestors at all were facts conveniently forgotten. Social mobility was as great in the South as elsewhere in America. One could become an aristocrat in two generations, and the securing of appropriate ancestors was, as Cash suggests, no difficult matter.

The Southern aristocrat trained his sons in a code of behavior which was self-consciously chivalric. The items in this code were *noblesse oblige,* a sense of personal and family honor, and, above all, a due and proper regard for the beauty and virtue of white women. Since the society was hierarchical, the young squire must learn to behave intuitively and with exactly the right tone—of deference or adoration or authority or benevolence or command—toward his elders, his mother and sisters and their friends, the overseer, the house Negroes, and the field-hands. His word of honor must be sacred even if his promise had been given orally in drink. If his word was doubted or if any insult was offered to his person, he must challenge the offender to a duel, provided they were social equals. Insults by those of lesser station could be cleared by administering a good caning or horsewhipping.

Since the women of his family were the keepers of the standards of Christian honor and of the purity of the white race, they must be protected against even the slightest freedom in glance or word. As Cash says:

> The upshot, in this land of spreading notions of chivalry, was downright gyneolatry. She was the South's Palladium, this Southern woman—the shield-bearing Athena gleaming whitely in the clouds, the standard for its rallying, the mystic symbol of its nationality in face of the foe. She was the lily-pure maid of Astolat and the hunting goddess of the Bœotian hill. And—she was the pitiful Mother of God. Merely to mention her was to send strong men into tears—or shouts. There was hardly a sermon that did not begin and end with tributes in her honor, hardly a brave speech

243

that did not open and close with the clashing of shields and the flourishing of swords for her glory. At the last, I verily believe, the ranks of the Confederacy went rolling into battle in the misty conviction that it was wholly for her that they fought.

"Woman!!! The center and circumference, diameter, and periphery, sine, tangent and secant of all our affections!" Such was the toast which brought twenty great cheers from the audience at the celebration of Georgia's one-hundredth anniversary in the 1830's.

The young aristocrat was also brought up to have a strong sense of obligation to his kin. The number of Southern words and expressions relating to the ties of family—kinfolks, blood kin, kissing kin, kissing cousins, connections, "Virginia cousins"—testifies to the strength of the code in this respect. In the early days planter families intermarried, as feudal houses always do, in order to bring two great fortunes together. Political power was also increased by these interfamily connections. The planter squire was obligated to help his less fortunate kin and was sometimes impoverished or made a bankrupt by assuming the debts of a brother or nephew. Female kin must be protected and assisted even if they arrived for a visit and stayed on in the family for years. In no respect was the code of kin more strongly exemplified than in the sense of obligation which a white master sometimes showed toward his children by a Negro mistress. If he did not provide for them during his lifetime, he was likely to leave them property or to manumit them in his will. On the reverse side, many a slave or free man of color took secret pride in being kin to the family in the great house.

It is useless to argue whether Southerners are more hospitable than the people of other parts of the country, but it is true that in plantation days they could afford to entertain guests lavishly. The stores of food raised on the place were not for export but were intended for the groaning table of the mansion. Visiting kin, neighbors from the other side of the county, the preacher, the stranger within the gates, were welcome. Some planters, it is recorded, had the roads patrolled by slaves on the lookout for acceptable travelers who might wish to dine and spend the night. There were house slaves in abundance to do the fetching and carrying, the laundering and barbering, and even to provide entertainment. The open-handed hospitality of some planters drove them into debt. F. B. Simkins notes, in *A History of the South*, that "George Washington, although an efficient and successful businessman and farmer, discovered that most of the profits of his Mount Vernon estate not consumed by his slaves were eaten up by the stream of relatives, friends, and distinguished travelers who passed his way."

1. ARISTOCRACY

The Southern Gentleman as He Saw Himself

When Daniel R. Hundley published his Social Relations in Our Southern States *in 1860 he especially invited the attention of Northern readers, who, he felt, were being completely misled by abolitionist propaganda. Though he pictures the Southern Gentleman, in the selections
given here, as a paragon of manhood and gentilesse, his work is not all
praise and no blame. He is careful to distinguish, in other chapters, the
deviations from the norm, particularly the Southern Yankee who is
tireless in his pursuit of riches as a trader (usually in Negroes) and a
speculator and the Cotton Snob who, nine cases out of ten, is the son
of a Southern Yankee. Hundley demarcates the other types and classes
as the Southern Yeoman, the Southern Bully (usually a loafing ex-
overseer), the Poor White Trash, and the Negro Slaves. In spite of the
extravagance of some of his statements—Hundley is often carried away
by his attempts to be witty and entertaining—*Social Relations in Our
Southern States *is a valuable pioneering sociological study.*

*Born in Alabama in 1832, Hundley received his education at the
University of Virginia and at Harvard, where he studied law. He
married a Virginian whose father had real-estate interests in Chicago.
Hundley settled in Chicago in 1856. A strong Union man and opposed
to Secession, he supported Douglas in the Presidential campaign of
1860. When war was imminent he returned to the South and helped
to organize the 31st Alabama Infantry, which elected him Colonel. He
fought in the east Tennessee campaign of 1862, was wounded at Vicksburg, and was captured during Sherman's advance on Atlanta. Taken
to the prison on Johnson's Island, in Lake Erie, two miles from San-
dusky, Ohio, he escaped just before the war ended, but was almost
immediately recaptured. His prison diary was published in 1874 as*
Prison Echoes of the Great Rebellion. *Meanwhile Hundley had returned to Alabama to practice law.*

The passages given here from Social Relations in Our Southern
States *(New York: Henry B. Price; 1860) are excerpted from pages
27–72.*

To begin with his pedigree, then, we may say, the Southern Gentleman comes of a good stock. Indeed, to state the matter fairly, he comes usually of aristocratic parentage; for family pride prevails to a greater extent in the South than in the North. In Virginia, the ancestors of the Southern Gentleman were chiefly English cavaliers, after whom succeeded the French Huguenots and Scotch Jacobites. In Maryland, his ancestors were in the main Irish Catholics—the retainers and associates of Lord Baltimore—who sought in the wilds of the New World religious tolerance and political freedom. In South-Carolina, they were Huguenots—at least the better class of them—those dauntless chevaliers, who, fleeing from the massacre of St. Bartholomew and the bloody persecutions of priests and tyrants, drained France of her most generous blood to found in the Western Hemisphere a race of heroes and patriots. In Florida, Louisiana, Texas, and other portions of the far South, the progenitors of the Southern Gentleman were chiefly Spanish Dons and French Catholics.

Thus it will be seen that throughout the entire extent of the South, (for the new Southern States have been settled almost wholly by emigrants from those named above,) wherever you meet with the Southern Gentleman, you find him *hijo dalgo,* as the Spaniards phrase it: however, there are many notable exceptions in every Southern State. For, owing to the repeal of the Law of Primogeniture, and the gradual decay of some of the old families, as well as the levelling effects of many of Mr. Jefferson's innovations, particularly the subsequent intermarriages between the sons and daughters of the gentry and persons of the middle class . . . there are scattered throughout all the Southern States many gentlemen of the genuine Southern character, whose ancestry was only in part of the cavalier stock. Indeed, Mr. Jefferson himself was a fit representative of these; for, while his mother was a Randolph, his father was only a worthy descendant of the sturdy yeomanry of England.

Besides being of faultless pedigree, the Southern Gentleman is usually possessed of an equally faultless physical development. His average height is about six feet, yet he is rarely gawky in his movements, or in the least clumsily put together; and his entire *physique* conveys to the mind an impression of firmness united to flexibility. . . .

We think we may attribute the good size and graceful carriage of the Southern Gentleman, to his out-of-doors and a-horseback mode of living. For we might as well here inform our readers, the genuine Southern Gentleman almost invariably lives in the country. But let them not conclude from this circumstance that he is nothing more than the simple-hearted, swearing, hearty, and hospitable old English or Virginia Country Gentleman, of whom we have all heard so repeatedly. The time has been when such a conviction could have been truthfully entertained; but that was long ago. In those good old times the Southern Gentleman had little else to do than fox-hunt, drink, attend the races, fight chicken-cocks, and grievously lament that he was owner of a large horde of savages whom he knew not how to dispose of.

But times change, *et nos mutamur in illis.* The new order of things which succeeded the innovations of Mr. Jefferson made it necessary for the Gentlemen of the South, for all the old families who had before lived upon their hereditary wealth and influence, to struggle to maintain their position, else to be pushed aside by the thrifty middle classes, who thought it no disgrace to work by the side of their slaves, and who were, in consequence, yearly becoming more wealthy and influential. Besides, after the repeal of the Law of Primogeniture, the large landed estates, the former pride and boast of the first families, very soon were divided up into smaller freeholds, and the owners of these, of necessity, were frequently forced to lay aside the old manners and customs, the air and arrogance of the grand seignor, and to content themselves with the plain, unostentatious mode of life which at present characterizes most gentlemen in the South. The result of all which has been, that the Southern Gentleman of to-day is less an idler and dreamer than he was in the old days, is more practical, and, although not so great a lover of the almighty dollar as his Northern kinsman, still is far from being as great a spendthrift as his fathers were before him.

But, notwithstanding the old style of Southern Gentlemen has in a measure passed away, the young South is nurtured in pretty much the same school as formerly—at least so far as physical education is concerned—and participates more or less in all those rollicking out-door sports and amusements still common in England to this day. Scarcely has he gotten fairly rid of his bibs and tuckers, therefore, before we find him mounted a-horseback; and this not a hobby-horse either, (which the poor little wall-flower of cities is so proud to straddle,) but a genuine live pony—sometimes a Canadian, sometimes a Mustang, but always a pony. By the time he is five years of age he rides well; and in a little while thereafter has a fowling-piece put into his hands, and a little black boy of double his age put *en croupe* behind him, (or in case mamma is particularly cautious, his father's faithful serving-man accompanies him, mounted on another horse,) and so accoutred, he sallies forth into the fields and pastures in search of adventures. At first he bangs away at every thing indiscriminately, and the red-headed woodpeckers more often grace his game-bag than quail or snipe; but by degrees he acquires the art and imbibes the spirit of the genuine sportsman, and ever after keeps his father's hospitable board amply supplied with the choicest viands the woods or fields or floods afford.

By floods, the reader will please understand rivers, creeks, and ponds; for our young Southerner is as much of a fisherman as a Nimrod. When he tires of his gun, he takes his fishing-rods and other tackle, and goes angling; and when he tires of angling, provided the weather is favorable, he denudes himself and plunges into the water for a swim, of which he tires not at all. Indeed, he will remain in the watery element until the sun blisters his back, and if thus forced to seek *terra firma*, he does it "upon compulsion," and under protest. As a general thing, the blue-noses of Nova Scotia, or the natives of South-America, are not greater lovers of the healthy exercise of swimming than the boys of the South, of all classes.

In his every foray, whether by flood or field, our young gentleman has for his constant attendant, Cuffee, junior, who sticks to him like his shadow. At the expiration of five years or so of this manner of living, (provided there is no family tutor, and in that case his mother has already learned him to read,) the master is sent to the nearest village, or district, or select school, returning home every night. Sometimes this school is from five to ten miles distant, and so he has to ride from ten to twenty miles every day, Saturdays and Sundays alone excepted. Again Cuffee is sent with his young master, and morning and evening the two are to be seen cantering to or from the school-house, the negro taking charge of their joint lunch for dinner, (to be eaten during "playtime,") and the master carrying on the pommel of his saddle or his arm the bag which contains his books and papers, and maybe a stray apple or peach to exchange with the village urchins for fishing-rods, or to present to some school-boy friend, who has a rosy-cheeked little sister, with a roguish black eye and a silvery laugh.

And although every day in the week, from Monday to Friday inclusive, is thus occupied, both master and slave sit up nearly all of Friday night, cleaning guns, arranging fishing-lines, and discussing enthusiastically the sports to be followed on the morrow. These change very materially, as our young Southerner begins to get higher and higher in his teens. He very soon surfeits of the tame pastime of shooting squirrels and ducks, woodcock and plover, or chasing of hares; when for a short while, say a couple of years, his chief delight is to hunt wild turkeys—a rare sport where turkeys are abundant and when one has a well-trained dog. But even this soon ceases to be attractive, and is succeeded by fox-hunting. Preparatory to entering upon the latter rare old English sport, our young gentleman gets some one of the many dusky uncles on his father's plantation, to procure him a deep intoned horn; which procured, he proceeds immediately to exchange his pony for the fleetest and most active of his father's stud. On a great many Southern plantations there are kept hunting horses, regularly trained for the sport as in England; and it is astonishing in what a little time they become as fond of the same as their riders. Even mules, after having been used a few times, will prick up their heavy ears at the sound of a merry horn, and will follow the hounds with all the eagerness of the best-blooded of their sires. . . .

When the Southern Gentleman has fully completed his academic labors—has honorably gone through the University Curriculum—if his means be ample, he seldom studies a profession, but gives his education a finishing polish by making the tour of Europe; or else marries and settles down to superintend his estates, and devotes his talents to the raising of wheat, tobacco, rice, sugar, or cotton; or turns his attention to politics, and runs for the State Legislature. Should, however, the patrimonial estate be small, or the heirs numerous, (and the generous clime of the South renders the latter supposition highly probable,) he then devotes himself to some one of the learned professions, or becomes an editor, or enters either the Army or the Navy. But of all things, he is most enamoured of politics and the Army; and it is owing to this cause, that the South has furnished us with all our great generals, from Washington to Scott, as well as most of our leading statesmen, from Jefferson to Calhoun. . . .

No matter what may be the Southern Gentleman's avocation, his dearest affections usually centre in the country. He longs to live as his fathers lived before him, in both the Old World and the New; and he ever turns with unfeigned delight from the bustle of cities, the hollow ceremonies of courts, the turmoil of politics, the glories and dangers of the battle-field, or the wearisome treadmill of professional routine, to the quiet and peaceful scenes of country life. The glare of gas and the glitter of tinsel, the pride, the pomp, the vanity, and all the grace and wit of *la bonne compagnie*, he surrenders without a sigh of regret, and joyfully retires to the seclusion of his own fireside, grateful for the auspicious and happy exchange. The old hall, the familiar voices of old friends, the trusty and well-remembered faces of the old domestics—these all are dearer to the heart of the Southern Gentleman than the short-lived plaudits of admiring throngs, or the hollow and unsatisfactory pleasures of sense. Indeed, with all classes in the South the home feeling is much stronger than it is in the North; for the bane of hotel life and the curse of boarding-houses have not as yet extended their pernicious influences to our Southern States, or at best in a very small degree. Nearly every citizen is a landholder, and therefore feels an interest in the permanency of his country's institutions. This is one reason why the South has ever been the ready advocate of war, whenever the rights of the nation have been trampled on, or the national flag insulted. But if the patriotic feeling is strong in the breast of even the poorest citizen, whose home is a log-cabin and whose sole patrimony consists of less than a dozen acres of land, how must it be intensified in the bosoms of those whose plantations spread out into all the magnificence of old-country manors! . . .

The natural dignity of manner peculiar to the Southern Gentleman, is doubtless owing to his habitual use of authority from his earliest years; for while coarser natures are ever rendered more savage and brutal by being allowed the control of others, refined natures on the contrary are invariably perfected by the same means, their sense of the responsibility and its incident obligations teaching them first to control themselves before attempting to exact obedience from the inferior natures placed under their charge. This is a fact which it were worth while to ponder thoughtfully, for herein lies the secret of the good breeding of the Gentlemen of the South, and the chief reason why they seldom evince that flurry of manner so peculiar to many of our countrymen; and why, also, they manifest on all occasions the utmost self-possession—that much coveted *savoir faire*, which causes a man to appear perfectly at home, whether it be in a hut or a palace. Hence in manners the Southern Gentleman is remarkably easy and natural, never haughty in appearance, or loud of speech—even when angry rarely raising his voice above the ordinary tone of gentlemanly conversation. Those boisterous good fellows, whom one meets constantly in the South, and sometimes even so far from home as New-York or Philadelphia, and whose wont is to monopolize all the talking, interlarding their speech with Southern provincialisms and Africanisms, are not in the remotest degree allied or akin to the real Southern Gentleman. He is ever well educated, and draws his language from the "well of pure English undefiled." Even though he may be poor, (which is neither an impossible nor improbable supposition,) he always manages to give his children the best opportunities for education the country affords: for it is one of his prejudices to detest boorishness and vulgarity—two inseparable companions of ignorance—and he would as heartily detest them in the persons of his own offspring, or other members of his family, as in the person of the most besotted drunkard that ever reeled into a gutter.

John Randolph Instructs His Young Cousin
in the Behavior Required of a
Virginia Aristocrat

Professor Dumas Malone has called John Randolph of Roanoke (1773–1833) "one of the most pathetic as well as one of the most brilliant figures that ever strutted and fretted his hour upon the American public stage." Born to wealth and position, as a young man he was contemptuous of the teachers who tried to educate him in the tradition of the Virginia gentleman, but the wide reading he did in those years later contributed to the amazing brilliance of his public speeches. He also sharpened the wit that would be his chief political and social weapon. By the time he was elected to Congress in 1800, Randolph's opponents had learned to fear his pointed abuse. A disciple of Jefferson until he quarreled with him and his administration, Randolph often declined to march under the party banner. He differed subsequently with Madison and Monroe so frequently that he called himself a "quiddist" or third-party man. The one principle he adhered to throughout was states' rights, though, as Henry Adams says, at the end this became "his hobby, his mania; he played tricks with it until his best friends were disgusted." He last held public office in the Senate, to which he was elected in 1825 to fill a vacancy.

A vast legend has grown up about this irascible and eccentric man. It is now known that much of his strange behavior can be ascribed to constant ill-health, insomnia, occasional lapses into madness, and the bitterness caused by sexual sterility. Yet he had his tender side, nowhere better shown than in his affection for his young cousin Theodore Bland Dudley, whom he called son. Randolph provided Dudley's early education in Virginia and his medical training in Philadelphia. From 1800 to 1810 Dudley lived at Randolph's plantation Bizarre and afterwards at Roanoke. There was a rift between them in 1818. Having suffered for two years from Randolph's "caprice and petulance," Dudley broke with his kinsman and mentor in 1820 and went to Richmond to practice medicine.

The year after Randolph's death Dr. Dudley published a selection of the letters he had received from his foster father: Letters of John Randolph to a Young Relative; Embracing a Series of Years, from Early Youth to Mature Manhood (*Philadelphia: Carey, Lea & Blanchard;*

251

1834). The letters cover the years between 1806 and 1822, when the final break between the two occurred. It is a remarkable correspondence, in which the older man poured out details of his public and private life which he hid from others. As the excerpts printed here show, it is also a "complete gentleman" intended for the instruction of the younger man in aristocratic behavior, and often, in the indirection of its maxims, a warning to young Dudley to avoid the mistakes that, through prejudice and irritability, John Randolph had committed.

❁

WHEN I asked whether you had *received* the bank notes I sent you, I did not mean to *inquire how you had laid them out.* Don't you see the difference? From your not mentioning that they had come to hand, (a careless omission; you should break yourself of this habit,) and your cousin informing me that she had not received two packets sent by the same mail, I concluded that the notes were probably lost or embezzled. Hence my inquiry after them. No, my son; whatever cash I send you (unless for some special purpose) is yours: you will spend it as you please, and I have nothing to say to it. That you will not employ it in a manner that you ought to be ashamed of, I have the fullest confidence. To pry into such affairs would not only betray a want of that confidence, and even a suspicion discreditable to us both, but infringe upon your rights and independence. For, although you are not of an age to be your own master, and independent in all your actions, yet you are possessed of rights which it would be tyranny and injustice to withhold, or invade. Indeed, this independence, which is so much vaunted, and which young people think consists in doing what they please, when they grow up to man's estate, (with as much justice as the poor negro thinks liberty consists in being supported in idleness, by other people's labour,)—this independence is but a name. Place us where you will,—along with our rights there must coexist correlative duties,—and the more exalted the station, the more arduous are these last. Indeed, as the duty is precisely correspondent to the power, it follows that the richer, the wiser, the more powerful a man is, the greater is the obligation upon him to employ his gifts in lessening the sum of human misery; and this employment constitutes happiness, which the weak and wicked vainly imagine to consist in wealth, finery, or sensual gratification. Who so miserable as the bad Emperor of Rome? Who more happy than Trajan and Antoninus? Look at the fretful, peevish, rich man, whose senses are as much jaded by attempting to embrace too much gratification, as the limbs of the poor post horse are by incessant labour. (Feb. 15, 1806).

Let me recommend to you another perusal of Lord Chatham's letters to his nephew. Attend to his precepts respecting *deportment* to inferiors, equals, and superiors. Let these words, also, be engraven on your mind—"Whatever you take from pleasure, amusement, or indolence, for these first few years of your life, will repay you a hundred fold in the pleasures, honours, and advantages, of all your remaining days." The candour with which you confess your indiscretion towards Dr. H., and your determination to avoid giving him future cause of displeasure, prevent my saying any thing on that subject, except to caution you against any indulgence of *sudden* suggestions of your feelings. Some impulse of this kind, I must persuade myself, and not boyish conceit, would have impelled you to lay down a regular exercise of your school. Remember that *labour is necessary to excellence.* This is an eternal truth, although vanity cannot be brought to believe, or indolence to heed it. I am deeply interested in seeing you turn out a respectable man, in every point of view; and, as far as I could, have endeavoured to furnish you with the means of acquiring knowledge and correct principles, and manners, at the same time. Self-conceit and indifference are unfriendly, in an equal degree, to the attainment of knowledge, or the forming of an amiable character. The first is more offensive, but does not more completely mar all excellence than the last; and it is truly deplorable that both flourish in Virginia, as if it were their native soil. A petulant arrogance, or supine, listless indifference, marks the character of too many of our young men. They early assume airs of manhood; and these premature men remain children for the rest of their lives. Upon the credit of a smattering of Latin, drinking grog, and chewing tobacco, these striplings set up for legislators and statesmen; and seem to deem it derogatory from their manhood to treat age and experience with any degree of deference. They are loud, boisterous, overbearing, and dictatorial: profane in speech, low and obscene in their pleasures. In the tavern, the stable, or the gaming-house, they are at home; but, placed in the society of *real* gentlemen, and men of letters, they are awkward and uneasy: in all situations, they are contemptible.

The vanity of excelling in pursuits, where excellence does not imply merit, has been the ruin of many a young man. I should, therefore, be under apprehensions for a young fellow, who danced uncommonly well, and expect more hereafter from his heels than from his head. Alexander, I think, was reproached with singing well, and very justly. He must have misapplied the time which he devoted to the acquisition of so great a proficiency in that art. I once knew a young fellow who was remarkably handsome; he was highly skilled in dancing and fencing—an exceedingly good skater, and one of the most dexterous billiard players and marksmen that I ever saw:—he sang a good song, and was

253

the envy of every foolish fellow, and the darling of every silly girl, who knew him. He was, nevertheless, one of the most ignorant and conceited puppies whom I ever beheld. Yet, it is highly probable, that if he had not been enamoured of the rare qualities which I have enumerated, he might have made a valuable and estimable man. But he was too entirely gratified with his superficial and worthless accomplishments to bestow a proper cultivation on his mind. (Jan. 8, 1807).

Your word ought to be dearer to you than your head: beware, then, how you put it into the lion's mouth. If it were proposed to you to save your lives by a *lie,* and either of you had the weakness to consent, I should pity him, but, at the same time, *despise him* from my very soul. (Oct. 6, 1807).

Do not, my dear boy, attempt too much at once: *festina lente.* If you have not time for fencing, discharge your master—after the quarter shall expire. Your object is not to become a gladiator, but to learn the use of arms—and that a few lessons will teach you; practice must do the rest. I would, also, advise laying aside the clarionet *pro tem.* You have, I believe, a turn for music, and it is an art that I would wish you to *excel* in, *if possible;* but any thing short of *excellence* (especially on the clarionet or violin) is *execrable.* (Dec. 18, 1810).

I am greatly pleased to learn that your strength and spirits are recruiting, and I highly approve of your pedestrian essays: but choose not *Virginians* for your companions. I have no doubt that many of the medical students of the south, leave Philadelphia as ignorant of every thing worthy to be known in that city, as when they entered it. This arises from a clannish spirit, which makes them associate exclusively with one another, and foster their ridiculous prejudices against the people of the middle and northern states, of whom, in fact, they know nothing. (Aug. 12, 1811).

I am shocked, and should be surprised, if any thing could surprise me that man can do, at the gross and cruel injustice done to the memory and family of our excellent friend, by his late employers: but it is not among money lenders, and, especially, monied corporations, that I should look for delicacy, feeling, or liberality; much less for justice. There is in all the combinations of nature and art, nothing so hard and callous as a trading company, of whatever description. They look to the dividend; to the profit and loss account of the leger; and, whether their gain flow from the blood of a Hindoo, or African; from the ruined reputation of an honest and amiable man, or the tears of his widowed companion and orphan offspring, it is all one to these *worthy personages.* (Oct. 6, 1811).

254

A Southern Gentleman Recalls His Training
in the Aristocratic Code

William C. Preston (1794–1860), from whose Reminiscences *these passages are taken, thoroughly exemplified the aristocratic attitudes and manners on which John Randolph gravely discoursed in his* Letters . . . to a Young Relative. *After graduating from South Carolina College, young Preston made the grand tour in Europe and studied for a time at the University of Edinburgh. In 1820 he was admitted to the bar in Virginia, but two years later he married and settled in Columbia, South Carolina. His political career in the state legislature and the United States Senate (1836–42) was distinguished. In 1845 he became president of his alma mater.*

As Preston began writing his memoirs shortly before he died, he was able to carry the account of his life only through the first months of his grand tour. They reveal a young Southern aristocrat of "sprightly parts" (though fastidious in his friendships) and a good talker and good listener who was equally at ease in the company of French noblemen and American Presidents.

Dr. Minnie Clare Yarborough edited The Reminiscences of William C. Preston *for the University of North Carolina Press in 1933. The excerpts given here are reprinted by permission of the publishers.*

I WAS born in Philadelphia on the 27th of Decem. 1794, the first child of my parents. My father was at that time a member of Congress from Virginia and thus it happened that I was born in Philadelphia instead of Washington County, Virginia. It was a tradition in my family that I was the first born of a government official at the seat of government and Washington being an acquaintance of my father and mother came to see the new born citizen. I can hardly persuade myself that I do not remember the scene of the illustrious man bending over my cradle and blessing the child, so vividly was it painted by my mother on my infant mind in childhood. My father was a member of Congress and his father a conspicuous Whig of the Revolution, being Col. of the County of Augusta and thus in command of the militia from the Blue

Ridge to the Mississippi. He commanded a regiment at Guilford. My mother was the only surviving child of Gen. Wm. Campbell of King's Mountain. She was a large heiress and my father too had hereditary wealth. My maternal grandmother was a sister of Patrick Henry. Thus I was well born and my mother in my childhood did not fail to let me understand it. She was a lady of beautiful person, a strong mind and a lofty character. Accustomed in her youth to the circle to which Washington gave the tone, her manners retained always a certain stateliness, which with her majestic person and high manners, made her a very conspicuous figure. Her wealth and her *manière à due* in some sort segregated her family from the poorer and plainer community in which she lived, and thus in my earlier childhood my associates were almost entirely domestic. . . .

[*Preston goes on to describe his early education. He recited his first lessons to an Irishman, a weaver who had come into his grandfather's family as far back as 1780 and who taught several generations to read in the Testament and cipher as far as the rule of three. Young Preston was next put under Mr. Hercules Whaley, a private tutor in the family. He was a good Latinist, knew some Greek, could play the violin well, and "read and recited poetry with exquisite power."*]

Whaley and I read together most of the Latin classics and many of the English, for my father had a very good library. But my parents thought (mistakenly as I have since believed) that their boy ought to be sent to a public school, and so at 14 I was sent to what was called the Washington College at Lexington,[1] a college superintended by lazy and ignorant Presbyterian preachers, and filled with dirty boys of low manners and morals. In six months at this place I unlearned as much as it was possible for a boy of sprightly parts to unlearn in six months, when being affected with some slight hemorrhage of the lungs my anxious parents thought it necessary for me to be sent into a Southern latitude and Florida was fixed on.

Mounted on horseback with a negro servant to wait on and to take charge of me, I proceeded on my lonely journey. Columbia lay in my way. There I put up at a tavern situated on the spot now occupied by the high sounding Congaree house—then bearing the most characteristic appellation of Goat-hall. There I met with several young men, Charleston boys who had come up to join the South Carolina College. These youngsters whose address and manners were very attractive very easily persuaded me that I was far enough South for my health and that the new and flourishing college which they were about to enter was a fit place to obtain an education. So after a night of anxious thought I acquiesced. I knew that my father's plan of education for

[1] Now Washington and Lee University.

me was that I should go thro' some Southern College, then to Yale or Princeton and complete my course in Europe. His notion, impressed upon me from my earliest days, was that I was to be a well educated man and then to study law as my life time profession. This was always his purpose and my own never deviated from it. I entered the Sophomore class, December 1809, being a few days under 15 years old, but looking several years older, so that no questions were asked as to my age.

[*Preston's education in manners continued in Richmond and in Washington, where, since he was a kinsman of Mrs. Madison, he was domesticated at the President's house and "there met with whatever was curious or conspicuous in the City." President Madison's cold and stiff manners young Preston took exception to, as also to the "foulness of conversation" in which the gentlemen of that generation indulged. But for the ladies of Madison's family he had the highest admiration. He was an "avowed pet" of Mrs. Madison. "The season was gay and I fully participated in it."*]

At the end of the winter I had got enough of this sort of life, and I was taken home to rusticate for a short time, thence the next winter, my father thinking that I should be quieted down in a law office for a while sent me to Richmond to be entered in Mr. Wirt's [2] office, that I might take one other step in the education he proposed for me. The winter was passed in a worse than stationary, it was a retrograde condition. The style of manners amongst the young Virginia gentlemen was that of riot and dissipation and I have always looked back to this period with shame and regret. It was time worse than lost. Our set in Richmond was occasionally put to shame by the transient presence of Wm. C. Rives, or Frank Gillmer, but very few of our habitués escaped a melancholy destiny in after life and I am persuaded that I escaped the ordinary fate by a constitutional incapacity for drinking, which is hereditary in my family. No Preston has ever been addicted to that fatal Virginia vice of drunkenness and thus I escaped. We lived fast, were much addicted to cards, and had an unceasing round of gaiety, in short were persons of "wit and pleasure about town," holding in utter scorn all sedate pursuits or grave occupations. We were roisterers and it is mournful to look back on what became of the members of that winter's society.

[*Preston's father wished that the young man's education should be completed in Europe. Before beginning the grand tour, however, he was required to see something of his own country. This journey took him through Tennessee, Kentucky, Indiana, Illinois, and Missouri.*]

[2] William Wirt (1772–1834), jurist and writer. He was Attorney General of the United States from 1817 to 1829.

In Kentucky I made acquaintance with all the principal families, most of whom were variously connected with my own. Portions of Kentucky as it came from the hands of nature are perfectly beautiful, the land apparently a rich alluvian, so that riding thro its magnificent forests of noble trees one has the feeling of being on a rich bottom near a large stream. The principal inhabitants being well born Virginians, retained much of their native and early characteristics, modified, however, by some touch of influence from their new and raw condition. I will not say that the modification was a defect, for that might be a matter of taste and opinion, but it was different from a staid and settled society. The Browns and the Breckenridges and the Howards had lost a portion of Virginia caste and assumed something of Kentucky esteem, an absence of reticence and a presence of presumptuousness. Amongst persons of my own age, who were native to the state, there was a self-dependence not to say self-assertion, and ostentatious suppression of the smaller courtesies of life and minute observances of convention, which was not pleasant. When emigration to a new country takes place even in masses, civilization is not transported or preserved. New physical circumstances induce new developments, and a fermentation of society must take place. An old state of society cannot be propagated in a new country. A certain loss of civilization is inevitable. Stranger and hardier qualities may be superinduced, but they supplant the gentler and more refined. In Indiana and Illinois, society had not begun to be organized.

2. CHIVALRY

"The role which woman should act in the great drama of life"

In this brief passage Professor Dew of William and Mary (later president of the college) introduces most of the arguments used in the Old South to elevate lovely woman to her pedestal and to keep her there. Thomas R. Dew (1802–46) was one of the leading defenders of slavery in the 1830's and 1840's. His Review of the Debate [*on the Abolition of Slavery*] *in the Virginia Legislature of 1831 and 1832, from which this selection is taken, was widely influential. It was reissued in 1849 as*

THOMAS R. DEW: *The Role Which Woman Should Act*

An Essay on Slavery *and again in that huge compendium of defenses of the "peculiar institution,"* The Pro-Slavery Argument *(1852). The excerpt printed here is taken from pages 31–3 of* An Essay on Slavery *(Richmond: J. W. Randolph; 1849).*

❁

IN the very first remove from the most savage state, we behold the marked effects of slavery on the condition of woman—we find her at once elevated, clothed with all her charms, mingling with and directing the society to which she belongs, no longer the slave, but the equal and the idol of man. The Greeks and Trojans, at the siege of Troy, were in this state, and some of the most interesting and beautiful passages in the Iliad relate to scenes of social intercourse and conjugal affection, where woman, unawed and in all the pride of conscious equality, bears a most conspicuous part. Thus, Helen and Andromache, are frequently represented as appearing in company with the Trojan chiefs, and mingling freely in conversation with them. Attended only by one or two maid servants, they walk through the streets of Troy, as business or fancy directs: even the prudent Penelope, persecuted as she is by her suitors does not scruple occasionally to appear among them; and scarcely more reserve seems to be imposed on virgins than married women. Mitford has well observed, that "Homer's elegant eulogiums and Hesiod's severe sarcasm, equally prove woman to have been in their days important members of society. The character of Penelope in the Odyssey is the completest panegyric on the sex that ever was composed; and no language ever gave a more elegant or more highly colored picture of conjugal affection, than is displayed in the conversation of Hector and Andromache, in the 6th book of the Iliad."

The Teutonic races who inhabited the mountains and fastnesses of Germany, were similarly situated to the Greeks; and even before they left their homes to move down upon the Roman Empire, they were no more distinguished by their deeds in arms, than for devotion and attention to the weaker sex: So much were they characterized by this elevation of the female sex, that Gilbert Stuart does not hesitate to trace the institution of chivalry, whose origin has never yet been satisfactorily illustrated, to the German manners. . . .

It is a most singular and curious fact, that woman whose sympathies are ever alive to the distress of others; whose heart is filled with benevolence and philanthropy, and whose fine feelings, unchecked by considerations of interest or calculations of remote consequences, have ever prompted to embrace with eagerness even the wildest and most destructive schemes of emancipation, has been in a most peculiar and

259

eminent degree indebted to slavery, for that very elevation in society which first raised her to an equality with man. We will not stop here to investigate the advantages resulting from the ameliorated condition of woman: her immense influence on the destiny of our race is acknowledged by all: upon her must ever devolve, in a peculiar degree, the duty of rearing into manhood a creature, in its infancy, the frailest and feeblest which Heaven has made—of forming the plastic mind—of training the ignorance and imbecility of infancy into virtue and efficiency. "There is perhaps no moral power the magnitude of which swells so far beyond the grasp of calculation, as the influence of the female character on the virtues and happiness of mankind: it is so searching, so versatile, so multifarious, and so universal: it turns on us like the eye of a beautiful portrait, wherever we take our position; it bears upon us in such an infinite variety of points, on our instincts, our passions, our vanity, our tastes, and our necessities; above all, on the first impressions of education and the associations of infancy." The *rule* [*role*] which woman should act in the great drama of life, is truly an important and an indispensable one; it must and will be acted, and that too, either for our weal or woe: all must wish then, that she should be guided by virtue, intelligence, and the purest affection; which can only be secured by elevating, honoring and loving *her*, in whose career we feel so deep an interest.

A Tournament in Honor of the Nuptials
of Miss ——, of Morven

The tournament, usually in the form of riding at the ring, became, about 1840, a fashionable entertainment in Virginia, Maryland, and the Carolinas, spreading later widely through the South. (The May fêtes celebrated in Southern schools and colleges today are a twentieth-century derivative.) The vogue was probably set by the famous tournament which, in 1839, Lord Eglinton staged at Eglinton Castle in Scotland, in the hope of reviving such "medieval" tests of skill, and which many Americans crossed the Atlantic to see. Tournaments became popular entertainments at the fashionable watering-places or were arranged by the owners of large estates, often in celebration of a wed-

ding, like that at Markham described below. One factor in the popularity of the tournament was the Southern interest in horses and horsemanship; another was the universal enthusiasm for the Waverley novels; even stronger was the opportunity the tournament offered for the romantic glorification of the female sex, whose favors the knights wore and in whose service they rode. Sometimes the ladies acted as judges; sometimes their hands bestowed the prizes; sometimes the victorious knight was privileged to crown his lady Queen of Love and Beauty; always there was occasion for eloquent speeches in praise of woman and her inspiration to deeds of honor and courage.

This account of a tournament in Virginia in 1857 appeared first in the Norfolk Herald *of September 5, 1857, with the heading: "Sports at Markham, Va." It was reprinted in James B. Avirett's* The Memoirs of General Turner Ashby and His Compeers *(Baltimore: Selby & Dulany; 1867), pp. 33–9.*

✸

It is a mistake to say that the age of chivalry has passed. It is true that in our lowland country, where we have, or think we have, a greater variety of amusements of a refined character, we never attempt even the semblance of a tournament, as it is practised in the mountains of our State. But a recent visit to the upper counties has convinced us that this once martial exercise, which had its origin in Roman or perhaps in Trojan times, and was so common in the feudal ages, still exists, and although *armes à outrance* are superseded by the rockets, yet the chivalric spirit of the descendants of the knights of the olden time is the same which stimulated the latter to deeds of greater danger.

It is fashionable to sneer at these imitations of the amusements of the middle ages; but when it is remembered that they are done in the daytime, and bring together from distant places the young and old of both sexes, and excite to courtly emulation, whilst they perfect our young men in the elegant accomplishment of horsemanship, they are far more worthy of commendation than the midnight revels of the ballroom, and other such like recreations (?) of our silken knights and faded damsels of the cities.

It was our good fortune to be present at a recent display of the kind, near Markham, in the County of Fauquier, which was held in honor of the nuptials of Miss ——, of Morven. All the beauty and bravery of that region seemed to have assembled on the occasion, if one might judge from the number of ladies who were ranged along the side of the mountain to witness the feats of the Knights, who were present, not to do battle as in the more barbarous times, but to prove their ability to bear the sword and lance in their behalf, if such necessity should ever arise.

Nothing can be more simple than the preparation as it appeared to us. In a dry meadow, or plain, at the foot of the mountain, two high posts were planted, about ten feet apart, from which was suspended a cord fastened to the top of each, and from the middle of this cord was hung a ring about six inches in diameter, slightly held by a hook. To dash at full speed from a point of some two hundred yards, and passing between the posts, to bear off the ring upon the point of a lance of six feet length, was one of the mysteries of the joust, and it would seem to be of easy accomplishment; but to do it all, and to do it gracefully, is a feat of horsemanship requiring fearlessness and hard practice.

In the present instance, we were struck with the whole of the arrangements. It was announced in the beginning that six young married ladies were to be the judges of the tournament and, beginning with the bride, they were successively called to their seats, which overlooked the field. A band of music, high up above the lady judges, sounded the approach of the Knights, who were then for the first time seen filing through the rocks and trees, and in good order soon displayed in line a few yards below where the ladies were seated. The Knights were nobly mounted, and dressed in the gay fashion and coloring which the fancy of each had selected. Richard Ashby, the Herald, one of the most manly-looking persons we ever beheld, then introduced the Knights, calling the roll as it were, thus: "The Knight of Avon"—"of Avenel"—"of the Lancet"—"of Aldenburg"—"of Frederick"—"Ali Pacha"—"Rob Roy"—"Roderick Dhu"—"McIvor"—"Knight of Markham"—and so on to the end of the list. A short address followed, stating the rules of the tilt, the duties of the contestants, and expressing confidence in their endeavors to win by their bravery the rewards which beauty was ready to bestow. The music sounded again, and the troop turned and passed along and away, until they were entirely concealed from view among the trees. And now the Herald, Mr. A. ——, of Markham, called to the Knight of Avon to come forth, and in an instant he was seen emerging from the forest and bounding upon his horse as fleetly as the spirited animal could bear him toward the ring, and, as gracefully as only he could do the deed, bore away the ring in triumph, amidst the shouts of the spectators and the strains of music. After, came one and another of the Knights, as well trained, and managing their horses as if they were centaurs, but with various success,—each successful one receiving the applause of the spectators in his turn.

There was one, however, who was a stranger, calling himself the Knight of Aldenburg, of moderate stature, simply attired, and indifferently mounted, who in spite of all his efforts, and he freely used his

262

spurs, could not force his steed to the lists, so that he was ruled out after three baffled attempts. The lady judges, however, overruled the rules, and admitted him to another trial, which he modestly accepted; and mounted upon another charger he came thundering along the plain, and bore away the prize from all competitors, having taken the ring seven times in succession.

The Knight of Avon, Rob Roy and Roderick Dhu were decided to be next in skill to him of Aldenburg, and entitled, after the victor had selected the Queen, to name the Maids of Honor—or, we believe, of love and beauty. This decree being announced, the Knights, with their Herald, rode up and again deployed before the judges, when the Knight of Aldenburg dismounted, and handing his bridle to his Esquire, knelt before Miss M. of Markham, and crowned her Queen. In quick succession the Knights of Avon, Rob Roy, and Roderick Dhu bowed lowly before Miss C. M. of Fauquier, Miss C. of Winchester, and Miss S. of Fredericksburg, as the selected Maids of Honor. Each lady replied with ease and fitly to the complimentary speeches of their respective knights. While this was being done, the echoes of the hills around were waked up by the trumpets of the musicians, and a most charming excitement prevailed among all—unless we except, perhaps, the Knights who had failed in the contest and the ladies to whom these Knights had vowed to do homage in case of success—for each Knight had knelt at his especial shrine that day, not excepting the turbaned representative of Ali Pacha.

The sun was setting behind the hill which made the western boundary of the lists, just as the act of coronation was finished—and so we might let the curtain drop upon them; but there was one incident that might have found fitting place even at the "passage of arms at Ashby." During the contest, a horseman rode up in the full costume of an Indian chief, painted and feathered, and calling himself Hiawatha. He rode an unbroken colt, without saddle or bridle; and without noticing the music or the crowd, he uttered the war-cry of his race, and passing like a flash along the line, he lifted the ring from its rest as if it were child's play, and continuing at full speed to the outer extremity of the plain, bounded over a high stone wall, and disappeared. This man of the forest, by the rules of the tournament, was not permitted to select and crown the Queen of Love and Beauty, nor was it his wish to do so, as it seemed; but in the judgment of the bride, tribunal, or ladies'-court, and of all who looked upon that scene, no Christian Knight was ever more fully entitled than he to the highest honors of Chivalry.

We have omitted much of this amusing spectacle, and incidents perhaps worthy of a place in the foreground of the picture; nor have we expatiated on the superb scenery of valley and mountain, embellished by the fine mansion of Mr. Marshall, (one of the sons of the late Chief

Justice,) which looked over upon the field of the tournament; nor of the surpassing beauty of the ladies, without whose smiles the gallant Knights would not have toiled for their spurs;—but we have said enough to show that "peace hath its triumphs as well as war," and to inspire our lowland youth with an honest desire to emulate their highland brethren in feats of manhood.

The Grandeur That Was Not

A distinguished scholar, Professor Odum, Kenan Professor of Sociology at the University of North Carolina, here passes judgment on the Southern myth of "lovely woman." This selection from Howard W. Odum's The Way of the South: Toward the Regional Balance of America *is copyright by The Macmillan Company and is used with The Macmillan Company's permission.*

IF the women of the South during the war and the tragic aftermath suffered beyond any man's estimate, there were also many who suffered much under the old system, where perchance they learned well a discipline which was to sustain them in the decades to come. There was the beautiful, heroic, and tragic case of several wives of one master, each taking up the load where the last one fell, each succeeding one bearing her quota of stalwart descendants of gentlemen. Thus rode forth a great master, married to a beautiful mistress, who begat near a score of children, some of whom died at birth or later. But even of those who remained there was still a large family. This mistress of the big house not only had her own family to look after, to supervise, to direct their nurture and education according to high standards, but also was called upon to supervise and direct the many industries of the great house and the large number of Negro families with children all about the place. In exchange for her efforts on behalf of these black folks she received of course much service, the nursing of her children, and many loyalties of the categorical sort. It may have been, too, however, that these servants were part and parcel of her family in other ways as mothers of the great master's black children who, added to the score of her own, created a remarkable family indeed.

Thus to the glory and splendor and beauty of the mistress of the big house, with her remarkable mastery, was added much that was improper in any institutional order which claimed recognition for its glory and perfection. This woman, alongside the written and spoken eulogies of her beauty and grace, had little freedom of any sort. Her work, like the work of the woman among the common people, was never done. She was chaperoned and bound in by conventions and great tasks. Education of the broader sort was not for her, and she, mistress that she was in many ways, was not supposed to interest herself in social, intellectual, and political movements. Many things she was not supposed to see or, if seeing, to record or, if recording, to let it see the light either in her own consciousness or in the records for posterity. Thus this remarkable character became a symbol for a certain type of hypocrisy, superficiality, and rationalization wherever reality was concerned, and this symbolism carried over into the reconstruction period and far into the twentieth century. For decades white children had been turned over to colored mammies, some through genuine continuation of the old custom, some through imitation, some through general unfitness, and some through the grand rationalization that children needed this discipline to make them gentlefolk.

So also had the women of the Confederacy preserved mass pictures of the Old South based upon romantic developments from individual incidences of beauty and glory, pictures that never were on land or sea or earth or sky. The Old South had nothing save perfection; its men were gentlemen; its women, ladies all. Any who criticized the old order or brought to light facts not conducive to its glorification either were not patriots or else were so uncultured as not to understand that all this new generation was neither to the manner nor to the manor born. Perhaps few things had militated so effectively against the South's facing reality as this pattern in which the lovely women of the South had tried to project an atmosphere of gentility, beauty, and glory through an overweening pride, bitterness, and narrowness.

Andrew Jackson Kills Charles Dickinson
at Twenty-four Paces

Dueling in the Old South was a function of the elaboration and acceptance of the chivalric code. Hundreds died, or conquered, on the field of honor—under the dueling oaks of New Orleans, on the Vidalia Sandbar near Vicksburg, at Foy's Point, across the river from Memphis —to repulse boldly spoken or whispered charges that they had lied, or stolen, or uttered slander, or to vindicate the honor of their women.

Everyone talked of the "code of honor" as if there were some official manual that settled all the minute points which gentlemen debated endlessly. But the only "codes" that existed were publications issued by individuals—such as Governor John Lyde Wilson's The Code of Honor *(Charleston, 1858). Under the hypothetical code a gentleman was not obligated to answer a challenge from a social inferior. An apology might be accepted from a social equal, though, as Harnett T. Kane notes in* Gentlemen, Swords and Pistols, *there could be no apology for a humiliating blow or a reflection on a woman. Once the exchanges had been made, the affair was in the hands of the seconds, who were supposed to try to prevent the duel from occurring—proper satisfaction having been given in some other way. (The efforts of the seconds seem to have led to more deaths than reconciliations.) If satisfaction was not acknowledged after the first or second fire, a third exchange might take place. To go farther than this was considered a violation of the code.*

Not every gentleman in the Old South believed in dueling as the best way of vindicating one's injured honor. Most of the states had statutes forbidding duels, though these were seldom enforced. Some prominent Southerners stood firmly against the practice—for example, Robert Barnwell Rhett, the political "fire-eater" of South Carolina, whose scruples were religious. George D. Prentice, the Louisville editor, once rejected a challenge in Little Rock with these words: "I have not the least desire to kill you, nor to harm a hair of your head, and I am not conscious of having done anything to entitle you to kill me. I do not want your blood on my hands, and I do not want my own on anybody's."

After the Civil War dueling declined rapidly. It had arrived in the South in the late colonial period as the chivalric code was taking shape, and was stimulated by the example of the French officers who served in the American Revolution. As the planter aristocrat, in Reconstruction days, turned to the cultivation of his fields with his own two hands and such Negroes as he could afford to employ, he became less sensitive to slights to his honor. By 1890 it was sufficient if he were prepared to "shoot on sight" anyone who aspersed him.

While dueling was in force editors and politicians found it especially difficult to avoid sending or accepting a challenge. In fighting Charles Dickinson in 1806 Andrew Jackson, by this time a politician of national reputation, was being true to the mores of his region, class, and calling. Dickinson was a young man of fashion who had been tutored in the law by John Marshall. In his cups he had spoken freely of Jackson's wife, whose divorce from her first husband was not obtained until two years after she and Jackson were married. Dickinson apologized for this offense. But he failed to keep his mouth shut and talebearers were soon telling Jackson that the young man had called him a coward and a liar and had dared him to challenge. Jackson's friends could not restrain him, and so the inevitable duel took place.

This account of the Jackson-Dickinson meeting is reprinted from The Life of Andrew Jackson, *by Marquis James (copyright 1933), pp. 115–18. It is used here by special permission of The Bobbs-Merrill Company, Inc.*

❁

ON Thursday, May 29, 1806, Andrew Jackson rose at five o'clock, and after breakfast told Rachel [his wife] that he would be gone for a couple of days and meanwhile he might have some trouble with Mr. Dickinson. Rachel probably knew what the trouble would be and she did not ask. Rachel had had her private channels of information concerning the Sevier affray. At six-thirty Jackson joined Overton at Nashville. Overton had the pistols. With three others they departed for the Kentucky line.

Mr. Dickinson and eight companions were already on the road. "Good-by, darling," he told his young wife. "I shall be sure to be at home to-morrow evening." This confidence was not altogether assumed. He was a snap shot. At the word of command and firing apparently without aim, he could put four balls in a mark twenty-four feet away, each ball touching another. The persistent tradition on the countryside, that to worry Jackson he left several such examples of his marksmanship along the road, is unconfirmed by any member of the Dickinson or Jackson parties. But the story that he had offered on the streets of Nashville to wager he would kill Jackson at the first fire was vouchsafed by John Overton, the brother of Jackson's second, a few days after the duel.

Jackson said he was glad that "the other side" had started so early. It was a guarantee against further delay. Jackson had chafed over the seven days that had elapsed since the acceptance of the challenge. At their first interview, Overton and Dr. Hanson Catlett, Mr. Dickinson's second, had agreed that the meeting should be on Friday, May thirtieth, near Harrison's Mills on Red River just beyond the Kentucky boundary. Jackson protested at once. He did not wish to ride forty miles to preserve the fiction of a delicate regard for Tennessee's unenforceable statute against dueling. He did not wish to wait a week for something that could be done in a few hours. Dickinson's excuse was that he desired to borrow a pair of pistols. Overton offered the choice of Jackson's pistols, pledging Jackson to the use of the other. . . .

As they rode Jackson talked a great deal, scrupulously avoiding the subject that burdened every mind. Really, however, there was nothing more to be profitably said on that head. General Overton was a Revolutionary soldier of long acquaintance with the Code. With his principal he had canvassed every possible aspect of the issue forthcoming. "Distance . . . twenty-four feet; the parties to stand facing each other, with their pistols down perpendicularly. When they are READY, the single word FIRE! to be given; at which they are to fire as soon as they please. Should either fire before the word is given we [the seconds] pledge ourselves to shoot him down instantly." Jackson was neither a quick shot, nor an especially good one for the western country. He had decided not to compete with Dickinson for the first fire. He expected to be hit, perhaps badly. But he counted on the resources of his will to sustain him until he could aim deliberately and shoot to kill, if it were the last act of his life.

On the first leg of the ride they traversed the old Kentucky Road, the route by which, fifteen years before, Andrew Jackson had carried Rachel Robards from her husband's home, the present journey being a part of the long sequel to the other. Jackson rambled on in a shrill voice. Thomas Jefferson was "the best Republican in theory and the worst in practice" he had ever seen. And he lacked courage. How long were we to support the affronts of England—impressment of seamen, cuffing about of our ocean commerce? Perhaps as long as Mr. Jefferson stayed in office. Well, that would be two years, and certainly his successor should be a stouter man. "We must fight England again. In the last war I was not old enough to be any account." He prayed that the next might come "before I get too old to fight."

General Overton asked how old Jackson reckoned he would have to be for that. In England's case about a hundred, Jackson said.

He spoke of Burr. A year ago, this day, Jackson had borne him from the banquet in Nashville to the Hermitage. He recalled their first meeting in 1797 when both were in Congress. Jackson also met General Hamilton that winter. "Personally, no gentleman could help liking Hamilton. But his political views were all English." At heart a monarchist. "Why, did he not urge Washington to take a crown!"

Burr also had his failings. He had made a mistake, observed Jackson with admirable detachment, a political mistake, when he fought Hamilton. And about his Western projects the General was none too sanguine. Burr relied over much on what others told him. Besides, there was Jefferson to be reckoned with. "Burr is as far from a fool as I ever saw, and yet he is as easily fooled as any man I ever knew."

The day was warm, and a little after ten o'clock the party stopped for refreshment. Jackson took a mint julep, ate lightly and rested until mid-afternoon. The party reached Miller's Tavern in Kentucky about eight o'clock. After a supper of fried chicken, waffles, sweet potatoes and coffee, Jackson repaired to the porch to chat with the inn's company. No one guessed his errand. At ten o'clock he knocked the ashes from his pipe and went to bed. Asleep in ten minutes, he had to be roused at five in the morning.

The parties met on the bank of the Red River at a break in a poplar woods. Doctor Catlett won the toss for choice of position, but as the sun had not come through the trees this signified nothing. The giving of the word fell to Overton. Jackson's pistols were to be used after all, Dickinson taking his pick. The nine-inch barrels were charged with ounce balls of seventy caliber. The ground was paced off, the principals took their places. Jackson wore a dark-blue frock coat and trousers of the same material; Mr. Dickinson a shorter coat of blue, and gray trousers.

"Gentlemen, are you ready?" called General Overton.

"Ready," said Dickinson quickly.

"Yes, sir," said Jackson.

"*Fere!*" cried Overton in the Old-Country accent.

Dickinson fired almost instantly. A fleck of dust rose from Jackson's coat and his left hand clutched his chest. For an instant he thought himself dying, but, fighting for self-command, slowly he raised his pistol.

Dickinson recoiled a step horror-stricken. "My God! Have I missed him?"

Overton presented his pistol. "Back to the mark, sir!"

Dickinson folded his arms. Jackson's spare form straightened. He aimed. There was a hollow "clock" as the hammer stopped at half-cock. He drew it back, sighted again and fired. Dickinson swayed to the ground.

As they reached the horses Overton noticed that his friend's left boot was filled with blood. "Oh, I believe that he pinked me," said Jackson quickly, "but I don't want those people to know," indicating the group that bent over Dickinson. Jackson's surgeon found that Dickinson's aim had been perfectly true, but he had judged the position of Jackson's heart by the set of his coat, and Jackson wore his coats loosely on account of the excessive slenderness of his figure. "But I should have hit him," he exclaimed, "if he had shot me through the brain."

With a furrow through his bowels Charles Dickinson tossed in agony until evening when friends eased him with a story that Jackson had a bullet in his breast and was dying. At ten o'clock he asked who had put out the light.

Rachel heard the news and fell on her knees weeping. "Oh, God have pity on the poor wife"—Mrs. Dickinson was with child—"pity on the babe in her womb."

Virility and Chivalry

John W. De Forest (1826–1906), Northern novelist, officer in the Civil War, and later (1866–7) an agent of the Freedmen's Bureau in Greenville, South Carolina, adds his shrewd comment on the "central trait of the 'chivalrous Southron.'" Shortly after his return to the North, De Forest published in Harper's Monthly, *the* Atlantic, *and* Putnam's *a series of perceptive articles based on his experiences and observations as the officer in charge of three counties, his "satrapy" as he called it. These articles were not collected into a book until 1948, when they were edited for the Yale University Press as* A Union Officer in the Reconstruction.

This passage is reprinted from the Harper's *article, "Chivalrous and Semi-chivalrous Southrons," (January 1869), pp. 196–7.*

It seems to me that the central trait of the "chivalrous Southron" is an intense respect for virility. He will forgive almost any vice in a man who is manly; he will admire vices which are but exaggerations of the masculine. If you will fight, if you are strong and skillful enough to kill your antagonist, if you can govern or influence the common herd, if you can ride a dangerous horse over a rough country, if you are a good shot or an expert swordsman, if you stand by your own opinions unflinchingly, if you do your level best on whisky, if you are a devil of a fellow with women, if, in short, you show vigorous masculine attributes, he will grant you his respect. I doubt whether a man who leaves behind him numerous irregular claimants to his name is regarded with disfavor at the South. He will be condemned theoretically; it may be considered proper to shoot him if he disturbs the peace of respectable families; but he will be looked upon as a nobler representative of his sex than Coelebs. The good young man, as pure as a young girl, whom one finds in the Abrahamic bosom of Northern Puritanism, would not be made a Grand Lama of in Dixie. The chivalrous Southron would unite with the aristocracy of Europe in regarding him as a sort of monster of neutral insipidity. I doubt whether even the women of our meridional regions admire that sort of youth. "I shouldn't fancy a hen-husband," said a lively Southern girl, alluding to a man without vices.

It may be taken for granted that a people which so highly prizes virility looks upon man as the lord of creation, and has the old fashioned ideas as to what is the proper sphere of woman. If the high-toned gentleman continues to be influential at the South, it will be a long time before the "strong-minded" obtain much of a following there, a very long time before they will establish female suffrage. Next to our supposed passion for putting the negro on an equality with the white, there is nothing in Northern life so abhorrent to the Southerners, of both sexes, as the movement in favor of woman's rights.

"I do think," said an emphatic old planter to me, "that your free-love business, and women's voting, and all that, is just the miserable-est mess that ever was invented. I don't see what ails you to go for such vile nonsense. But then you always were as full of whimsies as the devil."

It would have been useless to tell him that he was binding in one fagot ideas which had no connection. I did my wisest by him; I left him unanswered.

Editor Daniel Rebukes the Southern Generals
for Fighting a Chivalric War

John M. Daniel (1825–65) was one of the most remarkable of Virginia journalists. Misanthropic and with a certain streak of cruelty—he considered it entertaining sport to irritate his dogs until he set them fighting—solitary, dramatic in all his acts, and violent in his hatreds to the point where he was finally wounded in a duel by the Confederate Secretary of the Treasury, he was loved by his intimate friends and respected by his readers throughout the South. With the exception of a tour of duty as a diplomat in Sardinia and two brief periods of service in the Confederate forces, he was editor of the Richmond Examiner *from 1847 until his death, a few days before the* Examiner *plant was destroyed in the great fire that marked the fall of Richmond. Daniel had a genius for writing and could pull together the inept work of a junior journalist in a few moments of dashing revision. And he had the true journalist's understanding of the trends behind the great events going on around him. That understanding sometimes made his writing prophetic.*

He was prophetic when, in May 1863, almost two months before Gettysburg, he expressed something which many in the South were beginning to feel but none had so clearly said: that, for all the nobility of the Southern code of chivalry, the chivalric tradition had little place in a brutal modern war and might prove to be disastrous.

The following passage is selected from an editorial written by John M. Daniel for the Richmond Examiner *of May 12, 1863, and is quoted from Frederick S. Daniel (ed.):* The Richmond Examiner during the War; or, The Writings of John M. Daniel *(New York, printed for the author, 1868), pp. 83–5.*

We have had recently some remarkable returns for the pretty civilities showered by Stuart and Hampton on the Dutch farmers of Pennsylvania during their raid to Chambersburg. That souvenir of chivalry is forcibly brought to mind by the sharp contrast of recent occurrences. It has long been a laughing-stock for the North; and the narrative which was published by Colonel McClure, the Yankee commander at Chambersburg, of the polite phrases and punctilios of the "soft-mannered rebels" who invaded his military dominions, still survives among the Yankee humors of the war. We still have the picture before us of the sleek Yankee watching from the cover of his porch the wet, weary, and hungry "rebels" exposing themselves to a drenching rain, rather than invade the sanctity of the homes of the citizens of Chambersburg; "begging" a few coals to light their fires, and humbly asking permission to buy food from the negro wenches in the kitchens; while the officers made their salaams to Colonel McClure, and "thanked him for his candor" when he informed them that he was a red-hot abolitionist. It never seemed to have occurred to these damp knights that it was their duty to their men to take from an enemy what they wanted of food and shelter; they were too intent on pruning their manners, practising the knighthood of the middle ages in Pennsylvania, and establishing a chivalric fraternity with the Dutch civilization they had invaded.

We have had enough, in the recent Yankee raids, to put to the blush these recollections of "chivalry," and to teach us that the gentle knight-errantry of rose-water is but a poor way of opposing an enemy whose mission is that of savage warfare. . . .

Chivalry is a very noble quality. But we do not get our idea of it from the mincings of dandy preachers and parlor geldings. We do not derive our interpretation of the codes of war from sprigs dressed up in Confederate uniform of uncertain moral gender. We know that we are in a dreadful war; that we are fighting a base and deadly enemy. While it is not for the South to fight with any mean advantage, it is time for her to abandon those polite notions of war which she has got from the Waverley novels, and to fight with fire and sword. If any retaliation is to be made for the recent Yankee raids (and present opportunities invite it), its history should be written in broad tracks of blood and destruction. There should be no re-enactment of the scenes at Chambersburg. We must pay the enemy back in the savage coin of vengeance, and settle our accounts in blood.

3. KIN

Kin and the Love of Country

George Fitzhugh, one of the leading Southern apologists for slavery, believed passionately that civilization flowers from the "universal desire of white men to become aristocrats." For him, as for many of his class, pride of race and family was the primary motive that had operated to develop a unique and superior civilization in the Southern states. In the following excerpts from his "Family History and the Philosophy of Names" (De Bow's Review, *September 1860, pp. 269, 263–4*) *Fitzhugh introduces several of the concepts that were used over and over again, during the ante-bellum years, to support this argument.*

For a note on Fitzhugh, see p. 370.

FAMILIES are the most conservative of all institutions. The "son of nobody" belongs to no place or country. Men whose kin and ancestry for hundreds of years have resided in the same section, love their country and may be relied on in times of difficulty. Family pride begets patriotism, and is the only reliable source from whence it arises. Love of excitement, of adventure, of glory, or of plunder, may induce a man to fight bravely for any country or in any cause. But 'tis not the mercenary Swiss, nor the needy desperate adventurer, on whom a country can rely in times of peril. Those who have most ties, like the ancient oak, that has been putting forth [r]oots for centuries, are the men to cling to and defend their country. . . .

We know hardly a family most of whose members do not occupy the same social position which their ancestors held two hundred years ago. Pride of pedigree is the greatest stimulant to exertion, energy, industry, and economy. When by extravagance or misfortune one generation falls, it is not very difficult for the next generation, by industry and economy, in a new country like ours, to recover its normal ancestral position. This it usually does. Respectable connexion, as an incentive to virtuous exertion, will, ere long, cease to be under the ban of public opinion. Every man in America desires to be an aristocrat, for every man desires wealth, and wealth confers power and distinction, and makes its owner an unmistakable aristocrat. What vile hypocrisy, what malicious envy and jealousy, to censure and vilify in others, that which every man of us is trying with might and main to attain. Civilization would cease but for the universal desire of *white men* to become aristocrats. The negro rarely indulges such a wish, and hence, lacking this stimulant to exertion, can only be moved to industrious action by the fear of corporal punishment.

Men are not content with becoming aristocrats themselves, they moreover desire to found a family and make aristocrats of their posterity. Who is not ambitious to rear a distinguished race (a glorious ancestry) among his descendants. Ancestry is no more disgraceful in the past than in the future. The English Reviewer mentions several instances of great men, among them Dr. Franklin, who were very curious as to their ancestry. He might have added to the list the learned and pious Dr. Adam Clarke, who begins his autobiography with a disquisition on family and Christian names.

The recuperative elasticity of families is singularly exemplified by comparing the names on the roll of Battle Abbey with those of the leading families in Eastern Virginia. It will be found that very generally the old families of Virginia are of Norman descent: "Peckatone," a farm in Westmoreland county, belonged originally to the Corbins, or Corvins, their armorial device being a crow; next, by intermarriage, it fell to the Turbevilles, and by another marriage to the Taliaferros— "Corbin" and "Turberville" are names on the roll of Battle Abbey, and "Taliafer" was a chieftain and bard under the Conqueror, who was killed at the first onset in the Battle of Hastings.

Kin and Politics in Colonial Virginia

The following selection is excerpted from Chapter vi ("County Oligarchies") of Charles S. Sydnor's Gentlemen Freeholders: Political Practices in Washington's Virginia *(Chapel Hill: University of North Carolina Press; 1952). It is reprinted with the permission of the publishers. (In this selection Professor Sydnor's notes to the text have been omitted.)*

BIRTH into one of the ruling families was almost essential to the making of a political career in eighteenth-century Virginia. A man inherited local prominence from his father or uncle in much the same way that he inherited land and slaves and social position. It is difficult to recall the name of any Virginian of the Revolutionary generation who rose to high office without the aid of influential relatives. So it was with the Randolphs, Carters, Lees, Harrisons, and Nelsons; and so it was with men like Jefferson and Henry who are now known chiefly as revolutionists or as apostles of democracy. Thomas Jefferson's grandfather, who bore the same name, was a "gentleman justice" of Henrico County, a militia captain, and a sheriff. Peter Jefferson, father of the author of the Declaration of Independence, held the offices of justice, sheriff, surveyor, and county lieutenant, and he was a member of the House of Burgesses and a vestryman of the parish of St. James, Northam. Patrick Henry, another revolutionist and democrat, who, rightly or not, is often regarded as being more radical than Jefferson, was also born into a family of local prominence. His father was the presiding justice of the Hanover County Court, a militia colonel, and a vestryman, and his uncle was a clergyman of the Established Church. Thus, when Jefferson and Henry began their political careers, they were following in the footsteps of their fathers and kinsmen.

One can select at random from the prominent names of this generation and discover that in nearly every case the man rose to power on the shoulders of his father. James Madison's father was a justice, a county lieutenant, and a vestryman. George Wythe's father was a member of the House of Burgesses. George Washington's father, grandfather, and great grandfather were justices of the peace. His father also held the offices of churchwarden and sheriff, and his half-brother Lawrence of Mount Vernon was a burgess from Fairfax County and a trustee of Alexandria. The father of John Marshall was the principal vestryman of Leeds parish as well as justice of the peace, sheriff, and representative of Fauquier County in the House of Burgesses. Not his father but his uncle Joseph Jones, who held many important offices in colonial and revolutionary Virginia, aided James Monroe in his political beginnings.

Marriage into an influential family was also a distinct asset in politics. Thomas Jefferson's father improved his position by marrying Jane Randolph, a daughter of one of the largest and most powerful families in Virginia. John Marshall's marriage to Mary Willis Ambler, daughter of Jacquelin Ambler, brought him influential connections. There were, of course, other ways for a young man to gain the attention and approval of older and more powerful men besides kinship and marriage. The early and close association of George Washington with the Fairfaxes, especially with Colonel William Fairfax, was an important ele-

276

ment in the beginning of his political career. This political alliance began with Washington's supporting a son of Colonel Fairfax in an election held just three years before Lord Fairfax led the procession of voters to the poll that sent Washington to the House of Burgesses for the first time.

Whether won through birth, marriage, or friendship, support from the gentry was indispensable for the man who would rise in politics in eighteenth-century Virginia. With enough men of the gentry on his side, a candidate was almost unbeatable.

Reunion of the Kinfolks

This selection is taken from Ben Robertson's Red Hills and Cotton *(New York: Alfred A. Knopf; 1942), pp. 227–30. It is reprinted with the permission of the publisher. For a note on the author see p. 158.*

DURING laying-by time in August, on the second Monday in the month, we always held a reunion of all the kinfolks, usually at one of the houses over on Chauga Creek. About three hundred would attend, and we would arrive in carriages, in wagons pulled by mules, and on horseback and afoot; we would drive up in automobiles, and once one of our cousins landed in the bottoms in an airplane. During the morning we would sit in the shade of the trees and our cousin Unity and our Great-Aunt Narcissa and our cousin Ella would begin at the beginning of time, long before the Revolution, and trace the kinfolks from then until the moment of that reunion. They would tell us who had married whom, who had gone where, and what had happened. At noon someone would ring the yard bell and the three hundred of us would sit down on benches before long board tables—three hundred of us would eat an old-time dinner. About a hundred chickens would be fried and served on platters, and there would be fried steak, venison, fried fresh pork, whole boiled hams, sugared and spiced, and there would be roasted duck, baked turkey, cold veal, stuffed eggs, and beans, potatoes, roasting ear corn, cheese straws, lemon tarts, and bowls of highly seasoned chowchow pickles and peach preserves made from the wild clingstone peaches that grew on the cotton terraces, and there would be clingstone peach pickles, and blackberry jelly and apple jelly and pound cake, chocolate layer cake, coconut layer cake, marble cake, banana layer cake, caramel layer cake, sponge cake, angel-food cake, apple pie, peach pie, huckleberry pie, ambrosia, boiled frozen custard, fresh grapes, cold watermelons, cantaloupes, muskmelons, pomegranates. For drink there would be blackberry cordial, cider, hard cider, blackberry wine, sweet and deep purple in color, and there would be a dry scuppernong wine and muscadine wine, a strong elderberry wine and dandelion wine, clover-blossom wine, and pitchers filled with sweet milk, buttermilk, and water from the spring branch. Of course, we considered it outrageous and disgraceful for any of our kinfolks to drink corn liquor, so we did not serve white lightning at the dinner table. Those who drank that did so behind the barn.

Once I remember seeing my Great-Uncle John coming up the garden path smiling and talking to everyone and all the time mopping his fiercely flushed face. At the gate he started to walk toward the far edge of the yard, but at that moment my Great-Aunt Kate yelled to him from the front porch.

"John," she cried, "where did you get that liquor?"

"Why, Kate!" exclaimed my great-uncle, astonished.

"You heard me," continued my great-aunt. "Where did you get it?"

"I hardly touched it," said my great-uncle. "Just took a drop."

"You come on up here and sit down," said my great-aunt. Obediently my great-uncle went up on to the piazza, and from then on until time to go home he sat there in a chair. He sat there in silence—he did not say a word.

When we had eaten dinner at the reunions, somebody would talk about us and olden times, and then we would pack up and start early for our houses. All of our lives we had to start early from places, for we had stock at home to attend to. We had to milk and feed, and my kinfolks were the kind of people who believed that cows should be milked and mules fed at exactly the same hour, day after day. We might inconvenience ourselves, but not our livestock. It was low-down and trifling to inconvenience livestock.

4. HOSPITALITY

One Day of Southern Hospitality

When Henry Barnard, born in New England, made a tour of the South in 1833, three years after his graduation from Yale, he was delighted with the "manners and habits" and the "princely hospitality" he encountered there. During the five months of his journey he visited many of the important public figures of the day and recorded their conversation with a Boswell-like perseverance. Since Barnard was a handsome young man with an engaging personality, it is not surprising that his Southern hosts opened their hearts as well as their houses to him.

The narrative of Barnard's tour, from which this passage is excerpted, was put together from his notes and letters home and edited by Bernard C. Steiner. It was printed in Volume XIII of the Maryland Historical Magazine *(1918), pp. 267–386. Permission to reprint this excerpt was kindly granted by the magazine and Mr. Fred Shelley, Librarian of the Maryland Historical Society.*

Petersberg, March 15th 1833.

My Dear Betty

I think you would delight to visit this region, merely to observe the difference of manners and habits, from what you have been accustomed to, aye and to experience the princely hospitality of the *gentle* born families. For the last week I have had a succession of feasts. I accompanied Mrs. Campbell who is one of the most devoted mothers and well educated women I ever met with, and her daughter Miss Betty, a beautiful sprightly accomplished girl, to Shirley, the seat of the Carter family. Mrs. Carter, is of a high and wealthy family, and is one of the plainest most unassuming women, you will meet with any where. Now, that you may understand how we lived there, and how one of these large establishments are carried on. I will describe a single day there—I will suppose also that it is a day upon which company is expected etc, etc.

279

When you wake in the morning, you are surprised to find that a servant has been in, and without disturbing you, built up a large fire—taken out your clothes and brushed them, and done the same with your boots—brought in hot water to shave, and indeed stands ready to do your bidding—as soon as you are dressed, you walk down into the dining room—At eight o'clock you take your seat at the breakfast table of rich mahogany—each plate standing separate on its own little cloth—Mr. Carter will sit at one end of the table and Mrs. Carter at the other—Mrs. C. will send you by two little black boys, as fine a cup of coffee as you ever tasted, or a cup of tea—it is fashionable here to drink a cup of tea after coffee—Mr. Carter has a fine cold ham before him of the real Virginia flavor—this is all the meat you will get in the morning, but the servant will bring you hot muffins and corn batter cakes every 2 minutes—you will find on the table also, loaf wheat bread, hot and cold—corn bread—

After breakfast visitors consult their pleasure—if they wish to ride, horses are ready at their command—read, there are books enough in the Library,—write, fire, and writing materials are ready in his room—The Master and Mistress of the House are not expected to entertain visitors till an hour or two before dinner, which is usually at 3. If company has been invited to the dinner, they will begin to come about 1—Ladies in carriage and gentlemen horseback—After making their toilet, the company amuse themselves in the parlor—about a half hour before dinner, the gentlemen are invited out to take grog. When dinner is ready (and by the way Mrs. Carter has nothing to do with setting the table, an old family servant, who for 50 years has superintended that matter, does all that) Mr. Carter politely takes a Lady by the hand and leads the way into the dining room, and is followed by the rest, each Lady lead by a gentleman. Mrs. C. is at one end of the table with a large dish of rich soup, and Mr. C. at the other, with a saddle of fine mutton, scattered round the table, you may choose for yourself, ham—beef—turkey—duck—eggs with greens—etc—etc—for vegetables, potatoes, beets—hominy—This last you will find always at dinner, it is made of their white corn and beans and is a very fine dish—after you have dined, there circulates a bottle of sparkling champagne. After that off passes the things, and the *upper* table cloth, and upon that is placed the desert, consisting of fine plum pudding, tarts, etc, etc,—after this comes ice cream, West India preserves—peaches preserved in brandy, etc,—When you have eaten this, off goes the second table cloth, and then upon the bare mahogany table is set, the figs, raisins, and almonds, and before Mr. Carter is set 2 or 3 bottles of wine—Madeira, Port, and a sweet wine for the Ladies—he fills his glass, and pushes them on, after the glasses are all filled, the gentlemen pledge their services to the Ladies, and down goes the wine, after the first and second glass the ladies retire, and the gentlemen begin to circulate the bottle pretty briskly. You are at liberty however to follow the Ladies as soon as you please, who after music and a little chit chat prepare for their ride home.

A "Frolic" at Highland

Bennet H. Barrow (1811–54), owner of the substantial plantation High- land in the West Feliciana Parish of Louisiana, was a shrewd and care- ful planter, using up-to-date methods in his cotton fields and in his ex- periments with sugar-cane. Like his neighbors in this rich region of handsome houses, he was extremely fond of sports of all kinds—deer- hunting, fox-hunting, fishing, riding. With his brother William he raised, trained, and sold fine horses and raced them at courses as far away as Natchez and New Orleans. He also doted on balls and in- formal "frolics," like the one described in the passage below, which lasted for two days and nights, January 7–9, 1842.

Barrow kept a diary from 1836 to 1846, in which he recorded, in ec- centric spelling, all sorts of fascinating details of his business and social life. The entries are terse, but his language is strong and vivid and there is much to be read between the lines.

In 1943 Edwin A. Davis published a careful edition of Plantation Life in the Florida Parishes of Louisiana, 1836–1846 as Reflected in the Diary of Bennet H. Barrow *(New York: Columbia University Press). The passage extracted here is to be found on page 249. It is reprinted with the kind permission of Columbia University Press.*

7 Cloudy Verry warm, Went over to Ruffins this morning in my Cab. While there, Amanda & Miss Crab of Tennessee jumped in it & off they went without Bonnets. supposing them hid search was made evry Where, one hour or more they were seen returning from the swamp, I got in turned the cab & drove them as they were over to Mrs Wades —after being there some time, Who should come But Roberts wife &

Rosalie—after us in another Cab (without Bonnets,) remained at Cousin Olives few minutes. took Betsy Ratliff & Miss Laura Wade— Betsy in the Cab with Rosalie & Mary (& John Ruffins son) Miss Wade, Miss Carab, Amand, & myself in my Cab. only two seats in each Cab, Went on to Bennets found no one at Home, Came on to my House to dinner, sent & collected the neighbours. A. G. Barrow & family   Miss Swifts   Flower & family   Miss Mary Barrow   Miss Sophia Johnson   Mrs Collins   12 or 13 gentlemen—danced all night by the Piano & Violin

  8 Would not Let any Leave—got a violin player from Town "Norman" Let them rest & knap during the day some times. playing smut— at dark began to dance, at 12 Oclock their consciences made them refuse to dance any Longer, it Being Saturday night, to punish them fastened the doors 'till near two ok some blew the Lights out others tried to get out at the windows, Any thing, but dance they would'ent, retired at 2 Ok all nearly broke down, never have seen A collection so sudden and so perfectly free easy & happy for two days & nights, All restraint thrown aside never enjoyed myself as much

  9 Many Long & weary Looking faces sore feet &c. this morning however all regretting it was Sunday, none more than myself, without preparation it Began, plenty to Eate & drink is all they wanted, evry thing put down & each one helped himself When he wanted it, Cloudy spring day

Dr. Bagby on the Hospitality of Jeems Jimmison

George W. Bagby (1828–83), author of "Bacon and Greens," from which the following account of true, old-fashioned middle-class hospitality is taken, was a true Virginia gentleman of the old school. Though trained as a physician (at the University of Pennsylvania), he probably never tended half a dozen cases. Instead he spent most of his life writing sketches and editorials for the daily press.

  This selection from his "Bacon and Greens" (originally a lecture) is excerpted from Selections from the Miscellaneous Writings of Dr. George W. Bagby *(2 vols.; Richmond: Whittet & Shepperson; 1884), Vol. II, pp. 21–4. It was republished in* The Old Virginia Gentleman

GEORGE W. BAGBY: *Hospitality of Jeems Jimmison*

and Other Sketches, *with an introduction by Thomas Nelson Page* (*New York: Charles Scribner's Sons; 1910*).

❊

THE traveller enters [Jeems Jimmison's] domain through a rickety "big-gate," partly upheld by mighty posts, which remind him of the Druidical remains at Stonehenge. The road leads apparently nowhere, through thickets of old-field pine and scrub-oak. Here and there is an opening in the woods, with a lonely, crank-sided tobacco-house in the midst, looking as if it were waiting resignedly for the end of the world to come. He hears the crows cawing, the woodpeckers tapping and the log-cocks drumming, but sees no human being. Far away the roosters are crowing, and, perhaps, the scream of the peacock is heard. Slowly-sailing, white-billed buzzards eye him from on high and make him nervous. Over the trees, he can't tell where exactly, come the voices of the ploughers—"Gee," "Wo-haw," "Git up." He rides in the direction of the sound, but finds nobody. Anon he encounters an ox-cart, which turns aside for him. "Wo, Lamb!" "Come here, Darlin'!" "Back, Buck!" "Back! I tell you." The driver touches his hat and says, "Sarvunt, marster," but is too busy with his steers to give any directions. And, when his patience is fairly exhausted by a succession of dilapidated gates, tied up with grapevines, and complicated draw-bars, which compel him to get down from his horse and fill his hands with turpentine, (for Larkin's negroes won't half skin the poles which make the draw-bars)—when the traveller is thus bewildered and exhausted, and half tempted to turn back, he is suddenly relieved by an ebony apparition, resembling somewhat a kangaroo, clad in a solitary, mud-colored cotton garment, split up to the arm-pit on one side, and dexterously kept in position by a peculiar upward twist of the shoulder on the other side. This black-legged little spectre pops out of a gully, where he has been quietly eating dirt, darts over the broom-straw, knocks down the mullein stalks, crashes through the sassafras clump, "skeets" through the brier patch, shoots around the plum bushes and up the lane, under the morillo cherry-trees, disappears behind the fodder and straw stacks, winds in between the stable, corn-houses, hen-houses, the dairy, the smoke-house, and the kitchen; and so, like a varitable Jack-o'-my-lanthorn, with a nappy head, that resembles a diseased chestnut burr or part of the top of an old hair trunk, leads you up to the house itself.

There the native Virginian, with a Powhatan pipe in his mouth and a silver spectacle-case in his hand, awaits you, and asks you to "'light" and "come in" in the same breath. While a negro boy is running up from the "new ground" to take your horse, a mulatto girl is flying, with a pail on her head, to the spring for fresh water and a jug of milk. Two or three little negroes are chasing the chickens whose necks are soon to be twisted or chopped off with an axe at the wood-pile; ham is being sliced, eggs are frying in the frying-pan, a hoe-cake is on the fire, another head of cabbage is thrown into the pot, somebody is sheeting the bed upstairs, and (before your leggings are off) the case-bottle is at your elbow, and the native Virginian has taken possession of you, as if you were the Prodigal Son or the last number of the Richmond *Enquirer.*

Meantime your arrival has produced an excitement among the small Ebo-shins, as you will discover the first time you step out into the yard. A number of wild, black eyes are intently watching you through the panels of the fence, and the conversation which ensues on your appearance shows the estimation in which "Ole Marster," as the native Virginian is called, is held by his young barbarians. . . .

We will not stop to describe his old weather-boarded, often wainscoted, house, with its queer old furniture and its old family portraits, which indicate for Jeems Jimmison or his wife a better origin than his name would lead you to expect. One peculiarity, though, must not go unmentioned. No matter how small this house is, it is never full. There is always room for one more in it; and, on special occasions, such as a wedding or a Christmas frolic, the number of feather beds, straw beds, shuck beds, pallets, and shakedowns which this old house produces is literally incredible. To feed and lodge, if need be, the entire State is not a point of honor with Coonrod, but a matter of course—no other idea ever entered his head. What is called "hospitality" by other folks is with him so much a part of his nature that he has no name for it (unless he keeps an "Entertainment") and he never uses the word. How he managed, on a worn-out estate, to repeat, as it were, the miracle of the loaves and fishes is a mystery which must be charged, I fear, to the "barbarism of slavery," for the art of feeding and lodging everybody seems already to be passing away.

A Sour Note on Southern Hospitality

In his A Journey in the Back Country, *from which the passages below are taken, the northern agriculturist and travel-writer Frederick Law*

F. L. OLMSTED: *A Sour Note on Southern Hospitality*

Olmsted (see p. 162) gives a number of examples of the inhospitality he encountered on his journey in the back country of the middle South during the summer of 1854. These stories of rude behavior and wretched fare were much resented by Southern readers. Possibly De Bow, the New Orleans journalist, had a clue when he rebuked Olmsted as follows: "We have now grown accustomed to this [abuse from Northern travelers], and it is not at all surprising that here and there it is producing its effect in some violent exhibitions of feeling like that displayed by our worthy friend old Dr. Brewer, of Montgomery county, Maryland, who persistently refuses, on all occasions, to allow a Yankee even to cross his fields, or like that of John Randolph, who said in the House, 'Mr. Speaker, I would not allow one of my servants to buy as much as a toot-horn from one of these people.' "

The following extracts from A Journey in the Back Country *(New York: Mason Brothers; 1861) are taken from pages 407 and 409-11.*

PRESENTING myself and known only in the character of a chance traveler, most likely to be in search of health, entertainment and information, usually taken for and treated as a southerner, until I stated that I was not one, I journeyed nearly six months at one time (my second journey) through the South. During all this journey, I came not oftener than once a week, on an average, to public houses, and was thus generally forced to seek lodging and sustenance at private houses. Often it was refused me; not unfrequently rudely refused. But once did I meet with what northern readers could suppose Mr. De Bow to mean by the term (used in the same article), "free road-side hospitality." Not once with the slightest appearance of what Noah Webster defines hospitality, the "practice of receiving or entertaining strangers without reward."

Only twice, in a journey of four thousand miles, made independently of public conveyances, did I receive a night's lodging or a repast from a native southerner, without having the exact price in money which I was expected to pay for it stated to me by those at whose hands I received it. . . .

A naturalist, the author of a well known standard work, who has made several tours of observation in the slave States, lately confided to me that he believed that the popular report of southern hospitality must be a popular romance, for never, during all his travels in the South, had he chanced to be entertained for a single night, except by gentlemen to whom he was formally presented by letter, or who had previously been under obligations to him, without paying for it in money, and to an amount quite equal to the value received. By the wealthier, a night's entertainment had been frequently refused him, under circumstances which, as must have been evident to them, rendered his further progress seriously inconvenient. Once, while in company with a foreign naturalist—a titled man—he had been dining at the inn of a small county-town, when a certain locally distinguished judge had seen fit to be eloquent at the dinner-table upon the advantages of slavery in maintaining a class of "high-toned gentlemen," referring especially to the proverbial hospitality of southern plantations, which he described as quite a bewilderment to strangers, and nothing like which was to be found in any country unblessed with slavery, or institutions equivalent to it. It so happened that the following night the travelers, on approaching a plantation mansion in quest of lodging, were surprised to find that they had fallen upon the residence of this same judge, who recognized them, and welcomed them and bade them be at home. Embarrassed by a recollection of his discourse of hospitality, it was with some difficulty that one of them, when they were taking leave next morning, brought himself to inquire what he might pay for the entertainment they had received. He was at once relieved by the judge's prompt response, "Dollar and a quarter apiece, I reckon."

It is very true that the general custom of the South which leads a traveler to ask for a lodging at any private house he may chance to reach near nightfall, and to receive a favorable answer not merely as a favor but as a matter of business, is a convenient one, is one indeed almost necessary in a country so destitute of villages, and where, off certain thoroughfares of our merchants, there are so few travelers. It is a perfectly respectable and entirely sensible custom, but it is not, as it is commonly represented to be, a custom of hospitality, and it is not at all calculated to induce customs of hospitality with the mass of citizens. It is calculated to make inhospitality of habit and inhospitality of character the general rule; hospitality of habit and of character the exception. Yet the common misapplication of the word to this custom is, so far as I can ascertain, the only foundation of the arrogant assumption of superiority of character in this respect of the southerners over ourselves—the only ground of the claim that slavery breeds a race of more generous and hospitable citizens than freedom.

IX

MILITARY GLORY

THE Southerner has always thought of himself as a superior fighting man. He is born to the military tradition. He loves a good scrap and is proud of his ability to carry it off, usually with victory and always with honor.

The Southern military tradition began in the Indian wars and was strengthened by the Revolution. The colonies were led to victory by a Virginian experienced in the Indian fighting, and it was in Virginia that Cornwallis surrendered. After the Revolution the tradition was nourished by continuing warfare against the Indian long after he had ceased to be a threat in the North, and by the prominent part played by Southerners in setting up the Republic of Texas and in the later war against Mexico. It was nourished, too, by the Southerner's acceptance of violence as a part of life, by the aristocratic duel and the frontier gouging. And it was perpetuated by the survival of the militia system from colonial days. The county militia enrolled every able-bodied man and expected him to keep ready at home a musket and ammunition. Muster days were riotous holidays, and the local militia company became a matter of competitive civic pride.

The military tradition fed the military schools and was fed by them in turn. It was the conviction of the Southerner that military discipline was moral discipline, that it taught diligence, order, and restraint and was as necessary to the development of the successful gentleman as the training of the mind given by the more academic studies. Hence, beginning in the early 1800's, more and more military academies sprang up throughout the South. Virginia Military Institute was established at Lexington in 1839, South Carolina Military Academy, later to become The Citadel, in 1842, and Georgia Military Institute in 1851. By the Civil War, town after town in the South boasted a military academy, and many of them are still alive today.

Literature contributed to the tradition. The Southerner, partly out of a subconscious need to find justification for a distinctly feudal social and economic system, read heavily in Scott and in such Southern novels as Carruthers's *Knights of the Golden Horseshoe,* Kennedy's *Horseshoe Robinson,* and Simms's *The Partisan.* In them he found not only a reflection of his way of life but an idealized picture of chivalric warfare which went far to make acceptable the dashing bravado of such men as Jeb Stuart and the perhaps overgenerous chivalry of Lee.

The tradition is a continuous one. It began while the Southern states were still colonies, and it showed itself still alive in the last war when men from all over the South fought to defend a nation from which they had not been able to secede. But though it has by no means died, the tradition reached its fullest flowering in the Civil War. It produced then a galaxy of military leaders who, until the North had discovered the skill of Sherman and Grant, led the South from victory to victory. And in the Civil War the Southern military tradition showed most clearly the many different facets which, together, make it part of a way of life. All the selections in this section, therefore, deal with the Civil War. Much of what they reflect is true of the whole history of the South.

"Will you not be forced to submit?"—"Never!"

In spite of its title, Russell's My Diary North and South *(during the Civil War) is not a personal diary. It is, instead, vivid war reporting. William Howard Russell (1821–1907) was a special writer for the London* Times *and one of the first of the modern war correspondents. He was an honest reporter and a forceful writer—his exposures of mismanagement in the Crimea had helped to unseat a prime minister—and he had the born war correspondent's sense of the importance of what soldiers and civilians are feeling and thinking. He was also gifted with an intuitive eye for seemingly trivial details that would later prove important. Note, for example, how carefully he records the insubordination of the volunteers smoking on the hay, a minor incident here, but one indicative of a turn of mind which was to cost the Confederacy much. No reporter has given a more exciting picture of the confident war spirit that swept the South at the dawn of the Civil War than did Russell in writing his experiences in Charleston immediately after the fall of Sumter.*

The passage below is selected from William Howard Russell: My Diary North and South *(Boston: T. O. H. P. Burnham; 1863), pp. 97–108.*

THAT night I sat in the Charleston Club with John Manning. Who that has ever met him can be indifferent to the charms of manner and of personal appearance, which render the ex-Governor of the State so attractive? There were others present, senators or congressmen, like Mr. Chestnut and Mr. Porcher Miles. We talked long, and at last angrily, as might be between friends, of political affairs.

I own it was a little irritating to me to hear men indulge in extravagant broad menace and rodomontade, such as came from their lips. "They would welcome the world in arms with hospitable hands to bloody graves." "They never could be conquered." "Creation could not do it," and so on. I was obliged to handle the question quietly at first—to ask them "if they admitted the French were a brave and warlike people!" "Yes, certainly." "Do you think you could better defend yourselves against invasion than the people of France?" "Well, no;

but we'd make it pretty hard business for the Yankees." "Suppose the Yankees, as you call them, come with such preponderance of men and *matériel*, that they are three to your one, will you not be forced to submit?" "Never." "Then either you are braver, better disciplined, more warlike than the people and soldiers of France, or you alone, of all the nations in the world, possess the means of resisting physical laws which prevail in war, as in other affairs of life." "No. The Yankees are cowardly rascals. We have proved it by kicking and cuffing them till we are tired of it; besides, we know John Bull very well. He will make a great fuss about non-interference at first, but when he begins to want cotton he'll come off his perch." I found this was the fixed idea everywhere. The doctrine of "cotton is king,"—to us who have not much considered the question a grievous delusion or an unmeaning babble—to them is a lively all-powerful faith without distracting heresies or schisms. They have in it enunciated their full belief, and indeed there is some truth in it, in so far as we year after year by the stimulants of coal, capital, and machinery have been working up a manufacture on which four or five millions of our population depend for bread and life, which cannot be carried on without the assistance of a nation, that may at any time refuse us an adequate supply, or be cut off from giving it by war.

Political economy, we are well aware, is a fine science, but its followers are capable of tremendous absurdities in practice. The dependence of such a large proportion of the English people on this sole article of American cotton is fraught with the utmost danger to our honor and to our prosperity. Here were these Southern gentlemen exulting in their power to control the policy of Great Britain, and it was small consolation to me to assure them they were mistaken; in case we did not act as they anticipated, it could not be denied Great Britain would plunge an immense proportion of her people—a nation of manufacturers—into pauperism, which must leave them dependent on the national funds, or more properly on the property and accumulated capital of the district. . . .

April 17th.—The streets of Charleston present some such aspect as those of Paris in the last revolution. Crowds of armed men singing and promenading the streets. The battle-blood running through their veins—that hot oxygen which is called "the flush of victory" on the cheek; restaurants full, revelling in bar-rooms, club-rooms crowded, orgies and carousings in tavern or private house, in tap-room, from cabaret—down narrow alleys, in the broad highway. Sumter has set them distraught; never was such a victory; never such brave lads; never such a fight. There are pamphlets already full of the incident. It is a bloodless Waterloo or Solferino.

After breakfast I went down to the quay, with a party of the Gen-

eral's staff, to visit Fort Sumter. The senators and governors turned
soldiers wore blue military caps, with "palmetto" trees embroidered
thereon; blue frock-coats, with upright collars, and shoulder-straps
edged with lace, and marked with two silver bars, to designate their
rank of captain; gilt buttons, with the palmetto in relief; blue trousers,
with a gold-lace cord, and brass spurs—no straps. The day was sweltering, but a strong breeze blew in the harbor, and puffed the dust of
Charleston, coating our clothes, and filling our eyes with powder. The
streets were crowded with lanky lads, clanking spurs, and sabres, with
awkward squads marching to and fro, with drummers beating calls, and
ruffles, and points of war; around them groups of grinning negroes delighted with the glare and glitter, a holiday, and a new idea for them—
Secession flags waving out of all the windows—little Irish boys shouting
out, "Battle of Fort Sumter! New edishun!"—As we walked down towards the quay, where the steamer was lying, numerous traces of the
unsettled state of men's minds broke out in the hurried conversations of
the various friends who stopped to speak for a few moments. "Well,
governor, the old Union is gone at last!" "Have you heard what Abe
is going to do?" "I don't think Beauregard will have much more fighting for it. What do you think?" And so on. Our little Creole friend, by
the by, is popular beyond description. There are all kinds of doggerel
rhymes in his honor—one with a refrain—

> "With cannon and musket, with shell and petard,
> We salute the North with our Beau-regard"—

is much in favor. . . .

There was a large crowd around the pier staring at the men in
uniform on the boat, which was filled with bales of goods, commissariat stores, trusses of hay, and hampers, supplies for the volunteer
army on Morris' Island. I was amused by the names of the various
corps, "Tigers," "Lions," "Scorpions," "Palmetto Eagles," "Guards," of
Pickens, Sumter, Marion, and of various other denominations, painted
on the boxes. The original formation of these volunteers is in companies, and they know nothing of battalions or regiments. The tendency in volunteer outbursts is sometimes to gratify the greatest vanity
of the greatest number. These companies do not muster more than
fifty or sixty strong. Some were "dandies," and "swells," and affected to
look down on their neighbors and comrades. Major Whiting told me
there was difficulty in getting them to obey orders at first, as each man
had an idea that he was as good an engineer as anybody else, "and a
good deal better, if it came to that." It was easy to perceive it was the
old story of volunteer and regular in this little army.

As we got on deck, the Major saw a number of rough, long-haired-
looking fellows in coarse gray tunics, with pewter buttons and worsted

braid lying on the hay-bales smoking their cigars. "Gentlemen," quoth he, very courteously, "you'll oblige me by not smoking over the hay. There's powder below." "I don't believe we're going to burn the hay this time, kernel," was the reply, "and anyway, we'll put it out afore it reaches the 'bustibles," and they went on smoking. The Major grumbled, and worse, and drew off. . . .

When we had shipped all our passengers, nine tenths of them in uniform, and a larger proportion engaged in chewing, the whistle blew, and the steamer sidled off from the quay into the yollowish muddy water of the Ashley River, which is a creek from the sea, with a streamlet running into the head waters some distance up. . . .

[*The account continues with Russell's experiences on Morris Island.*]

The whole of the island was full of life and excitement. Officers were galloping about as if on a field-day or in action. Commissariat carts were toiling to and fro between the beach and the camps, and sounds of laughter and revelling came from the tents. These were pitched without order, and were of all shapes, hues, and sizes, many being disfigured by rude charcoal drawings outside, and inscriptions such as "The Live Tigers," "Rattlesnake's-hole," "Yankee Smashers," &c. The vicinity of the camps was in an intolerable state, and on calling the attention of the medical officer who was with me, to the danger arising from such a condition of things, he said with a sigh, "I know it all. But we can do nothing. Remember they're all volunteers, and do just as they please."

In every tent was hospitality, and a hearty welcome to all comers. Cases of champagne and claret, French *pâtés,* and the like, were piled outside the canvas walls, when there was no room for them inside. In the middle of these excited gatherings I felt like a man in the full possession of his senses coming in late to a wine party. "Won't you drink with me, sir, to the—(something awful)—of Lincoln and all Yankees?" "No! if you'll be good enough to excuse me." "Well, I think you're the only Englishman who won't." Our Carolinians are very fine fellows, but a little given to the Bobadil style—hectoring after a cavalier fashion, which they fondly believe to be theirs by hereditary right. They assume that the British crown rests on a cotton bale, as the Lord Chancellor sits on a pack of wool.

In one long tent there was a party of roystering young men, opening claret, and mixing "cup" in large buckets; whilst others were helping the servants to set out a table for a banquet to one of their generals. Such heat, tobacco-smoke, clamor, toasts, drinking, hand-shaking, vows of friendship! Many were the excuses made for the more demonstrative of the Edonian youths by their friends. "Tom is a little cut,

sir; but he's a splendid fellow—he's worth half-a-million of dollars."
This reference to a money standard of value was not unusual or perhaps unnatural, but it was made repeatedly; and I was told wonderful
tales of the riches of men who were lounging round, dressed as privates, some of whom at that season, in years gone by, were looked
for at the watering places as the great lions of American fashion. But
Secession is the fashion here. Young ladies sing for it; old ladies pray
for it; young men are dying to fight for it; old men are ready to demonstrate it. The founder of the school was St. Calhoun. Here his pupils
carry out their teaching in thunder and fire. States' Rights are displayed after its legitimate teaching, and the Palmetto flag and the red
bars of the Confederacy are its exposition. The utter contempt and
loathing for the venerated Stars and Stripes, the abhorrence of the very
words United States, the intense hatred of the Yankee on the part of
these people, cannot be conceived by any one who has not seen them.
I am more satisfied than ever that the Union can never be restored as
it was, and that it has gone to pieces, never to be put together again,
in the old shape, at all events, by any power on earth. . . .

As the boat touched the quay of the fort [Sumter], a tall, powerful-
looking man came through the shattered gateway, and with uneven
steps strode over the rubbish towards a skiff which was waiting to receive him, and into which he jumped and rowed off. Recognizing one
of my companions as he passed our boat he suddenly stood up, and
with a leap and a scramble tumbled in among us, to the imminent danger of upsetting the party. Our new friend was dressed in the blue
frock-coat of a civilian, round which he had tied a red silk sash—his
waistbelt supported a straight sword, something like those worn with
Court dress. His muscular neck was surrounded with a loosely-fastened
silk handkerchief; and wild masses of black hair, tinged with gray,
fell from under a civilian's hat over his collar; his unstrapped trousers
were gathered up high on his legs, displaying ample boots, garnished
with formidable brass spurs. But his face was one not to be forgotten—
a straight, broad brow, from which the hair rose up like the vegetation
on a river bank, beetling black eyebrows—a mouth coarse and grim,
yet full of power, a square jaw—a thick argumentative nose—a new
growth of scrubby beard and mustache—these were relieved by eyes
of wonderful depth and light, such as I never saw before but in the
head of a wild beast. . . . It was flashing, fierce, yet calm—with a
well of fire burning behind and spouting through it, an eye pitiless in
anger, which now and then sought to conceal its expression beneath
half-closed lids, and then burst out with an angry glare, as if disdaining
concealment.

This was none other than Louis T. Wigfall, Colonel (then of his
own creation) in the Confederate army, and Senator from Texas in

the United States—a good type of the men whom the institutions of the country produce or throw off—a remarkable man, noted for his ready, natural eloquence; his exceeding ability as a quick, bitter debater; the acerbity of his taunts; and his readiness for personal encounter. . . . The other day, when the fire against Sumter was at its height, and the fort, in flames, was reduced almost to silence, a small boat put off from the shore, and steered through the shot and the splashing waters right for the walls. It bore the Colonel and a negro oarsman. Holding up a white handkerchief on the end of his sword, Wigfall landed on the quay, clambered through an embrasure, and presented himself before the astonished Federals with a proposal to surrender, quite unauthorized, and "on his own hook," which led to the final capitulation of Major Anderson.

I am sorry to say, our distinguished friend had just been paying his respects *sans bornes* to Bacchus or Bourbon, for he was decidedly unsteady in his gait and thick in speech; but his head was quite clear, and he was determined I should know all about his exploit. Major Whiting desired to show me round the work, but he had no chance. "Here is where I got in," quoth Colonel Wigfall. "I found a Yankee standing here by the traverse, out of the way of our shot. He was pretty well scared when he saw me, but I told him not to be alarmed, but to take me to the officers. There they were, huddled up in that corner behind the brickwork, for our shells were tumbling into the yard, and bursting like—" &c. (The Colonel used strong illustrations and strange expletives in narrative.) Major Whiting shook his military head, and said something uncivil to me, in private, in reference to volunteer colonels and the like, which gave him relief; whilst the martial Senator—I forgot to say that he has the name, particularly in the North, of having killed more than half a dozen men in duels—(I had an escape of being another)—conducted me through the casemates with uneven steps, stopping at every traverse to expatiate on some phase of his personal experiences, with his sword dangling between his legs, and spurs involved in rubbish and soldiers' blankets.

"I hear the ringing laugh of Stuart—the Prince of Cavaliers!"

John Esten Cooke (1830–86) was a Virginian, and from first to last his love was Virginia's history and her traditions. His family lived near Winchester, in the Shenandoah Valley, and he spent his early boyhood there with his older brother, Philip Pendleton Cooke, who, like him, was to become a writer. Later, after the family had moved to Richmond, he studied law in his father's law office, but though he was admitted to the Virginia bar in 1851, he found law dull. He was constantly tempted away from it by the desire to write, and his early career was a succession of broken resolutions to write no more. Keeping the resolutions was made doubly difficult by the success of his writing. Before the age of thirty he established a nation-wide reputation, largely through The Virginia Comedians *(1854), a novel of late colonial life in Williamsburg.*

Cooke was a wholehearted Secessionist and fought from the beginning of the war until he surrendered with Lee at Appomattox Courthouse. At the same time, he brought his pen to the aid of the Confederacy and, mixing writing with campaigning, produced a Life of Stonewall Jackson *in 1863. After the war he gave up law for good and all, married, and settled down to farming and to writing. The Wearing of the Gray (1867) and Hammer and Rapier (1870) are collections of historical essays on military subjects. The Heir of Gaymount (1870) is generally accepted as the best of his postwar novels, and Stories of the Old Dominion (1879) still makes absorbing reading for boys.*

Cooke could have found no subject more fitted to his pen than James Ewell Brown Stuart's famous ride around McClellan. Cooke was very much a chronicler—at heart his novels are social history—and he was usually an accurate one. Douglas Southall Freeman, in his account of Stuart's ride in Lee's Lieutenants, *leans heavily on Cooke's account and makes only one minor correction. At the same time Cooke was very much a Cavalier, and what he was chronicling was a way of life that was fast turning into a dream. The epitome of that life was Jeb Stuart, the darling of the South, who rode his handsome horses at such a furious pace that he wore them out one after another, whose gray tunic was lined with red, and whose hat was cocked on one side with a gilt star and bore a plume. In the Confederate forces he developed so*

295

efficient and so spirited a cavalry corps that he rose rapidly to the rank of major general. He contributed much to the Confederate victory at First Manassas. He made his reconnaissance forces so indispensable as the eyes and ears of Lee's army that his absence at Gettysburg is generally considered to have been one of the decisive factors in Lee's failure to gain a victory. He was mortally wounded at Yellow Tavern in May 1864, when, with a force of 4,500 men, he stood between 12,000 of Sherman's Sabres and the city of Richmond.

The passage below is slightly condensed from John Esten Cooke: The Wearing of the Gray; Being Personal Portraits, Scenes and Adventures of the War (*New York: S. B. Treat & Company; 1867*), *pp. 174–90.*

I

Who that went with Stuart on his famous "Ride around McClellan" in the summer of 1862, just before the bloody battles of the Chickahominy, will ever forget the fun, the frolic, the romance—and the peril too—of that fine journey? Thinking of the gay ride now, when a century seems to have swept between that epoch and the present, I recall every particular, live over every emotion. Once more I hear the ringing laugh of Stuart, and see the keen flash of the blue eyes under the black feather of the prince of cavaliers!

If the reader will follow me he shall see what took place on this rapid ride, witness some incidents of this first and king of raids. The record will be that of an eye-witness, and the personal prominence of the writer must be excused as inseparable from the narrative. I need not dwell upon the "situation" in June, 1862. All the world knows that, at that time, McClellan had advanced with his magnificent army of 156,000 men, to the banks of the Chickahominy, and pushing across, had fought on the last day of May the bloody but indecisive battle of the Seven Pines. On the right it was a Confederate, on the left a Federal success; and General McClellan drew back, marshalled his great lines, darkening both the northern and southern banks of the Chickahominy, and prepared for a more decisive blow at the Confederate capital, whose spires were in sight. Before him, however, lay the Southern army, commanded now by Lee, who had succeeded Johnston, wounded in the fight of "Seven Pines." The moment was favourable for a heavy attack by Lee. Jackson had just driven before him the combined forces of Shields and Fremont, and on the bloody field of Port Republic ended the great campaign of the Valley at one blow. The veterans of his command could now be concentrated on the banks of the Chickahominy against McClellan; a combined advance of the forces under Lee and Jackson might save the capital. But how should the attack be made? In council of war, General Stuart told me he proposed an assault upon General McClellan's left wing from the direction of James River, to cut him off from that base. But this suggestion was not adopted; the defences were regarded as too strong. It was considered a better plan to attack the Federal army on the north bank of the Chickahominy, drive it from its works, and try the issue in the fields around Cold Harbour. The great point was to ascertain if this was practicable, and especially to find what defences, if any, the enemy had to guard the approach to their right wing. If these were slight, the attack could be made with fair prospects of success. Jackson could sweep around while Lee assailed the lines near Mechanicsville; then one combined assault would probably defeat the Federal force. To find the character of the enemy's works beyond the stream—his positions and movements—General Stuart was directed to take a portion of his cavalry, advance as far as Old Church, if practicable, and then be guided by circumstances. Such were the orders with which Stuart set out about moonrise on the night, I think, of June 12, upon this dangerous expedition.

As the young cavalier mounted his horse on that moonlight night he was a gallant figure to look at. The gray coat buttoned to the chin; the light French sabre balanced by the pistol in its black holster; the cavalry boots above the knee, and the brown hat with its black plume floating above the bearded features, the brilliant eyes, and the huge moustache, which curled with laughter at the slightest provocation—these made Stuart the perfect picture of a gay cavalier, and the spirited horse he rode seemed to feel that he carried one whose motto was to "do or die." I chanced to be his sole companion as he galloped over the broad field near his headquarters, and the glance of the blue eyes of Stuart at that moment was as brilliant as the lightning itself.

Catching up with his column of about 1500 horsemen, and two pieces of horse-artillery under Colonels William H. F. Lee, Fitz Lee, and Will. T. Martin, of Mississippi—cavaliers as brave as ever drew sabre—Stuart pushed on northward as if going to join Jackson, and reaching the vicinity of Taylorsville, near Hanover Junction, went that night into bivouac. He ambraced the opportunity, after midnight, of riding with Colonel W. H. F. Lee to "Hickory Hill," the residence of Colonel Williams Wickham—afterward General Wickham—who had been recently wounded and paroled. Here he went to sleep in his chair after talking with Colonel Wickham, narrowly escaped capture from the enemy near, and returning before daylight, advanced with his column straight upon Hanover Court-House. Have you ever visited this picturesque spot, reader? We looked upon it on that day of June—upon its old brick court-house, where Patrick Henry made his famous speech against the parsons, its ancient tavern, its modest roofs, the whole surrounded by the fertile fields waving with golden grain—all this we looked at with unusual interest. For in this little bird's nest, lost as it were in a sea of rippling wheat and waving foliage, some "Yankee cavalry" had taken up their abode; their horses stood ready saddled in the street, and this dark mass we now gazed at furtively from behind a wooden knoll, in rear of which Stuart's column was drawn up ready to move at the word. Before he gave the signal, the General dispatched Colonel Fitz Lee round to the right, to flank and cut off the party. But all at once the scouts in front were descried by the enemy; shots resounded; and seeing that his presence was discovered, Stuart gave the word, and swept at a thundering gallop down the hill. The startled "blue birds," as we used to call our Northern friends, did not wait; the squadron on picket at the court-house, numbering some one hundred and fifty men, hastily got to horse—then presto! they disappear in a dense cloud of dust from which echo some parting salutes from their carbines. Stuart pressed on rapidly, took the road to Old Church, and near a place called Hawes' Shop, in a thickly wooded spot, was suddenly charged himself. It did not amount to much, and seemed rather an attempt at reconnaissance. A Federal officer at the head of a detachment came on at full gallop, very nearly ran into the head of our column, and then seeing the dense mass of gray coats, fired his pistol, wheeled short about, and went back at full speed, with his detachment.

Stuart had given, in his ringing voice, the order: "Form fours! draw sabre! charge!" and now the Confederate people pursued at headlong speed, uttering shouts and yells sufficiently loud to awaken the seven sleepers! The men were evidently exhilarated by the chase, the enemy just keeping near enough to make an occasional shot practicable. A considerable number of the Federal cavalrymen were overtaken and captured, and these proved to belong to the company in which Colonel Fitz Lee had formerly been a lieutenant. I could not refrain from laughter at the pleasure which "Colonel Fitz"—whose motto should be *"toujours gai"*—seemed to take in inquiring after his old cronies. "Was Brown alive? where was Jones? and was Robinson sergeant still?" Colonel Fitz never stopped until he found out everything. The prisoners laughed as they recognised him. Altogether, reader, the interview was the most friendly imaginable.

The gay chase continued until we reached the Tottapotamoi, a sluggish stream, dragging its muddy waters slowly between rush-clad banks, beneath drooping trees; and this was crossed by a small rustic bridge. The line of the stream was entirely undefended by works; the enemy's right wing was unprotected; Stuart had accomplished the object of his expedition, and afterward piloted Jackson over this very same road. But to continue the narrative of his movements. The picket at the bridge had been quickly driven in, and disappeared at a gallop, and on the high ground beyond, Colonel W. H. F. Lee, who had taken the front, encountered the enemy. The force appeared to be about a regiment, and they were drawn up in line of battle in the fields to receive our attack. It came without delay. Placing himself at the head of his horsemen, Colonel Lee swept forward at the *pas de charge*, and with shouts the two lines came together. The shock was heavy, and the enemy—a portion of the old United States Regulars, commanded by Captain Royal—stood their ground bravely, meeting the attack with the sabre. Swords clashed, pistols and carbines banged, yells, shouts, cheers resounded; then the Federal line was seen to give back, and take to headlong flight. They were pursued with ardour, and the men were wild with this—to many of them—their first fight. But soon after all joy disappeared from their faces, at sight of a spectacle which greeted them. Captain Latanè, of the Essex cavalry, had been mortally wounded in the charge, and as the men of his company saw him lying bloody before them, many a bearded face was wet with tears. The scene at his grave afterward became the subject of Mr. Washington's picture, "The Burial of Latanè"; and in his general order after the expedition, Stuart called upon his command to take for their watchword in the future "*Avenge Latanè!*" Captain Royal, the Federal commandant, had also been badly wounded, and many of his force killed. I remember passing a Dutch cavalryman who was writhing with a bullet through the breast, and biting and tearing up the ground. He called for water, and I directed a servant at a house near by to bring him some. The last I saw of him, a destitute cavalryman was taking off his spurs as he was dying. War is a hard trade.

Fitz Lee immediately pressed on and burst into the camp near Old Church, where large supplies of boots, pistols, liquors, and other commodities were found. These were speedily appropriated by the men, and the tents were set on fire amid loud shouts. The spectacle was animating; but a report having got abroad that one of the tents contained powder, the vicinity thereof was evacuated in almost less than no time. We were now at Old Church, where Stuart was to be guided in his further movements by circumstances. I looked at him; he was evidently reflecting. In a moment he turned round to me and said: "Tell Fitz Lee to come along, I'm going to move on with my column." These words terminated my doubt, and I understood in an instant that the General had decided on the bold and hazardous plan of passing entirely round McClellan's army.

"I think the quicker we move now the better," I said, with a laugh.

"Right," was Stuart's reply; "tell the column to move on at a trot."
So at a rapid trot the column moved.

II

The gayest portion of the raid now began. From this moment it
was neck or nothing, do or die. We had one chance of escape against
ten of capture or destruction.

Stuart had decided upon his course with that rapidity, good judgment, and decision, which were the real secrets of his splendid efficiency as a leader of cavalry, in which capacity I believe that he has
never been surpassed, either in the late war or any other. He was now
in the very heart of the enemy's citadel, with their enormous masses
upon every side. He had driven in their advanced force, passed within
sight of the white tents of General McClellan's headquarters, burned
their camps, and ascertained all that he wished. How was he to return?
He could not cross the Pamunkey, and make a circuit back; he had no
pontoons. He could not return over the route by which he had advanced. As events afterward showed, the alarm had been given, and
an overpowering force of infantry, cavalry, and artillery had been
rapidly moved in that direction to intercept the daring raider. Capture
stared him in the face, on both of these routes—across the Pamunkey,
or back as he came; he must find some other loophole of escape.

Such was the dangerous posture of affairs, and such was the important problem which Stuart decided in five minutes. He determined to
make the complete circuit of McClellan's army; and crossing the
Chickahominy below Long Bridge, re-enter the Confederate lines from
Charles City. If on his way he encountered cavalry he intended to
fight it; if a heavy force of infantry barred his way he would elude,
or cut a path through it; if driven to the wall and debarred from escape
he did not mean to surrender. A few days afterward I said to him:

"That was a tight place at the river, General. If the enemy had come
down on us, you would have been compelled to have surrendered."

"No," was his reply; "one other course was left."

"What was that?"

"To *die game*."

And I know that such was his intention. When a commander means
to die game rather than surrender he is a dangerous adversary.

From Old Church onward it was *terra incognita*. What force of the
enemy barred the road was a question of the utmost interest, but adventure of some description might be safely counted on. In about
twenty-four hours I, for one, expected either to be laughing with my
friends within the Southern lines, or dead, or captured. Which of these

three results would follow, seemed largely to depend upon the "chapter of accidents." At a steady trot now, with drawn sabres and carbines ready, the cavalry, followed by the horse-artillery, which was not used during the whole expedition, approached Tunstall's Station on the York River railroad, the enemy's direct line of communication with his base of supplies at the "White House."

Everywhere the ride was crowded with incident. The scouting and flanking parties constantly picked up stragglers, and overhauled unsuspecting wagons filled with the most tempting stores. In this manner a wagon, stocked with champagne and every variety of wines, belonging to a General of the Federal army, fell a prey to the thirsty graybacks. Still they pressed on. Every moment an attack was expected in front or rear. Colonel Will. T. Martin commanded the latter. "Tell Colonel Martin," Stuart said to me, "to have his artillery ready, and look out for an attack at any moment." I had delivered the message and was riding to the front again, when suddenly a loud cry arose of "Yankees in the rear!" Every sabre flashed, fours were formed, the men wheeled about, when all at once a stunning roar of laughter ran along the line; it was a *canard*. The column moved up again with its flanking parties well out. The men composing the latter were, many of them, from the region, and for the first time for months saw their mothers and sisters. These went quite wild at sight of their sons and brothers. They laughed and cried, and on the appearance of the long gray column instead of the familiar blue coats of the Federal cavalry, they clapped their hands and fell into ecstasies of delight. One young lady was seen to throw her arms around a brother she had not before met for a long time, bursting into alternate sobs and laughter.

The column was now skirting the Pamunkey, and a detachment hurried off to seize and burn two or three transports lying in the river. Soon a dense cloud rose from them, the flames soared up, and the column pushed on. Everywhere were seen the traces of flight—for the alarm of "hornets in the hive" was given. Wagons had turned over, and were abandoned—from others the excellent army stores had been hastily thrown. This writer got a fine red blanket, and an excellent pair of cavalry pantaloons, for which he still owes the United States. Other things lay about in tempting array, but we were approaching Tunstall's, where the column would doubtless make a charge; and to load down a weary horse was injudicious. The advance guard was now in sight of the railroad. There was no question about the affair before us. The column must cut through, whatever force guarded the railroad; to reach the lower Chickahominy the guard here must be overpowered. Now was the time to use the artillery, and every effort was made to hurry it forward. But alas! it had got into a tremendous mudhole, and the wheels were buried to the axle. The horses were lashed, and jumped, almost breaking the traces; the drivers swore; the harness cracked—but the guns did not move. "Gat! Lieutenant," said a sergeant of Dutch origin to the brave Lieutenant McGregor, "it can't be done. But just put that keg on the gun, Lieutenant," pointing, as he spoke, to a keg of whiskey in an ambulance, the spoil of the Federal camp, "and tell the men they can have it if they only pull through!" McGregor laughed, and the keg was quickly perched on the gun. Then took place an exhibition of herculean muscularity which would have delighted Guy Livingston. With eyes fixed ardently upon the keg, the powerful cannoneers waded into the mudhole up to their knees, seized the wheels of gun and caisson loaded down with ammunition, and just simply lifted the whole out, and put them on firm ground. The piece whirled on—the keg had been dismounted—the cannoneers revelled in the spoils they had earned.

Tunstall's was now nearly in sight, and that good fellow Captain Frayser, afterward Stuart's signal officer, came back and reported one or two companies of infantry at the railroad. Their commander had politely beckoned to him as he reconnoitred, exclaiming in wheedling accents, full of Teutonic blandishment, "Koom yay!" But this cordial invitation was disregarded; Frayser galloped back and reported, and the ringing voice of Stuart ordered "Form platoons! draw sabre! charge!" At the word the sabres flashed, a thundering shout arose, and sweeping on in column of platoons, the gray people fell upon their blue adversaries, gobbling them up, almost without a shot. It was here that my friend Major F— got the hideous little wooden pipe he used to smoke afterward. He had been smoking a meerschaum when the order to charge was given; and in the rush of the horsemen, dropped and lost it. He now wished to smoke, and seeing that the captain of the Federal infantry had just filled his pipe, leaned down from the saddle, and politely requested him to surrender it.

"I want to smoke!" growled the Federal captain.

"So do I," retorted Major F—.

"This pipe is my property," said the captain.

"Oh! what a mistake!" responded the major politely, as he gently took the small affair and inserted it between his lips. Anything more hideous than the carved head upon it I never saw.

The men swarmed upon the railroad. Quick axes were applied to the telegraph poles, which crashed down, and Redmond Burke went in command of a detachment to burn a small bridge on the railroad near. Suddenly in the midst of the tumult was heard the shrill whistle of a train coming from the direction of the Chickahominy. Stuart quickly drew up his men in a line on the side of the road, and he had no sooner done so than the train came slowly round a wooded bend, and bore down. When within two hundred yards it was ordered to halt, but the command was not obeyed. The engineer crowded on all steam; the train rushed on, and then a thundering volley was opened upon the "flats" containing officers and men. The engineer was shot by Captain Farley, of Stuart's staff, and a number of the soldiers were wounded. The rest threw themselves upon their faces; the train rushed headlong by like some frightened monster bent upon escape, and in an instant it had disappeared.

Stuart then reflected for a single moment. The question was, should he go back and attack the White House, where enormous stores were piled up? It was tempting, and he afterwards told me he could scarcely resist it. But a considerable force of infantry was posted there; the firing had doubtless given them the alarm; and the attempt was too hazardous. The best thing for that gray column was to set their faces toward home, and "keep moving," well closed up both day and night, for the lower Chickahominy. So Stuart pushed on. Beyond the railroad appeared a world of wagons, loaded with grain and coffee—standing in the road abandoned. Quick work was made of them. They were all set on fire, and their contents destroyed. From the horse-trough of one I rescued a small volume bearing on the fly-leaf the name of a young lady of Williamsburg. I think it was a volume of poems—poetic wagon-drivers!

These wagons were only the "vaunt couriers"—the advance guard— of the main body. In a field beyond the stream thirty acres were covered with them. They were all burned. The roar of the soaring flames was like the sound of a forest on fire. How they roared and crackled! The sky overhead, when night had descended, was bloody-looking in the glare.

Meanwhile the main column had moved on, and I was riding after it, when I heard the voice of Stuart in the darkness exclaiming with strange agitation:

"Who is here?"

"I am," I answered; and as he recognised my voice he exclaimed:

"Good! where is Rooney Lee?"

"I think he has moved on, General."

"Do you *know* it?" came in the same agitated tone.

"No, but I believe it."

"Will you *swear to it?* I must know! He may take the wrong road, and the column will get separated!"

"I will ascertain if he is in front."

"Well, do so; but take care—you will be captured!"

I told the General I would "gallop on for ever till I found him," but I had not gone two hundred yards in the darkness when hoof-strokes in front were heard, and I ordered:

"Halt! who goes there?"

"Courier, from Colonel William Lee."

"Is he in front?"

"About a mile, sir."

"Good!" exclaimed the voice of Stuart, who had galloped up; and I never heard in human accents such an expression of relief. If the reader of this has ever commanded cavalry, moving at night in an enemy's country, he will understand why Stuart drew that long, deep breath, and uttered that brief word, "Good!" Once separated from the main column and lost—good-by then to Colonel Lee!

Pushing on by large hospitals which were not interfered with, we reached at midnight the three or four houses known as Talleysville; and here a halt was ordered to rest men and horses, and permit the artillery to come up. This pause was fatal to a sutler's store from which the owners had fled. It was remorselessly ransacked and the edibles consumed. This historian ate in succession figs, beef-tongue, pickle, candy, tomato catsup, preserves, lemons, cakes, sausages, molasses, crackers, and canned meats. In presence of these attractive commodities the spirits of many rose. Those who in the morning had made me laugh by saying, "General Stuart is going to get his command destroyed—this movement is mad," now regarded Stuart as the first of men; the raid as a feat of splendour and judicious daring which could not fail in terminating successfully. Such is the difference in the views of the military machine, unfed and fed.

III

In an hour the column moved again. Meanwhile a little incident had happened which still makes me laugh. There was a lady living some miles off in the enemy's line whom I wished to visit, but I could not obtain the General's consent. "It is certain capture," he said; "send her a note by some citizen, say Dr. H—; he lives near here." This I determined to do, and set off at a gallop through the monlight for the house, some half a mile distant, looking out for the scouting parties which were probably prowling on our flanks. Reaching the lonely house, outside the pickets, I dismounted, knocked at the front door, then the back, but received no answer. All at once, however, a dark figure was seen gliding beneath the trees, and this figure cautiously approached. I recognised the Doctor, and called to him, whereupon he quickly approached, and said, "I thought you were a Yankee!" and greeting me cordially, led the way into the house. Here I wrote my note and entrusted it to him for delivery—taking one from him to his wife, within our lines. In half an hour I rode away, but before doing so asked for some water, which was brought from the well by a sleepy, sullen, and insolent negro. This incident was fruitful of woes to Dr. H—! A month or two afterwards I met him looking as thin and white as a ghost.

"What is the matter?" I said.

"The matter is," he replied, with a melancholy laugh, "that I have been starving for three weeks in Fortress Monroe on your account. Do you remember that servant who brought you the water that night on Stuart's raid?"

"Perfectly."

"Well, the very next day he went over to the Yankee picket and told them that I had entertained Confederate officers, and given you all information which enabled you to get off safely. In consequence I was arrested, carried to Old Point, and am just out!"

I rejoined the column at Talleysville just as it began to move on the road to Forge Bridge. The highway lay before us, white in the unclouded splendour of the moon. The critical moment was yet to come. Our safety was to turn apparently on a throw of the dice, rattled in the hand of Chance. The exhaustion of the march now began to tell on the men. Whole companies went to sleep in the saddle, and Stuart himself was no exception. He had thrown one knee over the pommel of his saddle, folded his arms, dropped the bridle, and—chin on breast, his plumed hat drooping over his forehead—was sound asleep. His sure-footed horse moved steadily, but the form of the General tottered from side to side, and for miles I held him erect by the arm. The column thus moved on during the remainder of the night, the wary advance guard encountering no enemies and giving no alarm. At the first streak of dawn the Chickahominy was in sight, and Stuart was spurring forward *to the ford*.

It was impassable! The heavy rains had so swollen the waters that the crossing was utterly impracticable! Here we were within a few miles of McClellan's army, with an enraged enemy rushing on our track to make us rue the day we had "circumvented" them, and inflicted on them such injury and insult; here we were with a swollen and impassable stream directly in our front—the angry waters roaring around the half-submerged trunks of the trees—and expecting every instant to hear the crack of carbines from the rear-guard indicating the enemy's approach! The "situation" was not pleasing. I certainly thought that the enemy would be upon us in about an hour, and death or capture would be the sure alternative. This view was general. I found that cool and resolute officer, Colonel William H. F. Lee, on the river's bank. He had just attempted to swim the river, and nearly drowned his horse among the tangled roots and snags. I said to him:

305

"What do you think of the situation, Colonel?"

"Well, Captain," was the reply, in the speaker's habitual tone of cheerful courtesy, "I think we are caught."

The men evidently shared this sentiment. The scene upon the river's bank was curious, and under other circumstances would have been laughable. The men lay about in every attitude, half-overcome with sleep, but holding their bridles, and ready to mount at the first alarm. Others sat their horses asleep, with drooping shoulders. Some gnawed crackers; others ate figs, or smoked, or yawned. Things looked "blue," and that colour was figuratively spread over every countenance. When this writer assumed a gay expression of countenance, laughed, and told the men it was "all right," they looked at him as sane men regard a lunatic! The general conviction evidently was that "all right" was the very last phrase by which to describe the situation.

There was only one man who never desponded, or bated one "jot or tittle of the heart of hope." That was Stuart. I had never been with him in a tight place before, but from that moment I felt convinced that he was one of those men who rise under pressure. He was aroused, strung for the hard struggle before him, and resolute to do or die; but he was not excited. All I noticed in his bearing to attract attention was a peculiar fashion of twisting his beard, certain proof with him of surrounding peril. Otherwise he was cool and looked dangerous. He said a few words to Colonel Lee, found the ford impassable, and then ordering his column to move on, galloped down the stream to a spot where an old bridge had formerly stood. Reaching this point, a strong rear-guard was thrown out, the artillery placed in position, and Stuart set to work vigorously to rebuild the bridge, determined to bring out his guns or die trying.

The bridge had been destroyed, but the stone abutments remained some thirty or forty feet only apart, for the river here ran deep and narrow between steep banks. Between these stone sentinels, facing each other, was an "aching void" which it was necessary to fill. Stuart gave his personal superintendence to the work, he and his staff labouring with the men. A skiff was procured; this was affixed by a rope to a tree, in the mid-current just above the abutments, and thus a movable pier was secured in the middle of the stream. An old barn was then hastily torn to pieces and robbed of its timbers; these were stretched down to the boat, and up to the opposite abutment, and a foot-bridge was thus ready. Large numbers of the men immediately unsaddled their horses, took their equipments over, and then returning, drove or rode their horses into the stream, and swam them over. In this manner a considerable number crossed; but the process was much too slow. There, besides, was the artillery, which Stuart had no intention of leaving. A

306

regular bridge must be built without a moment's delay, and to this work Stuart now applied himself with ardour.

Heavier blows resounded from the old barn; huge timbers approached, borne on brawny shoulders, and descending into the boat anchored in the middle of the stream, the men lifted them across. They were just long enough; the ends rested on the abutments, and immediately thick planks were hurried forward and laid crosswise, forming a secure footway for the cavalry and artillery horses. Standing in the boat beneath, Stuart worked with the men, and as the planks thundered down, and the bridge steadily advanced, the gay voice of the General was heard humming a song. He was singing carelessly, although at every instant an overpowering force of the enemy was looked for, and a heavy attack upon the disordered cavalry.

At last the bridge was finished; the artillery crossed amid hurrahs from the men, and then Stuart slowly moved his cavalry across the shaky footway. A little beyond was another arm of the river, which was, however, fordable, as I ascertained and reported to the General; the water just deep enough to swim a small horse; and through this, as through the interminable sloughs of the swamp beyond, the head of the column moved. The prisoners, who were numerous, had been marched over in advance of everything, and these were now mounted on mules, of which several hundred had been cut from the captured wagons and brought along. They were started under an escort across the ford, and into the swamp beyond. Here, mounted often two on a mule, they had a disagreeable time; the mules constantly falling in the treacherous mud-holes, and rolling their riders in the ooze. When a third swamp appeared before them, one of the Federal prisoners exclaimed, with tremendous indignation, "How many d—d *Chicken*-hominies are there, I wonder, in this infernal country!"

The rear-guard, under Colonel W. H. F. Lee, had meanwhile moved down steadily from the high ground, and defiled across the bridge. The hoofs clattered on the hasty structure, the head of the column was turned toward the ford beyond, the last squadron had just passed, and the bridge was being destroyed, when shots resounded on the opposite bank of the stream, and Colonel Rush thundered down with his "lancers" to the bank. He was exactly ten minutes too late. Stuart was over with his artillery, and the swollen stream barred the way, even if Colonel Rush thought it prudent to "knock up against" the one thousand five hundred crack cavalry of Stuart. His men banged away at Colonel Lee, and a parting salute whizzed through the trees as the gray column slowly disappeared.

A lady of New Kent afterwards told me that Colonel Rush stopped at her house on his return, looking weary, broken down, and out of humour. When she asked him if he had "caught Stuart," he replied, "No, he has gone in at the back door. I only saw his rear-guard as it passed the swamp."

IV

Stuart had thus eluded his pursuers, and was over the Chickahominy in the hospitable county of Charles City. The gentlemen of the county, we afterwards heard, had been electrified by the rumour that "Stuart was down at the river trying to get across," and had built a hasty bridge for us lower down. We were over, however, and reaching Mr. C—'s, the General and his staff lay down on a carpet spread on the grass in the June sunshine, and went to sleep. This was Sunday. I had not slept since Friday night, except by snatches in the saddle, and in going on to Richmond afterwards fell asleep every few minutes on horseback.

Two hours of slumber, however, made Stuart as fresh as a lark; and having eaten Mr. C— very nearly out of house and home, we pushed on all day. At night the column stopped, and I thought the General would stop too; but he said, "I am going to Richmond to-night; would you like to ride with me?" I was obliged to decline; my horse was worn out. Stuart set out by himself, rode all night, and before daylight had passed over the thirty miles. An hour afterwards General Lee and the President knew the result of his expedition. The cavalry returned on the same day, moving slowly in front of the gunboats, which fired upon them; but no harm was done. Richmond was reached; and amid an ovation from delighted friends we all went to sleep.

Pickett's Charge at Gettysburg

Pickett's charge on Cemetery Hill has become legend. Every school-boy knows of it and recognizes it, however dimly, as a concentration of the South's long tradition of military glory in one brilliantly heroic and tragic moment. But Pickett's charge reflects the Southern military tradition in another way, less commonly known, for behind it lay a clash of judgment between two of the Confederacy's most capable

generals, Longstreet and Lee. Behind it too, almost regrettably, there lay Longstreet's unshaken loyalty to Lee, even in disagreement.

James Longstreet offers sharp contrast to the dashing Confederate generals of Jeb Stuart's stamp. He was a calm and quiet man who grew more quiet still after losing three of his children in an epidemic. There was nothing morose in his quietness, only a dominating sense of duty and an iron control of nerve. At the height of the battle the third day at Gettysburg, just before Pickett's crucial charge was to be launched, he lay down on the battlefield and slept. He was a capable administrator, solid and systematic in everything he did. His qualities won the respect of his subordinate officers, and his soldiers affectionately called him "Old Pete." To his superior, Lee, he rendered in turn the same affection and respect.

On the morning of July 3, 1863, when this account opens, the Confederate and Union armies lay facing each other on two of the long, gentle ridges that run south from the town of Gettysburg. The Union Army lay on Cemetery Ridge, stretching in a long line northward from strong emplacements in two rocky hills, Round Top and Little Round Top, until it looped eastward in a hook just south of Gettysburg itself. At about its center was Cemetery Hill, for which the ridge was named. The Confederate forces lay in a parallel line some 1,400 yards to the west on Seminary Ridge and, following the pattern of the Union lines, looped in a still larger hook eastward through the outskirts of Gettysburg. Lee felt that he had no alternative but to attack the Union center. Longstreet felt that such an attack was doomed to failure and that the most promising strategy was to swing Confederate forces around the end of the hook and attack the Union right, from behind. Unable to persuade Lee to change his plans, Longstreet was faced with having to order Pickett's division into an attack he was convinced would fail. It did fail, and that night the Confederate forces began the long retreat from Gettysburg.

The following account is Longstreet's own. It is an excerpt from "Lee in Pennsylvania," Longstreet's contribution to The Annals of the War Written by Leading Participants, North and South; *Originally Published in the Philadelphia Weekly Times (Philadelphia: The Times Publishing Company; 1879). It appears on pages 429–31.*

I DID not see General Lee that night. On the next morning he came to see me, and, fearing that he was still in his disposition to attack, I tried to anticipate him, by saying: "General, I have had my scouts out all night, and I find that you still have an excellent opportunity to move around to the right of Meade's army, and maneuvre him into attacking us." He replied, pointing with his fist at Cemetery Hill: "The enemy is there, and I am going to strike him." I felt then that it was my duty to express my convictions; I said: "General, I have been a soldier all my life. I have been with soldiers engaged in fights by couples, by squads, companies, regiments, divisions, and armies, and should know, as well as any one, what soldiers can do. It is my opinion that no fifteen thousand men ever arrayed for battle can take that position," pointing to Cemetery Hill. General Lee, in reply to this, ordered me to prepare Pickett's Division for the attack. I should not have been so urgent had I not foreseen the hopelessness of the proposed assault. I felt that I must say a word against the sacrifice of my men; and then I felt that my record was such that General Lee would or could not misconstrue my motives. I said no more, however, but turned away. The most of the morning was consumed in waiting for Pickett's men, and getting into position. The plan of assault was as follows: Our artillery was to be massed in a wood from which Pickett was to charge, and it was to pour a continuous fire upon the cemetery. Under cover of this fire, and supported by it, Pickett was to charge.

Our artillery was in charge of General E. P. Alexander, a brave and gifted officer. Colonel Walton was my chief of artillery; but Alexander, being at the head of the column, and being first in position, and being, beside, an officer of unusual promptness, sagacity, and intelligence, was given charge of the artillery. The arrangements were completed about one o'clock. General Alexander had arranged that a battery of seven eleven-pound howitzers, with fresh horses and full caissons, were to charge with Pickett, at the head of his line, but General Pendleton, from whom the guns had been borrowed, recalled them just before the charge was made, and thus deranged this wise plan. Never was I so depressed as upon that day. I felt that my men were to be sacrificed, and that I should have to order them to make a hopeless charge. I had instructed General Alexander, being unwilling to trust myself with the entire responsibility, to carefully observe the effect of the fire upon the enemy, and when it began to tell to notify Pickett to begin the assault. I was so much impressed with the hopelessness of the charge, that I wrote the following note to General Alexander: "If the artillery fire does not have the effect to drive off the enemy or greatly demoralize him, so as to make our efforts pretty certain, I would prefer that you should not advise General Pickett to make the charge. I shall rely a great deal on your judgment to determine the matter, and shall expect you to let Pickett know when the moment offers."

To my note the General replied as follows: "I will only be able to judge the effect of our fire upon the enemy by his return fire, for his infantry is but little exposed to view, and the smoke will obscure the whole field. If, as I infer from your note, there is an alternative to this attack, it should be carefully considered before opening our fire, for it will take all of the artillery ammunition we have left to test this one thoroughly; and, if the result is unfavorable, we will have none left for another effort; and, even if this is entirely successful, it can only be so at a very bloody cost." I still desired to save my men, and felt that if the artillery did not produce the desired effect, I would be justified in holding Pickett off. I wrote this note to Colonel Walton at exactly 1.30 P.M.: "Let the batteries open. Order great precision in firing. If the batteries at the peach orchard cannot be used against the point we intend attacking, let them open on the enemy at Rocky Hill." The cannonading which opened along both lines was grand. In a few moments a courier brought a note to General Pickett (who was standing near me) from Alexander, which, after reading, he handed to me. It was as follows: "If you are coming at all, you must come at once, or I cannot give you proper support; but the enemy's fire has not slackened at all; at least eighteen guns are still firing from the cemetery itself." After I had read the note, Pickett said to me: "General, shall I advance?" My feelings had so overcome me that I would not speak, for fear of betraying my want of confidence to him. I bowed affirmation, and turned to mount my horse. Pickett immediately said: "I shall lead my division forward, sir." I spurred my horse to the wood where Alexander was stationed with artillery. When I reached him, he told me of the disappearance of the seven guns which were to have led the charge with Pickett, and that his ammunition was so low that he could not properly support the charge. I at once ordered him to stop Pickett until the ammunition had been replenished. He informed me that he had no ammunition with which to replenish. I then saw that there was no help for it, and that Pickett must advance under his orders. He swept past our artillery in splendid style, and the men marched steadily and compactly down the slope. As they started up the ridge, over one hundred cannon from the breastworks of the Federals hurled a rain of canister, grape, and shell down upon them; still they pressed on until half way up the slope, when the crest of the hill was lit with a solid sheet of flame as the masses of infantry rose and fired. When the smoke cleared away, Pickett's Division was gone. Nearly two-thirds of his men lay dead on the field, and the survivors were sullenly retreating down the hill. Mortal man could not have stood that fire. In half an hour the contested field was cleared and the battle of Gettysburg was over.

"Will you falter now?"

As the war dragged on and the exuberant confidence with which the South had entered the battle ebbed away, more and more of the volunteers failed to join again when their enlistments ran out, more and more men overstayed leaves, and the desertion figures grew. The effort to keep the military spirit alive led to such appeals as the following plea to the men of Hood's division. It was printed as a small broadside.

Hd. Qrs. Hood's Division

Feb. 11th, 1864

Soldiers of Hood's Division: Your country calls you! Will you not give a willing response, in her hour of peril? Her insolent foemen proclaim her subjugation in the next six months; and their veterans are re-enlisting to insure this. Your sisters, your wives, and your mothers pray your protection from a fate too horrible to contemplate. Your comrades in Virginia are acting: Rhodes' Division has re-enlisted for the war, and the Congress of our country assures them "that their country will always bear in grateful remembrance the noble manner in which they have come to her assistance in the hour of her need." Will you, soldiers of a Division whose name is now a household word, be backward in giving assurance to the noble women of our common country, that you will CONTINUE to stand a bulwark against their hated foe! Will you falter now after daring so much; will you let it go down to posterity that any Division was MORE WILLING to serve than Hood's? In the name of our country I call upon you to re-enlist, confounding the confident enemy and showing to the world that you value freedom and will devote your lives to win it for your loved ones. Let us not await the law that forces service, but *give a willing offering to our country.*

Upon the re-enlistment of your Regiments your commanding General will feel strong enough to furlough ten per cent. of you, and a grateful country will bless you.

M. Jenkins, *Brig. Gen'l.*
Commanding.

"There was not a man in the Confederacy whose influence . . . was as great as his"

It may seem inappropriate, in a Southern reader, that Lee's surrender at Appomattox should be reported by Grant, but Lee wrote no memoir, and even had he done so, he could not have left us the most distinctive thing in Grant's account: the respect and admiration felt by a victor for the man whom he had beaten. The personality of Lee is alive beneath the simple restraint of Grant's words. The Union general had won a great military victory and was dictating the terms, but his own account makes it clear that Lee's quiet and gentlemanly bearing governed the way those terms were dictated.

Grant wrote his Personal Memoirs *in the last year of his life. From the beginning his career had been a succession of alternate brilliant successes and dismal failures, and in 1884, having been supreme commander of the Union forces and later President of the United States, he was penniless again. Encouraged by Mark Twain, he set about recouping his fortunes by writing his memoirs, though he was suffering under the torture of cancer and knew he was dying. He dictated the book at first, until his disease made it impossible for him to speak, and then he wrote. He finished the memoirs four days before he died, in July 1885.*

The passage below is selected from Personal Memoirs of U. S. Grant *(2 vols.; New York: Charles L. Webster & Company; 1885–6) Vol. II, pp. 489–98.*

WHEN I had left camp that morning I had not expected so soon the result that was then taking place, and consequently was in rough garb. I was without a sword, as I usually was when on horseback on the field, and wore a soldier's blouse for a coat, with the shoulder straps of my rank to indicate to the army who I was. When I went into the house I found General Lee. We greeted each other, and after shaking hands took our seats. I had my staff with me, a good portion of whom were in the room during the whole of the interview.

What General Lee's feelings were I do not know. As he was a man of much dignity, with an impassible face, it was impossible to say whether he felt inwardly glad that the end had finally come, or felt sad over the result, and was too manly to show it. Whatever his feelings, they were entirely concealed from my observation; but my own feelings, which had been quite jubilant on the receipt of his letter, were sad and depressed. I felt like anything rather than rejoicing at the downfall of a foe who had fought so long and valiantly, and had suffered so much for a cause, though that cause was, I believe, one of the worst for which a people ever fought, and one for which there was the least excuse. I do not question, however, the sincerity of the great mass of those who were opposed to us.

General Lee was dressed in a full uniform which was entirely new, and was wearing a sword of considerable value, very likely the sword which had been presented by the State of Virginia; at all events, it was an entirely different sword from the one that would ordinarily be worn in the field. In my rough traveling suit, the uniform of a private with the straps of a lieutenant-general, I must have contrasted very strangely with a man so handsomely dressed, six feet high and of faultless form. But this was not a matter that I thought of until afterwards.

We soon fell into a conversation about old army times. He remarked that he remembered me very well in the old army; and I told him that as a matter of course I remembered him perfectly, but from the difference in our rank and years (there being about sixteen years' difference in our ages), I had thought it very likely that I had not attracted his attention sufficiently to be remembered by him after such a long interval. Our conversation grew so pleasant that I almost forgot the object of our meeting. After the conversation had run on in this style for some time, General Lee called my attention to the object of our meeting, and said that he had asked for this interview for the purpose of getting from me the terms I proposed to give his army. I said that I meant merely that his army should lay down their arms, not to take them up again during the continuance of the war unless duly and properly exchanged. He said that he had so understood my letter.

Then we gradually fell off again into conversation about matters foreign to the subject which had brought us together. This continued for some little time, when General Lee again interrupted the course of the conversation by suggesting that the terms I proposed to give his army ought to be written out. I called to General Parker, secretary on my staff, for writing materials, and commenced writing out the following terms:

Appomattox C. H., Va.,
Apl 9th, 1865.

Gen. R. E. Lee,
    Comd'g C. S. A.

Gen: In accordance with the substance of my letter to you of the 8th inst., I propose to receive the surrender of the Army of

N. Va. on the following terms, to wit: Rolls of all the officers and men to be made in duplicate. One copy to be given to an officer designated by me, the other to be retained by such officer or officers as you may designate. The officers to give their individual paroles not to take up arms against the Government of the United States until properly exchanged, and each company or regimental commander sign a like parole for the men of their commands. The arms, artillery and public property to be parked and stacked, and turned over to the officer appointed by me to receive them. This will not embrace the side-arms of the officers, nor their private horses or baggage. This done, each officer and man will be allowed to return to their homes, not to be disturbed by United States authority so long as they observe their paroles and the laws in force where they may reside.

> Very respectfully,
> U. S. GRANT,
> Lt. Gen.

When I put my pen to the paper I did not know the first word that I should make use of in writing the terms. I only knew what was in my mind, and I wished to express it clearly, so that there could be no mistaking it. As I wrote on, the thought occurred to me that the officers had their own private horses and effects, which were important to them, but of no value to us; also that it would be an unnecessary humiliation to call upon them to deliver their side arms.

No conversation, not one word, passed between General Lee and myself, either about private property, side arms, or kindred subjects. He appeared to have no objections to the terms first proposed; or if he had a point to make against them he wished to wait until they were in writing to make it. When he read over that part of the terms about side arms, horses and private property of the officers, he remarked, with some feeling, I thought, that this would have a happy effect upon his army.

Then, after a little further conversation, General Lee remarked to me again that their army was organized a little differently from the army of the United States (still maintaining by implication that we were two countries); that in their army the cavalrymen and artillerists owned their own horses; and he asked if he was to understand that the men who so owned their horses were to be permitted to retain them. I told him that as the terms were written they would not; that only the officers were permitted to take their private property. He then, after reading over the terms a second time, remarked that that was clear.

I then said to him that I thought this would be about the last battle of the war—I sincerely hoped so; and I said further I took it that most of the men in the ranks were small farmers. The whole country had been so raided by the two armies that it was doubtful whether they would be able to put in a crop to carry themselves and their families through the next winter without the aid of the horses they were then riding. The United States did not want them and I would, therefore, instruct the officers I left behind to receive the paroles of his troops to let every man of the Confederate army who claimed to own a horse or mule take the animal to his home. Lee remarked again that this would have a happy effect.

He then sat down and wrote out the following letter:

> Headquarters Army of Northern Virginia.
> April 9, 1865
>
> General:—I received your letter of this date containing the terms of the surrender of the Army of Northern Virginia as proposed by you. As they are substantially the same as those expressed in your letter of the 8th inst., they are accepted. I will proceed to designate the proper officers to carry the stipulations into effect.
>
> R. E. LEE, General.
>
> Lieut.-General U. S. Grant.

While duplicates of the two letters were being made, the Union generals present were severally presented to General Lee.

The much talked of surrendering of Lee's sword and my handing it back, this and much more that has been said about it is the purest romance. The word sword or side arms was not mentioned by either of us until I wrote it in the terms. There was no premeditation, and it did not occur to me until the moment I wrote it down. If I had happened to omit it, and General Lee had called my attention to it, I should have put it in the terms precisely as I acceded to the provision about the soldiers retaining their horses.

General Lee, after all was completed and before taking his leave, remarked that his army was in a very bad condition for want of food, and that they were without forage; that his men had been living for some days on parched corn exclusively, and that he would have to ask me for rations and forage. I told him "certainly," and asked for how many men he wanted rations. His answer was "about twenty-five thousand:" and I authorized him to send his own commissary and quartermaster to Appomattox Station, two or three miles away, where he could have, out of the trains we had stopped, all the provisions wanted. As for forage, we had ourselves depended almost entirely upon the country for that.

Generals Gibbon, Griffin and Merritt were designated by me to carry into effect the paroling of Lee's troops before they should start for their homes—General Lee leaving Generals Longstreet, Gordon and Pendleton for them to confer with in order to facilitate this work. Lee and I then separated as cordially as we had met, he returning to his own lines, and all went into bivouac for the night at Appomattox.

Soon after Lee's departure I telegraphed to Washington as follows:

> Headquarters Appomattox C. H. Va.,
> April 9th, 1865, 4:30 P.M.
>
> Hon. E. M. Stanton, Secretary of War,
> Washington.
>
> General Lee surrendered the Army of Northern Virginia this afternoon on terms proposed by myself. The accompanying additional correspondence will show the conditions fully.
>
> U. S. GRANT,
> Lieut.-General.

When news of the surrender first reached our lines our men commenced firing a salute of a hundred guns in honor of the victory. I at once sent word, however, to have it stopped. The Confederates were now our prisoners, and we did not want to exult over their downfall.

I determined to return to Washington at once, with a view to putting a stop to the purchase of supplies, and what I now deemed other useless outlay of money. Before leaving, however, I thought I would like to see General Lee again; so next morning I rode out beyond our lines towards his headquarters, preceded by a bugler and a staff-officer carrying a white flag.

Lee soon mounted his horse, seeing who it was, and met me. We had there between the lines, sitting on horseback, a very pleasant conversation of over half an hour, in the course of which Lee said to me that the South was a big country and that we might have to march over it three or four times before the war entirely ended, but that we would now be able to do it as they could no longer resist us. He expressed it as his earnest hope, however, that we would not be called upon to cause more loss and sacrifice of life; but he could not foretell the result. I then suggested to General Lee that there was not a man in the Confederacy whose influence with the soldiery and the whole people was as great as his, and that if he would now advise the surrender of all the armies I had no doubt his advice would be followed with alacrity. But Lee said, that he could not do that without consulting the President first. I knew there was no use to urge him to do anything against his ideas of what was right.

I was accompanied by my staff and other officers, some of whom seemed to have a great desire to go inside the Confederate lines. They finally asked permission of Lee to do so for the purpose of seeing some of their old army friends, and the permission was granted. They went over, had a very pleasant time with their old friends, and brought some of them back with them when they returned.

When Lee and I separated he went back to his lines and I returned to the house of Mr. McLean. Here the officers of both armies came in great numbers, and seemed to enjoy the meeting as much as though they had been friends separated for a long time while fighting battles under the same flag. For the time being it looked very much as if all thought of the war had escaped their minds. After an hour pleasantly passed in this way I set out on horseback, accompanied by my staff and a small escort, for Burkesville Junction, up to which point the railroad had by this time been repaired.

X

THE NEGRO

THERE are 10,000,000 Negroes, among the total of 15,000,000 in America, to whom the South is home. In spite of the deprivations and humiliations their race has suffered since the earliest days of slavery, their ties are to the land that was made productive by the toil of their ancestors. Promises—not always fulfilled—of better wages and better living-conditions have lured hundreds of thousands of Negroes from the Southern land to such industrial centers in the North as Chicago and Detroit, and Harlem has gleamed like heaven to thousands more. But to the less adventuresome and the less bitter, life on Beale Street in Memphis or on South Rampart in New Orleans is still preferred to life in the Black Ghetto of South Chicago.

Wherever the visitor goes in the South today he will find that political leaders, businessmen, employers of labor, educators, editors, and clergymen are acutely aware of the immediacy of the Negro problem. There are many reasons why they are talking about solutions, wondering what the next stage in the evolution of the problem will be, wondering what the Negro wants and to what lengths he will go to get what he wants. For one thing, America's deep concern about the future of the uncommitted colored race in all parts of the world has forced an increased awareness of how our treatment of the Negro looks to the peoples of Africa and Asia. Again, businessmen know that the purchasing-power of American Negroes must be reckoned with. In 1951, in the whole of America, our Negro citizens spent $15,000,000,000, a sum that was nearly as much as the national income of Canada. Consumer power of this magnitude will not be denied attention and courtesy. Industrialists are thinking about eventual labor shortages in the South. How much longer, employers wonder, will it be possible to keep the Negro at the menial jobs? Will the time soon come when white labor-

ers will have to consent to taking orders from Negroes who are qualified to supervise their work?

Of all such pressing questions the most important is this: what is the
Negro problem in essence? Is it, as many argue, basically an economic
problem? Would the Negro be satisfied if he had a chance to rise in
the economic scale as far as his skill and intelligence, left unimpeded,
would permit him to go? Would the problem be solved if the tensions
between the Negroes and the poorer whites, so provocative of violence
in the past, could be relaxed by a general improvement in the Southern
economy?

Or is the question basically one of civil rights? The modern educated
Negro and those who follow him tell the world that Negroes in the
South are forced to accept second-class citizenship. They can instance
an infinite series of devices that have been invented to disfranchise the
colored man and keep him from the primary and the voting booth.
They can point to many Southern states which specifically deny to
the Negro rights that white Americans consider inalienable. If, then,
the Negro were accorded equal rights before the law, if he were permitted to enjoy first-class citizenship, would he be satisfied? Does he
want more?

The answer is that he does want more. Just what this is may be
found in the last item of a bill of particulars offered by a leading Negro
educator, Rayford W. Logan, Professor of History at Howard University:

> We want an equal share not only in the performance of re-
> sponsibilities and obligations but also in the enjoyment of rights
> and opportunities. We want the same racial equality at the ballot-
> box that we have at the income-tax window; the same equality
> before a court of law that we have before an enemy's bullet; the
> same equality for getting a job, education, decent housing, and
> social security that American kinsmen of our nation's enemies pos-
> sess. We want the Four Freedoms to apply to black Americans
> as well as to brutalized peoples of Europe and to the other under-
> privileged peoples of the world. We insist that insofar as the equal-
> ity asserted in the Declaration of Independence is applicable to all
> men, it should include us. We declare that our presence in this
> country for more than three hundred years, our toil, our honor-
> able service in all our nation's wars, our demonstrated capacity for
> progress warrant our aspirations for eventual first-class citizenship
> and eventual full integration into the public life of the American
> people.[1]

[1] "The Negro Wants First-Class Citizenship," in Rayford W. Logan, ed.: *What
the Negro Wants*, (Chapel Hill: University of North Carolina Press; 1944),
pp. 7–8.

The Negro

Eventual full integration into the public life of the American people.
The implication of this ultimate demand causes older Southerners to
dream of bloody race wars. It also discourages and alarms many Southern liberals who have for years supported the Negro's demands for
economic opportunity and civil rights.

Where can the line be drawn? Which areas in American life are
"public" and which are private? "Suppose," says the reluctant Southerner, "suppose we were to permit Negroes to eat in our restaurants,
sleep in our hotels, use our public toilets and waiting-rooms, sit where
we do in the theaters and ball-parks, would even this be enough?
Would they be content to draw the line finally at that point? Or does
'full integration into the public life' really mean the abolition of laws
against the intermarriage of whites and Negroes and consequently a
mongrelized South?"

Such fears are not quieted by pointing to the fact that in states where
there are no laws against the marriage of whites and Negroes the incidence of intermarriage is not great. Nor is the assertion of militant
Negroes that blacks will always prefer to marry blacks likely to be
believed. Where the old fear lingers it does not take much of an "incident" to cause it to explode into violence, in Miami, Florida—or in
Cicero, Illinois.

Fortunately there are many leaders in both races in the South who
are willing to let the future take care of ultimate demands. They
wisely prefer to work for practicable measures, perhaps realizable in
a lifetime—decent public housing for Negroes, adequate medical services, good schools, job opportunities. They know that the Negroes
will be less concerned about full integration and the whites will be less
fearful of what the demand for it may portend if the Negro is accorded everywhere in the South the civil rights that in certain cities
and states he has begun to win.

They know, too, that time is now on the side of decency and humanity. The millennium has by no means arrived, but changes are
taking place much more rapidly than some Southerners admit or even
realize. For example, in 1948 only 750,000 Negroes in the Southern
states were registered to vote. (Not all of them voted, by any means.)
It is estimated that by 1956, 3,000,000 will be permitted to register.
Almost overnight the most flagrant varieties of segregation were abolished in Washington, D.C., in part through the insistence of President
Eisenhower. Perhaps most remarkable of all has been the breakthrough
on the color front which has taken place in the Armed Forces. Quietly
and effectively such leaders as Navy Secretary Forrestal, Army Secretary Gray (a North Carolinian), Charles Fahy (Georgia-born Catholic
and former United States Solicitor General) set about abolishing segregation in the Services. By 1954 it was very nearly accomplished. But

one of the most extraordinary facts about this achievement is that it had the assent of many Southern congressmen who did not speak publicly for or against the measures taken but agreed in private to what they saw was inevitable. Integration had worked successfully during the Korean War, and the time had come when it could be prescribed for Army, Navy, and Air Force installations all over the world.

These Southern leaders in both races also know that thousands of white students in the colleges not only are ready for integration but are often impatient with their elders because they are fearful of its consequences. In those Southern universities to which Negroes have been admitted the attitude of the white students has been more than courteous; it has been friendly.

Most indicative of what the immediate future holds is the change taking place as a result of the movement of Southern Negroes from the country to the city. As Professor Henry A. Bullock of Texas Southern University has pointed out, the relationship between the white man and the Negro is transformed when the Negro goes to the city and finds a good job in business or industry. His relationship to the white man in a large measure ceases to be the traditional one which was once regulated by the subserviency of slave to master. His life is now on a "contractual" basis: all white men from whom he purchases goods and services, the real-estate man who sells him a lot, the housebuilder, his banker and insurance agent, the storekeeper with whom he trades, all these deal with him through policies, deeds, accounts, bills—in other words, through contracts. His life is no longer dependent on the good nature or the meanness of Mistah Snopes or on his word and whim. This far-reaching change in Southern mores may not increase the friendliness of one race toward the other, but it has brought the steadying and pacifying influence of the law into the area of race relations in a most effective way. There are not likely to be dynamitings or race riots in cities, North or South, where large numbers of Negroes are permitted to conduct their lives in this fashion.

1. THE NEGRO SPEAKS

A Slave Witness of a Slave Auction

The following account of a slave auction in New Orleans appears in Twelve Years a Slave: Narrative of Solomon Northup, a Citizen of New York, Kidnapped in Washington City in 1841, and Rescued in 1853, from a Cotton Plantation near the Red River, in Louisiana *(Auburn, N.Y., 1853), pp. 78–82. Northup's story of his years in slavery was edited by David Wilson, a lawyer in New York State and a minor writer of histories and biographies. Many slave narratives of this sort were published shortly before the Civil War, often with the aid of abolitionists who wished to use them for their propaganda value.* Twelve Years a Slave *is one of the least sensational and seemingly one of the most reliable. Northup regained his freedom when he contrived to get a letter through to friends in New York State in 1852. Governor Hunt then procured his liberation and Northup returned to his family in Glens Falls, New York.*

THE very amiable, pious-hearted Mr. Theophilus Freeman, partner or consignee of James H. Burch, and keeper of the slave pen in New-Orleans, was out among his animals early in the morning. With an occasional kick of the older men and women, and many a sharp crack of the whip about the ears of the younger slaves, it was not long before they were all astir, and wide awake. Mr. Theophilus Freeman bustled about in a very industrious manner, getting his property ready for the sales-room, intending, no doubt, to do that day a rousing business.

In the first place we were required to wash thoroughly, and those with beards, to shave. We were then furnished with a new suit each, cheap, but clean. The men had hat, coat, shirt, pants and shoes; the women frocks of calico, and handkerchiefs to bind about their heads. We were now conducted into a large room in the front part of the building to which the yard was attached, in order to be properly trained, before the admission of customers. The men were arranged on one side of the room, the women on the other. The tallest was

placed at the head of the row, then the next tallest, and so on in the order of their respective heights. Emily was at the foot of the line of
women. Freeman charged us to remember our places; exhorted us to appear smart and lively,—sometimes threatening, and again holding out
various inducements. During the day he exercised us in the art of "looking smart," and of moving to our places with exact precision.

After being fed, in the afternoon, we were again paraded and made
to dance. Bob, a colored boy, who had some time belonged to Freeman,
played on the violin. Standing near him, I made bold to inquire if he
could play the "Virginia Reel." He answered he could not, and asked
me if I could play. Replying in the affirmative, he handed me the violin.
I struck up a tune, and finished it. Freeman ordered me to continue
playing, and seemed well pleased, telling Bob that I far excelled him—
a remark that seemed to grieve my musical companion very much.

Next day many customers called to examine Freeman's "new lot."
The latter gentleman was very loquacious, dwelling at much length
upon our several good points and qualities. He would make us hold up
our heads, walk briskly back and forth, while customers would feel of
our hands and arms and bodies, turn us about, ask us what we could
do, make us open our mouths and show our teeth, precisely as a jockey
examines a horse which he is about to barter for or purchase. Sometimes a man or woman was taken back to the small house in the yard,
stripped, and inspected more minutely. Scars upon a slave's back were
considered evidence of a rebellious or unruly spirit, and hurt his sale.

One old gentleman, who said he wanted a coachman, appeared to
take a fancy to me. From his conversation with Freeman, I learned he
was a resident of the city. I very much desired that he would buy me,
because I conceived it would not be difficult to make my escape from
New-Orleans on some northern vessel. Freeman asked him fifteen
hundred dollars for me. The old gentleman insisted it was too much,
as times were very hard. Freeman, however, declared that I was sound
and healthy, of a good constitution, and intelligent. He made it a point
to enlarge upon my musical attainments. The old gentleman argued
quite adroitly that there was nothing extraordinary about the nigger,
and finally, to my regret, went out, saying he would call again. During
the day, however, a number of sales were made. David and Caroline
were purchased together by a Natchez planter. They left us, grinning
broadly, and in the most happy state of mind, caused by the fact of
their not being separated. Lethe was sold to a planter of Baton Rouge,
her eyes flashing with anger as she was led away.

The same man also purchased Randall. The little fellow was made
to jump, and run across the floor, and perform many other feats, exhibiting his activity and condition. All the time the trade was going
on, Eliza was crying aloud, and wringing her hands. She besought the

man not to buy him, unless he also bought herself and Emily. She promised, in that case, to be the most faithful slave that ever lived. The man answered that he could not afford it, and then Eliza burst into a paroxysm of grief, weeping plaintively. Freeman turned round to her, savagely, with his whip in his uplifted hand, ordering her to stop her noise, or he would flog her. He would not have such work—such snivelling; and unless she ceased that minute, he would take her to the yard and give her a hundred lashes. Yes, he would take the nonsense out of her pretty quick—if he didn't, might he be d—d. Eliza shrunk before him, and tried to wipe away her tears, but it was all in vain. She wanted to be with her children, she said, the little time she had to live. All the frowns and threats of Freeman, could not wholly silence the afflicted mother. She kept on begging and beseeching them, most piteously, not to separate the three. Over and over again she told them how she loved her boy. A great many times she repeated her former promises—how very faithful and obedient she would be; how hard she would labor day and night, to the last moment of her life, if he would only buy them all together. But it was of no avail; the man could not afford it. The bargain was agreed upon, and Randall must go alone. Then Eliza ran to him; embraced him passionately; kissed him again and again; told him to remember her—all the while her tears falling in the boy's face like rain.

Freeman damned her, calling her a blubbering, bawling wench, and ordered her to go to her place, and behave herself, and be somebody. He swore he wouldn't stand such stuff but a little longer. He would soon give her something to cry about, if she was not mighty careful, and *that* she might depend upon.

The planter from Baton Rouge, with his new purchases, was ready to depart.

"Don't cry, mama. I will be a good boy. Don't cry," said Randall, looking back, as they passed out of the door.

What has become of the lad, God knows. It was a mournful scene indeed. I would have cried myself if I had dared.

Frederick Douglass Learns to Read

Frederick Douglass (1817–95) was born near Easton, Maryland, of a slave woman and an unknown father who was, apparently, white. He was therefore a slave, and in his early life he suffered abuse and cruelty beyond the lot of most slaves. Once, when nearly destroyed in spirit by a slave-breaking master, he revolted suddenly and fought the man in a brutal, hand-to-hand struggle, which he won. The act was symbolic of his future, for he burned with an unquenchable ambition to be free. His first attempt to escape failed, but he succeeded in 1838, and became a laborer in New Bedford, Massachusetts.

When the abolitionists stumbled upon him in 1841, his true career began, and it proved to be a stellar one. His words ranked in power for the cause of abolition with those of William Lloyd Garrison and Harriet Beecher Stowe. He was an adviser to Lincoln, and during Reconstruction he was active in the fight for civil rights. He eventually became United States Minister to Haiti.

One of the determining experiences of his early career was his being taught to read as a child by an indulgent mistress in Baltimore. Teaching favorite slaves to read and even to write was not uncommon among some slaveholders before the Civil War, but there were others who strongly objected to the practice, and there were increasingly stringent laws against it. Those who objected saw all too clearly to what it would inevitably lead and, like Douglass's master, feared the result.

The following passage is chosen from Frederick Douglass: Life and Times of Frederick Douglass, Written by Himself, His Early Life as a Slave, His Escape from Bondage, and His Complete History to the Present Time . . . with an Introduction by Mr. George L. Ruffin of Boston (*Hartford, Conn.: Park Publishing Co.; 1882*), *pp. 87–8.*

THE frequent hearing of my mistress reading the Bible aloud, for she often read aloud when her husband was absent, awakened my curiosity in respect to this *mystery* of reading, and roused in me the desire to learn. Up to this time I had known nothing whatever of this wonderful art, and my ignorance and inexperience of what it could do for me, as well as my confidence in my mistress, emboldened me to ask her

326

to teach me to read. With an unconsciousness and inexperience equal
to my own, she readily consented, and in an incredibly short time, by
her kind assistance, I had mastered the alphabet and could spell words
of three or four letters. My mistress seemed almost as proud of my
progress as if I had been her own child, and supposing that her husband
would be as well pleased, she made no secret of what she was doing
for me. Indeed, she exultingly told him of the aptness of her pupil, and
of her intention to persevere in teaching me, as she felt her duty to do,
at least to read the Bible. And here arose the first dark cloud over my
Baltimore prospects, the precursor of chilling blasts and drenching
storms. Master Hugh was astounded beyond measure, and probably
for the first time proceeded to unfold to his wife the true philosophy
of the slave system, and the peculiar rules necessary in the nature of
the case to be observed in the management of human chattels. Of
course he forbade her to give me any further instruction, telling her
in the first place that to do so was unlawful, as it was also unsafe; "for,"
said he, "if you give a nigger an inch he will take an ell. Learning will
spoil the best nigger in the world. If he learns to read the Bible it will
forever unfit him to be a slave. He should know nothing but the will
of his master, and learn to obey it. As to himself, learning will do him
no good, but a great deal of harm, making him disconsolate and unhappy. If you teach him how to read, he'll want to know how to
write, and this accomplished, he'll be running away with himself."

Two Slave Narratives

*Among the many valuable activities of the Federal Writers' Project in
the 1930's was the assembling of the Slave Narrative Collection, most
of which is now permanently housed in the Library of Congress. Begun as a project for Negro workers under the Federal Emergency
Relief Administration, the interviewing of former slaves and the
gathering of documents about slavery days became in 1936 an important task of the Federal Writers' Project. White and Negro interviewers obtained their materials in eighteen states, recording over two
thousand narratives. To set the narrators thinking about their past the
interviewers had a number of questions to ask them—about their parents and masters, life in the quarters, the kind of work they had done,*

punishment, patrollers, the Ku-Klux and night riders, their later life, and their children. The interviews vary widely in reliability, vividness, and intrinsic interest, but the total record is extraordinary. The idea of rescuing this living testimony before it should vanish forever was a brilliant one.

A selection from the narratives was made by B. A. Botkin under the title Lay My Burden Down: A Folk History of Slavery (*University of Chicago Press; copyright 1945 by the University of Chicago). The two narratives reprinted here are found on pages 146–8 and 169–70 of this work.*

IF ALL SLAVES HAD BELONGED TO WHITE FOLKS
LIKE OURS

I WAS big enough to remember well us coming back from Texas after we refugeed there when the fighting of the war was so bad at St. Charles. We stayed in Texas till the surrender, then we all come back in lots of wagons. I was sick, but they put me on a little bed, and me and all the little children rode in a "Jersey" that one of the old Negro mammies drove, along behind the wagons, and our young master, Colonel Bob Chaney, rode a great big black horse. Oh! he nice-looking on that horse! Every once and a while he'd ride back to the last wagon to see if everything was all right. I remember how scared us children was when we crossed the Red River. Aunt Mandy said, "We crossing you old Red River today, but we not going to cross you any more, 'cause we are going home now, back to Arkansas." That day when we stopped to cook our dinner I picked up a lot little blackjack acorns, and when my mammy saw them she said, "Throw them things down, child. They'll make you wormy." I cried because I thought they were chinquapins. I begged my daddy to let's go back to Texas, but he said, "No! No! We going with our white folks." My mammy and daddy belonged to Colonel Jesse Chaney, much of a gentleman, and his wife, Miss Sallie, was the best mistress anybody ever had. She was a Christian. I can hear her praying yet! She wouldn't let one of her slaves hit a tap on Sunday. They must rest and go to church. They had preaching at the cabin of some one of the slaves, and in the summertime sometimes they had it out in the shade under the trees. Yes, and the slaves on each plantation had their own church. They didn't go gallivanting over the neighborhood or country like niggers do now. Colonel Chaney had lots and lots of slaves, and all their houses were in a row, all one-room cabins. Everything happened in that one room—birth, sickness, death, and everything, but in them days niggers kept their houses clean and their door yards too. These houses where they lived was called "the quarters." I used to love to walk down by that row of houses. It looked like a town, and late of an evening as you'd go by the doors you could smell meat a-frying, coffee making, and good things cooking. We were fed good and had plenty clothes to keep us dry and warm.

Along about time for the surrender, Colonel Jess, our master, took sick and died with some kind of head trouble. Then Colonel Bob, our young master, took care of his mama and the slaves. All the grown folks went to the field to work, and the little children would be left at a big room called the nursing-home. All us little ones would be nursed and fed by an old mammy, Aunt Mandy. She was too old to go to the field, you know. We wouldn't see our mammy and daddy from early in the morning till night when their work was done, then they'd go by Aunt Mandy's and get their children and go home till work time in the morning.

Some of the slaves were house Negroes. They didn't go to work in the fields. They each one had their own job around the house, barn, orchard, milkhouse, and things like that.

When washday come, Lord, the pretty white clothes! It would take three or four women a-washing all day.

When two of the slaves wanted to get married, they'd dress up nice as they could and go up to the big house, and the master would marry them. They'd stand up before him, and he'd read out of a book called *The Discipline* and say, "Thou shalt love the Lord thy God with all thy heart, all thy strength, with all thy might and thy neighbor as thyself." Then he'd say they were man and wife and tell them to live right and be honest and kind to each other. All the slaves would be there too, seeing the wedding.

Our Miss Sallie was the sweetest best thing in the world! She was so good and kind to everybody, and she loved her slaves, too. I can remember when Uncle Tony died how she cried! Uncle Tony Wadd was Miss Sallie's favorite servant. He stayed in a little house in the yard and made fires for her, brought in wood and water, and just waited on the house. He was a little black man and white-headed as cotton, when he died. Miss Sallie told the niggers when they come to take him to the graveyard, to let her know when they got him in his coffin, and when they sent and told her she come out with all the little white children, her little grandchildren, to see Uncle Tony. She just cried and stood for a long time looking at him, then she said, "Tony, you have been a good and faithful servant." Then the Negro men walked and carried him to the graveyard out in a big grove in the field. Every plantation had its own graveyard and buried its own folks and slaves right on the place.

If all slaves had belonged to white folks like ours, there wouldn't been any freedom wanted.

(*Narrator:* HARRIET MCFARLIN PAYNE, *aged 83; De Witt, Arkansas.*)

THE LAST TIME I SAW MASTER

No, sir, he wa'n't good to none of us niggers. All the niggers round hated to be bought by him 'cause he was so mean. When he was too tired to whup us, he had the overseer do it; and the overseer was meaner than the massa. But, mister, the peoples was the same as they is now. There was good ones and bad ones. I just happened to belong to a bad one. One day I remembers my brother January was cotched over seeing a gal on the next plantation. He had a pass, but the time on it done give out. Well, sir, when the massa found out that he was a hour late, he got as mad as a hive of bees. So when Brother January he come home, the massa took down his long mule skinner and tied him with a rope to a pine tree. He strip his shirt off and said: "Now, nigger, I'm going to teach you some sense."

With that he started laying on the lashes. January was a big, fine-looking nigger, the finest I ever seed. He was just four years older than me, and when the massa begin a-beating him, January never said a word. The massa got madder and madder 'cause he couldn't make January holler.

"What's the matter with you, nigger?" he say. "Don't it hurt?"

January, he never said nothing, and the massa keep a-beating till little streams of blood started flowing down January's chest, but he never holler. His lips was a-quivering and his body was a-shaking, but his mouth it never open; and all the while I sat on my mammy's and pappy's steps a-crying. The niggers was all gathered about, and some of 'em couldn't stand it; they had to go inside their cabins. After while, January, he couldn't stand it no longer hisself, and he say in a hoarse loud whisper: "Massa! Massa! have mercy on this poor nigger.". . .

Then the war came. The Yankees come in, and they pulled the fruit off the trees and et it. They et the hams and corn, but they never burned the houses. Seem to me like they just stay around long enough to git plenty something to eat, 'cause they left in two or three days, and we never seed 'em since. The massa had three boys to go to war, but there wasn't one to come home. All the children he had was killed. Massa, he lost all his money, and the house soon begin dropping away to nothing. Us niggers one by one left the old place, and the last time I seed the home plantation I was a-standing on a hill. I looked back on it for the last time through a patch of scrub pines, and it look so lonely. There wa'n't but one person in sight, the massa. He was a-setting in a wicker chair in the yard looking out over a small field of cotton and corn. There was four crosses in the graveyard in the side lawn where he was a-setting. The fourth one was his wife. I lost my old woman, too, thirty-seven years ago, and all this time, I's been a-carrying on like the massa—all alone.

(Narrator: WILLIAM COLBERT, *aged 93; Alabama; born 1844, Fort Valley, Georgia; slave in Georgia.)*

William Johnson, Free Negro of Natchez

In 1860 there were 250,000 Negroes in the South who were not slaves, more than half of whom lived in Maryland and Virginia. Though the plight of the freedman in the Old South has been called tragic, there were many, like the bold and enterprising William Johnson of Natchez from whose diary a passage is printed here, who made a more or less secure position for themselves in a society that in general feared them or at least resented their presence. The free Negroes tended to migrate to the towns where they worked as domestic servants, laborers, or artisans. Some made their living as blacksmiths or shoemakers, and they had a virtual monopoly of the barber's trade. A few acquired enough property to set themselves up as merchants or hotel-keepers. Some were themselves slaveholders: the 1860 Charleston tax returns, for instance, list 130 Negroes as owning 390 slaves. Some distinguished themselves in other ways than the primary business of staying alive and holding on to their status and meager property. John Chavis, a free Negro who conducted schools at Raleigh and Hillsborough, taught many white boys who later became eminent in North Carolina. Henry Evans preached to both races in a Methodist church in Fayetteville. In 1845 a group of Louisiana Negro writers published a collection of their poetry in Les Cenelles, Choix de Poésies Indigènes.

A Negro was free if he was born of a free mother. He might gain his freedom by manumission or, less often, by buying himself out of slavery, with his master's consent, of course. White fathers sometimes freed their mulatto children and gave them property. Gradually the laws governing manumission became more stringent. Most states required the consent of the county court before slaves could be freed. By the time of the Civil War, requirements of this kind had become so

331

numerous as to make manumission extremely difficult. Various restrictions were placed on the freedmen. In 1805 Virginia required them to leave the state immediately upon emancipation. Other states imitated this practice. There was always the danger that through fraud or force a free Negro might lose his status and once again become a slave.

By good fortune the diary of William Johnson, a free Negro of Natchez, has been preserved. One can learn a great deal about the life of the free man of color from its pages. Johnson's mother was freed by her master in 1814. Six years later her boy William was also freed. Young William learned barbering from his brother-in-law, and by 1827 he was well established in his own business. Eventually he owned three barbershops. He bought land, owned slaves, and did a thriving business as a moneylender. He liked to bet on the horses, bought liquor, enjoyed the theater, and took particular pleasure in the gossip and conversation of the white men who patronized his shop. In 1851 Johnson was murdered by a man who had lost to him in a lawsuit involving the boundaries of Johnson's plantation. The murderer eventually went free, but the sentiment in Natchez was strong for Johnson, whose "peaceable character" and "excellent standing" were well known in the region.

This passage from William Johnson's Natchez, the Ante-Bellum Diary of a Free Negro, *edited by William Ransom Hogan and Edwin Adams Davis (1951), is reprinted with the permission of the publishers, the Louisiana State University Press. Even so short a passage, comprising the entries for a little more than a month in 1837, gives a good idea of William Johnson's business ability, his love of sport and of gossip, and of his difficulties with his mulatto mother.*

MAY 25, 1837 I arose very Early in the morning and took Bill Nix and Bill Winston and mounted Our horses and crossed the River and went a Fishing in the Concordia and Cocodria Lake—Mc, J. Lacrose and G. Butler went along at the Same time and when we got Over to the Lake we found Messrs Levi Harrison, Pond, Rufner, Cambell, Stevenson, Noyes and Some Darkeys and after a short time young Bell and H. Austin Came Down. Young Bell got Drunk and Lye down and went to sleep and Caught no fish of course tho all the persons that were over there caught a Greate many. My two and myself Caught 4 Doz and 4 fish Mc Caught as many or more prehaps than we three did—I Left Mc at the Lake a fishing We Reached town quite Early in the Evening and got home in time to have Our fish Dressed for Supper—Mc and Mr Rufner, Harrison and a good many more Left Late in the evening and did not Get home until about 10 Oclock They treed a Coon on there way home Mc he took an active part in Killing the Coon He was Shot

Down by Rufner and Mc he Drew his Bucher Knife and was a spledge-ing it about in Greate stile over the Coon

27 Charles started Home this morning Early He Wrode on my Little mare

28 A very dull day in town Mr. Grafton Baker got pretty high—got into Several difficultys The one at the City Hotell I dont know any-thing about, but the One at the Mansion House He attempted o pull Dr Branders nose for refuseing to drink with him—When he made the attempt to pull his nose the Dr Knockd him Down with his stick, he struck him on Jaw or side of the face Mr Baker Recoved and struck him with his fist which Knocked the Dr Down

29 A Challenge passed To Day between Mr Armatt and Mr Besancon Mr Armatt Sent the Challenge, and Mr Besancon Accepted the Challenge and they were to have fought three feet a part Tis too Close I dont think they will fight, Mr B. it appears accused Mr Armatt of having been the author of Some piece that appeared in the Courrier and Journal office—this is said to have been the origin of it. To Day Mother paid me Sixty Dollars and She now owes me $600 towards the Girl Sharlot

30 To Day I Sent the Little Red Cow Down to New Orleans On the Steam Boat, Hail Columbia—the Cow and Calf was for Mrs Miller [1]— The Boat was to have gone at 10 Oclock but did not get away until 3 Oclock this Evening She had On Bourd Some of the finest Cattle that I have Ever Seen—Harden was on the Boat and as Bar Keeper and Fitzchue was on her also—I Sent a Letter by Harden and One by Louis Winsborough both to Mrs Miller—Whilst I was Down at the Landing to day I was told that those Gentleman that had Crossed the River was then about to fight a Duel. It was thot to be Besancon & Armatt that had gone across but it was a mistake for they had not gone over—I got in a Skifft and crossed the River but neither of the parties had gone over so I came directly back again—Mr Besancon told me this morning that he had been very much abusesd by the other party, and that he would fight the whole Concern of them, but what, he would be Satis-fied or Revenged He Seemed to have a good Strong Disposition to whale Mr Mellen if he met him any where and said also that Mr Black would get a fall through the course of the day

31 Nothing New that I know of To Day

June 1 Myself with Charles and Bill Crossed the River in Company with Mc To go over the River To fish We went over to the Concordia Lake and we caught a Greate many fish I had when I Got home ten Dozen and 4 fish and I had gave away and Lost about 2 Dozen Mr Eleck Bell hooked them from me Mc he Caught 7 Doz or near about it

[1] Johnson's free Negro sister, Adelia. In 1830 the Millers moved to New Or-leans, where they accumulated an estate, worth $21,000 in 1865.

We did not get over until Sun Down or night and we had to pay Double Ferryage—there were 7 horses & 8 or ten men Came over at the same time in the Boat.

3 In to days Free Trader we had a full Statement of all the corespondence between Mr Armat and Mr Besancon It was a Lengthy coresponace Quite so indeed but all Ended in peace[2] There were Seventeen persons Bathed to day in my Bath House. This Day I owe Mother $40 which Sum added to Sixty Dollars that She paid me on 29th of May is One Hundred Dollars that she has paid me on the money that I paid Mr Taylor for Her—She now owes me five Hundred and Sixty Dollars

4 Nothing has transpired that is worth a Comment. I gave French $2.25 to day and the Boys $3 both for Bath Buisness

5 Mr William H. Chambers Died Last night about 9 Oclock—Mrs Rebecka Bingham Died this evening Mr Chambers was buried out at the Family Burial Ground

10 I bought of young Mr Harris to day $10 Rail Road Scrip for Seven & ½ of our paper Currency

12 A fight took place this morning between Mr George Lancaster and Big Frank Little in the Market House, Frank Little it appears whiped Mary Lattimore[3] as she terms herself, for being at the Bench Drinking Coffee She was Left in Charge of Mr Lancaster and as soon as he herd that F Little had whiped her he went into market and commenced On F. Little as hard as he could with his fists They had a pretty sharp fight but was at Last Seperated by the bystanders, I herd Mr P. Gemmell walk past my Shop Door Cursing N. L. Williams He was about to Flake him and did attempt to Jump the counter after him and was prevented by Mr Neibut. He cursed him for a d—d scoundrell and a greate many more things.[4]

[2] The Natchez *Free Trader,* June 3, 9, 1837, carried accounts of the affair. Lorenzo A. Besancon was the editor of the *Free Trader,* and Thomas Armat was a local lawyer and politician. The June 9 issue contains four and one-half columns of correspondence regarding the proposed duel, and illustrates how duels were often averted by the intervention of friends who made a settlement satisfactory to both sides. The cause of the difficulty between the two men was political controversy. The distance between the parties in this proposed duel was to be thirty feet, and not three feet, as stated by Johnson in his May 29 entry.

[3] Mary Lattimore was a slave, the property of Dr. David Lattimore. On September 8, 1838, he swapped "a Mulatto woman named Mary," aged about twenty-one, to "Nancy [Lattimore] a free person of color" in exchange for another female slave, aged about eighteen, and $1.00. Adams County Deed Records, DD. 46.

[4] On May 6, 1836, Nathaniel L. Williams had purchased the three-story brick store building, occupied by the firm of Neibert & Gemmell and owned by Peter Gemmell and John G. Taylor. William Johnson's barbershop was immediately adjacent. Adams County Deed Records, X, 164–65. In 1837, Williams opened a new "Book and Drug Store," probably in the building he owned. Natchez *Courier,* November 27, 1837.

13 Nothing new worth recording—Mr Walker Gets the Girl that ran away from him some time ago

14 Mr Woodville P. Ward, the Post Master at Vicksburg, Died to day with Small pox—Extracted from N. Paper

15 To day Mr Melton, Scooth Meleene and William Reid in settling there accounts Disputes and had very near a fight. Mr Meleene Let Reid jab him in the abdomen with a gun seveal times and made no Resistance whatever—Sterns goes across the River to fish this Evening and intends fishing all day to morrow

16 The carpenters Commenced To repair the gallery the next Door at Capt Dossens, and very Glad I am to have thet place Stoped up. I Received a Letter from Captain Miller to day from Vicksburgh [5]

18 Mr A. Spielman owes me to this date the sum of three hundred Dollars

21 To day Mr N. L. Williams Came To me To know if I had made any arrangement with Mr Gemmell. I told him that I had not but was waiting for a tittle for the wall from Mr Gemmell, and he Said Mr Gemmell Cannot give you a title for the wall, for he has treated me very shabbyly Lately, and I will not do anything To oblige him in any way. He would Sooner put his head in the River and hold it there a half hour than ask me to Sign a deed for it You had better Seys he, waight untill I get back from the North, and then we will have the buisness fixed for He Cannot give you a tittle and I have not passed my deed to Captain Dossen yet but will do it when I return from the North. He gave me to understand that he would sell me the wall for the Same Sum that I was to pay Mr Gemmell for it.

22 To Days paper Announces the Ellction of Mr Izod to the Office of Sherriff—He had a majority of three hundred and fifty two over Col Woods—To Day Mr McGetrick paid me One months rent that was due on the 15th ins—the Amount of Rent was $79.00 I took 59 Dollars in Branch paper and $20 in Rail Road Scrip—He Left One hundred Dollars in Scrip—After taking Out the $20 it Leaves a Ballance of Eighty Dollars in Scrip in his favor of which I am to take Out Every month twenty Dollars as Long as it will Last To Day I herd Mr Paterson Driving Mr Abonette from his Store, saying go off! Go off—and I herd that they had takin him by the Collar and Led him to the door— Mr Bell had him put in Jail this Evening for debt

23 I Received a Letter this Morning by the Steam Boat Bunker Hill —The Letter Came from Mrs Miller, Mr Wiswall and Mr N L. Williams Leaves this place for the North.

24 To day I paid Mr Mark Breden & Spielman & Co. the Sum of One Hundred and fifty three Dollars for Building a Bake Oven—very high

[5] Johnson occasionally referred to Elisha Miller, the free Negro barber in Vicksburg, as "Captain Miller."

price Mother paid me twelve Dollars on the above Amount, This will Leave a Ballance of One hundred and forty One Dollars—I Loaned Mr McFadden $50 to be paid On Tuesday next, 27th instant

25 Buisness unusually dull, I wrode out and took Bill Winston with me To get Black Berrys. We got a greate many in a short time, Capt Pomp, or Mr Strickland is appointed Deputy Sherriff—Aunt F. Mc-Cary Stayd all night at our house

26 I Read a prety tight burlesque to day in the Jackson paper of the Duel that was to have Taken place between Mr Armatt & Besancon It apeared to be a Burlesque on Mr Armatt alone

27 Judge Rawlins called To Know Something Respecting my whish-ing to have a petition for a reduction of taxes on my Property—To Day we had a first rate fight between Bill Rushelow & Bill Winston—They made a Stand of[f]—Neither whiped

28 I herd this morning of the Dreadfull attack of Mr Rogers of Manchester on a Dr Reigna of the Same place, what the fight Grew Out of I Have not herd, but appears that Mr Rogers Saw Dr Reigna on his gallery and was in company with his family, ie, his wife and Chil-dren Mr Rogers drew a pistol and fired on him then Jumped To him, Knocked him down and stabed him clear through the body and screwed it around in his Dead Boddy—Latest accounts that he was put in Irons—to stand his tryal, Mr. R. Parker came in this Evening to Know how many Slaves I had about my yard as my property I told him that I had five and that I had Several Boys and they were not mine and they were not Bound to me yet.

29 I Caught old Mary to night with a Basket with 7 or 8 unbaked Buiscuit—I have reason to believe that she got them at the City Hotell, and the way I cursed her was the wright way and if Ever I can hear of her doing the Like again I will whip her untill I make her faint

30 This morning M[other] Commenced as usual to quarrell with Everything and Every body, I, Knowing perfectly well what it Grew Out of, I thought I would take the quickest way to stop it, and I ac-cordingly took a whip and gave her a few Cuts; As soon as that was done M. commenced to quarrell and abuse me Saying that I done it to oblige Sarah and advancing on me at the same time Dareing me to strike, which I would not do for anything in the world. I shoved her back from me three times

Booker T. Washington's Atlanta Exposition
Address

In Up from Slavery (*1901*), *a book that has become an American classic, Booker T. Washington (1856?–1915) told the story of his life. Like Frederick Douglass, he was born into slavery of a Negro mother and, it is believed, a white father. He worked as a child in salt furnaces and coal mines until he enrolled at Hampton Institute, penniless but anxious to learn. Later he studied at Wayland Seminary in Washington, D.C., and then returned to Hampton as an instructor.*

In 1881, when George W. Campbell, a former slaveowner, and Lewis Adams, a former slave, set about organizing a school for Negroes in Tuskegee, Alabama, Booker T. Washington was chosen to be its head. He began with a shanty and a Negro Methodist church, but by the time of his death, the school boasted over one hundred buildings, over fifteen hundred students, nearly two hundred faculty members, and an endowment of two million dollars. His reputation and influence had grown with his school. He was sought, all over the country, as a speaker on Negro education and race relations, and his simple sincerity, his direct humor, and the Biblical cadences of his speech had a profound effect.

He was of great assistance to the white men who were fighting to create a new South. Opposed to the conservative agrarians, they believed in forgetting the past, letting the plantation system die, and building a strong economy around small individual landholders and industrialization. In order to effect their program they needed to be able to assure Northern financial interests that the South would make some kind of decent settlement of the Negro problem, and it was here that Booker T. Washington was most helpful. For he was far more conservative than such "intellectual" Negro leaders as W. E. B. Du Bois, who demanded a measure of racial equality far greater than the South then was willing to grant. In Negro education he stressed practical training in the trades ahead of all else, and in social affairs he stressed the earning of respect and the maintenance of peace ahead of the winning of civil rights and social equality. This moderate position gave him leadership in the eyes of white and Negro alike.

Booker T. Washington stated his position again and again, but never more clearly than at Atlanta in 1895, and never with greater effect.

Speaking there at the Cotton States and International Exposition, he enunciated his doctrine: "In all things that are purely social we can be as separate as the fingers, yet one as the hand in all things essential to mutual progress." The speech came just at a moment when a note of compromise was seriously needed, and won him the position of Negro leadership left vacant by the recent death of Frederick Douglass. Some of his educational theories have since proved unworkable—the simple trades he taught his students turned out to be obsolete in an age of rapid technological progress. But his importance as the voice of moderation when moderation was essential cannot be denied.

The following selection is Chapter xiv of Booker T. Washington's Up from Slavery, *an Autobiography. The text used is that of the first edition, issued in 1901 by Doubleday, Page & Co.*

THE Atlanta Exposition, at which I had been asked to make an address as a representative of the Negro race, as stated in the last chapter, was opened with a short address from Governor Bullock. After other interesting exercises, including an invocation from Bishop Nelson, of Georgia, a dedicatory ode by Albert Howell, Jr., and addresses by the President of the Exposition and Mrs. Joseph Thompson, the President of the Woman's Board, Governor Bullock introduced me with the words, "We have with us to-day a representative of Negro enterprise and Negro civilization."

When I arose to speak, there was considerable cheering, especially from the coloured people. As I remember it now, the thing that was uppermost in my mind was the desire to say something that would cement the friendship of the races and bring about hearty coöperation between them. So far as my outward surroundings were concerned, the only thing that I recall distinctly now is that when I got up, I saw thousands of eyes looking intently into my face. The following is the address which I delivered:—

Mr. President and Gentlemen of the Board of Directors and Citizens.

One-third of the population of the South is of the Negro race. No enterprise seeking the material, civil, or moral welfare of this section can disregard this element of our population and reach the highest success. I but convey to you, Mr. President and Directors, the sentiment of the masses of my race when I say that in no way have the value and manhood of the American Negro been more fittingly and generously recognized than by the managers of this magnificent Exposition at every stage of its progress. It is a recognition that will do more to cement the friendship of the two races than any occurrence since the dawn of our freedom.

Not only this, but the opportunity here afforded will awaken among us a new era of industrial progress. Ignorant and inexperienced, it is not strange that in the first years of our new life we began at the top instead of at the bottom; that a seat in Congress or the state legislature was more sought than real estate or industrial skill; that the political convention or stump speaking had more attractions than starting a dairy farm or truck garden.

A ship lost at sea for many days suddenly sighted a friendly vessel. From the mast of the unfortunate vessel was seen a signal, "Water, water; we die of thirst!" The answer from the friendly vessel at once came back, "Cast down your bucket where you are." A second time the signal, "Water, water; send us water!" ran up from the distressed vessel, and was answered, "Cast down your bucket where you are." And a third and fourth signal for water was answered, "Cast down your bucket where you are." The captain of the distressed vessel, at last heeding the injunction, cast down his bucket, and it came up full of fresh, sparkling water from the mouth of the Amazon River. To those of my race who depend on bettering their condition in a foreign land or who underestimate the importance of cultivating friendly relations with the Southern white man, who is their next-door neighbour, I would say: "Cast down you bucket where you are"—cast it down in making friends in every manly way of the people of all races by whom we are surrounded.

Cast it down in agriculture, mechanics, in commerce, in domestic service, and in the professions. And in this connection it is well to bear in mind that whatever other sins the South may be called to bear, when it comes to business, pure and simple, it is in the South that the Negro is given a man's chance in the commercial world, and in nothing is this Exposition more eloquent than in emphasizing this chance. Our greatest danger is that in the great leap from slavery to freedom we may overlook the fact that the masses of us are to live by the productions of our hands, and fail to keep in mind that we shall prosper in proportion as we learn to dignify and glorify common labour and put brains and skill into the common occupations of life; shall prosper in proportion as we learn to draw the line between the superficial and the substantial, the ornamental gewgaws of life and the useful. No race can prosper till it learns that there is as much dignity in tilling a field as in writing a poem. It is at the bottom of life we must begin, and not at the top. Nor should we permit our grievances to overshadow our opportunities.

To those of the white race who look to the incoming of those of foreign birth and strange tongue and habits for the prosperity of the South, were I permitted I would repeat what I say to my own race, "Cast down your bucket where you are." Cast it down among the eight millions of Negroes whose habits you know, whose fidelity and love you have tested in days when to have proved treacherous meant the ruin of your firesides. Cast down your bucket among these people who have, without strikes and labour wars, tilled your fields, cleared your forests, builded your railroads and cities, and brought forth treasures from the bowels of the earth, and helped make possible this magnificent representation of the progress of the South. Casting down your bucket among my people, helping and encouraging them as you are doing on these grounds, and to education of head, hand, and heart, you will find that they will buy your surplus land, make blossom the waste places in your fields, and run your factories. While doing this, you can be sure in the future, as in the past, that you and your families will be surrounded by the most patient, faithful, law-abiding, and unresentful people that the world has seen. As we have proved our loyalty to you in the past, in nursing your children, watching by the sick-bed of your mothers and fathers, and often following them with tear-dimmed eyes to their graves, so in the future, in our humble way, we shall stand by you with a devotion that no foreigner can approach, ready to lay down our lives, if need be, in defence of yours, interlacing our industrial, commercial, civil, and religious life with yours in a way that shall make the interests of both races one. In all things that are purely social we can be as separate as the fingers, yet one as the hand in all things essential to mutual progress.

There is no defence or security for any of us except in the highest intelligence and development of all. If anywhere there are efforts tending to curtail the fullest growth of the Negro, let these efforts be turned into stimulating, encouraging, and making him the most useful and intelligent citizen. Effort or means so invested will pay a thousand per cent interest. These efforts will be twice blessed—"blessing him that gives and him that takes."

There is no escape through law of man or God from the inevitable:—

> The laws of changeless justice bind
> Oppressor with oppressed;
> And close as sin and suffering joined
> We march to fate abreast.

Nearly sixteen millions of hands will aid you in pulling the load upward, or they will pull against you the load downward. We shall constitute one-third and more of the ignorance and crime of the South, or one-third its intelligence and progress; we shall contribute one-third to the business and industrial prosperity of the South, or we shall prove a veritable body of death, stagnating, depressing, retarding every effort to advance the body politic.

Gentlemen of the Exposition, as we present to you our humble effort at an exhibition of our progress, you must not expect overmuch. Starting thirty years ago with ownership here and there in a few quilts and pumpkins and chickens (gathered from miscellaneous sources), remember the path that has led from these to the inventions and production of agricultural implements, buggies, steam-engines, newspapers, books, statuary, carving, paintings, the management of drug-stores and banks, has not been trodden without contact with thorns and thistles. While we take pride in what we exhibit as a result of our independent efforts, we do not for a moment forget that our part in this exhibition would fall far short of your expectations but for the constant help that has come to our educational life, not only from the Southern states, but especially from Northern philanthropists, who have made their gifts a constant stream of blessing and encouragement.

The wisest among my race understand that the agitation of questions of social equality is the extremest folly, and that progress in the enjoyment of all the privileges that will come to us must be the result of severe and constant struggle rather than of artificial forcing. No race that has anything to contribute to the markets of the world is long in any degree ostracized. It is important and right that all privileges of the law be ours, but it is vastly more important that we be prepared for the exercises of these privileges. The opportunity to earn a dollar in a factory just now is worth infinitely more than the opportunity to spend a dollar in an opera-house.

In conclusion, may I repeat that nothing in thirty years has given us more hope and encouragement, and drawn us so near to you of the white race, as this opportunity offered by the Exposition; and here bending, as it were, over the altar that represents the results of the struggles of your race and mine, both starting practically empty-handed three decades ago, I pledge that in your effort to work out the great and intricate problem which God has laid at the doors of the South, you shall have at all times the patient, sympathetic help of my race; only let this be constantly in mind, that, while from representations in these buildings of the product of field, of forest, of mine, of factory, letters, and art, much good will come, yet far above and beyond material benefits will be that higher good, that, let us pray God, will come, in a blotting out of sectional differences and racial animosities and suspicions, in a determination to administer absolute justice, in a willing obedience among all classes to the mandates of law. This, this, coupled with our material prosperity, will bring into our beloved South a new heaven and a new earth.

The first thing that I remember, after I had finished speaking, was that Governor Bullock rushed across the platform and took me by the hand, and that others did the same. I received so many and such hearty congratulations that I found it difficult to get out of the building. I did not appreciate to any degree, however, the impression which my address seemed to have made, until the next morning, when I went into the business part of the city. As soon as I was recognized, I was surprised to find myself pointed out and surrounded by a crowd of men who wished to shake hands with me. This was kept up on every street on to which I went, to an extent which embarrassed me so much that I went back to my boarding-place. The next morning I returned to Tuskegee. At the station in Atlanta, and at almost all of the stations at which the train stopped between that city and Tuskegee, I found a crowd of people anxious to shake hands with me.

The papers in all parts of the United States published the address in full, and for months afterward there were complimentary editorial references to it. Mr. Clark Howell, the editor of the Atlanta *Constitution*, telegraphed to a New York paper, among other words, the following, "I do not exaggerate when I say that Professor Booker T. Washington's address yesterday was one of the most notable speeches, both as to character and as to the warmth of its reception, ever delivered to a Southern audience. The address was a revelation. The whole speech is a platform upon which blacks and whites can stand with full justice to each other."

The Boston *Transcript* said editorially: "The speech of Booker T. Washington at the Atlanta Exposition, this week, seems to have dwarfed all the other proceedings and the Exposition itself. The sensation that it has caused in the press has never been equalled."

I very soon began receiving all kinds of propositions from lecture bureaus, and editors of magazines and papers, to take the lecture platform, and to write articles. One lecture bureau offered me fifty thousand dollars, or two hundred dollars a night and expenses, if I would place my services at its disposal for a given period. To all these communications I replied that my life-work was at Tuskegee; and that whenever I spoke it must be in the interests of the Tuskegee school and my race, and that I would enter into no arrangements that seemed to place a mere commercial value upon my services.

Some days after its delivery I sent a copy of my address to the President of the United States, the Hon. Grover Cleveland. I received from him the following autograph reply:—

Gray Gables, Buzzard's Bay, Mass.,
October 6, 1895.

Booker T. Washington, Esq.:

MY DEAR SIR: I thank you for sending me a copy of your address delivered at the Atlanta Exposition.

I thank you with much enthusiasm for making the address. I have read it with intense interest, and I think the Exposition would be fully justified if it did not do more than furnish the opportunity for its delivery. Your words cannot fail to delight and encourage all who wish well for your race; and if our coloured fellow-citizens do not from your utterances gather new hope and form new determinations to gain every valuable advantage offered them by their citizenship, it will be strange indeed.

Yours very truly,
GROVER CLEVELAND.

Later I met Mr. Cleveland, for the first time, when, as President, he visited the Atlanta Exposition. At the request of myself and others he consented to spend an hour in the Negro Building, for the purpose of inspecting the Negro exhibit and of giving the coloured people in attendance an opportunity to shake hands with him. As soon as I met Mr. Cleveland I became impressed with his simplicity, greatness, and rugged honesty. I have met him many times since then, both at public functions and at his private residence in Princeton, and the more I see of him the more I admire him. When he visited the Negro Building in Atlanta he seemed to give himself up wholly, for that hour, to the coloured people. He seemed to be as careful to shake hands with some old coloured "auntie" clad partially in rags, and to take as much pleasure in doing so, as if he were greeting some millionnaire. Many of the coloured people took advantage of the occasion to get him to write his name in a book or on a slip of paper. He was as careful and patient in doing this as if he were putting his signature to some great state document.

Mr. Cleveland has not only shown his friendship for me in many personal ways, but has always consented to do anything I have asked of him for our school. This he has done, whether it was to make a personal donation or to use his influence in securing the donations of others. Judging from my personal acquaintance with Mr. Cleveland, I do not believe that he is conscious of possessing any colour prejudice. He is too great for that. In my contact with people I find that, as a rule, it is only the little, narrow people who live for themselves, who never read good books, who do not travel, who never open up their souls in a way to permit them to come into contact with other souls— with the great outside world. No man whose vision is bounded by colour can come into contact with what is highest and best in the world. In meeting men, in many places, I have found that the happiest people are those who do the most for others; the most miserable are those who do the least. I have also found that few things, if any, are capable of making one so blind and narrow as race prejudice. I often say to our students, in the course of my talks to them on Sunday evenings in the chapel, that the longer I live and the more experience I have of the world, the more I am convinced that, after all, the one thing that is most worth living for—and dying for, if need be—is the opportunity of making some one else more happy and more useful.

The coloured people and the coloured newspapers at first seemed to be greatly pleased with the character of my Atlanta address, as well as with its reception. But after the first burst of enthusiasm began to die away, and the coloured people began reading the speech in cold type, some of them seemed to feel that they had been hypnotized. They seemed to feel that I had been too liberal in my remarks toward the Southern whites, and that I had not spoken out strongly enough for what they termed the "rights" of the race. For a while there was a reaction, so far as a certain element of my own race was concerned, but later these reactionary ones seemed to have been won over to my way of believing and acting.

While speaking of changes in public sentiment, I recall that about ten years after the school at Tuskegee was established, I had an experience that I shall never forget. Dr. Lyman Abbott, then the pastor of Plymouth Church, and also editor of the *Outlook* (then the *Christian Union*), asked me to write a letter for his paper giving my opinion of the exact condition, mental and moral, of the coloured ministers in the South, as based upon my observations. I wrote the letter, giving the exact facts as I conceived them to be. The picture painted was a rather black one—or, since I am black, shall I say "white"? It could not be otherwise with a race but a few years out of slavery, a race which had not had time or opportunity to produce a competent ministry.

What I said soon reached every Negro minister in the country, I think, and the letters of condemnation which I received from them were not few. I think that for a year after the publication of this article every association and every conference or religious body of any kind, of my race, that met, did not fail before adjourning to pass a resolution condemning me, or calling upon me to retract or modify what I had said. Many of these organizations went so far in their resolutions as to advise parents to cease sending their children to Tuskegee. One association even appointed a "missionary" whose duty it was to warn the people against sending their children to Tuskegee. This missionary had a son in the school, and I noticed that, whatever the "missionary" might have said or done with regard to others, he was careful not to take his son away from the institution. Many of the coloured papers, especially those that were the organs of religious bodies, joined in the general chorus of condemnation or demands for retraction.

During the whole time of the excitement, and through all the criticism, I did not utter a word of explanation or retraction. I knew that I was right, and that time and the sober second thought of the people would vindicate me. It was not long before the bishops and other church leaders began to make a careful investigation of the conditions of the ministry, and they found out that I was right. In fact, the oldest and most influential bishop in one branch of the Methodist Church said that my words were far too mild. Very soon public sentiment began making itself felt, in demanding a purifying of the ministry. While this is not yet complete by any means, I think I may say, without egotism, and I have been told by many of our most influential ministers, that my words had much to do with starting a demand for the placing of a higher type of men in the pulpit. I have had the satisfaction of having many who once condemned me thank me heartily for my frank words.

The change of the attitude of the Negro ministry, so far as regards myself, is so complete that at the present time I have no warmer friends among any class than I have among the clergymen. The improvement in the character and life of the Negro ministers is one of the most gratifying evidences of the progress of the race. My experience with them, as well as other events in my life, convince me that the thing to do, when one feels sure that he has said or done the right thing, and is condemned, is to stand still and keep quiet. If he is right, time will show it.

In the midst of the discussion which was going on concerning my Atlanta speech, I received the letter which I give below, from Dr. Gilman, the President of Johns Hopkins University, who had been made chairman of the judges of award in connection with the Atlanta Exposition:—

> Johns Hopkins University, Baltimore,
> President's Office, September 30, 1895.
>
> DEAR MR. WASHINGTON: Would it be agreeable to you to be one of the Judges of Award in the Department of Education at Atlanta? If so, I shall be glad to place your name upon the list. A line by telegraph will be welcomed.
>
> Yours very truly,
> D. C. GILMAN.

I think I was even more surprised to receive this invitation than I had been to receive the invitation to speak at the opening of the Exposition. It was to be a part of my duty, as one of the jurors, to pass not only upon the exhibits of the coloured schools, but also upon those of the white schools. I accepted the position, and spent a month in Atlanta in performance of the duties which it entailed. The board of jurors was a large one, consisting in all of sixty members. It was about equally divided between Southern white people and Northern white people. Among them were college presidents, leading scientists and men of letters, and specialists in many subjects. When the group of jurors to which I was assigned met for organization, Mr. Thomas Nelson Page, who was one of the number, moved that I be made secretary of that division, and the motion was unanimously adopted. Nearly half of our division were Southern people. In performing my duties in the inspection of the exhibits of white schools I was in every case treated with respect, and at the close of our labours I parted from my associates with regret.

I am often asked to express myself more freely than I do upon the political condition and the political future of my race. These recollections of my experience in Atlanta give me the opportunity to do so briefly. My own belief is, although I have never before said so in so many words, that the time will come when the Negro in the South will be accorded all the political rights which his ability, character, and material possessions entitle him to. I think, though, that the opportunity to freely exercise such political rights will not come in any large degree through outside or artificial forcing, but will be accorded to the Negro by the Southern white people themselves, and that they will protect him in the exercise of those rights. Just as soon as the South gets over the old feeling that it is being forced by "foreigners," or "aliens," to do something which it does not want to do, I believe that the change in the direction that I have indicated is going to begin. In fact, there are indications that it is already beginning in a slight degree.

Let me illustrate my meaning. Suppose that some months before the opening of the Atlanta Exposition there had been a general demand from the press and public platform outside the South that a Negro be given a place on the opening programme, and that a Negro be placed upon the board of jurors of award. Would any such recognition of the race have taken place? I do not think so. The Atlanta officials went as far as they did because they felt it to be a pleasure, as well as a duty, to reward what they considered merit in the Negro race. Say what we will, there is something in human nature which we cannot blot out, which makes one man, in the end, recognize and reward merit in another, regardless of colour or race.

I believe it is the duty of the Negro—as the greater part of the race is already doing—to deport himself modestly in regard to political

346

claims, depending upon the slow but sure influences that proceed from the possession of property, intelligence, and high character for the full recognition of his political rights. I think that the according of the full exercise of political rights is going to be a matter of natural, slow growth, not an over-night, gourd-vine affair. I do not believe that the Negro should cease voting, for a man cannot learn the exercise of self-government by ceasing to vote, any more than a boy can learn to swim by keeping out of the water, but I do believe that in his voting he should more and more be influenced by those of intelligence and character who are his next-door neighbours.

I know coloured men who, through the encouragement, help, and advice of Southern white people, have accumulated thousands of dollars' worth of property, but who, at the same time, would never think of going to those same persons for advice concerning the casting of their ballots. This, it seems to me, is unwise and unreasonable, and should cease. In saying this I do not mean that the Negro should truckle, or not vote from principle, for the instant he ceases to vote from principle he loses the confidence and respect of the Southern white man even.

I do not believe that any state should make a law that permits an ignorant and poverty-stricken white man to vote, and prevents a black man in the same condition from voting. Such a law is not only unjust, but it will react, as all unjust laws do, in time; for the effect of such a law is to encourage the Negro to secure education and property, and at the same time it encourages the white man to remain in ignorance and poverty. I believe that in time, through the operation of intelligence and friendly race relations, all cheating at the ballot box in the South will cease. It will become apparent that the white man who begins by cheating a Negro out of his ballot soon learns to cheat a white man out of his, and that the man who does this ends his career of dishonesty by the theft of property or by some equally serious crime. In my opinion, the time will come when the South will encourage all of its citizens to vote. It will see that it pays better, from every standpoint, to have healthy, vigorous life than to have that political stagnation which always results when one-half of the population has no share and no interest in the Government.

As a rule, I believe in universal, free suffrage, but I believe that in the South we are confronted with peculiar conditions that justify the protection of the ballot in many of the states, for a while at least, either by an educational test, a property test, or by both combined; but whatever tests are required, they should be made to apply with equal and exact justice to both races.

Of the Training of Black Men

When W. E. B. Du Bois, trained at Harvard and the University of Berlin, published in 1903 his The Souls of Black Folk, *from which the following passage is taken, his break with Booker T. Washington was for the first time openly acknowledged. Following the amazingly favorable reception of his Atlanta Exposition Address in 1895 (see p. 337), Washington had in a short time become the leader of the Negroes in America. His policy of accommodation and gradualism as the answer to the racial question appeased the white South and won the support of Northern politicians, businessmen, and philanthropists.*

During these same years the younger Du Bois, a trained sociologist, was making notable contributions to the scholarly study of the American Negro in Suppression of the African Slave Trade (1896), The Philadelphia Negro (1899), *and the series of monographs that began to appear in 1896 under the auspices of the Atlanta Conference. As a result of his scientific studies and his observations of the consequences of Washington's policy, Du Bois concluded that the "South ought to be led, by candid and honest criticism, to assert her better self and do her full duty to the race she has cruelly wronged and is still wronging. The North—her co-partner in guilt—cannot salve her conscience by plastering it with gold. . . . If worse comes to worst, can the moral fibre of this country survive the slow throttling and murder of nine millions of men?" The Negroes must insist on their civil rights. They must learn to exercise political power. If they were to have trained leaders in this crusade, the most capable and intelligent of their young men must receive the benefit of higher education. This—and more that was radical at the time—Du Bois said in "Of Mr. Washington and Others," the third essay in* The Souls of Black Folk.

Du Bois soon turned to action. In 1905 he was one of the organizers of the Niagara Movement, whose aims were the abolition of all distinctions based on race or color. This organization was short-lived but it prepared the way for the founding, in 1909, of the National Association for the Advancement of Colored People, whose principles are still, in the main, those which Du Bois enunciated in 1903 in his declaration of revolt against Washington and his "Tuskegee Machine." From 1910 to 1932 Du Bois edited The Crisis, *the official organ of the NAACP. He returned to Atlanta University (the only Negro graduate school in this country) to serve as Professor of Sociology from 1932 to 1944.*

348

As the following passage shows, Dr. Du Bois's leading idea from 1900 on has been that "no secure civilization can be built in the South with the Negro as an ignorant, turbulent proletariat." This excerpt is taken from "Of the Training of Black Men," the sixth essay in The Souls of Black Folk (*Chicago: A. C. McClurg & Co.; 1903*).

IF it is true that there are an appreciable number of Negro youth in the land capable by character and talent to receive that higher training, the end of which is culture, and if the two and a half thousand who have had something of this training in the past have in the main proved themselves useful to their race and generation, the question then comes, What place in the future development of the South ought the Negro college and college-bred man to occupy? That the present social separation and acute race-sensitiveness must eventually yield to the influences of culture, as the South grows civilized, is clear. But such transformation calls for singular wisdom and patience. If, while the healing of this vast sore is progressing, the races are to live for many years side by side, united in economic effort, obeying a common government, sensitive to mutual thought and feeling, yet subtly and silently separate in many matters of deeper human intimacy,—if this unusual and dangerous development is to progress amid peace and order, mutual respect and growing intelligence, it will call for social surgery at once the delicatest and nicest in modern history. It will demand broad-minded, upright men, both white and black, and in its final accomplishment American civilization will triumph. So far as white men are concerned, this fact is to-day being recognized in the South, and a happy renaissance of university education seems imminent. But the very voices that cry hail to this good work are, strange to relate, largely silent or antagonistic to the higher education of the Negro.

Strange to relate! for this is certain, no secure civilization can be built in the South with the Negro as an ignorant, turbulent proletariat. Suppose we seek to remedy this by making them laborers and nothing more: they are not fools, they have tasted of the Tree of Life, and they will not cease to think, will not cease attempting to read the riddle of the world. By taking away their best equipped teachers and leaders, by slamming the door of opportunity in the faces of their bolder and brighter minds, will you make them satisfied with their lot? or will you not rather transfer their leading from the hands of men taught to think to the hands of untrained demagogues? . . .

The dangerously clear logic of the Negro's position will more and more loudly assert itself in that day when increasing wealth and more intricate social organization preclude the South from being, as it so largely is, simply an armed camp for intimidating black folk. Such waste of energy cannot be spared if the South is to catch up with civilization. And as the black third of the land grows in thrift and skill, unless skilfully guided in its larger philosophy, it must more and more brood over the red past and the creeping, crooked present, until it grasps a gospel of revolt and revenge and throws its new-found energies athwart the current of advance. . . .

I insist that the question of the future is how best to keep these millions from brooding over the wrongs of the past and the difficulties of the present, so that all their energies may be bent toward a cheerful striving and co-operation with their white neighbors toward a larger, juster, and fuller future. That one wise method of doing this lies in the closer knitting of the Negro to the great industrial possibilities of the South is a great truth. And this the common schools and the manual training and trade schools are working to accomplish. But these alone are not enough. The foundations of knowledge in this race, as in others, must be sunk deep in the college and university if we would build a solid, permanent structure. Internal problems of social advance must inevitably come,—problems of work and wages, of families and homes, of morals and the true valuing of the things of life; and all these and other inevitable problems of civilization the Negro must meet and solve largely for himself, by reason of his isolation; and can there be any possible solution other than by study and thought and an appeal to the rich experience of the past? Is there not, with such a group and in such a crisis, infinitely more danger to be apprehended from half-trained minds and shallow thinking than from over-education and over-refinement? Surely we have wit enough to found a Negro college so manned and equipped as to steer successfully between the *dilettante* and the fool. We shall hardly induce black men to believe that if their stomachs be full, it matters little about their brains. They already dimly perceive that the paths of peace winding between honest toil and dignified manhood call for the guidance of skilled thinkers, the loving, reverent comradeship between the black lowly and the black men emancipated by training and culture.

The function of the Negro college, then, is clear: it must maintain the standards of popular education, it must seek the social regeneration of the Negro, and it must help in the solution of problems of race contact and co-operation. And finally, beyond all this, it must develop men. Above our modern socialism, and out of the worship of the mass, must persist and evolve that higher individualism which the centres of culture protect; there must come a loftier respect for the sovereign human soul that seeks to know itself and the world about it; that seeks a freedom for expansion and self-development; that will love and hate and labor in its own way, untrammeled alike by old and new. Such souls aforetime have inspired and guided worlds, and if we be not wholly bewitched by our Rhine-gold, they shall again. Herein the longing of black men must have respect: the rich and bitter depth of their experience, the unknown treasures of their inner life, the strange rendings of nature they have seen, may give the world new points of view and make their loving, living, and doing precious to all human hearts. And to themselves in these days that try their souls, the chance to soar in the dim blue air above the smoke is to their finer spirits boon and guerdon for what they lose on earth by being black.

"Poor Wayfarin' Stranger"

The author of No Day of Triumph, *from which the following incident is taken, has good reason to believe that for the white man as well as for the members of his race this is "not a day of triumph; it is a day of dedication. Here muster, not the forces of party, but the forces of humanity. Men's hearts wait upon us." The words are Woodrow Wilson's but they forge the theme and are the epigraph of J. Saunders Redding's account of his long journey among the Negroes of the South, undertaken in 1940 with the encouragement of the University of North Carolina and the Rockefeller Foundation.*

Dr. Redding was educated at Brown University; at present he is a professor at the Hampton Institute. His books include To Make a Poet Black *(1939), a novel,* Stranger and Alone *(1950),* They Came in Chains *(1950)—a volume in the People of America Series—and* On Being Negro in America *(1951).*

No Day of Triumph was published by Harper & Brothers, copyright, 1942, by J. Saunders Redding. The passage from it which is printed here will be found on pp. 168–75. It is reprinted by permission of the publishers.

OF course there is no typical southern white man, just as there is no typical southern Negro. There are niggers, darkies, and colored folks or nigrahs, terms which during slavery were based on differences in status in the social order, but which now imply only a nice discrimination on the part of the whites in such intangibles as attitudes and dispositions. Of course, to the vast majority of southern whites all Negroes are niggers. "All niggers look alike to me" is an axiom of great force, and the majority admit no exception to it. For them there is no mobility in social status and no elevating accomplishment among Negroes.

But also there are poor whites, plain crackers, and the good white folk. These distinctions were founded originally in economics, but they are less valid now than they were twenty years ago. Perhaps when the economy of the South progresses farther in the direction in which it seems to be going, these distinctions will be wiped out entirely. The plantation system is dying. The plantations themselves are passing into the ownership of companies and banks, and the *good white folk* who formerly lived on them (or off them, if you are opposed to a feudalistic society) are moving into the cities, where the crackers and landless poor whites have already been driven in great numbers by competition with progressively cheapened labor on impoverished soil. But though the distinctions were based in economics, they carried all the implications of the social pattern of relations between the races—a pattern that is breaking up also. The Negro can no longer tell his white friend from his white foe, the crackers from the good white folk on the basis of occupation or lack of it, economic position, or even on the basis of the constantly thinning personal relations between himself and somebody white. So complex have relations become in comparison with their earlier simplicity that in order to safeguard himself the Negro typifies all southern whites in gross, and when he comes across a deviation from this type he exaggerates the deviation as much as his concept of the norm is exaggerated. He does this in order to bring a more favorable balance into the picture, and not through either shock or surprise, for he knows that there are some good white people.

What is the southern white man? From childhood I had carried about in my heart and brain one picture of him. My grandmother's stories of Caleb Wrightson, her master; the Negro papers my father took; the cold fury of the editorials of Du Bois; the immature but gripping stories in the *Crisis* and *Opportunity;* bastardy, peonage, and lynching tales; and finally a little book of obscene cartoons, which came from heaven knows where, but which circulated surreptitiously through our school for weeks, all shaped my picture of the typical southern white. He was a soulless creature of the devil, drooling blood and venom, ignorant beyond belief, but also cunning beyond belief; filthy, lecherous, murderous, cowardly, superstitious, and by God accursed. He was gangling, raw-boned, pot-bellied, sandy-haired. He went about barefoot, in an undershirt and dirt-crusted blue denim breeches,

without which he never slept and within which he concealed a bottle
of red whisky, a horse pistol, and other lethal weapons. He was the
bogey-man with which a great many Negro mothers in the North
frightened their children into obedience. In short, he was the Negro
version of what (I discovered through Thomas Dixon and Fairfax
Craven) the Negro who was not a buffoon was to the white man.

I knew my picture was exaggerated and false, as composites are
always false, but experience and cold knowledge in the head seem to
have little power over images that well up from the vivid memories
of childhood fears. Six uninterrupted years in the South had not blotted
out that image of the southern white man. It lurked deep within me,
a gnawing, subconscious fear. On this journey through the South I was
constantly expecting to meet him, for now less than ever was I protected against chance contacts with him.

Indeed, I sought no protection, and often against my better judgment I picked up hitchhikers, who were generally harmlessly and de-
fensively voluble on such subjects as their colored friends (all of whom
nearly all of them expected me to know), Hitler, hitchhiking, animal
husbandry, fornication, money, and getting where they were going.
Many of them were looking for work, or merely going to the next
town to see a girl. One faded-eyed fellow, who was easily forty, was
going to Texas because he had "haid a eachin'" to go there since he
was a boy, and he had just seen Tom Mix and his wonder horse in a
"stage show," and so he was going. I did not mention to him that he
was sitting on a newspaper which carried an item relating Mix's accidental death in an automobile wreck in Michigan. I think it might
have killed him. Unlike most of them, he called me neither "Preacher,"
"Perfesser," nor "Docter."

Twice I thought I had met my typical southern white man.

Once when a bridge was out and a little three-car ferry was pressed
into service across the swollen St. Francis River in southeastern Missouri, I thought I had met him. My car was the third in line in the
narrow, improvised slipway. The other two drivers were white men,
one a young man driving an ancient, high-wheeled Dodge and the
other in his middle years, apparently prosperous and apparently on the
return end of a motor trip with his wife. His car, which bore a Kentucky license tag, was piled high with luggage and gaudy souvenirs,
and the windows were all stuck up with guest stickers.

I was standing looking at the swollen river when the older man
came up and then the young man. We fell into pleasant conversation
about cars, roads, and the little ferry, which we could see bobbing and
dancing frantically in mid-river. It was late afternoon, growing dark,
and the young man was worried that his old generator would not give
him sufficient power to run his lights in the night. We all went over

and looked at the generator. None of us knew anything about it, but the young man felt better for our looking.

"She's getting old," he said. "Anything's li'ble to happen. I sure hope she gets me where I'm goin'. She always has."

"She will," I said.

"Lotta life in her yet," the older man said. "Them old Dodges was good cars when Dodge made 'em."

"Mine's a Dodge," I said.

"'Tis, ain't it? What kinda car is it now?"

"Pretty good," I said.

"This here's been a durn good car," the young man said, putting the hood down. It had been painted recently and the brush strokes were pretty bad, but it had a certain dignity still.

"They made 'em to last when they built that'n. I knowed a feller in Versailles drove one twenty-some years."

"Versailles? Where's that at?" the young man asked.

"That's my home. That's in good old Kentuck."

"It's a funny thing, but your home state always looks good to you when you ain't in it," the young man said.

Just then we saw the boiling dust. The road off the highway where the damaged bridge was to the ferry slip was a bad dirt and gravel road. My own dust had not settled on it. We could not see what was coming, but we could see the dust whorling up and rolling thickly across the scraggly cotton fields.

"Here comes another car," I said.

"Yeah. I see it. He's got a hour to wait. Can't but three cars get on this ferry," the young man said, looking up the road. He was a good-looking young man, somewhat short and stocky, but with handsome eyes and a fine, mobile mouth.

"How you been finding the roads?" the older man asked me.

"Good."

"That's one thing. We got a system o' roads in this country, best in the world. All the way to California they're good. They tell me the army's going to build all the new roads. Gittin' ready for war, I reckon. Gittin' ready to fight that damn fool Hitler. War ain't no credit to nobody, but we can lick any nation on earth. Think we're ready?"

"I had to register," the young man said. "I'd's soon be in the damn army as doing what I'm doing."

"I never was in the army. I've come up between every war," the older man said.

Now we heard the rattling, metallic, machine-gun sound of gravel flying into fenders. We still could not see what was coming, but it sounded like more than one car, or a car traveling at high speed.

"Somebody sure is helling," the young man said.

354

"Goin'a bust a spring, too."

"Some guys is crazy." The young man hitched his thumbs in his belt.

The car poured out of the dust and in another second yelled to a stop just behind my car. It was a new car, one of the fast, light machines, but the left fender was smashed and the radiator grill and headlight entirely gone. A big, sloppy man got out, looked at my car, then across the river to the ferry, then at the other two cars and at us. He was dressed in khaki trousers and shirt, and just above the top of his trousers his shirt was open, exposing a mat of hair around his creased and startlingly white navel.

"Which one o' y-all does this yere car 'long to?" he asked, pointing to my car and walking toward us.

"Him. You sure was helling," the young man said.

"Big boy, yere?" the sloppy man said. "Big boy, you're goin'a hafter back up an' let me in 'er."

"Why?" I asked.

"Why? What the hell! Whare you from, boy?"

"None of your damned business," I said, hoping I was saying it quietly and without my voice trembling.

He turned his big bulk as if he were coming for me. His face, at first red with astonishment, was now white with anger. He looked at me and he also looked at the others. The young man and the older man looked at him impassively. The older man's wife was leaning across the seat under the wheel looking at us. The sloppy man licked his lips. I had made up my mind what I was going to do if I had to do it. I meant to send my foot plunging into his white belly.

"I ain't in no hurry," the older man said. "You can have my place."

"I'm goin' a have this yere niggah's place. Lis'en, you black . . ."

"For Christ's sake! Wallace Beery comes up an' wants to make trouble," the young man said.

The older man stopped going toward his car. Something passed out of me. It was as if stitches which had been tight and festering for a long time were being drawn. The something gathered in the top of my head and in the tips of my fingers and then ran up my arms and down through my chest and stomach and legs and into the ground. It was a sensation as real as pain. It left me feeling very light and free and no longer holding myself with that terrible, galvanizing concentration. I saw everything clearly, the lady watching us through the car window, the old man who had stopped in the middle of the road, the young man, and the white, hairy belly. I was not afraid.

"Damn'f I'd move for him," the young man said.

"I don't b'lieve I will now," the older man said, standing in the road. "No, sir. I don't b'lieve I will!"

The way he said it, suddenly flexing his arms in decision, seemed indescribably comic. The young man laughed. Then I laughed. The sloppy man licked his white lips. The lady got out of the car.

"What the hell is this?" the big man said.

"Wasn't nothin' but three cars waitin' for the ferry 'til you come," the young man said.

"Y-all side with a niggah 'gainst a white man?"

"What you wanta make trouble for?" The young man kept his thumbs hitched in his belt. He had not once raised his voice.

"Y-all mus' be niggah-lovers. This black bas . . ."

"Dick Eberle, you ain't a-goin'a move," the old lady said, "an' I ain't a-goin'a stand here an' listen to his swearing."

"If it wasn't for the ol' woman," the sloppy man said, threatening now also the young man.

"Yeah! You're Wallace Beery. You're Humphrey Bogart."

"Shut up, you!" And standing three feet away, the sloppy man drew back his hand.

"You stink!" the young man said, not moving.

Without another word, the big man went to his car, backed it furiously, and drove off in a great cloud of dust.

"He-hee," the older man said. After that there was an embarrassed silence.

Suddenly I was very tired and weak, and an almost psychopathic awareness multiplied my sensations to the point of pain. It seemed to me that a moment before, the young man, the older man, and I had been close together. Now we were apart. I did not try to think of a reason for this. I simply felt it like a vast steely emptiness in my stomach. The young man, his thumbs hitched in his brass-studded belt, stood looking at the ground. The old man had stooped and was intently studying a tire. He rubbed the dust off a space and looked, and then he rubbed the dust off another space and looked at the new tire. Still stooping, he duck-walked to another wheel and did the same thing. The lady stood in the road watching the approaching ferry. The young man turned and looked at the river.

"Dick, I reckon we better get in. It's about here," the lady said.

"I'm afraid it'll be dark by the time we get across. If you follow me, you won't have any trouble about your lights," I said to the young man.

"My car don't go so fast," the young man said, looking at the river and the sidling ferry. "I'm only goin' ten miles."

"I'd be glad to help you," I said.

"She'll kick up enough juice."

The ferry came in and a car bumped off, and then we drove on to the ferry. It was a dinky, flat-bottomed, homemade ferry, with an old automobile motor coughing under a piece of chicken wire in the stern.

It had no superstructure except a railing made of water piping along each side. We all sat in our cars on the trip over. Darkness came. When we reached the other side, I pretended to have trouble starting, and they pulled off. Then I pulled off very slowly, and they were gone.

Into a Strange New Land

Carl Thomas Rowan's great opportunity came when he was assigned to the Navy V-12 program during the Second World War and sent to study at Oberlin College. He had been born a Negro in Tennessee and had grown up in an environment of the small-town, Jim Crow South. To him the new freedom he found in the Navy, the responsibility he carried as an officer, and the new horizons opened by his studies at Oberlin were a revelation. After the war he went back to Oberlin to complete work for his bachelor's degree and then went on to the University of Minnesota to take a master's degree in journalism. He then became a highly successful writer for the Minneapolis Morning Tribune *and a respected leader among the younger men of the city.*

In 1952 he published South of Freedom, *stating that he had written it "because I do not believe that man was born to hate and be hated; I cannot believe that the race problem is an inevitable concomitant of democratic life." The book is a series of essays dealing with the race problem, some of which had already won him acclaim when they appeared as articles in the* Morning Tribune.

The following sensitive and honest portrayal of what it means to a young Negro to find himself breaking free of a restricting life that he has always known is reprinted from South of Freedom, *by Carl Thomas Rowan, by permission of Alfred A. Knopf, Inc., copyright 1952 by Carl T. Rowan.*

I REMEMBER 1943 as the year of the "great rebellion." For it was in the summer of 1943 that my mind, heart, and soul rebelled and ceased being part of a green, small-town Negro youth, well-schooled in the ways of his native South. During that summer, I broke all mental ties

357

with my home town; yet, physically, I was still very much a part of McMinnville, Tennessee, a farm-industrial community of about five thousand persons, at the foot of the Cumberland Mountains. It was a foolish and rather dangerous predicament for a young Southern Negro.

As I remember that Summer, I realize how fortunate I was to get out of McMinnville. Obviously, I had lost my usefulness to that middle-Tennessee community; and I cannot remember McMinnville ever being of particular usefulness to me. I had returned to McMinnville after spending my freshman year at Tennessee Agricultural and Industrial State College in Nashville. I felt that even in those nine months of college life I had outgrown my narrow life in McMinnville. I betrayed my feelings easily, much to the irritation of whites whose lawns I had mowed, whose windows I had washed, or whose basements I had scrubbed in past years.

During my year at Tennessee State, I had passed tests given by the United States Navy and was promised the opportunity to earn a commission, something the Navy had given no Negro at the time. After being sworn in at Nashville, I had returned to McMinnville, an apprentice seaman in the Naval Reserve. I was on inactive duty, awaiting assignment to what, in effect, was to be officers' candidate school.

For nearly eighteen years, practically all my life, I had lived in McMinnville. I had mowed lawns, swept basements, unloaded boxcars of coal, dug basements, hoed bulb-grass out of lawns, and done scores of other menial tasks that fell to Negroes by default. Until 1943, I did these jobs because almost all McMinnville Negroes did such jobs; the community expected it of us. In 1943, with Negro manpower already swept away by the draft board, I could see that I was expected to handle a greater-than-normal share of such jobs. But my year outside McMinnville, and my status as a Navy man, created revulsion within me and an air of haughtiness not designed to make me popular with the white citizens of my home town.

The Navy had put me outside the jurisdiction of draft boards, so, unlike many "rebellious" Negroes of the South, I could not be railroaded into the Armed Forces as punishment for offending some staunch citizen by rejecting his dirty chores. The Navy already had me, and I would be around until the Navy decided I should move elsewhere. I felt that, for the first time in my life, I was out of reach of all McMinnville and all her twenty-five-cents-an-hour jobs.

I became self-employed. I had learned to weave cane bottoms and backs for chairs in a shopwork class at Bernard High School, where the instructor had charged chair owners a very modest amount and the pupils did the work for sticks of peppermint candy. Since Bernard no longer was doing such work, I had a corner on the market. I tripled the charges and notified the "antique furniture" set that I was in business. Soon I had enough chairs piled up at my home to keep me busy most of the summer.

Tennessee summer days were not made for work; in fact, many a resident has doubted that they were made at all, but that they sprang to life from the caldrons of hell. In any event, I dressed more like a Southern Colonel than a Southern Negro, and spent the days reading. Occasionally I strolled through town, driving town and military policemen almost crazy in their efforts to understand how an apparently able-bodied Negro male had escaped the draft board. In three months they stopped me at least thirty times, demanding to see my draft-registration card.

That I was stopped so frequently was partially attributable to my conspicuous dress. Any Negro in a small Southern town is viewed with suspicion if he wears a tie and suit on weekdays, unless he is the principal of the Negro school, or perhaps a minister. I wore suits, which, though secondhand, were new to McMinnville. I had got them at the State Tuberculosis Hospital in Nashville, where I worked the summer of 1942 to earn tuition funds. I had left McMinnville for Nashville that summer—with seventy-seven cents in my pocket, and my clothes in a cardboard box—aboard a McBroom Lines truck on which I had wangled a ride from the white driver. I remember him only as a good Joe who drove me out to the college campus because he figured I could stand to save the bus fare.

At the hospital I carried food to the patients, bussed and washed dishes, swept ward floors and screens, and did almost everything but wash the nurses' feet. But I needed the thirty dollars a month—desperately. Occasionally, a doctor would complain that he had outgrown a suit. He would pass it to me, suggesting that I find someone who could use it. That was a fairly simple assignment. These suits made me one of the best-dressed freshmen on the Tennessee State campus; and but for my Naval Reserve card would have made me one of the best-dressed McMinnvillians ever jailed on a vagrancy charge.

After loafing through the blistering days that summer in McMinnville, I worked while the community slept. I weaved cane far into the cool night-hours, when the town was so silent that the rustle of wind in the pear tree behind the house was like the echo of a thousand chorus-girls, simultaneously swishing their taffeta skirts.

Early mornings, shortly after crawling into bed, and in the daze of half-sleep, I could smell boiling coffee and fried white salt-pork, and hear the splatter of hot grease as eggs were dropped into a frying-pan. Soon my father would be off to his job, stacking lumber at a near-by mill. And the rest of my family would be up, some heading for what work they could find, and my two younger sisters off to play. I would sleep until the sun's merciless rays curled the tin roof and drove me out of bed.

But morning after morning, before I arose, one or more cars pulled up in front of the house. A voice, obviously of a white person, would ask youngsters playing near by if "Tom Rowan's boy" lived there. "Yessir, Carl Rowan lives there," some child would reply, and, without further instructions, a clattering horde of kids would stampede into the house and to my bed to say: "Some white man wants you out there."

This irked me enough; but the whites always came with a half-demand, saying: "Somebody *has got* to do this job for me," and they irritated me until I acquired a smart-aleck disposition that was not part of my true nature. I had begun to love independence, and it pleased a part of me that I could not name, or even place, to be able to say that "Tom Rowan's boy" didn't *have* to do the job.

A man named Hunter, whose lawn I had mowed scores of times in previous years, several times for ten cents an hour, had me awakened early one morning. "Boy, they (he didn't say who) tell me uptown that you ain't doin' nothing. We're going to have a lawn party, and I gotta have my grass cut." With what now strikes me as boldness verging on recklessness, I told him that I had been so busy lately that I planned to hire someone to mow my lawn. He looked at my house, which sat about two feet off the gravel street, those two feet of yard containing not one blade of grass. He gave me a stare of contempt and drove away.

With reluctant thanks to man's greediness and inclination to war, I got out of McMinnville before I so provoked the whites as to jeopardize my physical well-being. One morning in late October I was ordered to active duty. On October 30, 1943, my secondhand clothes in a borrowed suitcase, I boarded a Jim Crow train and left the past and present of a life that I had begun to abhor. I had received more than the call of the United States Navy; as it turned out, I was answering the call of opportunity, for my hello to arms was farewell to the South in which I had been born and reared.

That I was leaving by Jim Crow train meant little to me then. Jim Crow was all I had known. For all the years that I had lived in the shadow of the Cumberland Mountains, two things were always certain: racial segregation and a steady stream of moonshine liquor out of the hills. I was a small-time youngster, off to a big-time war, riding the train for the first time in my life; and except for an accidental journey into Alabama aboard a lost bus, I was leaving Tennessee for the first time. Caught in a maelstrom of excitement, I could get little disturbed about Jim Crow—even when J was refused a Pullman berth from

Nashville to St. Louis, despite a Navy order. The ticket-seller told me none was available, and, even after my "great rebellion," I had not acquired the habit of challenging the word of a white man—not even after watching several whites get berths after my request was rejected. I took my first-class ticket and boarded a last-class coach, as Negroes had done for years.

I propped my head on my hand and dozed that Autumn night as my dirty, smoky Jim Crow coach rolled across Kentucky and southern Illinois. I was bound for Topeka, Kansas, and a Navy V-12 unit at Washburn Municipal University. There I found that I had crossed from my world of bare black feet on red clay and white perspiration on black brows into a strange new land. I had been snatched completely from a life of segregation; I was in a unit of 335 sailors, 334 of them white.

Remembering Nat Turner

Sterling A. Brown's poem on Nat Turner memorializes the leader of the most extensive slave revolt in the history of the Old South. From the earliest days of slavery white masters and their families lived in fairly constant fear of Negro insurrections, though they were surprisingly few in number when one considers the provocation and the opportunity.

The memory of such revolts as those led by Gabriel Prosser in Virginia (1800) and "Denmark" Vesey in Charleston (1822) persisted and, naturally enough, the number of the slaves involved and of their victims was exaggerated as the legends grew. After each outbreak the black codes were usually made more severe. Southerners were apprehensive lest the uprisings in Santo Domingo and Haiti induce slave revolts here. The abolitionists were particularly hated because their writings were incitements to rebellion. Southerners were quick to point out that the Nat Turner revolt occurred eight months after the publication of the first issue of William Lloyd Garrison's Liberator.

The strange personality of Nat Turner had much to do with the ferocity of the revolt named for him. He had on his head and breast marks which signified to the Negroes that he was "called" to lead them. Fanatically religious, he communed with voices and believed himself

*to be under the command of the Spirit. In May 1828 the great voice
told him that the time was near. An eclipse of the sun in February
1831 he took as a sign to begin the bloody work, but he twice postponed the day. The insurrection broke on August 21. Before troops
reached the seat of the trouble, Southampton County, Virginia, sixty
whites had been murdered, the first victims being the members of the
family of Turner's master, Joseph Travis. Of the more than fifty Negroes held for trial, seventeen were executed and twelve transported.
Many others had been killed during the revolt. Turner eluded his pursuers for more than two months. Although the revolt was quickly put
down, it spread terror through the South. Rumors abounded: that a
Negro band was marching on Macon, Georgia; that Wilmington,
North Carolina, had been burned.*

*Sterling A. Brown, who has graciously permitted me to reprint
"Remembering Nat Turner," was born in Washington, D.C., in 1901.
Educated at Williams College and at Harvard, he is now Professor of
English at Howard University. In 1937-8 he held a Guggenheim fel-
lowship. In 1939 he was a research worker on the Carnegie-Myrdal
study of the Negro. His books include* Southern Road *(1932), a vol-
ume of verse,* The Negro in American Fiction *(1938), and* Negro
Poetry and Drama *(1938).*

*A few explanatory notes to the poem are needed. Courtland (for-
merly Jerusalem), on the Nottaway River, is the county seat of
Southampton County, in which the Nat Turner insurrection took
place. Turner promised his followers that they would "go into Jerusalem."*

WE saw a bloody sunset over Courtland, once Jerusalem,
As we followed the trail that old Nat took
When he came out of Cross Keys down upon Jerusalem,
In his angry stab for freedom a hundred years ago.
The land was quiet, and the mist was rising,
Out of the woods and the Nottaway swamp,
Over Southampton the still night fell,
As we rode down to Cross Keys where the march began.

When we got to Cross Keys, they could tell us little of him,
The Negroes had only the faintest recollections:
"I ain't been here so long, I come from up roun' Newsome;
Yassah, a town a few miles up de road,
The old folks who coulda told you is all dead an' gone.
I heard something, sometime; I doan jis remember what.

STERLING A. BROWN: *Remembering Nat Turner*

'Pears lak I heard that name somewheres or other.
So he fought to be free. Well. You doan say."

An old white woman recalled exactly
How Nat crept down the steps, axe in his hand,
After murdering a woman and child in bed,
"Right in this house at the head of these stairs."
(In a house built long after Nat was dead.)
She pointed to a brick store where Nat was captured,
(Nat was taken in a swamp, three miles away)
With his men around him, shooting from the windows
(She was thinking of Harper's Ferry and old John Brown.)
She cackled as she told how they riddled Nat with bullets
(Nat was tried and hanged at Courtland, ten miles away)
She wanted to know why folks would come miles
Just to ask about an old nigger fool.
    "Ain't no slavery no more, things is going all right,
    Pervided thar's a good goober market this year.
    We had a sign post here with printing on it,
    But it rotted in the hole and thar it lays;
    And the nigger tenants split the marker for kindling.
    Things is all right, naow, ain't no trouble with the niggers.
    Why they make this big to-do over Nat?"

As we drove from Cross Keys back to Courtland,
Along the way that Nat came down from Jerusalem,
A watery moon was high in the cloud-filled heavens,
The same moon he dreaded a hundred years ago.
The tree they hanged Nat on is long gone to ashes,
The trees he dodged behind have rotted in the swamps.

The bus for Miami and the trucks boomed by,
And touring cars, their heavy tires snarling on the pavement.
Frogs piped in the marshes, and a hound bayed long,
And yellow lights glowed from the cabin windows.

As we came back the way that Nat led his army,
Down from Cross Keys, down to Jerusalem,
We wondered if his troubled spirit still roamed the Nottaway,
Or if it fled with the cock-crow at daylight,
Or lay at peace with the bones in Jerusalem,
Its restlessness stifled by Southampton clay.

We remembered the poster rotted through and falling,
The marker split for kindling a kitchen fire.

Thomas Jefferson on the Negro and the
Slavery Question

In his Notes on the State of Virginia, written in 1781 to answer queries put to him by the Marquis de Barbé-Marbois, Secretary of the French Legation, Jefferson made two remarkable pronouncements about the Negro and slavery. In his answer to Query XIV—"The administration of justice and the description of the laws"—he addresses himself to the ethnological and anthropological questions involved in the issues of slavery and emancipation. Though he is inclined to believe that the blacks are inferior to the whites "in the endowments both of body and mind," he advances this view as a "suspicion" only. He regrets that Americans have never considered the races of black and red men as "subjects of natural history." Consequently, Jefferson concludes, the opinion that the Negroes are "inferior in the faculties of reason and imagination must be hazarded with great diffidence."

The whole of his answer to Query XVIII—"The particular customs and manners that may happen to be received in that state"—Jefferson devotes to a consideration of the degrading effects of slavery on the white masters and their families. God's justice will not sleep forever. Sooner or later the evils of slavery will be done away with in America. Jefferson hopes that total emancipation, in the order of events, will come about "with the consent of the masters, rather than by their extirpation."

Although the forthrightness and eloquence of Jefferson's words in these two passages are epochal, one should not forget that many Southern leaders at the end of the eighteenth century were as determined as Jefferson was that the slaves should be freed, though few would have been as circumspect as he in discussing the capabilities of the Negro. George Washington emancipated his slaves in his will, as did John Randolph of Roanoke. If Jefferson had not been bankrupt at the end of his life, he would have done the same. Many Virginia leaders, among them Patrick Henry, George Wythe, James Madison, and George Mason, condemned slavery.

Foreseeing the difficulties of total and immediate emancipation if the freed slaves remained in the country, most of these men advocated colonization as the solution. When the American Colonization Society was founded in Washington in 1817, its first president was Bushrod Washington, a nephew of the general. A majority of its members were Southerners. In the first years of the anti-slavery societies there were more of these groups in the South than in the North.

Colonization failed as a solution, though the Republic of Liberia remains as a monument to this effort. Meanwhile the pro-slavery argument was growing in strength. The invention of the cotton gin in 1793 and the subsequent vast increase in cotton-planting convinced the majority of Southerners that slavery was indispensable to the prosperity of the region. By 1832 the enlightened ideas of Jefferson and like-minded men were submerged. In debating the slavery question the South turned from apology to defense.

The text of these two passages from the Notes on the State of Virginia *is that of the first London edition, issued by John Stockdale in 1787. This was, in effect, the first authorized public edition. The first of these passages is to be found on pages 229–35 and 238–40, the second on pages 270–3.*

It will probably be asked, Why not retain and incorporate the blacks into the state, and thus save the expence of supplying, by importation of white settlers, the vacancies they will leave? Deep rooted prejudices entertained by the whites; ten thousand recollections, by the blacks, of the injuries they have sustained; new provocations; the real distinctions which nature has made; and many other circumstances, will divide us into parties, and produce convulsions which will probably never end but in the extermination of the one or the other race.—To these objections, which are political, may be added others, which are physical and moral. The first difference which strikes us is that of colour. Whether the black of the negro resides in the reticular membrane between the skin and scarf-skin, or in the scarf-skin itself; whether it proceeds from the colour of the blood, the colour of the bile, or from that of some other secretion, the difference is fixed in nature, and is as real as if its seat and cause were better known to us. And is this difference of no importance? Is it not the foundation of a greater or less share of beauty in the two races? Are not the fine mixtures of red and white, the expressions of every passion by greater or less suffusions of colour in the one, preferable to that eternal monotony, which reigns in the countenances, that immovable veil of black which covers all the emotions of the other race? Add to these, flowing hair, a more elegant symmetry of form, their own judgment in favour of the whites, declared by their preference of them, as uniformly as is

the preference of the Oran-ootan for the black woman over those of
his own species. The circumstance of superior beauty, is thought
worthy attention in the propagation of our horses, dogs, and other
domestic animals; why not in that of man? Besides those of colour,
figure, and hair, there are other physical distinctions proving a difference of race. They have less hair on the face and body. They secrete
less by the kidnies, and more by the glands of the skin, which gives
them a very strong and disagreeable odour. This greater degree of
transpiration renders them more tolerant of heat, and less so of cold,
than the whites. Perhaps, too, a difference of structure in the pul-
monary apparatus, which a late ingenious experimentalist has discovered to be the principal regulator of animal heat, may have disabled
them from extricating, in the act of inspiration, so much of that fluid
from the outer air, or obliged them in expiration, to part with more of
it. They seem to require less sleep. A black, after hard labour through
the day, will be induced by the slightest amusements to sit up till midnight, or later, though knowing he must be out with the first dawn of
the morning. They are at least as brave, and more adventuresome. But
this may perhaps proceed from a want of forethought, which prevents
their seeing a danger till it be present. When present, they do not go
through it with more coolness or steadiness than the whites. They are
more ardent after their female: but love seems with them to be more
an eager desire, than a tender delicate mixture of sentiment and sensation. Their griefs are transient. Those numberless afflictions, which
render it doubtful whether heaven has given life to us in mercy or
in wrath, are less felt, and sooner forgotten with them. In general, their
existence appears to participate more of sensation than reflection. To
this must be ascribed their disposition to sleep when abstracted from
their diversions, and unemployed in labour. An animal whose body is
at rest, and who does not reflect must be disposed to sleep of course.
Comparing them by their faculties of memory, reason, and imagination, it appears to me that in memory they are equal to the whites; in
reason much inferior, as I think one could scarcely be found capable
of tracing and comprehending the investigations of Euclid; and that in
imagination they are dull, tasteless, and anomalous. It would be unfair
to follow them to Africa for this investigation. We will consider them
here, on the same stage with the whites, and where the facts are not
apocryphal on which a judgment is to be formed. It will be right to
make great allowances for the difference of condition, of education,
of conversation, of the sphere in which they move. Many millions of
them have been brought to, and born in America. Most of them, indeed, have been confined to tillage, to their own homes, and their own
society: yet many have been so situated, that they might have availed
themselves of the conversation of their masters; many have been

brought up to the handicraft arts, and from that circumstance have always been associated with the whites. Some have been liberally educated, and all have lived in countries where the arts and sciences are cultivated to a considerable degree, and all have had before their eyes samples of the best works from abroad. The Indians, with no advantages of this kind, will often carve figures on their pipes not destitute of design and merit. They will crayon out an animal, a plant, or a country, so as to prove the existence of a germ in their minds which only wants cultivation. They astonish you with strokes of the most sublime oratory; such as prove their reason and sentiment strong, their imagination glowing and elevated. But never yet could I find that a black had uttered a thought above the level of plain narration; never saw even an elementary trait of painting or sculpture. In music they are more generally gifted than the whites with accurate ears for tune and time, and they have been found capable of imagining a small catch.[1] Whether they will be equal to the composition of a more extensive run of melody, or of complicated harmony, is yet to be proved. Misery is often the parent of the most affecting touches in poetry.—Among the blacks is misery enough, God knows, but no poetry. Love is the particular œstrum of the poet. Their love is ardent, but it kindles the senses only, not the imagination. Religion, indeed, has produced a Phyllis Whately; but it could not produce a poet. The compositions published under her name are below the dignity of criticism. The heroes of the Dunciad are to her, as Hercules to the author of that poem. Ignatius Sancho has approached nearer to merit in composition; yet his letters do more honour to the heart than the head. They breathe the purest effusions of friendship and general philanthropy, and shew how great a degree of the latter may be compounded with strong religious zeal. He is often happy in the turn of his compliments, and his stile is easy and familiar, except when he affects a Shandean fabrication of words. But his imagination is wild and extravagant, and escapes incessantly from every restraint of reason and taste, and, in the course of its vagaries, leaves a tract of thought as incoherent and eccentric, as is the course of a meteor through the sky. His subjects should often have led him to a process of sober reasoning: yet we find him always substituting sentiment for demonstration. Upon the whole, though we admit him to the first place among those of his own colour who have presented themselves to the public judgment, yet when we compare him with the writers of the race among whom he lived, and particularly with the epistolary class, in which he has taken his own stand, we are compelled to enroll him at the bottom of the column. This criticism

[1] The instrument proper to them is the Banjar, which they brought hither from Africa, and which is the original of the guitar, its chords being precisely the four lower chords of the guitar. [Jefferson's note.]

supposes the letters published under his name to be genuine, and to have received amendment from no other hand; points which would not be of easy investigation. The improvement of the blacks in body and mind, in the first instance of their mixture with the whites, has been observed by every one, and proves that their inferiority is not the effect merely of their condition of life. . . .

The opinion, that they are inferior in the faculties of reason and imagination, must be hazarded with great diffidence. To justify a general conclusion, requires many observations, even where the subject may be submitted to the Anatomical knife, to Optical glasses, to analysis by fire, or by solvents. How much more then where it is a faculty, not a substance, we are examining; where it eludes the research of all the senses; where the conditions of its existence are various and variously combined; where the effects of those which are present or absent bid defiance to calculation; let me add too, as a circumstance of great tenderness, where our conclusion would degrade a whole race of men from the rank in the scale of beings which their Creator may perhaps have given them. To our reproach it must be said, that though for a century and a half we have had under our eyes the races of black and of red men, they have never yet been viewed by us as subjects of natural history. I advance it therefore as a suspicion only, that the blacks, whether originally a distinct race, or made distinct by time and circumstances, are inferior to the whites in the endowments both of body and mind. It is not against experience to suppose, that different species of the same genus, or varieties of the same species, may possess different qualifications. Will not a lover of natural history then, one who views the gradations in all the races of animals with the eye of philosophy, excuse an effort to keep those in the department of man as distinct as nature has formed them? This unfortunate difference of colour, and perhaps of faculty, is a powerful obstacle to the emancipation of these people. Many of their advocates, while they wish to vindicate the liberty of human nature, are anxious also to preserve its dignity and beauty. Some of these, embarrassed by the question, What further is to be done with them? join themselves in opposition with those who are actuated by sordid avarice only. Among the Romans emancipation required but one effort. The slave, when made free, might mix with, without staining the blood of his master. But with us a second is necessary, unknown to history. When freed, he is to be removed beyond the reach of mixture.

It is difficult to determine on the standard by which the manners of a nation may be tried, whether *catholic*, or *particular*. It is more difficult for a native to bring to that standard the manners of his own nation, familiarized to him by habit. There must doubtless be an unhappy influence on the manners of our people produced by the existence of slavery among us. The whole commerce between master and slave is a perpetual exercise of the most boisterous passions, the most unremitting despotism on the one part, and degrading submissions on the other. Our children see this, and learn to imitate it; for man is an imitative animal. This quality is the germ of all education in him. From his cradle to his grave he is learning to do what he sees others do. If a parent could find no motive either in his philanthropy or his self-love, for restraining the intemperance of passion towards his slave, it should always be a sufficient one that his child is present. But generally it is not sufficient. The parent storms, the child looks on, catches the lineaments of wrath, puts on the same airs in the circle of smaller slaves, gives a loose to the worst of passions, and thus nursed, educated, and daily exercised in tyranny, cannot but be stamped by it with odious peculiarities. The man must be a prodigy who can retain his manners and morals undepraved by such circumstances. And with what execration should the statesman be loaded, who, permitting one half the citizens thus to trample on the rights of the other, transforms those into despots, and these into enemies, destroys the morals of the one part, and the amor patriæ of the other. For if a slave can have a country in this world, it must be any other in preference to that in which he is born to live and labour for another; in which he must lock up the faculties of his nature, contribute as far as depends on his individual endeavours to the evanishment of the human race, or entail his own miserable condition on the endless generations proceeding from him. With the morals of the people, their industry also is destroyed. For in a warm climate, no man will labour for himself who can make another labour for him. This is so true, that of the proprietors of slaves a very small proportion indeed are ever seen to labour. And can the liberties of a nation be thought secure when we have removed their only firm basis, a conviction in the minds of the people that these liberties are of the gift of God? That they are not be be violated but with his wrath? Indeed I tremble for my country when I reflect that God is just: that his justice cannot sleep forever: that considering numbers, nature and natural means only, a revolution of the wheel of fortune, an exchange of situation, is among possible events: that it may become probable by supernatural interference! The Almighty has no attribute which can take side with us in such a contest.—But it is impossible to be temperate and to pursue this subject through the various considerations of policy, of morals, of history natural and civil. We must be contented to hope they will force their way into every one's mind. I think a change already perceptible, since the origin of the present revolution. The spirit of the master is abating, that of the slave rising from the dust, his condition mollifying, the way I hope preparing, under the auspices of heaven, for a total emancipation, and that this is disposed, in the order of events, to be with the consent of the masters, rather than by their extirpation.

George Fitzhugh on the "Free Slave Trade" of the North

George Fitzhugh (1806–81) was one of a group of Southern writers (he was a regular contributor to De Bow's influential Review) *who believed that the institution of slavery could be reasonably justified on sociological grounds. But he differed from most other defenders of slavery in that he was not content merely to justify it. He knew that the best defense is an attack, and that if slavery were to be saved, it would be saved only by converting those who believed in the powerful economic system that rivaled it—the laissez-faire, free-labor economy of the North. He had seen something of the Northern mills and had met abolitionists, among them Harriet Beecher Stowe. Northern capitalism and the zeal of the abolitionists confirmed him in the belief that the Southern way of life was threatened. He expressed his faith in the institution of slavery and his distrust of the free society that made the capitalists "cannibals" in* Sociology for the South; or, The Failure of Free Society (1854), *and in* Cannibals All! or, Slaves without Masters (1857).*

The following selection is the first chapter of Fitzhugh's Cannibals All! or, Slaves without Masters *(Richmond: A. Morris; 1857).*

THE UNIVERSAL TRADE

WE are all, North and South, engaged in the White Slave Trade, and he who succeeds best, is esteemed most respectable. It is far more cruel than the Black Slave Trade, because it exacts more of its slaves, and neither protects nor governs them. We boast, that it exacts more, when we say, "that the *profits* made from employing free labor are greater than those from slave labor." The profits, made from free labor, are the amount of the products of such labor, which the employer, by means of the command which capital or skill gives him, takes away, exacts or "exploitates" from the free laborer. The profits of slave labor are that portion of the products of such labor which the power of the master enables him to appropriate. These profits are less, because the master allows the slave to retain a larger share of the results of his own labor, than do the employers of free labor. But we not only boast that the White Slave Trade is more exacting and fraudulent (in fact, though not in intention) than Black Slavery; but we also boast, that it is more cruel, in leaving the laborer to take care of himself and family out of the pittance which skill or capital have allowed him to retain. When the day's labor is ended, he is free, but is overburdened with the cares of family and household, which make his freedom an empty and delusive mockery. But his employer is really free, and may enjoy the profits made by others' labor, without a care, or a trouble, as to their well-being. The negro slave is free, too, when the labors of the day are over, and free in mind as well as body; for the master provides food, raiment, house, fuel, and everything else necessary to the physical well-being of himself and family. The master's labors commence just when the slave's end. No wonder men should prefer white slavery to capital, to negro slavery, since it is more profitable, and is free from all the cares and labors of black slave-holding.

Now, reader, if you wish to know yourself—to "descant on your own deformity"—read on. But if you would cherish self-conceit, self-esteem, or self-appreciation, throw down our book; for we will dispel illusions which have promoted your happiness, and shew you that what you have considered and practiced as virtue, is little better than moral Cannibalism. But you will find yourself in numerous and respectable company; for all good and respectable people are "Cannibals all," who do not labor, or who are successfully trying to live without labor, on the unrequited labor of other people:—Whilst low, bad, and disreputable people, are those who labor to support themselves, and to support said respectable people besides. Throwing the negro slaves out of the account, and society is divided in Christendom into four classes: The rich, or independent respectable people, who live well and labor not at all; the professional and skillful respectable people, who do a little light work, for enormous wages; the poor hard-working people, who support every body, and starve themselves; and the poor thieves, swindlers and sturdy beggars, who live like gentlemen, without labor, on the labor of other people. The gentlemen exploitate, which being done on a large scale, and requiring a great many victims, is highly respectable—whilst the rogues and beggars take so little from others, that they fare little better than those who labor.

But, reader, we do not wish to fire into the flock. "Thou art the man!" You are a Cannibal! and if a successful one, pride yourself on the number of your victims, quite as much as any Feejee chieftain, who breakfasts, dines and sups on human flesh.—And your conscience smites you, if you have failed to succeed, quite as much as his, when he returns from an unsuccessful foray.

Probably, you are a lawyer, or a merchant, or a doctor, who have made by your business fifty thousand dollars, and retired to live on your capital. But, mark! not to spend your capital. That would be vulgar, disreputable, criminal. That would be, to live by your own labor; for your capital is your amassed labor. That would be, to do as common working men do; for they take the pittance which their employers leave them, to live on. They live by labor; for they exchange the results of their own labor for the products of other people's labor. It is, no doubt, an honest, vulgar way of living; but not at all a respectable way. The respectable way of living is, to make other people work for you, and to pay them nothing for so doing—and to have no concern about them after their work is done. Hence, white slave-holding is much more respectable than negro slavery—for the master works nearly as hard for the negro, as he for the master. But you, my virtuous, respectable reader, exact three thousand dollars per annum from white labor, (for your income is the product of white labor) and make not one cent of return in any form. You retain your capital, and never labor, and yet live in luxury on the labor of others. Capital commands labor, as the master does the slave. Neither pays for labor; but the master permits the slave to retain a larger allowance from the proceeds of his own labor, and hence "free labor is cheaper than slave labor." You, with the command over labor which your capital gives you, are a slave owner—a master, without the obligations of a master. They who work for you, who create your income, are slaves, without the rights of slaves. Slaves without a master! Whilst you were engaged in amassing your capital, in seeking to become independent, you were in the White Slave Trade. To become independent, is to be able to make other people support you, without being obliged to labor for *them.* Now, what man in society is not seeking to attain this situation? He who attains it, is a slave owner, in the worst sense. He who is in pursuit of it, is engaged in the slave trade. You, reader, belong to the one or other class. The men without property, in free society, are theoretically in a worse condition than slaves. Practically, their condition corresponds with this theory, as history and statistics every where demonstrate. The capitalists, in free society, live in ten times the luxury and show that Southern masters do, because the slaves to capital work harder and cost less, than negro slaves.

The negro slaves of the South are the happiest, and, in some sense, the freest people in the world. The children and the aged and infirm work not at all, and yet have all the comforts and necessaries of life provided for them. They enjoy liberty, because they are oppressed neither by care nor labor. The women do little hard work, and are protected from the despotism of their husbands by their masters. The negro men and stout boys work, on the average, in good weather, not more than nine hours a day. The balance of their time is spent in perfect abandon. Besides, they have their Sabbaths and holidays. White men, with so much of license and liberty, would die of ennui; but negroes luxuriate in corporeal and mental repose. With their faces upturned to the sun, they can sleep at any hour; and quiet sleep is the greatest of human enjoyments. "Blessed be the man who invented sleep." 'Tis happiness in itself—and results from contentment with the present, and confident assurance of the future. We do not know whether free laborers ever sleep. They are fools to do so; for whilst they sleep, the wily and watchful capitalist is devising means to ensnare and exploitate them. The free laborer must work or starve. He is more of a slave than the negro, because he works longer and harder for less allowance than the slave, and has no holiday, because the cares of life with him begin when its labors end. He has no liberty, and not a single right. We know, 'tis often said, air and water, are common property, which all have equal right to participate and enjoy; but this is utterly false. The appropriation of the lands carries with it the appropriation of all on or above the lands, *usque ad cœlum, aut ad inferos*. A man cannot breathe the air, without a place to breathe it from, and all places are appropriated. All water is private property "to the middle of the stream," except the ocean, and that is not fit to drink.

Free laborers have not a thousandth part of the rights and liberties of negro slaves. Indeed, they have not a single right or a single liberty, unless it be the right or liberty to die. But the reader may think that he and other capitalists and employers are freer than negro slaves. Your capital would soon vanish, if you dared indulge in the liberty and abandon of negroes. You hold your wealth and position by the tenure of constant watchfulness, care and circumspection. You never labor; but you are never free.

Where a few own the soil, they have unlimited power over the balance of society, until domestic slavery comes in, to compel them to pemit this balance of society to draw a sufficient and comfortable living from "terra mater." Free society, asserts the right of a few to the earth—slavery, maintains that it belongs, in different degrees, to all.

But, reader, well may you follow the slave trade. It is the only trade worth following, and slaves the only property worth owning. All other is worthless, a mere *caput mortuum*, except in so far as it vests the owner with the power to command the labors of others—to enslave them. Give you a palace, ten thousand acres of land, sumptuous clothes, equipage and every other luxury; and with your artificial wants, you are poorer than Robinson Crusoe, or the lowest working man, if you have no slaves to capital, or domestic slaves. Your capital will not bring you an income of a cent, nor supply one of your wants, without labor. Labor is indispensable to give value to property, and if you owned every thing else, and did not own labor, you would be poor. But fifty thousand dollars means, and is, fifty thousand dollars worth of slaves. You can command, without touching on that capital, three thousand dollars' worth of labor per annum. You could do no more were you to buy slaves with it, and then you would be cumbered with the cares of governing and providing for them. You are a slaveholder now, to the amount of fifty thousand dollars, with all the advantages, and none of the cares and responsibilities of a master.

"Property in man" is what all are struggling to obtain. Why should they not be obliged to take care of man, their property, as they do of their horses and their hounds, their cattle and their sheep. Now, under the delusive name of liberty, you work him, "from morn to dewy eve" —from infancy to old age—then turn him out to starve. You treat your horses and hounds better. Capital is a cruel master. The free slave trade, the commonest, yet the cruellest of trades.

H. R. Helper Compares the Free and
the Slave States

Few men have been guilty of a more intense or more unreasonable prejudice against the Negro than Hinton Rowan Helper (1829–1909) and at the same time few have done the race greater service. He was born in North Carolina of a poor family that owned a small farm and a few slaves, and he grew up in an impoverished household caught in the struggle for economic survival. His prejudice came out clear and unrestrained in Nojoque *(1867). There he denounced the Negro as a menace to the South and to white labor and freely stated that it was his purpose "to write the Negro out of America . . . and out of existence." His* Negroes in Negroland *(1868) is one of the bitterest expressions of racial hatred ever put in print.*

It was an irony of history that Helper should have already played no small part in freeing the Negro whom he hated, for in 1857 he had jumped into the slavery versus free-labor controversy with The Impending Crisis in the South *and the book eventually rivaled* Uncle Tom's Cabin *as one of the powerful contributing forces that led to war. It was violently and abusively abolitionist, not out of any sympathy for the slaves but simply because Helper believed that free white labor in the South was being destroyed by the competition of slavery. He supported his argument by an invidious comparison of the South with the North and by a convincing use of statistics. He proposed that the poorer Southern whites organize against the slaveholders, and suggested that if it came to open conflict they could count on the Negroes, who would usually "be delighted with the opportunity to cut their masters' throats."*

In 1858 Horace Greeley set about making The Impending Crisis *the campaign book for the Republican Party in the coming election, and it suddenly became the center of dissension. It provoked a long and bitter debate in the House of Representatives and it kept the Republican candidate for Speaker of the House, who had endorsed Greeley's idea, from election. To circulate it in the South was a crime and to own it was dangerous; in the North it was published in such numbers that it is still a common item on the shelves of second-hand-book stores.*

Helper died at eighty, a suicide, declaring: "There is no justice in this world." From first to last he had championed the Southern poor white laborer, and from first to last the Southern poor white laborer had lost. Even the Negro, who had reaped the benefit of Helper's labors, seemed part of the injustice.

The following passage is selected from Hinton Rowan Helper: Compendium of the Impending Crisis of the South (*New York: A. B. Burdick; 1860*), *pp. 12–16.*

IT is a fact well known to every intelligent Southerner that we are compelled to go to the North for almost every article of utility and adornment, from matches, shoepegs and paintings up to cotton-mills, steamships and statuary; that we have no foreign trade, no princely merchants, nor respectable artists; that, in comparison with the free states, we contribute nothing to the literature, polite arts and inventions of the age; that, for want of profitable employment at home, large numbers of our native population find themselves necessitated to emigrate to the West, whilst the free states retain not only the large proportion of those born within their own limits, but induce, annually, hundreds of thousands of foreigners to settle and remain amongst them; that almost everything produced at the North meets with ready sale, while, at the same time, there is no demand, even among our own citizens, for the productions of Southern industry; that, owing to the absence of a proper system of business amongst us, the North becomes, in one way or another, the proprietor and dispenser of all our floating wealth, and that we are dependent on Northern capitalists for the means necessary to build our railroads, canals and other public improvements; that if we want to visit a foreign country, even though it may lie directly south of us, we find no convenient way of getting there except by taking passage through a Northern port; and that nearly all the profits arising from the exchange of commodities, from insurance and shipping offices, and from the thousand and one industrial pursuits of the country, accrue to the North, and are there invested in the erection of those magnificent cities and stupendous works of art which dazzle the eyes of the South, and attest the superiority of free institutions!

The North is the Mecca of our merchants, and to it they must and do make two pilgrimages per annum—one in the spring and one in the fall. All our commercial, mechanical, manufactural, and literary supplies come from there. We want Bibles, brooms, buckets and books, and we go to the North; we want pens, ink, paper, wafers and envelopes, and we go to the North; we want shoes, hats, handkerchiefs, umbrellas and pocket knives, and we go to the North; we want furniture, crockery, glassware and pianos, and we go to the North; we want toys, primers, school-books, fashionable apparel, machinery, medicines, tomb-stones, and a thousand other things, and we go to the North for them all. Instead of keeping our money in circulation at home, by patronizing our own mechanics, manufacturers, and laborers, we send it all away to the North, and there it remains; it never falls into our hands again.

In one way or another we are more or less subservient to the North every day of our lives. In infancy we are swaddled in Northern muslin; in childhood we are humored with Northern gewgaws; in youth we are instructed out of Northern books; at the age of maturity we sow our "wild oats" on Northern soil; in middle-life we exhaust our wealth, energies and talents in the dishonorable vocation of entailing our dependence on our children and on our children's children, and, to the neglect of our own interests and the interests of those around us, in giving aid and succor to every department of Northern power; in the decline of life we remedy our eye-sight with Northern spectacles, and support our infirmities with Northern canes; in old age we are drugged with Northern physic; and, finally, when we die, our inanimate bodies, shrouded in Northern cambric, are stretched upon the bier, borne to the grave in a Northern carriage, entombed with a Northern spade, and memorized with a Northern slab!

But it can hardly be necessary to say more in illustration of the unmanly and unnational dependence, which is so glaring that it cannot fail to be apparent to even the most careless and superficial observer. All the world sees, or ought to see, that in a commercial, mechanical, manufactural, financial, and literary point of view, we are as helpless as babes; that, in comparison with the Free States, our agricultural recources have been greatly exaggerated, misunderstood and mismanaged; and that, instead of cultivating among ourselves a wise policy, of mutual assistance and coöperation with respect to individuals, and of self-reliance with respect to the South at large, instead of giving countenance and encouragement to the industrial enterprises projected among us, and instead of building up, aggrandizing and beautifying our own States, cities and towns, we have been spending our substance at the North, and are daily augmenting and strengthening the very power which now has us so completely under its thumb.

It thus appears, in view of the preceding statistical facts and arguments, that the South, at one time the superior of the North in almost all the ennobling pursuits and conditions of life, has fallen far behind her competitor, and now ranks more as the dependency of a mother country than as the equal confederate of free and independent States. Following the order of our tasks, the next duty that devolves upon us is to trace out the causes which have conspired to bring about this important change, and to place on record the reasons, as we understand them. . . .

And now to the point. In our opinion, an opinion which has been formed from data obtained by assiduous researches, and comparisons, from laborious investigation, logical reasoning, and earnest reflection, the causes which have impeded the progress and prosperity of the South, which have dwindled our commerce and other similar pursuits, into the most contemptible insignificance; sunk a large majority of our people in galling poverty and ignorance, rendered a small minority conceited and tyrannical, and driven the rest away from their homes; entailed upon us a humiliating dependence on the Free States; disgraced us in the recesses of our own souls, and brought us under reproach in the eyes of all civilized and enlightened nations—may all be traced to one common source, and there find solution in the most hateful and horrible word, that was ever incorporated into the vocabulary of human economy—*Slavery*.

Reared amidst the institution of slavery, believing it to be wrong both in principle and in practice, and having seen and felt its evil influences upon individuals, communities and states, we deem it a duty, no less than a privilege, to enter our protest against it, and, as a Southern man, to use all constitutional means and our most strenuous efforts to overturn and abolish it. . . .

The first and most sacred duty of every Southerner, who has the honor and the interest of his country at heart, is to declare himself an unqualified and uncompromising opponent of slavery. No conditional or half-way declaration will avail; no mere threatening demonstration will succeed. With those who desire to be instrumental in bringing about the triumph of liberty over slavery, there should be neither evasion, vacillation, nor equivocation. We should listen to no modifying terms or compromises that may be proposed by the proprietors of the unprofitable and ungodly institution. Nothing short of the complete abolition of slavery can save the South from falling into the vortex of utter ruin. Too long have we yielded a submissive obedience to the tyrannical domination of an inflated oligarchy; too long have we tolerated their arrogance and self-conceit; too long have we submitted to their unjust and savage exactions. Let us now wrest from them the sceptre of power, establish liberty and equal rights throughout the land, and henceforth and forever guard our legislative halls from the pollutions and usurpations of pro-slavery demagogues.

Christmas Night in the Quarters

Although the stereotype of the faithful Negro, a song always on his lips and loyalty to "Master" in his heart, had appeared in Southern novels written before the Civil War, it was left to such local-color writers as Joel Chandler Harris and Thomas Nelson Page to exploit this stereotype to the full. Northern magazines were eager to print dialect stories and poems with the faithful black servitor as a leading character—such as Page's "Marse Chan" and Harris's Uncle Remus stories.

One of the first of the poems in Negro dialect, and one that many white Southerners consider a true picture of Negro piety and high spirits, is Irwin Russell's "Christmas-Night in the Quarters." Joel Chandler Harris said that the most wonderful thing about Russell's dialect poetry is "his accurate conception of the Negro character. The dialect is not always the best,—it is often carelessly written,—but the Negro is there, the old-fashioned, unadulterated Negro, who is still dear to the

Southern heart. . . . I do not know where could be found to-day a happier or more perfect representation of Negro character."

Russell was born in 1853 in Port Gibson, Mississippi, the place he loved best and returned to after several roving adventures, including a brief try at a literary career in New York. As a boy he listened with delight to Negro talk and song and could imitate the dialect well. He began sending his Negro poems to local newspapers. Presently, when the "Bric-a-brac" department of Scribner's Monthly *took some of his work, Russell decided to desert the law and become a writer. He died at twenty-six while serving as a reporter on the* New Orleans Times.

Russell's famous poem is said to have been inspired by the Christmas celebrations at the home of friends, the Jeffries family of Greenwood. It was traditional in slavery times for the Negroes to hold a mild Saturnalia during the holidays. In Eliza Ripley's Social Life in Old New Orleans (1912) *there is a description of the customary distribution of presents on Christmas morning, the time when the festivities began.*

The following morning, Christmas Day, the field negroes were summoned to the back porch of the big house, where Marse Jim, after a few preliminary remarks, distributed the presents—a head handkerchief, a pocketknife, a pipe, a dress for the baby, shoes for the growing boy (his first pair, maybe), etc., etc., down the list. Each gift was received with a "Thankee, sir," and, perhaps, also a remark anent its usefulness. Then after Charlotte brought forth the jug of whiskey and the tin cups, and everyone had a comforting dram, they filed off to the quarters, with a week of holiday before them and a trip to town to do their little buying.

The text of "Christmas-Night in the Quarters" is that printed in Poems by Irwin Russell (New York: The Century Co.; 1888), pp. 1–15.

WHEN merry Christmas-day is done,
And Christmas-night is just begun;
While clouds in slow procession drift,
To wish the moon-man "Christmas gift,"
Yet linger overhead, to know
What causes all the stir below;
At Uncle Johnny Booker's ball
The darkies hold high carnival.
From all the country-side they throng,
With laughter, shouts, and scraps of song,—

Their whole deportment plainly showing
That to the Frolic they are going.
Some take the path with shoes in hand,
To traverse muddy bottom-land;
Aristocrats their steeds bestride—
Four on a mule, behold them ride!
And ten great oxen draw apace
The wagon from "de oder place,"
With forty guests, whose conversation
Betokens glad anticipation.
Not so with him who drives: old Jim
Is sagely solemn, hard, and grim,
And frolics have no joys for him.
He seldom speaks but to condemn—
Or utter some wise apothegm—
Or else, some crabbed thought pursuing,
Talk to his team, as now he's doing:

———————

Come up heah, Star! Yee-bawee!
    You alluz is a-laggin'—
Mus' be you think I's dead,
    An' dis de huss you's draggin'—
You's 'mos' too lazy to draw yo' bref,
    Let 'lone drawin' de waggin.

Dis team—quit bel'rin', sah!
    De ladies don't submit 'at—
Dis team—you ol' fool ox,
    You heah me tell you quit 'at?
Dis team's des like de 'Nited States;
    Dat's what I's tryin' to git at!

De people rides behin',
    De pollytishners haulin'—
Sh'u'd be a well-bruk ox,
    To foller dat ar callin'—
An' sometimes nuffin won't do dem steers,
    But what dey mus' be stallin'!

Woo bahgh! Buck-kannon! Yes, sah,
    Sometimes dey will be stickin';
An' den, fus thing dey knows,
    Dey takes a rale good lickin'.

De folks gits down: an' den watch out
   For hommerin' an' kickin'.

Dey blows upon dey hands,
   Den flings 'em wid de nails up,
Jumps up an' cracks dey heels,
   An' pruzently dey sails up,
An' makes dem oxen hump deysef,
   By twistin' all dey tails up!

In this our age of printer's ink
'Tis books that show us how to think—
The rule reversed, and set at naught,
That held that books were born of thought.
We form our minds by pedants' rules,
And all we know is from the schools;
And when we work, or when we play,
We do it in an ordered way—
And Nature's self pronounce a ban on,
Whene'er she dares transgress a canon.
Untrammeled thus the simple race is
That "wuks the craps" on cotton places.
Original in act and thought,
Because unlearned and untaught.
Observe them at their Christmas party:
How unrestrained their mirth—how hearty!
How many things they say and do
That never would occur to you!
See Brudder Brown—whose saving grace
Would sanctify a quarter-race—
Out on the crowded floor advance,
To "beg a blessin' on dis dance."

O Mahsr! let dis gath'rin' fin' a blessin' in yo' sight!
Don't jedge us hard fur what we does—you knows it's Chrismus-
   night;
An' all de balunce ob de yeah we does as right's we kin.
Ef dancin's wrong, O Mahsr! let de time excuse de sin!

We labors in de vineya'd, wukin' hard an' wukin' true;
Now, shorely you won't notus, ef we eats a grape or two,
An' takes a leetle holiday,—a leetle restin'-spell,—
Bekase, nex' week, we'll start in fresh, an' labor twicet as well.

Remember, Mahsr,—min' dis, now,—de sinfulness ob sin
Is 'pendin' 'pon de sperret what we goes an' does it in:
An' in a righchis frame ob min' we's gwine to dance an' sing,
A-feelin' like King David, when he cut de pigeon-wing.

It seems to me—indeed it do—I mebbe mout be wrong—
That people raly *ought* to dance, when Chrismus comes along;
Des dance bekase dey's happy—like de birds hops in de trees,
De pine-top fiddle soundin' to de bowin' ob de breeze.

We has no ark to dance afore, like Isrul's prophet king;
We has no harp to soun' de cords, to holp us out to sing;
But 'cordin' to de gif's we has we does de bes' we knows,
An' folks don't 'spise de vi'let-flower bekase it ain't de rose.

You bless us, please, sah, eben ef we's doin' wrong to-night;
Kase den we'll need de blessin' more'n ef we's doin' right;
An' let de blessin' stay wid us, untel we comes to die,
An' goes to keep our Chrismus wid dem sheriffs in de sky!

Yes, tell dem preshis anguls we's a-gwine to jine 'em soon:
Our voices we's a-trainin' fur to sing de glory tune;
We's ready when you wants us, an' it ain't no matter when—
O Mahsr! call yo' chillen soon, an' take 'em home! Amen.

The rev'rend man is scarcely through,
When all the noise begins anew,
And with such force assaults the ears,
That through the din one hardly hears
Old fiddling Josey "sound his A,"
Correct the pitch, begin to play,
Stop, satisfied, then, with the bow,
Rap out the signal dancers know:

Git yo' pardners, fust kwattillion!
Stomp yo' feet, an' raise 'em high;
Tune is: "Oh! dat water-million!
Gwine to git to home bime-bye."
S'lute yo' pardners!—scrape perlitely—
Don't be bumpin' gin de res'—
Balance all!—now, step out rightly;
Alluz dance yo' lebbel bes'.
Fo'wa'd foah!—whoop up, niggers!
Back ag'in!—don't be so slow!—

IRWIN RUSSELL: *Christmas Night in the Quarters*

Swing cornahs!—min' de figgers!
When I hollers, den yo' go.
Top ladies cross ober!
Hol' on, till I takes a dram—
Gemmen solo!—yes, I's sober—
Cain't say how de fiddle am.
Hands around!—hol' up yo' faces,
Don't be lookin' at yo' feet!
Swing yo' pardners to yo' places!
Dat's de way—dat's hard to beat.
Sides fo'w'd!—when you's ready—
Make a bow as low's you kin!
Swing acrost wid opp'site lady!
Now we'll let you swap ag'in:
Ladies change!—shet up dat talkin';
Do yo' talkin' arter while!
Right an' lef'!—don't want no walkin'—
Make yo' steps, an' show yo' style!

And so the "set" proceeds—its length
Determined by the dancers' strength;
And all agreed to yield the palm
For grace and skill to "Georgy Sam,"
Who stamps so hard, and leaps so high,
"Des watch him!" is the wond'ring cry—
"De nigger mus' be, for a fac',
Own cousin to a jumpin'-jack!"
On, on the restless fiddle sounds,
Still chorused by the curs and hounds;
Dance after dance succeeding fast,
Till supper is announced at last.
That scene—but why attempt to show it?
The most inventive modern poet,
In fine new words whose hope and trust is,
Could form no phrase to do it justice!
When supper ends—that is not soon—
The fiddle strikes the same old tune;
The dancers pound the floor again,
With all they have of might and main;
Old gossips, *almost* turning pale,
Attend Aunt Cassy's gruesome tale
Of conjurors, and ghosts, and devils,
That in the smoke-house hold their revels;
Each drowsy baby droops its head,

Yet scorns the very thought of bed:—
So wears the night, and wears so fast,
All wonder when they find it passed,
And hear the signal sound to go
From what few cocks are left to crow.
Then, one and all, you hear them shout:
"Hi! Booker! fotch de banjo out,
An' gib us *one* song 'fore we goes—
One ob de berry bes' you knows!"
Responding to the welcome call,
He takes the banjo from the wall,
And tunes the strings with skill and care,
Then strikes them with a master's air,
And tells, in melody and rhyme,
This legend of the olden time:

———

Go 'way, fiddle! folks is tired o' hearin' you a-squawkin'.
Keep silence fur yo' betters!—don't you heah de banjo talkin'?
About de 'possum's tail she's gwine to lecter—ladies, listen!—
About de ha'r whut isn't dar, an' why de ha'r is missin':

"Dar's gwine to be a' oberflow," said Noah, lookin' solemn—
Fur Noah tuk the "Herald," an' he read de ribber column—
An' so he sot his hands to wuk a-cl'arin' timber-patches,
An' 'lowed he's gwine to build a boat to beat de steamah *Natchez.*

Ol' Noah kep' a-nailin' an' a-chippin' an' a-sawin';
An' all de wicked neighbors kep' a-laughin' an' a-pshawin';
But Noah didn't min' 'em, knowin' whut wuz gwine to happen:
An' forty days an' forty nights de rain it kep' a-drappin'.

Now, Noah had done cotched a lot ob ebry sort o' beas'es—
Ob all de shows a-trabbelin', it beat 'em all to pieces!
He had a Morgan colt an' sebral head o' Jarsey cattle—
An' druv 'em 'board de Ark as soon's he heered de thunder rattle.

Den sech anoder fall ob rain!—it come so awful hebby,
De ribber riz immejitly, an' busted troo de lebbee;
De people all wuz drownded out—'cep' Noah an' de critters,
An' men he'd hired to work de boat—an' one to mix de bitters.

De Ark she kep' a-sailin' an' a-sailin' *an'* a-sailin';
De lion got his dander up, an' like to bruk de palin';

De sarpints hissed; de painters yelled; tell, whut wid all de fussin',
You c'u'dn't hardly heah de mate a-bossin' 'roun' an' cussin'.

Now, Ham, de only nigger whut wuz runnin' on de packet,
Got lonesome in de barber-shop, an' c'u'dn't stan' de racket;
An' so, fur to amuse he-se'f, he steamed some wood an' bent it,
An' soon he had a banjo made—de fust dat wuz invented.

He wet de ledder, stretched it on; made bridge an' screws an' aprin;
An' fitted in a proper neck—'twuz berry long an' tap'rin';
He tuk some tin, an' twisted him a thimble fur to ring it;
An' den de mighty question riz: how wuz he gwine to string it?

De 'possum had as fine a tail as dis dat I's a-singin';
De ha'r's so long an' thick an' strong,—des fit fur banjo-stringin';
Dat nigger shaved 'em off as short as wash-day-dinner graces;
An' sorted ob 'em by de size, f'om little E's to basses.

He strung her, tuned her, struck a jig,—'twuz "Nebber min' de
    wedder"—
She soun' like forty-lebben bands a-playin' all togedder;
Some went to pattin'; some to dancin': Noah called de figgers;
An' Ham he sot an' knocked de tune, de happiest ob niggers!

Now, sence dat time—it's mighty strange—dere's not de slightes'
    showin'
Ob any ha'r at all upon de possum's tail a-growin';
An' curi's, too, dat nigger's ways: his people nebber los' 'em—
For whar you finds de nigger—dar's de banjo an' de 'possum!

———————

The night is spent; and as the day
Throws up the first faint flash of gray,
The guests pursue their homeward way;
And through the field beyond the gin,
Just as the stars are going in,
See Santa Claus departing—grieving—
His own dear Land of Cotton leaving.
His work is done; he fain would rest
Where people know and love him best.
He pauses, listens, looks about;
But go he must: his pass is out.
So, coughing down the rising tears,
He climbs the fence and disappears.
And thus observes a colored youth

(The common sentiment, in sooth):
"Oh! what a blessin' 'tw'u'd ha' been,
Ef Santa had been born a twin!
We'd hab two Chrismuses a yeah—
Or p'r'aps *one* brudder'd *settle* heah!"

Cable's "Freed—Not Free"

George Washington Cable (1844–1925) was born and bred in New Orleans. He returned to the city after Civil War service with the Fourth Mississippi Cavalry—in the course of which he was once seriously wounded—and it was in New Orleans that he found his true profession when he began writing an immediately popular column for the Picayune. *And when* Scribner's Monthly *discovered him, published him, and set him on the road to a national reputation in 1873, the common subject of his romantic local-color stories was the Louisiana Creole. The best stories were the first, gathered in a single volume under the title* Old Creole Days *in 1879.*

But there was another side to George Washington Cable. While his father was a true Southerner of an old slaveholding family, his mother was a New Englander of the deepest Puritan dye, and her blood was strong in him. It showed itself in the way he imposed upon himself a severe study of mathematics, Latin, and the Bible at the same time that he was campaigning and fighting cavalry engagements; in the way, after the war, he rose daily at four in the morning to continue his studies, making up for the college education he had not had; and in the way, throughout his life, he drove his frail physique through tasks that would have broken stronger men.

His mother's blood showed itself, too, in the zeal with which he championed prison reform, better election laws, and, above all, justice for the Negro. Though Northern readers were delighted by his stories of Creole life, many citizens of New Orleans resented them deeply. This resentment was further aggravated when Cable published a volume of outspoken essays on some of the social problems of the day— The Silent South (1885). Partly as a result of the hostility that this book aroused, Cable turned at the age of forty to his mother's land and settled in Northampton, Massachusetts.

The following selection is from The Silent South together with The Freedman's Case in Equity and The Convict Lease System (*New York: Charles Scribner's Sons; 1885*), *pp. 15–20.*

❁

To be a free man is his still distant goal. Twice he has been a freedman. In the days of compulsory reconstruction he was freed in the presence of his master by that master's victorious foe. In these days of voluntary reconstruction he is virtually freed by the consent of his master, but the master retaining the exclusive right to define the bounds of his freedom. Many everywhere have taken up the idea that this state of affairs is the end to be desired and the end actually sought in reconstruction as handed over to the States. I do not charge such folly to the best intelligence of any American community; but I cannot ignore my own knowledge that the average thought of some regions rises to no better idea of the issue. The belief is all too common that the nation, having aimed at a wrong result and missed, has left us of the Southern States to get now such other result as we think best. I say this belief is not universal. There are those among us who see that America has no room for a state of society which makes its lower classes harmless by abridging their liberties, or, as one of the favored class lately said to me, has "got 'em so they don't give no trouble." There is a growing number who see that the one thing we cannot afford to tolerate at large is a class of people less than citizens; and that every interest in the land demands that the freedman be free to become in all things, as far as his own personal gifts will lift and sustain him, the same sort of American citizen he would be if, with the same intellectual and moral calibre, he were white.

Thus we reach the ultimate question of fact. Are the freedman's liberties suffering any real abridgment? The answer is easy. The letter of the laws, with a few exceptions, recognizes him as entitled to every right of an American citizen; and to some it may seem unimportant that there is scarcely one public relation of life in the South where he is not arbitrarily and unlawfully compelled to hold toward the white man the attitude of an alien, a menial, and a probable reprobate, by reason of his race and color. One of the marvels of future history will be that it was counted a small matter, by a majority of our nation, for six millions of people within it, made by its own decree a component part of it, to be subjected to a system of oppression so rank that nothing could make it seem small except the fact that they had already been ground under it for a century and a half.

Examine it. It proffers to the freedman a certain security of life and property, and then holds the respect of the community, that dearest of earthly boons, beyond his attainment. It gives him certain guarantees against thieves and robbers, and then holds him under the unearned contumely of the mass of good men and women. It acknowledges in constitutions and statutes his title to an American's freedom and aspirations, and then in daily practice heaps upon him in every public place the most odious distinctions, without giving ear to the humblest plea concerning mental or moral character. It spurns his ambition, tramples upon his languishing self-respect, and indignantly refuses to let him either buy with money, or earn by any excellence of inner life or outward behavior, the most momentary immunity from these public indignities even for his wife and daughters. Need we cram these pages with facts in evidence, as if these were charges denied and requiring to be proven? They are simply the present avowed and defended state of affairs peeled of its exteriors.

Nothing but the habit, generations old, of enduring it could make it endurable by men not in actual slavery. Were we whites of the South to remain every way as we are, and our six million blacks to give place to any sort of whites exactly their equals, man for man, in mind, morals, and wealth, provided only that they had tasted two years of American freedom, and were this same system of tyrannies attempted upon them, there would be as bloody an uprising as this continent has ever seen. We can say this quietly. There is not a scruple's weight of present danger. These six million freedmen are dominated by nine million whites immeasurably stronger than they, backed by the virtual consent of thirty odd millions more. Indeed, nothing but the habit of oppression could make such oppression possible to a people of the intelligence and virtue of our Southern whites, and the invitation to practice it on millions of any other than the children of their former slaves would be spurned with a noble indignation.

Suppose, for a moment, the tables turned. Suppose the courts of our Southern States, while changing no laws requiring the impaneling of jurymen without distinction as to race, etc., should suddenly begin to draw their thousands of jurymen all black, and well-nigh every one of them counting not only himself, but all his race, better than any white man. Assuming that their average of intelligence and morals should be not below that of jurymen as now drawn, would a white man, for all that, choose to be tried in one of those courts? Would he suspect nothing? Could one persuade him that his chances of even justice were all they should be, or all they would be were the court not evading the law in order to sustain an outrageous distinction against him because of the accidents of his birth? Yet only read white man for black man, and black man for white man, and that—I speak as an eye-witness—has been the practice for years, and is still so today; an actual emasculation, in the case of six million people both as plaintiff and defendant, of the right of trial by jury.

In this and other practices the outrage falls upon the freedman. Does it stop there? Far from it. It is the first premise of American principles that whatever elevates the lower stratum of the people lifts all the rest, and whatever holds it down holds all down. For twenty years, therefore, the nation has been working to elevate the freedman. It counts this one of the great necessities of the hour. It has poured out its wealth publicly and privately for this purpose. It is confidently hoped that it will soon bestow a royal gift of millions for the reduction of the illiteracy so largely shared by the blacks. Our Southern States are, and for twenty years have been, taxing themselves for the same end. The private charities alone of the other States have given twenty millions in the same good cause. Their colored seminaries, colleges, and normal schools dot our whole Southern country, and furnish our public colored schools with a large part of their teachers. All this and much more has been or is being done in order that, for the good of himself and everybody else in the land, the colored man may be elevated as quickly as possible from all the debasements of slavery and semi-slavery to the full stature and integrity of citizenship. And it is in the face of all this that the adherent of the old régime stands in the way to every public privilege and place—steamer landing, railway platform, theatre, concert-hall, art display, public library, public school, court-house, church, everything—flourishing the hot branding-iron of ignominious distinctions. He forbids the freedman to go into the water until *he* is satisfied that he knows how to swim, and for fear he should learn hangs mill-stones about his neck. This is what we are told is a small matter that will settle itself. Yes, like a roosting curse, until the outraged intelligence of the South lifts its indignant protest against this stupid firing into our own ranks.

"We would hunt him down and kill him"

In the passages that follow, excerpts from three speeches delivered in the United States Senate by Tillman of South Carolina (1847–1918), nothing was added to the battery of "arguments" that the advocates of white supremacy had at their command. The point is, rather, that Tillman's reasoning ran true to form and is still being used by latter-day

demagogues: that the Negro is an uncivilizable savage (or an animal— perhaps the "missing link"—or, at best, a child); that the blacks, who produced no civilization during centuries in Africa, profited in the days of slavery from the benign discipline and care of their white masters; that the license permitted the emancipated Negroes in the carpetbag days revealed their essential shiftlessness and their uncontrollable sexuality; that to educate the Negroes would only hasten a bloody war between the races, a war that would be made the more certain because education would train the blacks who would lead it.

From the time of the overthrow of the "Bourbon" rule in the South, around 1890, to the present these "facts" have been of great use to Southern demagogues—to Tillman and Cole Blease of South Carolina, Vardaman and Bilbo of Mississippi, Jeff Davis of Arkansas, Huey Long of Louisiana, and Talmadge of Georgia. In their appeal for the votes of the white farmers whose security was most immediately challenged by Negro competition, these old shibboleths brought out the voters and won elections.

Tillman was untiring in his efforts to "educate" the country to the terrible dangers of the mongrelization of the white race. Whenever he could, on the floor of the Senate, he contrived to introduce his views on the Negro question into the debate. Republicans turned their backs and left the chamber. When his Southern colleagues remained, they were likely to be embarrassed by such startling declarations as this: "As Governor of South Carolina I proclaimed that, although I had taken the oath of office to support the law and enforce it, I would lead a mob to lynch any man, black or white, who ravished a woman, black or white. This is my attitude calmly and deliberately taken, and justified by my conscience in the sight of God."

Tillman also carried on his negrophobic crusade outside the Senate. Using the Chautauqua platform as his instrument, he made the North resound with tirades that were even more crude and violent than those he delivered in the Senate. He received such applause from these Northern audiences that Professor Francis B. Simkins concludes that "the modern reactionary attitude toward the Negro dates from Ben Tillman and represents one of the most significant ways in which he influenced American life."

MR. PRESIDENT, I regret that I feel the necessity of bringing up again some parts of the speech of the Senator who has just taken his seat. However, he would not allow me to answer or interject an objection as he went along. It has reference to the race question in the South, the question which has been the cause of more sorrow, more misery, more loss of life, more expenditure of treasure than any and all questions which have confronted the American people from the foundation of the Government to the present day. Out of it grew the war, and after the war came the results of the war, and those results are with us now. The South has this question always with it. It can not get rid of it. It is there. It is like Banquo's ghost, and will not down. If I have felt called on to attack the Republican policy of this day and time and to accuse the Republicans in this Chamber with being hypocrites in regard to that issue, I have felt constrained to do so by reason of the facts and of the events of the past few years. . . .

There were numerous instances, possibly too numerous, of cruelty and wrongdoing, and I shall not apologize for the system, for, thank God, it is gone—torn up by the roots at a great cost of life and sacrifice of property. I would not restore it if I could by the waving of a hand. But I say to him when he parades that as a reason why we ought to be grateful—and I acknowledge that we ought—he at once convicts himself and those of his fellows who went on that crusade of blood and destruction for the purpose of liberating those people of having been misled and of having given Harriet Beecher Stowe's Uncle Tom's Cabin undue weight in inaugurating that crusade. I have already given due credit on this floor to the North for patriotism and honesty of purpose, and I realize that the love of the Union was a mighty factor in that great struggle. But it can not be denied that the slaves of the South were a superior set of men and women to freedmen of to-day, and that the poison in their minds—the race hatred of the whites—is the result of the teachings of Northern fanatics. Ravishing a woman, white or black, was never known to occur in the South till after the reconstruction era. So much for that phase of the subject. . . .

Mr. President, I have not the facts and figures here, but I want the country to get the full view of the Southern side of this question and the justification for anything we did. We were sorry we had the necessity forced upon us, but we could not help it, and as white men we are not sorry for it, and we do not propose to apologize for anything we have done in connection with it. We took the government away from [the carpetbag Negro government] in 1876. We did take it. If no other Senator has come here previous to this time who would acknowledge it, more is the pity. We have had no fraud in our elections in South Carolina since 1884. There has been no organized Republican party in the State.

We did not disfranchise the negroes until 1895. Then we had a constitutional convention convened which took the matter up calmly, deliberately, and avowedly with the purpose of disfranchising as many of them as we could under the fourteenth and fifteenth amendments. We adopted the educational qualification as the only means left to us, and the negro is as contented and as prosperous and as well protected in South Carolina to-day as in any State of the Union south of the Potomac. He is not meddling with politics, for he found that the more he meddled with them the worse off he got. As to his "rights"—I will not discuss them now. We of the South have never recognized the right of the negro to govern white men, and we never will. We have never believed him to be equal to the white man, and we will not submit to his gratifying his lust on our wives and daughters without lynching him. I would to God the last one of them was in Africa and that none of them had ever been brought to our shores. . . .

March 23, 1900

Some people have been ready to believe and to contend that the negro is a white man with a black skin. All history disproves that. Go to Africa. What do you find there? From one hundred and fifty million to two hundred million savages.

I happened in my boyhood, when I was about 12 years old, to see some real Africans fresh from their native jungles. The last cargo of slaves imported into this country were brought here in 1858 on the yacht *Wanderer,* landed on an island below Savannah, and sneaked by the United States marshal up the Savannah River and landed a little distance below Augusta, and my family bought some thirty of them.

Therefore I had a chance to see just what kind of people these were, and to compare the African as he is to-day in Africa with the African who, after two centuries of slavery, was brought side by side to be judged. The difference was as "Hyperion to a satyr." Those poor wretches, half starved as they had been on their voyage across the Atlantic, shut down and battened under the hatches and fed a little rice, several hundred of them, were the most miserable lot of human beings—the nearest to the missing link with the monkey—I have ever put my eyes on. . . .

Then if God in His providence ordained slavery and had these people transported over here for the purpose of civilizing enough of them to form a nucleus and to become missionaries back to their native heath, that is a question. . . . But the thing I want to call your attention to is that slavery was not an unmitigated evil for the negro, because whatever of progress the colored race has shown itself capable of achieving has come from slavery; and whether among those four million there were not more good men and women than could be found among the nine million now is to my mind a question. I would not like to assert it; but I am strongly of that belief from the facts I know in regard to the demoralization that has come to those people down there by having liberty thrust upon them in the way it was, and then having the ballot and the burdens of government, and being subjected to the strain of being tempted and misled and duped and used as tools by designing white men who went there among them. . . .

Well, Mr. President, I am done. I have treated this subject but imperfectly, but I have spoken from the soul, from my very heart, to tell you the truth, so help me God. I warn you that in proportion as you arouse false hopes in these people's minds as to their future, keeping the door of hope open by giving them offices, you are only sowing the wind which will whirl up into a whirlwind later on. You cannot keep that door open without shutting it on the whites. The Northern millions which have gone down there have gone into negro colleges and schools to equip these people to compete with their white neighbors.

All of the millions that are being sent there by Northern philanthropy has been but to create an antagonism between the poorer classes of our citizens and these people upon whose level they are in the labor market. There has been no contribution to elevate the white people in the South, to aid and assist the Anglo-Saxon Americans, the men who are descended from the people who fought with Marion and Sumter. They are allowed to struggle in poverty and in ignorance, and to do everything they can to get along, and they see Northern people pouring in thousands and thousands to help build up an African domination.

Senators I leave the subject with you. May God give you wisdom and light to "do as you would have others do unto you."

February 24, 1903

Now let me suppose a case. Let us take any Senator on this floor—I will not particularize—take him from some great and well-ordered State in the North, where there are possibly twenty thousand negroes, as there are in Wisconsin, with over two million whites. Let us carry this Senator to the backwoods in South Carolina, put him on a farm miles from a town or railroad, and environed with negroes. We will suppose he has a fair young daughter just budding into womanhood; and recollect this, the white women of the South are in a state of siege; the greatest care is exercised that they shall at all times where it is possible not be left alone or unprotected, but that can not always and in every instance be the case. That Senator's daughter undertakes to visit a neighbor or is left home alone for a brief while. Some lurking demon who has watched for the opportunity seizes her; she is choked or beaten into insensibility and ravished, her body prostituted, her purity destroyed, her chastity taken from her, and a memory branded on her brain as with a red-hot iron to haunt her night and day as long as she lives. . . .

In other words, a death in life. This young girl thus blighted and brutalized drags herself to her father and tells him what has happened. Is there a man here with red blood in his veins who doubts what impulses the father would feel? Is it any wonder that the whole countryside rises as one man and with set, stern faces seek the brute who has wrought this infamy? Brute, did I say? Why, Mr. President, this crime is a slander on the brutes. No beast of the field forces his female. He waits invitation. It has been left for something in the shape of a man to do this terrible thing. And shall such a creature, because he has the semblance of a man, appeal to the law? Shall men coldbloodedly stand up and demand for him the right to have a fair trial and be punished in the regular course of justice? So far as I am concerned he has put himself outside the pale of the law, human and divine. He has sinned against the Holy Ghost. He has invaded the holy of holies. He has struck civilization a blow, the most deadly and cruel that the imagination can conceive. It is idle to reason about it; it is idle to preach about it. Our brains reel under the staggering blow and hot blood surges to the heart. Civilization peels off us, any and all of us who are men, and we revert to the original savage type whose impulses under any and all such circumstances has always been to "kill! kill! kill!"

I do not know what the Senator from Wisconsin would do under these circumstances; neither do I care. I have three daughters, but, so help me God, I had rather find either one of them killed by a tiger or a bear and gather up her bones and bury them, conscious that she had died in the purity of her maidenhood, than have her crawl to me and tell me the horrid story that she had been robbed of the jewel of her womanhood by a black fiend. The wild beast would only obey the instinct of nature, and we would hunt him down and kill him just as soon as possible.

January 21, 1907

The Case of Eddie Mack

For Hodding Carter, crusading editor of the Greenville (Mississippi) Delta Democrat-Times, the pseudonymous "Eddie Mack" represents a class of Southern whites whose inherited prejudices toward the Negro both Northerners and Southerners must reckon with. Never a

*man to duck an important argument or fight, Carter here brings into
the open some unpleasant facts that have to be faced. For some readers,
Carter stops short of convictions to which they hold. But they should
remember that he has been threatened with violence and death for his
moderately liberal views on racial matters and on many other issues.*

"The Case of Eddie Mack" is Chapter vii of Mr. Carter's Southern
Legacy, *issued in 1950 by the Louisiana State University Press. The
chapter is reprinted here with the permission of the publishers.*

❀

EDDIE MACK, which was not his name, was a ne'er-do-well, a short,
gross man who usually needed a shave and who wore almost the year
round a hard straw hat and a collarless shirt, the neckband of which
was always held together with an incongruous, shiny collar button.
His decent, lower-middle-class parents lived not far from us; and their
household included Eddie's sad-faced wife, his children, who sometimes played with us, and intermittently Eddie himself. He would walk
past our house on his way to work, and after I knew about his secret
I felt ashamed and even wicked when I saw him.

The secret, which children whispered, was that Eddie was living on
the side with a light-skinned Negro woman whose home in that part
of the town known as the Quarters was familiar to many housewives
who brought her their lingerie and better linens for fine laundering.
They and everyone else knew about Eddie and the woman and about
others like them. Everyone condemned him and pitied his family, but
no one did anything about it. Some of the best citizens even hunted
with him on occasion, and his quadroon mistress—or high-yaller gal as
she was colloquially described—never lacked laundry business.

And later I knew other and more respectable Eddies who behaved
much as he did, only more circumspectly and with a less single-minded
devotion.

As we grew up we came to joke about the Eddie Macks, debating
with adolescent bravado the desirability or inevitability of their fleeting
alliances. They were surrounded by an obscene anatomical folklore,
and we laughed at this flagrant minority while publicly ignoring its
existence.

But there were other and less casual stories. About the Negro bellhop
in a Louisiana hotel who was a procurer of white women for the hotel
guests and whose horribly mutilated body was found in a swamp not
long after the talk got around that he received intimate favors from the
women he procured. About the Syrian girl who fell in love with a
Negro no darker than herself and who, after receiving repeated warn-

ings, saw him shot to death by a policeman who followed them down the railroad tracks one night to their trysting place. About the Arkansas plantation manager whose attachment to a Negro tenant's young daughter lasted many years, ending only when, an outcast and aging, he shot himself in the yard of the small home he had bought for her and their children. About the dispirited Negro teacher who divorced his handsome, easy wife when he learned that her finery had been acquired without cash payments from the manager of a ladies'-wear store. About the middle-aged Negro grocer, well-liked by his white patrons, who deserted his grocery and his family one night for a sluttish white woman and was caught and jailed—for auto theft—in Illinois, where a Mississippi automobile bearing a Negro man and a white woman aroused a policeman's suspicions.

The Southerner, conditioned to such departures from the norm, prefers not to discuss them except as isolated tidbits of scandal or tragedy. But the irrationality of conduct which these stories illustrate provokes the non-Southerner frequently to pungent comment. We are asked why we believe that laws forbidding sex relationships between the two races are necessary to keep them physically apart if natural selectivity or social repugnance separates man into ethnic groups. We are told the obvious, namely, that such laws have manifestly not succeeded in their purpose. We are criticized for the one-sidedness of their enforcement, since the white man is only rarely punished for miscegenation whereas the retribution is sure for the Negro man who is discovered. If racial purity is our objective, we are asked, what is the difference between a white and a Negro offender?

The mistake these questioners make, of course, is to insist upon rationality in the most irrational area of human behavior. The Southern attitude toward interracial sex relationships—and the attitude is by no means restricted to the South—is no more logical than are man's other wanderings through the whole confused labyrinth of sex itself. And there are certain realities, harsh or inconsistent as they may be, which have directed and still govern sex behavior in its interracial manifestations. They go back far beyond the time when the first Negroes were brought to Virginia or when the colonial authorities initially decided to legislate against cohabitation between white colonists and Negro slaves.

It is difficult to state harsh and often inconsistent realities without stepping on the toes both of the dominant group which imposes them and the submerged groups which must abide by them. They afford no pride for the white man nor comfort for the Negro. The unpleasant truth is that the Eddie Macks and the lynched bellhop are joint legatees of that illogical behavior which from the beginnings of recorded history has impelled the males of a dominant racial, national, or even

396

religious group to possess without compunction the women of dissimilar groups whom they have subjected or exploited, while setting apart their own women as inviolate. The pattern of duality is most apparent when the subjected people are economically submerged, culturally retarded, and profoundly different in physical appearance; it is then that one-way travel on miscegenation's somber street is most rigidly imposed. In effect, the dominant males assume that the bastard fruition of their own lust does not endanger ethnic integrity but that any reversal of the relationship debauches and imperils it.

Of course, it does not make sense in the abstract. The process of absorption is just as inevitable through the lightening of dark skins as it would be through the darkening of light skins. But the one method has met with tolerance, even sanction, and the other with violent disapproval and raw fear; and at the roots of the contradiction are instincts more real and enduring than race antipathies.

In no ethnic group has this illogical attitude persisted as strongly as among the Nordic and Celtic peoples of north Europe and the British Isles. From those areas came the principal colonizers of North America and the most persistent explorers and exploiters of the past 300 years. The English, the Scotch-Irish, the Germans, and the Scandinavians were far more rigid in their taboos than were the Spanish and French; but they were scarcely less industrious in begetting the half-caste offspring whom they would set apart—as witness the Eurasians of the Orient, the mixed bloods of the African coast and Polynesia and the five millions or more American Negroes of recognizably part-white ancestry. Obviously, there has also been unwitting assimilation when the person of mixed blood is physically indistinguishable from his white forebears.

All people who have been overcome by north-European and British expansion have been the victims of this bitter ambivalence, but none to such an uncompromising degree as the Negro. I believe that this is largely because the white man found the Negro in a state more savage by white tenets than that of any other people whose civilizations he modified or destroyed, and whose vast cultural lag he forthwith explained in terms of race. This is understandable, for even had the pillagers of the Gold Coast lived in an age of sociological detachment, they would scarcely have included anthropologists and sociologists in their slave- and treasure-ship companies. Moreover, the physical and color dissimilarities of the Negro were more pronounced, recognizable, and persistent. Perhaps also, the consistently menial position to which the Negro was reduced by slavery contributed to the contemptuous evaluation. And certainly the squalor in which the Negro masses have lived, the disproportionately high incidence of disease, crime, and illiteracy which has marred them, and their now-vanishing passivity and seeming moral numbness were wrongly but nigh universally interpreted as racial characteristics rather than as the results of racial mistreatment and neglect.

And, perhaps as a concomitant, there has lingered among most Anglo and Nordic Americans a profound and inexplicable fear that the Negro desires—and in the absence of segregation and miscegenation statutes would somehow be able—to merge biologically with a resisting white majority.

I repeat that these realities of attitudes and beliefs are harsh and inconsistent, but they are realities. The American South, more than any region in the Western world, is in its racial concepts the product of these realities.

Nowhere outside the British Isles is there so large a concentration of people of English and Scotch-Irish ancestry as in the South; a homogeneous, long-established people, their roots reaching back to the clannish, blood-conscious Sassenach and to the English, whose quietly arrogant assumption of superiority is an old and often provoking hallmark. Of our approximately 28 million white people, more than 95 per cent have these common origins, admixed with equally inflexible Germanic strains and leavened in only small degree by the subordinated Latin spirit of blood tolerance. Had the masters of the slave South been predominantly Spanish or even French, it is altogether probable that the South's population today would be as fused as are those of Brazil, Mexico, and Santo Domingo. But only a fringe of the South was settled by Latin adventurers, and these soon gave way, militarily and in their interracial patterns, before the Anglo-Saxon and Scotch-Irish onrush.

Among these blood-proud colonists of a hard frontier, the Negroes came unwillingly and in mounting numbers, not only as chattels but as primitives whose cultural inferiorities were interpreted as being related directly to their color. So it was that from the beginning the Negro's servile condition was condoned as proper and even helpful for a lower order of man; and, in order to maintain the system of slavery and to secure divine sanction for it, it was necessary to perpetuate the theory of superior and inferior races. I doubt that this effort was generally a conscious one, nor was it restricted to the South, either then or now. And we can hardly blame our forebears for accepting the theory that the naked Ashanti was in fact being aided through his forcible introduction to white civilization and to a limited sharing of Christianity. Even now the question can be argued with heat and futility and with a more decent intent than to rationalize a moral wrong.

Inevitably, the possessors had their way with the possessed, especially with those whose comeliness was enhanced in proprietary eyes by the blending of racial strains. Lust, loneliness, brutality, affection itself—

who can say in what proportions these emotions impelled the slave-holder to dishonor the slave, and who can decide now how much reluctance he met? If the joining of alien flesh was inevitable, so too was the ancient, irrational determination of the predatory male to keep his own womenfolk secure from the subjugated and the nonidentical.

The Negro male, slave and free, was forced into a baleful accommodation. He could not protest the use of his women, but, should he possess or seek to possess a white woman, forcibly or by agreement, his sure penalty was torture and death.

So it was that Eddie Mack could walk unmolested along our small-town street, and a plantation overseer could sit with his mulatto mistress and their fair-haired children in a house of his choosing. So it was that a Syrian girl's Negro lover died beside a railroad track and a Negro bellhop came to his death "at the hands of parties unknown." The psychologist must be summoned to evaluate the complex and related factors of fear and guilt, conviction of racial superiority, tradition and sex compulsions. But even the discerning layman recognizes that all these factors are present.

And it should be equally recognizable that segregation is essentially the product of the Southern male's determination that, except for the illicit and decreasingly condoned relationship of white man and Negro woman, the two races shall not be joined. When a Southerner protests something he calls social equality he really means sexual equality, whether he knows it or not, and his reaction is not likely to be modified by new laws or the repeal of old ones.

From this insistence that there shall be no intimacy on terms of equal acceptance have arisen the social taboos, wondrously complex and having as postulates not only the enforcement of racial separateness but of racial dominance.

Their extent and intensity are largely determined by numerical ratios and the degree of cultural development of the white enforcers. They are most meanly enforced where the white protagonists are least advanced economically, and most sternly where the pressure of numbers is acute. It is more than unfortunate happenstance that those Southern states whose white populations are the most retarded have also the largest Negro populations and resultantly give more emphasis to the extreme emotional expressions of white superiority.

A list of the taboos would be interminable. I can remember my humiliation as a small boy when I answered "ma'am" to someone who asked a question behind me, and turned to discover that the questioner was a Negro woman; and many years later, my inner misgivings when for the first time I addressed a Negro as "Mr." Although there is still a shockingly great likelihood that the Negro servant in a Southern kitchen is infected with syphilis or gonorrhea or tuberculosis, as long as her biscuits and behavior are good she can care for the children and prepare the meals until the bad blood carries her off; but the meals she prepares cannot be shared at a Southern table with the president of Howard University, the governor of the Virgin Islands, or the mediator for Palestine. It is fitting at Christmas time and on other symbolic occasions to give a drink to the yardman, but he takes his cheer standing up and after his employer. We Delta duck hunters find Negro handymen useful and entertaining company on a long hunting trip down river, and we will munch sandwiches with them in a muddy blind, but back on the boat they eat apart and remain inconspicuous. Gullible white and Negro patrons can mingle indiscriminately in the impersonal, foul-tent atmosphere of the carnival sideshow and the midway's sucker games, but not in the theater. If she has the purchase price, a Negro woman can buy hats, dresses, and shoes in many Southern urban shops, trying on, rejecting, and selecting, and the apparel she does not choose will be returned to the shelves for later sale; but she cannot wear her nonsegregated finery to a white church on Sunday even if she wants to. On the other hand, if she is a loved and longtime employee of a white family, she can attend in that church a wedding or a funeral of a member of the family.

In almost every expression of communal living—in the schools, the churches, the parks and playgrounds, the hospitals, the bus and railroad stations, the theaters—the taboos are maintained. Only the white and Negro slums slough off into each other. The taboos are contradictory only in a superficial sense. The determining point is simply that in the inescapable meeting of the races the superior-inferior status must be maintained.

The analytical observer may ridicule the inconsistencies and detest the human tragedies inherent in this uncompromising bracketing by race; but neither mockery nor protest nor legislation can, in the ascertainable future, change the white South's conviction that racial separateness at the mass levels of personal contact is the only acceptable way by which large segments of two dissimilar peoples can live side by side in peace. Any abrupt Federal effort to end segregation as it is practiced in the South today would not only be foredoomed to failure but would also dangerously impair the present progressive adjustments between the races.

More and more today the white man and the Negro are meeting at selective levels. But such communion is by choice and arises from interest in agreed-upon goals; and, more important, it is far removed from those murky human areas in which the feared and the fearing have the same submarginal denominators.

But as long as the white South continues to emphasize the inferior status of the Negro and makes separation synonymous with subordination, it unwittingly gives impetus to the thing it most fears. To the Negro, whiteness must be a contradictory symbol; on the one hand, a desirable characteristic and a conscious or unconscious goal, since without it he is denied the privileges of full citizenship; and, on the other hand, a hateful distinction which identifies his exploiter.

It is inescapably true that together with our uniform insistence upon racial separateness, we have consistently denied to the Negro the most precious intangible which man can possess. That is self-respect. And it is not necessary for the white South to strike at human dignity as a means of maintaining separation. More, it is not only morally wrong; it menaces the very principle of ethnic integrity upon which the structure of segregation theoretically rests.

Put it in the most human terms. In every town in the South there are Negroes who in their physical appearance are indistinguishable from white people. If they remain Negroes, they are subject to the multitude of discriminations that would make segregation intolerable to the militant and sensitive of any race. Certainly it is understandable that they sometimes move away and join the estimated 15,000 white-skinned Negroes who yearly cross over to the promised land of equal justice, unhindered franchise, unrestricted accommodations, adequate hospitalization, equal wage scales, and—so small and yet so great a thing—a handle to their names. Readily understandable, too, are baser and more vengeful attempts to attain the forbidden, and the pathetic success of the manufacturers of hair straighteners, and skin bleaches.

This thrusting toward whiteness is surely motivated primarily by an urge to escape from or avenge the penalties of blackness and not by any abstract considerations of the relative merits of various skin pigmentations. When men meet on equal terms, it is unnatural that any should experience shame because there are differences in physical appearances among them; the shame arises when stigma and subordination result from those differences; and with such humiliation comes inevitably the human urge to escape or retaliate.

It should be apparent that the very real economic and political progress which the Negro is making in the South has been accompanied by a decline in the traditional white man–Negro woman pattern of miscegenation itself. The slow expansion of a Negro middle class in the South has brought an ethical consciousness and a race pride that are evident in the decrease of common-law relationships among Negroes themselves and in the decline of *mésalliances* between white men and Negro women. There is no evidence that the educated, enfranchised Southern Negro is any more intent on marrying our daughters than was his slave great-grandparent. Nor, being a realist, does he share his Northern brother's gnawing preoccupation with segregation itself.

I believe that Savannah, Georgia, is an example of almost all the

401

Negro wants now to attain or can now attain as a citizen of the South. Savannah is not paradise, but it offers proof that seperation and subjugation need not go hand in hand. The Negro votes freely there although he represents 40 per cent of the population. In 1948 more business licenses were issued to Negro than to white businessmen. Negro doctors, lawyers, dentists, and bankers thrive professionally. The police force includes twelve Negroes and the post office employs fifty-four Negro mail carriers. Parks and playgrounds, schools and hospitals are more nearly equal in Savannah than anywhere else in the South.

I know that this explains the community and regional pride in the voice of the young Savannah Negro, a college graduate, who said to me: "I wouldn't live anywhere else than Savannah. We're treated like human beings here; and when we're treated like human beings, there's no reason for anybody to be afraid on either side."

That is something that Eddie Mack would not understand. But there are fewer Eddie Macks these days.

X I

VIOLENCE

Just as the United States is a lawless country when compared with the other democracies of the Western world, so the South is still the region in America where men most readily resort to violence when they should call in the law. A few statistics will indicate the differences at once. In 1951 the rate of murder and non-negligent manslaughter, per 100,000 of urban population, in the New England states was 1.24; in the Pacific states (Washington, Oregon, and California) it was 3.21; in the East South Central states (Kentucky, Tennessee, Alabama, and Mississippi) it was 12.45. Also in 1951 the state with the highest rate in the nation was Georgia (18.23). Other Southern states with comparatively high rates were Alabama (15.27), Tennessee (12.95), and South Carolina (12.51).[1] The average for all the states in the nation was 4.88. These figures bear out the impression of newspaper-reading visitors that Southerners, whites as well as Negroes, are still quick on the trigger and handy with the knife or razor and that the police are seldom on hand until there is mayhem or murder to report.

In accounting for the tradition of violence in the South one must note first that frontier survivals are still to be found there. Frontier life everywhere in America was reckless and lawless. Courts were too far away and too feeble to assert their authority. The frontiersman often had to protect his family and his property by his own fists and weapons or resort to vigilante action with his neighbors. As the plantation system was extended over most of the South between 1800 and 1860, the planter class, which controlled the county courts and the militia, suppressed, to some degree, frontier vigilantism. But the tradition was only dormant. It was easily awakened during the period of social disorganization following the Civil War.

[1] *Statistical Abstract of the United States*, 1953, published by the U.S. Department of Commerce, p. 142.

Meanwhile the aristocratic code of the planter class contributed its share to the tradition of violence. The planter was a proud and autocratic man, jealous of his personal honor and the good name of family and kin. Suits at law would not satisfy defamation or even insult. Duty demanded that the culprit be challenged, if he were the planter's social equal, or immediately caned or horsewhipped if he were an inferior. Toward his slaves the planter was usually no more severe in meting out physical punishment than he needed to be in order to secure obedience. A slave incapacitated by a beating would be of no use in the fields.

The breakdown of the old order after the war brought some strange reversals of behavior. The upper-class white man who before 1861 had been, as a slaveowner, the protector of the Negro, now often joined the poorer whites in enmity toward him. The emancipated Negro was resented because he was free, an incumbrance, and a potential threat to white supremacy. But part of the Southern vindictiveness was aimed indirectly at the Yankee invader, whether he was a carpetbagger or a do-gooder come south to educate the Negro or otherwise improve his lot. While Reconstruction lasted, the Yankee in the South could not be touched without fear of Northern reprisals, but a sassy Negro could be threatened, driven out of the community, or lynched. The quasi-military organization of the Ku-Klux Klan and other early night-riding groups suggests that some of their upper-class leaders wished to impose a partial restraint on race hatred and to select for punishment those Negroes who most flagrantly threatened white supremacy. But it was not long before many of these "better men," as W. J. Cash says, "let their own hate run, set themselves more or less deliberately to whipping up the hate of the common whites, and often themselves led these common whites into mob action against the Negro."

The years of the lynch mob may be over. In 1953 there were no lynchings in the United States. In the seventy years between 1882 and 1952 there were 4,730, the worst year being 1892, when 155 Negroes and 100 whites were murdered by vigilantes.[2]

In studying the psychopathology of lynching, the social psychologists have made some significant correlations. Lynching has been largely a rural phenomenon. The number of lynchings increased in depression years when cotton prices were low. The rate also climbed when the Populist leaders were most effectively stirring up the poor whites against the Negroes. Lynchings increased immediately following each of the two World Wars when the white population was made angry and apprehensive by the self-reliance and self-assertiveness of the

---

[2] Though the great preponderance of lynchings took place in the South, there were only six states—all of them in New England—in which there were no lynchings during this period.

returning Negro veterans. The active participants in the lynch mobs were young men of the uneducated classes who were not restrained in their gruesome fun by the often compliant officers of the law or the white leaders of the community. It must be admitted that for many of them the frenzied excitement of the stringing-up, the shooting, the sexual mutilation, the burning of the human torch, took the place, as H. L. Mencken said, "of the merry-go-round, the theatre, the symphony orchestra, and other diversions common to larger communities."

When violence breaks out in any community in the South today, its roots will usually be found deep in the past of the region. Hodding Carter illustrates this well in writing of "Bloody Tangipahoa" parish, in Louisiana, as he knew it twenty years ago (*Where Main Street Meets the River*, 1953). "Its gun readiness," he says, was "a hereditary compound of old feuds among the Kentucky and Tennessee families which had settled along the river bottoms, political enmities, racial conflicts and the tempers of a rural people who for generations had been their own policemen and personal avengers of insult. Undeniably, the people of the deep South, the rural South, are more inclined to violent retaliation than our Northern brothers, and more disinclined to punish a killer unless he also steals when he kills."

An Arkansas Fight

To the tradition of violence the boatmen who lived their riotous lives on the Mississippi contributed much. In the river towns their knifings and gougings were part of daily life, and among the rivermen the ornate hyperbole of the boasting which preceded the fight was refined until it became as much a convention as the bragging contest of the Anglo-Saxon heroes in the mead-hall.

The "bruising, Goughing, Biting, and ballocking" with which the ruder citizens of the South, and the rivermen in particular, amused themselves were a counterpart of the aristocratic duel. As time went on, the gougings aped the duels. It was the practice of Jim Bowie (inventor of the famous but ungentlemanly Bowie knife) to issue challenges or, having provoked a challenge, to insist on extravagant terms —that he and his opponent, for instance, should fight face to face with knives, astride a log, their britches nailed to the wood. This reduction of the duel to a point at which it began to seem absurd was in part responsible for its demise.

The following account is reprinted from the widely read humorous and sporting weekly journal The Spirit of the Times, *Vol. XII (February 18, 1843), p. 611.*

ONCE upon a time we were coming down the Mississippi River, on our way to this city. Bunyan has written about a certain delectable spot, situated somewhere in Utopia; but had the pilgrim seen the Arkansas landing we are just now speaking of, he would have thrown down his scallop shell and staff, and cut dirt as if the gentleman in black, on a streak of double-milled electricity, was after him. Two flatboats constituted the wharf, and they were continually butting their heads together. Such was the energy and regularity of their movement against each other, that for a moment we fancied the doctrine of Pythagoras was true, and that the departed spirits of two antagonistic rams had entered the timbers of the flatboats, and thence the combative symptoms above spoken of. As soon as the steamboat was moored alongside this floating wharf, the rush to board her was tremendous. One man, dressed in a hunting shirt of coarse homespun, and a coonskin cap, with a knife, something like that which sailors wear, sticking in his girdle, was the first to get on the plank that led from the flatboat to the steamer, and in his hurry to get on board he was pushed into the water, by a gigantic fellow in a bearskin coat, a coarse wool hat, and a pair of green baize leggings. The immersion of the gentleman in the hunting shirt was altogether accidental, but it was sufficient foundation, in the estimation of the cavaliers of Arkansas, for the tournament ground to be marked off, and the trumpets to blow "*largesse*" to the knights of the coonskin cap and the green baize leggings.

As soon as the ducked man arose from the top of the mulatto-colored river, he clenched one hand above his head, and hallowed, "Hold on there—you thin-milk-livered skunk! Hold on till I get on shore, and may I be cut up for shoe pegs if I don't make your skillet-faced phizcymahogany look like a cabbage made into sourkraut!"

"See here, stranger," replied the offender, "your duckin' was axesighdental; but if you want a tussel I am har—just like a fin on a cat-fish's back!"

"The plank was mine by seniority, as the doctors say, old cat skinner, and may I be ground up into gunpowder, if I don't light on to you like a bull bat on a gallinipper," remarked the dripping man, as he shook himself like a Newfoundland dog, and stepped on shore.

"Stranger," said the causer of the accident, while his eye gleamed like that of an enraged panther, and his fists clenched so forcibly that his nails were driven into the palms of his hands, "perhaps you don't know that I'm the man that fought with Wash. Coffee, and dirked wild Jule Lynch."

"May I run on a sawyer, and may my brains fall down into my boot heels as I am walking up a stony hill, if I care if you had a rough and tumble with the devil. You pushed me off the plank and you must fight," was the peaceable reply of the wet gentleman.

"See here, man," said the opponent of Wash. Coffee, as he bared his breast and pointed to a large scar that ran across three or four of his ribs, "Wild Jule done this, but I laid him up for a time—these big scratches on my face was got through my trying to hug a young bar— and this arm has been broken twice. I'm a cripple, but if you will fight, why strip and let's be at it."

In an instant a ring was made, and the two combatants, when doffed of their clothing, looked like middle-aged Titans, preparing for battle. The younger, who had fallen into the water was about twenty-eight years of age, and his opponent was thirty-four or five. With eyes made fiery by anger, and lips quivering with intense passion, the younger dealt his adversary a tremendous blow in the breast. Until this affront the elder man had maintained a strange coolness, and manifested a disposition rather in favor of an apology than anything else; but the

407

instant he felt the blow his nostrils became white, and twitched like a steed's scenting the battle. Closing his teeth hard together, he planted himself for the attack, and as his adversary approached him, he dealt him a fierce lick on the side of the face with his iron-bound knuckles, that laid his cheek bone as bare as though the flesh had been chopped off by an ax. Smarting with rage the other returned the compliment, and as the blood gushed in a torrent from his mouth, he turned around and spit out one or two of his teeth that were hanging by the gums, and with a "rounder" as it is technically termed, he hit the younger man [*sic*] a blow on the temple that laid him on the beach with a dead, heavy sound, like that of a falling tree.

"Thar, I hope he is got enough," said the elder of the two, at almost every word stopping to spit out some fragment of his broken jaw. One of his companions handed him a flask of brandy, and with a long deep-drawn swallow, like that of a camel at a spring on an oasis, he gulped down enough of the fiery liquor to have made a common man mad.

"Enough," cried the other party, who had been in a like manner attended by his friends. "Yes, when I drink your heart's blood I'll cry enough, and not till then, come on, you white-wired—"

"See here, stranger, stop thar. Don't talk of my mother—She's *dead —God bless her! I'm a man from A to izzard—and you—you thin gutted wasp, I'll whip you now if I die for it!*"

With a shout from the bystanders, and passions made furious by hate and deep draughts of liquor, with a howl the combatants again went to work. Disengaging his right hand from the boa constrictor grip of his opponent, the younger brute buried his long talon-like nails directly under the eyelid of his victim, and the orb clotted with blood hung by a few tendons to his cheek! As soon as the elder man felt the torture, his face for an instant was as white as snow, and then a deep purple hue overspread his countenance. Lifting his adversary in the air as though he had been a child, he threw him to the earth, and clutching his throat with both hands, he squeezed it until his enemy's face became almost black. Suddenly he uttered a sharp quick cry, and put his hand to his side, and when he drew it away it was covered with blood! The younger villain, while on his back, had drawn his knife and stabbed him. As the elder of the combatants staggered up, he was caught by some of his friends, and holding him in their arms, with clenched fists they muttered curses toward his inhuman opponent, who being shielded by his own particular clique, made for the river and plunged in. When about half way across, he gained a small island, and rising to his full height, he flapped his hands against his sides and crow'd like a cock.

"Ruo-ru—oo-o! I can lick a steamboat! My finger-nails is related to a saw mill on my mother's side, and my daddy was a doublebreasted catamount! I wear a hoop snake for a neck-handkerchief, and the brass buttons on my coat have all been boiled in poison! Who'll Ru—oo—ru—ooo!"

"We now shot them like dogs"

Davy Crockett (1786–1836), mighty hunter of bears, Congressman from the Tennessee frontier, and teller of tall tales, says he did not enjoy killing Indians. "I never liked this business with the Indians," he remarked, when the Creek War was over. "I'm glad I'm through with these war matters. They have no fun in them at all. It was nothing but dog eat dog." Still, Crockett's grandparents had been killed by Creeks; the Creeks, led by the Shawano chief Tecumseh, were out to get their revenge on the white men while the War of 1812 was on; and Davy's services as a scout were needed. He told Polly he had to go, and before long he and Andrew Jackson were war heroes.

Davy Crockett may not have had any fun killing Indians, but he was good at it and his words about the Indian boy stewing in his own grease suggest that the business did not disgust him as much as he says it did.

This passage is taken from A Narrative of the Life of David Crockett, of the State of Tennessee *(Philadelphia: E. L. Carey and A. Hart; 1834), pp. 86–9. This is one of the few accounts of Crockett's life which he undoubtedly had a hand in, though he admitted that he had the manuscript "run over by a friend or so."*

WE then marched to a place, which we called Camp Wills; and here it was that Captain Cannon was promoted to a colonel, and Colonel Coffee to a general. We then marched to the Ten Islands, on the Coosa river, where we established a fort; and our spy companies were sent out. They soon made prisoners of Bob Catala and his warriors, and, in a few days afterwards, we heard of some Indians in a town about eight miles off. So we mounted our horses, and put out for that town, under the direction of two friendly Creeks we had taken for pilots. We had also a Cherokee colonel, Dick Brown, and some of his men with us. When we got near the town we divided; one of our pilots going with each division. And so we passed on each side of the town, keeping near to it, until our lines met on the far side. We then closed up at both ends, so as to surround it completely; and then we sent Captain Hammond's company of rangers to bring on the affray. He had advanced near the town, when the Indians saw him, and they raised the yell, and came running at him like so many red devils. The main army was now formed in a hollow square around the town, and they pursued Hammond till they came in reach of us. We then gave them a fire, and they returned it, and then ran back into their town. We began to close on the town by making our files closer and closer, and the Indians soon saw they were our property. So most of them wanted us to take them prisoners; and their squaws and all would run and take hold of any of us they could, and give themselves up. I saw seven squaws have hold of one man, which made me think of the Scriptures. So I hollered out the Scriptures was fulfilling; that there was seven women holding to one man's coat tail. But I believe it was a hunting-shirt all the time. We took them all prisoners that came out to us in this way; but I saw some warriors run into a house, until I counted forty-six of them. We pursued them until we got near the house, when we saw a squaw sitting in the door, and she placed her feet against the bow she had in her hand, and then took an arrow, and, raising her feet, she drew with all her might, and let fly at us, and she killed a man, whose name, I believe, was Moore. He was a lieutenant, and his death so enraged us all, that she was fired on, and had at least twenty balls blown through her. This was the first man I ever saw killed with a bow and arrow. We now shot them like dogs; and then set the house on fire, and burned it up with the forty-six warriors in it. I recollect seeing a boy who was shot down near the house. His arm and thigh was broken, and he was so near the burning house that the grease was stewing out of him. In this situation he was still trying to crawl along; but not a murmur escaped him, though he was only about twelve years old. So sullen is the Indian, when his dander is up, that he had sooner die than make a noise, or ask for quarters.

Memorial of a Committee Appointed at a Meeting of Colored Citizens, of Frankfort, Ky., and Vicinity, Praying the Enactment of laws for the better protection of life

This document was presented to the United States Senate on March 25, 1871. It is printed in Index to the Miscellaneous Documents of the Senate of the United States for the First Session of the Forty-Second Congress *(Washington: Government Printing Office; 1871). It was ordered (on April 11, 1871) that the Memorial "lie on the table and be printed." The list of outrages given in the petition contains 116 items, of which 23 are printed here. The selection was made with the view of representing the different kinds of acts of violence reported in the Memorial.*

Immediately after the Civil War the Negroes of Kentucky were the victims of a curious political situation. In spite of the fact that Kentucky had been neutral during the war, the Federal government extended the Freedmen's Bureau to the state. Resenting its presence and the activities of its special courts, the state authorities refused to enact laws giving the Negroes status as free men. While attempts were being made to drive the Bureau from the state (it was removed in 1873), the Regulators and the Ku-Klux Klan took "the law" into their hands.

To the Senate and House of Representatives in Congress assembled:

We, the colored citizens of Frankfort and vicinity, do this day memorialize your honorable bodies upon the condition of affairs now existing in the State of Kentucky. We would respectfully state that life, liberty, and property are unprotected among the colored race of this State. Organized bands of desperate and lawless men, mainly composed of soldiers of the late rebel armies, armed, disciplined, and disguised, and bound by oath and secret obligations, have, by force, terror, and violence, subverted all civil society among colored people; thus utterly rendering insecure the safety of persons and property, overthrowing all those rights which are the primary basis and objects of the Government, which are expressly guaranteed to us by the Con-

411

stitution of the United States as amended. We believe you are not familiar with the description of the Ku-Klux Klans riding nightly over the country, going from county to county, and in the county towns, spreading terror wherever they go by robbing, whipping, ravishing, and killing our people without provocation, compelling colored people to break the ice and bathe in the chilly waters of the Kentucky River.

The legislature has adjourned. They refused to enact any laws to suppress Ku-Klux disorder. We regard them as now being licensed to continue their dark and bloody deeds under cover of the dark night. They refuse to allow us to testify in the State courts where a white man is concerned. We find their deeds are perpetrated only upon colored men and white republicans. We also find that for our services to the Government and our race we have become the special object of hatred and persecution at the hands of the democratic party. Our people are driven from their homes in great numbers, having no redress only the United States court, which is in many cases unable to reach them.

We would state that we have been law-abiding citizens, pay our taxes, and in many parts of the State our people have been driven from the polls, refused the right to vote; many have been slaughtered while attempting to vote. We ask, how long is this state of things to last?

We appeal to you as law-abiding citizens to enact some laws that will protect us, and that will enable us to exercise the rights of citizens. We see that the Senator from this State denies there being organized bands of desperadoes in the State; for information, we lay before you a number of violent acts, occurred during his administration. Although he, Stevenson, says half a dozen instances of violence did occur, these are not more than one-half the acts that have occurred. The democratic party has here a political organization composed only of democrats; not a single republican can join them. Where many of these acts have been committed, it has been proven that they were the men, done with arms from the State arsenal. We pray you will take some steps to remedy these evils.

Done by a committee of grievances appointed at a meeting of all the colored citizens of Frankfort and vicinity.

> HENRY MARRS,
> *Teacher Colored School,*
> HENRY LYNN,
> *Livery Stable Keeper,*
> H. H. TRUMBO, *Grocer,*
> SAMUEL DEMSEY,
> B. SMITH,
> B. J. CRAMPTON, *Barber,*
> *Committee.*

412

5. Sam Davis hung by mob at Harrodsburg, May 23, 1868.

6. William Pierce hung by a mob in Christian, July 12, 1868.

11. Cabe Fields shot and killed by disguised men near Keene, Jassemine County, August 3, 1868.

22. Mob attacked Cumins's house in Pulaski County; Cumins, his daughter, and a man named Adams killed in the attack, September 18, 1868.

27. Attack on negro cabin in Spencer County; a woman outraged, December, 1868.

28. Two negroes shot by Ku-Klux at Sulphur Springs, in Union County, December, 1868.

39. Ku-Klux whipped Lucien Green in Lincoln County, June, 1869.

40. Miller whipped by Ku-Klux in Madison County, July 2, 1869.

42. Mob decoy from Harrodsburg and hang George Bolling, July 17, 1869.

46. Mob tar and feather a citizen of Cynthiana, in Harrison County, August, 1869.

48. Ku-Klux burn colored meeting-house in Carroll County, September, 1869.

52. Ku-Klux ordered Wallace Sinthorn to leave his home near Parkville, Boyle County, October, 1869.

54. Regulator killed George Tankesley, in Lincoln County, November 2, 1869.

59. Regulators whipped Cooper, in Pulaski County, November, 1869.

62. Two negroes killed by mob while in civil custody, near Mayfield, Graves County, December, 1869.

69. Mob hung up, then whipped, Douglass Rodes, near Kingston, Madison County, February, 1870.

79. Three men hung by mob near Glasgow, Warren County, May, 1870.

86. Ku-Klux visited negro cabin, robbing and maltreating inmates, on Sand Riffle, in Henry County, June 10, 1870.

95. John Simes shot and his wife murdered by Ku-Klux, in Henry County, September, 1870.

102. Two negroes killed in Fayette County, while in civil custody, December 18, 1870.

105. A negro named George hung by a mob at Cynthiana, Harrison County, December, 1870.

106. Negro killed by Ku-Klux near Ashland, Fayette County, January 7, 1871.

116. Ku-Klux, to the number of 200, in February, came into Frank-

fort and rescued from jail one Scroggins that was in civil custody for shooting and killing one colored man named Strader Trumbo.

Three 1930 Lynchings

In 1930, when the number of lynchings took a sharp upward turn—there were twenty-one in that year—the Commission on Interracial Coöperation sponsored a thorough investigation of the lynching phenomenon. The director of this study, Dr. Arthur Raper, published the findings in The Tragedy of Lynching *(1933). The paragraphs printed below give the stark facts about three of the 1930 lynchings, as presented in Dr. Raper's book. An exhaustive etiological study, based on these facts, was made, of course, for each case.*

Between 1882 and the end of 1952 there were 4,730 lynchings in this country. Of the victims, 3,437 were Negroes. The states in which the largest number of lynchings took place were: Mississippi (574), Georgia (530), Texas (493), Louisiana (391), Alabama (347), Arkansas (284), Florida (282), Tennessee (251), Kentucky (205).

Since 1935, when there were twenty lynchings, this form of violence has decreased rapidly. In 1952 and 1953 there were no lynchings. As a result of this fortunate decline, Tuskegee Institute announced in December 1953 that it was discontinuing its annual report on lynchings. Other forms of violence against the Negro persist, but one may hope that this long and harrowing record is now closed.

These excerpts from The Tragedy of Lynching *are reprinted with the permission of the publisher, the University of North Carolina Press.*

TEXAS

In the afternoon of May 9, 1930, the Grayson County courthouse at Sherman, Texas, was on fire and George Hughes, Negro farm hand, was sweltering in the second-story vault. The Negro was accused of assaulting a white woman. After firing the courthouse, the rioters chased the militiamen from the square, blasted open the vault, dragged the Negro's body through the streets, and burned it along with the town's Negro business section.

OCILLA, GEORGIA

Protracted Tortures, Followed by Fire and Bullets. Upon reaching the place where the body of the girl was found, Irwin was tied to a tree with chains. The tortures began. Approximately a thousand people were present, including some women and children on the edge of the crowd. Members of the mob cut off his fingers and toes, joint by joint. Mob leaders carried them off as souvenirs. Next, his teeth were pulled out with wire pliers. When ever he expressed pain or tried to evade the approaches of his sadistic avengers, he was jabbed in the mouth with a pointed pole. Because of their nature, the remaining mutilations and tortures will not be described. Suffice it to say that they were indecent and brutal beyond belief.

After these mutilations, which lasted more than an hour, Irwin's mangled but living body was hung upon a tree by the arms. Logs and underbrush were piled beneath. Gasoline was poured on. A match was struck. As the flames engulfed the body, it was pierced by bullets.

James Irwin was dead. All day his body, burned past recognition, hung in the tree by the public road. Thousands of white people, including women and children, rode out to see the spectacle. At nightfall the county authorities took the body down and buried it.

OKLAHOMA

Henry Argo, nineteen-year-old Negro, was lynched at Chickasha, Grady County, Oklahoma, on May 31, 1930. He was accused of having criminally assaulted a white woman at her "dug out" home in a rural neighborhood near the city. The lynching occurred just three weeks after the mob disorders at Sherman, less than two hundred miles to the southeast. The major events at Chickasha came in rapid succession: It was about 4:30 P.M. when the alleged assault occurred, and within an hour the accused man was arrested; at six o'clock a mob was forming and soon numbered over a thousand; by eight thirty efforts were being made to enter the jail; about eleven the National Guardsmen were stoned and their truck burned; at 3:30 A.M. mob leaders shot the accused Negro in his cell; near seven he was stabbed, and at noon he died.

"Ride on, stranger"
The Kentucky Mountain Feud

Though he attended Harvard and did newspaper work for the New York Times, *John Fox, Jr. (1863–1919), novelist and war correspondent, never, in later life, deserted the Kentucky mountains for long. Eventually he published more than a dozen volumes—novels, novelettes, and collections of essays—whose great popularity made the Kentucky mountain life that he described familiar to the American people. He admired the clannish, proud, hospitable folk who lived high up in the valleys and coves of the Cumberland region. Though he knew they were more ignorant and thriftless than their pioneer ancestors, he said of them: "Americans to the core, they make the Southern mountains a store-house of patriotism." He also understood why they spent so much of their time feuding. He discussed the reasons in "The Kentucky Mountaineer," from which the following excerpt is taken. This is reprinted from* Blue Grass and Rhododendron, *by John Fox, Jr.; copyright 1901 by Charles Scribner's Sons, 1928 by Horace E. Fox; used by permission of the publishers.*

About thirty-five years ago two boys were playing marbles in the road along the Cumberland River—down in the Kentucky mountains. One had a patch on the seat of his trousers. The other boy made fun of it, and the boy with the patch went home and told his father. Thirty years of local war was the result. The factions fought on after they had forgotten why they had fought at all. While organized warfare is now over, an occasional fight yet comes over the patch on those trousers and a man or two is killed. A county as big as Rhode Island is still bitterly divided on the subject. In a race for the legislature not long ago, the feud was the sole issue. And, without knowing it, perhaps, a mountaineer carried that patch like a flag to victory, and sat under it at the capital—making laws for the rest of the State.

That is the feud that has stained the highland border of the State with blood, and abroad, has engulfed the reputation of the lowland blue-grass, where there are, of course, no feuds—a fact that sometimes seems to require emphasis, I am sorry to say. Almost every mountain county has, or has had, its feud. On one side is a leader whose authority is rarely questioned. Each leader has his band of retainers. Always he arms them; usually he feeds them; sometimes he houses and clothes them, and sometimes, even, he hires them. In one local war, I remember, four dollars per day were the wages of the fighting man, and the leader on one occasion, while besieging his enemies—in the county court-house—tried to purchase a cannon, and from no other place than the State arsenal, and from no other personage than the governor himself.

It is the feud that most sharply differentiates the Kentucky mountaineer from his fellows, and it is extreme isolation that makes possible in this age such a relic of mediæval barbarism. For the feud means, of course, ignorance, shiftlessness, incredible lawlessness, a frightful estimate of the value of human life; the horrible custom of ambush, a class of cowardly assassins who can be hired to do murder for a gun, a mule, or a gallon of moonshine.

Now these are the blackest shadows in the only picture of Kentucky mountain life that has reached the light of print through the press. There is another side, and it is only fair to show it.

The feud is an inheritance. There were feuds before the war, even on the edge of the blue-grass; there were fierce family fights in the backwoods before and during the Revolution—when the war between Whig and Tory served as a pretext for satisfying personal animosities already existing, and it is not a wild fancy that the Kentucky mountain feud takes root in Scotland. For, while it is hardly possible that the enmities of the Revolution were transmitted to the Civil War, it is quite sure that whatever race instinct, old-world trait of character, or moral code the backwoodsman may have taken with him into the mountains—it is quite sure that that instinct, that trait of character, that moral code, are living forces in him to-day. The late war was, however, the chief cause of feuds. When it came, the river-bottoms were populated, the clans were formed. There were more slave-holders among them than among other Southern mountaineers. For that reason, the war divided them more evenly against themselves, and set them fighting. When the war stopped elsewhere, it simply kept on with them, because they were more isolated, more evenly divided; because they were a fiercer race, and because the issue had become personal. The little that is going on now goes on for the same reason, for while civilization pressed close enough in 1890 and 1891 to put an end to organized fighting, it is a consistent fact that after the failure of Baring Brothers, and the stoppage of the flow of English capital into the mountains, and the check to railroads and civilization, these feuds slowly started up again. When I left home for the Cuban war, two companies of State militia were on their way to the mountains to put down a feud. On the day of the Las Guasimas fight these feudsmen fought, and they lost precisely as many men killed as the Rough Riders —eight.

Again: while the feud may involve the sympathies of a county, the number of men actually engaged in it are comparatively few. Moreover, the feud is strictly of themselves, and is based primarily on a privilege that the mountaineer, the world over, has most grudgingly surrendered to the law, the privilege of avenging his private wrongs. The non-partisan and the traveller are never molested. Property of the beaten faction is never touched. The women are safe from harm, and I have never heard of one who was subjected to insult. Attend to your own business, side with neither faction in act or word and you are much safer among the Kentucky mountaineers, when a feud is going on, than you are crossing Broadway at Twenty-third Street. As you ride along, a bullet may plough through the road ten yards in front of you. That means for you to halt. A mountaineer will come out of the bushes and ask who you are and where you are going and what your business is. If your answers are satisfactory, you go on unmolested. Asking for a place to stay all night, you may be told, "Go to So and So's house; he'll pertect ye"; and he will, too, at the risk of his own life when you are past the line of suspicion and under his roof.

There are other facts that soften a too harsh judgment of the mountaineer and his feud—harsh as the judgment should be. Personal fealty is the cornerstone of the feud. The mountaineer admits no higher law; he understands no conscience that will violate that tie. You are my friend or my kinsman; your quarrel is my quarrel; whoever strikes you, strikes me. If you are in trouble, I must not testify against you. If you are an officer, you must not arrest me, you must send me word to come into court. If I'm innocent, why, maybe I'll come.

Moreover, the worst have the list of rude virtues already mentioned; and, besides, the mountaineer is never a thief nor a robber, and he will lie about one thing and one thing only, and that is land. He has cleared it, built his cabin from the trees, lived on it and he feels that any means necessary to hold it are justifiable. Lastly, religion is as honestly used to cloak deviltry as it ever was in the Middle Ages.

A feud leader who had about exterminated the opposing faction, and had made a good fortune for a mountaineer while doing it, for he kept his men busy getting out timber when they weren't fighting, said to me, in all seriousness:

"I have triumphed agin my enemies time and time agin. The Lord's on my side, and I gits a better and better Christian ever' year."

A preacher, riding down a ravine, came upon an old mountaineer hiding in the bushes with his rifle.

"What are you doing there, my friend?"

"Ride on, stranger," was the easy answer. "I'm a-waitin' fer Jim Johnson, and with the help of the Lawd I'm goin' to blow his damn head off."

Even the ambush, the hideous feature of the feud, took root in the days of the Revolution, and was borrowed, maybe, from the Indians. Milfort, the Frenchman, who hated the backwoodsman, says Mr. Roosevelt, describes with horror their extreme malevolence and their murderous disposition toward one another. He says that whether a wrong had been done to a man peronally or to his family, he would, if necessary, travel a hundred miles and lurk around the forest indefinitely to get a chance to shoot his enemy.

But the Civil War was the chief cause of bloodshed; for there is evidence, indeed, that though feeling between families was strong, bloodshed was rare and the English sense of fairness prevailed, in certain communities at least. Often you shall hear an old mountaineer say: "Folks usen to talk about how fer they could kill a *deer*. Now hit's how fer they can kill a *man*. Why, I have knowed the time when a man would hev been druv outen the county fer drawin' a knife or a pistol, an' if a man was ever killed, hit wus kinder accidental by a Barlow. I reckon folks got used to weepons an' killin' an' shootin' from the bresh endurin' the war. But hit's been gettin' wuss ever sence, and now hit's dirk an' Winchester all the time." Even for the ambush there is an explanation.

"Oh, I know all the excuses folks make. Hit's fair for one as 'tis fer t'other. You can't fight a man f'ar and squar who'll shoot you in the back. A pore man can't fight money in the courts. Thar hain't no witnesses in the lorrel but leaves, an' dead men don't hev much to say. I know hit all. Looks like lots o' decent young folks hev got usen to the idee; thar's so much of it goin' on and thar's so much talk about shootin' from the bresh. I do reckon hit's wuss'n stealin' to take a feller critter's life that way."

Fighting the Ku Klux Klan in the 1920's

This account of the revival of the Klan and the courageous efforts to defeat it is excerpted from two chapters of Virginius Dabney's Liberalism in the South *(Chapel Hill: University of North Carolina Press;*

*1932). It is reprinted with the permission of the publishers. For a note
on Mr. Dabney see p. 208.*

❁

THE Klan was called back from the virtual oblivion which had envel-
oped it since reconstruction days by one William J. Simmons, a former
revivalist and traveling salesman and a "jiner" of parts, who seems to
have awakened to a keen realization of the commercial possibilities in
P. T. Barnum's estimate of the number of suckers born per minute. At
any rate, Simmons revived the Klan in 1915, with "white supremacy"
as one of its war cries. The going was heavy at first, but when Edward
Young Clarke, an able promoter, took charge of the situation in 1920,
things began to move at once, and the organization spread like wildfire
to all parts of the country. Negroes were the particular objects of the
Klan's wrath in the South, while in other sections Catholics, Jews, and
aliens were singled out for attack.

The Klan has now [1932] declined greatly in strength, and is moribund everywhere, but in the middle twenties its membership was well
up in the millions. The reasons for its remarkable growth are analyzed
by Frank Tannenbaum in his *Darker Phases of the South*. Mr. Tannenbaum feels that the habits of violence intensified by the war together
with the effect of the war upon the Negro were paramount in creating
a state of mind receptive to a secret, masked organization professing
devotion to the principles of "white supremacy" and "hundred per
cent Americanism." The South was a particularly lush field of operations for this Nordic crusade in view of the notions of "social equality"
thought to have been engendered in the minds of the half a million
blacks drafted into the army and paid the same wages as the white
soldiers. Besides, some two hundred thousand of these Negroes went
to France, where they were often received as the social equals of the
natives, and on their return many of them left the South for the North.
All in all, the South was ripe for the Klan after the war.

While the organization's membership was well distributed over the
country and was by no means confined to the South, it seems to have
had considerable strength in all the Southern states except Virginia and
the Carolinas. Texas boasted a larger number of Klansmen than any
other commonwealth in Dixie.

The Klan probably would have become practically extinct by 1928,
but the nomination of Governor Alfred E. Smith of New York for
the presidency revived the religious issue in such virulent form that the
organization's complete collapse was postponed. By 1930, however, the
K.K.K. was in such dire straits that the resourceful Mr. William J.

Simmons recognized the need for a change in nomenclature. He accordingly announced a "Caucasian Crusade," with himself and Congressman Robert Ramspect of Georgia among the sponsors, crusaders to be limited to "real, red-blooded white Americans, inside and out." This patriotic effort was without appreciable effect. . . .

Among the Southern public men who did not tremble before the Ku Klux Klan was Thomas T. Connally of Texas, who won his Senate seat from Earle B. Mayfield, the candidate of the Invisible Empire. Another who refused to truckle to the Klan was Governor Thomas W. Hardwick of Georgia, who ordered the organization to unmask and thereby signed his political death warrant. Curiously enough, Governor Hardwick had gone on record many times in his gubernatorial campaign for rigid enforcement of the Veazey Law, and had urged such amendments to that law as were needed to make it enforceable. This statute, which was drafted by the notorious anti-Catholic, Senator Thomas E. Watson, provided for the inspection of convents and monasteries and was bitterly resented by the Catholics of the state. Over against Mr. Hardwick's order unmasking the Klan must also be placed the fact that on international questions he is a rampant isolationist. It should be added, however, that as governor he abolished the lash in Georgia's prison camps and that until a short while ago he was one of the small number of Southerners on the national committee of the American Civil Liberties Union. Benjamin Meek Miller, the sitting governor of Alabama, should also be mentioned. He was retired from the Alabama Supreme Court by the K.K.K. and was elected to his present office on a platform calling for destruction of "Klan control of the jury box." He has turned a deaf ear to the wails of politicians and has fired numerous jobholders while instituting important governmental reforms. . . .

But there were still other ideas in Georgia. Soon the American Facist (sic) Association and Order of Blackshirts arose in Atlanta to assure tremulous Nordics that it would make the South safe for white supremacy. Not only so, but it would oust Negroes from their jobs and install sound Caucasian hundred per cent Americans in their stead. The Black Shirts were making headway in Atlanta and had enrolled twenty-one thousand members, thanks largely to the craven conduct of the Atlanta newspapers in permitting the order to grow unmolested, when the Macon *Telegraph* launched an editorial campaign which soon put them out of business.

"The best way Macon people can receive the Black Shirts is to keep their hands on their pocketbooks," said the editor of this fearless daily. "It is the custom of every sucker-tapping organization that ever existed to have a set of high-sounding principles and ambitious objectives with which to intrigue the man who has enough money to join, but not sense enough to stay out. . . . If the kluxing effort [Ku Klux Klan] had been shown up to start with, thousands of good Georgians would never have put on a mask or a nightshirt at $10 for a 35-cent garment and the order would have died aborning. . . ."

The *Telegraph* published a series of special news articles on the Black Shirts simultaneously with its editorial broadside against the order. The movement was unable to stand a thorough ventilation of its methods and purposes, and its demise was immediate.

While such exhibitions of racial bigotry as have been given by the Klan and the Black Shirts are profoundly discouraging to Southern liberals, it must be remembered that, after all, both organizations are virtually defunct at the present time. And if the probabilities are that similar societies will arise in the future, it seems reasonable to assume that the "racket" is getting stale, since the Black Shirts were unable in 1931 to rouse the populace at a dollar a head, one-tenth of the initiation fee which millions paid a few years previously to join the Klan.

XII

POLITICS

PROFESSOR V. O. KEY opens the last chapter of his monumental *Southern Politics* with this ominous statement: "A depressingly high rate of self-destruction prevails among those who ponder about the South and put down their reflections in books." Even though one may not subscribe to this gloomy view, it is necessary to warn the reader that he will encounter many paradoxes, ambiguities, and unbelievable situations in this note.

To begin with a few paradoxes. Southern politics has always been individualistic, earthy, "practical." Possibly because of the Calvinistic strain in Southern religion, one finds very little of the idealism which the Transcendentalists of New England or the Progressives of the Middle West injected into Northern politics. Yet the greatest liberal and idealist in American political life was a Southerner—Thomas Jefferson. Again, the South has originated no reform movements that have won the support of the whole nation. When it has been moved to social action, the impulse has come from outside, as when the South rode the wave of Populism in the 1880's or marched behind the New Deal in the 1930's. Yet the greatest political radical among our Presidents, a man who accomplished a bloodless revolution, was a Southern hero who commanded even greater allegiance than Jefferson did—Andrew Jackson of Tennessee. Again, though the South has furnished no President to the nation, except Woodrow Wilson, since General Zachary Taylor (1849–50), its influence in Congress has been great and indeed often paramount since the time of Grover Cleveland. And this, too, in spite of the fact that not even in the predictable future will a Southerner sit in the White House. Paradoxical, too, is the fact that the South, generally conservative in economic matters, has sent many liberal senators to Washington—Joseph T. Robinson of Arkansas, Hugo Black and Lister Hill of Alabama, Claude Pepper of Florida,

423

Frank Graham of North Carolina. It is also true that they are sometimes voted out of office before their years in the Senate have been
many.

From the earliest days a career in politics was the expected goal in
life of the Southern gentleman. In colonial times the wealthy planter
began this career as the local magistrate and colonel of the county
militia. In Virginia he then went on to the House of Burgesses and
aspired, finally, to a seat in the exclusive Governor's Council, where he
treated the King's representative as a peer and sometimes helped to
drive him out of office. Trained in the law, accustomed to command,
handsomely supported by his abundant acres, he was fit to rule and
entitled to ask for the votes of the merchants and small farmers. Little
wonder that the South should have furnished the nation with great
leaders in the time of the Revolution and the establishment of the Republic. From Virginia came Washington, Jefferson, Madison, Patrick
Henry, George Mason, and Richard Henry Lee. North Carolina contributed Joseph Hewes, Dr. Hugh Williamson, and Samuel Johnston.
From South Carolina came Henry Middleton and Henry Laurens
(both presidents of the Continental Congress), John Rutledge, Charles
Pinckney, and Pierce Butler. Georgia, youngest and weakest of the
colonies, was the fourth state to ratify the Constitution at the signing
of which she had been represented by William Few and Abraham
Baldwin. In the early days of the Republic the "Virginia dynasty"
dominated in national affairs. Of the first five Presidents, four were
from the Old Dominion: Washington, Jefferson, Madison, and Monroe.

Once the power of the rapidly waning Federalist Party was broken,
Jefferson and his followers held the destiny of the nation in their hands.
First of the great Southern politicians from the back country, he taught
his party how to unite the South and the West and to capture the votes
of the upcountrymen in all states. The name of Jefferson was powerfully evocative in the South until the time of the Civil War, but the
course of Jeffersonian democracy there was strange indeed. As William
E. Dodd describes it succinctly in *Statesmen of the Old South:*

> Jefferson contributed the idealistic democracy which grew to
> conservatism under Calhoun, who always insisted that he was a
> follower of the first Republican president but who nevertheless
> made slavery the basis of his system, "the stone rejected of the
> builders" thus becoming head of the corner, while Jefferson Davis,
> advancing yet a step further, set the world in arms on behalf of
> slavery—the property interests, the "privileged interests" of the
> time. It was a long and a deflected road from Jefferson to Jeffer-
> son Davis; but the South traveled it and thought it the king's high-
> way, just as the great Republican party has traveled from Lincoln

to McKinley, thinking the way perfectly plain and easy—a development almost identical with that of the Democrats from Jackson to Buchanan, from liberty and equality to privilege and property.

According to legend, the ante-bellum Southern politician who was the heroic incarnation of Jeffersonianism was Andrew Jackson. As Arthur M. Schlesinger, Jr., views the Jacksonian discipleship,[1] the "Hero of the Common Man" and his followers "moderated that side of Jeffersonianism which talked of agricultural virtue, independent proprietors, 'natural' property, abolition of industrialism, and expanded immensely that side which talked of economic equality, the laboring classes, human rights and the control of industrialism." The Jacksonians had to be realists in situations that Jefferson never had to face but prophetically foresaw might in time develop. "Jeffersonian democracy looked wistfully back toward a past slipping further every minute into the mists of memory, while Jacksonian democracy came straightforwardly to grips with a rough and unlovely present."

Where does Henry Clay of Kentucky, the man who never could be President, fit into this picture? Like Jefferson and Calhoun his youthful sympathies were with the upcountrymen, but when he became the powerful leader of the great Whig Party his brand of nationalism led him to champion internal improvements (at the expense of the Federal government), a protective tariff, and a national bank. In his own region he was "Prince Hal" or the "Cock of Kentucky"; to the Jacksonians he was the "Judas of the West." At first it seems strange that he should have drawn so much of his support from the rich planters of the South, but the reasons are not far to seek. They had their alliances with the commercial interests of the North. They hated the leveling measures of Jackson and feared the growing Southern clamor for separation from the Union. Clay was defeated in all his efforts save one—the staving off of civil war as long as his compromises could be made to work. Since the disappearance of his Whig Party in the 1850's, the South has never had a two-party system.

In the years between 1800 and 1860, as Southern influence in national affairs shifted from one dominant group to another, and thus from Virginia to South Carolina, to Tennessee, to Mississippi, the great political leaders continued to come up from the Southern courthouses and capitals to Washington City. Small wonder that the South felt it could make and govern a new nation even though the odds were against her in population and industry. When war came, the Confederacy could rely on the support of an extraordinary group of men who had once been or still were, on the eve of conflict, powerful in the nation's capital: Robert Toombs and Alexander Stephens of Georgia, Henry A.

[1] *The Age of Jackson* (1945), pp. 312–13.

Wise of Virginia (who, as Governor, signed the death warrant of John Brown), Robert Barnwell Rhett of South Carolina, William Lowndes Yancey of Alabama, Henry Foote and Jefferson Davis of Mississippi.

Perforce Southern politics was a regional affair for many years after the Civil War. At first the defeated white leaders struggled to oust the carpetbag regimes and regain control of the state governments. Known as Bourbons because there were many ex-Confederate leaders among them, they were "men so wedded to the ideals and practices of the past that they forgot nothing and learned nothing." [2] In one respect some of them did prepare for the future. Eager for the support of Northern capital, they adopted the principles embodied in Henry W. Grady's "New South." Businessmen and lawyers among them were frequently the agents of Northern industrialists and financiers.

Bourbon rule was challenged by the Populist movement of the 1880's. Beginning with the formation of the Farmers' Alliance in Texas (1875), Populist agitation was felt in most of the Southern states. In South Carolina Ben Tillman led the small farmers in demands for tax reforms, railroad regulation, and higher education in agriculture and engineering. The revolutionary language of Tillman, Tom Watson of Georgia, "Cyclone" Davis and "Stirrup" Ashby of Texas shocked their Bourbon opponents but taught the common people that they possessed power which they might learn to use. Since the days of these early demagogues most Southern politicians, no matter how extensively subsidized by the "interests," have habitually talked the language of the wool-hats and red-necks.

Populism became a dead issue in 1890 when the Lodge Force Bill, calling for Federal supervision of congressional elections, united the South in a solid front against Northern interference. Southern politicians of whatever stripe banded together in order to invent ingenious ways to eliminate the Negro as a political force. Thereafter "white supremacy" was continuously the real issue no matter under what guise it went to the polls.

The Northerner who has had little contact with the South is likely to know about six or eight words from which he builds his folklore of Southern politics.[3] Included in his limited vocabulary will be *Solid South, carpetbagger, white primary, grandfather clause, literacy test, filibuster, Southern demagogue.* But behind what seems to him to be the unvarying front of the Solid South are state and local variations in political practice, many of which are complex in the extreme and quite inexplicable unless one follows them down to their roots in history.

Certain political phenomena are frequently met with throughout the

[2] Francis B. Simkins: *A History of the South* (1953), p. 318.
[3] The information in this section is taken largely from V. O. Key's *Southern Politics* (New York: Alfred A. Knopf; 1949).

South. The Republican Party is, of course, feeble except in Texas, Florida, North Carolina, and east Tennessee. In most states "factionalism" is the rule; that is to say, the Democratic Party is actually composed of a group of factions, which shift in size and power as leaders come and go. Consequently the personal popularity of the leader of a faction is all-important. If he is seeking state-wide office or election to Congress, he must be able to count on the loyal support of his county and have alliances throughout the state. Often a great number of candidates, each representing a faction of some strength, have to be sorted out in the first primary. There were, for example, fourteen men contending for the governorship of Florida in 1936! Again, the Democratic primary is almost invariably the means by which a candidate is elected to office in the South. After the first primary, which selects the main contenders, comes the "second" or "run-off" primary. The candidate who wins in this is the Democratic nominee and will of course get the office.

At least one more generalization holds true in most parts of the South. In spite of the great interest in politics, the size of the electorate (not counting the Negroes) is smaller than it is in the North and West. The power of the Democratic primary will not explain this difference. As Key says, "the turnout at the primaries almost never reaches the level of participation in general elections in two-party states."

In examining the deviations from these norms in different Southern states, one finds a great variety of interesting situations. Each state has its unique political traditions. Virginia is controlled by the Byrd oligarchy, penny-pinching, autocratic, and free of corruption. This group of "not many more than a thousand professional politicians" governs the state. North Carolina, a progressive state with a well-balanced economy, is ruled by an economic oligarchy in which lawyers play an important part. Its government has traditionally been honest. South Carolina is a white-supremacy state. Millworkers and plantation-owners alike intend to keep the Negro in his place. In Florida it is every man for himself. The state is not only unbossed; it is unled. Georgia is another multifactional state where the urban-rural cleavage and the county-unit system can produce some extraordinary reversals. Within a few years it will turn out of office a liberal Ellis Arnall and give the governorship to "Hummon" Talmadge, better-educated but no-better-principled son of his pappy, "Old Gene."

In Alabama the frontier independence that survives in the rural areas often rises to challenge the "big mules," as the industrialists in Birmingham are called. Mississippi defies the political analysts. Rich where there is lumber or oil, rich for a long time in the cotton delta, desperately poor in the red hills, the chief battleground of the race question in the South, Mississippi seems to be mainly useful as a political scapegoat. At some time or other every Southern state has had reason to say: "Thank God for Mississippi." Louisiana is almost as complex. Longism still lingers there, and the perpetual dilemma of the voters is whether to vote for action and corruption or "good government" and apathy. No one seems willing to guess where Texas is headed politically. Given its wealth and the powerful influence of Northern capital, it might even turn Republican. Yet Arkansas, over the border, exhibits one-party Southern politics in its "purist" form. In few Southern states do local political potentates exercise such power. In Tennessee the Shelby County Crump machine has ruled for so long that men have difficulty in remembering when things were otherwise. This state exhibits, at the moment, two one-party systems. In east Tennessee the Republicans win local elections and send representatives to Congress. In middle and west Tennessee the Democrats, with or without Mister Crump, the "country boy who came to rule a commonwealth," are in control.

Observers agree that the touchstone of Southern politics is still the Negro question—how to keep the Negro from voting, how to control his vote if he does slip through the primary, how to nullify Northern efforts to compel the South to give him his civil rights. V. O. Key believes that an all-important clue to Southern politics is the fact "that the black-belt whites succeeded in imposing their will on their states and thereby presented a solid regional front in national politics on the race issue." A Southern senator or representative would commit political suicide if he dared to vote for a Federal anti-lynching bill or for FEPC legislation.

The greatest of all the paradoxes of Southern politics emerges with this issue. From 1865 until the 1930's the Negro was certain to be a Republican, the most genuine of Black Republicans. But since New Deal days the Southern Negro has often attached himself to the Democratic Party, the party to which his boss belongs and the party of the owner of his slave ancestors. If the new Negro intends to vote Democratic, why shouldn't he be permitted to vote? The logical answer is that he should. But Southern politics, like politics everywhere in America, is extra-logical. Then too, if Negroes voted in sizable numbers, they might, in a crucial situation, elect to high office a member of their own race.

Thomas Jefferson's First Inaugural Address

The election of Jefferson to the Presidency has sometimes been referred to as "the revolution of 1800." The defeated Federalists feared the worst, now that this man, Virginia aristocrat though he was, had been put in office by the upcountry people of the South and the voters in the new sections of all the states. As Professor William E. Dodd remarks in Statesmen of the Old South: *"Few men have been reviled as was Jefferson during the closing years of the eighteenth century. In Virginia a pious matron of a noted family wished that he might never have a son to succeed him, and in Massachusetts men prayed daily that the atheist, and arch-enemy of all good men and noble causes, might be brought to justice for his scandalous blasphemy."*

The First Inaugural was intended to be conciliatory. Behind Jefferson's simple statement—"we are all republicans; we are federalists"— was his determined purpose to unite all moderate men on the principles of democracy which he had written into the Declaration of Independence, the Virginia Bill for Establishing Religious Freedom, and the Kentucky Resolutions of 1798.

Though the address is a superb statement of Jefferson's principles of government, it enunciates many of the convictions of the agricultural party of the South whose leader he was. In particular, it stands for a "wise and frugal government, which shall restrain men from injuring one another" and shall "leave them otherwise free to regulate their pursuits of industry and improvement." It calls for "the support of the state governments in all their rights"; asserts that "the minority possess their equal rights" with the majority, "which equal laws must protect"; advocates the "encouragement of agriculture and of commerce as its handmaid" (saying nothing of infant industries); and speaks of a well-disciplined militia as "our best reliance in peace and for the first moments of war." During the years between 1800 and 1865 these principles would be reiterated and expanded by Southern apologists for the way of life of their region.

This text of the First Inaugural is derived from a facsimile of the original in Jefferson's hand. A few modifications of spelling and punctuation have been made.

FRIENDS AND FELLOW CITIZENS:—

Called upon to undertake the duties of the first Executive office of our country, I avail myself of the presence of that portion of my fellow citizens which is here assembled to express my grateful thanks for the favor with which they have been pleased to look towards me, to declare a sincere consciousness that the task is above my talents, and that I approach it with those anxious and awful presentiments which the greatness of the charge and the weakness of my powers so justly inspire. A rising nation, spread over a wide and fruitful land, traversing all the seas with the rich productions of their industry, engaged in commerce with nations who feel power and forget right, advancing rapidly to destinies beyond the reach of mortal eye, when I contemplate these transcendent objects, and see the honour, the happiness, and the hopes of this beloved country committed to the issue and the auspices of this day, I shrink from the contemplation, and humble myself before the magnitude of the undertaking. Utterly indeed should I despair, did not the presence of many, whom I here see, remind me, that in the other high authorities provided by our constitution, I shall find resources of wisdom, of virtue, and of zeal, on which to rely under all difficulties. To you, then, gentlemen, who are charged with the sovereign functions of legislation, and to those associated with you, I look with encouragement for that guidance and support which may enable us to steer with safety the vessel in which we are all embarked amidst the conflicting elements of a troubled world.

During the contest of opinion through which we have past, the animation of discussions and of exertions has sometimes worn an aspect which might impose on strangers unused to think freely and to speak and to write what they think. But this being now decided by the voice of the nation enounced according to the rules of the constitution, all will of course arrange themselves under the will of the law, and unite in common efforts for the common good. All too will bear in mind this sacred principle, that though the will of the majority is in all cases to prevail, that will, to be rightful, must be reasonable; that the minority possess their equal rights, which equal laws must protect, and to violate [which] would be oppression. Let us then, fellow citizens, unite with one heart and one mind, let us restore to social intercourse that harmony and affection without which liberty, and even life itself, are but dreary things. And let us reflect that having banished from our land that religious intolerance under which mankind so long bled and suffered, we have yet gained little if we countenance a political intolerance as despotic, as wicked, and capable of as bitter and bloody persecutions. During the throes and convulsions of the antient world, during the agonizing spasms of infuriated man, seeking through blood and slaughter his long-lost liberty, it was not wonderful that the agitation of the billows should reach even this distant and peaceful shore; that this should be more felt and feared by some and less by others; and should divide opinions as to measures of safety. But every difference of opinion is not a difference of principle. We have called by different names brethren of the same principle. We are all republicans: we are federalists. If there be any among us who would wish to dissolve this Union or to change its republican form, let them stand undisturbed as monuments of the safety with which error of opinion may be tolerated, where reason is left free to combat it. I know indeed that some honest men fear that a republican government cannot be strong, that this government is not strong enough. But would the honest patriot in the full tide of successful experiment abandon a government which has so far kept us free and firm, on the theoretic and visionary fear, that this government, the world's best hope, may, by possibility, want energy to preserve itself? I trust not. I believe this, on the contrary, the strongest government on earth. I believe it is the only one, where every man, at the call of the law, would fly to the standard of the law, and would meet invasions of the public order as his own personal concern. Sometimes it is said that man cannot be trusted with the government of himself. Can he then be trusted with the government of others? Or have we found angels, in the form of kings, to govern him? Let history answer this question.

Let us then, with courage and confidence, pursue our own federal and republican principles; our attachment to our union and representative government. Kindly separated by nature and a wide ocean from the exterminating havoc of one quarter of the globe; too high-minded to endure the degradations of the others; possessing a chosen country, with room enough for our descendants to the thousandth and thousandth generation; enjoying the most favourable temperateness of climate; entertaining a due sense of our equal right to the use of our own faculties, to the acquisitions of our industry, to honour and confidence from our fellow citizens, resulting not from birth but from our actions and their sense of them; enlightened by a benign religion, professed indeed and practiced in various forms, yet all of them inculcating honesty, truth, temperance, gratitude, and the love of man, acknowledging and adoring an overruling providence, which by all its dispensations proves that it delights in the happiness of man here, and his greater happiness hereafter; with all these blessings, what more is necessary to make us a happy and prosperous people? Still one thing more, fellow citizens, a wise and frugal government which shall restrain men from injuring one another, shall leave them otherwise free to regulate their own pursuits of industry and improvement, and shall not take from the mouth of labor the bread it has earned. This is the sum of good government, and this is necessary to close the circle of our felicities.

431

About to enter, fellow citizens, on the exercise of duties which comprehend everything dear and valuable to you, it is proper that you should understand what I deem the essential principles of our government, and consequently those which ought to shape its administration. I will compress them within the narrowest compass they will bear, stating the general principle, but not all its limitations. Equal and exact justice to all men, of whatever state or persuasion, religious or political; peace, commerce, and honest friendship with all nations, entangling alliances with none; the support of the state governments in all their rights, as the most competent administrations for our domestic concerns and the surest bulwarks against anti-republican tendencies; the preservation of the general government in its whole constitutional vigour as the sheet anchor of our peace at home and safety abroad; a jealous care of the right of election by the people, a mild and safe corrective of abuses which are lopped by the sword of the revolution where peaceable remedies are unprovided; absolute acquiescence in the decisions of the majority, the vital principle of republics, from which there is no appeal but to force, the vital principle and immediate parent of despotism; a well-disciplined militia—our best reliance in peace and for the first moments of war, till regulars may relieve them; the supremacy of the civil over the military authority; economy in the public expense, that labor may be lightly burthened; the honest payment of our debts and sacred preservation of the public faith; encouragement of agriculture, and of commerce as its handmaid; the diffusion of information and arraignment of all abuses at the bar of public reason; freedom of religion; freedom of the press; and freedom of person, under the protection of the habeas corpus; and trial by juries, impartially selected. These principles form the bright constellation which has gone before us and guided our steps through an age of revolution and reformation. The wisdom of our sages and blood of our heroes have been devoted to their attainment. They should be the creed of our political faith; the text of civil instruction, the touchstone by which to try the services of those we trust; and should we wander from them in moments of error or of alarm, let us hasten to retrace our steps and to regain the road which alone leads to peace, liberty, and safety.

I repair, then, fellow citizens, to the post you have assigned me. With experience enough in subordinate offices to have seen the difficulties of this, the greatest of all, I have learnt to expect that it will rarely fall to the lot of imperfect man to retire from this station with the reputation and the favor which bring him into it. Without pretensions to that high confidence you reposed in our first and greatest revolutionary character, whose preeminent services had entitled him to the first place in his country's love, and destined for him the fairest page in the volume of faithful history, I ask so much confidence only as may give firmness and effect to the legal administration of your affairs. I shall often go wrong through defect of judgment. When right, I shall often be thought wrong by those whose positions will not command a view of the whole ground. I ask your indulgence for my own errors, which will never be intentional; and your support against the errors of others who may condemn what they would not, if seen in all its parts. The approbation implied by your suffrage is a great consolation to me for the past; and my future solicitude will be to retain the good opinion of those who have bestowed it in advance, to conciliate that of others by doing them all the good in my power, and to be instrumental to the happiness and freedom of all.

Relying then on the patronage of your good will, I advance with obedience to the work, ready to retire from it whenever you become sensible how much better choices it is in your power to make. And may that infinite power which rules the destinies of the universe, lead our councils to what is best, and give them a favorable issue for your peace and prosperity.

Henry Clay Appeals to the South to Support His "American System"

Clay's famous speech "On American Industry," delivered in the House of Representatives on March 30 and 31, 1824, is one of the first public indications that the arguments dividing the North and the South, which would culminate in civil war, were growing into a quarrel. Although Clay is concerned throughout the entire speech to answer Southern objections to the protective tariff, which he was advocating as part of his "American system," the excerpt printed here is his direct appeal to the South to consider national rather than sectional interests in its voting.

The South abominated tariffs for the protection of native industries. Depending largely on the export of cotton, rice, and tobacco for its wealth, it regarded a high tariff as the chief means the Northern manufacturers and capitalists would use to exploit the planting class.

As a consequence of the depression that followed the War of 1812, a moderate protective tariff had been passed in 1816, there being twenty-five Southern votes for it in Congress and thirty-nine against it.

433

*At that time many leaders in the South, including John C. Calhoun
and William Lowndes of South Carolina, looked forward to the development of industry, particularly textile-manufacturing, in the region.
But by 1824 the opposition had stiffened. The new tariff passed, but the
margin in the Senate was four votes. In the course of the debate John
Randolph of Roanoke, loosing his bitter wit against the bill, spoke
prophetically. "We are the eel that is being flayed while the cook-maid
pats us on the head and cries with the clown in* King Lear, *'Down,
wantons, down' . . . a fig for the Constitution! When the scorpion's
sting is probing us to the quick, shall we stop to chop logic? . . .
There is no magic in the word* union."

*Increasingly the anger of the South at the protective tariffs "forced"
on it (the one of 1828 was called the Tariff of Abominations) turned
the thoughts of its leaders to dissolution of the Union. The first great
crisis came in 1832 in the Nullification controversy. The battle ended
in a draw. This time South Carolina was isolated in its threat to withdraw from the Union, but the price Calhoun and South Carolina exacted for the repeal of its nullification ordinance was Clay's Compromise Tariff of 1833.*

*Drawn by ties of birth and sentiment to the South, but by conviction
a spokesman for the industrial and commercial North and West, Clay
was led thereafter to many a compromise in order to save the Union.
The last time was in 1850. So enfeebled that he had to summon all his
spirit to the effort, he made his last great argument for the Compromise
of 1850 on July 22, speaking for three hours to a crowded Senate. His
eloquence and his influence were largely responsible for the passage of
the measure—and for a ten-year delay in the coming of the Civil War.*

This passage is reprinted from The Life and Speeches of the Hon.
Henry Clay, *compiled and edited by Daniel Mallory (2 vols.; New
York: A. S. Barnes & Company; 1857), Vol. I, pp. 513–15.*

HAVING called the attention of the committee to the present adverse
state of our country, and endeavored to point out the causes which
have led to it; having shown that similar causes, wherever they exist in
other countries, lead to the same adversity in their condition; and having shown that, wherever we find opposite causes prevailing, a high and
animating state of national prosperity exists, the committee will agree
with me in thinking that it is the solemn duty of government to apply
a remedy to the evils which afflict our country, if it can apply one. Is
there no remedy within the reach of the government? Are we doomed
to behold our industry languish and decay yet more and more? But

there is a remedy, and that remedy consists in modifying our foreign policy, and in adopting a genuine AMERICAN SYSTEM. We must naturalize the arts in our country; and we must naturalize them by the only means which the wisdom of nations has yet discovered to be effectual; by adequate protection against the otherwise overwhelming influence of foreigners. This is only to be accomplished by the establishment of a tariff, to the consideration of which I am now brought.

And what is this tariff? It seems to have been regarded as a sort of monster, huge and deformed—a wild beast, endowed with tremendous powers of destruction, about to be let loose among our people, if not to devour them, at least to consume their substance. But let us calm our passions, and deliberately survey this alarming, this terrific being. The sole object of the tariff is to tax the produce of foreign industry, with the view of promoting American industry. The tax is exclusively leveled at foreign industry. That is the avowed and the direct purpose of the tariff. If it subjects any part of American industry to burdens, that is an effect not intended, but is altogether incidental, and perfectly voluntary.

It has been treated as an imposition of burdens upon one part of the community by design, for the benefit of another; as if, in fact, money were taken from the pockets of one portion of the people and put into the pockets of another. But is that a fair representation of it? No man pays the duty assessed on the foreign article by compulsion, but voluntarily; and this voluntary duty, if paid, goes into the common exchequer, for the common benefit of all. Consumption has four objects of choice. First, it may abstain from the use of the foreign article, and thus avoid the payment of the tax. Second, it may employ the rival American fabric. Third, it may engage in the business of manufacturing, which this bill is designed to foster. Fourth, or it may supply itself from the household manufactures. But it is said, by the honorable gentleman from Virginia, that the south, owing to the character of a certain portion of its population, cannot engage in the business of manufacturing. Now, I do not agree in that opinion to the extent in which it is asserted. The circumstance alluded to may disqualify the south from engaging in every branch of manufacture, as largely as other quarters of the union, but to some branches of it, that part of our population is well adapted. It indisputably affords great facility in the household or domestic line. But, if the gentleman's premises were true, could his conclusion be admitted? According to him, a certain part of our population, happily much the smallest, is peculiarly situated. The circumstance of its degradation unfits it for the manufacturing arts. The well-being of the other, and the larger part of our population, requires the introduction of those arts. What is to be done in this conflict? The gentleman would have us abstain from adopting a policy called for by the interest of the greater and freer part of our popula-

435

tion. But is that reasonable? Can it be expected that the interests of the greater part should be made to bend to the condition of the servile part of our population? That, in effect, would be to make us the slaves of slaves. I went, with great pleasure, along with my southern friends, and I am ready again to unite with them in protesting against the exercise of any legislative power, on the part of congress, over that delicate subject, because it was my solemn conviction, that congress was interdicted, or at least not authorized, by the constitution, to exercise any such legislative power. And I am sure that the patriotism of the south may be exclusively relied upon to reject a policy which should be dictated by considerations altogether connected with that degraded class, to the prejudice of the residue of our population. But does not a perseverance in the foreign policy, as it now exists in fact, make all parts of the union, not planting, tributary to the planting parts? What is the argument? It is that we must continue freely to receive the produce of foreign industry, without regard to the protection of American industry, that a market may be retained for the sale abroad of the produce of the planting portion of the country; and that, if we lessen in all parts of America—those which are not planting as well as the planting sections—the consumption of foreign manufactures, we diminish to that extent the foreign market for the planting produce. The existing state of things, indeed, presents a sort of tacit compact between the cotton-grower and the British manufacturer, the stipulations of which are, on the part of the cotton-grower, that the whole of the United States, the other portions as well as the cotton-growing, shall remain open and unrestricted in the consumption of British manufactures; and, on the part of the British manufacturer, that, in consideration thereof, he will continue to purchase the cotton of the south. Thus, then, we perceive that the proposed measure, instead of sacrificing the south to the other parts of the union, seeks only to preserve them from being absolutely sacrificed under the operation of the tacit compact which I have described. Supposing the south to be actually incompetent, or disinclined, to embark at all in the business of manufacturing, is not its interest, nevertheless, likely to be promoted by creating a new and an American source of supply for its consumption? Now foreign powers, and Great Britain, principally, have the monopoly of the supply of southern consumption. If this bill should pass, an American competitor, in the supply of the south, would be raised up, and ultimately, I cannot doubt, that it will be supplied more cheaply and better.

Andrew Jackson Vetoes the Bill for Rechartering the Bank of the United States

Andrew Jackson was elected to the Presidency in 1828 as the champion of the common man—of the working classes in the Northern cities as well as the frontiersmen of the South and West. As a leader of the Jeffersonian wing of the Democratic Party, with its emphasis on the protection of human rights rather than property rights, he also swayed those voters in the South who had no liking for the "American system" of Henry Clay, soon to become the Whig Party's perpetual candidate for the Presidency.

As spokesman for the new democracy, Jackson early showed his hostility to the Bank of the United States, which, through its parent bank in Philadelphia and its twenty-seven branches scattered through the country, exercised great financial power. Jackson spoke against the bank in his first message to Congress, but his opportunity to move against it came almost providentially in 1832. The bank's charter was not due to expire until 1836, but this was a Presidential year and Henry Clay, planning to be a candidate, hoped to make the bank the decisive issue of the campaign. He and Daniel Webster, who were attorneys for the bank, easily persuaded its president, Nicholas Biddle, to try to obtain a renewal of the charter at this time.

This maneuver offered Jackson his chance. He gave no outward sign that he was disturbed by the way congressional votes in favor of recharter piled up. Several members of his Cabinet were sure that he would not veto the bill but would seek some compromise. But Jackson was ready to move when the bill came to him on July 4. Three of his closest associates were put to work drafting a veto message—Amos Kendall, a member of Jackson's private or "kitchen cabinet," Andrew J. Donelson, his private secretary, and Roger B. Taney, Attorney General and the one member of the Cabinet who was militantly opposed to recharter. While the work of composition went on, Jackson came and went in the room, weighing the arguments proposed and giving directions about what should be inserted or altered.

The veto message, with its moving declaration of Jackson's belief in the rights of the common man, was made public on July 10. Men of wealth throughout the country outdid themselves in charging Jackson with attempting to stir up the poor against the rich. Nicholas Biddle summoned up the horrors of the French Revolution to describe the iniquities of the veto message: "It has all the fury of a chained panther, biting the bars of his cage. It is really a manifesto of anarchy, such as Marat or Robespierre might have issued to the mob of the Faubourg St. Antoine."

But the Old Hero had won a solid victory. In the coming election he carried every state of the Old South except South Carolina, where 40,674 of the bank's shares were owned.

Jackson's decision to proceed at once with the destruction of the bank was unwise. The withdrawal of government funds from its vaults and the favoring of the fifteen state banks (known as "pet banks") increased speculation and led to unsound banking practices. Jackson's summary destruction of the bank was therefore in some degree responsible for the panic of 1837.

These excerpts from the veto message are reprinted from James D. Richardson: A Compilation of the Messages and Papers of the Presidents *(Washington: Government Printing Office; 1896), Vol. II.*

❁

Washington, July 10, 1832.

To the Senate:

The bill "to modify and continue" the act entitled "An act to incorporate the subscribers to the Bank of the United States" was presented to me on the 4th July instant. Having considered it with that solemn regard to the principles of the Constitution which the day was calculated to inspire, and come to the conclusion that it ought not to become a law, I herewith return it to the Senate, in which it originated, with my objections.

A bank of the United States is in many respects convenient for the Government and useful to the people. Entertaining this opinion, and deeply impressed with the belief that some of the powers and privileges possessed by the existing bank are unauthorized by the Constitution, subversive of the rights of the States, and dangerous to the liberties of the people, I felt it my duty at an early period of my Administration to call the attention of Congress to the practicability of organizing an institution combining all its advantages and obviating these objections. I sincerely regret that in the act before me I can perceive none of those modifications of the bank charter which are necessary, in my opinion, to make it compatible with justice, with sound policy, or with the Constitution of our country.

The present corporate body, denominated the president, directors, and company of the Bank of the United States, will have existed at the time this act is intended to take effect twenty years. It enjoys an exclusive privilege of banking under the authority of the General Government, a monopoly of its favor and support, and, as a necessary consequence, almost a monopoly of the foreign and domestic exchange. The powers, privileges, and favors bestowed upon it in the original charter, by increasing the value of the stock far above its par value, operated as a gratuity of many millions to the stockholders.

An apology may be found for the failure to guard against this result in the consideration that the effect of the original act of incorporation could not be certainly foreseen at the time of its passage. The act before me proposes another gratuity to the holders of the same stock, and in many cases to the same men, of at least seven millions more. This donation finds no apology in any uncertainty as to the effect of the act. On all hands it is conceded that its passage will increase at least 20 or 30 per cent more the market price of the stock, subject to the payment of the annuity of $200,000 per year secured by the act, thus adding in a moment one-fourth to its par value. It is not our own citizens only who are to receive the bounty of our Government. More than eight millions of the stock of this bank are held by foreigners. By this act the American Republic proposes virtually to make them a present of some millions of dollars. For these gratuities to foreigners and to some of our own opulent citizens the act secures no equivalent whatever. They are the certain gains of the present stockholders under the operation of this act, after making full allowance for the payment of the bonus.

Every monopoly and all exclusive privileges are granted at the expense of the public, which ought to receive a fair equivalent. The many millions which this act proposes to bestow on the stockholders of the existing bank must come directly or indirectly out of the earnings of the American people. It is due to them, therefore, if their Government sell monopolies and exclusive privileges, that they should at least exact for them as much as they are worth in open market. The value of the monopoly in this case may be correctly ascertained. The twenty-eight millions of stock would probably be at an advance of 50 per cent, and command in market at least $42,000,000, subject to the payment of the present bonus. The present value of the monopoly, therefore, is $17,-000,000, and this the act proposes to sell for three millions, payable in fifteen annual installments of $200,000 each.

It is not conceivable how the present stockholders can have any claim to the special favor of the Government. The present corporation has enjoyed its monopoly during the period stipulated in the original contract. If we must have such a corporation, why should not the Government sell out the whole stock and thus secure to the people the full market value of the privileges granted? Why should not Congress create and sell twenty-eight millions of stock, incorporating the purchasers with all the powers and privileges secured in this act and putting the premium upon the sales into the Treasury?

But this act does not permit competition in the purchase of this monopoly. It seems to be predicated on the erroneous idea that the present stockholders have a prescriptive right not only to the favor but to the bounty of Government. It appears that more than a fourth part of the stock is held by foreigners and the residue is held by a few hundred of our own citizens, chiefly of the richest class. For their benefit does this act exclude the whole American people from competition in the purchase of this monopoly and dispose of it for many millions less than it is worth. This seems the less excusable because some of our citizens not now stockholders petitioned that the door of competition might be opened, and offered to take a charter on terms much more favorable to the Government and country. . . .

It has been urged as an argument in favor of rechartering the present bank that the calling in its loans will produce great embarrassment and distress. The time allowed to close its concerns is ample, and if it has been well managed its pressure will be light, and heavy only in case its management has been bad. If, therefore, it shall produce distress, the fault will be its own, and it would furnish a reason against renewing a power which has been so obviously abused. But will there ever be a time when this reason will be less powerful? To acknowledge its force is to admit that the bank ought to be perpetual, and as a consequence the present stockholders and those inheriting their rights as successors be established a privileged order, clothed both with great political power and enjoying immense pecuniary advantages from their connection with the Government. . . .

Is there no danger to our liberty and independence in a bank that in its nature has so little to bind it to our country? The president of the bank has told us that most of the State banks exist by its forbearance. Should its influence become concentered, as it may under the operation of such an act as this, in the hands of a self-elected directory whose interests are identified with those of the foreign stockholders, will there not be cause to tremble for the purity of our elections in peace and for the independence of our country in war? Their power would be great whenever they might choose to exert it; but if this monopoly were regularly renewed every fifteen or twenty years on terms proposed by themselves, they might seldom in peace put forth their strength to influence elections or control the affairs of the nation. But if any private citizen or public functionary should interpose to curtail its powers or prevent a renewal of its privileges, it can not be doubted that he would be made to feel its influence.

Should the stock of the bank principally pass into the hands of the subjects of a foreign country, and we should unfortunately become involved in a war with that country, what would be our condition? Of

440

the course which would be pursued by a bank almost wholly owned by the subjects of a foreign power, and managed by those whose interests, if not affections, would run in the same direction there can be no doubt. All its operations within would be in aid of the hostile fleets and armies without. Controlling our currency, receiving our public moneys, and holding thousands of our citizens in dependence, it would be more formidable and dangerous than the naval and military power of the enemy. . . .

The bank is professedly established as an agent of the executive branch of the Government, and its constitutionality is maintained on that ground. Neither upon the propriety of present action nor upon the provisions of this act was the Executive consulted. It has had no opportunity to say that it neither needs nor wants an agent clothed with such powers and favored by such exemptions. There is nothing in its legitimate functions which makes it necessary or proper. Whatever interest or influence, whether public or private, has given birth to this act, it can not be found either in the wishes or necessities of the executive department, by which present action is deemed premature, and the powers conferred upon its agent not only unnecessary, but dangerous to the Government and country.

It is to be regretted that the rich and powerful too often bend the acts of government to their selfish purposes. Distinctions in society will always exist under every just government. Equality of talents, of education, or of wealth can not be produced by human institutions. In the full enjoyment of the gifts of Heaven and the fruits of superior industry, economy, and virtue, every man is equally entitled to protection by law; but when the laws undertake to add to these natural and just advantages artificial distinctions, to grant titles, gratuities, and exclusive privileges, to make the rich richer and the potent more powerful, the humble members of society—the farmers, mechanics, and laborers—who have neither the time nor the means of securing like favors to themselves, have a right to complain of the injustice of their Government. There are no necessary evils in government. Its evils exist only in its abuses. If it would confine itself to equal protection, and, as Heaven does its rains, shower its favors alike on the high and the low, the rich and the poor, it would be an unqualified blessing. In the act before me there seems to be a wide and unnecessary departure from these just principles.

Nor is our Government to be maintained or our Union preserved by invasions of the rights and powers of the several States. In thus attempting to make our General Government strong we make it weak. Its true strength consists in leaving individuals and States as much as possible to themselves—in making itself felt, not in its power, but in its beneficence; not in its control, but in its protection; not in binding the States more closely to the center, but leaving each to move unobstructed in its proper orbit.

Experience should teach us wisdom. Most of the difficulties our Government now encounters and most of the dangers which impend over our Union have sprung from an abandonment of the legitimate objects of Government by our national legislation, and the adoption of such principles as are embodied in this act. Many of our rich men have not been content with equal protection and equal benefits, but have besought us to make them richer by act of Congress. By attempting to gratify their desires we have in the results of our legislation arrayed section against section, interest against interest, and man against man, in a fearful commotion which threatens to shake the foundations of our Union. It is time to pause in our career to review our principles, and if possible revive that devoted patriotism and spirit of compromise which distinguished the sages of the Revolution and the fathers of our Union. If we can not at once, in justice to interests vested under improvident legislation, make our Government what it ought to be, we can at least take a stand against all new grants of monopolies and exclusive privileges, against any prostitution of our Government to the advancement of the few at the expense of the many, and in favor of compromise and gradual reform in our code of laws and system of political economy.

I have now done my duty to my country. If sustained by my fellow-citizens, I shall be grateful and happy; if not, I shall find in the motives which impel me ample grounds for contentment and peace. In the difficulties which surround us and the dangers which threaten our institutions there is cause for neither dismay nor alarm. For relief and deliverance let us firmly rely on that kind Providence which I am sure watches with peculiar care over the destinies of our Republic, and on the intelligence and wisdom of our countrymen. Through *His* abundant goodness and *their* patriotic devotion our liberty and Union will be preserved.

Calhoun on Nullification and the Concurrent Majority

John C. Calhoun (1782–1850) was not only the greatest statesman of the Old South after the Virginia dynasty passed from the scene; he was also a brilliant political theorist, some of whose ideas—in particular his theory of the "concurrent majority"—have relevance today.

JOHN C. CALHOUN: *The Concurrent Majority*

There are elements of tragedy in Calhoun's career. Born to be a leader, he sought the office of President time after time, only to have the nomination snatched from him by the intrigues of the Democratic leaders. Worse and more ironic was the perversion of Calhoun's political theories by the pro-slavery wing of his party.

Calhoun was the son of a small planter in the South Carolina up-country. He married into the Charleston aristocracy and became a planter on a much larger scale than his father. By inheritance he should have been a complete Jeffersonian and a defender of personal rights against property rights; he was, at least in his early years, an ardent nationalist. When he propounded his version of the theory of states' rights ("concurrent majority") he was really seeking a device to preserve the authority of the central government without infringing upon the liberty of minorities. His main intention was to help his beloved South Carolina in her refusal to approve the high tariffs insisted upon by the North. But the Southern Democrats pre-empted his doctrine for quite other ends, and Calhoun was increasingly and disastrously involved with the pro-slavery cause. Calhoun's "State Veto," or Nullification as it was generally called, became the warrant for Secession and, eventually, for civil war.

Calhoun's ideas on "State Veto" he set forth anonymously in the South Carolina Exposition and Protest, *an elaborate argument against the tariff of 1828. After the quarrel with Jackson which deprived him of the Presidential nomination in 1831, he acknowledged this document and then formally presented his arguments in two cogent statements: the "Fort Hill Address" (Fort Hill was the name of his plantation), issued as a campaign document, and the "Letter to General Hamilton on the Subject of State Interposition," in which he answered point by point the contentions of the opponents who had, he believed, misunderstood or misinterpreted his doctrines.*

During the remainder of his busy life—he was a member of the Senate from 1832 to 1850, except for a brief interval when he served as Tyler's Secretary of State—Calhoun found no time to publish any summations of his theories of democratic government, but he drew up two such documents, which were found among his papers and published after his death: A Disquisition on Government *and the much longer, unfinished* Discourse on the Constitution and Government of the United States.

The excerpts that follow are taken respectively from the "Letter to General Hamilton" and the Disquisition on Government *as printed in Richard K. Crallé:* The Works of John C. Calhoun *(6 vols.; New York: D. Appleton & Company; 1883), Vol. VI, pp. 181–2, and Vol. I, pp. 55–64.*

OF all the impediments opposed to a just conception of the nature of our political system, the impression that the right of a State to arrest an unconstitutional act of the General Government is inconsistent with the great and fundamental principle of all free states—that a majority has the right to govern—is the greatest. Thus regarded, nullification is, without farther reflection, denounced as the most dangerous and monstrous of all political heresies, as in truth, it would be, were the objection as well-founded as, in fact, it is destitute of all foundation, as I shall now proceed to show.

Those who make the objection seem to suppose that the right of a majority to govern is a principle too simple to admit of any distinction; and yet, if I do not mistake, it is susceptible of the most important distinction—entering deeply into the construction of our system, and, I may add, into that of all free States in proportion to the perfection of their institutions—and is essential to the very·existence of liberty.

When, then, it is said that a majority has the right to govern, there are two modes of estimating the majority, to either of which the expression is applicable. The one, in which the whole community is regarded in the aggregate, and the majority is estimated in reference to the entire mass. This may be called the majority of the whole, or the absolute majority. The other, in which it is regarded in reference to its different political interests, whether composed of different classes, of different communities, formed into one general confederated community, and in which the majority is estimated, not in reference to the whole, but to each class or community of which it is composed,—the assent of each taken separately,—and the concurrence of all constituting the majority. A majority thus estimated may be called the concurring majority.

When it is objected to nullification, that it is opposed to the principle that a majority ought to govern, he who makes the objection must mean the absolute, as distinguished from the concurring. It is only in the sense of the former the objection can be applied. In that of the concurring, it would be absurd, as the concurring assent of all the parts (with us, all the States) is of the very essence of such majority. Again, it is manifest, that in the sense in which it would be against nullification, it would be equally so against the Constitution itself; for, in whatever light that instrument may be regarded, it is clearly not the work of the absolute, but of the concurring majority. It was formed and ratified by the concurring assent of all the States, and not by the majority of the whole taken in the aggregate, as has been already stated. Thus, the acknowledged right of each State, *in reference to the Constitution,* is unquestionably the same right which nullification attributes to each *in reference to the unconstitutional acts of the Government;* and, if the latter be opposed to the right of a majority to govern, the former is equally so. I go farther. The objection might, with equal truth, be applied to all free States that have ever existed: I mean States deserving the name,—excluding, of course, those which, after a factious and anarchical existence of a few years, have sunk under the yoke of tyranny or the dominion of some foreign power. There is not, with this exception, a single free State whose institutions were not based on the principle of the concurring majority: not one in which the community was not regarded in reference its different political interests, and which did not, in some form or other, take the assent of each in the operation of the Government.

From A DISQUISITION ON GOVERNMENT

It follows, from what has been stated, that it is a great and dangerous error to suppose that all people are equally entitled to liberty. It is a reward to be earned, not a blessing to be gratuitously lavished on all alike; —a reward reserved for the intelligent, the patriotic, the virtuous and deserving;—and not a boon to be bestowed on a people too ignorant, degraded and vicious, to be capable either of appreciating or of enjoying it. Nor is it any disparagement to liberty, that such is, and ought to be the case. On the contrary, its greatest praise,—its proudest distinction is, that an all-wise Providence has reserved it, as the noblest and highest reward for the development of our faculties, moral and intellectual. A reward more appropriate than liberty could not be conferred on the deserving;—nor a punishment inflicted on the undeserving more just, than to be subject to lawless and despotic rule. This dispensation seems to be the result of some fixed law;—and every effort to disturb or defeat it, by attempting to elevate a people in the scale of liberty, above the point to which they are entitled to rise, must ever prove abortive, and end in disappointment. The progress of a people rising from a lower to a higher point in the scale of liberty, is necessarily slow;—and by attempting to precipitate, we either retard, or permanently defeat it.

There is another error, not less great and dangerous, usually associated with the one which has just been considered. I refer to the opinion, that liberty and equality are so intimately united, that liberty cannot be perfect without perfect equality.

That they are united to a certain extent,—and that equality of citizens, in the eyes of the law, is essential to liberty in a popular government, is conceded. But to go further, and make equality of *condition*

445

essential to liberty, would be to destroy both liberty and progress. The reason is, that inequality of condition, while it is a necessary consequence of liberty, is, at the same time, indispensable to progress. In order to understand why this is so, it is necessary to bear in mind, that the main spring to progress is, the desire of individuals to better their condition; and that the strongest impulse which can be given to it is, to leave individuals free to exert themselves in the manner they may deem best for that purpose, as far at least as it can be done consistently with the ends for which government is ordained,—and to secure to all the fruits of their exertions. Now, as individuals differ greatly from each other, in intelligence, sagacity, energy, perseverance, skill, habits of industry and economy, physical power, position and opportunity,—the necessary effect of leaving all free to exert themselves to better their condition, must be a corresponding inequality between those who may possess these qualities and advantages in a high degree, and those who may be deficient in them. The only means by which this result can be prevented are, either to impose such restrictions on the exertions of those who may possess them in a high degree, as will place them on a level with those who do not; or to deprive them of the fruits of their exertions. But to impose such restrictions on them would be destructive of liberty,—while, to deprive them of the fruits of their exertions, would be to destroy the desire of bettering their condition. It is, indeed, this inequality of condition between the front and rear ranks, in the march of progress, which gives so strong an impulse to the former to maintain their position, and to the latter to press forward into their files. This gives to progress its greatest impulse. To force the front rank back to the rear, or attempt to push forward the rear into line with the front, by the interposition of the government, would put an end to the impulse, and effectually arrest the march of progress.

These great and dangerous errors have their origin in the prevalent opinion that all men are born free and equal;—than which nothing can be more unfounded and false. It rests upon the assumption of a fact, which is contrary to universal observation, in whatever light it may be regarded. It is, indeed, difficult to explain how an opinion so destitute of all sound reason, ever could have been so extensively entertained, unless we regard it as being confounded with another, which has some semblance of truth;—but which, when properly understood, is not less false and dangerous. I refer to the assertion, that all men are equal in the state of nature; meaning, by a state of nature, a state of individuality, supposed to have existed prior to the social and political state; and in which men lived apart and independent of each other. If such a state ever did exist, all men would have been, indeed, free and equal in it; that is, free to do as they pleased, and exempt from the authority or control of others—as, by supposition, it existed anterior to society and government. But such a state is purely hypothetical. It never did, nor can exist; as it is inconsistent with the preservation and perpetuation of the race. It is, therefore, a great misnomer to call it *the state of nature*. Instead of being the natural state of man, it is, of all conceivable states, the most opposed to his nature—most repugnant to his feelings, and most incompatible with his wants. His natural state is, the social and political—the one for which his Creator made him, and the only one in which he can preserve and perfect his race. As, then, there never was such a state as the, so called, state of nature, and never can be, it follows, that men, instead of being born in it, are born in the social and political state; and of course, instead of being born free and equal, are born subject, not only to parental authority, but to the laws and institutions of the country where born, and under whose protection they draw their first breath. With these remarks, I return from this digression, to resume the thread of the discourse.

It follows, from all that has been said, that the more perfectly a government combines power and liberty,—that is, the greater its power and the more enlarged and secure the liberty of individuals, the more perfectly it fulfils the ends for which government is ordained. To show, then, that the government of the concurrent majority is better calculated to fulfil them than that of the numerical, it is only necessary to explain why the former is better suited to combine a higher degree of power and a wider scope of liberty than the latter. I shall begin with the former.

The concurrent majority, then, is better suited to enlarge and secure the bounds of liberty, because it is better suited to prevent government from passing beyond its proper limits, and to restrict it to its primary end,—the protection of the community. But in doing this, it leaves, necessarily, all beyond it open and free to individual exertions; and thus enlarges and secures the sphere of liberty to the greatest extent which the condition of the community will admit, as has been explained. The tendency of government to pass beyond its proper limits is what exposes liberty to danger, and renders it insecure; and it is the strong counteraction of governments of the concurrent majority to this tendency which makes them so favorable to liberty. On the contrary, those of the numerical, instead of opposing and counteracting this tendency, add to it increased strength, in consequence of the violent party struggles incident to them, as has been fully explained. And hence their encroachments on liberty, and the danger to which it is exposed under such governments.

So great, indeed, is the difference between the two in this respect, that liberty is little more than a name under all governments of the absolute form, including that of the numerical majority; and can only have a secure and durable existence under those of the concurrent or

447

constitutional form. The latter, by giving to each portion of the community which may be unequally affected by its action, a negative on the others, prevents all partial or local legislation, and restricts its action to such measures as are designed for the protection and the good of the whole. In doing this, it secures, at the same time, the rights and liberty of the people, regarded individually; as each portion consists of those who, whatever may be the diversity of interests among themselves, have the same interest in reference to the action of the government.

Such being the case, the interest of each individual may be safely confided to the majority, or voice of his portion, against that of all others, and, of course, the government itself. It is only through an organism which vests each with a negative, in some one form or another, that those who have like interests in preventing the government from passing beyond its proper sphere, and encroaching on the rights and liberty of individuals, can co-operate peaceably and effectually in resisting the encroachments of power, and thereby preserve their rights and liberty. Individual resistance is too feeble, and the difficulty of concert and co-operation too great, unaided by such an organism, to oppose, successfully, the organized power of government, with all the means of the community at its disposal; especially in populous countries of great extent; where concert and co-operation are almost impossible. Even when the oppression of the government comes to be too great to be borne, and force is resorted to in order to overthrow it, the result is rarely ever followed by the establishment of liberty. The force sufficient to overthrow an oppressive government is usually sufficient to establish one equally, or more, oppressive in its place. And hence, in no governments, except those that rest on the principle of the concurrent or constitutional majority, can the people guard their liberty against power; and hence, also, when lost, the great difficulty and uncertainty of regaining it by force.

It may be further affirmed that, being more favorable to the enlargement and security of liberty, governments of the concurrent, must necessarily be more favorable to progress, development, improvement, and civilization,—and, of course, to the increase of power which results from, and depends on these, than those of the numerical majority. That it is liberty which gives to them their greatest impulse, has already been shown; and it now remains to show, that these, in turn, contribute greatly to the increase of power.

In the earlier stages of society, numbers and individual prowess constituted the principal elements of power. In a more advanced stage, when communities had passed from the barbarous to the civilized state, discipline, strategy, weapons of increased power, and money,—as the means of meeting increased expense,—became additional and important elements. In this stage, the effects of progress and improvement on the increase of power, began to be disclosed; but still numbers and personal prowess were sufficient, for a long period, to enable barbarous nations to contend successfully with the civilized,—and, in the end, to overpower them,—as the pages of history abundantly testify. But a more advanced progress, with its numerous inventions and improvements, has furnished new and far more powerful and destructive implements of offence and defence, and greatly increased the intelligence and wealth, necessary to engage the skill and meet the increased expense required for their construction and application to purposes of war. The discovery of gunpowder, and the use of steam as an impelling force, and their application to military purposes, have for ever settled the question of ascendency between civilized and barbarous communities, in favor of the former. Indeed, these, with other improvements, belonging to the present state of progress, have given to communities the most advanced, a superiority over those the least so, almost as great as that of the latter over the brute creation. And among the civilized, the same causes have decided the question of superiority, where other circumstances are nearly equal, in favor of those whose governments have given the greatest impulse to development, progress, and improvement; that is, to those whose liberty is the largest and best secured. Among these, England and the United States afford striking examples, not only of the effects of liberty in increasing power, but of the more perfect adaptation of governments founded on the principle of the concurrent, or constitutional majority, to enlarge and secure liberty. They are both governments of this description, as will be shown hereafter.

But in estimating the power of a community, moral, as well as physical causes, must be taken into the calculation; and in estimating the effects of liberty on power, it must not be overlooked, that it is, in itself, an important agent in augmenting the force of moral, as well as of physical power. It bestows on a people elevation, self-reliance, energy, and enthusiasm; and these combined, give to physical power a vastly augmented and almost irresistible impetus.

These, however, are not the only elements of moral power. There are others, and among them harmony, unanimity, devotion to country, and a disposition to elevate to places of trust and power, those who are distinguished for wisdom and experience. These, when the occasion requires it, will, without compulsion, and from their very nature, unite and put forth the entire force of the community in the most efficient manner, without hazard to its institutions or its liberty.

All these causes combined, give to a community its maximum of power. Either of them, without the other, would leave it comparatively feeble. But it cannot be necessary, after what has been stated, to enter into any further explanation or argument in order to establish the superiority of governments of the concurrent majority over the numerical, in developing the great elements of moral power. So vast is this superiority, that the one, by its operation, necessarily leads to their development, while the other as necessarily prevents it,—as has been fully shown.

Davy Crockett Tells How to Win an Election

When Davy Crockett arrived in Washington in 1827 as Representative from western Tennessee, he was immediately named the "coonskin congressman." He liked the name and it stuck. Though he was not wearing his hunting shirt and fringed leggings as he had done while campaigning, he was willing to make political capital of his prowess as a bear-hunter and Indian-fighter and to let the tall tales that grew round him grow taller.

Historians have concentrated on Crockett's falling out with Andrew Jackson and the adroit use the Whigs made of this quarrel between the two best-known representatives of "coonskin democracy." But Crockett was not the frontier booby he sometimes let his opponents suppose he was. On two issues before Congress he fought with conviction: the attempt, unsuccessful in the end, to curb land speculation in his district, and the bill, which he unsuccessfully opposed, calling for the removal of the remnants of the five Indian tribes of the South to new territory across the Mississippi.

Crockett served in Congress from 1827 to 1831 and again from 1833 to 1835. He was defeated in his try for a fourth term by a man with a wooden leg whom Crockett referred to in his speeches as Old Timbertoes. The campaign was a savage one and was fought on this level of personalities and practical jokes. Fed up with politics and ready to move again, as always, Crockett turned his face toward Texas. He died there the next year, in the heroic defense of the Alamo.

Whether or not Crockett actually made the following speech to admirers in Little Rock, Arkansas, while on his way to Texas, does not much matter. It contains sentiments about coonskin campaigners and the tactics of suaver politicians which were undoubtedly his.

The passage is reprinted from Chapter xxvi of The Life of David

DAVY CROCKETT: *How to Win an Election*

Crockett, the Original Humorist and Irrepressible Backwoodsman
(*Philadelphia: Porter & Coates; 1865*). *For a note on this book, see
p. 640.*

❀

"ATTEND all public meetings," says I, "and get some friends to move
that you take the chair; if you fail in this attempt, make a push to be
appointed secretary; the proceedings of course will be published, and
your name is introduced to the public. But should you fail in both
undertakings, get two or three acquaintances, over a bottle of whiskey,
to pass some resolutions, no matter on what subject; publish them even
if you pay the printer—it will answer the purpose of breaking the ice,
which is the main point in these matters. Intrigue until you are elected
an officer of the militia; this is the second step towards promotion, and
can be accomplished with ease, as I know an instance of an election
being advertised, and no one attending, the innkeeper at whose house
it was to be held, having a military turn, elected himself colonel of
his regiment." Says I, "You may not accomplish your ends with as
little difficulty, but do not be discouraged—Rome wasn't built in a day.

"If your ambition or circumstances compel you to serve your country, and earn three dollars a day, by becoming a member of the legislature, you must first publicly avow that the constitution of the state
is a shackle upon free and liberal legislation; and is, therefore, of as
little use in the present enlightened age, as an old almanac of the year
in which the instrument was framed. There is policy in this measure,
for by making the constitution a mere dead letter, your headlong proceedings will be attributed to a bold and unshackled mind; whereas, it
might otherwise be thought they arose from sheer mulish ignorance.
'The Government' has set the example in his attack upon the constitution of the United States, and who should fear to follow where 'the
Government' leads?

"When the day of election approaches, visit your constituents far
and wide. Treat liberally, and drink freely, in order to rise in their
estimation, though you fall in your own. True, you may be called a
drunken dog by some of the clean shirt and silk stocking gentry, but
the real rough necks will style you a jovial fellow, their votes are certain, and frequently count double. Do all you can to appear to advantage in the eyes of the women. That's easily done—you have but
to kiss and slabber their children, wipe their noses, and pat them on
the head; this cannot fail to please their mothers, and you may rely
on your business being done in that quarter.

"Promise all that is asked," said I, "and more if you can think of anything. Offer to build a bridge or a church, to divide a county, create a batch of new offices, make a turnpike, or anything they like. Promises cost nothing, therefore deny nobody who has a vote or sufficient influence to obtain one.

"Get up on all occasions, and sometimes on no occasion at all, and make long-winded speeches, though composed of nothing else than wind—talk of your devotion to your country, your modesty and disinterestedness, or on any such fanciful subject. Rail against taxes of all kinds, office-holders, and bad harvest weather; and wind up with a flourish about the heroes who fought and bled for our liberties in the times that tried men's souls. To be sure you run the risk of being considered a bladder of wind, or an empty barrel, but never mind that, you will find enough of the same fraternity to keep you in countenance.

"If any charity be going forward, be at the top of it, provided it is to be advertised publicly; if not, it isn't worth your while. None but a fool would place his candle under a bushel on such an occasion.

"These few directions," said I, "if properly attended to, will do your business; and when once elected, why a fig for the dirty children, the promises, the bridges, the churches, the taxes, the offices, and the subscriptions, for it is absolutely necessary to forget all these before you can become a thoroughgoing politician, and a patriot of the first water."

Robert Toombs of Georgia Speaks His Farewell to the Senate on the Eve of the War of Rebellion

When Senator Toombs (1810–85) rose to speak in the Senate on January 7, 1861, the country was rushing headlong toward war. Many Southern statesmen had already sworn they would never accept Lincoln as President. A group of Southern senators and representatives had declared in an address to their constituents that "the honor, safety, and independence of the Southern people are to be found only in a Southern Confederacy"; and on December 20 South Carolina had seceded. One by one the senators from the South rose to speak their

farewells to the Union and to their colleagues. Among these the speech by Senator Toombs is noteworthy for both its eloquence and the care with which it reviewed the demands of the champions of Southern "rights." In it Toombs proudly accepted for his people the name of rebels. Five days later he left Washington to attend the convention at Milledgeville which would bring the keystone state of Georgia into the Confederacy.

The passage given here is Toombs's peroration. It is reprinted from the Congressional Globe, 36th Congress, 2nd session, p. 271.

You will not regard confederate obligations; you will not regard constitutional obligations; you will not regard your oaths. What, then, am I to do? Am I a freeman? Is my State, a free State, to lie down and submit because political fossils raise the cry of the glorious Union! Too long already have we listened to this delusive song. We are freemen. We have rights; I have stated them. We have wrongs; I have recounted them. I have demonstrated that the party now coming into power has declared us outlaws, and is determined to exclude four thousand million of our property from the common Territories; that it has declared us under the ban of the Empire, and out of the protection of the laws of the United States everywhere. They have refused to protect us from invasion and insurrection by the Federal Power, and the Constitution denies to us in the Union the right either to raise fleets or armies for our own defense. All these charges I have proven by the record; and I put them before the civilized world, and demand the judgment of to-day, of to-morrow, of distant ages, and of Heaven itself, upon the justice of these causes. I am content, whatever it be, to peril all in so noble, so holy a cause. We have appealed, time and time again, for these constitutional rights. You have refused them. We appeal again. Restore us these rights as we had them, as your court adjudges them to be, just as all our people have said they are; redress these flagrant wrongs, seen of all men, and it will restore fraternity, and peace, and unity to all of us. Refuse them, and what then? We shall then ask you to "let us depart in peace." Refuse that, and you present us war. We accept it; and inscribing upon our banners the glorious words, "liberty and equality," we will trust to the blood of the brave and the God of battles for security and tranquillity.

Journalist Pike Observes the "Black Parliament"
in South Carolina in the Spring of 1873

Though James Shepherd Pike (1811–82) was a northern-born news-paperman, an anti-slavery Whig and later a staunch Republican, and an associate editor of Greeley's New York Tribune *from 1852 to 1860, he was able to view events in South Carolina with considerable objectivity when he studied the effects of its Reconstruction government in 1873. In the book he wrote after his visit he is considerably more harsh with the Federal authorities, the venal press, and the Northern financial interests who were making money out of the corruption in the South Carolina legislature than he is with either the Negro legislators or the defeated Confederates. Inclined to be too pessimistic about the possible "Africanization" of the state, he was nevertheless concerned that justice should be done to both groups and that South Carolina should be relieved of its burden. The passages that follow are excerpted from Chapters i and ii of Pike's* The Prostrate State: South Carolina under Negro Government *(New York: D. Appleton & Company; 1874).*

In the place of this old aristocratic society stands the rude form of the most ignorant democracy that mankind ever saw, invested with the functions of government. It is the dregs of the population habilitated in the robes of their intelligent predecessors, and asserting over them the rule of ignorance and corruption, through the inexorable machinery of a majority of numbers. It is barbarism overwhelming civilization by physical force. It is the slave rioting in the halls of his master, and putting that master under his feet. And, though it is done without malice and without vengeance, it is nevertheless none the less completely and absolutely done. Let us approach nearer and take a closer view. We will enter the House of Representatives. Here sit one hundred and twenty-four members. Of these twenty-three are white men, representing the remains of the old civilization. These are good-looking, substantial citizens. They are men of weight and standing in the communities they represent. They are all from the hill country. The frosts of sixty and seventy winters whiten the heads of some among

454

them. There they sit, grim and silent. They feel themselves to be but loose stones, thrown in to partially obstruct a current they are powerless to resist. They say little and do little as the days go by. They simply watch the rising tide, and mark the progressive steps of the inundation. They hold their places reluctantly. They feel themselves to be in some sort martyrs, bound stoically to suffer in behalf of that still great element in the State whose prostrate fortunes are becoming the sport of an unpitying Fate. Grouped in a corner of the commodious and well-furnished chamber, they stolidly survey the noisy riot that goes on in the great black Left and Centre, where the business and debates of the House are conducted, and where sit the strange and extraordinary guides of the fortunes of a once proud and haughty State. In this crucial trial of his pride, his manhood, his prejudices, his spirit, it must be said of the Southern Bourbon of the Legislature that he comports himself with a dignity, a reserve, and a decorum, that command admiration. He feels that the iron hand of Destiny is upon him. He is gloomy, disconsolate, hopeless. The gray heads of this generation openly profess that they look for no relief. They see no way of escape. The recovery of influence, of position, of control in the State, is felt by them to be impossible. They accept their position with a stoicism that promises no reward here or hereafter. They are the types of a conquered race. They staked all and lost all. Their lives remain, their property and their children do not. War, emancipation, and grinding taxation, have consumed them. Their struggle now is against complete confiscation. They endure, and wait for the night.

This dense negro crowd they confront do the debating, the squabbling, the law-making, and create all the clamor and disorder of the body. These twenty-three white men are but the observers, the enforced auditors of the dull and clumsy imitation of a deliberative body, whose appearance in their present capacity is at once a wonder and a shame to modern civilization.

Deducting the twenty-three members referred to, who comprise the entire strength of the opposition, we find one hundred and one remaining. Of this one hundred and one, ninety-four are colored, and seven are their white allies. Thus the blacks outnumber the whole body of whites in the House more than three to one. . . . As things stand, the body is almost literally a Black Parliament, and it is the only one on the face of the earth which is the representative of a white constituency and the professed exponent of an advanced type of modern civilization. But the reader will find almost any portraiture inadequate to give a vivid idea of the body, and enable him to comprehend the complete metamorphosis of the South Carolina Legislature, without observing its details. The Speaker is black, the Clerk is black, the door-keepers are black, the little pages are black, the chairman of the Ways and

Means is black, and the chaplain is coal-black. At some of the desks sit colored men whose types it would be hard to find outside of Congo; whose costume, visages, attitudes, and expression, only befit the forecastle of a buccaneer. It must be remembered, also, that these men, with not more than half a dozen exceptions, have been themselves slaves, and that their ancestors were slaves for generations. Recollecting the report of the famous schooner Wanderer, fitted out by a Southern slave-holder twelve or fifteen years ago, in ostentatious defiance of the laws against the slave-trade, and whose owner and master boasted of having brought a cargo of slaves from Africa and safely landed them in South Carolina and Georgia, one thinks it must be true, and that some of these representatives are the very men then stolen from their African homes. If this be so, we will not now quarrel over their presence. It would be one of those extraordinary coincidences that would of itself almost seem to justify the belief of the direct interference of the hand of Providence in the affairs of men. . . .

The old stagers admit that the colored brethren have a wonderful aptness at legislative proceedings. They are "quick as lightning" at detecting points of order, and they certainly make incessant and extraordinary use of their knowledge. No one is allowed to talk five minutes without interruption, and one interruption is the signal for another and another, until the original speaker is smothered under an avalanche of them. Forty questions of privilege will be raised in a day. At times, nothing goes on but alternating questions of order and of privilege. The inefficient colored friend who sits in the Speaker's chair cannot suppress this extraordinary element of the debate. Some of the blackest members exhibit a pertinacity of intrusion in raising these points of order and questions of privilege that few white men can equal. Their struggles to get the floor, their bellowings and physical contortions, baffle description. The Speaker's hammer plays a perpetual tattoo all to no purpose. The talking and the interruptions from all quarters go on with the utmost license. Every one esteems himself as good as his neighbor, and puts in his oar, apparently as often for love of riot and confusion as for any thing else. It is easy to imagine what are his ideas of propriety and dignity among a crowd of his own color, and these are illustrated without reserve. The Speaker orders a member whom he has discovered to be particularly unruly to take his seat. The member obeys, and with the same motion that he sits down, throws his feet on to his desk hiding himself from the Speaker by the soles of his boots. In an instant he appears again on the floor. After a few experiences of this sort, the Speaker threatens, in a laugh, to call "the gemman" to order. This is considered a capital joke, and a guffaw follows. The laugh goes round, and then the peanuts are cracked and munched faster than ever; one hand being employed in fortifying the inner man with

456

this nutriment of universal use, while the other enforces the views of the orator. This laughing propensity of the sable crowd is a great cause of disorder. They laugh as hens cackle—one begins and all follow.

But underneath all this shocking burlesque upon legislative proceedings, we must not forget that there is something very real to this uncouth and untutored multitude. It is not all sham, nor all burlesque. They have a genuine interest and a genuine earnestness in the business of the assembly which we are bound to recognize and respect, unless we would be accounted shallow critics. They have an earnest purpose, born of a conviction that their position and condition are not fully assured, which lends a sort of dignity to their proceedings. The barbarous, animated jargon in which they so often indulge is on occasion seen to be so transparently sincere and weighty in their own minds that sympathy supplants disgust. The whole thing is a wonderful novelty to them as well as to observers. Seven years ago these men were raising corn and cotton under the whip of the overseer. To-day they are raising points of order and questions of privilege. They find they can raise one as well as the other. They prefer the latter. It is easier, and better paid. Then, it is the evidence of an accomplished result. It means escape and defense from the old oppressors. It means liberty. It means the destruction of prison-walls only too real to them. It is the sunshine of their lives. It is their day of jubilee. It is their long-promised vision of the Lord God Almighty.

Grady's "The New South"

Henry W. Grady (1850–89) was not a politician, though he has been called the "Warwick of Georgia Politics" because he made and unmade candidates for office. Few American politicians ever delivered so influential a speech as Grady's famous "The New South," given before the august New England Society of New York on the night of December 22, 1886.

At the moment relations between the North and the South were tense. The Republicans had lost the election in 1884 (to Cleveland), the first time the party had been out of power since Lincoln came into office. In their eagerness to regain the Presidency, they were "waving the bloody shirt" and some were even agitating for the revival of

Federal supervision of national elections in the South. The old sectional antagonisms were once more aroused. Northern capitalists who had begun to invest in Southern enterprises were particularly apprehensive of the outcome. At this juncture it was proposed to the officers of the New England Society in the City of New York that much good might be done if Henry W. Grady, editor of the Atlanta Constitution *and already known as the spokesman for the new South of industrial progress, were asked to make the speech at the society's annual dinner. The occasion was always widely reported in the press because many of the members were leaders in business and industry.*

Grady agreed to appear—the first Southerner who had ever been invited to make the annual address. He was an ideal choice for the occasion. He was in no way identified with the war, having been fifteen when the conflict ended. His Irish wit brightened his words, but he always spoke, as he did this night, with frankness and patriotic fervor.

When Grady rose, the audience had already listened to Dr. De Witt Talmage, a Brooklyn minister, who responded to the toast: "Forefathers' Day," and to General William T. Sherman, after whose words the orchestra had burst into "Marching through Georgia." As Grady's speech shows, he gracefully leaped these hurdles and went on to win the race of the evening. North and South alike praised the man and his speech. As his biographer Raymond B. Nixon has said, on this important occasion "Grady was the right man speaking the right word at the right time."

The text of "The New South" is that printed in Joel Chandler Harris' Life of Henry W. Grady. Including his Writings and Speeches *(New York: Cassell Publishing Company; 1890), pp. 83–93.*

❀

"THERE was a South of slavery and secession—that South is dead. There is a South of union and freedom—that South, thank God, is living, breathing, growing every hour." These words, delivered from the immortal lips of Benjamin H. Hill, at Tammany Hall, in 1866, true then and truer now, I shall make my text tonight.

Mr. President and Gentlemen: Let me express to you my appreciation of the kindness by which I am permitted to address you. I make this abrupt acknowledgment advisedly, for I feel that if, when I raise my provincial voice in this ancient and august presence, I could find courage for no more than the opening sentence, it would be well if in that sentence I had met in a rough sense my obligation as a guest, and had perished, so to speak, with courtesy on my lips and grace in my heart. Permitted, through your kindness, to catch my second wind, let me say that I appreciate the significance of being the first Southerner to speak at this board, which bears the substance, if it surpasses the semblance, of original New England hospitality—and honors the sentiment that in turn honors you, but in which my personality is lost, and the compliment to my people made plain.

I bespeak the utmost stretch of your courtesy tonight. I am not troubled about those from whom I come. You remember the man whose wife sent him to a neighbor with a pitcher of milk, and who, tripping on the top step, fell with such casual interruptions as the landings afforded into the basement, and, while picking himself up, had the pleasure of hearing his wife call out: "John, did you break the pitcher?"

"No, I didn't," said John, "but I'll be dinged if I don't."

So, while those who call me from behind may inspire me with energy, if not with courage, I ask an indulgent hearing from you. I beg that you will bring your full faith in American fairness and frankness to judgment upon what I shall say. There was an old preacher once who told some boys of the Bible lesson he was going to read in the morning. The boys, finding the place, glued together the connecting pages. The next morning he read on the bottom of one page, "When Noah was one hundred and twenty years old he took unto himself a wife, who was"—then turning the page—"140 cubits long—40 cubits wide, built of gopher wood—and covered with pitch inside and out." He was naturally puzzled at this. He read it again, verified it, and then said: "My friends, this is the first time I ever met this in the Bible, but I accept this as an evidence of the assertion that we are fearfully and wonderfully made." If I could get you to hold such faith tonight I could proceed cheerfully to the task I otherwise approach with a sense of consecration.

Pardon me one word, Mr. President, spoken for the sole purpose of getting into the volumes that go out annually freighted with the rich eloquence of your speakers—the fact that the Cavalier as well as the Puritan was on the continent in its early days, and that he was "up and able to be about." I have read your books carefully and I find no mention of that fact, which seems to me an important one for preserving a sort of historical equilibrium if for nothing else.

Let me remind you that the Virginia Cavalier first challenged France on the continent—that Cavalier, John Smith, gave New England its very name, and was so pleased with the job that he has been handing his own name around ever since—and that while Myles Standish was cutting off men's ears for courting a girl without her parents' consent, and forbade men to kiss their wives on Sunday, the Cavalier was courting everything in sight, and that the Almighty had vouchsafed great increase to the Cavalier colonies, the huts in the wilderness being as full as the nests in the woods.

But having incorporated the Cavalier as a fact in your charming little books, I shall let him work out his own salvation, as he has always done, with engaging gallantry, and we will hold no controversy as to his merits. Why should we? Neither Puritan nor Cavalier long survived as such. The virtues and good traditions of both happily still live for the inspiration of their sons and the saving of the old fashion. But both Puritan and Cavalier were lost in the storm of the first Revolution, and the American citizen, supplanting both and stronger than either, took possession of the republic bought by their common blood and fashioned to wisdom, and charged himself with teaching men government and establishing the voice of the people as the voice of God.

My friends, Dr. Talmage has told you that the typical American has yet to come. Let me tell you that he has already come. Great types, like valuable plants, are slow to flower and fruit. But from the union of these colonists, Puritans and Cavaliers, from the straightening of their purposes and the crossing of their blood, slow perfecting through a century, came he who stands as the first typical American, the first who comprehended within himself all the strength and gentleness, all the majesty and grace of this republic—Abraham Lincoln. He was the sum of Puritan and Cavalier, for in his ardent nature were fused the virtues of both, and in the depths of his great soul the faults of both were lost. He was greater than Puritan, greater than Cavalier, in that he was American, and that in his honest form were first gathered the vast and thrilling forces of his ideal government—charging it with such tremendous meaning and elevating it above human suffering that martyrdom, though infamously aimed, came as a fitting crown to a life consecrated from the cradle to human liberty. Let us, each cherishing the traditions and honoring his fathers, build with reverent hands to the type of this simple but sublime life, in which all types are honored, and in our common glory as Americans there will be plenty and to spare for your forefathers and for mine.

Dr. Talmage has drawn for you, with a master's hand, the picture of your returning armies. He has told you how, in the pomp and circumstance of war, they came back to you, marching with proud and victorious tread, reading their glory in a nation's eyes! Will you bear with me while I tell you of another army that sought its home at the close of the late war—an army that marched home in defeat and not in victory—in pathos and not in splendor, but in glory that equaled yours, and to hearts as loving as ever welcomed heroes home! Let me picture to you the footsore Confederate soldier, as buttoning up in his faded gray jacket the parole which was to bear testimony to his children of his fidelity and faith, he turned his face southward from Appomattox in April, 1865. Think of him as ragged, half-starved, heavy-hearted, enfeebled by want and wounds, having fought to exhaustion, he surrenders his gun, wrings the hands of his comrades in silence, and lifting his tear-stained and pallid face for the last time to the graves that dot old Virginia hills, pulls his gray cap over his brow and begins the slow and painful journey. What does he find—let me ask you who went to your homes eager to find, in the welcome you had justly earned, full payment for four years' sacrifice—what does he find when, having followed the battle-stained cross against overwhelming odds, dreading death not half so much as surrender, he reaches the home he left so prosperous and beautiful? He finds his house in ruins, his farm devastated, his slaves free, his stock killed, his barns empty, his trade destroyed, his money worthless, his social system, feudal in its magnificence, swept away; his people without law or legal status; his comrades slain, and the burdens of others heavy on his shoulders. Crushed by defeat, his very traditions are gone. Without money, credit, employment, material, or training; and beside all this, confronted with the gravest problem that ever met human intelligence—the establishing of a status for the vast body of his liberated slaves.

What does he do—this hero in gray with a heart of gold? Does he sit down in sullenness and despair? Not for a day. Surely God, who had stripped him of his prosperity, inspired him in his adversity. As ruin was never before so overwhelming, never was restoration swifter. The soldier stepped from the trenches into the furrow; horses that had charged Federal guns marched before the plow, and fields that ran red with human blood in April were green with the harvest in June; women reared in luxury cut up their dresses and made breeches for their husbands, and, with a patience and heroism that fit women always as a garment, gave their hands to work. There was little bitterness in all this. Cheerfulness and frankness prevailed. "Bill Arp" struck the key-note when he said: "Well, I killed as many of them as they did of me, and now I'm going to work." [Or] the soldier returning home after defeat and roasting some corn on the roadside, who made the remark to his comrades: "You may leave the South if you want to, but I am going to Sandersville, kiss my wife and raise a crop, and if the Yankees fool with me any more, I'll whip 'em again." I want to say to General Sherman, who is considered an able man in our parts, though some people think he is a kind of careless man about fire, that from the ashes he left us in 1864 we have raised a brave and beautiful city; that somehow or other we have caught the sunshine in the bricks and mortar of our homes, and have builded therein not one ignoble prejudice or memory.

But what is the sum of our work? We have found out that in the summing up the free Negro counts more than he did as a slave. We

461

have planted the schoolhouse on the hilltop and made it free to white and black. We have sowed towns and cities in the place of theories, and put business above politics. We have challenged your spinners in Massachusetts and your iron-makers in Pennsylvania. We have learned that the $400,000,000 annually received from our cotton crop will make us rich when the supplies that make it are home-raised. We have reduced the commercial rate of interest from 24 to 6 per cent., and are floating 4 per cent. bonds. We have learned that one northern immigrant is worth fifty foreigners; and have smoothed the path to southward, wiped out the place where Mason and Dixon's line used to be, and hung out [the] latchstring to you and yours. We have reached the point that marks perfect harmony in every household, when the husband confesses that the pies which his wife cooks are as good as those his mother used to bake; and we admit that the sun shines as brightly and the moon as softly as it did before the war. We have established thrift in city and country. We have fallen in love with work. We have restored comfort to homes from which culture and elegance never departed. We have let economy take root and spread among us as rank as the crabgrass which sprung from Sherman's cavalry camps, until we are ready to lay odds on the Georgia Yankee as he manufactures relics of the battlefield in a one-story shanty and squeezes pure olive oil out of his cotton seed, against any down-easter that ever swapped wooden nutmegs for flannel sausage in the valleys of Vermont. Above all, we know that we have achieved in these "piping times of peace" a fuller independence for the South than that which our fathers sought to win in the forum by their eloquence or compel in the field by their swords.

It is a rare privilege, sir, to have had part, however humble, in this work. Never was nobler duty confided to human hands than the uplifting and upbuilding of the prostrate and bleeding South—misguided, perhaps, but beautiful in her suffering, and honest, brave and generous always. In the record of her social, industrial and political illustration we await with confidence the verdict of the world.

But what of the Negro? Have we solved the problem he presents or progressed in honor and equity toward solution? Let the record speak to the point. No section shows a more prosperous laboring population than the Negroes of the South, none in fuller sympathy with the employing and land-owning class. He shares our school fund, has the fullest protection of our laws and the friendship of our people. Self-interest, as well as honor, demand that he should have this. Our future, our very existence depend upon our working out this problem in full and exact justice. We understand that when Lincoln signed the emancipation proclamation, your victory was assured, for he then committed you to the cause of human liberty, against which the arms of man cannot prevail—while those of our statesmen who trusted to make slavery the corner-stone of the Confederacy doomed us to defeat as far as they could, committing us to a cause that reason could not defend or the sword maintain in sight of advancing civilization.

Had Mr. Toombs said, which he did not say, "that he would call the roll of his slaves at the foot of Bunker Hill," he would have been foolish, for he might have known that whenever slavery became entangled in war it must perish, and that the chattel in human flesh ended forever in New England when your fathers—not to be blamed for parting with what didn't pay—sold their slaves to our fathers—not to be praised for knowing a paying thing when they saw it. The relations of the Southern people with the Negro are close and cordial. We remember with what fidelity for four years he guarded our defenseless women and children, whose husbands and fathers were fighting against his freedom. To his eternal credit be it said that whenever he struck a blow for his own liberty he fought in open battle, and when at last he raised his black and humble hands that the shackles might be struck off, those hands were innocent of wrong against his helpless charges, and worthy to be taken in loving grasp by every man who honors loyalty and devotion. Ruffians have maltreated him, rascals have misled him, philanthropists established a bank for him, but the South, with the North, protests against injustice to this simple and sincere people. To liberty and enfranchisement is as far as law can carry the Negro. The rest must be left to conscience and common sense. It must be left to those among whom his lot is cast, with whom he is indissolubly connected, and whose prosperity depends upon their possessing his intelligent sympathy and confidence. Faith has been kept with him, in spite of calumnious assertions to the contrary by those who assume to speak for us or by frank opponents. Faith will be kept with him in the future, if the South holds her reason and integrity.

But have we kept faith with you? In the fullest sense, yes. When Lee surrendered—I don't say when Johnson surrendered, because I understand he still alludes to the time when he met General Sherman last as the time when he determined to abandon any further prosecution of the struggle—when Lee surrendered, I say, and Johnson quit, the South became, and has since been, loyal to this Union. We fought hard enough to know that we were whipped, and in perfect frankness accept as final the arbitrament of the sword to which we had appealed. The South found her jewel in the toad's head of defeat. The shackles that had held her in narrow limitations fell forever when the shackles of the Negro slave were broken. Under the old regime the Negroes were slaves to the South; the South was a slave to the system. The old plantation, with its simple police regulations and feudal habit, was the only type possible under slavery. Thus was gathered in the hands of a splendid and chivalric oligarchy the substance that should have been diffused among the people, as the rich blood, under certain artificial conditions, is gathered at the heart, filling that with affluent rapture but leaving the body chill and colorless.

The old South rested everything on slavery and agriculture, unconscious that these could neither give nor maintain healthy growth. The new South presents a perfect democracy, the oligarchs leading in the popular movement—a social system compact and closely knitted, less splendid on the surface, but stronger at the core—a hundred farms for every plantation, fifty homes for every palace—and a diversified industry that meets the complex need of this complex age.

The new South is enamored of her new work. Her soul is stirred with the breath of a new life. The light of a grander day is falling fair on her face. She is thrilling with the consciousness of growing power and prosperity. As she stands upright, full-statured and equal among the people of the earth, breathing the keen air and looking out upon the expanded horizon, she understands that her emancipation came because through the inscrutable wisdom of God her honest purpose was crossed, and her brave armies were beaten.

This is said in no spirit of time-serving or apology. The South has nothing for which to apologize. She believes that the late struggle between the States was war and not rebellion; revolution and not conspiracy, and that her convictions were as honest as yours. I should be unjust to the dauntless spirit of the South and to my own convictions if I did not make this plain in this presence. The South has nothing to take back. In my native town of Athens is a monument that crowns its central hill—a plain, white shaft. Deep cut into its shining side is a name dear to me above the names of men—that of a brave and simple man who died in brave and simple faith. Not for all the glories of New England, from Plymouth Rock all the way, would I exchange the heritage he left me in his soldier's death. To the foot of that I shall send my children's children to reverence him who ennobled their name with his heroic blood. But, sir, speaking from the shadow of that memory which I honor as I do nothing else on earth, I say that the cause in which he suffered and for which he gave his life was adjudged by higher and fuller wisdom than his or mine, and I am glad that the omniscient God held the balance of battle in His Almighty hand and that human slavery was swept forever from American soil, the American Union was saved from the wreck of war.

This message, Mr. President, comes to you from consecrated ground. Every foot of soil about the city in which I live is as sacred as a battleground of the republic. Every hill that invests it is hallowed to you by the blood of your brothers who died for your victory, and doubly hallowed to us by the blow of those who died hopeless, but undaunted, in defeat—sacred soil to all of us—rich with memories that make us purer and stronger and better—silent but staunch witnesses in its red desolation of the matchless valor of American hearts and the deathless glory of American arms—speaking an eloquent witness in its white peace and prosperity to the indissoluble union of American States and the imperishable brotherhood of the American people.

Now, what answer has New England to this message? Will she permit the prejudice of war to remain in the hearts of the conquerors, when it has died in the hearts of the conquered? Will she transmit this prejudice to the next generation, that in their hearts which never felt the generous ardor of conflict it may perpetuate itself? Will she withhold, save in strained courtesy, the hand which straight from his soldier's heart Grant offered to Lee at Appomattox? Will she make the vision of a restored and happy people, which gathered above the couch of your dying captain, filling his heart with grace; touching his lips with praise, and glorifying his path to the grave—will she make this vision on which the last sigh of his expiring soul breathed a benediction, a cheat and delusion? If she does, the South, never abject in asking for comradeship, must accept with dignity its refusal; but if she does not refuse to accept in frankness and sincerity this message of good will and friendship, then will the prophecy of Webster, delivered in this very society forty years ago amid tremendous applause, become true, be verified in its fullest sense, when he said: "Standing hand to hand and clasping hands, we should remain united as we have been for sixty years, citizens of the same country, members of the same government, united, all united now and united forever." There have been difficulties, contentions, and controversies, but I tell you that in my judgment,

> "Those opened eyes,
> Which like the meteors of a troubled heaven,
> All of one nature, of one substance bred,
> Did lately meet in th' intestine shock,
> Shall now, in mutual well beseeming ranks,
> March all one way."

Huey Long Takes Up His Mortgage on Louisiana

The Southern demagogue is the regional counterpart of the machine boss of the Northern city. Just as a Tammany Hall sachem got much of his support from the bewildered poor in each ward, so the Southern

demagogue appealed largely to the rural voters. In bidding for the votes of the red-necks, the wool-hats, the crackers, the sand-hillers, and the lint-heads he could easily touch off their latent anger against the landowners and bankers who held their lives in fee and against the Negro sharecroppers or laborers who pressed them economically from below. He needed only about a half-dozen powerfully evocative tunes: the money power of the North, symbolized by Wall Street; Republican high tariffs; freight rates that discriminate against the South; Federal anti-lynching bills or other civil-rights legislation in behalf of the Negro; the un-Americanism of the attempts of the A.F. of L. and the C.I.O. to organize Southern labor. Again like his Northern counterpart, the demagogue has often enough stuffed his pockets with gifts for services rendered to the "interests" he raucously denounced.

Huey Long is the most notorious in the succession of Southern demagogues which begins with Pitchfork Ben Tillman of South Carolina and anti-Catholic, anti-Jewish, anti-Negro Tom Watson of Georgia. There is no doubt that Long "gave" the people of Louisiana benefits on which a decent economic existence could be built: good roads and new bridges (essential to a state in which there is water everywhere), lower telephone, gas, and electric rates. There is also no doubt that "the Kingfish" was a brawler who turned the state militia into a Sturmabteilung, an American Führer who did what he willed with Louisiana while he was Governor and continued to control it, through a subservient legislature, after he went to the United States Senate. Long might not have looked so dangerous and invincible if he had not risen to power in the time of Hitler and Mussolini. But his threat to American democracy made the thoughtful wonder, twenty years before Senator Joseph McCarthy arrived on the national scene, whether, in Sinclair Lewis's phrase, "it might happen here."

The following appraisal of Long's position at the time of his assassination is taken from Harnett T. Kane's Louisiana Hayride: The American Rehearsal for Dictatorship, 1928–1940, *copyright 1941 by Mr. Kane. It is reprinted here with the permission of the publishers, William Morrow & Company.*

A DULL silence was upon the state. Huey had foreclosed, taken up his mortgage. As T. O. Harris described it, he had become "owner in fee simple, with all reversionary rights and hereditaments, in full trust and benefit, to have and to hold, in paramount estate and freehold, for the balance of his days." No other man in America has had the powers he held in his hands.

He possessed the state government, the Governor, the university, all commissions and departments; the Legislature, the public schools, the treasury, the buildings, and the Louisianians inside them. The courts were his, except in isolated instances, and he had the highest judges. He had a secret police which did anything he asked: kidnaped men, held them incommunicado, inquired without check into private matters of opponents. He ran the elections. He counted the votes. He disqualified any man or woman whom he wanted disqualified. He could order the addition to the rolls of any number of voters that his judgment dictated. He was becoming local government in Louisiana. The officials of no town or city were secure. Let a brother or an uncle offend, and Huey would have a mayor or an alderman out of a job and his own man appointed in his place. He was reaching into local police affairs; he was controlling municipal finances by new boards. He could ruin a community by cutting off its taxes, preventing it from adopting substitutes, and then forcing new obligations to break its back. He was moving in upon the parish district attorneys, using his attorney-general as a club.

His power was becoming that of life and death over private business. His banking examiner, his homestead agents, his Dock Board, his Public Service Commission and State Tax Commission were instruments of financial salvation, or of ruin. He served as attorney for the state without hindrance, dug back far into the past records of companies on the wrong side, shook heavy payments from them and took a full third as a fee, by law. There was secrecy about most of the state's records. The law forbade officials to give out financial information; they could be put in jail for doing so. Others did not need a law to guide them in closing their records.

And government by thunderbolt had come, apparently, to stay. The Reichstag of the Nazis did what it was told. Huey's Reichstag did not know what it was doing when it did it, and had to ask afterward if it wanted to find out.

Huey's tax against the larger newspapers was under argument in the courts. If some technical flaw were found, he was ready to remedy that; to alter the tax but not the essential principle. Already he had taken over most of the smaller newspapers through the medium of new legislation regarding local public printing contracts, on which such journals depended. A state printing board saw that these newspapers behaved, or died.

A Louisiana man could lose a private position because the dictatorship decided that one of his friends or relatives had aggrieved it. He could be arrested on a faked charge and held as long as the machine wanted, without the knowledge of his friends. He could be tried before a machine judge, receive a sentence, appeal—and in the end find himself turned down by Huey's highest court. If he were on the other side, he could steal, gouge, maim, perhaps kill, and know that he was not in jeopardy; and he could grow rich without capital, without ability, with nothing to his credit except the "right connection."

A few examples of what favor meant: New Orleans bankers were charged with receiving deposits after they knew their institutions were in failing condition. The shifting of one legislator, brother of a banker, to Long, and all won legislative pardon. Again, a friend of Huey's committed an alleged forgery. Huey noded his head, and a law was passed outlawing criminal prosecutions after a short period; the friend went free. A strong-arm man followed orders by breaking the skull of an enemy at the Capitol. An unreconstructed judge convicted and sentenced him. The judge's words had not died away when the convicted man thrust his hand into a side pocket and drew out a pardon, signed and executed in advance by the dictator's Governor.

As the state lay quiet, Huey's appetite for power remained unappeased. Those last judges were comparatively harmless, encircled as they were; but they were irksome. He turned on Louisiana's Supreme Court: "That crooked legged chief justice" was a politician, said Huey. He and the other two minority members—"those three birds on the Supreme Court have got to be removed"; and with them "three rotten Ring judges down in New Orleans." A loyal attorney arguing a case threatened a judge: "Could you maintain yourself on the bench if the Legislature passed an act that rearranged the court and left you out? They did that very thing in my parish. Where did the judge go? He went to practicing law."

For amusement, Huey had the Regular Ring to toy with. He had reduced the city to abject surrender. Workers went without pay for weeks. Grass began to grow in some of the streets, as Huey had predicted. Roadwork, most other city work, halted. Garbage men went on strike. A majority of the Ring leaders went over to him. He kept them on their knees for months.

His last attack on the election rules brought a voice out of the silence, that of Mason Spencer, one of the last, lonely legislative opponents:

"When this ugly thing is boiled down in its own juices, it disfranchises the white people of Louisiana. I am not gifted with second sight. Nor did I see a spot of blood on the moon last night. But I can see blood on the polished floor of this Capitol. For if you ride this thing through, you will travel with the white horse of death. White men have ever made poor slaves."

As he spoke, the atmosphere was appropriate. The militia stood on guard over the Legislature. Baton Rouge was under the military heel. For the first time, the public had been moved out of the side galleries by armed men. Why? Could there have been fear of mass uprisings now? The explanation was that Huey Long feared murder at the hands of one of his subjects, or a cabal of them. For years he had talked of violent death. "Sure, I carry a gun. Sometimes I carry four. Can't tell when somebody's going to shoot the king," he joked. But generally he was solemn about it.

He had seen plots about him in his first days in the mansion at Baton Rouge. A mild-looking young man had walked past the residence twice a day at the same hour, looking up each time with marked interest. Huey called police, and they found that the "conspirator" had only been going to and from work a few squares away. In another instance Governor Huey had telephoned officials to arrest a man who was "driving round and round the place." The suspect had a new car and was accumulating mileage.

Open threats had been made, often, against Huey's safety. There were so many whose lives he had ruined, whose jobs he had taken away, whom he had abused in back-alley language. Such vows of vengeance were made generally in the heat of argument, of resentment against a particular trick. Huey met such talk with more protection, more bodyguards. For months the capital gossiped of hidden emplacements of machine guns that were ready in the state house, in case worst came to worst. To many men the military activities, the overcareful guard which Huey placed about himself, might have encouraged thoughts of gunplay. In his final months, Huey became more and more fearful.

Immediately after the Square Deal debacle, his attorney-general appeared in court to ask for an open hearing. Huey appeared as "special assistant attorney-general" to question witnesses regarding a "plot" against him. The Long man who had been "planted" in the Square Dealers' ranks described a scheme to force Huey's car to halt on the road, and then to shoot him to death. The opposition, declaring that the "plot" existed only in Huey's mind, cited the fact that, despite elaborate testimony, no charges were ever brought, and the matter was dropped. In Washington, Huey charged that the Standard Oil had tried to assassinate him. The Senate was discussing the World Court, and a fellow member suggested that Huey's war with Standard might be called to that organization's attention.

In July of 1935, the Kingfish rose again on the Senate floor, to allege that a plot to assassinate him had been discovered. He called attention to a caucus of oppositionists in a New Orleans hotel, declared that his men had installed a dictagraph and taken records of the conversation. There was talk, he asserted, of "one man, one gun, one bullet," and a question: "Does anyone doubt that President Roosevelt would pardon the man who rid the country of Huey Long?"

Angrily, the participants in the caucus denied a "plot" of any kind.

The meeting had been no secret at the time. It was a gathering of the remaining antis to discuss a ticket for 1936. Five Congressmen attended. Some said that in the course of long hours of informal conversation, some one may have talked at random of the benefits to the nation which might follow the death of the dictator. But, they added, it was hardly possible for any sizable group to get together in Louisiana any longer without some discussion of Huey's possible demise—Huey himself talked about it so often.

Back to Louisiana he came for yet additional extensions of power, further exercises of malice, tying up of loose ends. He called another special session for early September. A Congressional subcommittee was planning to go to Louisiana, to investigate charges made in connection with election affairs. Huey prepared a particularly curious law, making it an offense for any person to perform, in the name of the Federal Government, a function which the Federal Constitution did not specifically authorize. He was turning to States' Rights with a vengeance. Then there were two other bills, these against judges. One abolished a position held by a Baton Rouge jurist, W. Carruth Jones, an oppositionist. The other gerrymanded the anti-Long St. Landry-Evangeline district of South Louisiana, to link part of it with a predominantly Long area near by. This would thrust out another hostile judge, Benjamin F. Pavy. Judge Pavy had presided for thirty years in that district. He had enjoined the use of the dummy election commissioners; Huey had marked him down and was now getting around to the matter. It was a minor affair, as such retaliations went.

Sunday, September 8, however, was a Sabbath of travail for Dr. Carl Austin Weiss, a young doctor of Baton Rouge, son of another doctor, son-in-law of Judge Pavy. He was a quiet, gentle scholar, a man who "had nothing to do with politics," but who felt deeply on the subject of dictators and dictatorships. He had done postgraduate work in Vienna when the Social Democratic movement was crumbling, when Dollfuss ordered the destruction of the workers' co-operative apartments. He remembered those days, and he thought bitterly of the days that were now upon Louisiana. Two relatives, one a teacher, and a patient who was a close friend, were victims of Huey's spite. The bill against Judge Pavy was certain to pass. And shocking word came to friends. Long was making unfounded remarks, as he had made them about others, that Judge Pavy had Negro blood. He might go at any time on the radio to vent his utterances. It was a stain that might mark the life of the judge's grandson, Dr. Weiss's young child.

Eight years earlier, Carl Austin Weiss's class book at Tulane University had declared that he would "go out and make the world take notice." On this day he said good-by, quietly, and started on what his family thought was a professional call. In his Capitol, Huey was ending a smoothly functioning night meeting. Walking out, he gave his final order: "Everybody be here in the morning." His black-and-white sports shoes tapped along an ornate corridor, along a marble hallway toward the office of his Governor. Several Long men were there, one of them Supreme Court Justice Fournet. Huey paused to pass a few words. According to Long witnesses, a slight, bespectacled man in white came from behind one of the pillars. From under the bottom of his coat a hand moved, thrust a small gun into Huey's side, and fired one shot.

But others in Louisiana insist that, despite his mental state, Dr. Weiss did not go to Long with the deliberate intent to kill him. Instead, they argue, he sought only to talk with him; and the panicky guards precipitated the shooting, perhaps killed the Kingfish themselves in the scuffle. This is the story that at least one third of Louisiana believes; and it can cite unexplained facts and circumstances to support its contention. In any event, the first bullet hit Huey, and he clutched his side and cried out.

The bodyguards lost no more time. Huey staggered away, hand to his side. One man dived at Weiss, felled him, and they grappled. The guard backed off, firing. Weiss fell forward on his face, the gun slipping along the polished floor, out of his hand. Half a dozen of the guards poured lead into him from all directions. There was no sound from his lips. The body stiffened, but still the guns spat out in vengeance. Sixty-one bullet holes were found by the coroner: thirty in front, twenty-nine in back, two through the head.

Huey was on his way, at once, to a near-by hospital. "I wonder why he shot me?" he asked, as he was driven up. For thirty-one hours he fought for his life, in as determined a manner as he had fought for the gubernatorial chair and for the Presidency. The first person to give him attention was Arthur Vidrine, the country doctor whom he had elevated to the superintendency of Charity Hospital. The bullet had passed through three loops of the intestine and taken part of the kidney before it left the body. The dangers were shock and internal hemorrhage, one almost equal to the other. Should an operation, with the resultant shock, be performed at once, or later? Two outstanding surgeons were called from New Orleans, efforts made to rush them by plane. But no airship was available. They started by automobile; on the way, they met with an accident. Vidrine operated. Huey remained part conscious, part delirious. He talked of his autobiography, which he had decided was to be a best seller, and he talked of his end: "Oh, Lord, don't let me die. I have a few more things to do. . . . My work for America is not finished. . . ."

With his family and the leading men of his régime about him, Huey Pierce Long slipped into death on September 10, 1935.

In the main hallway of his skyscraper Capitol the body lay on its bier for two days. Eighty thousand persons passed before it and saw the former country boy in his tuxedo. On the second day the coffin was lowered into a hastily dug grave in the sunken garden before the Capitol. An estimated 125,000 to 150,000 men, women and children— from the hollows, from the swamps, from New Orleans, from Dry Prong, from DeQuincy, from Maringouin—packed the area, climbed trees, stood on roofs to watch. Old women cried. Men wiped away tears. Their man had died, for them. The Rev. Gerald L. K. Smith of the share-the-wealth organization pealed to his listeners: "The blood which dropped upon our soil shall seal our hearts. . . . His body shall never rest as long as hungry bodies cry for food, as long as lean human frames stand naked, as long as homeless wretches haunt this land of plenty. . . ." And the red-eyed O. K. Allen called upon Huey's followers to carry on his program by "perpetuating ourselves in office."

As in its unwinding, so in its final moments, did the story of Huey Long do violence to American tradition. Assassination has never been a political method that stirred anything but revulsion in this nation. But Long's death came as a not illogical sequel to the life he had chosen to lead. The full account of those last days has never been revealed. Some believe that if, at a future date, the proper persons may be persuaded to speak, a sensation may result. This much can be said now: No evidence has yet been offered to connect Carl Austin Weiss with a plot of any kind; and there has been no disclosure of the full circumstances leading up to the moment when the young doctor stepped from behind the pillar, nor of the immediate events that followed. An autopsy was not performed on the body of the dictator.

It was not an uprising of an aggrieved populace that stopped the tyrant's breath. Despite the grim note, the heightened cynicism of the latter excesses, he and his men could still claim that the Louisiana electorate was generally with him and them. He had come close to political disaster on several occasions, but he had always convinced his commoners that he was on their side. He had rigged the election machinery against an unimpeded choice at the polls; he had clearly violated the law, as in the Fournet election and other cases; he had made mock of the democratic process in instance after instance. But he persuaded his followers that only through him could they receive the fulfillment of their needs. He had given sufficient tangible benefits, he had kept enough of his promises, to reassure them that he meant what he said.

"At least we got *something*," a North Louisiana farmer said. "Before him, we got nothing. That's the difference."

Likewise, on the national scene, he could suffer ignominious loss; he could be hooted at and warned against as a hazard to the country. But each week seemed to bring more men and women to his banner. They believed what he told them.

He had aroused in Louisiana an army that might have become a revolutionary one; he was recruiting on the national scene a force that might have turned into a revolutionary one. But he was not a revolutionary leader, despite his spleen and his hill man's resentment toward those who were above him in rank. . . .

Essentially the same forces that had produced the other Southern hillbilly governors and senators had produced Huey Long. What qualities enabled him to reach a status on the American scene achieved by none before him?

Once, in the middle of a discussion of his attributes, Huey yawned: "Just say I'm *sui generis*, and let it go at that." This flattering description was not far removed from the truth. The Kingfish fitted no mold. He was a mixture of types: the original hill-country rebel, the egotist demanding constant satisfaction, the evangelist who backslid, the overlord of a city gang. He had a single-track mind, if ever man had one. It ran from and then back to one object, Huey. He knew what he wanted, one thing above all, and of that he could never get enough: absolute control.

He had one of the keenest brains in the South; for that matter, in the nation: a hard-driving intelligence and a sharp ingenuity. Two United States Supreme Court justices declared him one of the outstanding attorneys to appear before them. He knew human nature from the bottom; he was an almost intuitive observer. He recognized few rules, even those of cold politics. "Unpredictable" was a weasel word for him; his about-faces were stupendous, his ability to halt himself in mid-action was sometimes incredible. He was ruthless; he was amoral; ethics, to him, was a word that was used in class when he went to Tulane. He was the politician-organizer without peer, a genius in manipulation, in planning and conduct of the drive. "The best campaigner America ever saw," Washington veterans termed him.

Above all, he recognized one principle: that he had to produce something in order to keep in power—jobs and money, money and benefits, benefits and jobs. He must make promises, and keep enough of those promises to maintain his hold; and at all times he must take care that another did not outpromise him.

"He did more good, and more evil, than any man in the history of his state," Dr. H. C. Nixon has declared in evaluation. He left the state with gains that will advantage it for generations to come; and with a heritage from which it will suffer for that same period.

X I I I

RELIGION

S OUTHERNERS are a churchgoing people. In many states half the population is identified with one or another of the multitudinous sects available to the pious. A visitor to the South will notice at once the power that religion has in the lives of the people. Newspapers print church news *in extenso*, carry the Sunday-school lesson for the week, and columns of pastoral advice from local preachers or syndicated religious writers in the North. The churches are big and the newest ones in the larger cities are often multi-million-dollar "plants" equipped with schoolrooms, kitchens, and marriage-chapels. It may startle a Northern visitor to see eighty thousand spectators in the stadium of a Southern university rise and stand with heads bowed just before the whistle blows for the kick-off. In a moment he will hear over the loudspeaker the voice of a Baptist or Methodist preacher asking God to permit his Holy Spirit to descend on the spectacle.

By far the largest denomination in the South is the Southern Baptist Convention. This is the "official" Baptist church, but those who prefer some other variety of the Baptist religion may choose from a multitude of splinter-groups, some of which were formed in the early eighteenth century and claim to be the "original" Baptist church in America: Free Will Baptists, Separate Baptists, Regular Baptists, Primitive Baptists (extreme Calvinists), Missionary Baptists, Free Baptists, United Baptists, Seventh-Day Baptists, Church of Christ Baptists (who practice foot-washing), Duck River Baptists (a Tennessee specialty), Two-Seeds-in-the-Spirit Predestinarian Baptists. The schisms have continued down into this century. In North Carolina the Christian Unity Baptists were organized in 1909. In 1925 a Texas-Arkansas group formed the American Baptist Association.

There are many reasons, historical and intrinsic, why the Baptist faith has flourished in the South. In frontier times, when the sectarian

474

missionaries were preaching in the wilderness, the Baptists usually got to the new settlement first, though the Methodists followed soon after and the Presbyterians were not far behind. The Baptist churches appealed to the frontiersmen. They did not require a learned clergy as the Presbyterians and Episcopalians did. Baptist farmer preachers were encouraged to carry the word ever farther into the forest depths. The Baptist congregations curbed the ungodly among their members with as much firmness as did the early New England ministers and thus helped to keep life orderly in the new settlements. When the Great Revival in the West (on the Kentucky-Tennessee border) began to spread to other Southern states, the Baptists, who had at first been reluctant to endorse camp-meeting emotionalism soon outstripped the other denominations in bringing souls to Christ by revivalistic methods. As the Baptists until recently were loosely organized, secession after secession took place. If a Baptist congregation didn't like the theology or the particular kind of immersion practiced by its leader, it could form a new Baptist association and begin bringing in the converts.

The Methodists have done nearly as well, but in the early days they suffered reverses. Since they were a schismatic denomination, they were attacked and sometimes driven out of communities where the Church of England was strong. At the time of the Revolution there was some feeling against them because their church was of recent English origin. The Presbyterians have been entrenched wherever the migrating Scotch-Irish settled: in the valley of Virginia, in North Carolina, in the Watauga and Holston settlements in east Tennessee.

In the earliest days the Church of England was the established church in Virginia only, but by 1706 it had captured South Carolina and became the official church of the colony. From 1700 to 1814 every Governor was an Anglican or Episcopalian. Shortly before the Revolution acts of establishment were put into effect in North Carolina and Georgia. When the Great Migration into the Mississippi territory began after the War of 1812, there were many Episcopalians among the emigrant planters who had left the Eastern states in search of new and rich acres.

One important reason why the various Protestant sects, and even Catholics in some instances, were able to gain a foothold early was that several of the colonies had extremely liberal laws regarding religious toleration. Unlike Massachusetts, which drove out all dissenters from the Covenant theology, the Carolinas, by the decree of the Proprietors, gave the dissenting religious sects the privilege of free worship, and even the Catholics were treated generously in South Carolina until 1696. Georgia permitted the free exercise of religion to all except the Catholics, and they were excluded only because it was feared they might serve as spies for the French in Louisiana and the Spanish in

475

Florida. European Protestants of all varieties were welcomed. An Anglican clergyman arrived with Oglethorpe's first party of settlers in 1733. (Oglethorpe himself was a High-churchman.) In the following year forty-two families of Salzburger Lutherans came to the colony with their spiritual leader. Moravians landed at Savannah in 1735, and in the next year, when Oglethorpe made his second voyage to the colony, in the ship with him were another band of Moravians and the brothers Charles and John Wesley, then ordained Anglican clergymen, but soon to be founders of Methodism.

In the colonies that were under French or Spanish rule the situation was reversed. Catholic governors did their best to run out the intrepid Protestant missionaries who tried to make converts within their domain. Not until 1763 did Protestants venture into the Mobile area. In the Mississippi region early Protestants had to hold secret meetings in their houses or in forest hide-outs. In Louisiana, Bienville's Black Code of 1724 proscribed all religions except the Catholic. At the time America acquired the Louisiana Territory there were very few Protestants in New Orleans. The situation in Texas was more favorable to Protestant colonizers though Catholicism was the prescribed religion. When the Mexican authorities began to permit bands of settlers from the States to take up land in the region, all Protestants were required by law to become Catholics—which they quite cynically did. But the officials were not very strict in enforcing the law. When in 1832 the commandant at Nacogdoches learned that a Methodist and a Presbyterian preacher had held a meeting in Sabine County, he is reported to have shrugged the trouble off in this manner:

"Are they stealing horses?" the commandant inquired. "No, Señor Commandant." "Are they killing anybody?" "No, Señor Commandant." "Are they doing anything bad?" "No, Señor Commandant." "Then leave them alone," the commandant ordered.[1]

Though the Baptists are the largest religious group in Texas today, the Catholics hold second place.

Strangely enough, Catholics are also a strong group in Kentucky. (Again the Baptists are in the lead.) For once, the Catholics arrived in a section of the upper South as soon as the Baptists did. There was a Catholic church near Rohan Knobs in the 1780's. The Catholics have continuously been active in the state. Hundreds of tourists arrive every year to have a look at the outside of the awesome Trappist monastery near Bardstown. The first Catholic Bishop of Louisville invited the monks to settle there in 1848 when their abbey at La Meilleraye in France was fearful of what might happen to it in the year of revolutions.

[1] *Texas, a Guide to the Lone Star State* (New York: Hastings House; 1940), p. 107.

Another religious organization that is strong in Kentucky and Tennessee is the Christian Church, sometimes known as the Campbellites. (Officially it is now the Church of the Disciples.) Founded in the early nineteenth century by an alliance between the followers of Barton W. Stone, who had been suspended from the Presbyterian Synod of Kentucky, and the flock of Alexander Campbell, a Presbyterian who had joined the Baptists and then seceded, this church also has many congregations in the Middle West.

As the Methodists and Baptists have grown staid and wealthy in the South, members of their congregations who long for the good old days of revivalism have found their way into various new Pentecostal sects where they can sing and shout and confess in public as joyfully as their ancestors did. Defections also sometimes take place because the Southern clergy today—and this applies to Presbyterians and Episcopalians as well as Baptists and Methodists—are often liberal in their social thinking. As Southern preachers have always told their congregations how to live their lives, these more radical ministers run into trouble when they preach world unity or the right of labor to organize or invite the Negroes to desert the Colored Baptist Association or the African Methodist Episcopal Church and worship with the white brethren in unsegregated pews. As elsewhere in America, when a family rises on the social ladder, it is fairly certain to transfer its allegiance to St. Mark's or St. Paul's (P.E.).

Thomas Jefferson's "Bill for Establishing
Religious Freedom"

Shortly after the Declaration of Independence was signed, Thomas Jefferson returned to Virginia, where he was soon one of the leaders in the exacting task of revising the laws of the Old Dominion. The Bill for a General Revision of the Laws passed on October 26, 1776, but the five revisors (Edmund Pendleton, George Wythe, George Mason, Thomas Ludwell Lee, and Jefferson) would need nearly three years for their work.

Among the 126 bills reported to the General Assembly in 1779 (by which time Jefferson was Governor of Virginia) in order to legalize the "Revised Laws," the most controversial was the "Bill for Establishing Religious Freedom." Because of his work on this bill, Jefferson was accused of infidelity and impiety. But he was justly proud of it and ranked it in importance with the Declaration of Independence.

The Episcopal Church in Virginia fought the bill. Although it did not explicitly deprive the church of its ancient privileges—this had already been done in part by the Assembly in 1776—the bill, with its ringing declaration of religious freedom and its doctrine of the necessary separation of church and state, was naturally anathema to a body that had once been the Established Church in Virginia in more than name.

Because of the controversy it provoked, the bill did not become law until 1786. James Madison led the fight that secured its passage. Jefferson was then absent as Minister in France.

The text of the bill given here is from the first printing, a broadside issued, probably without official sanction, in 1779. In its final form, as passed by the Assembly, some passages of the bill were modified.

❁

A BILL *for establishing* RELIGIOUS FREEDOM, *printed for the consideration of the* PEOPLE.

WELL aware that the opinions and belief of men depend not on their own will, but follow involuntarily the evidence proposed to their minds, that Almighty God hath created the mind free, and manifested his Supreme will that free it shall remain, by making it altogether insusceptible of restraint: That all attempts to influence it by temporal punishments or burthens, or by civil incapacitations, tend only to beget habits of hypocrisy and meanness, and are a departure from the plan of the holy author of our religion, who being Lord both of body and mind, yet chose not to propagate it by coercions on either, as was in his Almighty power to do, but to extend it by its influence on reason alone: That the impious presumption of legislators and rulers, civil as well as ecclesiastical, who, being themselves but fallible and uninspired men, have assumed dominion over the faith of others, setting up their own opinions and modes of thinking, as the only true and infallible, and as such, endeavouring to impose them on others, hath established and maintained false religions over the greatest part of the world, and through all time: That to compel a man to furnish contributions of money for the propagation of opinions which he disbelieves and abhors, is sinful and tyrannical: That even the forcing him to support this or that teacher of his own religious persuasion, is depriving him of the comfortable liberty of giving his contributions to the particular pastor whose morals he would make his pattern, and whose powers he feels most persuasive to righteousness, and is withdrawing from the Ministry those temporal rewards which, proceeding from an approbation of their personal conduct, are an additional incitement to earnest and unremitting labour for the instruction of mankind: That our civil rights have no dependence on our religious opinions, any more than on our opinions in physicks or geometry: That therefore the proscribing any citizen as unworthy the publick confidence, by laying upon him an incapacity of being called to offices of trust and emolument, unless he profess or renounce this or that religious opinion, is depriving him injuriously of those privileges and advantages to which, in common with his fellow citizens he has a natural right: That it tends also to corrupt the principles of that very religion it is meant to encourage, by bribing with a monopoly of wordly honours and emoluments, those who will externally profess and conform to it: That though indeed these are criminal who do not withstand such temptation, yet neither are those innocent who lay the bait in their way: That the opinions of men are not the object of civil government, nor under its jurisdiction: That to suffer the civil Magistrate to intrude his powers into the field of opinion, and to restrain the profession or propagation of principles on supposition of their ill tendency, is a dangerous fallacy, which at once destroys all religious liberty; because he being of course Judge of that tendency will make his own opinions the rule of judgment, and approve or condemn the sentiments of others only as they shall square with, or differ from his own: That it is time enough for the rightful

purposes of civil government for its officers to interfere when principles break out into overt acts against peace and good order: And
finally, that truth is great and will prevail if left to herself; that she is
the proper and sufficient antagonist to errour, and has nothing to fear
from the conflict, unless by human interposition, disarmed of her
natural weapons, free argument and debate; errours ceasing to be dangerous when it is permitted freely to contradict them

WE the General Assembly of *Virginia* do enact, that no man shall be
compelled to frequent or support any religous Worship place or Ministry whatsoever, nor shall be enforced, restrained, molested, or
burthened in his body or goods, nor shall otherwise suffer on account
of his religious opinions or belief, but that all men shall be free to
profess, and by argument to maintain their opinions in matters of religion, and that the same shall in no wise diminish, enlarge, or affect
their civil capacities.

AND though we well know that this Assembly, elected by the people for the ordinary purposes of legislation only, have no power to
restrain the acts of succeeding Assemblies, constituted with powers
equal to our own, and that therefore to declare this act irrevocable
would be of no effect in law; yet we are free to declare, and do declare, that the rights hereby asserted are of the natural rights of mankind, and that if any act shall be hereafter passed to repeal the present,
or to narrow its operation, such act will be an infringement of natural
right.

The War of the Churches in Virginia

*When the publishing firm of Houghton, Mifflin was looking for a
writer to prepare the volume on Virginia in its American Commonwealths series, it naturally turned to John Esten Cooke (1830–86).
From the appearance of his first novels,* Leather Stocking and Silk *and*
The Virginia Comedians (*both in 1854*), *he had been known as the
novelist of Virginia. His work in preparing* Stories of the Old Dominion (*1879*), *though this was a book for boys, had carried him back to
some of the sources he made use of in* Virginia: A History of the People
(*1883*). *In this volume Cooke wrote with particular feeling about "The
War of the Churches." The tribulations of the Episcopal Church in*

Virginia during the late eighteenth century (for which Jefferson's "Bill for Establishing Religious Freedom" was in part responsible) affected deeply a man who had written in his diary, while at work on The Virginia Comedians: *"Last Sunday—March 5—I joined St. James's Church. It is the greatest event of my life and I devoutly thank God for having changed my heart and made me see the sublime light of heaven."*

The passage given below is slightly condensed from pages 390–6 in the 1891 edition of Virginia: A History of the People. *For further notes on Cooke and another example of his historical writing, see above, p. 295.*

THREATENING hands were raised in every quarter against the Established Church, and the attacks of her combined enemies, the non-conformists of all descriptions, began in earnest. They were to overthrow the Establishment at last, and destroy it, root and branch, but as yet it was too strong for them; and the civil authorities, acting in its supposed interests, resorted to persecution. This was directed chiefly at the Baptists, who had recently become a strong communion. The first church was formally established in 1760, but soon there were numbers of others in Spotsylvania, Orange, Louisa, and Fluvanna. A passionate impulse swayed the preachers of the Baptist faith. The propaganda went on without rest. They saw visions which spurred them to call others to repentance, and the true form of baptism. James Read, in North Carolina, had a mysterious call by night. In his sleep he was heard crying "Virginia! Virginia!" and obeying the heavenly voice he set out and reached Orange, where great crowds flocked to listen to him. Soon the Establishment took alarm. The clergy denounced the new sect, calling them followers of the German Anabaptists, and predicting a repetition of the horrors of Munster. But this the Baptists indignantly denied, asserting that they were preachers of the true Gospel only; if they disturbed the lethargy of the Establishment it was not their fault. Persecution followed. In June, 1768, three preachers of the new church, John Waller, Lewis Craig, and James Childs, were arrested by the sheriff of Spotsylvania. They were offered their liberty if they would promise to discontinue preaching; but that had no more effect in their case than in the case of John Bunyan. They gloried in their martyrdom. As they went to prison through the streets of Fredericksburg, they raised the resounding hymn, "Broad is the road that leads to death." Through the windows of the jail they preached to great throngs of people. When this had gone on for more than a month they were released; they had resolutely persisted in making no promises to discontinue their efforts. Their persecutors were even ashamed. When they were arraigned for "preaching the Gospel contrary to law," Patrick Henry, who had ridden fifty miles to witness the trial, suddenly rose and exclaimed:

"May it please your worships, what did I hear read? Did I hear an expression that these men whom your worships are about to try for misdemeanor are charged with *preaching the Gospel of the Son of God?*"

The solemn voice is said to have deeply moved all who heard it. The State prosecutor "turned pale with agitation," and the court were near dismissing the accused. Elsewhere the persecution went on; in Chesterfield, Middlesex, Caroline, and other counties. Men were imprisoned for their faith; it was a reproduction of the monstrous proceedings in the Mother Country. But the result was what might have been foreseen by any but the judicially blind. The Baptists only grew stronger. In 1774 the *Separates* had fifty-four Churches, and the *Regulars* were steadily increasing also. One and all, these and other Dissenters, were actuated, says one of their advocates, by two strong principles—love of freedom and "hatred of the Church Establishment." They were "resolved never to relax their efforts until it was utterly destroyed," and they lived to see the wish fulfilled.

In this bitter antagonism to the Establishment the Methodists had no part; they were "a society within the Church," and advocated only a more evangelical spirit in worship. But the Quakers and Presbyterians cooperated with the Baptist Dissenters and were unresting in their hostility to the union of Church and State. The noble memorial from the Presbytery of Hanover, which may yet be seen on the yellow old sheet in the Virginia Archives, sums up the whole case with admirable eloquence and force. It is trenchant and severe, but that was natural. It is the great protest of Dissent in all the years. . . .

The immemorial hostility thus pursued the Episcopacy to the end. The dislike of the Episcopal clergy had terminated in dislike of the Episcopal tenets, which Samuel Davies had thought so admirable. In demanding their incontestable rights, which it was a shame to have so long withheld from them, the opponents of the Establishment demanded them with outcries against the Episcopacy, which were neither discriminating nor just. The vestries had been largely responsible for that ill-living in the clergy. Few good men would come to preach in Virginia when their places in the parishes depended upon the whim of the "parson's masters"; when they were scanned with critical eyes, to be dismissed at a moment's warning. The Church, too, had now come to be hated by its old adversaries. It was treated without mercy when it was disabled and powerless. It is not a pleasant spectacle, looking back to those old times. One fancies, while reading the story, some poor animal with legs broken, dragging its bleeding body along, pursued by relentless enemies, who worry it with sharp teeth in the very death agony. The law for exempting Dissenters overthrew the Establishment; that was just. But this was not enough. When the Church, on its petition (1784), was made a body corporate to manage its own affairs, new excitement arose. It was in vain to point out that other communions were at full liberty to become corporations. The Presbytery of Hanover were implacable, and protested against the law. They would have nothing to do with it. They cried with comic alarm that the old Establishment, which was deadest of the dead, was coming to life again; and the law was repealed.

Lastly the Bill for Religious Freedom, the darling project of Jefferson, consolidated the policy of non-intervention in matters of faith into a compact system. There was no longer any Establishment or shadow of such a thing; at the end of the century it was dead in all its parts. But even that was not enough. We have set forth its persecuting spirit; let us see how it was persecuted in turn. The modern principle that the spoils belong to the victors was applied to it. The old hostility was not dead, it had only gone to sleep; and now it woke and struck a last blow. The glebe lands of the Church were directed to be sold (1802). It was not to keep its parsonages, the donations made to it, or the vessels used in Baptism and the Holy Communion. The question came before the Court of Appeals, of which Edmund Pendleton was now president. He was bitterly opposed to the sale of the Church property, which he considered a great wrong. But just before the decision, while he was writing his opinion, he suddenly expired. His vote would have prevented it; and doubtless his sudden death was regarded by zealots as the intervention of Providence.

The Court decided against the Church. It is true the law forbade the sale of the Church edifices and the property in them; but this provision protected neither. The parishes were obliterated and the clergy scattered. Thus all fell into the hands of persons who had small respect for religious things. The Church buildings were put to profane uses. "A reckless sensualist," says Dr. Hawks, "administered the morning dram to his guests from the silver cup" used in the Holy Communion. Another "converted a marble baptismal font into a watering-trough for horses."

What to say of these things? There is nothing to say. It was simply a phase of this poor human nature which all the years reproduce. It was not, however, a misfortune to the Church thus to fall before its enemies. It had persecuted and reaped the harvest; it was persecuted in turn, and its day of adversity was better for it than its day of prosperity. Its adversaries overthrew it utterly, tearing up, as they supposed, its very roots; and through all the long years of the first quarter of the new century "the dust lay an inch thick" on the unused Prayer Books. The old church buildings were closed or had fallen into the hands of vandals. The ancient tombstones were defaced, the holy vessels profaned; ministers and people were dispersed, and worshiped only in private; and when Bishop Meade applied to Chief Justice Marshall for a subscription he gave it, but said that it was useless to attempt to revive so dead a thing as the Episcopal Church.

Nevertheless it revived. Excellent Dr. Griffith had been elected the first Virginia bishop (1786); James Madison the second (1790); and Richard Channing Moore the third (1814). It was left for the pure apostle, William Meade, to labor without ceasing and raise the prostrate Church from the dust. In the years preceding and following his ordination as bishop (1829), he was unresting. He went to and fro on horseback, an itinerant apostle preaching the faith. He was a man of great ability, pure in heart and resolute of will. At his call the old worshipers came back to the ruined places, and the dismantled churches, half overgrown with brambles and ivy, were once more thronged. Life had still been in the body, an obstinate vitality which refused to be trodden out. What the Church had lost was the impure blood, and it rose purified and invigorated.

Bishop Asbury Rides the Methodist Circuits in the South

It fairly makes one's bones ache to read even a few pages of Francis Asbury's journal. Indefatigable in the Lord's work from his arrival in America in 1771 until his death in 1816, the good Bishop is said to have covered more than three hundred thousand American miles on horseback and, when age advanced on him, in his battered old sulky pulled by an ancient gray mare.

Soon after the Wesleyan movement began in England, in 1739, lay preachers arrived in the colonies. In 1766, Methodist societies were formed in New York and Maryland. But the work of conversion was carried on in a rather haphazard fashion and a strong organizer was needed in the colonies. John Wesley found the man he wanted in young Francis Asbury, who was only twenty-six when he volunteered for service in America. Born near Birmingham, the son of a pious mother who encouraged her son's religious precocity, Asbury had traveled as a lay preacher in the Black Country circuits near his birthplace before he was twenty-one. In 1767 he was admitted to the ministry by the Wesleys, a few days before his twenty-second birthday.

Once in America, Asbury began to show his remarkable powers of leadership and organization. In a series of adroit moves he became by 1782 the virtual head of American Methodism. Wesley tried several times to put him in his place, but Asbury was determined that the Church in America should be autonomous and he was not to be checked even by the anger of the founder, who wrote to him in 1788: "I study to be little; you study to be great. I creep; you strut along. . . . How can you, how dare you suffer yourself to be called bishop? I shudder, I start at the very thought! Men may call me a knave or a fool, a rascal, a scoundrel, and I am content; but they shall never, by my consent, call me a bishop. For my sake, for God's sake, for Christ's sake, put an end to this!"

But Wesley's American "superintendent" was always Bishop Asbury to the thousands upon thousands to whom he preached, in fields, barns, cabins, meeting-houses, from New Hampshire to the Mississippi Territory. Suffering from ill-health much of the time, as well as from self-medication and the strange diets he invented for himself, Asbury was not to be stopped by hostile members of other sects, by flooded rivers or unpassable mountains, by filthy houses or filthy beds. There were souls to be saved even in the remotest settlements.

Asbury lived to see the Methodists established as one of the three dominant religious groups in the South—the others being the Presbyterians and the Baptists. During the Revolution Methodism was associated with Toryism (John Wesley was outspokenly hostile to the American cause). The sect was persecuted by the Established Church in Virginia and had to fight the Baptists in Kentucky and Tennessee. The gentry disliked the Methodists because they early took a stand against slavery, an issue that led in 1844 to the breaking apart of the Church into Northern and Southern divisions. Among the people of the backwoods the strictness of the Methodist Discipline was often a handicap, though the Church's emphasis on free grace won converts among those who had turned their backs on the Calvinism of their Eastern bringing-up.

As a preacher Asbury was austere and dignified, winning souls by his message rather than his eloquence. Yet he rejoiced in the fervor of the new camp meetings and did little to curb the excesses of revivalism.

*All was evidence of the outpouring of the Lord's grace in America.
When the old man died he was characteristically "making all possible
haste" to reach Baltimore for the Conference of 1816.*

*Asbury resolved to keep a diary when he embarked for America in
1771. It was published in three volumes in 1852 as* Journal of Rev.
Francis Asbury (*New York: Lane & Scott*).

❁

Thursday, 11 [January 1787]. Rode through the snow to Fairfield
[Virginia]. Here a Captain R. had turned the people out of the barn in
which worship was held, and threatened to take brother Paup to jail if
he did not show his authority for preaching; after all this vapouring of
the valiant Captain, when the affair was brought before the court,
Captain R— found it convenient to ask pardon of our brother, although
he sat upon the bench in his own cause:—so the matter ended. The
Lord is at work in the Neck: [1] more than one hundred have been added
to the society since conference, who are a simple, loving, tender people.

We had a good time on *Friday*, the 12th; I spoke on Acts xxvi, 18. I
think God has spoken by me to S—s, a wild man—but the Lord can
tame him. O Lord, speak for thyself!

Sunday, 14. We had a crowd at the Presbyterian meetinghouse in Lancaster, to whom I delivered a very rough discourse: it was a close and
searching time, and we had many communicants, both white and
coloured. . . .

Friday, 14 [March 1788]. Our conference began, and we had a very
free, open time. On *Saturday* night I preached on "I have set watchmen
upon thy walls," &c. On the *Sabbath*, on "The Lord turned and looked
on Peter," &c. It was a gracious season, both in the congregation, and
in the love-feast. While another was speaking in the morning to a very
crowded house, and many outside, a man made a riot at the door; an
alarm at once took place; the ladies leaped out at the windows of the
church, and a dreadful confusion ensued. Again, whilst I was speaking
at night, a stone was thrown against the north side of the church; then
another on the south; a third came through the pulpit window, and
struck near me inside the pulpit.[2] I however continued to speak on; my
subject, "How beautiful upon the mountains," &c.

Upon the whole, I have had more liberty to speak in Charleston this
visit than I ever had before, and am of opinion that God will work
here: but our friends are afraid of the cross. . . .

[1] The region in Virginia between the Potomac and Rappahannock rivers is
called the Northern Neck.

[2] Asbury's preaching against slavery angered the Charlestonians.

FRANCIS ASBURY: *Riding the Methodist Circuits*

Thursday, 10 [July 1788]. We had to cross the Alleghany mountain again, at a bad passage. Our course lay over mountains and through valleys, and the mud and mire was such as might scarcely be expected in December. We came to an old, forsaken habitation in Tyger's Valley.[3] Here our horses grazed about, while we boiled our meat. Midnight brought us up at Jones's, after riding forty, or perhaps fifty miles. The old man, our host, was kind enough to wake us up at four o'clock in the morning. We journeyed on through devious lonely wilds, where no food might be found, except what grew in the woods, or was carried with us. We met with two women who were going to see their friends, and to attend the quarterly meeting at Clarksburg [West Virginia]. Near midnight we stopped at A—'s, who hissed his dogs at us: but the women were determined to get to quarterly meeting, so we went in. Our supper was tea. Brothers Phoebus and Cook took to the woods; old —— gave up his bed to the women. I lay along the floor on a few deerskins with the fleas. That night our poor horses got no corn; and next morning they had to swim across the Monongahela. After a twenty miles' ride we came to Clarksburg, and man and beast were so outdone that it took us ten hours to accomplish it. I lodged with Col. Jackson. Our meeting was held in a long, close room belonging to the Baptists. Our use of the house it seems gave offence. There attended about seven hundred people, to whom I preached with freedom; and I believe the Lord's power reached the hearts of some. After administering the sacrament, I was well satisfied to take my leave. We rode thirty miles to Father Haymond's, after three o'clock, Sunday afternoon, and made it nearly eleven before we came in. About midnight we went to rest, and rose at five o'clock next morning. My mind has been severely tried under the great fatigue endured both by myself and my horse. O, how glad should I be of a plain, clean plank to lie on, as preferable to most of the beds; and where the beds are in a bad state, the floors are worse. The gnats are almost as troublesome here, as the mosquitoes in the lowlands of the seaboard. This country will require much work to make it tolerable. The people are, many of them, of the boldest cast of adventurers, and with some the decencies of civilized society are scarcely regarded, two instances of which I myself witnessed. The great landholders who are industrious will soon show the effects of the aristocracy of wealth, by lording it over their poorer neighbours, and by securing to themselves all the offices of profit or honour. On the one hand savage warfare teaches them to be cruel; and on the other, the preaching of Antinomians poisons them with error in doctrine: good moralists they are not, and good Christians they cannot be, unless they are better taught.

Tuesday, 15. I had a lifeless, disorderly people to hear me at Morgan-

[3] Tygart's, in Greenup County, Kentucky.

town [West Virginia], to whom I preached on "I will hear what God the Lord will speak." It is matter of grief to behold the excesses, particularly in drinking, which abound here. I preached at a new chapel near Colonel Martin's, and felt much life, love, and power. Rode to the widow R—'s, and refreshed with a morsel to eat; thence to M. Harden's, where, though we had an earth floor, we had good beds and table entertainment. . . .

TENNESSEE.—*Tuesday*, 6 [April 1790]. We were compelled to ride through the rain, and crossed the Stone Mountain: those who wish to know how rough it is may tread in our path. What made it worse to me was, that while I was looking to see what was become of our guide, I was carried off with full force against a tree that hung across the road some distance from the ground, and my head received a very great jar, which, however, was lessened by my having on a hat that was strong in the crown. We came on to the dismal place called Roan's Creek, which was pretty full. Here we took a good breakfast on our tea, bacon, and bread. Reaching Watauga, we had to swim our horses, and ourselves to cross in a canoe; up the Iron Mountain we ascended, where we had many a seat to rest, and many a weary step to climb. At length we came to Greer's, and halted for the night.

Wednesday, 7. We reached Nelson's chapel about one o'clock, after riding about eighteen miles. Now it is that we must prepare for danger, in going through the wilderness. I received a faithful letter from brother Poythress in Kentucky, encouraging me to come. This letter I think well deserving of publication. I found the poor preachers indifferently clad, with emaciated bodies, and subject to hard fare; yet I hope they are rich in faith.

Friday, 9. After receiving great kindness from dear sister Nelson, we came on to brother Bull's, who wrought for us, *gratis*, what we wanted in shoeing our horses. Thence we went on to brother Gott's, and to brother P—'s; and thence, groping through the woods, to brother Easley's; depending on the fidelity of the Kentucky people, hastening them, and being unwilling they should wait a moment for me. We crossed Holstein at Smith's ferry, and rode thirty miles to Amie's, where we were well entertained for our money. Coming along, I complained that the people would take no pay for their food or services; that complaint has ceased. Very unwell as I was we pushed down Holstein to the last house; here we had no hope of company from the eastern or western side. We turned out our horses to graze, and they strayed off; so here we are anchored indeed.

The unsettled state of my stomach and bowels makes labour and life a burden. We are now in a house in which a man was killed by the savages; and O, poor creatures! they are but one remove from savages themselves. I consider myself in danger; but my God will keep me whilst thousands pray for me.

Sunday, 11. My soul is humbled before God, waiting to see the solution of this dark providence. The man of the house is gone after some horses supposed to be stolen by Indians. I have been near fainting; but my soul is revived again, and my bodily strength is somewhat renewed. If these difficulties, which appear to impede my path, are designed to prevent my going to Kentucky, I hope to know shortly. I spent the *Sabbath* at Robert Bean's. In the evening, a company of eleven came to go forward. Our horses were not to be found without a great sum.

Monday morning, 12. We loaded brother Anderson's little horse with my great bags, and two pair smaller; four saddles, with blankets and provender. We then set out and walked ten miles, and our horses were brought to us, and those who brought them were pleased to take what we pleased to give. Brother A— sought the Lord by fasting and prayer, and had a strong impression that it was the will of God that I should not go with that company.

Tuesday, 13. We came back to A—'s,—a poor sinner. He was highly offended that we prayed so loud in his house. He is a distiller of whisky, and boasts of gaining £300 per annum by the brewing of his poison. We talked very plainly; and I told him that it was of necessity, and not of choice, we were there; that I feared the face of no man. He said, he did not desire me to trouble myself about his soul. Perhaps the greatest offence was given by my speaking against distilling and slave-holding.

Having now been upon expenses from *Friday* until this day, for four horses and three men, I judged it high time to move.

Thursday, 15. We rode fifty miles; and next day preached at Owens's.

Saturday, 17. We rode on with great violence, which made me feel very serious.

Sunday, 18. Brother W. preached at General Russell's, on the birth, character, and office of John the Baptist.

Monday, 19. I resolved on taking a *proper* dose of Tartar-emetic; this has wrought me well, and I hope for better health.

From *December* 14, 1789, to *April* 20, 1790, we compute to have travelled two thousand five hundred and seventy-eight miles. Hitherto hath the Lord helped. Glory! glory to our God! . . .

Tuesday, 29 [January 1793]. We reach Savannah. Next day I rode twelve miles along a fine, sandy road to view the ruins of Mr. Whitefield's Orphan-House:[4] we found the place, and having seen the cop-

[4] Bethesda still stands, the oldest existing orphanage in America. It was founded in 1740 by George Whitefield, the great preacher who succeeded John Wesley as minister in Savannah. On the death, in 1791, of Selina, Countess of Huntingdon, who had aided the orphanage, it was permitted to fall into decay. The institution suffered many other vicissitudes. Finally, in 1867, it was restored to its original use.

perplate, which I recognised, I felt very awful; the wings are yet stand-ing, though much injured, and the school house still more. It is reported that Mr. Whitefield observed, whilst eating his last dinner in the house, "This house was built for God; and cursed be the man that puts it to any other use." The land for the support of the school is of little value, except two rice plantations, which we passed in our route.

I returned to Savannah, and preached on Luke xix, 10, to a serious people, with whom I had liberty.

Friday, February 1. I came to Ebenezer, and had a pleasing interview with Mr. Bergman; he cannot speak much English. The Lord has cer-tainly something in design for this man, more than to be buried in this place. We rode through rice plantations for nearly two miles, and were entangled in the swamp. O, how dreadful to be here in the dark!

Saturday, 2. I am not enough in prayer. I have said more than was for the glory of God concerning those who have left the American con-nexion, and who have reviled Mr. Wesley, Mr. Fletcher, Doctor Coke, and poor *me.* O that I could trust the Lord more than I do, and leave his cause wholly in his own hands!

This being *Saturday,* we rest to read and write, having ridden, since *Monday* morning, about one hundred and twenty-four miles.

I reflect upon the present ruin of the Orphan-House; and taking a view of the money expended, the persons employed, the preachers sent over, I was led to inquire, where are they? and how was it sped? The earth, the army, the Baptists, the Church, the Independents, have swal-lowed them all up at this *windmill end of the continent.* A wretched country this!—but there are souls, precious souls, worth worlds. . . .

TENNESSEE.—*Saturday,* 25 [April 1797]. We were escorted by three brave young Dutchmen. After riding three miles we began to scale the rocks, hills, and mountains, worming through pathless woods, to shun a deep ford. I thought, ride I must; but no—the company concluded to walk. I gave my horse the direction of himself, under Providence. I had to step from rock to rock, hands and feet busy; but my breath was soon gone, and I gave up the cause, and took horse again, and resolved that I would ride down the hills, although I had not ridden up them. At last (hit or miss, Providence is all) into the path we came, and thence kept down the river and over to Little Toe, bearing down the stream. When we had passed the Gap, we wished to feed; but the man had no corn to sell. We tried, man and horse, to reach Nathan Davies's; where we ar-rived, and were made comfortable. I was much spent with the labours of this day. Hearing of the quarterly meeting at Dunworth's, I rode on *Sunday,* 26th, twelve miles, and arrived time enough for me to give them a feeble, yet faithful talk, on Isa. i, 9. I am of opinion it is as hard, or harder, for the people of the west to gain religion as any other. When I consider where they came from, where they are, and how they are, and how they are called to go farther, their being unsettled, with so many objects to take their attention, with the health and good air they enjoy; and when I reflect that not one in a hundred came here to get religion, but rather to get plenty of good land, I think it will be well if some or many do not eventually lose their souls. I was met by our brethren, Kobler, Burke, and Page. I rested on *Monday* and *Tuesday,* to take breath and medicine. I find myself so hardly put to it at times that I can only journalize a little. We concluded, as there are not proper stations on the Cumberland path, it will not do for me to lodge on the ground: the general opinion is against it. We are to try to go to Kentucky next week. . . .

Tuesday, 6 [February 1798]. My fever was very light last night. I received a most loving letter from the Charleston conference; there is great peace and good prospects there. I hope to be able to move next week. I have well considered my journal: it is inelegant; yet it conveys much information of the state of religion and country. It is well suited to common readers; the wise need it not. I have a desire that my journals should be published, at least after my death, if not before. I make no doubt but others have *laboured:* but in England, Scotland, and Ireland, and those kingdoms which have been civilized and improved one thousand years, and which are under such improvements, no ministers could have *suffered* in those days, and in those countries, as in America, the most ancient parts of which have not been settled two hundred years, some parts not forty, others not thirty, twenty, nor ten, and some not five years. I have frequently skimmed along the frontiers, for four and five hundred miles, from Kentucky to Green Brier, on the very edge of the wilderness; and thence along Tigers Valley to Clarksburgh on the Ohio. These places, if not the haunts of savage men, yet abound with wild beasts. I am only known by name to many of our people, and some of our local preachers; and unless the people were all together, they could not tell what I have had to cope with. I make no doubt the Methodists are, and will be, a numerous and wealthy people, and their preachers who follow us will not know our struggles but by comparing the present improved state of the country with what it was in our days, as exhibited in my journal and other records of that day.

The "Great Revival in the West" or the "Second Awakening"

In the 1740's the Presbyterian and Congregational churches in America were struck by a tidal wave of revivalism which divided congregations and often set minister against minister, and synod against synod. This "Great Awakening" or the "Great Work" was marked in both the North and the South by thousands of conversions brought about by the fervent exhortations of the preachers and the public confessions of the converted sinners, who in their ectasy often fell into fainting fits and convulsions. The remarkable sermons of George Whitefield, a disciple of the Wesleys then in America, helped send the revival fever-high. By the time it had subsided the issue of emotionalism in conversion had so divided the churches that conservatives who deprecated revivalism were called the Old Sides and those who saw in it the work of God had got the name of New Lights. The New Light ministers were as well educated as their conservative opponents, the greatest of them being Jonathan Edwards, the best theologian of his time. The New Lights presently founded colleges of their own, chiefly Princeton in the North, and, in Virginia, Hampden-Sydney and Liberty Hall, now Washington and Lee.

The "Second Awakening" or the "Great Revival in the West," described in the passage printed below, was a very different movement from the "Great Awakening." It took place sixty years later in the "West"—that is, on the Kentucky-Tennessee frontier—and then spread to many other states. The leaders were not men of the intellectual caliber of Jonathan Edwards or Samuel Davies, but exhorters with little theological training. The sinners they converted were frontiersmen, hungry for the frenzied "exercises" of the camp meetings which soon became a feature of the revival. Further, several sects were soon involved, at first the Presbyterians and Methodists, then the Baptists, and finally the Shakers, who, when they heard the "good news" at their colony in New York State, sent out a delegation of missionaries, in 1805, to share in the great work.

The following account of the "Great Revival" was written many years after the events described and by a man who had not witnessed them. But he was brought up in the country in which the orgies of conversion took place and his father, the Elder Reuben Ross, was a famous

Baptist preacher who had known many of the participants. His description has the virtue of objectivity (which many of the partisan contemporary accounts lack). It also relies heavily on the statements made by such important witnesses as Elder Stone, the Presbyterian, Peter Cartwright, the Methodist "local" preacher, and Lorenzo Dow, one of the most powerful of the camp-meeting exhorters.

This account of the "Great Revival" is taken from pages 233–41 of James Ross's Life and Times of Elder Reuben Ross *(Philadelphia: Grant, Faires & Rodgers; 1882).*

❁

IN the year 1799, several ministers of the Presbyterian Church, Elders McGready, Hodge, and Rankin, and one belonging to the Methodist Episcopal Church, Elder John McGee, held a sacramental meeting, at the old Red River Church, which stood on or near the same site as the church of that name now does. The meeting drew together a large congregation, considering the thinly settled country.

On Sunday Elder Hodge preached and, as he was often heard to say afterwards, addressed the assemblage with a freedom and power, never before felt. The hearers though riveted in their attention, remained silent and quiet. As he closed his discourse, Elder John McGee rose, singing,

> Come, Holy Spirit, Heavenly Dove,
> With all thy quickening powers,
> Kindle a flame of sacred love,
> In these cold hearts of ours.

He had not sung more than the verse quoted, when an aged lady, Mrs. Pacely, sitting quite across the congregation to the left, and Mrs. Clark, also advanced in years, seated to the right, began in rather suppressed but distinct tones, to hold a sort of dialogue with each other, and to reciprocate sentiments of praise and thanksgiving to the Most High, for his grace in redemption. Still the preacher sang on, and the venerable ladies praised God, in louder tones. The preacher, still singing came down from the pulpit, intending to take the hands of these two happy old sisters; shaking hands, however, as he passed along, with all those within his reach. Suddenly persons began to fall as he passed through the crowd—some as dead; some most piteously crying for mercy; and a few, here and there, lifting their voices high, in the praise of the Redeemer. Among these last was Elder William McGee, who fell to the floor, and, though shouting praises, was for some time so overpowered as to be unable to rise. The other ministers, McGready,

493

Hodge, and Rankin, were so surprised and astonished at this apparent confusion in the house of the Lord, that they made their way out of the door, and stood asking each other in whispers, "what is to be done." Elder Hodge looking in at the door, and seeing all on the floor, praising or praying, said, "We can do nothing. If this be of Satan, it will soon come to an end; but if it is of God, our efforts and fears are in vain. I think it is of God, and will join in ascribing glory to his name."

He walked into the house where the others presently followed. Rapidly those who had fallen to the floor mourning and crying for mercy, arose, two or more at a time, shouting praise, for the evidences felt in their own souls, of sins forgiven—for "redeeming grace and dying love." So there remained no more place that day, for preaching or administering the Supper. From thirty to forty, that evening professed to be converted.

Thus began that wonderful religious movement, which not only pervaded Kentucky, Tennessee, and Ohio, but crossed the mountains, and spread over many of the states on the Atlantic seaboard. On account of the strange bodily agitations attending it, it was considered the most wonderful event of the times.

"The next appointment was for the Saturday and Sunday following, at what is to this day called the Beach Meeting House, situated a little south of the Cumberland Ridge, ten miles west of Gallatin, Sumner County, Tennessee." Here a vast crowd assembled, and scenes similar to those at Red River Meeting house transpired. But the most wonderful meeting was at Muddy River Church, a few miles north of Russellville, Kentucky, the Sunday after. "The people came in from the two states twenty, thirty, fifty, and even a hundred miles. Some came in tented wagons, some in open wagons, some in carts, some on horse back, and many on foot."

The meeting house, hours before preaching commenced, could not seat the third part of those on the ground. And still they came by dozens, fifties, and hundreds. A temporary pulpit was quickly erected under the shady trees, and seats made of large trees felled and laid upon the ground. The preaching commenced, and soon the presence of the all-pervading Power was felt, throughout the vast assembly.

"As night came on it was apparent the crowd did not intend to disperse. What was to be done? Some took wagons, and hurried to bring in straw from barns and treading-yards. Some fell to sewing the wagon sheets together, and others to cutting forks and poles, on which to spread them. Counterpanes, coverlets, and sheets were also fastened together, to make tents or camps. Others were dispatched to town and to the nearest houses to collect bacon, meal, flour, with cooking utensils to prepare food for the multitude. In a few hours it was a sight to see how much was gathered together for the encampment."

"Fires were made, cooking begun; and by dark, candles lighted, and fixed to a hundred trees; and here was the first, and perhaps the most beautiful camp ground the world ever saw." (See Smith's *Legends of the War of the Revolution.*)

Barton W. Stone, at that time in the fellowship of the Presbyterian Church, and Pastor of the Cane Ridge and Concord congregation, in Bourbon County, Kentucky, heard of the mighty work going on in southern Kentucky, and determined to go down and see for himself. He seems to have been a man of fine talents, respectable learning, spotless character, and childlike simplicity; but easily attracted by what was strange and marvelous. Early in the spring of 1801, he set out for Logan County, to attend one of the great camp meetings.

"On arriving," he writes, "I found the multitude assembled on the edge of a prairie, where they continued encamped many successive days and nights, during all which time, worship was being conducted in some parts of the encampment. The scene to me was passing strange. It baffles description. Many, very many, fell down, as men slain in battle, and continued, for hours together, in a comparatively breathless and motionless state. Sometimes for a few moments reviving and exhibiting symptoms of life, by a deep groan, or piercing shriek, or by a prayer for mercy most fervently uttered. After lying thus for hours, they obtained deliverance. The gloomy cloud that had covered their faces, seemed gradually and visibly to disappear; and hope, in smiles, to brighten into joy. They would then arise, shouting deliverance, and address the surrounding multitude in language truly eloquent and impressive. With astonishment did I hear women and children declaring the wonderful works of God and the glorious mysteries of the gospel. Their appeals were solemn, heart-rending, bold, and free. Under such addresses, many others would fall down in the same state, from which the speakers had just been delivered.

"Two or three of my particular acquaintances from a distance, were struck down. I sat patiently by one of them, whom I knew to be a careless sinner, for hours, and observed with critical attention, every thing that passed, from the beginning to the end. I noticed the momentary revivings as from death, the humble confession, the fervent prayer and ultimate deliverance; then, the solemn thanks and praise to God, the affectionate exhortation to companions and to the people round to repent and come to Jesus. I was astonished at the knowledge of gospel truth displayed in these exhortations. The effect was that several sank down into the same appearance of death. After attending to many such cases, my conviction was complete, that it was a good work, nor has my mind wavered since on the subject."

Elder Stone, in chapter sixth of his book, enumerates six kinds of bodily agitations during this great excitement. The falling exercise; the jerks; the dancing exercise; the barking exercise; the laughing exercise; and the singing exercise.

"The falling exercise," he says, "was very common among all classes both saints and sinners of every age, and every grade, from the philosopher to the clown. The subject of this exercise, would generally, with a piercing scream, fall, like a log, on the floor, earth, or mud, and appear as dead.

"The jerks cannot be so easily described. Sometimes, the subject of the jerks would be affected in the whole system. When the head alone was affected, it would be jerked backward and forward, or from side to side, so quickly that the features of the face could not be distinguished. When the whole system was affected, I have seen a person stand in one place, and jerk backwards and forward, in quick succession, their hands nearly touching the floor behind and before. All classes, saints as well as sinners, strong as well as weak, were thus affected. They could not account for it, but some have told me, these were among the happiest moments of their lives.

"The dancing exercise generally began with the jerks, and was peculiar to professors of religion. The subject, after jerking awhile, began to dance, and then the jerks would cease. Such dancing was indeed *heavenly* to the spectators. There was nothing in it like levity, or calculated to excite levity in beholders. The smile of heaven shone in the countenance of the subject, and assimilated to angels, appeared the whole person. [Rather highly colored!]

"The barking, as opposers contemptuously called it, was nothing but the jerks. A person afflicted with the jerks, especially in the head, would often make a grunt or a bark, (if you please) from the suddenness of the jerk. This name "barking," seems to have had its origin from an old Presbyterian preacher of East Tennessee. He had gone into the fields for private devotion, and was seized with the jerks. Standing near a sapling, he caught hold of it, to prevent his falling, and as his head jerked back, he uttered a grunt or kind of noise similar to a bark, his face being turned upward. Some wag discovered him in this position, and reported that he found him barking up a tree.

"The laughing exercise was frequent, confined solely to the

religious. It was a loud, hearty laughter, but one *sui generis*. It excited laughter in no one else. The subject appeared rapturously solemn, and his laughter excited solemnity in saint and sinner. It was truly indescribable.

"The running exercise, was nothing more than that persons, feeling something of these bodily agitations, through fear attempted to run away, and thus escape from them, but it commonly happened that they ran not far before they fell or became so greatly agitated, they could proceed no farther.

"The singing exercise is more unaccountable than anything I ever saw. The subject, in a very happy state of mind, would sing most melodiously, not from the mouth or nose, but from the breast entirely, the sound issuing thence. Such music silenced everything and attracted the attention of all. It was most heavenly. None could ever be tired of hearing it. Dr. J. P. Campbell and myself, were together at a meeting, and were attending to a pious lady thus exercised, and concluded it to be something beyond anything we had ever known in nature."

This is, in part, what Elder Stone saw and heard, when he visited Southern Kentucky, in 1801, at the commencement of these strange exercises, expressed in his *naive,* or artless way. Lorenzo Dow, while on tour of preaching in 1804, says:

"I passed by a meeting house, where I observed the undergrowth had been cut down for a camp-meeting, and from fifty to one hundred saplings cut off about breast high, and on inquiring about it, learned that they had been left for the people to jerk by.

This excited his curiosity, and on going round, he "found where the people had laid hold of them and jerked so powerfully that, they had kicked up the earth, like horses in fly-time"! He believed the jerking was "entirely involuntary, and not to be accounted for, on any known principle."

Peter Cartwright, in his book, speaks of the strange bodily exercises of the times, and seems to have been rather amused at what he sometimes saw.

"Just in the midst of our controversies on the subject of the powerful exercises among the people under preaching, a new exercise broke out among us called the *jerks,* which was overwhelming in its effects upon the bodies and minds of the people. No matter whether they were saints or sinners, they would be taken under a warm song or sermon and seized with a convulsive jerking all over, which they could not by any possibility avoid. And the more they resisted, the more violently they jerked. If

497

they would not strive against it and pray in good earnest, it would usually abate. I have seen more than five hundred persons jerking at once in my large congregations. Most usually, persons taken with the jerks, to obtain relief, as they said, would rise up and dance—some would run, but could not get away—some would re-sist,—on such the jerks were most severe.

"To see those proud young gentlemen and ladies, dressed in their silks, jewelry, and prunella from top to toe, take the jerks, would often excite my risibility. The first jerk or two you would see their fine bonnets, caps, and combs fly, and their long, loose hair crack almost as loud as a wagoner's whip."

He tells an amusing story of two young men who brought their sisters to meeting one day, each armed with a horsewhip, and told the crowd that if Cartwright gave their sisters the jerks, they intended to horse-whip him. The girls went in, took their seats, and the youngsters stood at the door. Being a little unwell that day, and having a vial of peppermint in his pocket, just as he rose to commence preaching he drank a little of it. The young fellows, keeping their eyes on him steadily, saw this. While in the midst of his sermon the girls fell to jerking violently. When he had finished, and came down from the pulpit, he was told by a friend to be on his guard, as there were some fellows at the door who intended to whip him. On hearing this, he went to them, and asked why they were going to whip him? They answered, because he had given their sisters the jerks. He told them he had not given them the jerks. They replied he had, for they saw him with the medicine he carried about with him for the purpose. He then said, if he had given the girls the jerks he reckoned he could give it to them too, and commenced taking his peppermint out. At this the young fellows wheeled, took to their heels, and he saw no more of them.

Elder Stone tells us he had never seen anyone injured by the jerks; but Elder Cartwright says:

"During a camp-meeting, at a place called the Ridge, in William McGee's congregation, there was a very large, drinking man, curs-ing the jerks and all religion together. Soon he commenced jerking himself and started to run, but could not get away. He then took out his bottle of whisky and swore he would drink the jerks to death, but jerked so violently he could not get the bottle to his mouth, though he tried very hard to do so. At length he fetched a very violent jerk, snapped his neck, fell, and soon expired, sur-rounded by a very large crowd."

After Elder Stone had spent some time in Southern Kentucky, he returned to Cane Ridge, and related the strange things he had seen and heard. The people seemed to be solemnly impressed, and much feeling was manifested. During the second sermon he preached, after his return, two little girls were struck down, and the most intense excitement ensued, which overspread the whole country. At some of the great camp-meetings that followed, it was thought that from twenty to twenty-five thousand people were present, and bodily exercises of the most wonderful character were there likewise.

Thus far, no one, in public, had ventured to say aught against these strange phenomena, every one being as it were overawed by what they saw and heard. But at length, during a great camp-meeting near Paris, Kentucky, a Presbyterian minister arose and in the strongest terms denounced what he saw as extravagant and monstrous. A party took ground against it immediately. A bitter opposition arose, and from that day the wonderful movement began sensibly to decline.

B. W. Stone, Richard McNamar, John Dunlavy, John Thomson, Robert Marshall, and David Purviance, the leading spirits of the revival, finally seceded from the mother church and formed a new organization called the Springfield Presbytery. A year or two after, they abandoned this enterprise and Presbyterianism likewise, and formed a new body which they called the "Christian Church," but which others called New Lights, if I remember rightly.

This body held many of the views which characterized Elder Campbell's Reformation; and Elder Stone intimates pretty clearly, in his book, that they had adopted his views, or stolen his thunder, especially the famous dogma, "baptism for the remission of sins."

The Shakers came along, however, and took off two of his preachers, Dunlavy and McNamar. Marshall and Thomson went back to the Presbyterians and Elders Stone and Purviance united with the Reformers; and thus the old "Christian Church" finally disappeared in Elder Campbell's Reformation, which has adopted the old name again, "Christian Church."

A Swedish Lady Novelist Inspects a Camp Meeting

By the time Fredrika Bremer visited a camp meeting near Charleston in 1850, elders and preachers had the goings-on under better control than in the early days of this singularly American institution—or else Miss Bremer did not see all that may have been happening in the farthest reaches of the campground.

The origins of the camp meeting are still not altogether clear though it is believed that the first of these gatherings took place on the Kentucky-Tennessee border at the time of the Great Revival in 1799. Itinerant ministers found that they got surprising results if they held protracted meetings, lasting sometimes four or five days. Some kind of lodging and eating arrangements had to be made for the huge crowds that flocked in to hear the exhorters, hence the name—camp meeting. Gradually a kind of routine was evolved. There were usually three services during the day, besides other sessions for prayer. The night service, spectacular with flaming torches of pine knots and the blackness of the surrounding forest, often went on till dawn, while the sinners and the saved sang, shouted, "called on the Lord," groaned, danced, laughed the "holy laugh," and usually gave way to the bodily convulsions called the "jerks."

The less respectable elements of the frontier population were attracted by the opportunities offered by the dense crowds and the darkness. Whisky was sold in the bushes and the newly saved often got gloriously drunk. Whores did a good business and even the holy sometimes lapsed from the arms of Jesus into human embraces.

The first camp meetings were Presbyterian, but they soon became almost exclusively Methodist. By 1812 at least four hundred camp meetings were being held annually in the United States, each organized by the presiding elder of a Methodist district.

The camp meeting has survived in modern Methodism, but the tents and shacks of the early days have been replaced by resort-like houses, the stumps on which the early preachers shouted and exhorted by a tabernacle, the pine torches by electric lights. Some even have swimming pools and tennis courts. Bush-sports are not permitted.

Fredrika Bremer (1801–65) was at the height of her international fame as a novelist when she visited America in 1849. An inveterate traveler, she had come to these shores expecting to find a real land of promise and perhaps to write a novel about American life. An ardent feminist, she had been led to believe that American men held their women in high regard. Her main purpose in turning her travel-letters into an extended account of her two years in America was to better woman's lot in Sweden. Mary Howitt, an English devotee of Scandinavian literature, translated the work as The Homes of the New World; Impressions of America. *It was issued by Harper & Brothers in 1853, in two volumes. The book was so popular that five printings were required within a month. The selection given here is printed from the edition of 1858, Vol. I, pp. 306–17.*

❁

FREDRIKA BREMER: *Camp Meeting*

AWAY we go, through forest and field, eighteen miles from Charleston. It is late in the afternoon and very warm. We stop; it is in the middle of a thick wood. There is wood on all sides, and not a house to be seen. We alight from the carriages and enter a fir-wood. After we have walked for an hour along unformed paths, the wood begins to be very animated. It swarms with people, in particular with blacks, as far as we can see among the lofty tree-stems. In the middle of the wood is an open space, in the centre of which rises a great long roof, supported by pillars, and under which stand benches in rows, affording sufficient accommodation for four or five thousand people. In the middle of this tabernacle is a lofty, square elevation, and in the middle of this a sort of chair or pulpit. All round the tabernacle, for so I call the roofed-in space supported on pillars, hundreds of tents, and booths of all imaginable forms and colors, are pitched and erected in a vast circle, and are seen shining out white in the wood to a great distance, and every where, on all sides, near and afar off, may be seen groups of people, mostly black, busied at small fires, roasting and boiling. Children are running about or sitting by the fires; horses stand and feed beside the carriages they have drawn thither. It is a perfect camp, with all the varied party-colored life of a camp, but without soldiers and arms. Here every thing looks peaceful and festive, although not exactly joyful.

By degrees the people begin to assemble within the tabernacle, the white people on one side, the black on the other; the black being considerably more numerous than the white. The weather is sultry; thunder-clouds cover the heavens, and it begins to rain. Not a very agreeable prospect for the night . . . but there is nothing for it, we must pass the night here in the wild wood. We have no other resource. But stop; we have another resource. That excellent young Mr. R. employs his eloquence and a tent is opened for us, and we are received into it by a comfortable bookseller's family. The family are red-hot Methodists, and not to be objected to. Here we have coffee and supper.

After this meal I went to look around me, and was astonished by a spectacle which I never shall forget. The night was dark with the thunder-cloud, as well as with the natural darkness of night; but the rain had ceased, excepting for a few heavy drops, which fell here and there, and the whole wood stood in flames. Upon eight fire-altars, or fire-hills, as they are called—a sort of lofty table raised on posts, standing around the tabernacle—burned, with a flickering brilliance of flame, large billets of firewood, which contains a great deal of resin, while on every side in the wood, far away in its most remote recesses, burned larger or smaller fires, before tents or in other places, and lit up the lofty fir-tree stems, which seemed like columns of an immense natural temple consecrated to fire. The vast dome above was dark, and the air was so still that the flames rose straight upward, and cast a wild light, as of a strange dawn upon the fir-tree tops and the black clouds.

Beneath the tabernacle an immense crowd was assembled, certainly from three to four thousand persons. They sang hymns—a magnificent choir! Most likely the sound proceeded from the black portion of the assembly, as their number was three times that of the whites, and their voices are naturally beautiful and pure. In the tower-like pulpit, which stood in the middle of the tabernacle, were four preachers, who, during the intervals between the hymns, addressed the people with loud voices, calling sinners to conversion and amendment of life. During all this, the thunder pealed, and fierce lightning flashed through the wood like angry glances of some mighty invisible eye. We entered the tabernacle, and took our seats among the assembly on the side of the whites.

Round the elevation, in the middle of which rose the pulpit, ran a sort of low counter, forming a wide square. Within this, seated on benches below the pulpit, and on the side of the whites, sat the Methodist preachers, for the most part handsome tall figures, with broad, grave foreheads; and on the side of the blacks their spiritual leaders and exhorters, many among whom were mulattoes, men of a lofty, noticeable, and energetic exterior.

The later it grew in the night, the more earnest grew the appeals; the hymns short, but fervent, as the flames of the light-wood ascended, like them, with a passionate ardor. Again and again they arose on high, like melodious, burning sighs from thousands of harmonious voices. The preachers increase in the fervor of their zeal; two stand with their faces turned toward the camp of the blacks, two toward that of the whites, extending their hands, and calling on the sinners to come, come, all of them, *now* at this time, at this moment, which is perhaps the last, the only one which remains to them in which to come to the Savior, to escape eternal damnation! Midnight approaches, the fires burn dimmer, but the exaltation increases and becomes universal. The singing of hymns mingles with the invitations of the preachers, and the exhortations of the class-leaders with the groans and cries of the assembly. And now, from among the white people, rise up young girls and men, and go and throw themselves, as if overcome, upon the low counter. These are met on the other side by the ministers, who bend down to them, receive their confessions, encourage and console them. In the camp of the blacks is heard a great tumult and a loud cry. Men roar and bawl out; women screech like pigs about to be killed; many, having fallen into convulsions, leap and strike about them, so that they are obliged to be held down. It looks here and there like a regular fight; some of the calmer participants laugh. Many a cry of anguish may be heard, but you distinguish no words excepting, "Oh, I am a sinner!" and "Jesus! Jesus!"

During all this tumult the singing continues loud and beautiful and the thunder joins in with its pealing kettledrum.

While this spectacle is going forward in the black camp we observe a quieter scene among the whites. Some of the forms which had thrown themselves on their knees at the counter have removed themselves, but others are still lying there, and the ministers seem in vain to talk or to sing to them. One of these, a young girl, is lifted up by her friends and found to be "in a trance." She now lies with her head in the lap of a woman dressed in black, with her pretty young face turned upward, rigid, and as it appears, totally unconscious. The woman dressed in black, and another, also in the same colored attire, both with beautiful, though sorrowful countenances, softly fan the young girl with their fans, and watch her with serious looks, while ten or twelve women— most of them young—stand around her, singing softly and sweetly a hymn of the resurrection; all watching the young girl, in whom they believe that something great is now taking place. It is really a beautiful scene in that thunderous night, and by the light of the fire-altars.

After we had contemplated these scenes, certainly for an hour, and the state of exaltation began to abate, and the principal glory of the night seemed to be over, Mrs. W. H. and myself retired to the tent to rest. . . .

It was sultry and oppressive in the tent. Our kind hostess did all in her power to make it comfortable for us; and Mrs. W. H. thought merely of making all comfortable for me, taking all the inconvenience to herself. I could not get any rest in the tent, and therefore wished at least yet once more to take a look at the camp before I lay down for the night.

It was now past midnight; the weather had cleared, and the air was so delicious and the spectacle so beautiful, that I was compelled to re- turn to the tent to tell Mrs. Howland, who at once resolved to come out with me. The altar-fires now burned low, and the smoke hung within the wood. The transparently bright and blue heaven stretched above the camp. The moon rose above the wood, and the planet Jupiter stood brilliantly shining just over the tabernacle. The singing of hymns still ascended, though much lower; still the class-leaders exhorted; still the young girl slept her mysterious sleep; still the women watched, and waited, and fanned her, in their attire of mourning. Some op- pressed souls still lay bowed upon the counter, and still were the preachers giving consolation either by word or song. By degrees the people assembled in the tabernacle dispersed, scattered themselves through the woods, or withdrew to their tents. Even the young sleep- ing girl awoke, and was led by her friends away from the assembly.

Mr. R. had now joined us, and accompanied by him we went the round of the camp, especially on the black side. And here all the tents were still full of religious exaltation, each separate tent presenting some new phasis. We saw in one a zealous convert, male or female, as it might be, who with violent gesticulations gave vent to his or her newly-awakened feelings, surrounded by devout auditors; in another we saw a whole crowd of black people on their knees, all dressed in white, striking themselves on the breast, and crying out and talking with greatest pathos; in a third women were dancing "the holy dance" for one of the newly converted. This dancing, however, having been forbidden by the preachers, ceased immediately on our entering the tent. I saw merely a rocking movement of women, who held each other by the hand in a circle, singing the while. In a fourth, a song of the spiritual Canaan was being sung excellently. In one tent we saw a fat negro member walking about by himself and breathing hard; he was hoarse, and, sighing, he exclaimed to himself, "Oh! I wish I could hollo!" In some tents people were sitting around the fires, and here visits were received, greetings were made, and friendly, cheerful talk went on, while every where prevailed a quiet earnest state of feeling, which we also experienced whenever we stopped to talk with the people. These black people have a something warm and kind about them which I like much. One can see that they are children of the warm sun. The state of feeling was considerably calmer in the camp of the whites. One saw families sitting at their covered tables eating and drinking. . . .

The principal sermon of the [next] day was preached about eleven o'clock by a lawyer from one of the neighboring states, a tall, thin gentleman, with strongly-marked, keen features, and deep-set, brilliant eyes. He preached about the Last Judgment, and described in a most lively manner "the fork-like cloven flames, the thunder, the general destruction of all things," and described it as possibly near at hand. "As yet, indeed," exclaimed he, "I have not felt the earth tremble under my feet; it yet seems to stand firm," and he stamped vehemently on the pulpit floor; "and as yet I hear not the rolling of the thunder of doom; *but* it may, nevertheless, be at hand," and so on; and he admonished the people, therefore, immediately to repent and be converted.

Spite of the strength of the subject, and spite of the power in the delineation, there was a something dry and soulless in the manner in which it was presented, which caused it to fail of its effect with the congregation. People seemed to feel that the preacher did not believe, or rather, did not livingly feel that which he described and preached. A few cries and groans were heard, it is true, and some sinners came forth; but the assembly, upon the whole, continued calm, and was not agitated by the thunder of the Last Judgment. The hymns were, as on the former occasion, fervent and beautiful on the side of the negroes' camp. This people seem to have a keen perception of the most beautiful doctrines of religion, and understand particularly well to how to apply them. Their musical talents are remarkable. Most of the blacks have beautiful, pure voices, and sing as easily as we whites talk.

After this service came the hour of dinner, when I visited various tents in the black camp, and saw tables covered with dishes of all kinds of meat, with puddings and tarts; there seemed to be a regular superfluity of meat and drink. Several of the tents were even furnished like rooms, with capital beds, looking-glasses, and such like.

The people seemed gay, happy and gentle. These religious camp-meetings . . . are the saturnalia of the negro slaves. In these they luxuriate both soul and body, as is their natural inclination to do; but on this occasion every thing was carried on with decency and befitting reverence. These meetings have of late years greatly improved in moral character, and masters allow their servants and slaves to be present at them, partly for pleasure, and partly because they are often productive of good results. I did not observe the slightest circumstance which was repugnant to my feelings or unbecoming, except, if people will, the convulsive excitement. I had some conversation on this subject with the leader of the meeting, the amiable and agreeable Mr. Martin, the Methodist preacher, and he disapproved of it, as I had already heard. These excited utterances, however, said he, appear to belong to the impulsive negro temperament, and these sudden conversions, the result of a moment of excitement, have this good result, that such converts commonly unite themselves to churches and ministers, become members of a so-called class, and thus obtain regular instruction in the doctrines of religion, learn hymns and prayers, and become generally from that time good Christians and orderly members of society.

In the great West, as well as here in the South, and in all places where society is as yet uncultivated, it is the Methodists and the Baptists who first break the religious ground, working upon the feelings and the senses of these children of nature. Afterward come the Calvinists, Lutherans, and many others, who speak rather to the understanding. Missionaries who assemble the people and talk to them under God's free heaven, who know how to avail themselves of every circumstance presented by the time, the scenery around them, and their own free positions, are likely to produce the most powerful results; and I have heard extraordinary instances related of their influence over the masses, and of the contagious effect of that excitement of mind which frequently occurs on these occasions. These camp-meetings continue from three to seven days. The one at which we were present was to break up on the following day, and it was expected that a great number of conversions would take place on the following night. Nevertheless, this seemed to depend on casual circumstances, and probably more than any thing else upon a preacher whose sermon had that tendency.

The "Great Iron Wheel" Controversy

The Protestant sects in the United States, North as well as South, have often warred with one another in a most un-Christian fashion. A particularly bitter Baptist-Methodist fight—called the "Great Iron Wheel" Controversy—broke out in Tennessee in the 1850's. The row was touched off by the publication of J. R. Graves's The Great Iron Wheel; or Republicanism Backwards and Christianity Reversed, in a Series of Letters Addressed to J. Soule, Senior Bishop of the M. E. Church, South (*Nashville: Graves & Marks; 1855*).

"Dr." Graves (his LL.D. is dubious) was "set apart" for the Baptist ministry at the age of twenty-four. He was then living in Kentucky, having gravitated south from Vermont by way of Ohio. Within two years Elder Graves had migrated to Tennessee and become editor of the Tennessee Baptist, *with which journal he began an editorial career that lasted nearly fifty years. He was also a prolific writer of polemical and controversial works, the most sensational of which was* The Great Iron Wheel. *This book was reissued at least thirty times and reached a sale of 100,000 copies. A lurid account of Methodism as a great conspiracy against honest and pious Americans, the work pictures the Methodist Church as a "clerical despotism," the very "Popery of Protestantism," controlled by bishops who are as nefarious as Jesuits in their subversive schemes.*

The next year Elder Graves was given a verbal thrashing when Parson Brownlow came to the rescue of the Methodists with his equally abusive The Great Iron Wheel Examined; or Its False Spokes Extracted. *W. G. Brownlow, Virginia-born Whig who was to become the Unionist "martyr" of east Tennessee during the Civil War, disposes of the character of Graves in his first chapter and then goes on to demolish his many heresies, taking 331 pages for his congenial task.*

The passages printed here from The Great Iron Wheel *are to be found on pages vii–viii, 169–70, 180–1 of the first edition. The brief excerpts from Brownlow's reply are taken from pages 23–4 and page 26 of* The Great Iron Wheel Examined (*Nashville, published for the author, 1856*).

ELDER GRAVES ON THE METHODIST "DESPOTISM"

THE "Great West" is to-day one great battle-field; and indeed the whole South is intensely agitated upon these questions, and the publications of the Book Concern, and numberless others, issuing from the Methodist press, South and West, more shameless even than the above, are brought into the field. The ten thousand circuit-riders echo and iterate and reiterate these sentiments in the ear of the multitude, and scatter these books and tracts broadcast, as the winds scatter the autumnal leaves. The Author then appeals to the press and to the world to decide, if Baptists do not owe it to themselves and to the principles they represent and most conscientiously believe, to defend themselves from undeserved contumely, and their principles from unmerited reproach? If these Letters are considered an attack, let them be looked upon as an attempt to *spike the enemy's guns*, in which effort, the aid of the Baptist press of America is most affectionately and earnestly invoked. . . .

Methodism the Popery of Protestantism—as absolute and all-controlling as Jesuitism—Papal Bishops
Dear Sir:—In my last, I asserted that the Methodism of the Discipline was a naked clerical despotism, and, in *essence*, *Popery* itself, and the worst form of Popery, *Jesuitism*.

Let us impartially compare them. The Edinburgh Encyclopædia says: "Loyola (the founder of the Jesuits) resolved that the government of the Jesuits should be absolutely monarchical. A General, chosen for life by deputies from the several provinces, possessed supreme and independent power, extending to every person, and applying to every case. Every member of the order, the instant that he entered its pale, surrendered all freedom of thought and action; and every personal feeling was superseded by the interests of that body to which he had attached himself. He went wherever he was ordered; he performed whatever he was commanded; he suffered whatever he was enjoined; he became a mere passive instrument incapable of resistance. The gradation of rank was only a gradation in slavery; and as perfect a despotism over a large body of men, dispersed over the face of the earth, was never before realized."

Now, will you turn back to the Wheel-illustration by your own

Cookman? The great outer wheel—the bishops answer to the General of the Society of Jesuits. Methodism has *many* Generals instead of *one;* so that it is Jesuitism in this respect, only "a great deal more so!" The power of the bishops, like that of the General of the Jesuits, extends *over* and *through the whole* Society—over all its agents and officers.

The second feature is also alike. Every minister or member, the instant he enters Methodism, surrenders *all religious freedom!* Think of this, Americans—think of it! He is no longer his own, but the *servant,* if a member, of all the clergy, and the leaders or petty overseers they appoint over him besides. The most ignoble sort of thraldom! If a minister, while he rules those *under* him, he himself is a slave of *his chief ministers*—those above him in rank! Therefore the third feature holds good—*"gradation in rank is only gradation in slavery!"*

The fourth general feature of Jesuitism is also perfect in Methodism. The minister who joins the Society of Mr. Wesley is compelled to go wherever he is ordered, without asking any *cause* or *questions;* return when commanded; to perform whatever is enjoined by his chief ministers; is a mere passive *tool* in the hands of his masters, to do their gracious wills and biddings! You may say that Methodist ministers elect their bishops—so do the Jesuits elect their General! And many a slave chooses his master; nothing is more common. But is he any the less a slave?

American Christians have heard much of the *awful* oath taken by Catholic priests and bishops to the Pope; many never saw it. I lay it before you, and place by its side the *oath you enjoin* upon all your ministers to obey you, together with your fellow-bishops, the *Popes* of Methodism; and I humbly ask you to point out to me any important difference. . . .

Be assured, sir, it affords me no pleasure to write these things—to portray these awful, and to my mind, abominable features of your system. I am painfully shocked as each unscriptural feature develops itself before me—as the system passes in review before my mind.

My heart sickens at these sentiments—at the picture of spiritual bondage and degradation, enjoined and achieved by these chief ministers—these Methodist "principalities and powers," and all these unhallowed and impious pretensions claimed by the *especial grace* of God to their word! I am sad and pained to think that professed Protestant ministers should, in the name of religion, assert such fearful Antichristian authority and jurisdiction over their brethren. I am grieved to think that American Christians can be found blindly and servilely to bow down to such a degrading spiritual and temporal vassalage. I close each paragraph, as I do each letter, humbled with a sense of the weakness of human nature, with a fervent prayer that His light and truth may go forth until this darkness shall be illumined, and this blindness be dispelled—and priestcraft and spiritual wickedness, that has enthroned itself in high places, and became proud and insolent with authority, may be overthrown, and all the friends of Christ be made to rejoice in the glorious liberty wherewith Christ makes us free.

PARSON BROWNLOW ON ELDER GRAVES

The whole tenor of Graves's course, editorially, has been that of a vagabond politician who expected to live only by excitement—making ruffian-like attacks upon private character, committing all manner of excesses, standing preëminent in selecting themes for lying, and the lowest and most scurrilous abuse of Methodist preachers. He has made repeated attacks upon me, through his paper, with a view to engage me in a controversy upon points of doctrine and Church polity. I was engaged in defence of one of the political parties of the country, and in promoting the internal improvement schemes of our State, and did not choose to occupy my columns in a controversy of this kind with a humiliating spectacle of vice and depravity literally crawling in the dust of contention! This unwillingness of mine to bandy epithets with an inflated *gasometer*, whose brain I believed to be a mass of living, creeping, crawling, writhing, twisting, turning, loathsome vermin, he politely construed into a want of *courage* on my part to encounter the *caitiff* of the "Tennessee Baptist." I confess to a want of moral courage to meet one who eats carrion like the buzzard, and then vomits the mass of corruption upon decent human beings!

There *is* a point, however, at which even such assaults become harmful, and deserve rebuke. The appropriate quarter from which such rebuke should emanate would seem to be a member of the Church this bad man has sought to vilify, and a member of the editorial fraternity. Under this conviction, I have taken him in hand; and by the time I am through with the task, I flatter myself that I will be able to satisfy the candid and impartial of every sect, that the aforesaid editor of the "Tennessee Baptist," and author of the "Great Iron Wheel," has no reverence whatever for truth, and that his warped and biased soul has been steeped in infamous falsehoods and vile calumnies during the greater part of his inglorious career. . . .

Take *J. R. Graves* in his length and breadth, in his height and depth, in his convexity and concavity, in his manners and in his propensities, and he is a very little man; but in that littleness there is combined all that is offensive and disagreeable among Christian gentlemen. For several years past, in portions of several States, with an unearthly din, this man has been barking, neighing, bleating, braying, mewing, puffing, swaggering, strutting; and in every situation, an offensive *smell*, to

509

gentlemen of refined tastes and Christian habits, has gone out from him! And believing the homely old adage, that "he who lies down with dogs must rise up with fleas," he has been permitted to pass unwhipped by justice.

The Scriptural Defense of Slavery

The ante-bellum South was even more of a "Bible belt" than it is today. To Methodists, Baptists, and Presbyterians particularly, the words of the Old and New Testaments were not only sacred but literally true. Inevitably, therefore, as the intersectional argument over slavery rose to fever pitch in the 1850's, pro-slavery arguments from scriptural authority were sought—and abundantly found. Of the many ingenious defenses of slavery—sociological, economic, ethnological, and "anthropological"—the apologia *worked up from the text of the Bible was probably the most effective—in the South. It appears in many of the tracts and books produced by the controversy, but the Reverend Thornton Stringfellow, of Culpeper County, Virginia, was the polemicist who gave this argument exhaustive treatment in his* Scriptural and Statistical Views in Favor of Slavery (*Richmond: J. W. Randolph; 4th ed., 1856). This work, an expansion of an essay he had published in 1841, was reprinted in 1860 in a huge compendium, 900 pages in length, which brought together what were thought to be the most cogent writings in defense of slavery—*Cotton is King, and Pro-Slavery Argument.*

The Reverend Mr. Stringfellow's treatise is 149 pages long, but fortunately he summarizes his argument in the passage reprinted here (from pages 81–3). The points he makes were iterated in hundreds of sermons below Mason and Dixon's Line.

My reader will remember that the subject in dispute is, whether involuntary and hereditary slavery was ever lawful in the sight of God, the Bible being judge.

1. I have shown by the Bible, that God decreed this relation be-

tween the posterity of Canaan, and the posterity of Shem and Japheth.

2. I have shown that God executed this decree by aiding the posterity of Shem, (at a time when "they were holiness to the Lord,") to enslave the posterity of Canaan in the days of Joshua.

3. I have shown that when God ratified the covenant of promise with Abraham, he recognized Abraham as the owner of slaves he had bought with his money of the stranger, and recorded his approbation of the relation, by commanding Abraham to circumcise them.

4. I have shown that when he took Abraham's posterity by the hand in Egypt, five hundred years afterwards, he publicly approbated the same relation, by permitting every slave they had bought with their money to eat the passover, while he refused the same privilege to their *hired servants*.

5. I have shown that God, as their national lawgiver, ordained by express statute, that they should buy slaves of the nations around them, (the seven devoted nations excepted,) and that these slaves and their increase should be a perpetual inheritance to their children.

6. I have shown that God ordained slavery by law for their captives taken in war, while he guaranteed a successful issue to their wars, so long as they obeyed him.

7. I have shown that when Jesus ordered his gospel to be published through the world, the relation of master and slave existed by law in every province and family of the Roman Empire, as it had done in the Jewish commonwealth for fifteen hundred years.

8. I have shown that Jesus ordained, that the legislative authority, which created this relation in that empire, should be obeyed and honored as an ordinance of God, as all government is declared to be.

9. I have shown that Jesus has prescribed the mutual duties of this relation in his kingdom.

10. And lastly, I have shown, that in an attempt by his professed followers to disturb this relation in the Apostolic churches, Jesus orders that fellowship shall be disclaimed with all such disciples, as seditious persons—whose conduct was not only dangerous to the State, but destructive to the true character of the gospel dispensation.

This being the case, as will appear by the recorded language of the Bible, to which we have referred you, reader, of what use is it to argue against it from moral requirements?

They regulate the duties of this and all other lawful relations among men—but they cannot abolish any relation, ordained or sanctioned of God, as is slavery.

Tongues and Snakes

With no little persistence and with the admonition of a Negro café-owner: "I'd leave 'em alone if I was you, boss," Archie Robertson found snake-handlers near Lookout Mountain in Tennessee. In his book from which the following passage is taken, That Old-Time Religion *(1950), Robertson traces the sect, an offshoot of the rapidly growing Pentecostal or Holiness churches, back to George Hensley, a follower of "Holiness," who in 1909, on White Top Mountain in Tennessee, began to practice what he found in the last chapter of the Gospel of Mark:*

> *17. And these signs shall follow them that believe: In my name shall they cast out devils; they shall speak with new tongues.*
> *18. They shall take up serpents; and if they drink any deadly thing, it shall not hurt them; they shall lay hands on the sick, and they shall recover.*

Most of the members of the Holiness groups or Churches of God are content to be healed with the laying on of hands and, in their "tarrying" services, to wait, amidst the clamor of shouts, hymns, and cymbals, for the heavenly fire to descend so they may speak with tongues. Not so the disciples of Hensley, who preached snake-handling "until the cult has spread by word of mouth through the whole Appalachian region." State officials have tried to stamp out the practice, but inquirers who hunt far enough in the night can still find Preacher Ramsay and his box of dry-land moccasins.

This selection from Archie Robertson's That Old-Time Religion *(pages 176–81) is reprinted by permission of and arrangement with Houghton Mifflin Company, the authorized publishers.*

On the last night of my sojourn among them, the church had erected a new and better tent in another part of Chattanooga. A metalworks sent a bright blast into the sky, and neighborhood Negroes stood outside the tent-flaps and murmured uneasily. Preacher Ramsay came to the door, a short, spry old man with a few white hairs on his head, rimless glasses, and a genial shrewd face, which suggested a fox. He wore a sleeveless sweater, without a necktie.

He invited the colored people to come in.

"We're a-goin' to praise God together and preach about a place where there'll be no white or black. In Heaven when we meet up yonder we'll all be children of God."

He told me that there had been a little trouble in getting snakes. The rattlers were going back into their holes at the approach of cold weather; and the law had confiscated some which they had planned to fatten up during the winter.

"But once in a while some feller brings us one." He smiled encouragingly.

I entered the tent with the colored people, who filled all but the front benches.

As before, the Signs Following church people occupied forward seats at right angles to the pulpits. There was a real mourner's bench, T-shaped and varnished. On it throughout the evening Elaine, very pretty in pink, folded and unfolded a pink blanket, endlessly making her bed, lying down, getting up, and starting over. Elaine was nineteen months old.

"All I ask is order on the grounds," said Preacher Ramsay. (His remarks were not addressed to Elaine, who played unmolested all evening.) "I mean you colored people, and you white people too."

He issued a call to prayer for the sick.

"Any colored child of God, hit's just the same as a white child of God, come forward if you will."

No one came; the church members knelt down in a body at the altar and began to pray and burst out into a tumult of "the tongues." A handsome black-haired girl in a red dress began to jerk so violently it seemed she might dislocate a vertebra. The middle-aged woman who had read Scripture for Brother Henry jerked also, holding her hand to her neck as if she had a toothache. Two girls in blue began to dance; and a tall young man, who I was told was a preacher of the sect, began to jump up and down, wordlessly, his eyes closed, his face in a trance, and his fingers opening and closing as if his hands were hungry.

They sang to guitar and mandolin "They Called My Name on the Radio," a new popular hymn inspired by the "give-away" programs of the time.

Gradually I learned to understand some of their other songs:

> *When first I went to holiness,*
> *I thought it was a shame,*
> *To see the people jump and shout,*
> *In praisin' Jesus' name.*

And

> *The Devil tried to tell me*
> *My Bible was a lie,*
> *That Jesus didn't love me,*
> *And I was sure to die.*

Elaine stopped making her bed on the altar and began to jump and clap with the cheerful tunes. Then she turned to stuffing saw-dust down the shirt-tail of a boy friend of like age.

Her parents turned to me and smiled, a foreman in a local mill and his wife. She was of hill stock, with delicate fair skin, blue eyes, and a firm set to her jaw; her husband might have had Welsh or Irish blood, for his smile was quicker, and his face had a round, candid mold. They were visiting Baptists.

"Of course, we don' go along with all they do, but we think they're good people and we like to help out," he said.

Preacher Ramsay now asked Elaine's parents to sing a duet. They sang a Baptist missionary hymn, "Send the Light," while the Holiness people listened respectfully. The Signs Following band struck up, "I'm Gettin' Ready to Leave This World, I'm Gettin' Ready for Gates of Pearl."

They followed this with "What a Beautiful Thought I am Thinking." The tall man's hands opened and closed hungrily.

The preacher stretched a rope across the front. "All you unbelievers and little children, stay back." Elaine's parents pulled her to safety, as a man walked down the aisle with a small box covered with a wire mesh. The preacher took out a dry-land moccasin, not quite full-grown. His face was transported; the two girls in blue went into a dance, the girl in red began her violent jerks, the man with hungry fingers began to jump higher, higher. The preacher made the serpent into a crown for his bald head and leaned over the rope, his glasses blazing. Several of the colored people, and a white Episcopalian from the front row, left the tent.

"This makes you feel *good*, children!" the preacher shouted. "Hit's the best feelin' you ever had in your life! Hit puts you way upon a high place where you look down on ever'thing that's gone before!" He slipped the snake in his pocket, placed it under his shirt, and passed it to one of the dancing girls in blue, who coiled it closely in her hand.

A ten-year-old in my pew whispered proudly, "That's my sister up there!" The man with the hungry fingers held the poisonous snake over his heart.

"Hit's the Word of God!" cried Preacher Ramsay. "The Bible don't say you *can* handle serpents, it says they *shall* handle serpents!"

After a few minutes the moccasin was returned to his box. (Elaine's parents held her up for a quick look.) The box was taken out into the street, where a police whistle blew.

The little boy whispered, his eyes big. "Ever' policeman that kills one of our snakes, dies."

Brother Ramsay continued to preach. He gave the altar call, but no one came.

Now he asked the Negroes if they would sing. They were silent. He picked out a buxom stolid woman on the back row and told her to lead; she began slowly, in a rich, rocking rhythm:

> *He got His eyes on you, He got His eyes on you;*
> *My Lawd settin' in de Kingdom, got His eyes on you.*

All the Negroes joined in the chorus, the rich voices warming the tent. The snake excitement was all gone.

> *You better mind, my sister, you better mind what you say,*
> *My Lawd settin' in de Kingdom, got His eyes on you.*

Now she sang and solemnly, "Gimme That Old Time Religion." The chorus grew in volume and intensity, verse by verse.

> *It will make us love one another,*
> *And it's good enough for me.*

Elaine's parents joined in.

> *It was good for the Hebrew Children.*

The Signs Following people, their guitars silent, were singing too. The tent began to rock.

> *It will make me love my enemy.*

"Glory to God!" shouted the preacher. "Makes me feel good to see white and colored praisin' God together!"

> *It was good for Paul and Silas.*

Brother Ramsay leaped over the rope. "I tell you, children, if we can't work and pray together in this world, we'll never get to that world up yonder!" His face was shining.

Elaine's father turned to me, flushing slightly, "I don' care what folks say—the Lord must be with 'em—else that moccasin would have bit."

Faith of Our Fathers

The following passage is excerpted from the third chapter of Hodding Carter's Southern Legacy, *published by the Louisiana State University Press in 1950. It is reprinted with the permission of the publisher.*

Editor of the Greenville (Mississippi) Delta Democrat-Times, *Pulitzer Prize winner, and the author of several books on the South, Hodding Carter is a member of a notable group of Southern liberals which includes Virginius Dabney of Richmond and Mark Ethridge of Kentucky.*

THE South may be described as the Bible belt in the same offhand and derisive way that the Eastern seaboard can be identified as the barbiturate belt, the roaring, raw cities of the Midwest the tommy-gun belt, and the West Coast the divorce belt.

But the religious identification goes deeper. Though the citadels crumble, the South remains the great western-world stronghold of Protestant, fundamentalist Christianity. As such it is the legatee of the spiritually zestful, mystic, and masochistic soul of its largely Celtic forebears.

In Tennessee, devout folk still sing praises to the hero of their brush with monkey-minded sons of darkness:

William Jennings Bryan is dead, he died one Sabbath day.
So sweetly was the king asleep, his spirit passed away;
He was at Dayton, Tennessee, defending our dear Lord,
And as soon as his work on earth was done, he went to his reward.
He fought the evolutionists, the infidels and fools
Who are trying to ruin the minds of our children in the schools,
By teaching we came from monkeys and other things absurd
By denying the works of our blessed Lord and God's own holy word.

In Mississippi, Tennessee, and Arkansas, the teaching of evolutionary theories is still technically illegal; and, in the spring of 1948, the University of Arkansas turned down a proposed course which listed the first chapter of Genesis under "Myths of Creation." The camp meeting, brought up to date with loud-speakers and cooling systems, can, in rural Southern localities, outdraw Betty Grable and break even with Jim Folsom, Herman Talmadge, and John Rankin. The political pressures, in certain material directions, of the Baptist and Methodist churches, and to some extent the Presbyterian, are powerful and not uniformly misapplied. New churches continue to be built, though it is somewhat more difficult now to fill the pulpits than the pews. There is in the South an unexhausted reservoir of simple piety, which, if directed toward true acceptance of the Sermon on the Mount and the Christian concept of man's brotherhood, could and may yet effect a more profound change in regional social-racial patterns than any legislation devised toward that end.

Few Southerners find it easy to look upon these facts with detachment. That thing called the old-time religion is in the blood of most of us, and if it is laughed at, the laughter has as accompaniment an almost inescapable inner, esoteric warning that the ways of God are not to be mocked by man. A little over a century ago, the South of the Scotch-Irish farmer and frontiersman was swept by an evangelical flood that submerged the gentlemanly Jeffersonian skepticism and Anglican liberalism, leaving on the Southeastern seaboard alone an isolated high ground of doubt and investigation.

Through the back country rode the indomitable Methodist circuit riders. Rough-tongued men and women were propelled below the surface of rushing rivers and obscure streams by the sanctified hands of self-discovered Baptist preachers, and rose choking, to scream the glory of God and their temporary abnegation of red liquor, eye gouging, and painted Jezebels. This was the Second Awakening, primitive, democratic, and certain, and religious liberalism in the South died before its surge. Victim, too, but of secular and sectional considerations, was the early revivalist concern with the black man's freedom; the Protestant churches of the South became the inspired spokesmen for the institution of slavery, entrenching themselves the more solidly thereby, and Christianity, Northern version, a distorted, satanic misinterpretation of the gospel that doomed the sons of Ham. God had providentially placed the poor, heathen African in the charge of the South. God was on the South's side. It was as simple as that.

"The parties in this conflict are not merely abolitionists and slaveholders," proclaimed the Reverend James Henley Thornwell, Presbyterian divine and president of South Carolina College in 1850. "They are atheists, socialists, communists, red republican jacobins on the one side, and the friends of order and regulated freedom on the other. In one word, the world is the battleground, Christianity and atheism the combatants; and the progress of humanity at stake."

Organized religion in the South became the mighty fortress of the *status quo;* the revival exhorters assumed the dignity and the defense of the ruling classes, uncompromising as ever in their castigation of the sins of the flesh but equally adamant in their justification of man's ownership of man. A Calvinistic God had ordained slavery; those who rebelled against it were in rebellion against God. Narrow fanaticism, strict and literal interpretation of the Bible, defense of the established order and its apostles, orthodoxy discernible even among the anarchical multitude of sects—these were the South's religious answer to the abolitionist, the hell-damned skeptic, the new, restless scientist, and the worldly outsider.

And that, to a lessening and challenged degree, is the religious South's position today.

Yet, it is unfair to so limit the impact of Protestantism upon the South. God was an anthropomorphic Hebraic avenger, with terrible lightning in his eyes, but the Christ child was gentle and forgiving, loving man, loving even the least of these, even the retarded black, God-ordained to be a hewer of wood and drawer of water. A tribal God punished the wrongdoer, but it was the tender Christ who illumined the path of righteousness, who waited beside the still waters, who whispered in the ear of the tempted, who cried out in agony, "Father, forgive them; for they know not what they do." . . .

The vengeful tradition persists. Once . . . I suggested editorially that a Holy Roller revival in our town remove itself beyond the city limits because the noise was disturbing to Christians and sinners alike. The participants were handling snakes and white-hot coal-oil-lamp chimneys, getting the shakes and the shouts, and it was not pleasant. So, the next day it was noised around that I was to be denounced in the Unknown Tongue that night. I went to hear it. My Holy Roller friends made certain that their listeners would know who was being denounced. In the middle of the unintelligible jabber-jabber-jabber of the Unknown Tongue, they would occasionally shout my name or that of my newspaper.

Such performances mean religion yet to too many Southerners. Some powerful denominations in Mississippi still conduct state-wide days or hours of prayer whenever the legislature undertakes gingerly to repeal or modify our unavailing liquor laws; but I have not known them to concentrate similarly when forward social legislation is being considered. We have an eighteen-year-old printer's apprentice in my newspaper plant who, in the name of religion, refuses to go to a movie, play cards, dance, or drink even a Coca-Cola. And I know two Protestant ministers to whom inclusion of a rabbi in a ministerial alliance is repugnant because they hold the Jews eternally responsible for the death of Christ.

Tragedy lies in this mean dissipation of the tremendous Southern reservoir of faith. Fortunately, that tragedy is being increasingly perceived by churchmen and laymen, particularly the younger men and women, and from their awareness comes not only future hope but present action. In seeming contradiction to the constant evidence of misdirected zeal, many churches of the South—Protestant and Catholic alike—are far ahead of their memberships in the areas of social action, which is as it should be and must be. It is not uncommon today for ministers to espouse constitutional rights for Negroes or to bespeak applied Christianity in economic relationships. Some of them pay for their daring. There is much muttering in the South against radical tendencies in the churches, the Federal Council of the Churches of Christ and the YMCA and the YWCA being especial targets, and the spirit of schism is strong. But by the very fact that the minister is still a man apart, ordained by God, his courage and vision can command respect if not emulation. As an example, I can cite the experience of a devoted young clergyman, who less than a year after he came to our town preached a blunt, biting sermon on racial discrimination. He was violently criticized, some members left his congregation, and it was predicted that he would not last a month longer. He is still here and I know that he has won converts.

And where could be found more fertile fields for crusading than the churches of the essentially rural South? There the communal stream runs strong. There, as much as human frailties and human concerns permit, men and women dwell for a short time beyond themselves, seeking refreshment of the spirit, warming themselves in the bright sunlight of the churchyard beneath a brighter if uncomprehended sun. There, fleetingly, they are malleable to good; there the inheritance of ardent faith could pry open the hearts to the words of the preacher who finds his text in Galatians:

"There is neither Jew nor Greek, there is neither bond nor free, there is neither male nor female: for ye are all one in Christ Jesus."

XIV

CITIES AND TOWNS

WHEN Mr. Ellwood Fisher spoke in 1849 on "The North and the South" before the Mercantile Library Association of Cincinnati, he brought to his listeners a proposition that was widely acclaimed thereafter in the South as just and true. The South, he said, was the first region ever to build a high culture on agriculture. In earlier times men had assumed that large cities were necessary to the development of a civilization. But, Mr. Fisher opined, cities cause inequality of condition, great depravity of morals, great increase in want, and of crime. This evil, the preference for city life, in the belief that only in cities could culture flourish, was, according to Fisher, "for the first time successfully encountered and conquered by the institutions of the South."

This characteristic dislike of cities lingers in the South today, in spite of the zeal of booster clubs, Rotary, and Committees of 100. There are few large cities in the South. In 1950 only one even quasi-Southern city, St. Louis, was in the group of the ten largest cities in the country. In the next group of ten, Houston and New Orleans take their place. If we move back to the period just before the Civil War and review the figures for 1860, we find that out of 102 American cities with a population of 10,000 or more, only ten were in the states that would soon form the Confederacy, with North Carolina, Florida, Mississippi, Arkansas, and Texas having none. By the standard of those days New Orleans was a metropolis, with its population of 168,675, but it was four times as large as any other Southern city.

Aside from Charleston, Savannah, Mobile, New Orleans, and Nashville, few large Southern cities have much characteristic charm save that of location. They grew in size after the blight of standardized American life had begun to descend on cities everywhere in the nation. If the voices and manners of the people did not tell you the city is Southern, you might think you were almost anywhere in urban America. The telltale marks face you as you walk the streets: the Beaux Arts courthouse, Roman-temple banks, Tudor "taverns," hotel coffeeshoppes, modernistic movie marquees, neon-lighted night clubs, Coca-Cola signs, drugstores with their counters filled with everything marketable except drugs.

To find the distinctive Southern charm one must seek it in the old villages and smaller cities: in Alexandria, Virginia, with its narrow "flounder" houses; in aristocratic Beaufort, South Carolina; in romantic Demopolis, Alabama, founded in 1817 by Napoleonic refugees; in Natchez, of course, when the tourists are gone (which is seldom); in Biloxi, Mississippi, which fishes and entertains seekers after the hot Gulf sunshine; in Bayou La Batre, Alabama, where you can loaf your troubles away and eat the best crab omelet in the world. Children in Bayou La Batre used to be a-feared of Lafitte the pirate. They were told that he would pull them down into the bayou if they went out after dark.

Thirty years ago Southern cities were dingy. Visitors were depressed by the Negro sections with their tumbledown, unpainted hovels, broken sidewalks, and unpaved streets. These slums were almost invariably on the outskirts of town so that the traveler by car encountered them as he entered and as he left. In New Deal days many of the worst of these sections were replaced with good public housing, and more recently the cities themselves have undertaken to remove those which remain. Prosperity, paint, and civic consciousness have done wonders for Southern cities. The decay left by the jerry-building of frontier days and boom years is gradually being removed in the South, as elsewhere in America.

"These cities differ radically among themselves"

Professor Edd Winfield Parks, from whose Segments of Southern Thought *this discriminating account of the principal Southern cities is taken, described himself in 1938 as a "distributist-agrarian" in his social thinking. Brought up in the environment of a Tennessee small town, as he grew up he realized, with a sense of shock, that to many Americans* "city, *when used as an adjective, means all that is fine and desirable,* country *all that is backward and crude." Because he later lived in such big cities as Los Angeles, Boston, and Nashville, he could survey urban life in the South with a double vision. At present he is at home in one of the most charming of the smaller Southern cities, Athens, Georgia (pop., in 1950, 28,180), where he is Professor of English at the University of Georgia.*

This excerpt from Professor Parks's chapter on "Southern Towns and Cities" in Segments of Southern Thought *(1938) is reprinted with the permission of the University of Georgia Press.*

AT once the largest and most picturesque city in all the South is New Orleans—which, as Lyle Saxon has discerningly pointed out in *Fabulous New Orleans,* is in reality two cities. There is the old French city —the Vieux Carré—and the newer "American city." Here, more clearly than in any other town, can one observe the incessant yet rarely noticeable struggle between progress and tradition. For the two sections pay allegiance to strangely dissimilar gods, and it is with regret that one notices unmistakable signs of predominance of the god of business.

The streets in the old city are narrower; in the newer section they frequently have a center drive, which is planted with palms or evergreen trees. Canal Street, the business center, is neutral ground; in "old town," as it is frequently called, the houses are predominantly French or Spanish, closely joined together, with much graceful ironwork around small balconies, and with inner courtyards. The entire atmosphere is leisurely and cosmopolitan: in part the work of artists and Bohemians who inhabit the Vieux Carré, in part the survival of French and Spanish family life. Here, too, are memories and realities: of

E. W. PARKS: *"These cities differ radically"*

Antoine's, Galatoire's, La Louisianne, and older, not-quite-forgotten restaurants that made of eating and drinking a fine art; the St. Louis cemetery and cathedral; the old Ursuline Convent that served also as an archbishop's palace; the great "dueling oaks," that belong in spirit, if not in location, to the old town—all these, and a score of blocks of houses, a few fine government buildings, are relics of French and Spanish days. Yet, as I write this, newspapers chronicle the doom of the old and famous French Market House—*Halle des Boucheries*. In a few months it will be torn down and replaced with a new and up-to-date building. Fire, also, has taken its toll, in the old Opera House, and, caught between these twin agents of destruction, the Vieux Carré seems fated, soon, to disappear.

Yet the subtle forces of tradition permeate even the new city, with its wide streets and miscellaneous architecture. Men work in leisurely fashion, and go out, each morning and afternoon, for coffee that, according to legend, will help to ward off malaria. And New Orleans bears the imprint of river and of ocean. It is distinctly a Mississippi river town, although commerce on the river has lost its economic importance, and adds, today, little more than a touch of color and strangeness. But floods are ever-threatening, and men can never forget that the city is often ten feet below the level of the Mississippi, and dependent on levees for its safety. Once, too, the great bend in the river gave to the city a rounded shape and the name of the "Crescent City"—a name without meaning today, save that its principal streets running north and south curve to follow the bend in the river. New Orleans remains a great seaport, a gateway for such southern products as cotton, grain, and lumber, and a center for imports from South America. But there is little manufacturing: New Orleans, as much today as before the Civil War, depends upon the surrounding country for its support. It is a clearing-house for the lower South.

Men have turned the brilliant social life of an older day into a first-rate tourist attraction. Mardi Gras has become an institution, with its Rex, its Mystic Krewe of Comus, Knights of Momus, and Crewe of Proteus. There are balls and street parades, river carnivals, and both organized and impromptu revelry, but the ancient flavor has gone, to a large extent, in the modern effort to entertain visitors. True, business stops while society plays . . . but business reaps in the end, one feels, a two-fold harvest. Yet in this, as in so many other instances, the old and the new are in combat.

Far removed from such conflict is Birmingham, city of the new South. It is the one industrial center between New Orleans and Atlanta, the center of the iron and coal industry south of Pennsylvania. The buildings are all of a kind: relatively new, with a preponderance of modern skyscrapers dwarfing the more ordinary store-buildings and the semi-classic governmental and institutional structures. Situated on the slope of Red Mountain, it escapes a monotonous regularity chiefly through this natural ruggedness of the terrain. For Birmingham is predominantly a child of the twentieth century, and it has no old traditions that cause men to regret the passing of old landmarks.

In physical location Richmond possesses one likeness to Birmingham: the capital of Virginia was originally built on seven hills, and once it was called the "modern Rome." But the hills, overhanging the James River, are small—and there, abruptly, the resemblance ceases. For Richmond, like New Orleans, is a blend of old and new; even the principal industry—the preparation of tobacco for use—far antedates the Revolutionary War. Few towns possess more definitely the intangible stamp of historical associations. The public buildings have one quality even rarer than tradition: they have architectural merit. The capitol building was designed by Thomas Jefferson after the model of the ancient Roman temple, the Maison Carrée, of Nîmes, and the later additional wings have conformed to the same general type. All the public buildings in Richmond have, in fact, conformed to this adapted classical style, and the statuary commemorating notable men of yesteryear adds to this impression of Richmond as a classical American city. Prominent landmarks and historic buildings recall memories of Washington, Jefferson, Marshall, Madison, Lee, and a veritable host of men only slightly less famous. One cannot easily forget such names, or forget that in 1730 Richmond was known as "Byrd's Warehouse," or that once it was the capital of the Confederacy. But Richmond is sorely divided, one group feeling that memories can be bought at too high a price, and striving desperately for business growth; the other prizing an older way of living that seems inevitably in conflict with modern progress.

"No city should be a museum, kept intact under glass." That statement was hurled at Richmond some years ago; with even more justice can it be applied to Charleston. Although it has an extremely fine port and is an important commercial city, this phase of its life has been rather largely neglected. All historic places and features have been carefully preserved: the Battery, with its magnificent view of the harbor and of Fort Sumter; wooded White Point Garden, with its monuments to great men of another day; the Powder Magazine, the Slave Market, and the old residential houses that recall days when Pringles and Heywards and Hugers ruled the community. Twelve miles from town are the Magnolia Gardens, perhaps the principal attraction to tourists, and certainly an integral part of the community. Like New Orleans, it possesses one of the few really important social events of the nation, but Charleston has retained for its St. Cecilia's Ball an exclusiveness that commercial prosperity has never tarnished. Here family is all-important, and relatives are counted to the "nth" generation; yet here, too, is a Gallic lightness of manner, and at times a fiery zeal bringing a recollection that Charleston is tempered with a large group of people of French Huguenot descent. That zeal once led the state into nullification and, again, led the South into a war. But today it seems dormant—primarily interested in preserving faded but imperishable glories.

Although Savannah was founded by James Oglethorpe in 1733, it seems to have less of history and somewhat more of humanity, than Charleston. The tang of the marsh is in the air, and the picturesque scenes native to any port town are constantly in view. For Savannah remains undeniably a small town, though an exceedingly busy port, and its air of leisurely dignity seems far more in keeping with Georgia than do the bustling ways of Atlanta.

Perhaps it is not by accident that two of our most prosperous cities have little connection with the agrarian South. Unlike Birmingham, Atlanta did not spring up over night. Before the Civil War the first name of the village, Marthasville, was changed to Terminus, because increasingly the railroads centered round that town. And Terminus in due time became Atlanta, the central goal of General Sherman, who described it as "the wrist of a hand whose fingers reach the five principal ports of the Gulf and South Atlantic coasts." During the days of reconstruction, Atlanta became capital of the state; since that time, its valuable central location and its easy accessibility have made it, in sober truth, the "New York of the South." For Atlanta also is new, with broad streets and a metropolitan air, and it has become a center of manufacturing as well as of distribution. Rural Georgia has little tangible connection with it, save to supply it with food, and the city quite evidently is not proud of Georgia. All emphasis is thrown on its fine buildings and educational institutions, and, above all, on the fact that Atlanta is the metropolis of the South and, basically, a branch of New York. Although a leisureliness, an old-time courtesy and gentility, pervades the atmosphere, the casual visitor is rarely allowed to forget, in his business contacts, that this way of life is less important than the city's commerce.

Compared with Atlanta, Nashville seems an overgrown small town, with narrow and out-moded streets, grimy old buildings, and the settled placidity of middle age. This, however, is only a half-picture. Once it was a frontier town, but those days are completely past, and long since forgotten; today it is "the Athens of the South," boasting of fine educational institutions and of grand old days, yet reaching somewhat reluctantly for new commercial projects. It has Vanderbilt, Peabody, Ward-Belmont, and Fisk: the four extremes in modern education. For Vanderbilt represents the old-time classical college that has branched out into a large university; Peabody, the modernized institution that believes men can be transformed into teachers if they are taught the correct methods; Ward-Belmont remains an outstanding boarding school for well-to-do young ladies; and Fisk is preëminent in the field of cultural education for Negroes. Here are four radically different schools, in a city that rebuilds the Greek Parthenon, and now puts on, through its Chamber of Commerce, a five-year plan to lure new industries from the North. A divided city, that prizes on the one side, Friendly Five shoes—and, on the other, the Hermitage. Like every southern city, it lives on inconsistencies: allows baseball on Sundays, yet forbids movies; prides itself on culture, but has no decent theatre and is shunned even by road shows; points with pride to historical tradition while it seeks the very things that, inevitably, must destroy the value and the validity of those traditions.

Memphis, like Atlanta, owes much of its development to the accident of location. It is the trade center for the upper Mississippi Delta and other less famous, but hardly less rich, valleys. Distinctly a river town in pre-Civil War days, Memphis retains a picturesque quality through its location on the bluffs of the Mississippi, and the dock and river-boats give it something of the appearance of a port town. No longer is the river an important commercial adjunct of the city, however; but railroads have kept it a focal point for trade in the old Southwest. Unlike most cities today, Memphis is directly dependent on the surrounding country, for practically all of its commerce and industry revolve around cotton and hardwood. It is the largest inland market handling actual cotton in the country and the greatest center for the manufacture of cottonseed products. An open city, with wide streets and many handsome buildings, it has remained a type of the old plantation center —and its attempt to rival larger cities in the North and the West received one tangible check quite recently when its newest skyscraper was sold at auction under the bankruptcy law. When the surrounding country is prosperous, Memphis thrives; when, as at present, the farmer and the planter are poverty-stricken, the city suffers in proportion.

There are other cities that might, with equal justice, be sketched in greater detail. The industrial cities of Chattanooga and Knoxville; the pleasant port of Mobile; the resort city of Asheville, and the tobacco town of Durham. But any sketches of this nature must be inconclusive and unsatisfactory. I have omitted, deliberately, the Texas cities, for Dallas and Fort Worth belong to the Southwest; and San Antonio, though a fascinating blend of Spanish, Mexican, southern, western, and military life, seems outside the scope of this discussion. For a similar reason, I have omitted Louisville, though it might well be labelled "southern"—Louisville seems clearly comparable with St. Louis, and far removed, somehow, from Memphis or New Orleans. With equal arbitrariness I have neglected with regret ancient and picturesque St.

Augustine; without remorse the tourist cities of Florida. They represent a transplanted East. Some day this culture may bulk large in a study of southern life; at the present moment it is quite negligible. These arbitrary distinctions were unfortunate, but necessary, in any attempt to describe or to analyze the southern city as a type that is representative and that has become, in some instances, a section within the larger section that is the South.

Mobile in 1844

The author of this pungent description of Mobile was a young Northerner in search of health in the South when he wrote these words. Henry Benjamin Whipple, born in 1822, was destined to become one of the most famous men of his day in the upper Northwest. Ordained as an Episcopal minister in 1850, he was consecrated Bishop of Minnesota in 1859. Builder of churches and schools, friend of the workingman and especially of the Indians in his pastoral care, Bishop Whipple was as widely known in England as in America. Though he became the counselor of governors and Presidents, Bishop Whipple never lost his keen delight in new adventures and the ability to write engagingly about them, which this youthful diary shows. He was fond of the South and in later years he was accustomed to spend part of the winter season there in order to escape the prolonged cold and snow of Minnesota.

This excerpt from Bishop Whipple's Southern Diary, 1843–1844, *edited by Lester B. Shippee in 1937, is reprinted with the permission of the publishers, the University of Minnesota Press.*

MOBILE is a town of about 15,000 inhabitants in the winter & 2,500 in summer situated on the Mobile River about 30 miles from the Gulf of Mexico. The land about Mobile is very low, and much of it is exceedingly swampy, which during the hot months renders the city very sickly. Much of the business part of the city is made land and during the rainy season the streets are nearly impassable on account of the mud. At such times the streets resemble miry stage roads more than the pavements of the city. This city was settled first by the Spaniards and has still quite a considerable trade with Havana & a large number of Spanish & French population. Ferdinand DeSoto visited this part of the south at or about the year 1540. In 1819 this was only a small town of 800 inhabitants & its business was very light, as but a small part of Alabama was settled. The business of Mobile is very extensive indeed— probably greater than of any town of its size in the United States. It is generally a wholesale jobbing business with the surrounding country— altho a large retail business is done here with the fashionables of the town. During the summer months the business nearly ceases and all who can, leave the city. The deaths for the year 1842 were as per the sexton's report 683. Last year the crop of cotton at this port during the season amounted to about 480 thousand bales but this year the crop will be lighter altho' it will bring a larger price. There are but few fine buildings in the city and it appears to be a place of business rather than of pleasure. Its streets are thronged at this season of the year. Some of the back streets are beautiful and out of the city in the piny woods are some beautiful residences of the aristocracy of the city. The morals of this place are bad, altho' great credit is due to the Alabamians for the passage of a law making it a penetentiary offence and $500 fine to carry concealed weapons in the streets, and this law has had an excellent effect altho it is broken daily. A theatre, a circus & several minor per- formances meet with a very good encouragement here. Gamblers and others of similar stamp and character infest this as well as many other southern cities, and meet with but little to intimidate them. A few nights since two gentlemen were robbed & knocked down in the street—and one of them his life is despaired of. The streets of Mobile appear to me worse than any I have ever seen. The transition from wet to dry is so sudden that one is either wading in mud or suffocating with dust. I visited today the planters' press for compressing cotton for shipping. The machinery is simple and yet so admirably calculated for the object that one steam engine working two presses is able to com- press 1000 bales of cotton per day. It is done by means of heavy blocks of wood worked on screws. The lazy laughing singing negroes about the wharves make you laugh in spite of yourself. Such an array of flat noses and ivory you will seldom see—and then the merry sound of their voices as they sing "Ole Dan Tucker" "Yaller Girls" &c &c. There are a few of the tribe of Choctaws who still linger about their old hunting grounds & visit the city daily for selling of light wood. They are wretched & degraded looking objects, the miserable remnants of the nobility of the Indian race. The civilization of the white men has done but little for your people except to effect your ruin.

You can see as great varieties of character in the streets of Mobile as in any city of its size in the union. Clerks of all shapes and sizes; white & red haired men, staid thinking men, and brainless fops. Here goes a staid, demure faced priest & behind him is a dashy gambler. Here goes a quiet Quaker merchant and there is your Mississippi "buster," "half horse & half alligator with a touch of snapping turtle & a cross of lightning." Here is a walking tailor's advertisement and there is backwoods "Chickasaw hayman" all dressed "in yaller, pink & blue." Here is perambulating gin Cask, yclept a sot and yonder is an onion eyed Grahamite.[1] Here is a sailor just on shore with a pocket full of rocks ready for devilment of any kind and there is a beggar in rags. Pretty Creoles, pale faced sewing girls, painted vice, big headed & little headed men, tall anatomies & short Falstaffs, all are seen each full of himself & as if isolated from the world, so full do all seem of themselves. Oh! what an array of knowledge boxes, what a diversity in bread baskets, a great country this and no mistake. . . .

The military of Mobile were out today the 22ond of February. It was a grand gala day with them and they made a fine show, the uniforms & equipage was in good taste & in good order & they drilled very well. Such independent companies are an honor to any place. The tone of society in Mobile is very gay and to a certain extent dissipated, altho' there are many here who prefer literature & its rational enjoyments to the theatre & gay revels. Many young men come here every winter in search of business and leaving behind them the restraints of home they become dissipated & rush madly to destruction.

The boarding houses in Mobile & its hotels except the Mansion House are far worse than those of Savannah. Indeed I have sat down at some hard meals since I left Savannah & were it not that the meals are harder where there is none, I should have gone hungry. Especially in the up country of Georgia I ate meals that would disgrace John Brown's track. Such a destitution of good beef and pretty women I have never seen as in Georgia up country. At the first boarding house I tried at Mobile I suffered. Roast pigs came on the table & such pigs. Could they have talked they would have said, "I am o'er young to take me from me mammy yet," and fish, oh! more like chips than fish. Oh! tell it not in Gath & publish it not, that I have eaten of such a bill of fare. I am now very comfortably located at Mrs. Jones and we have a good table and Mrs. Jones is an agreeable lady. I have been much amused at some of the countrymen dressed in red, green or blue homespun whom I daily see here. A gentleman told me a good story of his giving one of these fellows a Sedlitz powder. The cracker saw the gentleman drink a Sedlitz powder and supposing that it was some kind of liquor to make drunk come, said "I say, stranger, will you give me

[1] A follower of Sylvester Graham (1794–1851), whose writing on dietetics persuaded many to become vegetarians.

one of them blue & white things." "Oh! yes" said he & gave him one & went out. The cracker, not knowing how to drink it, mixed one in one tumbler & one in the other & first drank one & then the other. As soon as he felt it begin to work & effervesce he began to run about the room & holding on to his stomach, cried "I'm a dead hos & no mistake, he's pisoned me, he's pisoned me." The stranger had to explain & make apologies to save himself a flogging which the cracker's friends promised him.

They have a fine market here and I see daily all kinds of vegetables offered for sale, tomatoes not excepted, and I see by today's paper that strawberries have been seen here. Sunday morning is the great market day & then you may see all kinds of flesh, fish, and fowl, wild game, vegetables & fruits, eatables and drinkables of all sorts and descriptions —and then, too, all classes may be seen wending their way to the market. Black and white, rich and poor, all seem bent on making the Sabbath morning a day of toil, of merchandise, of money spending & money getting instead of a time for quiet reflection & meditation. The Sabbath is very indifferently kept here. Eating houses, groceries, apple stands & many other shops are open on this day, which shows that that solemn reverence for the day is not felt here which characterizes it at the north. This is to a great degree the case over most parts of the south, altho I have seen many places where the Sabbath is honored & cherished by all.

I attended church today at the 1st Presbyterian Church and was much pleased with the sermon from Rev. W. T. Hamilton. Mr. H. is a powerful preacher altho he has an affected way with him which detracts from his eloquence. I believe his peculiar manners are natural to him, yet to me they are unpleasant. The text was "The people are too many that I sh^d give the Midianites into their hand lest they vaunt themselves and say our own hands have done this" and he made a beautiful application of the subject to the church.

I have felt quite sick today on account of the extreme heat and the suffocating air impregnated with dust. When the streets are dry, it is almost impossible for one to breathe or move. I never have been in a place where the atmosphere was as disagreeable.

Edward King Takes Time Off to Enjoy the Beauty
of Charleston

When the able reporter Edward King was sent on his long tour through the South by Scribner's Monthly *in 1873, he was supposed to pay particular attention to the condition of agriculture and industry. He therefore begins his two chapters on Charleston with an account of the rebuilding of bridges and railroads, the revival of shipping and the export trade in cotton, rice, and lumber, and the opportunities the region afforded to Northern capital. But he is soon seduced into writing the nostalgic description of the city itself which is given here. It is reprinted from pages 439–43 of King's* The Great South *(Hartford: American Publishing Company; 1875).*

VERY lovely is the old city, lying confidingly on the waters, at the confluence of the broad Ashley and Cooper rivers, and fronting on the spacious harbor, over whose entrance the scarred and ever memorable Sumter keeps watch and ward. Nature has lavished a wealth of delicious foliage upon all the surroundings of the city, and the palmetto, the live and water oaks, the royal magnolias, the tall pines, the flourishing hedges, and the gardens filled with rich, tropical blooms, profoundly impress the stranger. The winter climate is superb, and the sunshine seems omnipresent, creeping into even the narrowest lanes and by-ways.

In 1680, the people who had been encouraged to remove from the badly chosen site of a settlement which they had selected on the banks of the Ashley river in 1671, laid the foundations at Charleston, and the town at once sprang into activity. It began its commerce in dangerous times, for pirates hovered about the mouth of the Ashley, and many a good ship, laden with the produce of the plantations, and bound for Great Britain, was plundered, and its crew set on shore, or murdered, if resistance was offered. A hurricane also swept over the infant town, half ruining it; and then began a series of destructive fires, which, from 1680 to 1862, have, at fearfully short intervals, carried havoc and destruction into the homes of the wealthiest.

In later years, too, the fleets of hostile Spaniards or Frenchmen sometimes brought panic even to Charleston bar; and the beacon fires on Sullivan's Island, in the harbor, warned the citizens to be on their guard. In 1728, a hurricane created an inundation, which overflowed the town and lowlands, forced the inhabitants to take refuge on the roofs of their dwellings, drove twenty-three fine ships ashore, and leveled many thousands of trees. In the same year came the yellow fever, sweeping off multitudes of whites and blacks. After the surrender, by the proprietary government, of its control of the province, into the hands of the sovereign of Great Britain, on the payment of a round sum of purchase money, Charleston became more prosperous than ever before. In 1765 it was described as "one of the first cities in British America, yearly advancing in size, riches and population."

The approaches to Charleston from the sea are unique, and the stranger yields readily to the illusion that the city springs directly from the bosom of the waves. The bar at the harbor's mouth will allow ships drawing seventeen feet of water to pass over it. The entrance from the sea is commanded on either side by Morris and Sullivan's Islands, the former the scene of terrific slaughter during the dreadful days of 1863, and subsequently one of the points from which the Union forces bombarded Charleston; and the latter at present a fashionable summer resort, crowded with fine mansions. On the harbor side of Sullivan's Island, Fort Moultrie, a solid and well-constructed fortification, frowns over the hurrying waters. Passing Sumter, which lies isolated and in semi-ruin, looking, at a distance, like some coral island pushed up from the depths, one sails by pleasant shores lined with palmettoes and grand moss-hung oaks, and by Castle Pinckney, and anchors at the substantial wharves of the proud little city.

Many ships from many climes are anchored at these wharves, and the town seems the seaport of some thriving commercial State, so little does it represent the actual condition of South Carolina. The graceful Corinthian portico and columns of the new Custom-House, built of pure white marble, rise up near the water-side. There is a jolly refrain of the clinking of hammers, the rattling of drays, and the clanking of chains, which indicates much activity. Here some foreign vessel, which has come for phosphates, is unloading her ballast; here a rice-schooner is unloading near a pounding-mill. On one hand are lumber-yards; on another, cotton-sheds, filled with bales. Hundreds of negroes, screaming and pounding their mules, clatter along the piers and roadways; a great Florida steamer is swinging round, and starting on her ocean trip to the Peninsula, with her decks crowded with Northern visitors. Along "East Bay" the houses are, in many places, solid and antique. The whole aspect of the harbor quarter is unlike that of any of our new and smartly painted Northern towns. In Charleston the houses and streets have an air of dignified repose and solidity. At the foot of Broad street, a spacious avenue lined with banks and offices of professional men, stands the old "Post-office," a building of the colonial type, much injured during the late war, but since renovated at considerable expense. Most of the original material for the construction of the edifice was brought from England in 1761. Within its walls the voices of Rutledge, Pinckney, Gadsden, Lowndes and Laurens were raised to vehemently denounce the Government against whose tyranny the "Thirteen original States" rebelled; from the old steps Washington addressed the Charlestonians in 1791; and for many years during this century it was an Exchange for the merchants of Charleston and vicinity. When the British occupied Charleston, the building was the scene of many exciting episodes. The basement was taken for a prison, and all who were devoted to the cause of American liberty were confined therein. From that prison the martyr, Isaac Hayne, was led to execution; and in the cellar one hundred thousand pounds of powder lay safely hidden from the British during the whole time of their occupation. On the site of this building stood the old council-chamber and watch-house used in the days of the "proprietary government."

The original plan of Charleston comprised a great number of streets running at right angles, north and south, east and west, between the two rivers. But many of these streets were very narrow, being, in fact, nothing more than lanes; and they have remained unchanged until the present day. The darkness and narrowness of the old lanes, the elder colonists thought, would keep away the glare of the bright sun; but the modern Charlestonians do not seem of their opinion, for they open wide avenues, and court the sun freely in their spacious and elegant mansions on the "Battery." Some of the Charleston avenues present a novel appearance, bordered as they are on either side by tall, weather-stained mansions, whose gable-ends front upon the sidewalks, and which boast verandas attached to each story, screened from the sun and from observation by ample wooden lattices, and by trellised vines and creepers. The high walls, which one sees so often in France and England, surround the majority of the gardens, and it is only through the gate, as in New Orleans, that one can catch a glimpse of the loveliness within. In some of the streets remote from the harbor front, the stillness of death or desertion reigns; many of the better class of mansions are vacant, and here and there the residence of some former aristocrat is now serving as an abode for a dozen negro families.

On King street one sees the most activity in the lighter branches of trade; there the ladies indulge in shopping, evening, morning, and afternoon; there is located the principal theatre, the tasty, little "Academy of Music," and there also, are some elegant homes. Along that section of King street, near the crossing of Broad, however, are numerous little shops frequented by negroes, in which one sees the most extravagant array of gaudy but inexpensive articles of apparel; and of eatables which the negro palate cannot resist. The residence streets of the "Palmetto City," on the side next the Ashley river, are picturesque and lovely. They are usually bordered by many beautiful gardens. A labyrinth of long wooden piers and wharves runs out on the lagoons and inlets near the Ashley, and the boasted resemblance of Charleston to Venice is doubtless founded on the perfect illusion produced by a view of that section from a distance. The magnificent and the mean jostle each other very closely in all quarters.

New Orleans: Decatur Street

This essay is reprinted from The Collected Essays of John Peale Bishop, *edited by Edmund Wilson; copyright 1933, 1936, 1948 by Charles Scribner's Sons; used by permission of the publishers. For a note on Bishop see p. 3.*

A BLANK sun stares down at Decatur Street. The sky is high and, as always here, shows clouds which, strangely, do not affect the intensity of light. The air hangs heavy, with no perceptible stir, except that occasionally there is a strong odor from the docks, where coffee is being unloaded from boats of Brazil.

This is the Vieux Carré of New Orleans, with houses that date from the docks, where coffee is being unloaded from boats of Brazil, shutters opening on narrow galleries. All have fine railings: festoons of cast-iron grapes and black twining leaves are looped along a second story with wet wash; formal intricacies of the early eighteen hundreds project over the pavement signs of Jax and Regal Beer. Under the galleries, Decatur Street garishly rots in the sun. In the afternoon, the dubious barbershops, red-striped and fly-specked, are not drowsier than the riverfront saloons. But at night the latter waken with sinister entertainment. An eleven-year-old boy, his face racked by sleeplessness (he is said to support a mother and four younger children), sings to the music

534

of a hammered piano *On the Isle of Capri*, with the mechanical gestures of a suffering doll. Monotonous jazz is provided by Negroes, liquor by bars; sailors come here from the ends of the world, the girls mostly from the hill-country of the surrounding states. They are not called hostesses, for they order these things more directly in the South; after Prohibition, there was never any hint that the saloon would not return. The darkness of backrooms is alive, on a good night, with crowded shapes of love in the making.

Painted invitations outside saloons are for seamen: "Sink Your Hook in Here." Doorways opening on tobacco-colored corridors advertise "Rooms for Spanish and Filipino Sailors," with prices from fifteen to fifty cents. Popeye and the native pirate, Jean Laffitte, lend their names to places of amusement. Blank's Place declares that it is "Famous from Coast to Coast." Inside, it has between bar and backrooms the usual white lattice, inscribed "Tables for Ladies" and surmounted by seven white stars each inscribed with a girl's name—Doris, Nora, Edna, Dorothy, Helen, Marie, Mary Ann. New Orleans is a Southern port, and in this aspect resembles an American Marseilles, expurgated, it is true, from time to time, for this is, after all, America. The latest purge, which was begun something over a year ago, came as a result of the controversy between the late Huey Long and the city government of New Orleans. The underworld, which was with the state dictator almost to a man, quite faithfully believed, as long as he was alive, that once the Hillbilly Napoleon was triumphant and the last remnants of the Bourbon regime were destroyed, everything would be wide open again. Huey is dead by assassination. And his interdiction stands against the famous old district, through which generations of great Creole ladies drove on their way to the opera. It closed most of the houses and all of the shutters. It also overcrowded the waterfront.

The French Market begins with the Creole Café du Monde, which also allows itself to be known as the Original Coffee Stand. It looks, beyond the corner of Decatur Street, at the only baroque square in this America. In Jackson Square the general on horseback, uprearing in bronze, is surrounded by a staff—in constant attendance—of bench-warmers, panhandlers and river bums. They look across a green luxuriance of tropical vegetation to a waste of railroad-tracks and the great warehouses on the docks. The Mississippi runs below them, a swift, deep, yellow, muddy flood. Nowhere, not even at New Orleans, did the Americans of the last century know how to put their water-ways to any but commercial uses. Water traffic is always pleasant to watch: white paddle-boat ferries, the unloadings from the tropics to the concrete docks. But the Mississippi is romantic only to the mind; here it is an ugly river, in its lower stretches between levees, the only ugly river I remember ever to have seen in America.

Once, if we may judge by the small model in the Cabildo, the old Halle des Boucheries of the French Market must have looked extraordinarily like a primitive Greek temple, on squat columns, all the space under the roof open to the air. Progress in the nineteenth century half enclosed the arcades with bathroom tiles, without thereby increasing the cleanliness, half screened them with wire, to accumulate more dirt, and painted the almost hidden pillars a dull oxblood red. A still more progressive twentieth century proposes to demolish it altogether and replace it by something not less sightly and a little more sanitary. This should not be hard. But the proposed change is resented by all who remember it in some happier romantic stage before the war, when Choctaw women sold herbs and sassafras-bark from grass-woven baskets and Negresses in tropically gay chignons dispensed hot drip-coffee with a flavor of chicory.

The sheds beyond have, also, I am told, parts from the past; but all that can be seen of them is a haphazard construction of time, more patched than repaired. Outside, a drowsiness of Southern sun falls on a grey man asleep on a chicken-coop. His dishevelled socks are grey above his cut shoes, his forlorn hat pulled over his eyes. An old Negro sits bent in a witless doze over his cart, in a somnolence only less deep than that of his donkey dozing in the shafts. Sleep pervades the market; at any hour of the day or night one finds Negroes in blue jeans stretched on sacks and lost to the world, or shelved in twos and threes on high-piled crates. Cajun boys curl in their carts to snore on beds of kale and cabbage; snoozing farmers dangle their legs over dropped backboards, undisturbed by the crap game in the next truck.

The booths are Sicilian, hung with red peppers, draped with garlic, piled with fruit, trayed with vegetables, fresh and dried herbs. A huge man, fat as Silenus, daintily binds bunches for soup, while his wife quarters cabbages, ties smaller bundles of thyme, parsley, green onions, small hot peppers and sweet pimientos to season gumbos. Another Italian with white mustache, smiling fiercely from a tanned face, offers jars of green filé powder, unground allspice, pickled onions in vinegar. Carts and trucks flank the sidewalk; one walks through crates of curled parsley, scallions piled with ice, wagonloads of spinach with tender mauve stalks, moist baskets of crisp kale; sacks of white onions in oyster-white fishnet, pink onions in sacks of old rose; piles of eggplant with purple reflections, white garlic and long sea-green leeks with shredded roots, grey-white like witches' hair. Boxes of artichokes fit their leaves into a complicated pattern. Trucks from Happy Jack, Boothville and Buras have unloaded their oranges; a long red truck is selling cabbages, green peppers, squashes long and curled like the trumpets of Jericho. There is a more than Jordaens profusion, an abundance more glittering in color than Pourbus. A blue truck stands in sunlight, Negroes clambering over its sides, seven men in faded jeans, washing-blue overalls; the last over is a mulatto in a sweater of pure sapphire. A mangy cat steps across a roadway of crushed oranges and powdered oyster-shells.

Two women pick wood from the waste between market and rail-road-tracks; three slum-boys quarrel among the stands over the division of five rotting oranges. Here, as elsewhere, penury in a land of abundance. From their covered wagons of unsold produce two Cajun lads look out with an air of hopeless poverty. On this narrow but rich alluvial soil, accumulated through a million years of flood, the new Sicilian survives; the older stock of whatever race, whatever color, diminishes toward starvation.

In the fish-market, a black man huge as an executioner hacks the meat of snapping-turtles from giant shells. Red-snappers, rose-scaled, lie beside the slender silver-foil Spanish mackerel and pompano from the Gulf of Mexico. Lake trout from Pontchartrain are tied together by strips of palmetto; carried on nappy heads, great round baskets of crabs go by, bedded in Spanish moss. Vast piles of shrimps, transparent shells from Barataria, are cooled under shovels of crushed ice. In their wire confines, the mahogany-red crawfish are in constant crawling motion; the monster swamp frogs squat under continual streams of water.

Once again on the sidewalk of Decatur Street, I am offered for sale a short-eared owl. And without turning my head, as the owl in his cage of withes is amazingly able to do until he blinks painfully between his shoulders, looking backward, I find myself listening to a conversation between a Negro man and two women: "This nigger wanted to commit suicide. But then *he* come in and found him. And then *he* got mixed up and pretty near killed *hisself*." I remember the old superstition that no black man ever does away with himself. The man's voice is soft, high, uncomplaining, almost gay. His speech is confusing until I make out that the dead man is always "that nigger" and that the live one is simply "he." " 'Cause they was good alcohol and they was wood alcohol. See? And the bottles was mixed up and he pretty near got a swallow of bad alcohol. They was that great big demijohn of creosote, and that nigger just turned it up and drank. He wanted to die, see? That nigger, he wanted to die. And then when he felt the pains in his stummock, he began hollerin', 'Lordy, Lordy! Get me sumpin' quick! I didn't mean to do it.' But he did, see? That nigger wanted to die. And he did. They give him some milk. And he drunk too much of it. Then he didn't even talk any more, he had such cramps, but he was sufferin' with his eyes. That was when *he* come in and almost killed hisself mixin' up that bad alcohol. It scared him when he seed him on that bed. He was sufferin' so it upset him sumpin' awful. And he got that bad alcohol. But that other nigger, he wanted to die."

The owl had quite closed his eyes. And looking up, at the corner, in the bright sunlight, I saw a sign, "Poor Boy Sandwich: Grande Dame Coffee: J. Battistella." At the moment, it seemed to me to resume much of Louisiana: a neon sign, unlit in the sun, ending with an Italian name.

Birmingham

The following piece is condensed from an article by Harold H. Martin which appeared in the Saturday Evening Post *of September 6, 1947. It was one of a series of articles on "The Cities of America." Mr. Martin, who is an associate editor of the* Post, *has graciously permitted these excerpts from his article to be reprinted here.*

BIRMINGHAM is young. When New Orleans was full of years and grace and mellow culture, wildcats were chasing rabbits through the brier patches where Birmingham's tallest buildings now stand. When Atlanta was already big and busy enough to attract the rude attention of Gen. William Tecumseh Sherman, farmers were calling their cattle home across the swamps where Birmingham's steel mills smoke today. Memphis was a proud and prosperous river port when squirrels were hiding hickory nuts above the untapped wealth of iron and coal upon which Birmingham was to grow. She is the brash newcomer among the cities of the South. In consequence, her achievements, which have been prodigious, are a matter of pride to her when she measures them by the brief span of her years. Her citizens are fond of calling her "the youngest of the world's great cities." Sometimes they turn the phrase around and call her "the greatest of the world's young cities." When feeling particularly expansive they speak of her in deep-chested chamber-of-commerce tones as "The Magic City" or "The City of Destiny."

But somehow, for all her pride in the great labors which converted a cornfield into a metropolis in little more than the span of one man's life, Birmingham is haunted by a sense of great promise unfulfilled. She is troubled by a vision of the city which might have been—a finer, fairer place by far, richer not alone in wealth and population but in those things of the mind and the spirit which she feels she lacks today. . . .

538

The same forces which have built her so rapidly, many believe, have served to choke and throttle her. In the Age of Steel, rich cities grew where iron and coal and limestone could be cheaply brought together. In no other known spot in the nation do these ingredients of steel lie so close together in great quantities as in the Birmingham district. On a rare day when the air is clear the visitor may mount Red Mountain to the towering statue of Vulcan—god of the gorge, and the city's symbol—to see this one basic reason for Birmingham's existence dramatically presented. There in the valley below may be seen, all in a distance of fifteen miles, the black tipples of the coal mines, the red-stained mouths of the ore shafts, the loaded limestone cars and the web of rails along which these raw materials flow to the great mills and furnaces which lie in the valley, breathing flame.

There, her citizens say, in one panoramic glance may be seen her strength and her weakness. The valley is her basket, and all her eggs are in it. When the mines are busy and the furnaces roaring, Birmingham rides the crest.[1] When the mines are down and the fires are cold, the depression which stalks Birmingham makes the depression which other cities know seem like Mardi Gras. "Hard times," says an old adage of the town, "come here first and stay longest.". . .

The peculiar properties of the region's minerals had been known generations before the founding of the city. In wilderness days, Indians from as far as Mississippi journeyed there to get its red earth, which made a durable war paint. Andy Jackson's old soldiers, first settlers of the valley, used the hematite ore to dye their buckskins. During the Civil War a scattering of little mines produced the iron that Gadsden foundries made into Confederate cannon. And ever since 1827, geologists had been touting the area as one of the world's richest known mineral beds, but making little impression on a state largely dominated by wealthy cotton planters, who looked upon mining and manufacturing as Yankee enterprises, unfit pursuits for gentlemen. So it was late in the 1850's before two railroads, known somewhat confusingly as the South and North Alabama, and the Northeast and Southwest Alabama, began to make their way over humpbacked grades and rickety trestles toward a junction in the mineral valley.

During the Civil War all work stopped, Alabama being busy with more pressing matters, but shortly after Appomattox a young Confederate veteran named John T. Milner, who had made the original survey for the South and North, again began poking the right-of-way of that railroad through a hungry land that by now was ready to do anything to make a dollar. About the same time, John C. Stanton, a Boston capitalist, got control of the Northeast and Southwest, renamed it the

[1] Since 1950 Birmingham's Committee of 100 has been working to bring new and diversified industry to the city.

539

Alabama and Chattanooga Railroad, and with Chinese labor imported from California began to push toward a junction with Milner's line somewhere in Jones Valley, a tranquil pastoral area bounded by a mountain of iron to the south and the coal fields along the Warrior River to the north. Being smart men, they both realized that where the railroads crossed, a city would form. So they jointly bought up 7000 acres of land surrounding the junction point agreed upon, laid out a town, and went back to building their railroads.

Soon disquieting news reached Milner. Mr. Stanton, he learned, along with a wealthy Montgomery banker named Josiah Morris, had obtained options on another site, some miles away from the one they had already surveyed. Alarmed by this seeming chicanery, Milner immediately began to muddy the waters a bit himself. He started new surveys for his road's route that wandered over the face of the valley, crossing Stanton's proposed roadbed both above and below the valley's only existing municipality, a drowsy hamlet once known as Frog Level, but now dignified by the title of Elyton. Milner's subterfuge had the effect he wanted. Stanton was so confused that he failed to take up his options, and Milner, with Morris, grabbed them.

Milner and Morris lost no time getting their real-estate development started on the new site. Aided by a white-maned old gentleman named James Robert Powell, a stagecoach tycoon, they laid out the streets and avenues of their town across the fields, swamps, brier patches and wood lots of the farmlands two miles east of Elyton, which looked on with some alarm at all this bustle. They formed a stock company, named it the Elyton Land Company, sold two thousand shares at $100 a share, elected Powell president of the company and turned over to him the promotion of the town which they had named for England's huge steel center. . . .

It was fourteen years before the hopeful Elyton Land Company paid its first dividend. By that time Colonel Powell, the booming, swaggering "Duke of Birmingham," was gone. Discouraged, he had retired to his Mississippi plantation, where soon he was killed, in a tavern squabble on the Yazoo.

But Milner didn't give up. Knowing that cheap iron would put the town on its feet again, he instigated experiments in using the Birmingham coal for coking. The tests proved that the days of expensive iron, made with charcoal, were over. Birmingham's coal made good coke. New life was breathed into the town, and a new prophet came to cry its glorious future. His name was Henry F. DeBardeleben, forebear of a family still prominent in the city. Believing, and frequently saying, that "Life is just one big poker game," he wheedled extra capital from English and Northern bankers to start mines and furnaces and rolling mills. He founded the town of Bessemer, in his haste to get it going buying and hauling to its site the old exhibit building of the New Orleans Exposition. Iron-masters flocked in from the East. Land speculators came. The Elyton Land Company, nearly broke in 1880, from 1883 to 1887 paid more than $5,500,000 in dividends. Its stock, once down to seventeen dollars a share, was held at $4000 a share.

Then the price of pig iron began to fall. Fabulous land-promotion ventures crashed. Struggling mines and mills began to merge. Out of the welter of speculations four companies came safely, though so enfeebled financially they had trouble buying groceries to stock their commissaries.

With pig iron nearly worthless, the struggling town finally found a way out. She learned how to make steel. And just as coke pig iron had rescued her from one disaster, steel saved her again. Huge U. S. Steel came in in 1907 to add the Tennessee Coal, Iron and Railroad Company to its empire just as that struggling company, which had moved hopefully down from Tennessee during the boom, was about to go under. Republic came in. Since then, Birmingham's biggest industries have been Northern-owned and the reins that guided her have been largely held in outside hands.

Her growth has surged and ebbed with the rise and fall of steel. She has grown as steel has grown, lain hungrily dormant through depressions, fared well or badly according to fortunes of the huge industry of which, in actuality, she has been a by-product, able or willing to exercise little control over her own civic destiny.

This sometimes happy, sometimes dolorous ride on the coattails of industry has created a city of violent contrasts. Among her citizens she could once count fifty millionaires, but until the last depression brought the final tight unionization of her mines and mills after years of bitter, sometimes bloody, labor strife, even boom times brought to the majority of her population only a subsistence living.

In her outer areas, when spring brings out the lilacs, she is a city of dramatic, even breath-taking beauty. She is also, despite the clearing up of many blighted areas, still a city checkerboarded with teeming and unkempt slums, some of which snuggle embarrassingly close to her finest downtown buildings.

She is a friendly and most generous city. Her Red Cross and Community Fund drives never fail to go beyond their goals. Yet over-all projects for the city's good—such as the smoke-abatement campaign— find the going rough. In the smoke drive, one indignant industrialist submitted only after threat of arrest, and the campaign was said to be only 50 per cent effective. Before the smoke was controlled, you could not see your hand a foot before your face on a morning when the smog was thick. Now it is visible two feet before your face.

Birmingham's government is honest and has been since her old aldermanic system, controlled largely by saloon-keepers and contractors, was thrown out around the turn of the century in favor of a three-man commission. She has no dives, no gambling dens and no open houses of joy to tempt the weak, a tribute to the watchfulness of the 452 churches which make her the strongest church-going, Sunday-school-supporting town of her size in the nation. Yet her crimes of violence are so numerous that she is periodically embarrassed by leading the nation in homicides per capita.

Her schools are among the country's best, scholastically, and her garbage collection is so swift and efficient that sanitary engineers from other cities have visited Birmingham to look upon it with awe. Yet her parks need more attention than they have received in the past, the auditorium is sadly in need of repair, and the town is without a zoo, since a depression-ridden city administration failed to provide funds to feed Miss Fancy, an amiable female elephant who was once ridden through the town by a keeper full of joyous waters.

Some of her downtown buildings, notably the Electric Building, have received wide acclaim for their architectural beauty, but the current city hall is a mouldering old relic of the Iron Age, from which the ceiling plaster falls so frequently the average citizen is afraid to enter it unless he is wearing a miner's hat.

For decades little groups in the town have busied themselves with matters more of the mind and the spirit than of the mine and the mill. Clubs devoted to the arts, to music, painting, literature and the theater have existed sporadically over the years and are currently sponsoring Starlight Opera, an outdoor program of light summer music, and a series of plays. But in the field of literature Birmingham's most famous son is still Octavus Roy Cohen, whose humorous stories about Negroes were considered to be exaggerated until the residents of 18th Street started reading about themselves and faithfully mimicking Florian Slappey, Sis Callie Flukers and Lawyer Chew. In music, her outstanding contribution has been Tuxedo Junction, a jump tune, and a melodious lament in which an unknown resident of the town calaboose (said by Birmingham to be the nation's largest) implores his love to write him a letter, send it by mail, send it in care of Birmingham Jail. The town remembers East Lynne and a Maurice Evans' Hamlet, but the brightest memory of her stage centers around the time a prominent citizen, appearing in a home-talent production of Julius Caesar, strode from the wings, stumbled and in his confusion bellowed: "Where is Cassius at?". . .

Despite her willingness to denounce outsiders for mentioning the shortcomings of which local residents freely complain, there is definite evidence that the city is now stirred by a new vision of what she wants to be. In the past two years the once moribund chamber of commerce has set out to capture any and all small industry which might fit in around big steel. Poking its head up above the smoke, the chamber also has inaugurated a program of livestock development in the surrounding counties, luring the cattle-growing youth by offering free hay and shavings and a nickel more per pound than Montgomery pays, all wrapped up in a big show and sale featuring Gene Autry and a genuine Wild West Rodeo.

A new and stronger drive to bring outlying municipalities and un-incorporated areas into the city's fold has begun, with city and county fathers, the town's three newspapers and 45,000 members of the CIO unions all trumpeting for consolidation. If consolidation goes through, the population will rise from the present estimated figure of 315,000 to about 503,000. Another ancient evil is also being attacked—the failure of the legislature to reapportion itself on a basis of population, a reform which would give Birmingham three senators and eighteen repre-sentatives at Montgomery, instead of the one senator and seven repre-sentatives which she now has. Since soft persuasion has so long failed, one group of young businessmen is ready to go to law to force a show-down.

Already proud of being the first city to require all her people be-tween the ages of fifteen and fifty to undergo an examination for syphilis, Birmingham within the next few years will complete a $20,-000,000 medical center. On the shelf in Mayor Cooper Green's office there are plans for spending some $75,000,000 more on badly needed civic enterprises. Of this, $7,000,000 will go for schools, to be divided be-tween white and colored on a population basis; $4,000,000 to get rid of the grade crossings which make driving hazardous; $1,000,000 for a "Cow Coliseum" at old Fairgrounds Park; a civic center to be built up around Woodrow Wilson Park. (It was called Capitol Park a long time, until Birmingham gave up trying to spirit the Statehouse away from Montgomery.) Here a fine new city hall will stand [2] and a renovated auditorium, perhaps even a Museum of Arts and Sciences. After that there's talk of boring a tunnel through Red Mountain to connect the downtown section with the highways to the South.

The Southern Research Institute, conceived in Birmingham, is a product of the new spirit. Bringing together the biggest collection of scientific brains in the South, its laboratories seek new ways of giving added value to Southern raw materials and better ways to make the things the South now makes.

There are a few signs, considerably smaller than a man's hand, which indicate that Birmingham's big industries at long last are becoming a

[2] This has now been built.

little embarrassed by the fact that many Birminghamians, though grateful for their presence, feel that they are citizens more in name than in spirit.

In years past they have ignored such talk. Today they will reply, though unofficially, through spokesmen with a familiar passion for anonymity.

"We are here to make steel," they explain plaintively. "We are not here to build a city. We sell our products throughout the South. If a plant that uses steel wants to set up in Chattanooga or Atlanta or Jackson, Mississippi, that's their business, not ours. If Birmingham wants them, it's Birmingham's business to go out and get them."

Heretofore big steel has taken no part in the going out and getting. Last year, though, Ervin Jackson, the new president of the chamber of commerce, went out on the town with a war cry, "We've got the big diamond. Now let's get some little diamonds to cluster around it." He found, to his surprise, that big steel was willing to help. He came out of the Brown-Marx Building, Tennessee Coal & Iron's headquarters, dazedly carrying a check for $10,000. TCI's annual contribution to the chamber in the past had been $1800.

TCI makes no bones, though, about its lack of enthusiasm for the expansion of the city limits which would take in its Fairfield and Ensley mills and make them subject to a city ad valorem tax.

They say they will not fight against consolidation, but they have no intention of fighting for it. "Just what," they inquire bluntly, "can a city do for a steel mill?"

So it is too early yet to say for sure that a new day has dawned in Birmingham. That glow on the horizon may be only the glare of a furnace going into blast out on the edge of town. But many things are in the wind. Years ago a social-minded writer said of her: "Here then is the measure of her civic leadership—to rise above the ways of small places, and neither by local brigandage, nor by clinging dependency, but by the sheer strength of her democracy, show that a fairer balance may be struck between self-government and corporate industry . . . a better city be made in which man can live and work."

When that was written, in 1912, Birmingham didn't quite get what the man was driving at. She was still content then to grow with steel, and she saw nothing shameful in a clinging dependency. From 1910 to 1930 she was one of the fastest-growing cities in the United States, through no particular effort of her own. Then something happened to stop that growth. She wants to start it again. She thinks that by striking that "fairer balance" some of the old magic—which wasn't magic at all, but opportunity—will come back to work for her. As her iron-masters might put it, she is anxious to go into blast again.

County Court Day in Kentucky

*Even the casual traveler can see at once how important the county
town is in Southern life. The main roads coming into it from the four
points of the compass lead straight to the courthouse square. In its
center is the courthouse: small, of mellow red brick and white wood-
trim in the old counties of Virginia; columned in Greek-revival style
farther south; Second Empire mansard in counties that somehow prospered in the 1880's; raw modernistic in the Texas ranch towns.*

*On the four streets facing the courthouse all of man's material needs
are catered to. Here you can find the principal (or only) hotel, the old
opera house, now showing movies, the best restaurant, the "package
store," unless—as usually happens—the town is dry. In front of the
courthouse the Confederate soldier stands on his pedestal. Children play
round him while parents and kin gossip on the benches in the little park
or shop in the stores across the street.*

*In the courtroom on the second floor of the courthouse there seems
always to be a trial in progress. Those who have come to town for
business or pleasure climb the stairs for a few minutes of the show, and
a show it is indeed if the contending lawyers are working on a case that
stretches their wit and oratory.*

*Sooner or later every Southern novelist sends his characters to the
county town on some decisive errand. For this reason many Southern
county towns, real or imaginary, have become famous—none more so
than Faulkner's Jefferson, which many of his fellow townsmen consider a libelous caricature of their Oxford, Mississippi, which can be
found on a road map.*

*Things have changed very little in the more remote Southern county
towns since the Kentucky novelist James Lane Allen (1849–1925)
wrote delightfully of them in* The Blue-Grass Region of Kentucky
*(New York: Macmillan Company; 1900), the book from which this se-
lection is reprinted (pp. 88–110).*

It may be that some stranger has sojourned long enough in Kentucky
to have grown familiar with the wonted aspects of a county town. He
has remarked the easy swing of its daily life: amicable groups of men

545

sitting around the front entrances of the hotels; the few purchasers and promenaders on the uneven brick pavements; the few vehicles of draught and carriage scattered along the level white thoroughfares. All day the subdued murmur of patient local traffic has scarcely drowned the twittering of English sparrows in the maples. Then comes a Monday morning when the whole scene changes. The world has not been dead, but only sleeping. Whence this sudden surging crowd of rural folk—these lowing herds in the streets? Is it some animated pastoral come to town? some joyful public anniversary? some survival in altered guise of the English country fair of mellower times? or a vision of what the little place will be a century hence, when American life shall be packed and agitated and tense all over the land? What a world of homogeneous, good-looking, substantial, reposeful people with honest front and amiable meaning! What bargaining and buying and selling by ever-forming, ever-dissolving groups, with quiet laughter and familiar talk and endless interchange of domestic interrogatories! You descend into the street to study the doings and spectacles from a nearer approach, and stop to ask the meaning of it. Ah! it is county court day in Kentucky; it is the Kentuckians in the market-place.

II

They have been assembling here now for nearly a hundred years. One of the first demands of the young commonwealth in the woods was that its vigorous, passionate life should be regulated by the usages of civil law. Its monthly county courts, with justices of the peace, were derived from the Virginia system of jurisprudence, where they formed the aristocratic feature of the government. Virginia itself owed these models to England; and thus the influence of the courts and of the decent and orderly yeomanry of both lands passed, as was singularly fitting, over into the ideals of justice erected by the pure-blooded colony. As the town-meeting of Boston town perpetuated the folkmote of the Anglo-Saxon free state, and the Dutch village communities on the shores of the Hudson revived the older ones on the banks of the Rhine, so in Kentucky, through Virginia, there were transplanted by the people, themselves of clean stock and with strong conservative ancestral traits, the influences and elements of English law in relation to the county, the court, and the justice of the peace.

Through all the old time of Kentucky State life there towers up the figure of the justice of the peace. Commissioned by the Governor to hold monthly court, he had not always a court-house wherein to sit, but must buy land in the midst of a settlement or town whereon to build one, and build also the contiguous necessity of civilization—a jail. In the rude court-room he had a long platform erected, usually running its whole width; on this platform he had a ruder wooden bench placed, likewise extending all the way across; and on this bench, having ridden into town, it may be, in dun-colored leggings, broadcloth pantaloons, a pigeon-tailed coat, a shingle-caped overcoat, and a twelve-dollar high fur hat, he sat gravely and sturdily down amid his peers; looking out upon the bar, ranged along a wooden bench beneath, and prepared to consider the legal needs of his assembled neighbors. Among them all the very best was he; chosen for age, wisdom, means, weight and probity of character; as a rule, not profoundly versed in the law, per-haps knowing nothing of it—being a Revolutionary soldier, a pioneer, or a farmer—but endowed with a sure, robust common-sense and rectitude of spirit that enabled him to divine what the law was; shaking himself fiercely loose from the grip of mere technicalities, and de-ciding by the natural justice of the case; giving decisions of equal authority with the highest court, an appeal being rarely taken; per-petuating his own authority by appointing his own associates: with all his shortcomings and weaknesses a notable, historic figure, high-minded, fearless, and incorruptible, dignified, patient, and strong, and making the county court days of Kentucky for well nigh half a cen-tury memorable to those who have lived to see justice less economically and less honorably administered.

But besides the legal character and intent of the day which was thus its first and dominant feature, divers things drew the folk together. Even the justice himself may have had quite other than magisterial reasons for coming to town; certainly the people had. They must interchange opinions about local and national politics, observe the workings of their own laws, pay and contract debts, acquire and trans-fer property, discuss all questions relative to the welfare of the com-munity—holding, in fact, a county court day much like one in Vir-ginia in the middle of the seventeenth century.

III

But after business was over, time hung idly on their hands; and being vigorous men, hardened by work in forest and field, trained in foot and limb to fleetness and endurance, and fired with admiration of physical prowess, like riotous school-boys out on a half-holiday, they fell to playing. All through the first quarter of the century, and for a longer time, county court day in Kentucky was, at least in many parts of the State, the occasion for holding athletic games. The men, young or in the sinewy manhood of more than middle age, assembled once a month at the county-seats to witness and take part in the feats of muscle and courage. They wrestled, threw the sledge, heaved the bar, divided and played at fives, had foot-races for themselves, and quarter-races for their horses. By-and-by, as these contests became a more prominent feature of the day, they would pit against each other the champions of different neighborhoods. It would become widely known beforehand that next county court day "the bully" in one end of the county would whip "the bully" in the other end; so when court day came, and the justices came, and the bullies came, what was the county to do but come also? The crowd repaired to the common, a ring was formed, the little men on the outside who couldn't see, Zaccheus-like, took to the convenient trees, and there was to be seen a fair and square set-to, in which the fist was the battering-ram and the biceps a catapult. What better, more time-honored proof could those backwoods Kentuckians have furnished of the humors in their English blood and of their English pugnacity? But, after all, this was only play, and play never is perfectly satisfying to a man who would rather fight; so from playing they fell to harder work, and throughout this period county court day was the monthly Monday on which the Kentuckian regularly did his fighting. He availed himself liberally of election day, it is true, and of regimental muster in the spring and battalion muster in the fall—great gala occasions; but county court day was by all odds the preferred and highly prized season. It was periodical, and could be relied upon, being written in the law, noted in the almanac, and registered in the heavens.

A capital day, a most admirable and serene day for fighting. Fights grew like a fresh-water polype—by being broken in two: each part produced a progeny. So conventional did the recreation become that difficulties occurring out in the country between times regularly had their settlements postponed until the belligerents could convene with the justices. The men met and fought openly in the streets, the friends of each standing by to see fair play and whet their appetites.

Thus the justices sat quietly on the bench inside, and the people fought quietly in the streets outside, and the day of the month set apart for the conservation of the peace became the approved day for individual war. There is no evidence to be had that either the justices or the constables ever interfered.

These pugilistic encounters had a certain law of beauty: they were affairs of equal combat and of courage. The fight over, animosity was gone, the feud ended. The men must shake hands, go and drink together, become friends. We are touching here upon a grave and curious fact of local history. The fighting habit must be judged by a wholly unique standard. It was the direct outcome of racial traits powerfully developed by social conditions.

IV

Another noticeable recreation of the day was the drinking. Indeed, the two pleasures went marvellously well together. The drinking led up to the fighting, and the fighting led up to the drinking; and this amiable co-operation might be prolonged at will. The merchants kept barrels of whiskey in their cellars for their customers. Bottles of it sat openly on the counter, half-way between the pocket of the buyer and the shelf of merchandise. There were no saloons separate from the taverns. At these whiskey was sold and drunk without screens or scruples. It was not usually bought by the drink, but by the tickler. The tickler was a bottle of narrow shape, holding a half-pint—just enough to tickle. On a county court day well nigh a whole town would be tickled. In some parts of the State tables were placed out on the sidewalks, and around these the men sat drinking mint-juleps and playing draw-poker and "old sledge."

Meantime the day was not wholly given over to playing and fighting and drinking. More and more it was becoming the great public day of the month, and mirroring the life and spirit of the times—on occasion a day of fearful, momentous gravity, as in the midst of war, financial distress, high party feeling; more and more the people gathered together for discussion and the origination of measures determining the events of their history. Gradually new features incrusted it. The politician, observing the crowd, availed himself of it to announce his own candidacy or to wage a friendly campaign, sure, whether popular or unpopular, of a courteous hearing; for this is a virtue of the Kentuckian, to be polite to a public speaker, however little liked his cause. In the spring, there being no fairs, it was the occasion for exhibiting the fine stock of the country, which was led out to some suburban pasture, where the owners made speeches over it. In the winter, at the close of the old or the beginning of the new year, negro slaves were regularly hired out on this day for the ensuing twelvemonth, and sometimes put upon the block before the court-house door and sold for life.

But is was not until near the half of the second quarter of the century that an auctioneer originated stock sales on the open square, and thus gave to the day the characteristic it has since retained of being the great market-day of the month. Thenceforth its influence was to be more widely felt, to be extended into other counties and even States; thenceforth it was to become more distinctively a local institution without counterpart.

To describe minutely the scenes of a county court day in Kentucky, say at the end of the half-century, would be to write a curious page in the history of the times; for they were possible only through the unique social conditions they portrayed. It was near the most prosperous period of State life under the old regime. The institution of slavery was about to culminate and decline. Agriculture had about as nearly perfected itself as it was ever destined to do under the system of bondage. The war cloud in the sky of the future could be covered with the hand, or at most with the country gentleman's broad-brimmed strawhat. The whole atmosphere of the times was heavy with ease, and the people, living in perpetual contemplation of their superabundant natural wealth, bore the quality of the land in their manners and dispositions. . . .

The town is packed. It looks as though by some vast suction system it had with one exercise of force drawn all the country life into itself. The poor dumb creatures gathered in from the peaceful fields, and crowded around the court-house, send forth, each after its kind, a general outcry of horror and despair at the tumult of the scene and the unimaginable mystery of their own fate. They overflow into the by-streets, where they take possession of the sidewalks, and debar entrance at private residences. No stock-pens wanted then; none wanted now. If a town legislates against these stock sales on the streets and puts up pens on its outskirts, straightway the stock is taken to some other market, and the town is punished for its airs by a decline in its trade.

As the day draws near noon, the tide of life is at the flood. Mixed in with the tossing horns and nimble heels of the terrified, distressed, half-maddened beasts, are the people. Above the level of these is the discordant choir of shrill-voiced auctioneers on horseback. At the corners of the streets long-haired—and long-eared—doctors in curious hats lecture to eager groups on maladies and philanthropic cures. Every itinerant vender of notion and nostrum in the country-side is there; every wandering Italian harper or musician of any kind, be he but a sightless fiddler, who brings forth with poor unison of voice and string the brief and too fickle ballads of the time, "Gentle Annie," and "Sweet Alice, Ben Bolt." Strangely contrasted with everything else in physical type and marks of civilization are the mountaineers, who have come down to "the settlemints" driving herds of their lean, stunted cattle, or bringing, in slow-moving, ox-drawn "steamboat" wagons, maple-sugar, and baskets, and poles, and wild mountain fruit—faded wagons, faded beasts, faded clothes, faded faces, faded everything. A general day for buying and selling all over the State. What purchases at the dry-goods stores and groceries to keep all those negroes at home fat and comfortable and comely—cottons, and gay cottonades, and gorgeous turbans, and linseys of prismatic dyes, bags of Rio coffee and barrels of sugar, with many another pleasant thing! All which will not be taken home in the family carriage, but in the wagon which Scipio Africanus is driving in; Scipio, remember; for while the New-Englander has been naming his own flesh and blood Peleg and Hezekiah and Abednego, the Kentuckian has been giving even his negro slaves mighty and classic names, after his taste and fashion. But very mockingly and satirically do those victorious titles contrast with the condition of those that wear them. A surging populace, an in-town holiday for all rural folk, wholly unlike what may be seen elsewhere in this country. The politician will be sure of his audience to-day in the court-house yard; the seller will be sure of the purchaser; the idle man of meeting one still idler; friend of seeing distant friend; blushing Phyllis, come in to buy fresh ribbons, of being followed through the throng by anxious Corydon.

And what, amid this tumult of life and affairs—what of the justice of the peace, whose figure once towered up so finely? Alas! quite out-grown, pushed aside, and wellnigh forgotten. The very name of the day which once so sternly commemorated the exercise of his authority has wandered into another meaning. "County court day" no longer brings up in the mind the image of the central court-house and the judge on the bench. It is to be greatly feared his noble type is dying. The stain of venality has soiled his homespun ermine, and the trail of the officer-seeker passed over his rough-hewn bench. So about this time the new constitution of the commonwealth comes in, to make the autocratic ancient justice over into the modern elective magistrate, and with the end of the half-century to close a great chapter of wonderful county court days.

But what changes in Kentucky since 1850! How has it fared with the day meantime? What development has it undergone? What contrasts will it show?

Undoubtedly, as seen now, the day is not more interesting by reason of the features it wears than for the sake of comparison with the others it has lost. A singular testimony to the conservative habits of the Kentuckian, and to the stability of his local institutions, is to be found in the fact that it should have come through all this period of upheaval and downfall, of shifting and drifting, and yet remained so much the same. Indeed, it seems in nowise liable to lose its meaning of being the great market and general business day as well as the great social and general laziness day of the month and the State. Perhaps one feature has taken larger prominence—the eager canvassing of voters by local politicians and office-seekers for weeks, sometimes for months, before-hand. Is it not known that even circuit court will adjourn on this day so as to give the clerk and the judge, the bar, the witnesses, an opportunity to hear rival candidates address the assembled crowd? And yet we shall discover differences. These people—these groups of twos and threes and hundreds, lounging, sitting, squatting, taking every imaginable posture that can secure bodily comfort—are they in any vital sense new Kentuckians in the new South? If you care to understand whether this be true, and what it may mean if it is true, you shall not find a better occasion for doing so than a contemporary county court day.

The Kentuckian nowadays does not come to county court to pick a quarrel or to settle one. He *has* no quarrel. His fist has reverted to its natural use and become a hand. Nor does he go armed. Positively it is true that gentlemen in this State do not now get satisfaction out of each other in the market-place, and that on a modern county court day a three-cornered hat is hardly to be seen. And yet you will go on defining a Kentuckian in terms of his grandfather, unaware that he has changed faster than the family reputation. The fighting habit and the shooting habit were both more than satisfied during the Civil War.

Another old-time feature of the day has disappeared—the open use of the pioneer beverage. Merchants do not now set it out for their customers; in the country no longer is it the law of hospitality to offer it to a guest. To do so would commonly be regarded in the light of as great a liberty as to have omitted it once would have been considered an offence. The decanter is no longer found on the sideboard in the home; the barrel is not stored in the cellar.

Some features of the old Kentucky market-place have disappeared. The war and the prostration of the South destroyed that as a market for certain kinds of stock, the raising and sales of which have in consequence declined. Railways have touched the eastern parts of the State, and broken up the distant, toilsome traffic with the steamboat wagons of the mountaineers. No longer is the day the general buying day for the circumjacent country as formerly, when the farmers, having great households of slaves, sent in their wagons and bought on twelve-months' credit, knowing it would be twenty-four months' if they desired. The doctors, too, have nearly vanished from the street corners, though on the highway one may still happen upon the peddler with his pack, and in the midst of an eager throng still may meet the swaying, sightless old fiddler, singing to ears that never tire gay ditties in a cracked and melancholy tone.

Through all changes one feature has remained. It goes back to the most ancient days of local history. The Kentuckian *will* come to county court "to swap horses"; it is in the blood. In one small town may be seen fifty or a hundred countrymen assembled during the afternoon in a back street to engage in this delightful recreation. Each rides or leads his worst, most objectionable beast; of these, however fair-seeming, none is above suspicion. It is the potter's field, the lazar-house, the beggardom of horse-flesh. The stiff and aged bondsman of the glebe and plough looks out of one filmy eye upon the hopeless wreck of the fleet roadster, and the poor macerated carcass that in days gone by bore its thankless burden over the glistening turnpikes with the speed and softness of the wind has not the strength to return the contemptuous kick which is given him by a lungless, tailless rival. Prices range from nothing upward. Exchanges are made for a piece of tobacco or a watermelon to boot. . . .

Perhaps you will not accept it as an evidence of progress that so many men will leave their business all over the country for an idle day once a month in town—nay, oftener than once a month; for many who are at county court in this place to-day will attend it in another county next Monday. But do not be deceived by the lazy appearance of the streets. There are fewer idlers than of old. You may think this quiet group of men who have taken possession of a buggy or a curb-stone are out upon a costly holiday. Draw near, and it is discovered that there is fresh, eager, intelligent talk of the newest agricultural implements and of scientific farming. In fact, the day is to the assembled farmers the seedtime of ideas, to be scattered in ready soil—an informal, unconscious meeting of grangers.

Annals of Possum Trot

In Possum Trot, Rural Community, South, *Herman C. Nixon, Vanderbilt professor of the social sciences, wished to find out if he could "get down to earth in attempting a regional understanding" by writing about the Alabama small town he knew as a boy. After recounting the annals of Possum Trot and describing its present dormant condition, in which there is more idleness than leisure, Professor Nixon goes on to discuss its potential revivification. Possum Trot, and communities like it, could "produce more milk and drink it. It could produce more food and eat it. It could provide more shelter and use it. It could provide more beauty and see it." It needs a community house and folk school, "with some attention to the local community and community ways." An intercommunity council, bringing together the other hamlets in the region, might "stimulate the use, and check the waste, of economic resources, of scenic resources, and of human resources." In short, in Professor Nixon's view, which he shares with the "Southern Agrarians," the whole of the present South "might think of fulfilling prophecy, the prophecy of Thomas Jefferson, architect and planner of a rural society."*

Possum Trot was first settled by white men and a few slaves some sixty years before the beginnings of these observations. Those sixty years can be briefly reviewed through word-of-mouth stories and a few scraps from recorded annals. The community is in the northern part of Calhoun County. This county was first called Benton in honor of Thomas Hart Benton, the Missouri statesman, but was changed in 1858 to its present name in honor of John C. Calhoun, since Benton's views on slavery had become distasteful to ardent Southerners, though yeomen they might be. In Rome, Georgia, my Grandpa Green in those early days once saw and heard a semi-drunk six-footer announce on the street and repeat, "I am from Benton county and can whip any man in Rome." He was unmolested and had no chance to make good his boast.

The red hills of my boyhood were near the upper border of the Creek Indian empire and near the lower border of the Cherokees' upland fields. The locality was thus among the Alabama lands opened up to settlers as the Indians were removed into the bounds of what is now Oklahoma when Andrew Jackson was President. One of General Jackson's officers, General John Coffee, with his troops, had surprised and defeated a band of Indians about fifteen miles from the Possum Trot scene early one morning during the war with the Creeks in 1813. It was early morning hot Coffee to the Indians. The town which was for seventy years the county seat of Benton or Calhoun was named Jacksonville in honor of Indian Fighter Jackson.

The Indians left traces behind. An ex-slave, when an old man, once gave me a story he got when a young man from an old Indian of our region. This Indian said that there were four races, and he ranked them in order as white man, Indian, dog, and Negro. The red men left many names for places in this part of the country. Across the mountain from Possum Trot and Tallahatchee Creek is Choccolocco Creek, both streams being tributaries of Coosa River, which is formed by the junction of the Etowah and the Oostanaula and which, in turn, joins the Tallapoosa to form the Alabama. The village of Ohatchie is only fifteen miles west of Possum Trot, and ten miles to the northeast is a hamlet bearing the Indian name of Ladiga. The adjacent county on the north is Cherokee, which recently celebrated the centennial of its founding with a party of Cherokees as special guests.

The early settlers came to this community and county largely from the Carolinas and Georgia. My mother's people, the Greens, came from the district around Greenville, South Carolina. My grandfather Nixon was born in North Carolina and lived in Georgia, where my father was born, before coming to Alabama. Possum Trot settlers had relatives who established themselves farther south or west on better lands nearer the river. There were many Green kinsmen in different parts of the county. To distinguish one Jake Green from another Jake Green, who

554

had sought gold in California, the latter was called "California Jake." There were relatives of early Tennesseans, and also Virginia connections. Early settlers' names included Moreland, Huffard, McCain, Harris, Carpenter, Boozer, Rowland, Scott, Price, Prater, Reaves, and others.

Long after the Civil War a family from Pennsylvania came to Possum Trot and prospected for iron ore and farmed. The man became known as the "Yankee," later as the "Old Yankee," few neighbors ever learning or remembering his three-syllable name. After his time the farm he had owned continued to be designated as the "Old Yankee Place." A one-time hamlet, where there was once a tannery, two miles from Possum Trot, was called Germania for a German who operated the "tan yard." The post office, railway station, tannery, and German family many years ago disappeared. The most notable thing remaining there is a large spring, Germania Spring, patronized by picnickers, transients, washwomen, and field hands.

Many stories of slavery and slavery days were handed down in this community. There were stories of droves of slaves coming from points northeast and going south or west, of a local master who fed slave tots "potlicker" in a wooden trough, of slaves shouting in church with white people in front, of a slave woman asking to join the Episcopal church in town, so that when the minister talked she could "talk back at him." There were stories of slave-visitings and of contacts at night with the patrol. To escape punishment or interference from the hands of the neighborhood patrol at night, the slaves wishing to visit off the farm at night sought passes from their master or members of his family. "Let John Green pass and repass," on the date specified, was a frequent form. Not infrequently a master's name was signed by a son or daughter without his knowledge, but it worked. Lacking a pass and meeting a patrol, a slave might take to his heels. Hence the refrain, known in Possum Trot and elsewhere,

> *"Run, nigger, run, pat (a)rol'l ketch you,*
> *Run, nigger, run, you'd better git home!"*

There was the couplet,

> *"Oh, oh, master, don't ketch me!*
> *Ketch that nigger behind that tree."*

And another,

> *"Nigger run, nigger flew,*
> *Nigger tore his shirt in two."*

The patrol often consisted of young men who did not seriously mind riding around the community at night. They at times undertook to waylay slaves and have a little fun at their expense, as when they administered a whipping to some of Warren Harris's slaves, who nevertheless had passes properly signed. They told the victims that a law had been passed to abolish passes and to whip regardless of their having passes. But Warren Harris had the tongue of a steamboat captain, or a stronger one, if possible, and he administered a verbal lashing, which the young patrol members took without protest.[1]

Corn shuckings were not peculiar to slavery, but there were corn shuckings in Possum Trot in slavery times. On such occasions, following the work of harvesting, a whole crop of corn was shucked by the slaves from the different farms of the neighborhood, and a good time seemingly was had by all. The accompanying singing and shouting on calm nights actually attracted visitors from distances of five miles, visitors who had no other way of knowing what was going on. The crowd generally divided into two teams, with leaders and, maybe, a jug of liquor at the bottom of the pile of corn for the winner. The teams started at opposite sides of the pile and raced to the middle, shucking the corn in front of them. They shucked, sang, and shouted until no shucks were left on the corn. Then came a big supper and perhaps a little liquor and singing, with such improvised words as

"Drink, puppy, drink, slobber, puppy, slobber;
Come, brave boys, let's foller."

Afterwards there was dancing, except for the over-religious, but even they did not go home until morning.

The Civil War left stories in Possum Trot, which is only fifty miles southwest of Sherman's line of march to Atlanta. "The Yankees are coming!" was a warning that was not soon forgotten. One of my mother's grandfathers refused to halt at a Yankee command, while he was crossing a field on foot to my mother's other grandfather's house, and was shot in the leg, but kept moving and reached the house with gold in his pocket. Before the war was over, Possum Trot heard the critical comment that it was "a rich man's war and a poor man's fight." But Possum Trot had farmers and farm boys in the war to the end. Mark Weaver told me stories about "Fighting Joe" Wheeler. Sanford Harmon let me feel a bullet hole in the top of his head as he described his experiences in the battle of Antietam. Gus Ledbetter was a one-arm veteran, with memories preceding the war. John Patterson always and inevitably got shouting happy when Dixie was played or sung.

The Ku Klux Klan rode after the war in Possum Trot. Peter Hunt, a Negro, whose life extended into my day, could tell of being visited at night by robed riders. They called for water and drank it by the

---

[1] There could have been a connection in spirit, method, and personnel between the patrol and the subsequent Klan, which has been described as a "sort of patrol."

bucketful, one member remarking that it was the best he had drunk since being killed at the battle of Shiloh, and then adding that it was important to hurry, since they were due in Montgomery (125 miles away) in ten minutes. A few words, significant words, of advice and warning were left with the bewildered host. At Cross Plains, nine miles northeast of Possum Trot, a Canadian schoolteacher, William C. Luke by name, and four other men, including three Negroes, were lynched by men in disguise on a July night in 1870, as a result of race friction that seemingly grew out of an ordinary fist fight between a white boy and a colored boy. That episode was well remembered in my rural community. It was linked with the Klan, and it has been given as the reason for changing the name of Cross Plains to Piedmont, with the coming of northern capital for its development.

Possum Trot first saw a railroad in 1867, or, in the words of a Negro construction worker, "two years after the surrender." This line was once the Selma, Rome and Dalton, then the East Tennessee, Virginia and Georgia, and finally and permanently, the Southern. In the early eighties another rail line came through under the name of East and West, or "E & W." It was started between Atlanta and Birmingham and did not reach either city until it was lenghtened, straightened, and improved as part of the Seaboard system two decades later. The E & W crossed the other road overhead near Possum Trot, and the crossing point was first named East and West Junction, long known as the "Junction," though the new post office and station soon took the name of Merrellton, a modification of Merrill, the name of a daughter of a neighboring postmistress, who was asked by postal officials to name the place. President Chester A. Arthur appointed my father, a Democrat, as the Merrellton postmaster, and there was never another until the office was discontinued to yield to a rural route. The Republican administration did not practice spoils or patronage at Possum Trot, which in one election was the banner beat in the banner county for Democracy. There was one Republican vote cast in the precinct, according to definite tradition, in that election, but the vote was disregarded in favor of a perfect score, as the story was later told. That was after Reconstruction and before the coming of the populist movement. Even a boomlet for the hamlet with the coming of the second railroad did not threaten its traditional politics.

The railroads gave temporary urban hopes to a few at the Junction, and a few lots were staked off and sold. Anniston, sixteen miles away, was being developed under the initial leadership of Sam Noble, a Connecticut Yankee, and was on the way to becoming an industrial center of thirty thousand population. There were men in Possum Trot who had made sorghum syrup with a portable mill and cooking pan right on what became the main street (Noble Street) in Anniston. Why could not the Junction grow? It did, but it was not to become a town or city. Piedmont was to become the new urban center in that part of the county and the world. The Junction–Possum Trot community was to remain rural, though furnishing opportunities for merchandising, saw-milling, charcoal production, rock-quarrying, and other non-farming enterprises, at times including iron-ore mining. Many laborers could live on the farm without working on the farm. They could leave the farm for local non-farm labor, which they generally called "following public works." Charcoal was shipped by the carload to iron furnaces before stone coal became the universal source of fuel for that purpose. Many a car went to Rock Run, between Possum Trot and Rome, to the "Rock Run Furnace." One of the earliest memories I have is of the black faces of white men loading charcoal. I was later to learn that this was the reason for scarred hillsides and mountainsides.

The railroads ran parallel nine miles between the Junction and Piedmont, and in the old days there were occasional train races. One time, with the engineers betting their hats on the outcome, the little E & W won the race, as they arrived at the Junction, and went west "round the bend" from the station with both hats. During one of the races, in a drizzling rain, a Possum Trot fellow, Wiley Garrett, was walking along one of the tracks in the same direction the trains were going. He looked back, seeing only one train, and crossed over a few steps to the other track. He cursed at the enginemen of the first train for yelling as the train pulled up alongside him. He recognized the second train barely in time to jump, though getting hit in his mid-section in mid-air and becoming crippled for life.

The road stretch is fairly straight from Piedmont to Possum Trot, but long fluctuating grades, especially on the older road, were causes of trouble for long freight trains before the use of automatic coupling and air brakes. Trains not infrequently broke into two sections, and the engineer had to race the front section down grade and far enough from the foot of the grade to be safe. With no telephone or telegraph service available, it was not easy to get the sections quickly together again. Once, while such a process was taking place near Possum Trot, after the rear section had stopped and sent a flagman to the rear, an oncoming train crashed into the caboose, killing the conductor. The flagman, said to have been steadily on duty for more than forty hours, fell asleep on the job and let the accident happen.

The farm boys, white and colored, knew the leading railroaders of the lines, by name and sight, and admired them, especially John Thomas, who was years a passenger engineer and wrote a book, *Fifty Years on the Rail*. "Pa" Hagan, longtime a freight conductor was known by his friendly nickname by many of both races. There were stories of Wirt Hall, large Negro brakeman from Ladiga, who could carry a bale of cotton on his back and shoulders, and who could swing on to a fast-moving train. Luke Hudson, the Negro who gave me much local lore, once asked me if I ever chanced up North to run into his older brother, who years ago was a Pullman porter between New York and Chicago. These departures from farms were in days of rural expansion, before so much timber was cut, so much land cleared, and so many farms turned over to cultivation by tenants.

The Farmers' Alliance movement of the eighties and early nineties touched Possum Trot and left for many years an influence of irregularity among the voters. An Alliance banner stood in a corner of an upstairs room of the Butler Green house for years after there was no Alliance for it to wave over. A local Alliance general store gave up the ghost after a short experiment, partly, it was said, because of poor management. The community was divided on the Alliance issue, and there was at least one hopeful spirit who cited economic laws as barriers to the movement. If there were debtors, with mortgaged farms, there also were those who farmed debt-free lands, with corn in the crib, hogs in the woods, meat in the smokehouse, and sweet potatoes in storage to last to the next crop. This was more widely true among families living on poorer lands some miles west and north of the Junction and away from the railroads.

There were cotton patches and a few cotton gins around Possum Trot since early times. I saw two abandoned gin establishments which had been operated locally by horsepower, or, more strictly speaking, by two mules going round and round. Each establishment had one gin of only forty saws, instead of a series of eighty-saw machines. There was hand-feeding of seed cotton into the saws for years after the Civil War, and, after the coming of the mechanical feeder, cotton was placed into the feed hopper by hand up into the twentieth century. The lint was, in turn, transferred by hand from gin to press and first tramped down by human foot-power, generally by a Negro laborer. Two or three bales a day, not an hour, constituted the maximum capacity, if there was no trouble. The cottonseed was removed from the gin floor entirely by hand. This by-product had lost its nuisance feature by the eighties and was becoming an important item of commerce and industry. A local ginner came back from a business visit to Rome with the startling news that at the hotel he had eaten bread seasoned with cottonseed oil, instead of hog lard, and could not tell the difference.

Old land deeds tell a story of activities and dealings in this neighborhood. Wood Moreland through purchase secured a United States "grant" to lands in Section 31, Township 13, in 1841. This original document, which I have, is signed for President John Tyler by "R. Tyler." Wood Moreland sold land to the Huffard family, who in turn sold land to B. P. Moreland in 1856 at five dollars an acre. The land came into the possession of Berry Moreland, and a deed of 1870 conveys the land to J. D. Arnold, of Jacksonville. On this deed Berry Moreland made "his X mark," and his wife Elizabeth made "her X mark" to dispose of the two hundred acres. George Arnold, of Jacksonville, bought the land from J. D. Arnold and in 1886 mortgaged it to the "New England Mortgage and Security Company," a Connecticut corporation, for a loan of $500. In 1887 William D. Nixon purchased the tract from George Arnold for $1,000 and also assumed that mortgage as well as another claim of seventy-five dollars. In 1868 William Scott sold to William Green a neighboring tract, which later became the "Jim Green Farm." This deed also conveys the perpetual right to use water from the "White Oak Spring" just across the line on other Scott lands.

Many Possum Trot farmers went to town to trade before the establishment of the Junction and even afterwards. Trading "on time" for autumn payment through sale of cotton had come to be the practice of many. It was rather customary in those days for various families from that whole part of the county to make "time" purchases at Rowan and Dean's in the county-seat town of Jacksonville. This firm had a bank account in New York, there being no bank in the town for years. It sold merchandise on credit at a high "mark-up" above cash prices. It bought cotton for shipment and sale through a New York account. It loaned money. It took mortgages on crops, livestock, and farms. Members of the firm ended up by owning not only hundreds, but thousands, of acres, including homesteads in the Possum Trot community. Many an agrarian critic in the days of the Farmers' Alliance spoke his mind on the subject of Rowan and Dean. There was a report that a Negro preacher had prayed in the pulpit, thanking God that they were going to a heavenly country where there would be

"No more mortgages and liens,
An' no more Rowans and Deans."

The Jacksonville weekly *Republican* came to several citizens in the Possum Trot region for tens of years, when Jacksonville was the county seat and Anniston was not old enough and large enough to win the courthouse. The weekly edition of the Atlanta *Constitution* was read with religious regularity by many in the eighteen-eighties and eighteen-nineties and later. John Patterson, when once in Atlanta, called at the *Constitution* offices and complained because the paper printed so much bad news and no good news. He brought back to Possum Trot the answer, "There is no good news; if it is good, it isn't news."

Possum Trotters read the *Constitution* in those days for more than news. There were editorials by Henry W. Grady, spokesman of the

New South, of which Possum Trot wanted to be a part. There were writings by Joel Chandler Harris, creator of "Uncle Remus." There were stories of Alabama country life by Betsy Hamilton. There were comments by "Bill Arp" (Charles H. Smith), a one-time Rome lawyer, who was a cracker-box philosopher and a Georgia Cracker humorist. He was Bill Martin, Bud Medders, and Charley Maner combined in print. There was the pioneer column of Frank L. Stanton, the "Riley of the South," who served up homely anecdotes, jingles of joy, "Songs of the Soil," and repetitions of "never mind the weather." Stanton, who went to the *Constitution* from the Rome *Tribune*, could have been a Possum Trot poet, for he was ever paying tribute to water-melons, blackberries, "possum and taters," barbecues, "fishing time," religious revivals, and barn dances. Possum Trot understood him when he made "The Rattlesnake" say,

"You just push the button, and I'll do the rest."

The *Constitution* was such an accepted institution in this community that I once thought it was started by a convention in 1787.[2]

The *Hearth and Home*, a monthly of Augusta, Maine, had a few Possum Trot subscribers for years, and so had *Comfort*, another Augusta low-priced monthly, laden with patent-medicine advertising. Later there were a few readers of the different Chicago publications of W. D. Boyce and Company. Uncle Robert McCain for years "took" the New York *Christian Herald*.[3]

Stories of old-time school days have come down. One is about a double whipping two generations ago received by a twin brother, before the teacher realized that he was applying the second hickory switch to the same boy, with the other momentarily escaping punishment for their joint devilment. Short split sessions were held at Green's School House, a mile and a half from the Junction, and this one-room house was also used as the voting place for the precinct, or beat eight. Salem Church, over near the railroads, was not only a meeting place for Presbytrians and for union-church purposes, but it was also for some years used for a neighborhood school. Miss Ella Rhine around 1880 sometimes taught school in a little house in the yard of the Rhine farm home. Negroes had recourse to churches for schooling.

Besides the Presbyterians on the main highway, there were many Methodists and Baptists in the community, both white and colored.

The white Methodists had established Asbury, a mile and a half from Salem, at the junction of two highways reaching different points on the Coosa River. The Negro Methodists built a house on a spot

[2] Not long ago an observer remarked that Possum Trot people used to swear by the *Constitution*, but now they swear at it.

[3] My earliest reading habit started through my reading newspapers and periodicals in the post office between their arrival and their delivery.

given them on the McCain farm and called it McCain's Chapel. Their Baptist brothers had a makeshift meeting place two miles up the road. The white Baptists had to go farther than any others to worship, except the "Hardshell" Baptists, who had to go several miles into the backwoods northwestward to Pilgrim's Rest. The latter were strong for the ancient rite of foot-washing, for the doctrine of predestination, and for a God-called, uneducated ministry. Some of the striking language of the Pilgrim's Rest pulpit has been handed down. One preacher at an all-day meeting said that before being "converted" he felt "like a dead dog floating on a millpond." Another said that before being saved he was "like a sack of sand open at both ends." The annual "foot-washing day" was a great day at Pilgrim's Rest, not only for "Hardshells" for miles around, but also for spectators, who came to visit and have a share of the "dinner on the groun'." There was a handed-down story that once a lone old Negro "Hardshell" member in the region was observed participating in the foot-washing service. A white man washed the Negro's feet after the Negro had washed the white man's feet.

All the churches, especially the Baptists, had all-day Sunday singings, with "dinner on the groun'" and visitors crowding in from "fifteen mile aroun'." A sixty-dollar organ eventually supplanted the tuning fork. For such occasions an unmarried field hand would sometimes use a week's wages to "hire" a horse and buggy and "haul some calico." A preacher denounced the buggy factories as being run by the devil, since the seat was so narrow. But that style of courting was one way to win a "dough-baker."

The Methodists held their own in revival meetings, with early enthusiasm that at times grew into shouting. Besides shouters, there were sometimes crying babies on hand. Stirring revivals were held at Asbury before, and in, my time. The spiritual gains were accompanied by social contacts and good times, especially on the part of the young. The younger groups in those days hated to see a revival series, a "protracted meeting," come to an end. When one was about to end too soon to suit the socially minded—the preachers in charge thinking the spiritual harvest was complete—a special scheme was designed to continue the meeting and the good time. A group of young men, by conspiracy, accepted the invitation to come to the "mourners' bench" on what might have been the last night. The plan worked and the revival continued. The Salem Presbyterians were the first to break the rigid custom of dividing the men and women worshipers by the aisle. This church led in social life for the young.

All of Possum Trot knew about Sam Jones, the "mountain evangelist," who had shifted from law to a drunkard's gutter and then to a regional pulpit. The Reverend Sam P. Jones lived at Cartersville, Georgia, forty miles away, at one end of the E & W railroad. He gave sermons and addresses in Calhoun County, and many traveled on the E & W to hear this stirring Methodist in his home town. It was told and believed that he had received his first revealing vision of hell while drunk and looking into the glow of a blast furnace between Cartersville and our community. Vivid were the memories of the Sam Jones comments on drinking, card-playing, Sabbath-breaking, dancing, and even low-neck dresses. In rural eyes he had no equal, either for religion or entertainment.

I have heard much shouting around the "mourners' bench" at Negro revivals. I heard a Negro cotton-picker say that he was once at the "mourners' bench" and kneeling for prayer, when suddenly a pistol fell out of his pocket. His fellow picker across the cotton row said, "That same thing happened to me, excepting it was a razor."

Possum Trot, especially in the eighties and nineties, had its share of candy-pullings, box-suppers, breakdowns, and picnics, with kissing games and "lemonade stirred with a spade." The Negroes too had these activities. At an old-time big wedding supper, a hog cooked whole was propped up on the table with an apple in its mouth. School "exhibitions" included Paul Bunyan stories. Barnyard rest-time comment included stories of "Buffalo Bill," "Wild Bill," and Jesse James, as well as "real" ghost stories, touched up with "raw head and bloody bones."

Possum Trot knew the taste of corn liquor, especially at election times, sometimes at house-raisings and well-diggings, and sometimes at dances. White men knew. Black men knew. Possum Trot knew illegitimate children, illegitimates who were black, who were white, and who were half black and half white. Isaac Teague, ex-slave, knew who was his white father. Soon after the rise of Anniston to cityhood, many Possum Trot men learned the way to Nora's house, west of the city's railway station. One time after cotton was sold and money was left over, a gang of men from down the creek below Possum Trot chipped in and gave Nora $200 for an exclusive night's rental of her house and all the women. (They could not do that now on Possum Trot cotton money, and they would not do that now in that community.)

It has been frequently true, however, that money cleared above debts, after selling cotton, was spent for wholesome purposes. Such money has gone for shoes, schoolbooks, preachers' support, fiddles, guitars, organs, buggies, home needs, Santa Claus items, and the like. More recently cotton money has paid for automobiles and radios.

So was the mixed life of labor and play in Possum Trot in its early days and in its middle period. If the story of those days were enlarged, it would be more of the same life among rural hills. The annals would be simple, for Possum Trot and the world were not yet causing trouble to each other. The recent history of Possum Trot brings up more talk of growth and change and problems. The old days did not linger, and neither can this story.

X V

BUSINESS AND INDUSTRY

A saying current in the South sums up the changes in the balance between industry and agriculture which have been going on during the past twenty years: "Cotton's going West, cattle's coming East, the Negro's going North, the Yankee's coming South." In no part of the country, except the Pacific coast region, is there such an industrial upsurge. The traveler watching from a Pullman window sees one gigantic plant after another, all of the most modern construction, rush by. Nearly every Southern state is moving to the front in at least one product: Virginia in synthetic fibers; North Carolina in furniture-making; South Carolina in textiles; Mississippi in wood pulp made from slash pine; Texas in natural gas, petroleum, sulphur, and the new petrochemicals. This most recent upsurge follows another industrial boom earlier in the century. Between 1900 and 1939 the volume of manufactured products in North Carolina increased 1,397.4 per cent. The rate of increase for Texas in the same period was 1,181.4 per cent. Even Arkansas, at the bottom of the list, showed an increase of 254.4 per cent.

Northern industry continues to move South, a process that has been going on, of course, since the 1880's. But even more significant is the volume of the newer industrial products that are coming from below Mason and Dixon's line. By 1951 du Pont, manufacturing orlon at Camden, South Carolina, neoprene rubber at Louisville, nylon yarn at Chattanooga, had placed half its investment in the South, having built twenty plants there, in nine states.

The picture is by no means as rosy as these facts might indicate. The most significant statistics one can look at are the per capita income figures, by states, for the year 1952. In North Carolina the figure was $1,049; in Texas, $1,452. In most Northern and Western states these sums were exceeded, often by substantial amounts. The Connecticut

564

figure, for example, was $2,080; in New York, it was $2,038; in California, $2,032. Evidently the South still has a long way to go before its total income will be equal to that of other regions comparable in size.

Before the industrial revolution arrived in America, the South had developed domestic manufactures suited to its needs. The wheels of gristmills turned in the swiftly moving streams and small ironworks produced the tools required by an agrarian economy. As the plantations grew in size, a large number of articles were produced by slaves who were trained as carpenters, cabinetmakers, brickmakers, and wheelwrights. Only luxuries and objects that required taste and great skill in their making had to be imported.

In the early years of the nineteenth century Southern commerce flourished in the ports of Charleston, Savannah, Mobile, and New Orleans, into which poured the products of the whole Mississippi Valley. For nearly ten years, beginning in 1834, New Orleans outranked New York in the volume of its exports. But the Southern factors, who handled the plantation products of their clients, and the shipping merchants gradually let their advantages slip from their hands. Cotton was shipped direct to Europe from Southern ports, but the ships laden with European goods on the homeward voyage put in at New York. From New York, European and Northern products were sent South in coastal vessels. Gradually the Southern ports lost to New York in the whole export-import trade. Clement Eaton notes in his *History of the Old South* that even as early as 1822 "Southern products, rice, cotton, tobacco, and naval stores, made up 55 per cent of the exports of New York port, and as late as 1860 cotton ranked an easy first in New York's exports."

Unfortunately, too, the profits made by the Southern planters were more likely to go into the purchase of more land and more slaves than into the necessitous banks of the South and its infant industries. Thus the South came increasingly to depend on Northern capital for whatever industrial enterprises it did undertake. And this meant, of course, that the profits from these enterprises had to be shared with the North.

The reasons for the slow growth of ante-bellum manufacturing are well summarized by Eaton.[1]

The progress of manufactures below the Mason and Dixon line was impeded by a number of psychological and physical handicaps. The agrarian ideal caused many Southerners of the ante-bellum period to hold prejudices against trade and manufacturing and to regard planting and politics as more honorable occupations. Southern capital was largely monopolized in buying more land and slaves. The accumulation of capital needed to start manufac-

[1] *A History of the Old South* (New York: Macmillan Company; 1949), p. 424.

tures was retarded also by the indirect method of selling the Southern agricultural staples, which enabled Northern business men to exploit the South and which contributed largely to perpetuating the colonial status of that region. Lesser reasons for the industrial lag of the South were the necessity of supporting a relatively larger dependent population of children and old people than existed in the North, the avoidance of the South by European immigrant laborers, the aversion of yeomen farmers to give up the independence of the farm and become "mill hands," the belief that Negroes were not suited to the handling of machinery, and the argument that the rise of manufactures would weaken the slave system and the opposition in the South to the protective tariff. Consequently, in 1860 the South produced slightly less than 10 per cent of the manufactures of the United States (measured in terms of value).

A few modifications of this statement are needed. Actually a fair number of Southerners were eager to see their region move ahead industrially. Notable among them were William Gregg and James Dunwoody Brownson De Bow, whose valiant efforts are reported on below (see pp. 574 and 569). At the Southern Commercial Conventions held between 1837 and 1860, the growing industrial might of the North was decried in florid speeches, but when the commercial men returned home, they did little to offset it except to join in the general clamor for "non-importation" agreements against Northern Products.

In one particular, the extension of its railroad system, the South made remarkable advances. During the decade 1850–60 it surpassed the North in the rate of construction. The first railroad uniting the upper South with the Middle West, the Baltimore & Ohio, was begun as early as 1828, but the magnificent dream of ex-Senator Hayne of South Carolina, of a railroad connecting Charleston with Cincinnati, which was to reach the Ohio by way of the Cumberland Gap, was never fulfilled. And the plans of Jefferson Davis, then Secretary of War, for a Southern Pacific railroad with its eastern terminus at Memphis, were headed off by Senator Stephen A. Douglas, who was taking care of the interests of the Chicago capitalists. (Neither man won. The first transcontinental railroad was not completed until 1869.)

When the Civil War came, the South was seriously lacking in plants that could manufacture essential war materials. Though handicapped by lack of manpower, machinery, and capital, the leaders in charge of supply accomplished some remarkable feats, as for example the expansion of Richmond's Tredegar Iron Works, which became the chief arsenal of the Confederacy. But for many items, among them much-needed drugs and surgical supplies, the South had to depend on the precarious fortunes of the blockade-runners.[2] By the war's end Northern generals had learned the first principle of modern warfare: destroy the enemy's transportation lines and his capacity to produce. Atlanta, railroad center of the deep South, was a blackened ruin and the naval foundry at Selma, Alabama, had been destroyed. There was little left of the South's industry when Lee surrendered to Grant at Appomattox.

In the 1880's Southern industry began to revive and expand under the impetus of the leaders in the New South movement. Such men as Henry W. Grady of Atlanta, Richard H. Edmonds of the Baltimore *Manufacturer's Record*, and Walter Hines Page called on the South to lift itself out of the ruin of war by the "real reconstruction which active trade will inaugurate." They sought an end to recriminations against the North and urged Northern capital to help rebuild the shattered Southern economy. The invigorating idea took hold with all save the "unreconstructed" and the older leaders in politics and business who could not adjust to the new order.

As a result, something like a mania for the building of textile mills swept the upper South. In most instances these new factories were brought into existence by Southerners themselves, the capital often coming from a host of small subscribers. The marvels of urban life in Gastonia and Spartanburg compensated the operatives lured from the mountain valleys for the disadvantages of long hours and low wages. Most of the new mill towns that sprang up between 1880 and 1900 were small feudal dynasties controlled by the millowners, who kept their workers in line by various means—from the company store to the sermons of the preachers whose salaries they paid. But no one considered that the owner was grinding the faces of the poor. Rather, he was a hero because he gave work to those who had seldom seen cash money. The loyalty of the workers to the owners persisted for years and later made it difficult for the textile unions to get a foothold in the South. Not until the time of the great textile strikes of 1929 and 1934 did the workers experience for the first time the full force of strikebreaking techniques well known in the North—evictions, arrests, injunctions, the black-list, mayhem and murder committed by the police, hired thugs, and the state militia.

In the early twentieth century the South continued to expand its traditional industries—tobacco-processing (in Durham and Winston-Salem), the manufacturing of oil, cattle-feed, and fertilizer from the versatile cottonseed, and the spinning and weaving of cotton textiles. (In 1923 the number of spindles in the South for the first time exceeded those in the North.) The inducements that attracted Northern capital southward were many. All of the Southern states except North Caro-

[2] For an account of how the South suffered during the war from a lack of ordinary household goods, see "The Pinch of Necessity," p. 106.

lina and Texas offered new industries tax-exemption for a specified period. The labor supply was abundant. Employees would work for lower wages than in the North and were usually indifferent to the propaganda of labor-organizers. For a long time laws regulating hours of work and the employment of women and children were very lax.

In the years of the Great Depression the Federal government did much to strengthen the Southern economy, and when World War II came, it located about one fifth of war-plant construction in the South. Much of the money that the soldiers in the training-camps brought into the South stayed there, as anyone can see if he will notice the spruced-up appearance of many small towns which serviced now vanished military installations.

Not all Southerners are complacent about the extraordinary industrial expansion that began with the outbreak of World War II. There are several weaknesses in the situation. Many of the handsome new plants are Northern-owned or are branches of Northern concerns. Many Southern railroads and electric holding-companies are also in large part owned and directed by "outsiders." In these respects the long-existing industrial "colonialism" of the South still continues. Two inducements to industrial migration southward will not persist much longer: the abundant labor supply and the favorable differential in wages. In steel, for example, the differential was 17½ cents an hour in 1937. In 1953 it had dropped to 5 cents. In June 1954, 40,000 workers in Southern steel mills at last secured, through the effort of the United Steel Workers of America, C.I.O., the abolition of the remaining differential. This is fine for the workers, but it may give pause to companies in the North which still think they can solve their labor problems by migrating to the South.

Yet it is a fact of the greatest significance that the Southern wage-earners are catching up with their fellow workers in other parts of the country. For this means that consumer purchasing-power in the South has created a big market for housing, automobiles, and household appliances. The wealth that comes into the South today in the form of wages will stay there and multiply, even if some of the industrial dividends still flow into Northern tills.

De Bow on the Southern Industrial Revolution

James Dunwoody Brownson De Bow (1820–67) was the Old South's most vocal champion of industrialization and commercial expansion. The son of an impoverished merchant of Charleston, he struggled to gain an education. When he was graduated as valedictorian of his class at Charleston College, in 1843, he was already marked as a young man whose seriousness, ambition, and literary gifts would take him far. The turning-point of his life came in 1845 when he attended the Memphis Convention and listened with excitement to the debates on the question of internal improvements in the South. He resolved to found a review, which would be commercial in the highest sense, for commerce, as he conceived it, ramified into many aspects of life, even agriculture, the professions, fortifications, transportation, legislation, and art. Though he found encouragement for his venture among Charlestonians, De Bow decided to launch his review in New Orleans because of the great commercial activity in the Southwest. In January 1846 the first number of his Commercial Review of the South and Southwest *was off the press. Under various names and published in different cities, the* Review *continued to be published until 1880.*

At first De Bow's views were national in scope, but he gradually became more partisan and pro-Southern. He drifted on the tide of Secession, and after war came he did important work for the Confederacy as its chief agent for the purchase and sale of cotton. Though De Bow was a strong advocate of industrialization, commercial expansion, and internal improvements—especially railroad-building—he considered that the South would always be predominantly agricultural. In his efforts to convince the planter class that gentlemen did not demean themselves by engaging in commerce and industry, he proposed that Southern colleges should teach economics and business. In 1845 he was made Professor of Public Economy, Commerce, and Statistics at the University of Louisiana, but as the New Orleans historian Gayarré says: "It was a professorship without students, and no ability could have commanded an audience. The time had not yet come when any interest could have been taken in such subjects."

De Bow's knowledge and influence brought him frequent requests to address commercial conventions. The passage given below is excerpted from a speech he delivered before the Jackson Railroad Convention in January 1852. It was published in De Bow's huge compendium entitled

The Industrial Resources, Statistics, Etc., of the United States, and more particularly of the Southern and Western States: embracing a view of their Commerce, Agriculture, Manufactures, Internal Improvements, Slave and Free Labor, Slavery Institutions, Products, etc., of the South. *This three-volume work, running to more than 1,600 pages, was first printed in 1852. The text used here is from the third edition (New York: D. Appleton & Co.; 1854), Vol. III, pp. 76–82.*

❀

THE Committee who were entrusted with the duty of inviting the assembling of this Convention, has instructed me, one of its members, to recapitulate a few of the advantages which were proposed from its action: and also to suggest some practicable means, if such exist, of making that action felt widely, generally, and beneficially, throughout our limits, in the future. . . .

But what shall we say of the South—the old South, which fought the battles of the Revolution—which gave the statesmen, the generals, and the wealth of those early times—which concentrated then the agriculture, the commerce, and, even to some extent, the manufactures of the continent, but which has lost, or is losing everything else, save that agriculture; and even this last resource growing less and less remunerative, threatens in the event to complete her beggary? How much has the South promised, and how little has she fulfilled? Her manufactures originated coeval with those of the North, and when there were not fifteen cotton factories in the whole Union, she had constructed an immense one in her limits. Nearly half a century has passed since then, and yet the South, though growing nearly all of the cotton required for the world's consumption, leaves 29–30ths of the profitable business of its conversion into fabrics to other and to foreign hands!

And how has it been with our commerce? When New-England struggled with the whale in northern seas, the rich argosies of the South, laden with abundant products, were seeking the markets of all Europe. Seventy years before the Revolution, Maryland, Virginia, and Carolina, as the chronicles tell us, furnished the entire exports of the colonies, and imported more largely than New-England or New-York. Fifty years before the Revolution things had but slightly changed, and the exports of New-York, New-England, and Pennsylvania together, were less in amount than those of the single colony of Carolina. Even in 1775, the exports of New-York were £187,000; Carolina, £579,000; Virginia, £758,000. Imports of New-York, £1,200; Virginia and Maryland, £2,000; Carolina, £6,000. Georgia, a new plantation, equaled New-York! As late as the close of the century, Charleston continued to contest the palm with New-York. But how has that struggle ended? Who dares grapple with that colossal city, without the certainty of being ground into powder? What has become of southern commercial competition, now that New-York and New-England conduct nine-tenths of the imports of the country and one half of its exports, though nearly all of these exports, with which, of course, the imports are purchased, are of southern material, and more than an equal proportion of the imports are for southern consumption? Thus it is calculated that the South lends from year to year a trading capital to the North amounting to nearly one hundred millions of dollars, and upon which the North receives the entire profits! Can it be wondered at, then, that the North grows rich, and powerful, and great, whilst we, at best, are stationary? . . .

The South had within her limits once the longest rail-road in the world, and projected and actually commenced constructing the first great rail-road across the mountains to the teeming West; and how has she pursued this movement? Whilst the North has opened innumerable communications with the valley, and is draining it of the most valuable products, in return inundating it with the products of her workshops and her commerce, enriching herself beyond the dreams of her own enthusiasts, what single communication has the South to that valley, except what nature has given her—the great river and its tributaries—a communication which must soon be superseded by the works of art. After twenty years' experience, notwithstanding our early promise, and with equal population with the North, we have but one-third the actual miles of rail-road constructed, though our territory is five times as great. In other words, the North has twelve times, or including Texas, eighteen times the extent of railroads to the square mile that the South has; and each mile of northern territory has expended thirty times as much upon such roads as each mile of southern territory. . . .

We have been content to be solely agriculturists, and to exhaust the fertility of an abundant soil, believing that all other pursuits being derivative only, were of less importance, and even dignity. The fashion of the South has been to consider the production of cotton, and sugar, and rice, the only rational pursuits of gentlemen, except the professions, and like the haughty Greek and Roman, to class the trading and the manufacturing spirit as essentially servile. I admit the day is passing away, but it is passing too late to save us, unless we display a degree of vigor and energy far beyond what past experience would bid us hope. The planters of the South perceive the position of peril in which they are placed. They have a slave force which has increased in numbers

711,085 in ten years, and which must be shut up forever within its present limits, though the productions of these slaves have not increased in value in proportion, or in anything like it. . . .

The planters of the South have lately met in convention, at Macon, Ga., and propose another convention in May next, in Montgomery. Some of their delegates were sent to this convention. But what is it they propose? It is not to create a demand for their labor in its present exercise, or to create new results for that labor, but letting things remain as they are, to affix a certain arbitrary standard of price, and by a combination among themselves, preserve that standard, in defiance of all extraneous influences. It is barely possible that something may come off this scheme that shall tell upon their future prosperity. It is possible that there are other plans which may be adopted, more promising of success, or at least that something is practicable to relieve the planters, as things now stand; yet we must be allowed to entertain some doubt in the matter.

Gentlemen of the South and the West, the true mischief under which we labor stands upon the surface, and requires no probing to discover. Four times the number of grain growers find but a two-fold increased market for their products, and 750,000 additional slaves are becoming consumers in a larger degree than producers. Here is labor expended without profit—lost to all the purposes of improvement, and of advanced prosperity and wealth. Where, then, shall we look for a practical remedy? We must diversify, or find new employment for labor. And how is this to be done? I answer,

I. *In the construction of a system of rail-roads through our limits.*— It is a merit of rail-roads that they have the highest influence in diversifying the industry of a people. They open a country and extend population, thus creating the very trade that supports them. They raise the price of lands by bringing them into more immediate connection with market, and thus pay back the investment, without reference to their actual earnings, which, in addition, are usually as large as those of other descriptions of investment. They build up cities, as all experience shows, and, by giving certainty, speed and economy to communication, make manufactories practicable where otherwise we in vain would look for them. . . .

No people on earth have the means of building rail-roads so economically, so speedily, and with such certainty of success, as we of the South and West. As compared with the North, what we have already built has cost, on the average, not half so much. Our country is level— we have no right of way to purchase. We have abundance of timber on the spot, and will only pay the expense of working it, and, throughout the South, have an available cheap negro labor, which, if diverted from agriculture into this field, would diminish nothing of the money value of our crops, and thus make the rail-roads a clear gain to the wealth of the country.

Wherever negro labor has been applied, it has been with great success. Of the 700,000 negroes, whose labor has added nothing to the wealth we had ten years ago, could 100,000 be diverted to the construction of rail-roads, the South might open several thousand miles every year, and would have the same means of ironing them that she has now from her other resources. . . .

Another advantage enjoyed by the South and the West is, that there is an immense public domain belonging to the government, and will soon belong to the states, which can be procured for the mere asking, and which will go a great way towards building our rail-roads. The grant to the Mobile road, it is thought, will iron the whole route. Texas and Louisiana, and Mississippi and Alabama, are peculiarly favored in this manner. . . .

II. Having constructed a system of rail-roads netting every section of our territory, the South and West will naturally resort to manufactures, which is our second great remedy for the evils which the present shows and the future foreshadows. Hamilton Smith, of Kentucky, has demonstrated, that where the coal and the iron, and the provisions are, there will be the seat of manufacturing empire; and by a calculation as close as it is perfect, has demonstrated for the Ohio Valley the prospective Manchesters and Lowells of the Union. We think this the truth, but not the whole truth. The South has only to make a systematic and combined movement to break down northern supremacy in this particular. What practical difficulty is there in the way of her supplying the whole demand of America, at least, for coarse cottons and yarns? The material may be used upon the spot where it is grown, thus saving all the expense of shipment and insurance, and interest and commissions, equivalent to two or three cents a pound, or to a protective tariff enjoyed by the South over the North of from 25 to 33 per cent. Our experiments, when fairly tested, have been successful; and it is worthy of remark, that the embarrassments of northern mills during the last year, were not in the same degree felt by those of the South, whilst southern cotton goods already take the palm even in northern markets. Our surplus negro labor has here a wide field open; and every one familiar with the mere mechanical and unintelligent operation of tending the machinery of a cotton-mill, will admit that negro labor, properly organized and directed, can be as effective as the ignorant and miserable operatives of Great Britain. . . . But, says one, we have not the capital to spare. I admit we have not at present, because it is diverted into different channels; but if we will withdraw it, we shall find there is quite enough among us. Or even if we had not the capital, it will be easy to invite it from all sections of the Union, and the world, if we can demonstrate, as we can, a higher degree of profit for it here. But we must have laws to favor such organizations, and a sound and liberal system of financial credit and banking. How much of the mighty capital of the North is foreign, accumulated by debt, or invited by the hope of profit? The South can have as much, if she will but make the effort. . . .

Gentlemen, a great reform, like that which is necessary in our position, is not to be achieved in a day. It requires organization, agitation, the dissemination of information, the frequent meeting of practical men, memorials and addresses. The day of deliberation is at last followed by the day of action. It is thus that conventions have their great value. They bring about an association of effort, arouse dormant energies, stimulate emulation. They are a blessed invention of our popular institutions, and are not less in importance than the meeting of our constituted authorities.

William Gregg: Factory Master of the Old South

William Gregg (1800–67) has rightly been called the "Father of Southern Cotton Manufacturing." This energetic, farsighted, kindly man was of Scotch descent. At the age of ten young William was placed with his uncle, Jacob Gregg, who made a fortune as a watchmaker, but later engaged in the manufacture of cotton machinery and operated one of the first cotton factories in the South. As Gregg's biographer, Broadus Mitchell, says: "Hargreaves stumbled over his wife's spinning wheel and began the Industrial Revolution. William Gregg happened on his Uncle's tiny plant in Georgia, and became the father of the cotton manufacture in the cotton States."

William Gregg was already a man of substance in Charleston when he began working on his plan for a large textile plant and a village for its operations. He had studied at first hand the cotton mills in New England and had given much thought to the problem of the relationship of industry to agriculture in the South. In 1845 he set forth his views in a pamphlet entitled Essays on Domestic Industry. *In this work Gregg looked far beyond such issues of the moment as the tariff question. He was, among other matters, much concerned over the precariousness of the Southern economy, agricultural as well as industrial.*

574

He boldly contrasted the way in which Northern states utilized their resources with the conditions prevailing in South Carolina, "in which a man hesitates about building a comfortable dwelling-house, lest the spirit of emigration deprive him of its use—in which the cream of a virgin soil is hardly exhausted, before the owner is ready to abandon it, in search of a country affording new and better lands,—in which our forest lumber cutters fell, with ruthless hand, the finest timber trees on the face of the globe, selecting those portions which are most easily turned into merchantable lumber, and leaving the balance to rot on the ground."

Gregg pushed ahead with his plans for a well-equipped and well-organized cotton factory. In the year of the publication of his Essays on Domestic Industry *he obtained a South Carolina charter for the Graniteville Manufacturing Company. This was no routine accomplishment. Corporations were unpopular in the state at that time because they were associated in the public mind with speculation.*

Graniteville, located five miles from Aiken, prospered under Gregg's vigorous management, and the mill was soon exporting thousands of bales of its "fine, honestly-made domestics" to Northern and foreign customers. When war came, the Graniteville products were of immense value to the Confederacy. Gregg brought his factory through the difficult days that followed the defeat of the South. Worn-out machinery had to be replaced, dams and canal banks repaired, at a time when working capital was almost impossible to obtain.

Today at Graniteville one of the mill buildings and many of the old mill houses are still in use.

The following account of Gregg's work at Graniteville is excerpted from Broadus Mitchell's William Gregg, Factory Master of the Old South (*1928*). *It is reprinted with the permission of the publishers, the University of North Carolina Press.*

IT was essential to Gregg's plan that his mill should be a native product —in inspiration, in capital, in work-people, and in actual building material as well. The blue granite, of which mill and dams were built, was quarried from beside the stream, a few hundred yards away from the factory site. An expert judge says that Gregg must have obtained the plan of the old mill building, however, from New England; there are any number like it in the Blackstone Valley. He was undoubtedly influenced by James Montgomery's estimate of the cost of buildings and machinery for a cotton factory. This contemplated a "brick, or stone-house, four stories and attic, 142 by 42 feet," 4,992 throstle spindles, and 128 looms; Montgomery thought the building and power equipment could be had more cheaply in South Carolina than in New England, for which he gave prices. . . .

Though there is some doubt about the matter, it would appear that the mill was driven at first by a single water wheel; however, evidences of this original arrangement were obliterated by changes in the power system made in 1854 and again in 1866. In the former year a second wheel was installed in a new wheel pit, and a conducting pipe was constructed to serve a third wheel should it be required. In the latter year a new turbine wheel, more powerful than those of 1854, was installed, and what remains to be seen now goes back to both of these periods of improvement. An examination of the wheel pit at the lower end of the mill would indicate that the wheel once housed here was of some sixty feet diameter and twelve feet on the face. The space in which the wheel revolved has now been floored over at several levels, but the hollowed out stones sunk into each wall, in which the 30-inch axle rested, are still to be seen; imbedded in one of them are the stumps of the iron bolts which held the capstone on. . . .

One who saw the first granite blocks of the factory laid described the bustle of those days at the outset. People came eager to get the work. There was no one but found a job congenial to his country training, though it be no better than ditching. Gregg was in the midst of them every day, called upon for a hundred decisions. After dams were built, a saw mill was erected and in two years cut over 5,000,000 feet of lumber; while the mill itself and the warehouses took much of this, the cottages for future operatives took more. . . .

Gregg had the operatives' cottages, for the most part, dotted about irregularly on the forested slopes. All of those he built are standing and in good condition, except five which burned.

It should be remembered that Gregg "devoted three years of laborious and assiduous attention" to the construction of Graniteville, and then operated the business for five years more before he accepted a penny from the company for his services. It is true that he was a rich man with leisure to give to any project that took his interest, and certainly all he performed for Graniteville was done *con amore;* it is further true that for a while he did not expect to let the work engross all his time and energies, but his service was nonetheless uncalculatingly generous. No amount of money could have procured from any one else but Gregg the eagerness, the consummate care, the many-sided practical effectiveness which he gave freely. Like the creator he was, he did not set a price on the product of his art. His engineering achievement, particularly considering the fact that he was not a technical specialist, was as remarkable as his unpaid devotion. At the stockholders' meeting at the end of the first year of construction work, it was decided to pay the treasurer $500 a year. There was no thought of paying Gregg.

When Graniteville began to take tangible shape its appeal to investors was more general. After this year of building and digging the number of stockholders had increased from 23 to 30, and the number of shares from 391 to 600, making the capital subscribed ($500 a share) $300,000 instead of $195,500. A manuscript list of share owners, dated March 19, 1847, shows that two former members of the company had dropped out, S. S. Farrar and Alex. McDonald, while nine new ones had been added.

Fortunately, we have several detailed descriptions of Graniteville at the time of its erection and first completion. These differ in some particulars, but no attempt has been made here to reconcile them. The earliest dates from the spring of 1848, and is by a representative of a Charleston newspaper who was one of a party invited by Gregg to view the rising village. The company began by buying 11,000 acres of land in Edgefield District, embracing Horse Creek. In October, 1846, the foundation stone of the main factory building was laid, and the first works of improvement commenced. "It would inspire the visitor," wrote the correspondent, "to see how much has been done since that time. The rude forest has been cleared, streets laid out, canals cut, and embankments thrown up, malls graded and beautifully laid out, saw mills, machine shops, stores, offices, dwellings for operatives, and factory houses erected; and all put in such a state of forwardness as already to present the appearance of a flourishing and busy village."

The canal was almost a mile long, 15 feet wide at the bottom, 37 on the surface, and about 5 feet deep. It commenced at Horse Creek, where it was protected by a substantial granite dam. . . .

On the opposite side of the canal, which was crossed by several bridges, ran Canal Street, on which were to be boarding houses; twelve of these were completed—a hotel of about twenty rooms, three houses of sixteen rooms each, and eight others of eight rooms each. "Fronting upon the canal, and having handsome porticoes or piazzas, they afford residences which would not detract from the beauty of any village in the Union." On the street back of this, forty cottages were to be built, in the Gothic order, each with five rooms; of these four had been completed. "Determined to impart an entirely religious and moral tone to the community of Graniteville," the company had granted sites to Baptists and Methodists if they would erect churches designed by good architects. The Baptist church, in the Gothic style, was nearing completion; the Methodist was a modification of the Gothic, by J. B. White, a Charleston architect. A handsome school house was to be erected and teachers employed by the company. . . .

The company-owned cotton mill village is now almost peculiar to the South, where it is well-nigh universal. There is reason to believe that Gregg set a precedent at Graniteville which has been controlling. . . .

Graniteville heralded a new day for the Poor Whites of the South. Of English, German, and Scotch-Irish stock, they were blood kin to the dominant class in the low country; they were only a few generations removed from the frontiersmen who cleared the land they occupied; but, expelled by negro slavery, they were strangers in their own land. The first great cotton mill welcomed them back into the body social. The good beginning that Gregg made would have been more closely followed but for the crescendo of pro-slavery argument, the Civil War, and the desperate decade and a half that ensued upon the conflict. After 1880 Gregg's purpose came to the minds of thousands, and, through the founding of scores of mills and villages, was applied widespread. Reentrance into the life of the South through the industrial door has brought its hardships to the Poor Whites—in long hours, stagnating routine, low wages, and a paternalism which some think has, through several generations, smothered the divine spark of independence. But it is impossible for a ruling society to turn its back on the mass of the people for long years, without recovery of the neglected being painful. On a despoiled field the first poor crops must be turned under before better ones are raised to yield fruit. Faithful and uncomplaining, the Poor Whites have learned a new standard of living, and in a spiritual as well as an economic sense, are catching step with our times. When they were far, far behind the van, William Gregg placed himself at the head of the moving column. He declared that "it is only necessary to make comfortable homes in order to procure families that will afford laborers of the best kind. A large manufacturing establishment located anywhere in the State, away from a town and in a healthy situation, will soon collect around it a population who, however poor, with proper moral restraints thrown around them, will soon develop all the elements of good society. Self-respect, and attachment to the place will soon find their way into the minds of such, while intelligence, morality, and well directed industry, will not fail to acquire position."

Graniteville was like a feudal village, with the great stone factory substituted for the turreted castle, and the wooden houses in place of thatched cots; the Poor Whites came in for the protection of their overlord just as eagerly as did the peasants of centuries earlier, and if they gave up something of an unmeaning freedom, they gained in the substantial asset of security. Gregg was to be to his retainers landlord, employer, teacher, clergyman, and judge.

The wages paid seem low to us now, but compared favorably with the practice in contemporary neighboring mills. It must always be remembered that before taking industrial employment these people had handled scarcely any cash, having existed under a credit system which kept them barely even with their obligations or plunged them chronically into debt. The money wages Gregg gave them, coupled with the "rights" (to continue the feudal figure) which they enjoyed in garden and woods, and the privileges of school and church and medical service, undoubtedly amounted to more than they had received in their old country environment. Rentals of company houses ran from $16 to $25 a year. The average wage of the 300 men, women, and children employed at Graniteville in April, 1849 was $3.05 per week. Men made from $4 to $5, women from $3 to $4, and children from $1 to $2. Most of the work was done by the piece. The hours were long—from twelve to twelve and a half—about the same working day as in England and the North at this time. A rising bell was rung from the factory tower, and, it was said, "the system of labor requires the attendance of every one in the mill and office, at the ringing of the second bell in the morning. Work is begun as soon as there is light sufficient for running the machines. The instant the bell ceases to ring the gates are locked, and tardy ones are required to pass through the office." Lateness to work was rare. At 7 o'clock (at least this was the time in winter) the mill was stopped for three quarters of an hour, when the operatives had breakfast, undoubtedly going to their homes. Work was resumed then until 1 o'clock, when three quarters of an hour was allowed for dinner. Then work was continued until 7:30. After dark the operatives worked by solar burners. Nothing indicates a short day Saturday. Under this scheme of labor the workers, it was said, were "as cheerful and well disposed as any in the world." . . .

Gregg and Graniteville were identical terms. He made the place out of hand, and it reflected, in every department of its life, his affectionate care. There have been mill men in the South since who, while no less despotic over their communities, have been less benevolent. A later generation of managers has maintained welfare programs first for profit, and second for the happiness and progress of the workpeople. With William Gregg the human motive ran *pari passu* with the commercial. He acted, in all his plans for the life of the people of Graniteville, from a profound sense of social obligation, and a finer patriotism than answers to war trumpets. *Noblesse oblige* was his intuition. He set a pattern for the industry which, in our more complex day, can never be quite returned to. The subjects over whom he ruled in his little kingdom were economically as weak as he was strong, and yet no hint of exploitation ever entered his consciousness.

"Mr. Gregg was the boss of this place as long as he lived," said an octogenarian who beamed at the name as he commenced his reminiscences. And another assured me that "his memory is very green at

Graniteville now. There is no person of any age in the town who hasn't something to tell you of William Gregg."

He presents many similarities with Robert Owen, yet with a difference. Gregg's work at Graniteville was like Owen's at New Lanark in that he meant to make it a type for the whole of society. But Owen reached out into utopian fancies as noble as they were impracticable, while Gregg planned a social reorganization through the steady implanting of industry in an agricultural economy. Owen found an industrial revolution demanding remedy on its human side. Gregg, in the midst of slavery and stagnation, believed that only the introduction of manufactures would lift the Poor Whites into an admirable standard of living.

After 1854, Gregg lived the year 'round on the hilltop overlooking the village and so could give it the closest supervision. Just as at New Lanark, so at Graniteville, the school lay very near the proprietor's heart. When Gregg was working out the plans for his venture it is certain that the teaching of reading, writing, and arithmetic to the children was as definitely a part of his program as the industrial training of operatives, the profits of the company, or the indirect advantages that were to accrue to the community from the manufacturing enterprise. "How easy would it be for the proprietors of such establishments," he had written, looking forward to the planting of industrial villages, "with only a small share of philanthropy, to make good use of the school fund in ameliorating the condition of this class of our population, now but little elevated above the Indian of the forest. . . . It is, perhaps, not generally known, that there are *twenty-nine thousand* white persons in this State, above the age of twelve years, who can neither read nor write—this is about one in every five of the white population."

When he could put his purpose into practice, he inaugurated the first compulsory education system (albeit informal and limited, yet surprisingly effective) in the South, and perhaps in this country. He described it briefly himself: "All parents are required to keep their children, between the ages of six and twelve, at school—good teachers, books, etc., are furnished by the company, free of charge." And he added that this requirement was "willingly acquiesced in by the people."

In 1850 the school already had a hundred pupils. The recollection of old inhabitants of Graniteville is that if every urging of Gregg's did not suffice to secure attendance of the children, the offending family was fined by him five cents a day for every day a child stayed away from school. Not only did he insist that the children of the village proper go to school, but he was anxious to have neighboring families benefit from it. One of the early scholars, now a very old man, told of

580

Gregg's solicitude in this connection with lively appreciation. Mr. Perdue's father was a small farmer two miles from Graniteville, and could not pay to keep all of his children at school at once. Gregg came to see the family one morning, and noting children playing about the house, asked why they were not in the classes. The father told him. "Tut-tut-tut-tut-tut, Wylie," he rejoined (he had a way of doing this when a little provoked), "send them all up to the school, you hear!" And so it was.

The school, at any rate after it had been in operation a few years, had three teachers, two of them ladies from Charleston, and the third a man. Gregg would usually include the school in his daily visits to the mill; when he would drive his bob-tailed horse up at recess time, the children would flock against the fence, and spill through and over it into the road until they blocked the way. Gregg liked this, and would laugh and play with them as they climbed over his buggy. Very often he would go in and talk to the pupils. One of those who sat as a little tot under these instructions told me that "he was always impressing lessons of politeness ('if one of you boys sees a lady drive up, run out and offer to hold her horse'). There was one boy in the school said never to be polite. Gregg would always ask for him, ('if George Crocker is here, let him stand up!'). Then he would lecture directly at George."

Sometimes he would conclude his remarks by telling the boys that he did not take his workman's apron off until he was worth $50,000. "Now go to work, boys" he would admonish them.

Gregg not only had his compulsory school attendance law, but he was his own enforcement officer. If he came across a truant, he would return the boy to school, or, if the offense was repeated, would take him to the office for a licking. Nobody wanted to be taken to the office! One day Gregg learned that a boy who had often fallen under his displeasure for truancy had sneaked off from school and gone fishing. The old man lay in wait for him on the road, and as the culprit emerged from the bushes beside the stream, seized him, lifted him into the buggy and drove to the mill office. Instead of the customary whipping, the boy got a new punishment. Gregg stood him on the high bookkeeper's desk and left him there without a word. He had tipped off the office employees to ask questions, and as each one passed through the room, Gregg would explain, "There stands the boy that would rather go fishing than get an education." After this was many times repeated the little fellow begged to be let down, and he would never run away from school again.

Once when Gregg suddenly appeared at the verge of the swimming hole, buggy whip in hand, the boys were so frightened they clutched up their clothes and, without stopping to put them on, ran right into the schoolroom. He devised still another method of punishment. Once at the end of the war when lead was scarce, the boys ripped the metal from the valley gutters of the schoolhouse to make bullets for their hunting excursions. Gregg was very angry, but calmed down by the time he had got them to the mill. Here he organized a jury and "tried" them.

Though he wanted the children to stay in school in school hours, he was fond of taking them on picnics and giving them all the pleasure he could. Every spring there was a special outing, when the youngsters of the village and the near-by country were taken on the millpond in flatboats. These were equipped with seats run across them. Gregg would be full of fun, explaining that all were as safe as on the deck of a ship going into New York harbor. Once, after thus assuring them, he gave them a scare. He always tried to give repair work about the buildings and grounds to the people of the vicinity when he could. One of his firm friends among these folk was an old Irish ditcher, who had very early come to Graniteville, named Fagin. Fagin was a careless old fellow, in summer never bothering to wear shoes. If Gregg saw him he would hail him, take him in the buggy and drive about to explain what was to be done. Fagin would break stone and throw it in behind the dam, and keep the canal banks in shape. Gregg took an undisguised pleasure in his old retainer; they were called "very thick." Gregg had taken Fagin along on this picnic. When the rest were not looking, and by previous arrangement, he pushed Fagin off the "flat" and into the pond. There was a great scrambling and shouting, Gregg waving his arms in mock dismay, before the old fellow, with much spluttering, was drawn aboard.

Every little episode connected with these excursions is likely to be remembered and treasured by some one in Graniteville today. Once Mrs. Gregg, who was likewise the friend of the village, made gingerbread horses for the picnic, and Gregg threw them into the crowd for the children to scramble after. . . .

Gregg enforced a strict rule of prohibition upon liquor in Graniteville. His Quaker tradition may have influenced him, but more powerful considerations were his regard for industrial efficiency and his sense of responsibility for the orderliness and good name of his village. The mill had scarcely started when he wrote that "The use of alcohol is not permitted in the place—young people, particularly males, are not allowed to remain in the place in idleness." . . . This restraint was "willingly acquiesced in by the people, and we have one of the most moral, quiet, orderly, and busy places to be found any where." In every lease to property in Graniteville the tenant engaged not to have or sell liquor on the premises. Solon Robinson reported that "if any one is disposed to make a brute of himself over the whisky cup, he must go to some other place, for neither in store or tavern in that village has that curse of the earth ever entered, or can ever enter until owners change."

"I'd Take the Mill Anytime"

In the late 1930's the Federal Writers' Project in North Carolina began collecting and writing the "life histories of tenant farmers, farm own-ers, textile and other factory workers, persons in service occupations in towns and cities . . . and persons in miscellaneous occupations such as lumbering, mining, turpentining, and fishing." From the materials collected an informative book was made, These Are Our Lives, *issued in 1939 by the University of North Carolina Press.*

The interviewer-author of "I'd Take the Mill Anytime" is Muriel Wolff. She was instructed, as were all those who worked on this proj-ect, to gather as much information about her subject's family, educa-tion, politics, religion, and attitudes toward his occupation and kind of life as she could. But, above all, the men and women interviewed were to be encouraged to speak for themselves. The interviewer was required to keep his "own opinions and feelings in the background" and to get his "story" in the words of the person interviewed. Miss Wolff was particularly fortunate in her session with Smith Coon (not his real name, of course). He wanted to talk and he talked to the point.

"I'd Take the Mill Anytime" is reprinted from These Are Our Lives *(pp. 180–7) with the permission of the publishers. The interview has been condensed.*

In 1886 Camden was a village with a red mud main street, a few stores clustered about a square, and one cotton mill, the McDonald. How-ever, at that time young H. J. Filmer, a partner in Filmer-Holmes Dry Goods Store, was building another cotton mill. Among the workmen on this job, as bricklayer and carpenter, was a stolid "Dutch" farmer from the Hickory Hill section of Culpepper County. His name was Coon.

Today two of this man's sons have been with Filmer Mills longer than any other employees. I talked with Smith, the younger son, who has worked in the mill for forty-nine years. At fifty-nine he is wiry, healthy, young looking. He owns his own home, a comfortable two-story bungalow on Ashboro Street. The house is spacious and furnished in better taste than many so-called middle class houses in town.

"I don't know what good hit'll do you to talk to me," Smith said modestly, "for I ain't done nothing much." But he was really pleased that he had been sought out and once he started talking he forgot his shyness.

"When Mr. H. J. got ready to open up his mill back in '86, he didn't have but thirteen houses for his hands. That don't sound like many nowadays when many a house jest has one hand in it, but Mr. H. J. figured if he hired big families, he could get enough hands in them thirteen houses to work his mill.

"I reckon that's howcome he wanted us. Anyway he wrote my father a letter asking him to move his force to the mill—hit was ready to start work. My sister had that letter, but when she was a-cleaning up sometime back, she burnt it up. I sure hated that; I'd a-give most anything for that letter.

"I won't never forget that day in the fall of '86 when we moved in to Camden. We started out before daylight and hit was way after dark when we got here. Hit don't look like it could take that long to come sixteen miles, but back then there jest wasn't anything you'd call a road; why two teams always went together so if one got stuck the other could pull it out. I was six year old whenever we moved and what I mainly remember about that trip is hanging my head over the side of the wagon so that I got my chin bumped underneath when we hit the pine log road.

"Soon as the mill opened, my father and all the younguns that was old enough commenced to work. There was nine of us younguns, five girls and four boys and everyone of us 'ceptin' one got their start in that same mill—hit's the one they call plant number one now. I was too little to go to work right away, but whenever I was nine or ten I began. At first I doffed. I got ten cents a day for working from six o'clock in the morning to five minutes until seven o'clock in the evening. Course you keep a-goin' up, so I went to the spinning room and on to the weaving room. Then they put me to fixing looms. I've always been a good hand to fix any kind of machinery and after while they made me the overseer of the shop. Well, I stayed at that till fifteen year ago when they give me the job I've got now—the overseer of the yard. And believe me hit *is* a job too! I have to weigh ever bit of cotton goin' in and out and see to the loadin' and unloadin' of it. Why jest today we handled close to 500 bales—that's somethin', let me tell you, and the worst part of it is bossing the niggers that handle it. You have to talk to 'em like you're a-goin' to kill 'em or they'll lay down on you and not do a lick of work. I've got so I can talk jest as mean and hateful as anything—oh I don't mean it, but I have to git the work out of 'em.

"Since the cut I'm not a-makin' but 56¢ a hour. That sounds like a lot more than what I started out at, but money don't go nowheres any more. Back when I was a-gettin' ten and twenty-five cent a day you could take your money to the store and have something to show fer it. Why my father, before he died, had a pile of gold pieces he had saved from way back yonder when we used to git paid off in gold money. A body could save then, but it takes everything you make now to live.

"Education? Don't ask me about that 'cause I never did have none to amount to anything. They didn't have no city schools then like they has now. Mr. H. J. had a school that run in the daytime for the young'uns too little to go to the mill and at night for them that worked. Well I went to his school some before I commenced to work and at night for a while too, but it didn't amount to so much. . . .

"I'll tell you hit's a pleasure to work for a company that treats you like the Filmers does. I've know'd all of 'em well. Many's the time back yonder that I hitched up Mr. H. J.'s buggy for him, drove him up town or down to the mill, and went to the postoffice to get his mail. Jack and Reeves is the boys I know the best and they've turned out the best. Why I consider Reeves Filmer jest as good a friend as I've got in this world.

"I've got a picture of Mr. H. J. in with my insurance policy—I'll show it to you if you'd like to see it. Yessir, he was a fine looking man and a good man too. See this insurance policy? He give every hand down at Culpepper then one of these, and if I was to die tomorrow, my wife would git $500. There ain't but four or five of us has these any more because they took the policies away from all the hands that walked out during that big strike some years back.

"Yes, me and a few others kept right on going to the mill all the time they was having the strike. It took nerve too to walk in that gate with all the crowd standin' there hollerin' at you. They'd call us all kinds of names, but I didn't say a word back to 'em—that was the best way to do. The mill wasn't running, but we got our pay fer going there.

"Plenty of 'em that walked out was sorry they had, some of 'em didn't want to go out in the first place but they was threatened. You couldn't begin to git me to join one of them unions. All they want is the dues they can git from you, and you don't never know what they do with the money because they won't give a report on it. I read in the paper not long ago where they wanted some union to show its books and it wouldn't do it.

"In this last strike every mill here and up at Filmerton kept a-running all the time and no hands quit. I jest wisht you could've seen Filmerton. Law it looked like a war, guns and soldiers all about. The mill had a airplane flying around to watch all the main highways and when it seen a band of cars (flying squadron) starting out from some town, it would fly right low and drop a note down to let us know what was coming. At our mill we never was bothered by anybody. The funniest thing happened up at Filmerton when one of them squadrons went there. You know the mill owns the whole town. Well, the sheriff was on the lookout for these folks from out of town and every time they started off the main street—hit's a State highway—the sheriff would say, "This is private property, you can't come on it." So that squadron couldn't do a thing but go up and down main street till they got so wore out they jest give up and went back home.

"What party do I belong to? Well I served two terms on the city Board of Aldermen so you know I'm not no Republican. I think what the government's been a-doing is all right. I tell you what's a fact, I believe we'd a had a rebellion back when Roosevelt come in if the government hadn't done like it did. A man jest couldn't hardly keep going when Hoover was in; you can't live on no dollar a day like he said to do. You know, there's a sight of folks down at the mill has changed over to being Democrats in the last couple years.

"You take when they had that NRA, Mr. Filmer made us keep all the rules to the letter. If a man worked overtime one day, I had to allow him that much time off the next. Mr. Filmer is mighty particular about all sich rules. . . .

"I'm the sexton up at the church. I git $10 a month for cleaning up, running the furnace, fixing the organ if it gits out of order, opening the church and ringing the bell whenever they're a-going to have a meeting, but I declare hit's more trouble to me than what I git out of it. If they could git anybody else who could run the furnace right, I don't reckon I'd keep the job, but them young boys they had been getting to fire it just nearly 'bout ruint it.

"Yes ma'm, this here house is mine; I saved up to build it and I planned it myself. Well now, I like these big rooms too—I was determined that when I built me a house I was going to have plenty of space about me, so when I planned this one, I made it like I wanted hit to be. If there's anything I despise it's to be scrouged into little bitty rooms. My wife and the girls see to keeping the rooms fixed up this a-way—that there music box (piano) is a real old timey one my sister bought somewhere.

"I've got an electric refrigerator that cost me $200—that's a lot of money and I hated to put it out at the time, but law, now I wouldn't begin to take what I paid fer it. I jest wouldn't be without it since I've got used to it. Something else I like mighty well is my automatic hot water heater. Hit keeps the water hot all the time, all you have to do is jest open any tap and you've got hot water right now, day or night.

"I would sure hate to go back to living like folks used to. Didn't nobody have things then the way we do now, living wasn't as good. There's a lot of people feel they can't git along without a automobile and some of 'em can't so well. I don't have one fer I ain't got no use fer it; I walk down to the mill, to the church, or uptown when I'm obliged to go.

"Well I've sure enjoyed talking to you and I hope you'll come back again when my wife's here fer I know she'd like to talk to you.

"I'll just walk across the street with you. I told Sam Heilig I would come over sometime tonight and work on his stove fer him. Cold weather'll catch us soon."

Geyser of Oil

The oil money of the Southwest began to flow on the day Captain Anthony Lucas's gusher erupted on Spindletop, near Beaumont, Texas. After years of setbacks—discouraging advice from "experts," difficulties in getting financial backing, failure to find a rig that would do the tough drilling job—the vision of Pattillo Higgins was fulfilled. Nine years after his Gladys City Oil, Gas and Manufacturing Company was organized, the heavy green oil spouted. Because of the persistence of Pattillo Higgins, George Carroll, a lumber man, Captain Lucas, Dalmatian-born mining engineer, John Galey, wildcatter, and the Hamill brothers, drilling contractors, Beaumont was to become the oil center of the Southwest. Scores of companies would go up on the board of the Beaumont exchange. Most would perish, but such giants as the Magnolia Petroleum Company, the Texas company (Texaco), and Humble Oil were also born in Beaumont.

Texas still keeps its lead as the chief oil-producing state of the Southwest, but the wells of Louisiana and Oklahoma are making those states rich. Mississippi is on the way.

The following passage is reprinted from J. A. Clark and M. T. Halbouty's Spindletop, *pp. 52–6 (with omissions). Reprinted by permission of Random House, Inc. Copyright 1952 by James A. Clark and Michel T. Halbouty.*

THERE wasn't a trace of a cloud in the sky. The weather was cold and invigorating and smoke was rising from every chimney in Beaumont on the morning of January 10, 1901.

Pattillo Higgins rode off into the north wind toward Hardin County to complete a deal that would get him out of debt. He had located a strip of timberland that Frank Keith would buy.

Al Hamill was in the freight depot early to pick up the new fishtail bit from Corsicana. It was barely daylight when he and Higgins exchanged greetings as they passed each other on Park Street.

After a brief visit to the well, Captain Lucas returned to his home on the way to town to tell Caroline he would be in Louie Mayer's store on Crockett Street.

The morning *Enterprise* gave its usual reports of the local, national and world events. The district attorney, who had been supported by George Carroll in the recent election, would start a war on gambling. A big diamond discovery was reported from Capitan near El Paso. Dr. Walter Reed announced his famous discovery of the carrier of yellow fever. Old Tom Sharkey was crying for another crack at Kid McCoy. William Jennings Bryan was due to visit Houston, and Al. G. Fields' minstrels and Sousa's band were booked into the Goodhue Opera House. Mayor Wheat returned from Washington without selling the city's improvement bonds. Governor Sayers was to open the new session of the state legislature in Austin. . . .

On the hill the crew of three had put on the new fishtail bit. That done, the drill stem was lowered back into the hole. With the pipe down about 700 feet and Curt Hamill steering it from the double boards forty feet above the derrick floor, something began to happen.

Mud started to bubble up over the rotary table. Al and Peck backed away when suddenly the force increased and mud spurted high up the derrick. Curt, drenched with mud and gumbo, grabbed for the ladder and slid down it to safety. All three scampered in different directions. This was a new experience for these old hands of the Corsicana field. As they ran, six tons of four-inch pipe came shooting up through the derrick, knocking off the crown block. Then the pipe leapt, like activated spaghetti, on over the top of the derrick and broke off in sections, falling around the camp like giant spikes driven into the earth.

Then everything was quiet. The Hamills and Peck Byrd cautiously returned to the derrick floor. It was a shambles, with mud, muck and water standing a foot deep. The disgusted crew looked over the situation, started cleaning up the debris, and expressed themselves in a manner of eloquence reserved for men of the oil fields.

"What the hell are we going to do with the damn thing now?" Peck Byrd asked Al as he shut off the boiler fires.

"Well, Peck," Al was saying, "I guess we'll just have to shovel this mud away and see if . . ."

His words were interrupted by a roar like the shot of a heavy cannon. Then again the flow of mud started up through the hole, followed by a terrific column of gas. The startled crew scattered again. Peck missed his footing and tumbled headlong into the slush pit. Within seconds, the gas was followed by a solid flow of oil—green and heavy.

"Peck, run to the house and get the Captain," Al shouted, "while Curt and me try to figure this thing out. It looks like oil! Hurry! Hurry!"

The mud-soaked Peck Byrd ran to the Lucas home. When he got there he was out of breath and sat holding his side, panting a few minutes, before he could deliver the message to Mrs. Lucas.

"Get the Captain! Tell him to come right now!" Peck shouted in excitement. "Look, Mrs. Lucas, look," he said, pointing to the well. But before she could find out what had happened, Peck was off on a run back to the well.

She looked toward the hill and saw a great plume of black liquid spouting over the derrick. The sight was fantastic. She could not explain what had happened, but she implored the Captain to lose no time in getting back to the hill.

"Hurry, Anthony, something awful has happened. The well is spouting," she shouted into the telephone.

The Captain turned and fled from the store without explanation. He mounted his gig, as Louie Mayer watched in astonishment, and stood on the floor-boards whipping his horse as he raced out Park Street, past the O'Brien and Carroll homes, out Highland Avenue and past his own home without even looking toward his wife, who was trying to attract his attention by waving from the porch.

The phenomenon was in full view now. It was frightening to the Captain. His eyes had never beheld such a sight before. Could it be oil?

When he reached the hill, Lucas' excitement was too much and the horse was too slow. At the apex of the hill, he tried to jump from the buggy and tumbled down the slope. Al Hamill saw the fall and started toward him, but the Captain rolled forward and came to his feet on a dead run.

"Al, Al," he was shouting, "what is it? What is it?"

"Oil, Captain! Oil, every drop of it," the jubilant Al replied.

Grabbing Al Hamill by the waist and swinging him around, Lucas looked up toward the gray skies and said, "Thank God. Thank God, you've done it! You've done it!"

"It came in at ten-thirty, almost an hour ago, and it has been shooting a steady six-inch stream of oil more than a hundred feet above the top of the derrick, just like it is now. I can't understand it," Al said. "But I don't think we are going to pay George Carroll for that derrick."

Captain Lucas was exultant. He stood under the shower of green oil, felt it, smelled it and tasted it to make certain he wasn't dreaming.

Then he backed off and looked up to the top of the great plume. Oil, shale, and rocks were raining down. Almost to himself he whispered hoarsely, with a rising inflection, "A geyser of oil! A geyser of oil!". . .

A roustabout working in Perry McFaddin's crew building the levees turned to one of the reporters and simply said, "Mister, that's some gusher, ain't it?" From that day on the well was referred to as the Lucas gusher and the dictionaries soon had a new application for the word.

Chemical Treasure Trove

Mr. Williams Haynes, author of Southern Horizons, *from which this account of the newest Southern industries is taken, was stating sober fact when he said in his "Warning to the Reader": "This book needed to be written. . . . A revolution is brewing in Southern farms and factories, and it is high time that all of us look into its causes and consider its effects." Mr. Haynes was well equipped to survey this revolution and report on its progress. He was for many years the publisher of* Chemical Industries *and he has written extensively on the history of the chemical industry in this country.*

Southern Horizons, *W. Haynes. Copyright 1946, D. Van Nostrand Company, Inc. The passage given here is excerpted from pages 252–69.*

By precept and example Doctor A. P. Beutel furnishes one perfect answer to that question of Southern chemical raw materials processed in the South. He was born in Ohio. In Michigan, starting at a draftsman's desk, he climbed up the ladder to general manager. But during the past five years he has become as Texan as a barbecued pig.

"Dutch" Beutel—almost nobody calls him "Doctor Beutel" and even good friends do not know what his initials "A. P." stand for—is in charge of the $90,000,000 colony of the Dow Chemical Company at the mouth of the Brazos River. Here magnesium, the lightest of structural metals, is extracted from sea water, and styrene is turned out in vast quantity for synthetic rubber and plastics. In a third new plant a number of Dow's other chemicals are made from Texas salt, sulfur, and petroleum. The general manager of this, the biggest chemical operation in all the South, is a plain, honest, outspoken engineer. "Dutch" is as forthright as a sledgehammer. He is also a shining example.

I had been warned of the miraculous transformation in this old friend of mine. So, when I found him entrenched behind his horseshoe desk that is built into his modernistic, air-conditioned office, I hailed him with a raucous request, "Let me see your feet."

"Hell's bells!" he exploded, "you've been talking to that dizzy bunch in the New York office. No," he went on with slow emphasis, showing me his shoes, "I do not wear cowbow boots to the office. But," he added with a grin, "I do wear them Sundays."

"Dutch" is inordinately proud that over the week end he is entitled to wear both his trouser bottoms tucked into the tops of said boots. According to the niceties of range etiquette this means that he has a thousand head of steers on his ranch.

"I sure do like it down here," he went on in the true Tajos vernacular, "and do I like running a chemical plant in the South! Why, I wouldn't go back to that frozen Michigan, not for—" He broke off, not able to name a price that did not sound too ridiculous.

Right here Doctor Beutel becomes a symbolic figure. His pro-South ideas are shared by hundreds of Northern chemical operating men who have been playing headline roles in the chemicalization of the South. These ideas are grounded on dollars and good sense. They are the good reasons why three out of four of the four billion dollars put into new chemical plants during the past four years has been spent south of the Potomac. For war needs or for postwar expansion plans this was one point upon which Army and Navy, Government officials and industrial executives, all agreed. The American chemical industry is moving South.

Down South a chemical plant can be built in the open. It needs no weatherproof building; even a tent-like roof is often quite unnecessary. Its stills and autoclaves, joined by a network of pipes, need no thick layers of insulation. If gas or liquid is to be carried from one unit to another, there is no need to forestall freezing by burying the pipes deep below the frostline.

At Baton Rouge I was discussing these climatic advantages with Marion Boyer, who immediately staged a neat demonstration. From the window of his office he pointed to the neighboring plant where du Pont makes tetraethyl lead.

"See that fine building down by the river," he said. "That is their original unit. We told them they did not have to build a fine university hall like that. But no, they knew how to build a chemical plant, and they did. They learned quickly enough. Just look at the rest of the property."

Like any Southern oil refinery, it is spotted with apparatus all exposed to the elements. The saving is considerable—more than half of the original investment in construction, and "Dutch" Beutel estimates that the savings in time, labor, and materials for repairs and current maintenance are a third. Some of his contemporaries say that this is high, since he is comparing Texas with northern Michigan where at both ends conditions are extreme, but at least the saving is substantial.

These climatic advantages are enticing and profitable. They make a persuasive appeal to those who know that in the big half-moon from Jacksonville to Corpus Christi is the most complete collection of chemical raw materials on earth. Over a century ago a brilliant Irishman, who was the father of the English chemical industry, said, "The foundations of my business rest on salt, lime, and sulfur, and the greatest of these is sulfur." No other region combines these three basic inorganic chemical materials in such abundance.

Sulfur, melted underground with hot water, is pumped in golden streams from half a dozen great deposits scattered from the marshy bayous of the lower Mississippi Delta all along the flat coastal plains of Texas. Beneath the whole Gulf Coast lie colossal beds of pure rocksalt. Time and again wildcatters for oil have bored for a thousand feet into these beds, and disgusted, drawn their drills still in the salt. Limestone is barged down the Mississippi from Alabama, or better, the Gulf Coast is fringed with great reefs of oystershells, beds of almost pure calcium carbonate, to be dredged up in two-ton clamshell buckets.

Close by in New Mexico is potash. In Florida, Tennessee, and South Carolina is phosphate rock. Both are raw materials for fertilizers and for an increasing number of important chemical products. There is mercury in the Big Bend of Texas; bauxite for alum in Arkansas or across the Gulf of Mexico from British Guiana; fine clays and ochres in Georgia and Alabama; native gypsum and fine silica in many locations. This sector of the South has almost everything, and what is lacking can come in by barge or boat, the cheapest of all transportation. This last asset completes the economic combination. Most chemical raw materials are bulky or heavy and low priced. They cannot afford high freight that can be absorbed by finished products.

The South has also a vast store of organic materials needed in the synthesis of textile fibers, plastics and resins, waxes and glues, perfumes and medicines. Here are to be had two forms of cellulose, from cotton linters and from pine wood, for manufacturing paper, transparent wrapping sheets, photographic film, smokeless powder, the finest of lacquers. At hand, too, are vegetable oils from cottonseed and peanuts; proteins from cottonseed meal, soybeans, and grain sorghums; carbohydrates from sweet potato or rice starch or the sugar cane of Louisiana. Southern rosin and turpentine are already the base of exciting chemical developments. Lignin, tall oil, and furfural, recovered wastes that have chemical futures, are all available.

Most important of all, petroleum and natural gas, perfectly able to replace coal, coke, and coal tar, both as fuel (chemical manufacturing needs lots of power and heat) and as chemical raw materials, are here in bountiful supply. They are undoubtedly the strongest magnets drawing chemical enterprises to the Gulf Coast area. And quite recently this attraction has been made stronger. . . .

As the exploring drills have bored deeper and deeper into the earth's crust, a very heavy, very light-colored oily liquid and a colorless gas have gushed forth. There is nothing new in this underground alliance of gas and oil, but this gas and oil are different from ordinary natural gas and petroleum. In fact, they are so distinctive that conservation commissioners had trouble making up their minds whether to rate these operations as petroleum or gas wells. The drillers call them "gasoline wells," the chemists, "gas-condensates." You will hear a lot about these gas-condensates in the near future, for they are going to do things to high-octane gasoline and give us some new Southern industries. . . .

For twenty years gas has been returned to oil wells to maintain the underground pressure so that as much petroleum as possible can be brought from the reservoir to the surface. Cycling a gas-condensate is not quite so simple. The rich gases from underground are collected and are literally scrubbed with an absorption oil which sops up the heavier hydrocarbons which are then removed by distilling. The denuded oil goes back to the absorbers while the stripped dry gas is compressed again and returned to the reservoir. The recovered condensate, distilled out of the absorption oil, is then processed by regular refinery methods, to gasoline, kerosene, and heavy oil fractions, and the gases—butane, propane, and ethane—are separated out for enriching fuel gas, or making aviation gasoline, or as chemical raw materials.

This cycling operation is no penny-ante game. Though but six years old, already there are forty such plants, chiefly in Louisiana and coastal Texas. More are being built. Every day nearly four billion cubic feet of gas-condensates are being cycled, recovering some ninety thousand barrels of liquid products which give us a quarter of all our natural gasoline and allied products. No wonder the experts declare that cycling is the most important of all the startling wartime developments in the oil and gas industries. . . .

In grandfather's time the dyers used vinegar as a mild, impure acetic

593

acid. At the time of World War I, acetic acid came as a joint product with wood alcohol—of evil Prohibition days' reputation—when wood is charred in a tightly closed iron retort. Twenty years ago synthetic acetic acid was first prepared from acetylene, the gas which blazed in the Prest-O-Lite headlights of the Gay Nineties and which today burns hotly with oxygen in the welding torch. Now acetic acid is being made from acetaldehyde cracked out of recycled gas-condensates. It is the same old acetic acid, but the Celanese people think it will be cheaper. If it is, it will cut the costs of rayon and plastics.

Logic as straightforward as a gun barrel backs this new chemical operation. Cellulose plus acetic acid equals cellulose acetate, which is Celanese. The operation is not a war baby, for the process had been worked out at the home plant in Cumberland, Maryland, where an output of ten tons a day had been on schedule. But the new plant in Texas is also turning out thirty-five tons of butadiene a day. That process, too, is a Celanese development, with some novel short-cuts, aimed at lower costs.

Butadiene suggests synthetic rubber, so I asked the manager, Arthur E. Peterson, about the postwar program. He answered in his deep English voice, quite a shock to ears atuned to the soft Texas drawl, and his reply was no less startling than his accent. "The future of butadiene isn't hitched tight to synthetic rubber. It makes some rather fascinating new plastics."

This hints that the new Celanese plant at Guadalajara, Mexico, may not be the only postwar expansion planned by astute Camille Dreyfus for this company. It reminded me of the new low-cost plastic from butylene and sulfur dioxide about which Ross Thomas and Richard Alden, top Phillips petroleum chemists, are so enthusiastic. . . .

However tempting the prospects in petro-chemicals, the oil executives declare flatly that they do not intend to get into what they are pleased to call "the chemical gadget business." They say they will make only basic chemical intermediates, raw materials you can ship by the tankcar, leaving to the rubber and chemical manufacturers the job of working these up into finished products. But the rubber and chemical people just cannot help wondering.

It may be true that the petroleum leaders, their eyes focused on markets for twenty-five billion gallons of gasoline and five hundred million barrels of fuel oil, cannot see such microscopic figures as one hundred thousand pounds of some chemical with a tongue-twisting name. Yet rubber and plastics are not peanuts and popcorn on anybody's sales counter, and these men are not blind to the figures on a balance sheet. The dollar sign says that petroleum companies earn two, four, six, sometimes eight per cent on their net worth, while chemical companies earn ten, twelve, sometimes more than fifteen per cent. That

594

is language any company president understands. And the petroleum companies have the raw materials, the apparatus, the technical staffs to launch forth as chemical manufacturers. . . .

Meanwhile some of these puzzled executives have found a way out of the petro-chemical dilemma by alliances. Phillips Petroleum and Goodrich Rubber started it when they organized the Hycar Chemical Company and long before Pearl Harbor produced a new, strictly American type of Buna synthetic rubber. A wartime version of the same idea is the Port Neches butadiene plant operated by the so-called Port Arthur group of oil companies; Texas, Gulf, Socony-Vacuum, Pure Oil, and Magnolia. Near by at Texas City, the Carbide and Carbon Chemicals Corporation has a working agreement to take ethylene and propane from the adjoining refinery of Pan-American. The newest petro-chemical alliance is the Jefferson Chemical Company, owned jointly by American Cyanamid and Texas Oil. . . .

More effectively than the wisest State Industrial Commission or the most energetic Chamber of Commerce, such joint chemical enterprises will promote the postwar industrialization of the South. Just as raw materials draw chemical makers Southward, so their products are a magnet attracting other industries. . . .

In the South a lot of new chemicals will presently be available for many kinds of industries, and much Southern postwar planning is predicated on these materials. Synthetic resins will be made at Memphis, at Tuscaloosa, and at Mobile, and while today there is but one important Southern plastics fabricator making cups and electrical sockets and such like, I was told of enthusiastic plans afoot in Atlanta, New Orleans, and Mobile to enter this promising field. I read the blueprints for at least two big plastic-plywood operations. Both these have been drawn by Southern lumber companies which prewar only shipped "rough stuff" to be finished in Northern planing mills. With all the raw materials now locally available and big market at the front door, new paint and lacquer plants are projected at Houston, Jacksonville, Savannah, Vicksburg, and, I dare say, a dozen other Southern cities.

Most of these projects are fathered by Southern men financed by local capital. In the main the new petro-chemical industry will be a big-boy game, played by the strong petroleum, chemical, and rubber companies. But these new "associated enterprises" are the idea of hometown talent. This is a type of Southern industrialization quite distinct from that which depends upon a branch factory of a Northern company bribed by a free plant site or lured by the delusive prospect of a low wage scale. It is at once the promise and pledge of the South's chemical future.

X V I

THE ARTS

THE South's claim to having contributed anything remarkable to the artistic life of America has often been challenged, frequently by critics within its borders. The harsh judgment pronounced by W. J. Cash will be found in the second selection in this volume (p. 12). Broadus Mitchell, another Southerner by birth, in the chapter he contributed to *Culture in the South* (1935) is almost as devastating:

> We affected to believe that the way of life of the old South needed no defense, but awoke admiration. If it had drawbacks in general illiteracy, lack of inventiveness, absence of economic incentive, and the banishing of political democracy, these were minor debits. The great fact was that we developed "culture." If we did, it was so elusive that the observer today cannot find it. It did not take form in music, poetry, prose, building, works of engineering, jurisprudence, science or theology, let alone the infinitely more difficult matter of decent human comfort and independence for the average man within the South.

In 1920 H. L. Mencken, whose home-town, Baltimore, wishes to be considered a Southern city, opened his famous attack on Southern culture—"The Sahara of the Bozart"—with J. Gordon Coogler's immortal couplet (and went on from there):

> Alas for the South! Her books have grown fewer—
> She was never much given to literature.

In fending off such attacks, the Southern Agrarians, and other champions, have often taken the line that Professor Mitchell scornfully rejected. They have talked about a homogeneous culture based on traditional religious and political values, abundant leisure, hospitality, and manners, about the Southerner's sense of responsibility for others—in short, about the enviable way of life developed by the Old South in contrast to the commercial spirit striped with Puritan piety which was the Northern way.

This line of argument is really beside the point, and for two reasons. We do not judge the artistic culture of any other section of the country solely by what it produced before the Civil War. Why do Southern defenders go on talking as if no one had sung ballads or written a novel in their land since the fall of Richmond? During the past thirty years the South has experienced a literary renaissance greater than any that has been seen in America since the days of Emerson and Melville. The time has come to talk about the writers who brought about this renaissance rather than the deficiencies of William Gilmore Simms's prose style.

The second fallacy is one that critics of American life often slip into. While we have been waiting anxiously for an American Shakespeare and the writer of "the great American novel," artistic happenings have been taking place here which we fail to mention until Europeans inquire about them. Donald Davidson comes near to the heart of this matter—where we can profitably look for evidences of artistic culture in the South—in his "A Mirror for Artists," the chapter he contributed to *I'll Take My Stand*, the 1930 manifesto of the Southern Agrarians:

> So far as the arts have flourished in the South, they have been, up to a very recent period, in excellent harmony with their milieu. The South has always had a native architecture, adapted from classic models into something distinctly Southern; and nothing more clearly and satisfactorily belongs where it is, or better expresses the beauty and stability of an ordered life, than its old country homes, with their pillared porches, their simplicity of design, their sheltering groves, their walks bordered with boxwood shrubs. The South has been rich in the folk-arts, and is still rich in them—in ballads, country songs and dances, in hymns and spirituals, in folk tales, in the folk crafts of weaving, quilting, furniture-making. Though these are best preserved in mountain fastnesses and remote rural localities, they were not originally so limited. They were widepread; and though now they merely survive, they are certainly indicative of a society that could not be termed inartistic.

Of course Mr. Davidson finds greatness in the writers he approves of among the contributors to the modern Southern literary renaissance. Others he banishes to outer darkness: Paul Green and DuBose Heyward, whose "studies of negro life [are] so palpably tinged with latter-day abolitionism," and T. S. Stribling, who writes "like a spiritual companion of Harriet Beecher Stowe." One doubts, too, if Mr. Davidson, in reckoning up the artistic achievements of the modern South, would count the Negro's contribution of jazz and the blues.

Has the multifactionalism of Southern politics affected those who write about the arts in the South?

1. BUILDING

The South has originated no distinctive style of architecture, but in the two hundred and fifty years before the Civil War it adapted to its own purposes the domestic and public building-styles which came to it from abroad and even from the North. Southerners built well and with an eye to posterity. When a plantation-owner was ready to tear down the old log dwelling or the small cottage-style brick dwelling his grandfather had erected and was making his plans for his great house, he built it with the hope that it would never pass from his family. Since the upper South was proud of its Anglo-Saxon legal institutions and valued highly the art of politics, its public buildings, from the crossroads courthouse to the state capitol, were designed as monuments of which later generations would be proud.

In the upper South during colonial times new styles in architecture followed, at the distance of years, the succession of the styles that prevailed in England. One of the last of the Gothic churches in the Western world survives in Smithfield County, Virginia—St. Luke's, built, according to legend, in 1632. Several Virginia houses, including Stratford, the home of the Lees, show traces of the Jacobean style. The traditional small brick or frame house of Virginia, with one or two dormers in its roof, derives from the cottage of Tudor and Stuart times. In the eighteenth century the English Georgian arrived, and prevailed until the Greek revival came into favor in the 1830's. But just as many of the simple, pedimented early Georgian houses show traces of the earlier baroque style in their magnificent doorways, so do many of the early Greek-revival houses, built a century later, betray the lingering Georgian influence in moldings, cornices, and fireplaces.

In the colonial South that had ties to France and Spain a quite different kind of domestic architecture prevailed, adapted to the subtropical climate of the lower Mississippi region. The houses were high off the ground—to offset dampness and possible flooding. Thick walls kept out the heat, and the long sloping roof, carried out over the two-storied gallery, made deep shade in the long summers. The later examples were augmented with flanking pavilions. Often the outside stairway leading to the lower gallery was divided and made to curve gracefully toward the center of the house. Few examples of Spanish colonial survive.

So thoroughly is the white-columned Greek-revival style of architecture associated with the South that many people must believe it originated there. Actually the earliest important example of this style, which swept over all of America between 1820 and 1850, is Latrobe's Bank of Pennsylvania, erected in Philadelphia in 1798. The style caught on rather slowly in the South, possibly because there was so much justifiable pride in the buildings already in existence.

The wave of enthusiasm for the new style reached Richmond in the 1820's. In North Carolina it attained its apogee when the new Capitol was built, between 1838 and 1840, in Raleigh. Greek revival came late to Charleston, South Carolina. Several buildings erected there in the 1850's are more Roman than Greek in their inspiration. Meanwhile Gideon Shryock had done magnificent work in the style in Frankfort, the old capital of Kentucky. His design for the Capitol building won the competition in 1825.

Shryock's master, the eminent Philadelphia architect William Strickland, was called to Nashville, Tennessee, in 1845 to plan and supervise the construction of the state Capitol. When this was completed, it was the handsomest Greek-revival building in the South. Strickland died in Nashville in 1854 after having completed many works in the new style.

While the Greek-revival temples and columns and capitals were spreading through the South, another style, inspired by the Gothic Middle Ages, received some attention. The old state capitols at Baton Rouge, Louisiana, and Milledgeville, Georgia, are important monuments in this Gothic revival.

For many years after the war the South was too poor to afford buildings of any size, though the churches often managed to raise enough money to build new edifices in the eclectic styles fashionable in the 1870's and 1880's. The general conservatism of the South has warded off the modern styles of this century, though in thriving commercial centers like Houston a few bold spirits have been willing to experiment with designs inspired by the work of Gropius or Frank Lloyd Wright.

The traveler in the South must be enterprising if he wishes to see the glories of Southern architecture. Many of the surviving great plantation houses must be pursued up unmarked country roads and along rivers on which boats no longer navigate. The Civil War destroyed many public buildings: Columbia, South Carolina, was burned, almost certainly by the Federal troops, and the retreating Confederates who set fire to war supplies at Richmond inadvertently burned down a large part of the old city. As many Southern cities, now grown large, had only a few thousand inhabitants at the time of the war, the traveler will look in vain for splendid ante-bellum banks, taverns, customs-houses, and churches. Aside from Charleston, Savannah, Mobile, and New Orleans, the most rewarding cities are the old and diminished state capitals such as Edenton and New Bern in North Carolina, Milledgeville in Georgia, and Frankfort in Kentucky, or other small cities whose commercial prosperity was once great.

Following page 614 is a series of photographs illustrating various aspects of Southern architecture.

2. COOKING

The rapid tourist who "does" the South in five days will keep himself alive by consuming the universal American foods—cheeseburgers, Coca-Colas (ask for a "dope"), and Dairy Queens. If he puts up at a chain hotel, he will be mildly surprised to find that his standard American breakfast is supplemented by a soggy white mess called (incorrectly) grits and more sausages in more forms than he has ever encountered. At lunch he will try the Southern fried chicken and decide that it is as tendinous as the Northern variety. If he is lucky enough to get a seat at Antoine's (after standing in line for the privilege), he will return to Worcester, Mass., and tell his friends that only in New Orleans does the reality of Southern cooking match the myth.

The trouble is that, as with all rapid tourists, he doesn't meet any of the local inhabitants. If someone in Charleston would take him home to dinner and serve him baked guinea squash and spoon bread, his life would be made happier.

Unless our Worcesterian meets the right people and finds the right restaurants, he will never know that Southerners even now eat better than the inhabitants of any other section of the country. In every family someone cherishes the ancestral receipts for Brunswick stew and fatty cornbread and someone still demands that ambrosia shall be served once a week.

Southerners ate well in the past because they had all the foods the plantation grew to load their tables with. They were far more ingenious in devising things to do with corn meal (water-ground of course) than the New Englanders, who never got farther in this department than Indian pudding and lye hominy. (Corn flourished in Southern soils, whereas wheat grew tall and produced little grain.) They also had better ideas about the hog and used every inch of him, from maws to chitterlings.

Your Southerner still eats high on the hog. If you suspect that the foods and feasts described below belong to history, rest assured that they can be met with today—if you are invited to dine in Selma or

Savannah. You can also experiment with some of them if you will get
your hands on the following cookbooks: Marion Brown: *The Southern
Cook Book* (Cardinal Edition, 1953); *Charleston Receipts Collected by
the Junior League of Charleston* (published by Walker, Evans, &
Cogswell, 1950); and Lena Richard: *New Orleans Cook Book*
(Houghton Mifflin, 1940).

Mr. Rutledge's Oyster Roast

John Rutledge (1739–1800) was twenty-one and a half years old when he was elected a member of the South Carolina Assembly. Newly returned from England, where he had studied at the Middle Temple, young Mr. Rutledge at once began his career as lawyer and politician, and the mending of his fortunes. His political oyster roast persuaded the influential voters of Christ Church parish to let him represent them in the Assembly. This was the first stage in a long career of service to his colony, state, and nation. From 1789 to 1791 Rutledge was an Associate Justice of the United States Supreme Court, from which office he resigned to become Chief Justice of South Carolina.

Feasting one's constituents was fairly common in the Old South, though few provided such an overwhelming menu as Rutledge did on this occasion. It is known that Patrick Henry, Edmund Randolph, George Mason, and George Washington were not above offering this kind of inducement to the voters.

This passage is taken from Richard Barry's Mr. Rutledge of South Carolina *(New York: Duell, Sloan & Pearce; 1942), pp. 41–5. It is reprinted here with the permission of the publishers.*

THE day of the oyster roast arrived.

At dawn the wagons were on the road, bringing supplies from various parts of the plantation to the greensward in front of the Great House, set at the end of its avenue of live oaks that stretched a mile to the main highway. The oak trees were more than three hundred feet apart.

The slaves brought utensils, dug pits, and set up a number of ovens, in parallel lines, two hundred yards apart. The house wenches, directed by the butler, set the long cypress tables which the carpenters had erected midway between the ovens and just at the side of the road. They used the ancestral napery, china, silverware, linen some of which had been brought by Hugh Hext from England in 1684 when he came with his original grant from the Lords Proprietors.

The feast was spread under a bright sky. It was shaded by the Spanish moss which festooned in long spirals from the hoary oaks. The brisk

January air was pervaded by the tantalizing odors of the cooking.

Before noon the guests began to arrive by buggy, by horseback, or by canoe. The Horrys came from St. Phillips' Parish, across two rivers. They had to start at dawn, but Mrs. Rutledge had made sure that Miss Horry and her parents should be present. When she suggested guests who lived in other parishes, John had objected. She noted that he had asked, almost exclusively, their neighbors from Christ Church Parish, but he would not give her his reasons.

At noon John offered his arm to his mother and together they walked from the Great House down to the tables to inspect the service. After it was approved, to the proud satisfaction of the butler, the fine linen, silver, glass, china, and cutlery were removed to wicker baskets at the side.

The bare boards were then spread with individual linen mats, wooden oyster platters, oyster knives, and, for each guest, a protective arm-rest clamped to the table. There was also a large tumbler for each guest.

At noon the fires were started. Soon the pits on either side were glowing with hickory coals and the thin smoke was curling up into the tall fronds of the live oaks. Shortly after twelve more guests arrived. Everyone knew that promptness was important to the proper preparation of a roasted oyster, so all came before one o'clock.

In Christ Church there were sixty male communicants and about a hundred and fifty voters. More than half of these, with their wives and grown children, were present that day. The carpenters waited near-by with extra cypress lumber to add new tables if needed—and before long they were needed. The tables spread down the avenue for a quarter of a mile; but there was no crowding; everyone had plenty of elbow room. The effect was certainly baronial. The lord of the manor was "at home."

Precisely at one o'clock John blew a hunter's horn from the steps of the Great House. This was the signal for the "hands" to pour the oysters, by the barrelful, on the live coals. Simultaneously the guests were seated and the butler appeared, with his assistants, bearing silver pitchers of hot drinks—whiskey punch for the men, eggnog with a dash of nutmeg and a little Barbados rum for the women. The tumblers were filled.

No one tasted the punch, however, before John rose from the head of the first table, glass in hand, and offered the toast: "To our friends, neighbors and guests from Christ Church Parish—and elsewhere, welcome!" They all drank.

Instantly, a battalion of pickaninnies ran from the fires bearing platters of sputtering oysters straight from the hot coals. There followed a clatter of knives struggling with oysters. There was a pickaninny for every two guests. They were trained to watch and keep everyone supplied with sizzling oysters, one at a time. The purpose was to get the freshly steamed oysters from the fire to the gullet with all the juices intact.

This went on for the better part of an hour. Then a male guest near the head of the table gave the signal—it was not thought seemly for the host to suggest any pause in the eating—and the men withdrew by stepping over the stationary benches.

When they had withdrawn, the women also rose. It was not so easy for them, especially the young ones who wore long bouffant skirts, to get out without confusion. They, too, had to get over the benches, and if a girl's or a woman's foot showed, beyond the toe, her embarrassment was intense. The men chivalrously avoided the dangerous chance of seeing a glint of hose above a shoe top. The matrons got themselves out, without help, and then assisted the girls.

The guests strolled along the creek or wandered over to the Negro cabins and watched the "picks" dance or otherwise rested for an hour, while the butler's assistants removed the rough tools of the oyster massacre and set the formal table.

About three o'clock they all came back from the creek or the cabins or the Great House, where some took their midday siesta, and sat down again at the long tables, now transformed to gleaming cascades of napery, crystal, china, and silver, with the early buds of January roses sprinkled down the middle.

Now it was apparent how ridiculous it was to call this an oyster roast. There were crayfish in aspic, shrimp and watercress salad, red snapper baked whole in Bordeaux Sauce; there was a terrapin stew and venison patty, with a pudding made of palmetto hearts and yams baked so tenderly they fell into the mold of any hand they touched. There was Madeira for the men and schnapps for the women, or Bordeaux if they preferred. There were biscuit beaten hard and thin; each only a bite, but served plentifully. Everything was trundled to the tables in huge pannikins, which acted like fireless cookers to keep the food warm.

The eating went on for all of two hours. With the cardinals chattering above in the oak leaves, the winter sun sifting through, the Madeira softening any sense of haste, everyone felt free of time and space. Who wanted to hurry when confronted by a deep-sea red snapper baked in Bordeaux? Or a swamp terrapin who jumped from his diamond back so recently into the soup of beef stock set in rum? Or a plentiful helping of palmetto marrow?

The venison patty was the chef d'œuvre. The women wanted to know what the game cook had put in it. The Indian had brought in the deer, but venison was only the base of a patty like this.

604

John Rutledge called his game cook, a wrinkled, dried-up old darky woman, black as coal, with kinky white hair. Her beady amber eyes glowed with suppressed excitement. She held herslf aloof, proud, and dignified. She was not haughty, but she was equal to the best of them in personal distinction. The white folks—rulers of all the empire she ever knew—hung on her words, quizzing her in soft voices. What did she put in it? She shrugged her shoulders—"O, a little of this, a little of that." How long for the hanging, how long for the salting, how long for the boiling? "O, not too long—but long nuf." And where had she learned this momentous secret? From her "gran'maw, who'd it f'm 'er pappy," who got it "f'm Chicasaw—in part—an' part f'm a game cook who die sixty years afo'. She live Waccamaw plantation—she ol' 'oman afo' she wrastle deer patty—yel gotta be ol'."

At last they gave it up and she went off to her kitchen—an empress with authority possessed by none other. She would not admit she felt herself better than anyone else on the plantation, but no one else approached her just the same.

Between John Rutledge and his game cook there was a strange bond. She never lived with anyone but Rutledges and Hexts. His father had chosen her and she was a possession that he cherished.

At last it was nearly sundown. The roast was almost over. John rose and told them, most casually, that he wanted to be a member of the Commons; and asked them to vote for him at the next election.

What with the Madeira, the rum, the whiskey, and all the rest of the roast, there may have been confusion in grasping what he meant. Apparently he made no particular point of it. The guests agreed offhand that whatever he asked for he should have.

Juleps before Breakfast

The English war-correspondent W. H. Russell was visiting at Houmas, the extensive sugar plantation of Mr. Burnside, when he ate this breakfast and survived. He describes it on pages 276–7 of My Diary North and South (*Boston: T. O. H. P. Burnham; 1863*). *For a note on Russell see p. 289.*

June 6th [1861]—My chattel Joe, *"adscriptus mihi domino,"* awoke me to a bath of Mississippi water with huge lumps of ice in it, to which he recommended a mint-julep as an adjunct. It was not here that I was first exposed to an ordeal of mint-julep, for in the early morning a stranger in a Southern planter's house may expect the offer of a glassful of brandy, sugar, and peppermint beneath an island of ice—an obligatory panacea for all the evils of climate. After it has been disposed of, Pompey may come up again with glass number two: "Massa say fever very bad this morning—much dew." It is possible that the degenerate Anglo-Saxon stomach has not the fine tone and temper of that of an Hibernian friend of mine, who considered the finest thing to counteract the effects of a little excess was a tumbler of hot whiskey and water the moment the sufferer opened his eyes in the morning. Therefore, the kindly offering may be rejected. But on one occasion before breakfast the negro brought up mint-julep number three, the acceptance of which he enforced by the emphatic declaration, "Massa says, sir, you had better take this, because it'll be the last he make before breakfast."

Breakfast is served: there is on the table a profusion of dishes—grilled fowl, prawns, eggs and ham, fish from New Orleans, potted salmon from England, preserved meats from France, claret, iced water, coffee and tea, varieties of hominy, mush, and African vegetable preparations. Then come the newspapers, which are perused eagerly with ejaculations, "Do you hear what they are doing now—infernal villains! that Lincoln must be mad!" and the like.

Edibles and Potables

If you wish to start an argument among your Southern friends, show them this list. They will instantly quarrel with many of the items. They will also add ten new ones in ten minutes. Meanwhile your education in the mysteries of Southern cooking will be rapidly advanced. Some of the edibles and potables were English to begin with. Some of them the North has so long shared with the South that their Southern origins have been forgotten. Some are distinctly subregional or are identified with particular cities. Through the whole list those persistent Southern staples "hog and hominy" appear in many guises.

ambrosia
artichoke pickle
ash cake
barbecued spareribs
batter bread
batter cakes
beaten biscuit
black-eyed peas
black-strap
Brunswick stew
burgoo
butter beans
café brulot
chess pies
chickasaw peas
chitlins (chitterlings)
cimlins
collards
corn cakes
corn pone
cow peas
crab gumbo
cracklin' bread
crayfish bisque
creole fried chicken
creole gumbo
cush
daube glacé
egg bread
fat-back
fatty cornbread
field peas
flannel cakes
flip
fried okra
fried pies
ginger ice
goobers
grits (boiled, fried, baked)
gumbo filé
hoe cakes
hog jowls
hog maws
hoppin'-john
hush puppies

jumbalaya
light bread
lye hominy
minced oysters
mint julep
molasses pie
Mulatto rice
okra
okra gumbo
okra pilau
orange wine
oyster loaf
oysters Rockefeller
pain perdu
pecan pie
pompano
pot liquor
potted doves
pralines
Ramos gin fizz
red fish
red snapper
Saint Cecilia punch
Sally Lunn
Sangeree punch
Sazerac cocktail
scuppernong wine
she-crab soup
short'nin' bread
shrimp pie
shrimp rémoulade
side meat
Smithfield ham
soft cornbread
sorghum
sowbelly
spiced beef
spoon bread
strawberry shrub
sugar pie
sweet pickled watermelon
sweet-potato pie
syllabub
terrapin soup
turnip greens

3 . MUSIC-MAKING

More than any of the other arts, except that of the theater, music needs the support of an audience. A composer works by himself, as a novelist does, but his symphony or suite must eventually be performed in a concert hall if his name is to become known. One does not find concert halls in the lonely places of the South, in the piney woods or the sandhills or the bayou country. Thus it is that music as a formal art has flourished only recently in the South, as the cities of the region have become large enough to support composers and performers. There have been a few exceptions to this rule. In its inception the St. Cecilia Society of Charleston was a musical organization, patterned after similar societies that originated in England in the late seventeenth century. And in New Orleans, while the Creole culture dominated the city, French opera had a vigorous life. Of late several symphony orchestras have been firmly established in Southern cities—notably in New Orleans, Chattanooga, Knoxville, Birmingham, Dallas, and Houston. This development is part of the increased nation-wide interest in symphonic music.

In earlier days music was not an art in which Southern gentlemen indulged, though Robert Carter III, of Nomini Hall, enjoyed playing his harpsichord and Thomas Jefferson was an accomplished violinist. Music was in the hands of the women of the family or was left to itinerants of German, French, or Italian origin. In the female seminaries of the South music had an important place in the curriculum. In some of them the standards of accomplishment required more than the ability to accompany the singer of a tender ballad or "render" a few arpeggios on the harp. It startles one to learn, for instance, that when the Amite Female Academy was burned by Federal troops thirteen pianos were destroyed. They had been hauled through the wilderness to the academy in Liberty, Mississippi, with great cost and effort.

Turning to the folk music of the South, one finds riches beyond those of any other region of the country. At last, through the efforts of several generations of collectors, we know how vast is this treasury of hymns and spirituals (of both of the whites and the Negroes), of ballads and work songs, shouts and blues, the Gumbo songs (of the slaves of the Creoles) and the Cajun songs of Louisiana.

And in New Orleans, as everybody knows, jazz had its beginnings. To Europeans this is the greatest contribution America has made to music. Parisians who would have no interest in the fact that memories of his years in Florida inspired Frederick Delius's opera *Koanga* know that Sidney Bechet, Jelly Roll Morton, and Louis Armstrong are identified with New Orleans. To them, too, Memphis means W. C. Handy, "father of the blues," and Bessie Smith, greatest of the blues-singers.

A "Sacred Harp" Convention

Slowly and belatedly the rich stores of folk music in the South have been uncovered. First to be appreciated, collected, and written about were the Negro spirituals (see note p. 627). Then the ballad-collectors, hunting for American survivals of the English ballads, began their rewarding search in the Southern Appalachians. Solely intent on finding the so-called "Child ballads" (so named for Harvard Professor F. J. Child's English and Scottish Popular Ballads, *1883–98), these early collectors paid no attention to the secular and religious folk-songs which were of American origin. They also ignored another kind of native religious music—the "Psalm and Hymn Tunes, Odes and Anthems" of the* Sacred Harp.

It was left for a professor of German at Vanderbilt University, George Pullen Jackson (1874–1953) to discover the Sacred Harp *singers and their traditional music. Yet, as he has noted, no act of "discovery" was required. The music of the* Sacred Harp *is sung just as devotedly in the South today as it was more than a hundred years ago when the first edition of this collection of religious songs was printed. But no folklorist or musical scholar had ever thought to listen in at a* Sacred Harp *meeting or convention. Professor Jackson was the first to heed what his ears told him.*

This extraordinary musical tradition goes back more than two hundred years to a time when the "Old Baptists," who had previously had little music of their own, began to use the hymn tunes collected by other sects and to fit well-loved secular folk tunes to the words of favorite hymns. In 1844 B. F. White, editor of a newspaper in Harris County, Georgia, and a leading teacher in singing schools in the region, published in Philadelphia the first edition of The Sacred Harp. *This book, in its familiar oblong form, with its characteristic "shaped" notes, became the treasured possession of thousands and was passed down through generations. It is still in print, the latest edition being the "Denson Revision" of 1936.*

The music of The Sacred Harp *is genuine four-part music in which each of the four voices is equally "eventful." Since the major tunes often omit the fourth and the seventh tones of the scale and the naturalminor tunes omit the second and the sixth, the* Sacred Harp *music sounds strangely primitive to unaccustomed listeners. There is every reason why it should, since this, like other varieties of folk song, pre-serves and carries down the ancient musical modes.*

This account of a Sacred Harp *convention in Texas is excerpted from George Pullen Jackson's* White Spirituals in the Southern Up-lands *(1933). It is reprinted with the permission of the publisher, the University of North Carolina Press.*

I ARRIVED in Mineral Wells, Texas, toward the end of the Great Drouth of 1930. The clerk of the sky-scraping Baker Hotel in the Lone Star State's favorite spa could not direct me to the Interstate Sacred Harp Convention. He knew nothing of it. He was able, however, to direct me to the municipal convention hall. The Friday morning session was just starting with a song as I entered. After the song the chaplain read from the scriptures, offered a prayer, and then singing, nothing but singing, filled the forenoon from nine to twelve excepting for a short recess in the middle.

I observed the singers. There were about two hundred of them, men, women, and children. They were all country folk, of course, though some of them lived, as I learned, in Texas cities. They were the same type, precisely, that I had met in many other Sacred Harp conventions. This was evident from their work-browned faces and their absence of "style." Galluses were much in evidence.

The singers were what is commonly called "pure Anglo-Saxon stock," but what is in reality . . . Celtic, Teutonic, and Anglo-Saxon, and hence Nordic. If they are to be dubbed "poor whites," the term should be used to signify those people who have not yet turned from their ancient attitudes toward life values and adopted the current com-mercially standardized ones. . . .

The singers occupied the level floor space of the auditorium, leaving the tiers of seats, rising to both sides, for the sparsely assembled lis-teners. These listeners were also country people. The singers sat in folding chairs on four sides of a rectangular open space where the leader stood. The men and women "tenors" (sopranos) were in front of the leader, the men and women "trebles" (tenors) at his left, the women altos behind him, and the basses at his right. Each singer had a copy of the big *Sacred Harp* on his lap. Some of these were of the 1930 printing. But here and there I saw yellowed copies of an edition that had appeared two generations ago, heirlooms that were brought along, mayhap, when the singers' forebears moved into the new state of Texas. But this difference in edition brought no confusion, for the song on any given page was the same for all the printings of this 86-year-old survival in musical culture.

Each singer wore a ribbon badge which showed him to be an accredited delegate from some other singing convention or singing school. They had gathered, as I learned later, largely from Texas and the adjoining states to the north and east. Though Alabama organizations were represented by over twenty delegates, one hailed from Georgia and one from Tennessee.

The president, W. H. Coston of Dallas, announced the "brother" who was to "sing." (In Alabama he "led" a "lesson." And in the *Harmonia Sacra* singings of the Shenandoah Valley he "entertained us.") His time on the floor was three songs long. He called the page of his first song and then "keyed" the tune by singing its tonic and other opening tones without the help of even a tuning fork. "Faw, law, sol!" The singers of all four parts got their pitch instantly and, after the one deliberate chord with which all the *Sacred Harp* songs begin, the whole chorus was on its way singing the song once through by "notes" (solmization syllables) only, a practice which is unique today with these four-shapers and is clearly recognizable as the survival of a custom started two hundred years ago in the first American singing schools. Then came the words, one to three stanzas. Some leaders stood still. But most of them walked around the open space giving the entrance cues—in the often-sung "fuguing" songs—successively to the different sections. The leader's beat was with both arms, for he was seldom encumbered with a book; and his arm movements were simply down and up. The songs seldom demanded anything else, and if they did it made no difference. The response of the singers was usually vigorous and rhythmically precise, for they, making little use of the book, kept their eyes on the leader and beat time also, always with one arm or merely the hand. And if that hand held a fan, it was given a little twist, half a revolution, each time it came up. The reading ability of these singers was nothing short of astounding. There are 550 pages of four-part music in the *Sacred Harp*, and they tackled and mastered, by solmization as well as by text, anything that any leader put up. This meant either that they had, by long years of singing, learned the entire book practically by heart, or that they were sight readers of what we could call "professional" stature. I came to the conclusion that both memorization and sight-reading ability were responsible for this remarkable accomplishment.

The women were not declassed in this *Sacred Harp* convention. While male singers were perhaps more numerous, still the womenfolk were an important element in the ranks and as leaders. Owing to the lack of volume in their voices, it was customary for some man to "key" the tune for them. But otherwise their conductorial work was on a par with that of the males.

This singing went on busily for over two hours. And one session was much like all the others, but for the choice of leaders and songs. The program committee strove to make it possible for each delegate who was a leader—and most of them were—to have his or her turn on the floor. The patriarchs like the Alabama Densons and C. J. Griggs, delegate from the United Sacred Harp Convention of Georgia, were accorded special leadership privileges. Thus during the seven sessions at least fifty delegates led one or more "lessons." I have no record of the number of songs sung on this occasion. But the figures for similar meets held in Birmingham in 1924 and 1925 show an average of forty songs sung each session, or two hundred and eighty during the seven sessions of three days. The most industrious singing seems to have been done at the 1925 convention of the B. F. White organization in Birmingham, where one session showed as many as fifty-three songs sung, one full day of three sessions, one hundred and forty-one songs, and for the entire three-day meet three hundred and twenty. . . .

May I stress the importance of the emotional element in this singing by quoting from a declaration made to me by Charles Martin, an inveterate Sacred Harper of Atlanta:

"Every time I go to one of these singings I feel that I am attending a memorial to my mother. Twenty years ago she floated out into the harbor of eternal rest. Today she is taking part in the Royal Band. This singing takes me back to the dearest spot known to humanity, that of a mother's knee. It never fails, on such occasions, that some song or some voice amongst the singers reminds me of my dear old mother. And then it just seems as if the purest joys nearest heaven were bidding clouds give way to sun and light and as if heaven itself hovered over the place.

"You'll have to put up a mighty high fence," the old singer declared convincingly after a little pause, "to keep me out of a Sacred Harp Singing."

Jazz from Storyville, New Orleans

The following colorful account of the origins of New Orleans jazz is taken from A History of Jazz in America, *by Barry Ulanov, copyright 1952 by Barry Ulanov, reprinted by permission of The Viking Press, Inc., New York. The passages will be found on pages 38 and 44–8.*

It was only in 1897, in a new ordinance sponsored by Alderman Story, that a specific district was set up to limit prostitution geographically. The earlier ordinance had restricted only operations, and had actually given the brothels and unaffiliated whores an unmistakably large swathe through the city in which to work. It was, then, from 1897 to 1917 (when the Secretary of the Navy shut down all red-light districts) that tourism descended upon prostitution in New Orleans and jazz came alive.

The district, a sizable chunk of New Orleans, was at first open to Negroes and mulattos, at least in certain sections, and they brought their trade and their music with them. In the last eight months of organized Storyville a restricted Negro district about half the size of Storyville proper was established. But for most of the two important decades Negro and white women, Negro and white musicians, worked side by side. Here in what their owners and residents invariably called palaces, chateaux, and maisons, in what are accurately named honky-tonks, in saloons, and in all the other entertainment places—except perhaps the "cribs," the tiny dwellings of the cheapest prostitutes—jazz was played. The well-placed white man in New Orleans looked down upon Storyville, publicly regarded it as a civic disgrace, whatever his private behavior; but at Carnival time, and especially on the day of Mardi Gras, this Orleanian lost none of his propriety and gained much in warmth by joining with the district in a celebration long since world-famous. The white Carnival had its King Rex, and the Negroes their King Zulu and their music, easily the most distinguished contribution to the jubilant festivities. . . .

[In the five pages omitted here Mr. Ulanov describes the famous guide to the New Orleans bordellos, The Blue Book, *and the two principal establishments of Storyville—Miss Lulu White's New Mahogany Hall and Countess Willie Piazza's mansion at 317 N. Basin.]*

The Countess apparently was the first to hire a pianist, and there is a story, perhaps apocryphal, that his name, self-adopted or conferred by the customers ("club boys"), was John the Baptist. Another of the Countess's pianists was Tony Jackson, a showmanly musician who brought vaudeville into the brothel, and after 1908 became an established name in New York. He will be forever associated with his song, "I've Got Elgin Movements in My Hips with Twenty Years' Guarantee." Lulu White could also boast some fine pianists, notably Richard M. Jones, who died during the 1940s in Chicago, and Clarence Williams, who when he came to New York probably brought more of New Orleans with him than any other man, in his song-writing, record-making, and public performances. The most famous of the Anderson Annex pianists was Ferdinand Joseph (Jelly Roll) Morton, the

613

Gulfport, Mississippi, musician, who will be remembered as long for his spoken jazz narratives as for his piano-playing and composing.

Lulu White's Mahogany Hall and adjoining saloon, at the corner of Bienville and Basin Streets, makes a good starting point for a tour of the area where jazz flourished from the late 1880s to 1917. Right before us, as we face south, is the Southern Railroad, a stretch of tracks leading along Basin Street to the terminal on Canal. A block east, on Iberville, is Tom Anderson's Annex, and back of it, on Franklin Street, the 101 Ranch, which had changed by 1910 from a kind of waterfront saloon, though some distance from the river, into one of the most impressive of the jazz hangouts, where King Oliver and Sidney Bechet and Pops Foster and Emanuel Perez played some of their strong early notes. Billy Phillips, owner of the 101, opened the Tuxedo Dance Hall diagonally across from the Ranch. The Tuxedo was the scene of many police raids and ultimately of Phillips's killing. Freddie Keppard played his driving cornet at the Tuxedo, and later Johnny Dodds was the featured clarinetist and Oscar Celestin led the band named after the hall, the Tuxedo Band, which in a later edition was still playing on Bourbon Street in New Orleans in 1951. Two blocks away from Lulu White's, at Liberty and Bienville, was the Poodle Dog Cafe—a name used in city after city; it was popular from 1910 through the early twenties as far north as Washington, D. C., where a cafe of the same name was the scene of Duke Ellington's first piano-playing job. North one block and east another, on Iberville, was Pete Lala's Cafe, much patronized for the music as well as the barrels of liquor, and where, at one time or another, Kid Ory and King Oliver and Louis Armstrong led bands. Lala also owned "The 25" club, a block down from the Tuxedo, another of the sometime jazz places.

Down the railroad tracks, as one goes away from the center of town on Basin Street, are cemeteries. Up Iberville and Bienville and Conti, going north, are cemeteries. If you follow the tracks, past the cemeteries, past St. Louis Street and Lafitte Avenue, you reach what is now called Beauregard Square, where now squats the Municipal Auditorium, graced with flowers and grass shrubbery. Now, in season, there are band concerts and rallies and public events of all sorts here. In 1803, Fort St. Ferdinand, built by the Spaniards on this spot, was destroyed in an attempt to wipe out yellow fever, thought to be caused by the stagnant water of the moats and the abundant filth of the city's ramparts. The park which replaced the fort was at first used as a circus ground, then enclosed with an iron fence and made into a Sunday-afternoon promenade ground and pleasance for Orleanians. For the city's Negro slaves, granted a half-holiday every Sunday, the new park was a wonderful gathering-place. Named Congo Square, the great open area was used by the Negroes for games, for singing to the ac-

Westover

WESTOVER on the James, home of William Byrd II, is one of the most magnificent houses of the Old Dominion. Its construction was begun in 1729. Interior and exterior details, though eclectic, are harmonized by a consistent delicacy of parts and execution. The baroque doorway is the commanding feature of the river front of the house.

The State Capitol, Richmond

THE design for the Capitol in Richmond was developed in Paris in 1785 by Jefferson and Clérisseau, the leading French architectural authority of his day. Reflecting a close study of the Roman temple in Nîmes, the so-called Maison Carrée, Virginia's Capitol pre-dates the Madeleine in Paris, first great European temple reproduction, by twenty years.

Photograph by Wayne Andrews

Ormond

THE great house of Ormond Plantation stands beside the Mississippi at Good Hope, Louisiana, within easy distance of New Orleans. The middle section was built by a French planter, Pierre Trépagnier, about 1800. It shows an interesting blending of French and Spanish influences. Later owners, the Irish Butlers, gave the house its present name.

Greenwood

THE building of Green-
wood, in 1830, was super-
vised by its owner, William
Ruffin Barrow, Jr. The
house is completely enclosed
by thirty-foot columns with
Doric capitals, and is
crowned with a roof belvedere. Notable for such interior luxuries as silver door-
knobs and gold-leaf cor-
nices, Greenwood is a model
of ante-bellum Louisiana
elegance.

Old Capitol, Baton Rouge

WHEN James H. Dakin designed the first Capitol (1847–50) for Louisiana, he deliberately avoided the classical styles which, he said, were in favor "in every city and town in our country" and chose the newly fashionable Tudor-Gothic. His building was destroyed by fire during the Civil War, but was reconstructed in 1882. In his *Life on the Mississippi* Mark Twain said of the Old Capitol: "Sir Walter Scott is probably responsible for the Capitol building; for it is not conceivable that this little sham castle would ever have been built if he had not run the people mad, a couple of generations ago, with his medieval romances."

Longwood

Designed by the fashionable Philadelphia architect Samuel Sloan, Longwood, near Natchez, was only half completed when the Civil War broke out. More than a hundred thousand dollars had already been spent on it by Dr. Haller Nutt. He had planned this Moorish extravaganza as the great house of his plantation, which was supported by eight hundred slaves. "Nutt's Folly" marks the close of the most opulent era in Southern architecture.

A "Cracker Cabin"

Photograph by Brown Brothers

Stadium of the Rice Institute, Houston, Texas

THIS magnificent example of modern architecture at its best was designed by Milton McGinty, Hermon Lloyd, and William B. Morgan. All Texans, they received their architectural training at the Rice Institute.

companiment of tom-toms, for Voodoo ritual and ceremony. Here such of Africa as remained passed into Negro Creole life in America. Here were uttered the strange chants, the curious sounds, the ancient cries of the tribes, transformed, subtly but unmistakably, by French and Spanish culture: "*Pov piti Lolotte à mouin*"—softly, not clearly; "*Pov piti Lolotte à mouin*"—more firmly now, and clearer to the ear, repeated like the first line of the blues; then, twice, "*Li gagnin bobo, bobo,*" the second time with a variation, "*Li gagnin doulè*"; then, again, the first line, sung twice; and finally, "*Li gagnin bobo, Li gagnin doulè.*" The hypnotic effect must have been irresistible. The affinity with the remaining traces of Voodoo in Haiti, and in the rites of the Candomblé in Brazil is unmistakable—music, incantatory words, and dancing. The dancing, before the half-holiday celebrations ceased during the Civil War, attracted its share of tourists to sway and be moved in spite of themselves by the hypnotic beat.

The bamboulas, huge tom-toms made of cowhide and casks, were the bass drums, pummeled with long beefbones. Bamboo tubes produced a skeletal melody. Staccato accents were made by the snapping together of bones—the castanets. An ass's jawbone was rattled; the instrument is still used in Latin-American music and is known as the *guajira*, a word that means "rude" or "boorish," "rustic" or "rural" in present-day Cuban Spanish. Many Negro instruments, rhythms, and dances came to be used in Central and South America, leading eventually to the rhumba and the conga, the samba and the mambo, in Cuba, Argentina, and Brazil, where, as in New Orleans, music developed in numbers of Congo Squares, half-holiday games and chants and dances. The effect of Congo Square was twice felt in jazz; once directly, as it filtered through the tonks and the barrelhouses, the Storyville parlors and ballrooms; again indirectly, when bebop musicians went to Cuba to reclaim their earlier heritage.

By the end of the 1880s New Orleans Negro musicians were no longer playing jawbones, hide-covered casks, or bamboo tubes. As they grew more interested in the meaning and mechanics of music, they became more interested in the white man's instruments, which offered broader, fuller expression. These men, like many members of the American Federation of Musicians today, were part-time instrumentalists, who by day cut hair or served food or lifted bales or ran errands, but by night or on Saturdays or Sundays, for special or ordinary celebrations, played the instruments of the white man. The instrumentation of jazz at the end of the nineteenth century was in a sense conventional, although it was not the dance-music instrumentation familiar to most Orleanians. For the string trio (heard even in brothels) and the larger polite organization of bows and gut, Negro musicians substituted brass-band horns, cornet and clarinet and trombone, with an occasional

615

roughening contributed by a tuba. Rhythm came, naturally enough, from drums and the string bass (more often than the tuba), and sometimes from the piano. These were the logical instruments, for the first large contribution to the new music was made by marching bands.

They marched (without the bass and piano) to wakes and from them in Negro New Orleans. They marched for weddings and for political rallies, when they were summoned away from their ghetto precincts. They marched again and again, just to march, for the pleasure of the members of the fraternal organizations and the secret orders with which their culture abounded. There were always plenty of other parades too—for the Fourth of July and Labor Day and Jackson Day and Carnival, for funerals and during election campaigns. And when the bands got going and the beat became irresistible, the followers, chiefly youngsters, fell in, dancing behind the musicians and keeping up the friendly, informal infernality. The bands played all the standard hymns, such as "Rock of Ages" and "Nearer, My God, to Thee" and "Onward, Christian Soldiers," and they made of some of them immortal jazz compositions, lifted forever from the parade or the funeral to the night club and the recording studio and the concert hall. And such a transfiguration as they turned out of "When the Saints Go Marching In" deserved the larger audience it finally found for its humors, at once delicate and assaulting, satirical and deeply religious. There were the "Saints" and the "Rock" and the "Soldiers" to move the deceased nearer to his God as he was brought to his resting place in the special section of the cemetery reserved for Negroes. Once he was interred, the music changed. "Didn't He Ramble?" the bandsmen asked rhetorically and followed the tale of a rambling townsman with their freely improvised, booming, blasting choruses, one after another, leading from the "Ramble" to Alphonse Picou's polka-like "High Society" and Jelly Roll Morton's tribute to a fellow Mississippian pianist, King Porter, after whom "King Porter Stomp" was named. Maybe they'd finish off with a rag, Scott Joplin's "Maple Leaf" perhaps, or the most famous of all, "Tiger Rag," fashioned from an old French quadrille. Whatever they played, the bands blew a mighty sound along the streets and through the alleys and into the squares of New Orleans. And when they were finished with parades they played for dances, little and big, and they brought with them into the makeshift and the more solidly constructed ballrooms and into the parks all the atmosphere of the marching band. Their dances looked and sounded almost like the big ballroom blowouts of the twenties and thirties in Harlem at the Savoy or the Renaissance, or in Chicago or St. Louis or any other town where Negroes gathered to listen and to dance to their music.

Jazz was absorbed into Negro New Orleans and passed on to interested whites. It was taken up with that mixture of casual acceptance

616

and rabid enthusiasm that is always found when an art form becomes an integrated part of a culture. Whole bands were hired to advertise excursions on the river, picnics by the lake, prize fights, and dances; whole bands were lifted onto furniture wagons, bass, guitar, cornet, clarinet, and drums, with the trombonist's slide hanging behind as he sat on the back edge, feet hanging down, slide hanging down, forming the "tailgate" of the wagon. Music was everywhere in the last years of Storyville and the first years of jazz.

4. SONG AND STORY

Folk Songs

One of the richest cultural possessions of America is its vast treasure of folk songs. The conditions of life in this country were ideally suited for the transmission and origination of thousands of ballads (narrative songs), revival hymns, "shouts," jail-house songs, work songs, and blues, a treasure to which white Americans and Negroes alike have contributed. The immigrant hordes, from the Continent as well as England and Scotland, brought their songs with them and carried them to their place of settlement. Their sons and daughters, even when they moved on, continued to sing the old songs, and thus it is that a ballad which a collector discovers in the Cumberland Mountains and thinks is indigenous to that region may turn up later a thousand miles away. Meanwhile it will have been supplied with a new cast of characters and new place names. And as the folk have passed down their songs to sons and grandsons, they have modified tunes as well as texts.

In the remote region of the South collectors, equipped nowadays with sensitive recording devices, can still find singers who know dozens of the old songs and will sing them freely and unaffectedly for strangers. Inevitably the influence of the hillbilly radio music has begun to destroy this tradition, but generations of devoted if not always well-trained collectors have gathered in much of the rich harvest. Fortunately, the great Archive of American Folk Song, a collection of thousands of master records maintained by the Library of Congress, was built up while there was still an abundance of singers who had never been near a loud-speaker. Of late, too, folk-music festivals have been held in various places in the South at which native singers, fiddlers, and performers on the "dulcimoor" are made to feel that they can be proud of the ballads and tunes they know.

It is wrong, of course, to separate folk songs from their tunes, as has been done here. The tune, which often uses a "gapped" scale (five or six notes instead of the now usual seven), sounds delightfully strange to modern ears. And the experienced singer will introduce changes of his own by varying the underlying rhythm or dwelling arbitrarily on certain notes in the melody. Cecil Sharp, the English collector who recorded folk songs in the Southern Appalachians in 1917, remarked of the singers he heard there: "The wonderful charm, fascinating and well-nigh magical, which the folk-singer produces upon those who are fortunate enough to hear him is to be attributed very largely to his method of singing, and this, it should be understood, is quite as traditional as the song itself. The genuine folk-singer is never conscious of his audience—indeed, as often as not, he has none—and he never, therefore, strives for effect, nor endeavors in this or in any other way to attract the attention, much less the admiration of his hearers."

Barbey Ellen

For more than two hundred years the pathetic ballad of Barbara Allan, who refused comfort to her lover (identified in America as Sweet William or Young Johnny or Willie or Sweet Jimmy or Young Jamie Grove) has delighted both Englishmen and Americans. Pepys noted in his diary, in January 1666: "In perfect pleasure I was to hear her [Mrs. Knipp, the actress] sing, and especially her little Scotch song of Barbary Allan." A century later Goldsmith asserted that "the music of the finest singer is dissonance to what I felt when our old dairy-maid sung me into tears with . . . 'The Cruelty of Barbara Allen.'" Of all the ballads that the Scotch and English brought to America, this story of "Barbey" and her woeful lover (known to professional folklorists as "Child, No. 84") leads in number of versions and tunes. This version was recorded in Cade's Cove, Blount County, Tennessee, in 1928. It is reprinted from Mellinger Edward Henry's Folk Songs from the Southern Highlands *(1938) with the kind permission of the publisher, J. J. Augustin.*

Barbey Ellen

WAY down South where I came from
Is where I got my learning.
I fell in love with a pretty little girl,
And her name is Barbey Ellen.

I courted her for seven years,
And I asked her if she would marry.
With a bowed down head and a sweet little smile,
She never made no answer.

Early along in the spring,
When the red roses were blooming,
A young man on his death bed lay
For the love of Barbey Ellen.

He sent his servant down to town
To a place where she was dwelling:
"My master is love-sick and sent for you,
If your name is Barbey Ellen."

She slightly talked and slowly walked
And slowly went unto him.
"Young man, young man, I heard you were sick,
For the love of me, your darling."

"Yes, I am sick, and very sick
And with me death is dwelling
And none the better will I be,
Till I get Barbey Ellen."

"Yes, you are sick, and very sick,
And with you death is dwelling,
But none the better will you be
While my name is Barbey Ellen.

"Don't you remember the other day
When we were all a-drinking,
You passed the glass to the ladies all around,
But you slighted me, your darling?"

"Yes, I remember the other day,
When we were all a-drinking:
I passed the glass to the ladies all around,
But all for you, my darling."

He turned his pale face to the wall,
His back he turned towards them:
"Adieu, adieu, to all this world,
But be kind to Barbey Ellen."

She had not rode five miles from town,
Till she heard the death bells ringing,
And every lick, it seemed to strike:
"Hard hearted Barbey Ellen."

She looked east, she looked west,
Till she saw the pale corpse coming:
"Lay him down, lay him down,
And let me look upon him."

The more she looked, the worse she got
Till she bursted out in crying:
"Young man, young man, you died for me.
I will die for you tomorrow."

They buried Sweet Willie in one church yard,
And Barbey in the other,
And out of Barbey's breast sprang a red, red rose,
And out of his a brier.

They grew and grew to such a length of height,
Till they could not grow no higher;
And there they tied in a true-lover's knot
And the rose run around the brier.

Old Smoky

*Most of the versions of this ballad have turned up, naturally enough,
in the North Carolina Smokies, but it has also been found in Georgia.
This version was obtained in Avery County, North Carolina, in 1929
and was first printed in Mellinger Edward Henry's* Folk Songs from
the Southern Highlands *(1938). It is reprinted here with the kind permission of the publisher, J. J. Augustin.*

Old Smoky

On top of Old Smoky, all covered with snow
I lost my true lover by courting too slow.

While courting is pleasure and parting is grief,
A false hearted lover is worse than a thief.

A thief they will rob you and take what you have,
But a false hearted lover will take you to the grave.

The grave will decay you, will turn you to dust,
Only one boy out of a hundred a poor girl can trust.

They'll tell you they love you to give your heart ease;
As soon as your back's turned, they'll court who they please.

'Tis raining, 'tis hailing, this dark stormy night;
Your horses can't travel for the moon gives no light.

Go, put up your horses and give them some hay;
Come, sit down beside me as long as you can stay.

My horses aren't hungry; they won't eat your hay;
My wagon is loaded; I'll feed on my way.

As sure as the dewdrops fall on the green corn,
Last night he was with me; tonight he is gone.

I'll go back to Old Smoky, to the mountain so high,
Where the wild birds and turtle doves can hear my sad cry.

Way down on Old Smoky all covered in snow,
I lost my blue eyed boy by courting too slow.

I wrote him a letter of roses and lines;
He sent it back to me all twisted in twine.

He says, "You keep your love letters, and I'll keep mine;
You write to your true love and I'll write to mine.

"I'll go to old Georgia; I'll write you my mind;
My mind is to marry you and leave you behind."

The Hunters of Kentucky [1]

A contemporary of the age of Jackson remembered that in 1828 "the land rang with 'The Hunters of Kentucky.'" The land rang because Old Hickory had taken over for campaign purposes the ballad that celebrated his famous victory at New Orleans in 1815.

The lyrics to "The Hunters of Kentucky" were written by Samuel Woodworth (1785–1824), better remembered as the author of "The Old Oaken Bucket." The tune was taken from the song "Miss Bailey," from a comic opera, Love Laughs at Locksmiths. *Who set the words to the tune is not known for sure. Noah Ludlow (1795–1886), who was prominent in the beginnings of the theater in the old West, claims to have done so at New Orleans in the spring of 1822. Whoever was responsible for joining the words and the tune, "The Hunters of Kentucky" was widely known and sung by 1824.*

The song celebrates the exploits of the Kentucky militia in its astounding victory over the regular troops of Britain and sings the superiority of the strength of the American frontier to the martial pomp of Europe. It thus confirmed the national pride of the American people. The version given here is taken from the Amateur's Song Book *(Boston, 1843).*

1. YE gentlemen and ladies fair who grace this famous city,
   Just listen if you've time to spare, while I rehearse a ditty;
   And for an opportunity, conceive yourselves quite lucky,
   For 'tis not often here you see a hunter from Kentucky,
   O Kentucky, the hunters of Kentucky.
   O Kentucky, the hunters of Kentucky.

2. We are a hardy freeborn race, each man to fear a stranger,
   Whate'er the game, we join in chase, despising toil and danger,
   And if a daring foe annoys, whate'er his strength and forces,
   We'll show him that Kentucky boys are "alligator horses."
                              O Kentucky, &c.

---

[1] This note was contributed by Professor John W. Ward of Princeton University, an authority on the Jackson legend.

622

3. I s'pose you've read it in the prints how Packenham attempted
   To make old hickory Jackson wince, but soon his schemes repented;
   For we with rifles ready cock'd, thought such occasion lucky,
   And soon around the hero flock'd the hunters of Kentucky.
   O Kentucky, &c.

4. You've heard I s'pose how New Orleans is fam'd for wealth and
     beauty,
   There's girls of ev'ry hue it seems, from snowy white to sooty,
   So Packenham he made his brags, if he in fight was lucky,
   He'd have their girls and cotton bags, in spite of old Kentucky.
   O Kentucky, &c.

5. But Jackson he was wide awake, and wasn't scar'd at trifles,
   For well he knew what aim we take with our Kentucky rifles;
   So he led us down to Cypress swamp, the ground was low and
     mucky,
   There stood John Bull in martial pomp, and here was old Kentucky.
   O Kentucky, &c.

6. A bank was rais'd to hide our breast not that we thought of dying,
   But that we always like to rest, unless the game is flying:
   Behind it stood our little force—none wish'd it to be greater,
   For ev'ry man was half a horse, and half an alligator.
   O Kentucky, &c.

7. They did not let our patience tire, before they show'd their faces—
   We did not choose to waste our fire, so snugly kept our places:
   And when so near to see them wink, we thought it time to stop 'em;
   And 'twould have done you good I think, to see Kentuckians drop
     'em.
   O Kentucky, &c.

8. They found at last 'twas vain to fight, where lead was all their
     booty;
   And so they wisely took a flight, and left us all our beauty,
   And now if danger e'er annoys, remember what our trade is;
   Just send for us Kentucky boys, and we'll protect you, ladies.
   O Kentucky, &c.

Turnip Greens

The text for this version of "Turnip Greens" was gathered by Professor A. P. Hudson and published in his Folk Songs of Mississippi and Their Background (*Chapel Hill: University of North Carolina Press; 1936*). *It is printed here with the permission of the publishers. The text of the ballad was furnished by Miss Lois Womble of Water Valley, Mississippi. It appears to be indigenous to that state. As Professor Hudson says: "It is a heavenly-vision poem satirizing Mississippians who live above their means, and singing the praises of turnip greens."*

HAD a dream the other night—
    Dreamed that I could fly,
Flapped my wings like a buzzard
    And flew up to the sky.

St. Peter stood at the Golden Gate.
    "From what place did you fly?"
I told him from Mississippi
    I flew up to the sky.

He showed me through a telescope—
    I don't know what that means—
I saw ten thousand people
    Living on turnip greens.

They all looked so sassy,
    Been living above their means,
And he kicked them down to the hot place
    For stealing turnip greens.

Turnip greens, turnip greens,
    Good old turnip greens,
Cornbread and buttermilk,
    And good old turnip greens.

Confederate Songs

The Civil War was a singing war. Soldiers in the field and their kin back home shared the sentiment of "Lorena" and the patriotic fervor of "Strike for the South." But the troops on both sides shared each other's songs as well—"Just before the Battle, Mother," "All Quiet along the Potomac," "When This Civil War Is Over," "Home, Sweet Home," and especially the ballads of Stephen Foster. In his Songs of the Confederacy *(1951) Dr. Richard Harwell quotes a Confederate who wrote of the music that drifted across from the Federal lines during Sherman's campaign: "Softly and sweetly the music from their bands as they played the national airs [was] wafted up and over the summit of the mountains. Somehow, some way, in some inexplicable and unseen manner 'Hail Columbia,' 'America' and 'The Star Spangled Banner' sounded sweeter than I had ever before heard them, and filled my soul with feelings I could not describe or forget."*

Regimental bands were maintained to play marches, for reviews and parades, and gayer pieces during times when the business of war was relaxed. Men sang as they marched, harmonized around the campfire, and occasionally put on "jubilees," which were alcoholic as well as musical.

The two Confederate songs that follow represent a large number which were popular. "Dixie" should be here, though it was written in 1859 by Daniel Decatur Emmett, a Northerner, for Bryant's Minstrels. So should "Maryland, My Maryland," "The Yellow Rose of Texas," and "The Volunteer."

According to Dr. Harwell (see above), "The Bonnie Blue Flag" was introduced into the program of Harry Macarthy's "Personation Concerts" in 1861. It is said that General Ben F. ("Beast") Butler confiscated the plates for "The Bonnie Blue Flag" and threatened to punish anyone caught even whistling it. The song was inspired by the Confederacy's single-starred first flag.

When "Goober Peas" was published in 1866, the words were credited to "A. Pindar" and the music to "P. Nutt," obviously pseudonyms. ("Pinda" is a Gullah Negro word for the goober or peanut.) Harwell suggests that the song was of spontaneous origin, finally put on paper by Blackmar, the New Orleans music-publisher.

THE BONNIE BLUE FLAG

WE are a band of brothers, and native to the soil,
Fighting for our liberty, with treasure, blood and toil;
  And when our rights were threatened, the cry rose near and far:
  Hurrah for the Bonnie Blue Flag that bears a Single Star!

Chorus
    Hurrah! Hurrah! for Southern rights, Hurrah!
    Hurrah for the Bonnie Blue Flag that bears a Single Star!

As long as the Union was faithful to her trust,
Like friends and like brethren kind were we and just;
  But now when Northern treachery attempts our rights to mar,
  We hoist on high the Bonnie Blue Flag that bears a Single Star.

First gallant South Carolina nobly made the stand;
Then came Alabama, who took her by the hand;
  Next, quickly Mississippi, Georgia, and Florida,
  All raised on high the Bonnie Blue Flag that bears a Single Star.

Ye men of valor, gather round the banner of the right,
Texas and fair Louisiana, join us in the fight:
  Davis, our loved President, and Stephens, statesman rare,
  Now rally round the Bonnie Blue Flag that bears a Single Star.

And here's to brave Virginia! The Old Dominion State
With the young Confederacy at length has linked her fate;
  Impelled by her example, now other States prepare
  To hoist on high the Bonnie Blue Flag that bears a Single Star.

Then cheer, boys, cheer, raise the joyous shout,
For Arkansas and North Carolina now have both gone out;
  And let another rousing cheer for Tennessee be given—
  The Single Star of the Bonnie Blue Flag has grown to be eleven.

Then, here's to our Confederacy; strong we are and brave,
Like patriots of old, we'll fight our heritage to save;
  And rather than submit to shame, to die we would prefer—
  So cheer again for the Bonnie Blue Flag that bears a Single Star!

Chorus
    Hurrah! Hurrah! for Southern rights, Hurrah!
    Hurrah! for the Bonnie Blue Flag has gained the Eleventh Star.

626

GOOBER PEAS

Sitting by the roadside on a summer day,
Chatting with my messmates, passing time away,
Lying in the shadow underneath the trees,
Goodness, how delicious, eating goober peas!

Chorus
    Peas! Peas! Peas! Peas! eating goober peas!
    Goodness, how delicious, eating goober peas!

When a horseman passes, the soldiers have a rule,
To cry out at their loudest, "Mister, here's your mule,"
But another pleasure enchantinger than these,
Is wearing out your grinders, eating goober peas!

Just before the battle the General hears a row,
He says, "The Yanks are coming, I hear their rifles now,"
He turns around in wonder, and what do you think he sees?
The Georgia militia eating goober peas!

I think my song has lasted almost long enough,
The subject's interesting, but the rhymes are mighty rough,
I wish this war was over, when free from rags and fleas,
We'd kiss our wives and sweethearts and gobble goober peas!

Negro Spirituals and Songs

Negro slaves carved out the plantations and tilled the fields of the
Old South. Slave artisans, skilled as carpenters and bricklayers, did
much of the work in building the mansion on the hill. The house slaves
made possible the hospitality for which the region was famous. To
lighten their tasks and to comfort themselves under the humiliation of
slavery, the Negroes sang while working in the fields, at camp meetings, wherever they gathered and were permitted the solace of song.
    Sometimes their masters encouraged them to sing, knowing that the
slaves turned out more work when they worked together rhythmically,
and believing that the consolations of religious expression were harmless enough. In the days of slavery visitors from abroad and from the
North were sometimes invited to hear the Negroes sing or heard them

by chance in the fields and around the cabins. A few slave songs, most of them spirituals, were written down before the Civil War, but only after slavery was abolished did it become evident that the songs of the Negro, sacred and secular, constituted one of the richest folk treasures a people ever possessed. Even now we do not know just how rich that treasure is.

First to be discovered were the spirituals. Colonel Thomas Wentworth Higginson, who led a regiment of freed slaves in the Federal Army, remembering how his soldiers sang round their campfires, included a chapter on the spirituals in his *Army Life in a Black Regiment* (1870). When Fisk University, the Negro college in Nashville, was struggling into existence, the Fisk Jubilee Singers undertook to raise money for their institution by concert tours in the North and abroad. After the initial astonishment at their programs died away—many attended thinking they were going to see a minstrel show—the Jubilee Singers delighted and moved their audiences. The Reverend Theodore Cuyler wrote to the *New York Tribune*, after hearing them in 1872:

> Allow me to bespeak, through your journal . . . a universal welcome through the North for these living representatives of the only true, native school of American music. We have long enough had its coarse caricature in corked faces: our people can now listen to the genuine soul music of the slave cabins, before the Lord led his "children out of the land of Egypt, out of the house of bondage."

As the spirituals grew in favor, scholars began to argue about their origins. Some found them to be the pure and spontaneous expression of a race in bondage. Others thought they could detect definite memories of Africa in them, particularly in the melodies. Finally, in 1934, Professor George Pullen Jackson in *White Spirituals of the Southern Uplands* pointed out many similarities in melody and text between the white and Negro spirituals. When the slaves adopted the religion of the white man, it was only natural that they should also appropriate for their own uses his hymns and spiritual songs. What the Negro did with these songs is another matter, as a single example should prove. These lines from a Negro spiritual:

> Went down to the rocks to hide my face,
> The rocks cried out no hiding place,

are much more vigorous and imaginative than the lines in the white spiritual from which they were derived:

> To hide yourself in the mountain top
> To hide yourself from God.

One of the spirituals quoted in Colonel Higginson's book demonstrates to what a high poetical level their authors could rise:

> I know moon-rise, I know star-rise,
> I lay dis body down.
> I walk in de moonlight, I walk in de starlight,
> To lay dis body down.
> I walk in de graveyard, I walk throo de graveyard,
> To lay dis body down.
> I lie in de grave an' stretch out my arms,
> I lay dis body down.
> I go to de jedgment in de evenin' of de day
> When I lay dis body down,
> An' my soul an' your soul will meet in de day
> When I lay dis body down.

There are several reasons why the secular folk-songs of the Negroes have only recently been brought to light. In the first place, the spirituals obscured them. Northern audiences were much taken with the spirituals because their deep-felt piety proved that the Negro religion had inspired a great number of superb sacred songs. In the spirituals, too, one could find both the Negro's longing for the promised land of freedom and his Christian patience under the burden placed upon him.

As for the secular songs themselves, Negroes were often reluctant to sing them before white men; consequently it was necessary for skilled and determined collectors like Newman I. White and Alan Lomax to go after them. Most of the rowing songs and other work songs of slavery days survive only in remnants, so that not much is known about their contents; but the work songs of the gang laborers since freedom are full of taunting though covert references to the boss and the gang leader. The jail songs are openly rebellious. A further reason why the collecting of the secular songs came late is that many of them are obscene or would once have been thought so. Others, belonging to a class White called "upstart crows," make fun of religion in the fashion of this example, reported from Alabama:

> Jesus, lover of my soul,
> How many chickens have I stole?
> One last night, two night before,
> Going back to-night to get two more.

Most popular with the white public, both in this country and abroad, have been the blues. A blues song is the expression of a single individual, telling of his unhappiness in love or reporting some calamity or tragedy in his home or community. The form of the blues song is simple. It begins with one line sung three times or a line sung twice, either with or without a modification the second time. (In this line the singer states the cause of his troubles.) Then follows the final line, which gives the situation a cynical or sardonic turn. Thus in the famous "Memphis Blues" the lead line states:

> Some folks say Memphis Blues ain't bad.

The "punch line" concludes:

> It must not a been the Memphis Blues I had.

The blues originated in the Negro underworld and the first singers were usually men. Because the imitation blues songs have been for the most part about misfortunate love and have been sung by women, many white Americans associate the blues with Negro women and their unhappy love-affairs. But as the editors of the *Negro Caravan* state, such male blues singers as Jim Jackson, Lonnie Johnson, and Huddie Ledbetter (Leadbelly), whose songs are not exclusively about love, have been "enthusiastically received by the Negro masses."

Steal Away to Jesus

The versions of "Steal Away to Jesus," "Go Down, Moses," and "Joshua Fit de Battle ob Jerico" which are given here are those which James Weldon Johnson used in The Book of American Negro Spirituals *(1923). They are reprinted with the kind permission of the publishers, The Viking Press.*

> STEAL away, steal away, steal away to Jesus!
> Steal away, steal away home,
> I ain't got long to stay here.
> Steal away, steal away, steal away to Jesus!
> Steal away, steal away home,
> I ain't got long to stay here.
>
> My Lord, He calls me,
> He calls me by the thunder,

The trumpet sounds within-a my soul,
I ain't got long to stay here.

Steal away, steal away, steal away to Jesus!
Steal away, steal away home,
I ain't got long to stay here.
Steal away, steal away, steal away to Jesus!
Steal away, steal away home,
I ain't got long to stay here.

Green trees a-bending, po' sinner stand a-trembling,
The trumpet sounds within-a my soul,
I ain't got long to stay here,
Oh, Lord I ain't got long to stay here.

GO DOWN, MOSES

Go down, Moses,
  'Way down in Egypt land,
Tell ole Pharaoh,
  To let my people go.
Go down, Moses,
  'Way down in Egypt land,
Tell ole Pharaoh,
  To let my people go.

    When Israel was in Egypts land:
      Let my people go,
    Oppressed so hard they could not stand,
      Let my people go.

  "Thus spoke the Lord," bold Moses said;
      Let my people go,
    If not I'll smite your first born dead,
      Let my people go.

Go down, Moses,
  'Way down in Egypt land,
Tell ole Pharaoh,
  To let my people go.
O let my people go.

JOSHUA FIT DE BATTLE OB JERICO

Joshua fit de battle ob Jerico, Jerico, Jerico,
Joshua fit de battle ob Jerico,
An' de walls come tumblin' down.

You may talk about yo' king ob Gideon,
You may talk about yo' man ob Saul,
Dere's none like good ole Joshua
At de battle ob Jerico.

Up to de walls ob Jerico,
He marched with spear in han'
"Go blow dem ram horns" Joshua cried,
"Kase de battle am in my han'."

Den de lam' ram sheep horns begin to blow,
Trumpets begin to soun',
Joshua commanded de chillen to shout,
An' de walls come tumblin' down.

Dat mornin'
Joshua fit de battle ob Jerico, Jerico, Jerico,
Joshua fit de battle ob Jerico,
An' de walls come tumblin' down.

John Henry

The researches of Professor L. W. Chappell indicate that this famous ballad originated as a work song at the time of a spectacular contest between the then new steel-drill and a Negro steel-driver during the building of the Big Bend Tunnel on the Chesapeake & Ohio railroad (1870–3). Apparently the ballad elements were added later. Though John Henry is a Negro folk-hero, the song about his great exploit is current among whites as well as Negroes. This particular version is the second in a group of thirty printed in Louis W. Chappell's John Henry,

John Henry

a Folk-lore Study (*Jena, 1933*), *pp. 104–5. Permission to reprint it here was graciously given by Professor Chappell.*

JOHN HENRY was a very small boy,
He sat on his daddy's knee;
He picked up a hammer, a little piece of steel,
Says, "This hammer'll be the death of me."

Captain told John Henry,
Says, "A man ain't nothin' but a man;
If you beat that steam drill down,
I'll lay a hundred dollars in your hand."

John Henry told the captain,
Says, "When you go to town
Bring John back a twelve-pound hammer,
And he'll sure whip your steam drill down."

John Henry told the captain,
"A man ain't nothin' but a man,
And if I don't beat your steam drill down
I'll die with a hammer in my hand, Lawd, Lawd."

John Henry went up on the mountain,
He came down on the side;
The rock was so tall, John Henry was so small,
That he laid down his hammer and he cried, "Lawd, Lawd."

Put John Henry on the right hand side,
That old steam drill on the left;
"Before I'll let that steam drill beat me down
I'll hammer my fool self to death."

John Henry said to his shaker boy,
Says, "Boy, you'd better pray,
For if I miss this six-foot steel
Tomorrow'll be your burying day."

The man that owned that old steam drill
Thought it was mighty fine,

But John Henry drove fourteen long feet
While the steam drill only made nine.

John Henry said to his loving little woman,
Says, "I'm sick and I want to go to bed;
Fix me a place to lay down, chile,
I got a rolling in my head."

John Henry had a pretty little woman,
The dress she wore was red;
She went down the track and she looked back,
Says, "I'm going where John Henry fell dead."

John Henry had a loving little woman,
The dress she wore was blue;
She went down the track, she never looked back,
Says, "John Henry, I've been true to you."

John Henry had a loving little woman,
The dress she wore was blue;
She went down the track, she never looked back,
Says, "John Henry, I'm leaving you."

John Henry had a loving little woman,
Her name was Polly Ann;
John Henry got sick and had to go to bed,
Polly bucked steel like a man.

"I had a good woman"

*This famous blues song, of which there are many variants, is reprinted
by permission of the publishers from Newman I. White:* American Negro Folk-Songs *(Cambridge, Mass.: Harvard University Press; 1928).
This version was reported from Auburn, Alabama, in 1915–16.*

I HAD a good woman, I had a good woman,
But the fool laid down and died;
I had a good woman, but the fool laid down and died.
If you got a good woman, you better pin her to your side.

When a man gets the blues, when a man gets the blues,
He jes' catches a train and rides;
When a man gets the blues, he catches a train and rides.
But when a woman gets the blues, she lays her little head and cries.

A blond woman, a blond woman,
Make a tadpole hug a whale,
A blond woman make a tadpole hug a whale;
But a dark-haired woman make you go right straight to jail.

Some folks say, oh, some folks say
That the nigger blues ain't bad.
Oh, some folks say that the nigger blues ain't bad.
Well, it must not have been the nigger blues I had.

Oh, some niggers like, oh, some niggers like
A yaller or a brown.
Oh, some niggers like a yaller or brown.
But for my choice, I'll take the blackest woman in town.

Tall Tales and Short

In any gathering of Southerners someone, sooner or later, tells a story and the competition begins. The stories flow on and on, for the rest of the evening—stories about a gambling great-grandfather who diced away three plantations, about an old colored woman who ruled the lives of her white folks, about famous hunts and hounds and horses, about Old Man So-and-So and his five wives, about battles, murders, floods, and wrecks, about Jean Lafitte and Mike Fink, Stonewall Jackson and Jeb Stuart and "Old Hickory" and the "Swamp Fox," Bilbo and Blease and Huey Long. Any Yankee who has been lucky enough to be present when Paul Green or A. P. Hudson or Archibald Henderson or Robert Penn Warren or Roy P. Basler or Sterling Brown begins a story understands why the tall tales invented by A. B. Longstreet and G. W. Harris and J. J. Hooper and J. G. Baldwin delighted the whole nation in the 1850's and why the modern Southern novel is so rich in character and incident and the lore and humor of the folk.

Why are Southerners the best tellers of stories in the country? For one thing, boys are bred to it, just as they learn to hunt and shoot and ride. There seem to be more convenient places for story-telling in the South—the kitchen, the parlor, the gallery, the shady porch of the store, the curb in front of the bank, the steps of the courthouse. And there has always been more leisure. A Vermonter would be wasting time, his own and his neighbor's, if he stopped for more than one story while they are "mending wall" together. In Evergreen, Alabama, it would be impolite to withdraw from a story-telling session until everyone has had a chance at capping the story just told—several times around. And, as B. A. Botkin says in his *Treasury of Southern Folklore,* in no other region are "land and lore more perfectly suited and wedded to each other. The rural South is a land of the out-of-doors come up to the door and even indoors . . . where the climate and the open sky make a man expansive and enduring of lung and tongue when it is his 'night to howl' or when he is haranguing his 'friends and feller-citizens' or 'sistern and brethren.' "

Of the thousands of Southern tall tales and short which have found their way into print, the smallest representation by class is from the Negroes. Yet the Southern Negro has a rich folk-literature. There are two reasons why not much of it has been printed. Few Negro writers have made use of it.[1] (James Weldon Johnson, Zora Neale Hurston, and Sterling Brown are notable exceptions.) The other reason is that many stories which Negroes tell one another disclose "the sharpened sense of struggle and protest inherent in [their] anomalous position as the least alien yet the most separate of American minorities." Negroes do not care to tell these stories to white men.

Yet there is one variation among the stories of this kind over which both whites and Negroes can laugh together—the retort of the not-so-dumb old Negro which excuses him from the white man's wrath. Mr. Botkin reports a good example from South Carolina.

An old Negro man kept driving his model-T Ford through red lights, while stopping every time at a green light. A motorcycle cop stopped him to find out why.

"Lord, white folks," he said. "I ain't mean to do no harm. When that there light come on, I seed all the white folks goin', so I just naturally thought that that red light was for us colored folks to go on."

[1] One of the best collections of Negro anecdote and folk-say is E. C. L. Adams's *Nigger to Nigger* (1928). Though the book was compiled by a white man, Negroes agree that the tone of these stories is authentic.

The Bell "Witch"

Professor A. P. Hudson of the University of North Carolina has followed the ghostly track of the Bell "Witch" of Tennessee and Mississippi for years. He first learned about the "Witch" from Miss Lois Womble of Water Valley, Mississippi. Later he garnered many details of the legend from Miss Ethel Lewellen and Mr. Fonnie Black Ladd. From the stories as told by Miss Lewellen and Mr. Ladd, Professor Hudson put together the account printed here. It was first published in his Specimens of Mississippi Folk-Lore *(Ann Arbor: Edwards Brothers; 1928), pp. 158–60. In 1934 Professor Hudson and Mr. Pete Kyle McCarter published in the* Journal of American Folk-Lore *(January-March, pp. 45–63) an expanded version of the legend, recovered from oral tradition in Mississippi and based on variants and fragments as told by many people who remembered the story. This version may also be found in Professor Hudson's* Humor of the Old Deep South *(New York: Macmillan Company; 1936), pp. 433–46. Professor Hudson has graciously given permission for the reprinting of his 1928 version here.*

"To Panola County, about a half century ago," Miss Lewellen begins, "there moved with the Bell family a 'witch' that tormented one of the Bell girls and caused a great deal of suspicion to arise among the other members of the family and the community."

Mr. Fonnie Black Ladd, from recollections of the story as he heard it in his childhood at Oakland, adds some details about the circumstances in which the family moved to Mississippi. The Bells were living at Bell, Tennessee. Becoming dissatisfied, the father of the family expressed his desire to sell his farm and go somewhere else. The mother was opposed to going. One of the daughters agreed with her father and argued in favor of going to Mississippi. One night the *lar familiaris* of the family spoke to her and warned her against going. The daughter nevertheless persisted in her arguments and finally persuaded her father to sell out and move to Mississippi. Before the family left, the *lar* addressed her again and threatened to pursue her with its vengeance.

When they got to Mississippi, Miss Lewellen's account proceeds, "the members of the family talked of sending this girl away so that they might be free from the 'Witch's' awful presence. They also hoped that the girl might rid herself of the unspeakable torture which the 'Witch' visited upon her. 'There's no use for you to do this,' said a Voice, 'for no matter where she goes I will follow.'

"No one was ever able to see the 'Witch'; but often some member of the family would see food disappear as the 'Witch' carried it from the cupboard to 'his' mouth. 'His' favorite food was cream, and 'he' took it from every jar of milk. The Bells were never able to get any butter from the milk they churned.

"An old negro woman once hid under a bed and tried to see the 'Witch.' But ere she had long been there, something began to bite, scratch, and pinch her; and she was almost killed before she could get out.

"Although the 'Witch' treated the girl very cruelly, 'he' was not entirely inimical to other members of the family; on the contrary, 'he' proved very helpful on several occasions.

"One day Mr. Bell was talking of visiting a family in which every one was ill. 'I have just come from there,' said a Voice from nowhere, and proceeded to describe the physical condition of every member of the family, and also to tell what every member of the family was doing on that particular day. Investigation showed that the report of illness was false and proved the accuracy of every detail of the Voice's account of the state and activities of the family.

"On another occasion Mr. Bell was preparing to go for a doctor to attend one of his sick children. The Voice said, 'There's no need for you to go; I can get the doctor.' No one else went, but in due time the doctor came.

"One day the 'Witch' caused the wagon in which the Bells were going to church to stop on level ground. After vain efforts to get their horses to start the wagon again, the unseen hand of the 'Witch' lifted the wagon and horses off the road, transported it through the air a short distance, and set it down again without harming any one."

Mr. Ladd tells another story of the wagon which may be merely a variant of the foregoing, but which has some circumstances indicating that it is independent. To understand its proper connection beyond Miss Lewellen's remark that the "Witch's" attentions to other members of the family were not always malignant but were sometimes benevolent, the reader will remember that Mrs. Bell, according to Mr. Ladd's account of the circumstances attending the removal of the family to Mississippi, opposed leaving the Tennessee home. Thus, according to Mr. Ladd, the "Witch" was always kind to the mother. Mr. Ladd's story runs like this:

One day the whole family was invited to attend a quilting bee. Mrs.

Bell was ill; there was therefore some discussion about the propriety of leaving Mammy at home sick. As Daddy was invited too, the children all insisted on his going. There was a family row, the upshot of which was that everybody piled into the wagon and started, leaving Mammy at home sick. But before the happy party had proceeded far, the "Witch," champion of Mammy's rights, asserted himself. One of the wheels of the wagon flew off and let the axle down into the road with a bump. Not much disturbed by what seemed to be a mere accident, the boys and the old man piled out and replaced wheel and "tap." They had gone but a short distance when another wheel mysteriously flew off. Again they replaced the wheel and proceeded, somewhat sobered. Then one of the children saw a spectral hand pull another wheel off. When they had put it back in place, they held council, turned the team around, and drove back home, going softly. On the way back not another wheel came off.

Another story by Mr. Ladd illustrates the puckish character which the Bell "Witch" sometimes assumed. On several occasions when the old man and the boys went out to catch the mules and horses in preparation for a day's work or a trip to town, the animals would resist bridling like mustangs, plunging around in the stable as if stung by invisible hornets or possessed of evil spirits. When finally harnessed or saddled, they would buck like bronchos. These antics were always explained as the work of the Bell "Witch."

Miss Lewellen's account continues, showing that Mr. Bell had something of the scientific spirit:

"Mr. Bell was very curious about the 'Witch,' and finally persuaded 'him' to permit the familiarity of a handshake. He promised not to squeeze the hand. The hand that Mr. Bell shook was as small, soft, and chubby as a baby's. One day Mr. Bell raised a discussion of how the 'Witch' entered the house. 'I raise a certain corner of the house and come in,' said a Voice outside. 'Watch.' The house top was raised several inches and then let down.

"Other people of the community reported that they often met what appeared to be a riderless horse; but the horse would stop, and some one on his back would carry on a conversation with the person met."

To return to the girl, the devoted object of the "Witch's" vengeance. Mr. Ladd was unable to recall concrete details of the general statement that the "Witch" tormented her and tortured her. Miss Lewellen gives only one instance:

"One time the girl whom the 'Witch' tortured was getting ready to go to a party. As she was combing her hair, it suddenly became full of cockleburs. The 'Witch' explained, 'I put these in your hair; you have no business going to the party.' The men-folks came in and fired

639

shots in the direction from which the voice came; but every shot was met by one from the invisible hand of the 'Witch,' and the engagement proved a draw."

Miss Lewellen concludes her account of the Bell "Witch" with the statement: "The girl grieved her life away; and after her death the 'Witch' never returned either to torment or to comfort the Bells."

Mr. Fonnie Black Ladd supplies the final detail describing the funeral of the unhappy girl. The coffin containing the body was conveyed to the country graveyard in a farm wagon. As the little procession drove out of the yard of the homestead, some one looked up and saw a great black bird, something like a buzzard or the bird which the negroes call a "Good God," with a bell around its neck slowly ringing. This great bird flew with miraculous slowness above and just ahead of the lumbering wagon all the way to the graveyard, and poised in air over the grave while the funeral service was being held. Then it flew away, the bell still slowly ringing. And the Bell "Witch" never visited the family again.

Colonel Crockett Shoots for His Supper

Davy Crockett was on his way to Texas—where he would soon die in the defense of the Alamo—when this shooting match occurred, or perhaps didn't occur. The story of the two bullets in the bull's-eye is legendary. It was certain to attach itself to Davy, just as almost every other legend of frontier bravado did, sooner or later. This particular exploit is reprinted from Chapter xxvi of the Life of David Crockett, the Original Humorist and Irrepressible Backwoodsman *(Philadelphia: Porter & Coates; 1865). This work was a compilation that joined together, with a few additions, the three Crockett autobiographies (A Narrative of the Life of David Crockett, 1834; An Account of Col. Crockett's Tour to the North and Down East, 1835; Col. Crockett's Exploits and Adventures in Texas, 1836) in the composition of which, so Constance Rourke believed, Crockett had some share.*

Colonel Crockett Shoots for His Supper

THE public mind having been quieted by the exhibition of the puppet show, and allowed to return to its usual channel, it was not long before the good people of Little Rock began to inquire what distinguished stranger had come among them; and learning that it was neither more nor less than the identical Colonel Crockett, the champion of the fugitive deposites, then straight they went ahead at getting up another tempest in a teapot; and I wish I may be shot if I wasn't looked upon as almost as great as a Punch and Judy.

Nothing would answer, but I must accept of an invitation to a public dinner. Now as public dinners have become so common, that it is enough to take away the appetite of any man, who has a proper sense of his own importance, to sit down and play his part in the humbug business, I had made up my mind to write a letter declining the honor, expressing my regret, and winding up with a flourish of trumpets about the patriotism of the citizens of Little Rock, and all that sort of thing; when the landlord came in, and says he, "Colonel, just oblige me by stepping into the back yard a moment."

I followed the landlord in silence, twisting and turning over in my brain, all the while, what I should say in my letter to the patriotic citizens of Little Rock, who were bent on eating a dinner for the good of their country; when he conducted me to a shed in the yard, where I beheld, hanging up, a fine fat cub bear, several haunches of venison, a wild turkey as big as a young ostrich, and small game too tedious to mention. "Well, Colonel, what do you think of my larder?" says he. "Fine!" says I. "Let us liquor." We walked back to the bar. I took a horn, and without loss of time I wrote to the committee, that I accepted of the invitation to a public dinner with pleasure,—that I would be always found ready to serve my country, either by eating or fasting; and that the honor the patriotic citizens of Little Rock had conferred upon me, rendered it the proudest moment of my eventful life. The chairman of the committee was standing by while I wrote the letter, which I handed to him; and so this important business was soon settled.

As there was considerable time to be killed, or got rid of in some way, before the dinner could be cooked, it was proposed that we should go beyond the village, and shoot at a mark, for they had heard I was a first-rate shot, and they wanted to see for themselves, whether fame had not blown her trumpet a little too strong in my favor: for since she had represented "the Government" as being a first-rate statesman, and Colonel Benton as a first-rate orator, they could not receive such reports without proper allowance, as Congress thought of the post-office report.

Well, I shouldered my Betsey, and she is just about as beautiful a piece as ever came out of Philadelphia, and I went out to the shooting ground, followed by all the leading men in Little Rock, and that was a clear majority of the town, for it is remarkable, that there are always more leading men in small villages than there are followers.

I was in prime order. My eye was as keen as a lizard, and my nerves were as steady and unshaken as the political course of Henry Clay; so at it we went, the distance, one hundred yards. The principal marksmen, and such as had never been beat, led the way, and there was some pretty fair shooting, I tell you. At length it came to my turn. I squared myself, raised my beautiful Betsey to my shoulder, took deliberate aim, and smack I sent the bullet right into the center of the bull's eye. "There's no mistake in Betsey," said I, in a sort of careless way, as they were all looking at the target, sort of amazed, and not at all overpleased.

"That's a chance shot, Colonel," said one who had the reputation of being the best marksman in those parts.

"Not as much chance as there was," said I, "when Dick Johnson took his darkie for better for worse. I can do it five times out of six any day in the week." This I said in as confident a tone as "the Government" did, when he protested that he forgave Colonel Benton for shooting him, and he was now the best friend he had in the world. I knew it was not altogether as correct as it might be, but when a man sets about going the big figure, halfway measures won't answer no how; and "the greatest and the best" had set me the example, that swaggering will answer a good purpose at times.

They now proposed that we should have a second trial; but knowing that I had nothing to gain and everything to lose, I was for backing out and fighting shy; but there was no let off, for the cock of the village, though whipped, determined not to stay whipped; so at it again we went. They were now put upon their mettle, and they fired much better than the first time; and it was what might be called pretty sharp shooting. When it came to my turn, I squared myself, and turning to the prime shot, I gave him a knowing nod, by way of showing my confidence; and says I, "Look out for the bull's eye, stranger." I blazed away, and I wish I may be shot if I didn't miss the target. They examined it all over, and could find neither hair nor hide of my bullet, and pronounced it a dead miss; when says I, "Stand aside and let me look, and I warrant you I get on the right trail of the critter." They stood aside, and I examined the bull's eye pretty particular, and at length cried out, "Here it is; there is no snakes if it ha'n't followed the very track of the other." They said it was utterly impossible, but I insisted on their searching the hole, and I agreed to be stuck up as a mark myself, if they did not find two bullets there. They searched for my satisfaction, and sure enough it all come out just as I had told them; for I had picked up a bullet that had been fired, and stuck it deep into the hole, without any one perceiving it. They were all perfectly satisfied, that fame had not made too great a flourish of trumpets when speaking of me as a marksman; and they all said they had enough of shooting for that day, and they moved that we adjourn to the tavern and liquor.

Lawyer Prentiss and the Bedbug Trial

Sergeant Smith Prentiss (1808–50) was born in Maine and was gradu-ated from Bowdoin College, but before he was twenty-one he had taught school in Natchez, Mississippi, and had been admitted to the bar. He soon became one of the most celebrated criminal lawyers in the Southwest. Though briefly a member of Congress, Prentiss was not a distinguished politician. But as an orator and trial lawyer before a jury he was famous in the Old South. He was also an extravagant gambler and drinker. His eloquence and wit, as well as his flamboyant behavior, made him an almost legendary figure. Stories adhered to him, like the one told here—an extract (pp. 211–12) from "Reminiscences of Sargent [sic] S. Prentiss," in L. J. Bigelow: Bench and Bar: a Com-plete Digest of the Wit, Humor, Asperities, and Amenities of the Law *(New York: Harper & Brothers; 1868).*

MANY years ago, when Prentiss was engaged in his large practice in Mississippi, he and his friend, Judge Gohlson, were on the circuit in some of the eastern counties of the state, and stopped for the night at Hernando. Late at night Prentiss discovered that Judge Gohlson and himself were not the only claimants for possession of the bed, as he was vigorously beset by a description of vermin which do not make very comfortable bed-fellows. Accordingly he awoke Gohlson, and a consultation was had whether they should beat a retreat, or make an effort to exterminate their assailants. The latter course was, however, adopted, and for this purpose they took from their saddlebags a brace of pistols, with caps, powder, and other munitions of warfare. With pistol in hand, they proceeded to raise the bed-clothing, and as one of the creeping reptiles started from his hiding-place, "bang! bang!" would go the pistols. This, of course, aroused and alarmed the worthy landlord, who came in hot haste to the room, and, when he learned the facts, was in great rage. Prentiss demanded he should leave the room, claiming that he was only "exercising the right of self-defense—the right which the law of God and the law of man had given him." Both the entreaty and the threats of the landlord proved unavailing. The firing continued until bed, bedstead, and bedding were completely riddled with balls. At last they succeeded in capturing one of the enemy, when a difference of opinion arose between Prentiss and Judge Gohlson as to what should be his fate. At length it was agreed that the offending vermin should be "fairly and impartially tried by *a jury of his countrymen*." Three of the landlord's sons were brought in, and forced to sit as members of the jury, and a third lawyer who was present acted as judge. The prisoner was then pinned to the wall. Judge Gohlson (who was a very able lawyer) opened for the prosecution in a speech of two hours in length. Prentiss followed for the defense in a speech of four hours. There were those present who had known Prentiss intimately, and had heard him on great occasions of his life, and who now assert that this was perhaps the most brilliant speech he ever delivered.

5. WRITING

Whatever the causes may be (and there will be occasion to look into them later in this introduction), the South in recent years has furnished the country with more good writers than any other region. This Renascence, as it has been called,[1] is a belated one. New England has long since experienced its literary flowering and Indian summer. There was once a "literary frontier" in San Francisco, and in the 1920's one talked about a "Chicago school." Meanwhile the South pretty well neglected what authors it did raise up. Schoolchildren memorized "Excelsior" and "Old Ironsides"; only by chance did they hear about Timrod or Cable. Many able Southern writers left home to find a publisher and a public in the North.

Yet we know that Southern gentlemen read books and that many of them possessed remarkable libraries—that of William Byrd of Westover is said to have been the largest private collection in the colonies. Southern academies and colleges held firmly to the classical curriculum. Southern political leaders—Jefferson, John Taylor of Caroline, Calhoun, Alexander Stephens—were cultivated men and could quote the classical writers on civil polity as readily as an Oxford scholar.

Why, then, did the Southern writer lack recognition at home? For

[1] Louis D. Rubin, Jr., and Robert D. Jacobs, eds.: *Southern Renascence: The Literature of the Modern South* (Baltimore, 1953).

one thing, Southerners sent to Europe and particularly to England for their books and their literary standards. The colonialism in the arts which persisted in America until the late nineteenth century was markedly evident in the South. In succession Addison, Pope, Burke, Tom Moore, Byron, Scott, and Carlyle were read, admired, and imitated. In the second place, a young Southerner with ambitions to succeed as a poet or novelist had to reckon with the fact that the artist had no place in the hierarchy of Southern society. If he indulged himself in verse-making or essay-writing, he must do so strictly as an amateur. Writing was not a profession.

Almost every Southern writer in ante-bellum days attempted to conform to this requirement by first establishing his professional respectability, and the profession he chose was almost invariably the law. He had before him the approved example of William Wirt (1772–1834), whose Addisonian *Letters of the British Spy* (1803) were highly regarded. But Mr. Wirt was an eminent lawyer, orator, and statesman whose professional career guaranteed the respectability of his essays. Other writers who tried to follow his example were not so fortunate. The poets Edward Coote Pinkney (1802–28), Philip Pendleton Cooke (1816–50), and Henry Timrod (1828–67) dutifully made a try at the law but found they had no taste for it. Even Paul Hamilton Hayne (1830–86), after Poe the Southern poet who was most determined to live by his pen, practiced law for a time. He was just beginning to succeed as a poet (in defiance of the custom of his region) when the Civil War came. Yet two of his three volumes of verse issued before the War were published by a Northern firm, Ticknor & Fields of Boston.

Like the poets, the ante-bellum Southern novelists generally had to conform to the requirement of a profession or defy the tradition. Virginia-born William Caruthers (1802–46), whose three novels are still readable today, was a physician. John Esten Cooke (1830–86), brother of the poet, practiced law until the Civil War and wrote his early novels between the visits of clients. Even William Gilmore Simms, most distinguished of this generation of novelists, studied law, but avoided the life of a lawyer by years of editing and hack-writing before the sale of his novels was profitable.

Ante-bellum writers who cared to be more than amateurs were often very bitter about the indifference of Southerners to their efforts. Philip Pendleton Cooke reveals in one of his letters what a hunting friend thought of his verse-making: "What do you think of a friend of mine, a most valuable, and worthy, and hard-riding one, saying gravely to me a short time ago. 'I wouldn't waste time on a damned thing like poetry; you might make yourself, with your sense and judgment, a useful man in settling neighborhood disputes and differences.'" Simms had even more reason to be bitter. In his Border Romances and Revolutionary Romances he had endowed the South with an exciting legend. The worth of what he had done was recognized in the North and even in Europe, but Southerners showed little appreciation of his achievement. In 1847 Simms bursts out in a letter to his friend James Henry Hammond, South Carolina Governor and Senator: "The South dont care a d—n for literature or art. Your best neighbour & kindred never think to buy books. They will borrow from you & beg, but the same man who will always have his wine, has no idea of a library. . . . At the North, the usual gift to a young lady is a book—in the South, a ring, a chain, or a bottle of Eau de Cologne." Hammond agreed with him thoroughly, adding, in a letter written five years later: "However Authors may get on at the North—& I doubt if it is very comfortably, it is a settled fact I think—settled by your case that the South will not encourage & sustain them."

It is pointless to ask whether the ante-bellum poets of the South would have accomplished more if they had commanded at home the kind of respect which Longfellow and Lowell won for themselves in the North. But one must admit that what they did contrive to publish is not memorable, if one excepts Poe and possibly Thomas Holley Chivers. Even such anthology pieces as Richard Henry Wilde's "To the Mocking-Bird," Cooke's "Florence Vane," and Timrod's "The Cotton Ball" are exercises rather than poems. Occasionally a faint fragrance rises from them, as if one had lifted the lid from a forgotten potpourri of rose petals. It is believable, for example, that Southern gentlemen once raised their glasses and vibrated to the manly sentiments voiced for them in Pinkney's famous "A Health":

> I fill this cup to one made up
>   Of loveliness alone,
> A woman, of her gentle sex
>   The seeming paragon;
> To whom the better elements
>   And kindly stars have given
> A form so fair, that, like the air
>   'Tis less of earth than heaven.

With the novel the story is brighter. Beginning with John P. Kennedy's *Swallow Barn* in 1832, the "plantation novel" makes its entrance. Northern readers and perhaps some Southerners delighted in these Irvingesque pictures of life in the great house and in the quarters. Characters and plots were stock, but the descriptions of race-meets, hunts, tourneys, Christmas feasts, and visits to the Springs were authentic and novel. At the same time Scott was transplanted to the South, and year by year the legend of a glorious past grew more extravagant in color and deed. Southern historical novels were shipped out of Northern publishing houses along with packages of pirated copies of Scott and Dickens. By the time of the Civil War nearly every famous event in the history of the South had been made glamorous by Caruthers, Kennedy, Simms, John Esten Cooke, and their imitators.

Southern readers, except gentlemen who subscribed to Porter's sporting weekly, the *Spirit of the Times*, were generally unaware of the extraordinary literature of humor which A. B. Longstreet, J. J. Hooper, W. T. Thompson, J. G. Baldwin, and G. W. Harris produced between 1835, the year of Longstreet's *Georgia Scenes*, and the war. Even today few Americans know Harris's *Sut Lovingood's Yarns* (collected in 1867), Hooper's *Some Adventures of Captain Simon Suggs, late of the Tallapoosa Volunteers* (1845), and Baldwin's *Flush Times of Alabama and Mississippi* (1853). Yet here is the Old South that the plantation novelists disdained—the South of gander-pullings, match dogfights, militia drills, courtroom duels, gouging and ballocking, and frontier practical jokes. Many of these tales possess a lustiness that would not reappear in American literature for nearly a century. This Southern humor surpasses its Northern counterpart, the work of Seba Smith and Artemus Ward, because it depends less on parody and on verbal tricks of bad grammar and misspelling. From it real characters emerge who speak the authentic idiom of the folk.

Though it is a verifiable fact that Lee surrendered unconditionally at Appomattox, the notion prevails with many Americans today that the South would have won if Grant hadn't been a butcher, if Jefferson Davis hadn't interfered with his generals, and if the North hadn't sent newly arrived immigrants into the lines. For this rearrangement of history a group of Southern novelists writing between 1865 and 1920 is largely responsible. One year after the war ended, John Esten Cooke, who had served in the Confederate cavalry under Stuart, was ready with his immensely popular *Surry of Eagle's Nest*, a tale which apotheosized "Jackson, that greater than the leader of the Ironsides—Stuart, more fiery than Rupert of the Bloody Sword—Ashby, the pearl of chivalry and honor—Lee, the old Roman, fighting, with a nerve so splendid, to the bitter end." This was the first of a long line of novels written by Southerners who took for their themes the bravery of officers and butternut-clad privates and the beauty and fortitude of their women or the iniquities of carpetbaggers, bushwhackers, and scalawags or the necessitous activities of the early Ku-Klux Klan. Far from resenting this covert revenge on the North for having won the war, Northern readers could not get enough of these stories. They kept Thomas Nelson Page (1853–1922) employed writing tales of faithful slaves who refused to take advantage of their freedom. James Lane Allen (1849–1925) and John Fox, Jr. (1863–1919), glorified the past and the people of Kentucky, and Mary Johnston (1870–1936) rewrote the history of Virginia in fifteen of her twenty-two popular romances. It is not accidental that Margaret Mitchell's *Gone with the Wind* has been the most widely read book in America, after the Bible. Miss Mitchell merely cashed in on the legend of Southern bravery, gallantry, and gracious manners which these earlier novelists had so magnified that by 1936 it had become one of the dominant American myths.

From the end of the First World War until the middle 1930's writing in the South experienced a flowering such as America had not known since the decade of the 1850's, which produced *Moby-Dick, The Scarlet Letter, Walden,* and *Leaves of Grass.* A list of the important first books or first works in a significant mode written by Southerners between 1919 and 1931 is truly amazing. John Crowe Ransom's *Poems about God* (1919), Elizabeth Madox Roberts's *The Time of Man* (1926), Allen Tate's *Mr. Pope and Other Poems* (1928), William Faulkner's *The Sound and the Fury* (1929), Thomas Wolfe's *Look Homeward, Angel* (1929), Robert Penn Warren's first volume of verse (1930), Katherine Anne Porter's *Flowering Judas* (1930), Caroline Gordon's *Penhally* (1931) are by no means all the works that can be put into this record. In addition, because Southern writing had at last come into its own, certain writers of an older generation seemed to find new energy and hope. James Branch Cabell had been writing since 1904, but only with *Jurgen* (1919) did he have his first popular success. Ellen Glasgow had tried a variety of modes since her first novel in 1897—the problem novel, historical fiction, the novel of manners—but in the twenties she discovered her true vein, social satire, and produced two memorable works, *The Romantic Comedians* (1926) and *They Stooped to Folly* (1929).

Ever since critics and literary historians began to realize that much of our best contemporary writing was coming from the South, they have tried to find the reason why. Of course, no satisfactory answer can be found. Literary efflorescence cannot be correlated with business cycles and population graphs. Still, a few observations are pertinent and will stand inspection. The decade of the twenties was a remarkable one in American literature, even if we disregard the South. Some of the impulses that "account for" Sherwood Anderson, Sinclair Lewis, F. Scott Fitzgerald, Ernest Hemingway, John Dos Passos, and Hart Crane operated in the lives of Southern as well as Northern and Western writers. But for the Southern writers the work they did amounted to a kind of coming home again (quite literal in the instance of Faulkner) and a rediscovery of their region. It was as if a spring had been released and a new land revealed. Where Faulkner's great-grandfather (also a novelist) had seen only the White Rose of Memphis, the great-grand-son, recently returned from the First World War and in search of his métier, began to discover the Sartorises, the Compsons, the Bundrens, and the Snopeses. These new writers could bring the Southern past, which was close to them and dear, into focus with the realities of the present. In their novels irony, depth of psychological understanding, faithfulness to historical fact, a sense of tragedy and doom replaced the sentimentalities of a Page and the rodomontades of a Mary Johnston. One notices, too, that in the early years of this flowering many a young poet or novelist could count on the support and admiration of a group of his peers. In Nashville one such group came to be known as the Fugitives because of the title of the little magazine of verse they issued. There were similar groups in New Orleans, Charleston, Richmond, and Chapel Hill.

But the most important fact is that finally the hopes of the defeated ones—Timrod, Hayne, Poe—were realized. At last Southern writing had come into its own and was a part of world literature. In the Paris bookstores, alongside the novels of Gide and Mauriac stood *La Route au Tabac*, *Les Ancêtres*, and *Tandis j'agonise*.

Edgar Allan Poe

The most remarkable fact about the short, unhappy life of Edgar A. Poe (1809–49) is that he accomplished as much as he did, in spite of poverty, drink, the loss of editorial positions, and the vilifications of other critics. His collected works fill sixteen volumes in the Virginia Edition of 1902.

The mysteries that long obscured the various stages of Poe's life have at last been fairly well resolved and the story which emerges is at least credible. Poe's parents were actors. When his mother died during an engagement in Richmond, the boy, then two years old, was taken into the household of John Allan, a tobacco-exporter who eventually became a wealthy man. Allan did not adopt the child, and as Poe grew up, the tensions between them increased until there was a final break soon after Poe was dismissed from West Point in 1831.

Meanwhile Poe had received his early schooling in England, where the Allans lived from 1815 to 1820. In 1826 Allan sent Poe to the newly founded University of Virginia, but did not provide him with enough money so that he could live there as a young Southern gentleman should do. The years 1827–9 Poe spent in the United States Army. Though Allan helped to procure his discharge, it was evident to Poe that he must now fend for himself. He settled in Baltimore, where he began to make his way as a writer, with the assistance of John P. Kennedy, a lawyer who was also a novelist. Poe had already published, obscurely, his first three volumes of poetry: Tamerlane (*1827*), Al Aaraaf, Tamerlane, and Minor Poems (*1829*), *and* Poems (*1831*).

In 1835 Poe was made assistant editor of the Southern Literary Messenger, *which was published in Richmond. There a pattern in his life was formed that would be several times repeated. Poe was an excellent editor. He discovered and encouraged writers and wrote vigorous reviews whose quality was far above the general level of the reviewing of the day. But bouts of drinking and quarrels with the owner of the journal caused his discharge from the* Southern Literary Messenger *at the end of 1836. From 1838 to 1843 Poe lived in Philadelphia, supporting himself as well as he could by magazine-editing and free-lance writing. It was the most productive period of his career, marked especially by the publication, in two volumes, of* Tales of the Grotesque and Arabesque (*1840*).

When Poe moved to New York in 1844, he had hopes of at last directing a magazine of his own. He was famous—or notorious—in literary circles there as the author of a weird poem, "The Raven," which he used to recite in company. He was also feared because of his slashing attacks on his contemporaries in a series of "profiles" called "The Literati."

When Poe's child-wife, Virginia, died in 1847, he pretty much went to pieces. On October 3, 1849 he was found lying unconscious outside Ryan's Fourth Ward polls in Baltimore. He died four days later.

To the French poets Baudelaire, Mallarmé, and Valéry, who made a cult of Poe, he seemed the supreme example of the alienated artist, shunned by the society in which he must earn his bread and having his real life in the world of his dreams and visions. That Poe was a strange genius for mid-century commercial America to have produced is incontestable, but his interest in the America of his day was closer than his early biographers wished to believe. He reviewed expertly and thoroughly the work of American writers from Hawthorne down to Thomas Dunn English. Possibly as many as half his stories were based to some degree on events of the times or were suggested by the works of writers contemporary with him.

In spite of his parade of cosmopolitan learning a good case can be made for Poe as a Southern author. As a Southerner he disliked the members of the ascendant New England school of writers, with the exception of Lowell, who was his friend. He spoke of the "odious old woods of Concord" and called Boston "Frogpondium." He once called *Virginian society as "absolutely aristocratical as any in Europe." He was as sensitive to slights to his honor and as chivalric toward women as the code of the Old South demanded. Though he attended Mr. Jefferson's university, he was as anti-democratic as a Fitzhugh or a Dew and he had no faith in human perfectibility. It may well be that because he did not inherit or achieve a secure place in the Southern hierarchical society, the traits of the Southern gentleman were exaggerated in Poe almost to the point of burlesque.*

TO HELEN

HELEN, thy beauty is to me
  Like those Nicéan barks of yore,
That gently, o'er a perfumed sea,
  The weary, way-worn wanderer bore
  To his own native shore.

On desperate seas long wont to roam,
  Thy hyacinth hair, thy classic face,
Thy Naiad airs, have brought me home
  To the glory that was Greece
And the grandeur that was Rome.

Lo! in yon brilliant window-niche
  How statue-like I see thee stand,
  The agate lamp within they hand!
Ah, Psyche, from the regions which
  Are Holy-Land!

ISRAFEL

And the angel Israfel, whose heart-strings are a lute, and who has the sweetest voice of all God's creatures.—Koran.

In Heaven a spirit doth dwell
  "Whose heart-strings are a lute";
None sing so wildly well
As the angel Israfel,
And the giddy stars (so legends tell),
Ceasing their hymns, attend the spell
  Of his voice, all mute.

Tottering above
  In her highest noon,
  The enamoured moon
Blushes with love,
  While, to listen, the red levin
  (With the rapid Pleiads, even,
  Which were seven,)
  Pauses in Heaven.

And they say (the starry choir
  And the other listening things)
That Israfeli's fire
Is owing to that lyre
  By which he sits and sings—
The trembling living wire
  Of those unusual strings.

But the skies that angel trod,
  Where deep thoughts are a duty,
Where Love's a grown-up God,
  Where the Houri glances are
Imbued with all the beauty
  Which we worship in a star.

Therefore, thou art not wrong,
  Israfeli, who despisest
An unimpassioned song;
To thee the laurels belong,
  Best bard, because the wisest!
Merrily live, and long!

The ecstasies above
  With thy burning measures suit—
Thy grief, thy joy, thy hate, thy love,
  With the fervour of thy lute—
  Well may the stars be mute!

Yes, Heaven is thine; but this
  Is a world of sweets and sours;
  Our flowers are merely—flowers,
And the shadow of thy perfect bliss
  Is the sunshine of ours.

If I could dwell
Where Israfel

Hath dwelt, and he where I,
He might not sing so wildly well
A mortal melody,
While a bolder note than this might swell
From my lyre within the sky.

ULALUME—A BALLAD

The skies they were ashen and sober;
The leaves they were crispèd and sere—
The leaves they were withering and sere;
It was night in the lonesome October
Of my most immemorial year;
It was hard by the dim lake of Auber,
In the misty mid region of Weir—
It was down by the dank tarn of Auber,
In the ghoul-haunted woodland of Weir.

Here once, through an alley Titanic,
Of cypress, I roamed with my Soul—
Of cypress, with Psyche, my Soul.
These were days when my heart was volcanic
As the scoriac rivers that roll—
As the lavas that restlessly roll
Their sulphurous currents down Yaanek
In the ultimate climes of the pole—
That groan as they roll down Mount Yaanek
In the realms of the boreal pole.

Our talk had been serious and sober,
But our thoughts they were palsied and sere—
Our memories were treacherous and sere—
For we knew not the month was October,
And we marked not the night of the year—
(Ah, night of all nights in the year!)
We noted not the dim lake of Auber—
(Though once we had journeyed down here)—
Remembered not the dank tarn of Auber,
Nor the ghoul-haunted woodland of Weir.

And now, as the night was senescent
And star-dials pointed to morn—
As the star-dials hinted of morn—

At the end of our path a liquescent
  And nebulous lustre was born,
Out of which a miraculous crescent
  Arose with a duplicate horn—
Astarte's bediamonded crescent
  Distinct with its duplicate horn.

And I said—"She is warmer than Dian:
  She rolls through an ether of sighs—
  She revels in a region of sighs:
She has seen that the tears are not dry on
  These cheeks, where the worm never dies
And has come past the stars of the Lion
  To point us the path to the skies—
  To the Lethean peace of the skies—
Come up, in despite of the Lion,
  To shine on us with her bright eyes—
Come up through the lair of the Lion,
  With love in her luminous eyes."

But Psyche, uplifting her finger,
  Said—"Sadly this star I mistrust—
  Her pallor I strangely mistrust:—
Oh, hasten!—oh, let us not linger!
  Oh, fly!—let us fly!—for we must."
In terror she spoke, letting sink her
  Wings till they trailed in the dust—
In agony sobbed, letting sink her
  Plumes till they trailed in the dust—
  Till they sorrowfully trailed in the dust.

I replied—"This is nothing but dreaming:
  Let us on by this tremulous light!
  Let us bathe in this crystalline light!
Its Sibyllic splendor is beaming
  With Hope and in Beauty to-night:—
  See!—it flickers up the sky through the night!
Ah, we safely may trust to its gleaming,
  And be sure it will lead us aright—
We safely may trust to a gleaming
  That cannot but guide us aright,
Since it flickers up to Heaven through the night."

Thus I pacified Psyche and kissed her,
  And tempted her out of her gloom—

654

And conquered her scruples and gloom,
And we passed to the end of the vista,
But were stopped by the door of a tomb—
By the door of a legended tomb:
And I said—"What is written, sweet sister,
On the door of this legended tomb?"
She replied—"Ulalume—Ulalume—
'Tis the vault of thy lost Ulalume!"

Then my heart it grew ashen and sober
As the leaves that were crispèd and sere—
As the leaves that were withering and sere;
And I cried—"It was surely October
On *this* very night of last year
That I journeyed—I journeyed down here—
That I brought a dread burden down here!
On this night of all nights in the year,
Ah, what demon has tempted me here?
Well I know, now, this dim lake of Auber—
This misty mid region of Weir—
Well I know, now, this dank tarn of Auber,
This ghoul-haunted woodland of Weir."

Said we, then—the two, then: "Ah, can it
Have been that the woodlandish ghouls—
The pitiful, the merciful ghouls—
To bar up our way and to ban it
From the secret that lies in these wolds—
From the thing that lies hidden in these wolds—
Have drawn up the spectre of a planet
From the limbo of lunary souls—
This sinfully scintillant planet
From the Hell of the planetary souls?"

THE MASQUE OF THE RED DEATH [1]

The "Red Death" had long devastated the country. No pestilence had ever been so fatal, or so hideous. Blood was its Avatar and its seal—the redness and the horror of blood. There were sharp pains, and sudden

---

[1] This particular story has been chosen to represent Poe's work in the genre for a number of reasons. First, in a small compass it exemplifies one of his salient literary theories, applicable to poems as well as stories. "Nothing is more clear than that every plot, worth the name, must be elaborated to its *dénouement* before anything be attempted with the pen. It is only with the *dénouement* constantly in view that

dizziness, and then profuse bleeding at the pores, with dissolution. The scarlet stains upon the body and especially upon the face of the victim, were the pest ban which shut him out from the aid and from the sympathy of his fellow-men. And the whole seizure, progress, and termination of the disease, were the incidents of half an hour.

But the Prince Prospero was happy and dauntless and sagacious. When his dominions were half depopulated, he summoned to his presence a thousand hale and light-hearted friends from among the knights and dames of his court, and with these retired to the deep seclusion of one of his castellated abbeys. This was an extensive and magnificent structure, the creation of the prince's own eccentric yet august taste. A strong and lofty wall girdled it in. This wall had gates of iron. The courtiers, having entered, brought furnaces and massy hammers and welded the bolts. They resolved to leave means neither of ingress or egress to the sudden impulses of despair or of frenzy from within. The abbey was amply provisioned. With such precautions the courtiers might bid defiance to contagion. The external world could take care of itself. In the meantime it was folly to grieve, or to think. The prince had provided all the appliances of pleasure. There were buffoons, there were improvisatori, there were ballet-dancers, there were musicians, there was Beauty, there was wine. All these and security were within. Without was the "Red Death."

It was toward the close of the fifth or sixth month of his seclusion, and while the pestilence raged most furiously abroad, that the Prince Prospero entertained his thousand friends at a masked ball of the most unusual magnificence.

It was a voluptuous scene, that masquerade. But first let me tell of the rooms in which it was held. There were seven—an imperial suite. In many palaces, however, such suites form a long and straight vista, while the folding doors slide back nearly to the walls on either hand, so that the view of the whole extent is scarcely impeded. Here the case was very different; as might have been expected from the duke's love of the

---

we can give a plot its indispensable air of consequence or causation, by making the incidents, and especially the tone at all points, tend to the development of the intention." By working back step by step from the *dénouement* of *The Masque of the Red Death* one can see how adroitly Poe built his story. Further to be noted is the pervasive symbolism, a characteristic ingredient in his method: the color red, to distinguish this plague (undoubtedly the cholera, newly arrived in America) from the black death (bubonic plague) of the Middle Ages; the sequence of colors in the rooms; the menacing ebony clock and the attitude of the masquers toward it, symbolizing the forced gaiety that seeks to kill time by forgetting it. There is also a remarkable and characteristic dream sequence in which the grotesque figures of the masquers stalk to an fro in the seven chambers like a "multitude of dreams." Noteworthy, too, is the careful attention to décor. By all these means Poe attempts, as always in his most serious work, to "elevate the soul" of his reader to the "contemplation of the beautiful."

bizarre. The apartments were so irregularly disposed that the vision embraced but little more than one at a time. There was a sharp turn at every twenty or thirty yards, and at each turn a novel effect. To the right and left, in the middle of each wall, a tall and narrow Gothic window looked out upon a closed corridor which pursued the windings of the suite. These windows were of stained glass whose color varied in accordance with the prevailing hue of the decorations of the chamber into which it opened. That at the eastern extremity was hung, for example, in blue—and vividly blue were its windows. The second chamber was purple in its ornaments and tapestries, and here the panes were purple. The third was green throughout, and so were the casements. The fourth was furnished and lighted with orange—the fifth with white—the sixth with violet. The seventh apartment was closely shrouded in black velvet tapestries that hung all over the ceiling and down the walls, falling in heavy folds upon a carpet of the same material and hue. But in this chamber only, the color of the windows failed to correspond with the decorations. The panes here were scarlet —a deep blood color. Now in no one of the seven apartments was there any lamp or candelabrum, amid the profusion of golden ornaments that lay scattered to and fro or depended from the roof. There was no light of any kind emanating from the lamp or candle within the suite of chambers. But in the corridors that followed the suite, there stood, opposite to each window, a heavy tripod, bearing a brazier of fire, that projected its rays through the tinted glass and so glaringly illumined the room. And thus were produced a multitude of gaudy and fantastic appearances. But in the western or black chamber the effect of the firelight that streamed upon the dark hangings through the blood-tinted panes was ghastly in the extreme, and produced so wild a look upon the countenances of those who entered, that there were few of the company bold enough to set foot within its precincts at all.

It was in this apartment, also, that there stood against the western wall, a gigantic clock of ebony. Its pendulum swung to and fro with a dull, heavy, monotonous clang; and when the minute-hand made the circuit of the face, and the hour was to be stricken, there came from the brazen lungs of the clock a sound which was clear and loud and deep and exceedingly musical, but of so peculiar a note and emphasis that, at each lapse of an hour, the musicians of the orchestra were constrained to pause, momentarily, in their performance, to hearken to the sound; and thus the waltzers perforce ceased their evolutions; and there was a brief disconcert of the whole gay company; and, while the chimes of the clock yet rang, it was observed that the giddiest grew pale, and the more aged and sedate passed their hands over their brows as if in confused revery or meditation. But when the echoes had fully ceased, a light laughter at once pervaded the assembly; the musicians

657

looked at each other and smiled as if at their own nervousness and folly, and made whispering vows, each to the other, that the next chiming of the clock should produce in them no similar emotion; and then, after the lapse of sixty minutes (which embrace three thousand and six hundred seconds of the Time that flies), there came yet another chiming of the clock, and then were the same disconcert and tremulousness and meditation as before.

But, in spite of these things, it was a gay and magnificent revel. The tastes of the duke were peculiar. He had a fine eye for colors and effects. He disregarded the *decora* of mere fashion. His plans were bold and fiery, and his conceptions glowed with barbaric lustre. There are some who would have thought him mad. His followers felt that he was not. It was necessary to hear and see and touch him to be *sure* that he was not.

He had directed, in great part, the movable embellishments of the seven chambers, upon occasion of this great *fête;* and it was his own guiding taste which had given character to the masqueraders. Be sure they were grotesque. There were much glare and glitter and piquancy and phantasm—much of what has been since seen in "Hernani." There were arabesque figures with unsuited limbs and appointments.

There were delirious fancies such as the madman fashions. There were much of the beautiful, much of the wanton, much of the *bizarre,* something of the terrible, and not a little of that which might have excited disgust. To and fro in the seven chambers there stalked, in fact, a ·multitude of dreams. And these—the dreams—writhed in and about, taking hue from the rooms, and causing the wild music of the orchestra to seem as the echo of their steps. And, anon, there strikes the ebony clock which stands in the hall of the velvet. And then, for a moment, all is still, and all is silent save the voice of the clock. The dreams are stiff-frozen as they stand. But the echoes of the chime die away—they have endured but an instant—and a light, half-subdued laughter floats after them as they depart. And now again the music swells, and the dreams live, and writhe to and fro more merrily than ever, taking hue from the many-tinted windows through which stream the rays from the tripods. But to the chamber which lies most westwardly of the seven there are now none of the maskers who venture; for the night is waning away; and there flows a ruddier light through the blood-colored panes; and the blackness of the sable drapery appalls; and to him whose foot falls upon the sable carpet, there comes from the near clock of ebony a muffled peal more solemnly emphatic than any which reaches *their* ears who indulge in the more remote gaieties of the other apartments.

But these other apartments were densely crowded, and in them beat feverishly the heart of life. And the revel went whirlingly on, until at length there commenced the sounding of midnight upon the clock. And then the music ceased, as I have told; and the evolutions of the waltzers were quieted; and there was an uneasy cessation of all things as before. But now there were twelve strokes to be sounded by the bell of the clock; and thus it happened, perhaps, that more of thought crept, with more of time, into the meditations of the thoughtful among those who revelled. And thus too, it happened, perhaps, that before the last echoes of the last chime had utterly sunk into silence, there were many individuals in the crowd who had found leisure to become aware of the presence of a masked figure which had arrested the attention of no single individual before. And the rumor of this new presence having spread itself whisperingly around, there arose at length from the whole company a buzz, or murmur, expressive of disapprobation and surprise —then, finally, of terror, of horror, and of disgust.

In an assembly of phantasms such as I have painted, it may well be supposed that no ordinary appearance could have excited such sensation. In truth the masquerade license of the night was nearly unlimited; but the figure in question had out-Heroded Herod, and gone beyond the bounds of even the prince's indefinite decorum. There are chords in the hearts of the most reckless which cannot be touched without emotion.

Even with the utterly lost, to whom life and death are equally jests, there are matters of which no jest can be made. The whole company, indeed, seemed now deeply to feel that in the costume and bearing of the stranger neither wit nor propriety existed. The figure was tall and gaunt, and shrouded from head to foot in the habiliments of the grave. The mask which concealed the visage was made so nearly to resemble the countenance of a stiffened corpse that the closest scrutiny must have had difficulty in detecting the cheat. And yet all this might have been endured, if not approved, by the mad revellers around. But the mummer had gone so far as to assume the type of the Red Death. His vesture was dabbled in *blood*—and his broad brow, with all the features of the face, was besprinkled with the scarlet horror.

When the eyes of Prince Prospero fell upon this spectral image (which, with a slow and solemn movement, as if more fully to sustain its *rôle*, stalked to and fro among the waltzers) he was seen to be convulsed, in the first moment with a strong shudder either of terror or distaste; but, in the next, his brow reddened with rage.

"Who dares"—he demanded hoarsely of the courtiers who stood near him—"who dares insult us with this blasphemous mockery? Seize him and unmask him—that we may know whom we have to hang, at sunrise, from the battlements!"

It was in the eastern or blue chamber in which stood the Prince Prospero as he uttered these words. They rang throughout the seven rooms loudly and clearly, for the prince was a bold and robust man, and the music had become hushed at the waving of his hand.

It was in the blue room where stood the prince, with a group of pale courtiers by his side. At first, as he spoke, there was a slight rushing movement of this group in the direction of the intruder, who, at the moment was also near at hand, and now, with deliberate and stately step, made closer approach to the speaker. But from a certain nameless awe with which the mad assumptions of the mummer had inspired the whole party, there were found none who put forth hand to seize him; so that, unimpeded, he passed within a yard of the prince's person; and, while the vast assembly, as if with one impulse, shrank from the centres of the rooms to the walls, he made his way uninterruptedly, but with the same solemn and measured step, which had distinguished him from the first, through the blue chamber to the purple—through the purple to the green—through the green to the orange—through this again to the white—and even thence to the violet, ere a decided movement had been made to arrest him. It was then, however, that the Prince Prospero, maddening with rage and the shame of his own momentary cowardice, rushed hurriedly through the six chambers, while none followed him on account of a deadly terror that had seized upon all. He bore aloft a drawn dagger, and had approached, in rapid impetuosity, to within three or four feet of the retreating figure, when the latter, having attained the extremity of the velvet apartment, turned suddenly and confronted his pursuer. There was a sharp cry—and the dagger dropped gleaming upon the sable carpet, upon which, instantly afterward, fell prostrate in death the Prince Prospero. Then, summoning the wild courage of despair, a throng of the revellers at once threw themselves into the black apartment, and, seizing the mummer, whose tall figure stood erect and motionless within the shadow of the ebony clock, gasped in unutterable horror at finding the grave-cerements and corpse-like mask, which they handled with so violent a rudeness, untenanted by any tangible form.

And now was acknowledged the presence of the Red Death. He had come like a thief in the night. And one by one dropped the revellers in the blood-bedewed halls of their revel, and died each in the despairing posture of his fall. And the life of the ebony clock went out with that of the last of the gay. And the flames of the tripods expired. And Darkness and Decay and the Red Death held illimitable dominion over all.

George W. Harris

In the years between 1835, when Augustus Baldwin Longstreet's Georgia Scenes was published, and the Civil War a group of writers in the South were delighting the readers of local papers and those who subscribed to William T. Porter's (New York) Spirit of the Times with their earthy, humorous tales of life on the semi-frontier. Presently these scattered stories were gathered into books and thus had a wider audience. But only for a short time. Sophisticated Americans after the war began to look down on the supposed crudities of William T. Thompson's Major Jones's Courtship (1843), Johnson J. Hooper's Adventures of Simon Suggs (1845), and Thomas B. Thorpe's Hive of the Bee Hunter (1854).

When Henry Watterson tried, in 1882, to revive interest in these forgotten writers by publishing selections from their work in Oddities in Southern Life and Character, he felt it was necessary to deprecate what he was offering. In presenting this humor it was not his purpose, he noted, "to make much boast of its quality, but to offer it as in some sort a picture of a day that is gone, of a race which has passed into history, of a region whose swamps and ridges, mountain passes and vast cotton lands [were] given over for a century to song and dance and sunburnt mirth."

Watterson need not have apologized. Though the life they depicted was boisterous and sometimes Rabelaisian and their characters illiterate, the writers themselves were skilled in the Southern art of telling a story. They were versatile men—Harris was, for example, at various times a silversmith, riverboat captain, political writer, and inventor. They knew at first hand the practical jokes and rough horseplay that enlivened barbecue and camp meeting, muster days and quarter races. And they liked to hear the rogues and village rakes they had created tell their tall stories. Mark Twain learned to write in this school, but, save for him, Americans would have to wait until the 1910's for stories so close to the earth and so true to the spoken word.

The best of these Southern humorists is George W. Harris, creator of Sut Lovingood, that "queer-looking, long legged, short bodied, small headed, white haired, hog eyed, funny sort of genius" who rides up to Pat Nash's grocery (saloon) in the first of the Sut Lovingood yarns, "Sut Lovingood's Daddy, Acting Horse," starts talking a blue streak, and never stops until 280 pages later when he finishes telling about

661

"Dad's Dog-School." Harris excels because he had as great a gift for language (both word and metaphor) as he did for story-telling. Once the reader gets by Sut's thick east Tennessee dialect, he will enjoy this little fabliau from the Great Smokies as much for the way Sut tells his story as for its matter.

"Rare Ripe Garden-seed" is the twenty-first of the twenty-four stories in Sut Lovingood: Yarns Spun by a Nat'ral Born Durn'd Fool. Warped and Wove for Public Wear (*New York: Dick & Fitzgerald; 1867*), *pp. 227–39. The last five pages of the story are omitted here because they are anticlimactic.*

RARE RIPE GARDEN-SEED (FOR NEWLY MARRIED FOLKS)

"I TELL yu now, I minds my fust big skeer jis' es well as rich boys minds thar fust boots, ur seein the fust spotted hoss sirkis. The red top ove them boots am still a rich red stripe in thar minds, an' the burnin red ove my fust skeer hes lef es deep a scar ontu my thinkin works. Mam hed me a standin atwixt her knees. I kin feel the knobs ove her jints a-rattlin a-pas' my ribs yet. She didn't hev much petticoats tu speak ove, an' I hed but one, an' hit wer calliker slit frum the nap ove my naik tu the tail, hilt tugether at the top wif a draw-string, an' at the bottom by the hem; hit wer the handiest close I ever seed, an' wud be pow'ful cumfurtin in summer if hit warn't fur the flies. Ef they was good tu run in, I'd war one yet. They beats pasted shuts, an' britches, es bad es a feather bed beats a bag ove warnut shells fur sleepin on.

"Say, George, wudn't yu like tu see me intu one 'bout haf fadid, slit, an' a-walkin jis' so, up the middil street ove yure city chuch, a-aimin fur yure pew pen, an' hit chock full ove yure fine city gal friends, jis' arter the people hed sot down frum the fust prayer, an' the orgin beginin tu groan; what wud yu du in sich a margincy? say hoss?"

"Why, I'd shoot you dead, Monday morning before eight o'clock," was my reply.

"Well, I speck yu wud; but yu'd take a rale ole maid faint fus, rite amung them ar gals. Lordy! wudn't yu be shamed ove me! Yit why not ten chuch in sich a suit, when yu hesn't got no store clothes?

"Well, es I wer sayin, mam wer feedin us brats ontu mush an' milk, wifout the milk, an' es I wer the baby then, she hilt me so es tu see that I got my sheer. Whar thar ain't enuf feed, big childer roots littil childer outen the troff, an' gobbils up thar part. Jis' so the yeath over: bishops eats elders, elders eats common peopil; they eats sich cattil es me, I eats possums, possums eats chickins, chickins swallers wums, an' wums am content tu eat dus, an' the dus am the aind ove hit all. Hit am all es regilur es the souns frum the tribil down tu the bull base ove a fiddil in good tchune, an' I speck hit am right, ur hit wudn't be 'lowed.

" '*The Sheriff!*' his'd mam in a keen tremblin whisper, hit sounded tu me like the skreech ove a hen when she sez 'hawk,' tu her little roun-sturn'd, fuzzy, bead-eyed, stripid-backs.

"I actid jis' adzacly as they dus; I darted on all fours onder mam's petticoatails, an' thar I met, face tu face, the wooden bowl, an' the mush, an' the spoon what she slid onder frum tuther side. I'se mad at mysef yet, fur rite thar I show'd the fust flash ove the nat'ral born durn fool what I now is. I orter et hit all up, in jestis tu my stumick an my growin, while the sheriff wer levyin ontu the bed an' the cheers. Tu this day, ef enbody sez 'sheriff,' I feels skeer, an' ef I hears constabil menshun'd, my laigs goes thru runnin moshuns, even ef I is asleep. Did yu ever watch a dorg dreamin ove rabbit huntin? Thems the moshuns, an' the feelin am the rabbit's.

"Sheriffs am orful 'spectabil peopil; everybody looks up tu em. I never adzacly seed the 'spectabil part mysef. I'se too fear'd ove em, I reckon, tu 'zamin fur hit much. One thing I knows, no country atwix yere an' Tophit kin ever 'lect me tu sell out widders' plunder, ur poor men's co'n, an' the tho'ts ove hit gins me a good feelin; hit sorter flashes thru my heart when I thinks ove hit. I axed a passun onst, what hit cud be, an' he pernounced hit tu be *onregenerit pride,* what I orter squelch in prayer, an' in tendin chuch on colleckshun days. I wer in hopes hit mout be 'ligion, ur sence, a-soakin intu me; hit feels good, enyhow, an' I don't keer ef every suckit rider outen jail knows hit. Sheriffs' shuts allers hes nettil dus ur fleas inside ove em when they lies down tu sleep, an' I'se glad ove hit, fur they'se allers discumfortin me, durn em. I scarcely ever git tu drink a ho'n, ur eat a mess in peace. I'll hurt one sum day, see ef I don't. Show me a sheriff a-steppin softly roun, an' a-sorter sightin at me, an' I'll show yu a far sampil ove the speed ove a express ingine, fired up wif rich, dry, rosiny skeers. They don't ketch me *much,* usin only human laigs es wepuns.

"Ole John Doltin wer a 'spectabil sheriff, monsusly so, an' hed the bes' scent fur poor fugatif devils, an' wimen, I ever seed; he wer sure fire. Well, he toted a warrun fur this yere skinful ove durn'd fool, 'bout that ar misfortnit nigger meetin bisness, ontil he wore hit intu six seperit squar bits, an' hed wore out much shoe leather a-chasin ove me. I'd foun a doggery in full milk, an' hated pow'ful bad tu leave that settilment while hit suck'd free; so I sot intu sorter try an' wean him off frum botherin me so much. I suckseedid so well that he not only quit racin ove me, an' wimen, but he wer tetotaly spiled es a sheriff, an' los' the 'spectabil seckshun ove his karacter. Tu make yu fool fellers onderstan how hit wer done, I mus' interjuice yure minds tu one Wat Mastin, a bullit-headed yung blacksmith.

"Well, las' year—no hit wer the year afore las'—in struttin an' gob-blin time, Wat felt his keepin right warm, so he sot intu bellerin an' pawin up dus in the neighborhood roun the ole widder McKildrin's. The more dus he flung up, the wus he got, ontil at las' he jis cudn't stan the ticklin sensashuns anutner minnit; so he put fur the county court clark's offis, wif his hans sock'd down deep intu his britchis pockets, like he wer fear'd ove pick-pockets, his back roach'd roun, an' a-chompin his teef ontil he splotch'd his whiskers wif foam. Oh! he wer yearnis' hot, an' es restless es a cockroach in a hot skillit."

"What was the matter with this Mr. Mastin? I cannot understand you, Mr. Lovingood; had he hydrophobia?" remarked a man in a square-tail coat, and cloth gaiters, who was obtaining subscribers for some forthcoming Encyclopedia of Useful Knowledge, who had quartered at our camp, uninvited, and really unwanted.

"What du yu mean by high-dry-foby?" and Sut looked puzzled.

"A madness produced by being bit by some rabid animal," explained Squaretail, in a pompous manner.

"Yas, hoss, he hed high-dry-foby *orful,* an' Mary McKildrin, the widder McKildrin's only darter, hed gin him the complaint; I don't know whether she bit 'im ur not; he mout a-cotch hit frum her bref, an' he wer now in the roach back, chompin stage ove the sickness, so he wer arter the clark fur a tickit tu the hospital. Well, the clark sole 'im a piece ove paper, part printin an' part ritin, wif a picter ove two pigs' hearts, what sum boy hed shot a arrer thru, an' lef hit stickin, printed at the top. That paper was a splicin pass—sum calls hit a par ove licins—an' that very nite he tuck Mary, fur better, fur wus, tu hev an' tu hole tu him his heirs, an'—"

"Allow me to interrupt you," said our guest; "you do not quote the marriage ceremony correctly."

"Yu go tu *hell,* mistofer; yu bothers me."

This outrageous rebuff took the stranger all aback, and he sat down.

"Whar wer I? Oh yes, he married Mary tight an' fas', an' nex day he wer abil tu be about. His coat tho', an' his trousis look'd jis' a skrimshun too big, loose like, an' heavy tu tote. I axed him ef he felt soun. He sed yas, but he'd welded a steamboat shaftez the day afore, an' wer sorter tired like. Thar he tole a durn lie, fur he'd been a-ho'nin up dirt mos' ove the day, roun the widder's garden, an' bellerin in the orchard. Mary an' him sot squar intu hous'-keepin, an' 'mung uther things he bot a lot ove *rar ripe garden-seed,* frum a Yankee peddler. Rar ripe co'n, rar ripe peas, rar ripe taters, rar ripe everything, an' the two yung durn'd fools wer dreadfully exercis'd 'bout hit. Wat sed he ment tu git him a rar ripe hammer an' anvil, an' Mary vow'd tu grashus, that she'd hev a rar ripe wheel an' loom, ef money wud git em. Purty soon arter he hed made the garden, he tuck a noshun tu work a spell down tu Ataylanty,

in the railroad shop, es he sed he hed a sorter ailin in his back, an' he
tho't weldin rail car-tire an' ingine axiltrees, wer lighter work nur
sharpinin plows, an' puttin lap-links in trace-chains. So down he went,
an' foun hit agreed wif him, fur he didn't cum back ontil the middil ove
August. The fust thing he seed when he landid intu his cabin-door, wer
a shoebox wif rockers onder hit, an' the nex thing he seed, wer Mary
herself, propped up in bed, an' the nex thing he seed arter that, wer a
par ove littil rat-eyes a-shinin abuv the aind ove the quilt, ontu Mary's
arm, an' the nex an' las' thing he seed wer the two littil rat-eyes afore-
sed, a-turnin intu two hundred thousand big green stars, an' a-swingin
roun an' roun the room, faster an' faster, ontil they mix'd intu one
orful green flash. He drap't intu a limber pile on the floor. The durn'd
fool what hed weldid the steamboat shaftez hed fainted safe an' soun
es a gal skeered at a mad bull. Mary fotch a weak cat-scream, an'
kivered her head, an' sot intu work ontu a whifflin dry cry, while littil
Rat-eyes gin hitssef up tu suckin. Cryin an' suckin bof at onst ain't far;
mus' cum pow'ful strainin on the wet seckshun ove an' 'oman's con-
stitushun; yet hit am ofen dun, an' more too. Ole Missis McKildrin,
what wer a-nussin Mary, jis' got up frum knittin, an' flung a big gourd
ove warter squar intu Wat's face, then she fotch a glass bottil ove swell-
skull whiskey outen the three-cornered cupboard, an' stood furnint
Wat, a-holdin hit in wun han, an' the tin-cup in tuther, waitin fur Wat
tu cum to. She were the piusses lookin ole 'oman jis' then, yu ever seed
outside ove a prayer-meetin. Arter a spell, Wat begun tu move,
twitchin his fingers, an' battin his eyes, sorter 'stonished like. That pius
lookin statue sed tu him:

" 'My son, jis' take a drap ove sperrits, honey. Yu'se very sick,
dumplin, don't take on darlin, ef yu kin help hit, ducky, fur poor
Margarit Jane am mons'ous ailin, an' the leas' nise ur takin on will kill
the poor sufferin dear, an yu'll loose yure tuckil ducky duv ove a sweet
wifey, arter all she's dun gone thru fur yu. My dear son Watty, yu mus'
consider her feelins a littil.' Sez Wat, a-turnin up his eyes at that vartus
ole relick, sorter sick like—

" 'I is a-considerin em a heap, rite now.'

" 'Oh that's right, my good kine child.'

"Oh dam ef ole muther-in-lors can't plaster humbug over a feller, jis'
es saft an' easy es they spreads a camrick hanketcher over a three hour
ole baby's face; yu don't feel hit at all, but hit am thar, a plum inch
thick, an' stickin fas es court-plaster. She raised Wat's head, an' sot the
aidge ove the tin cup agin his lower teef, an' turned up the bottim slow
an' keerful, a-winkin at Mary, hu wer a-peepin over the aidge ove the
coverlid, tu see ef Wat *tuck the perskripshun,* fur a heap ove famerly
cumfort 'pended on that ar ho'n ove sperrits. *Wun* ho'n allers saftens a
man, the yeath over. Wat keep a-battin his eyes, wus nur a owl in day-

light; at las' he raised hissef ontu wun elbow, an' rested his head in that han, sorter weak like. Sez he, mons'ous trimblin an' slow: 'Aprile—May —June—July—an' mos'—haf—ove—August,' a-countin the munths ontu the fingers ove tuther han, wif the thumb, a-shakin over his head, an' lookin at his spread fingers like they warn't his'n, ur they wer nastied wif sumfin. Then he counted em agin, slower, Aprile—May—June— July—an', mos' haf ove August, an' he run his thumb atwixt his fingers, es meanin mos' haf ove August, an' look'd at the pint ove hit, like hit mout be a snake's head. He raised his eyes tu the widder's face, who wer standin jis' es steady es a hitchin pos', an' still a-warin that pius spression ontu her pussonal feturs, an' a flood ove saft luv fur Wat, a-shinin strait frum her eyes intu his'n. Sez he, 'That jis' makes four months, an' mos' a half, don't hit, Missis McKildrin?' She never sed one word. Wat reached fur the hath, an' got a dead fire-coal; then he made a mark clean acrost a floorplank. Sez he, 'Aprile,' a-holdin down the coal ontu the aind ove the mark, like he wer fear'd hit mout blow away afore he got hit christened Aprile. Sez he, 'May'—an' he marked across the board agin; then he counted the marks, one, two, a-dottin at em wif the coal. 'June,' an' he marked agin, one, two, three; counted wif the pint ove the coal. He scratched his head wif the littil finger ove the han holdin the charcoal, an' he drawed hit slowly acrost the board agin, peepin onder his wrist tu see when hit reached the crack, an' sez he 'July,' es he lifted the coal; 'one, two, three, four,' countin frum lef tu right, an' then frum right tu lef. 'That haint but four, no way I kin fix hit. Ole Pike hissef cudn't make hit five, ef he wer tu sifer ontu hit ontil his laigs turned intu figger eights.' Then he made a mark, haf acrost a plank, spit on his finger, an' rubbed off a haf inch ove the aind, an' sez he, 'Mos' haf ove August.' He looked up at the widder, an' thar she wer, same es ever, still a-holdin the flask agin her bussum, an' sez he 'Four months, an' mos' a haf. *Haint enuf, is hit mammy?* hits jis' 'bout (lackin a littil) *haf enuf*, haint hit, mammy?'

"Missis McKildrin shuck her head sorter onsartin like, an' sez she, 'Take a drap more sperrits, Watty, my dear pet; dus yu mine buyin that ar rar ripe seed, frum the peddler?' Wat nodded his head, an' looked 'what ove hit,' but didn't say hit.

" 'This is what cums ove hit, an' four months an' a haf am rar ripe time fur babys, adzackly. Tu be sure, hit lacks a day ur two, but Margarit Jane wer allers a pow'ful interprizin gal, an' a yearly rizer.' Sez Wat,

" 'How about the 'taters?'

" 'Oh, *we* et 'taters es big es goose aigs, afore ole Missis Collinze's blossomed.'

" 'How 'bout co'n?'

" 'Oh we shaved down roasin years afore hern tassel'd—'

" 'An' peas?'

" 'Yes son, we hed gobs an' lots in three weeks. Everything cums in adzackly half the time hit takes the ole sort, an' yu *knows*, my darlin son, yu planted hit waseful. I tho't then yu'd rar ripe everything on the place. Yu planted *often,* too, didn't yu luv? fur fear hit wudn't cum up.'

" 'Ye-ye-s-s he—he did,' sed Mary a-cryin. Wat studied pow'ful deep a spell, an' the widder jis' waited. Widders allers wait, an' allers win. At las, sez he, 'Mammy.' She looked at Mary, an' winked these yere words at her, es plain es she cud a-talked em. 'Yu hearn him call me *mammy twiste*. I'se *got him* now. His back-bone's a-limberin fas', he'll own the baby yet, see ef he don't. Jis' hole still my darter, an' let yer mammy knead this dough, then yu may bake hit es brown es yu please.'

" 'Mammy, when I married on the fust day ove Aprile'—The widder look'd oneasy; she tho't he mout be a-cupplin that day, his weddin, an' the idear, dam fool, tugether. But he warn't, fur he sed 'That day I gin ole man Collins my note ove han fur a hundred dullars, jew in one year arter date, the balluns on this lan. Dus yu think that ar seed will change the *time* eny, ur will hit alter the *amount?*' An' Wat looked at her powerful ankshus. She raised the whisky bottil way abuv her head, wif her thumb on the mouf, an' fotch the bottim down ontu her han, spat. Sez she, 'Watty, my dear b'lovid son, pripar tu pay *two* hundred dullars 'bout the fust ove October, fur hit'll be jew jis' then, *es* sure es that littil black-eyed angel in the bed thar, am yer darter.'

"Wat drap't his head, an' sed, *'Then hits a dam sure thing.'* Rite yere, the baby fotch a rattlin loud squall, (I speck Mary wer sorter figetty jis' then, an' hurt hit.) 'Yas,' sez Wat, a-wallin a red eye to'ards the bed; 'my littil she—what wer hit yu called her name, mammy?' 'I called her a sweet littil angel, an' she is wun, es sure es yu're her daddy, my b'loved son.' 'Well,' sez Wat, 'my littil sweet, patent rar ripe she angel, ef yu lives tu marryin time, yu'll 'stonish sum man body outen his shut, ef yu don't rar ripe lose hits vartu arter the fust plantin, that's all.' He rared up on aind, wif his mouf pouch'd out. He had a pow'ful forrid, fur-reachin, bread funnel, enyhow—cud a-bit the aigs outen a catfish, in two-foot warter, wifout wettin his eyebrows. 'Dod durn rar ripe seed, an' rar ripe pedlers, an' rar ripe notes tu the hottes' corner ove—'

" 'Stop Watty, *darlin,* don't swar; 'member yu belongs tu meetin.'

" 'My blacksmith's fire,' ainded Wat, an' he studied a long spell; sez he,

" 'Did you save eny ove that infunnel doubil-trigger seed?' 'Yas,' sez the widder, 'thar in that bag by the cupboard.' Wat got up ofen the floor, tuck a countin sorter look at the charcoal marks, an' reached down the bag; he went tu the door an' called 'Suke, muley! Suke, Suke, cow, chick, chick, chicky chick.' 'What's yu gwine tu du now, my dear son?' sed Missis McKildrin. 'I'se jis' gwine tu feed this actif *smart* truck tu the cow, an' the hens, that's what I'se gwine tu du. Ole muley haint hed a calf in two years, an' I'll eat sum rar ripe aigs.' Mary now venter'd tu speak: 'Husban, I ain't sure hit'll work on hens; cum an' kiss me my luv.' 'I haint sure hit'll work on hens, either,' sed Wat. 'They's powerful onsartin in thar ways, well es wimen,' an' he flung out a hanful spiteful like. 'Takin the rar ripe invenshun all tugether, frum 'taters an' peas tu notes ove han, an' childer, I can't say I likes hit much,' an' he flung out anuther hanful. 'Yer mam hed thuteen the ole way, an' ef this truck stays 'bout the hous', yu'se good fur twenty-six, maybe thuty, fur yu'se a pow'ful interprizin gal, yer mam sez,' an' he flung out anuther hanful, overhandid, es hard es ef he wer flingin rocks at a stealin sow. 'Make yere mine easy,' sed the widder; 'hit never works on married folks only the fust time.' 'Say them words agin,' sed Wat, 'I'se glad tu hear em. Is hit the same way wif notes ove han?' 'I speck hit am,' answer'd the widder, wif jis' a taste ove strong vinegar in the words, es she sot the flask in the cupboard wif a push. . . .

Sidney Lanier

Sidney Lanier (1842–81) is best known as the leading poet of the South in the years just after the Civil War. Though his "The Marshes of Glynn" can still evoke the mysterious beauty of the marshland near Brunswick, Georgia, and his poems on contemporary themes—for example, "Corn" and "The Symphony"—recall the issues of agrarianism versus industrialization, most of Lanier's verse is too "poetical" for modern taste.

Lanier's one novel, Tiger-Lilies (1867), deserves to be better remembered than it is. In part autobiographical, it reflects the ideas and aspirations of a romantic young Southerner, in love with music (Lanier was a flutist of distinction), transcendental Nature, and the writings of Carlyle, Richter, and Novalis. But the second book of the novel takes some of the characters into the Civil War and in this section one finds several admirably realistic chapters, including the one printed here describing life in a Northern prison camp.

Lanier is writing out of his own experience. After the blockade-runner Lucy, to which Lanier had been assigned in 1864, was captured in the *Gulf Stream by the Federal cruiser* Santiago-de-Cuba, *Lanier knew the inside of several prisons, first at Fortress Monroe, then at Camp Hamilton, and for three months at Point Lookout, Maryland. The prison was badly overcrowded and diarrhea, dysentery, typhoid fever, and scurvy were prevalent. Lanier had never been robust, and at Point Lookout he contracted the lung trouble which developed into tuberculosis, the disease he fought the rest of his life. Lanier's fictionalized account of his prison experiences is lightened by the humor that men are capable of under such conditions, but the horrors are evident enough.*

The chapter is reprinted from Tiger-Lilies (*New York: Hurd & Houghton; 1867*), *pp. 198–206.*

❁

A SOLDIER-POET IN A NORTHERN PRISON

To go into a prison of war is in all respects to be born over.

For, of the men in all the prisons of the late war, it might be said, as of births in the ordinary world,—they came in and went out naked. Into the prison at Point Lookout, Maryland, were born, at a certain time, of poor and probably honest parents, twelve thousand grown men. Their inheritance with which they had to begin life *de novo* was the capability of body or soul wherewith each happened to be endowed at the moment of this second birth. And so, in this far little world, which was as much separated from the outer world as if it had been in the outer confines of space, it was striking to see how society immediately resolved itself into those three estates which invariably constitute it elsewhere.

For there were here, first, the aristocrats, who lived well but did not labor; second, the artisans, who lived well by laboring; third, the drones, who starved by not laboring. Moreover one could find here all the subdivisions of these great classes which occur in the regions of crowded civilization. For instance, of the aristocrats, there were the true-gentlemanly sort, the insulting-obtrusive sort, the philanthropic sort, the fast sort; of the artisans, there were the sober-citizenly sort, the mind-your-own-business-and I-mine sort, the gloomy brooding-over-oppression sort, the cheerful workers, the geniuses, together with those whose labor was spiritual, such as the teachers of French, and arithmetic, and music, including those who lived by their wits in the bad sense; and of the drones, the kind who swear that the world owes them a living, but who are too lazy to collect the debt; the sentimental-vulgar kind, whose claims are based upon a well-turned leg or a heavy

669

moustache, and are consequently not appreciated by a practical world; the self-deprecatory sort, who swear that Nature has been unkind in endowing them, and who then *must* starve for consistency's sake or forswear themselves; and lastly, the large class of out-and-out unmitagated drones, who, some say, serve the mere purpose of inanimate clay chinked into the cracks of this great log-cabin which we all inhabit, and who, poor men! must endure much bad weather on the wrong side of the house.

Was there then no difference between life in the prison and life in the world?

It is to be answered,—none, generically; the difference was one of degree merely.

For instance, if our every-day world had a catechism, its first question, What is the chief end of man? might be answered, "The chief end of man is either end of Pennsylvania Avenue." Whereas this question in the prison-world catechism would be answered, "The chief end of man is the West End";—which at Point Lookout was (for the pleasure of the paradox-loving) at the eastern extremity of the Peninsula.

In the one case the aim was to be President or Congressman, with honor and luxury; in the other, the aim was to get into a cracker-box cabin, where rain and vermin were not free of the house, as they were in the tents in which ten out of the twelve thousand resided.

So, the stature of the men and the burning of their passions remained the same inside the prison as out of it, only the objects of these passions and exertions were immeasurably diminished in number and dignity. To Philip Sterling this was the terrible feature in the prison-changed behavior of his old army friends. They did not crowd to shake joyful hands with him and hear the news from outside, but met him with smiles that had in them a sort of mournful greasiness, as if to say: Ah, old boy, mighty poor eating in here! Their handshakes were not vigorous, their souls did not run down and meet Philip's at the finger-tips. How could they? These same souls were too busy in devising ways and means to quiet the stomachs and intestines,—a set of dependents who show their born inferiority to the soul by always crying out to it when they are in distress, and by always endeavoring to dethrone it when they have waxed fat on its labor.

Some such thoughts crossed Philip's mind, as on the loveliest morning of May, a few days after his night in the cell at Fortress Monroe, he found himself inside the great gate of the prison at Point Lookout. He had recognized and spoken to some friends as they passed by, but had not yet left the rank in which his squad of seventy fellow-captives had been drawn up after being marched into the prison.

A Federal sergeant told them off into smaller squads. Philip stood in the last.

670

—"Four, five, six, seven, eight," finished the sergeant. "Plenty o' room in eleventh division. Corporal, Eleventh!"

"Here, sir."

"Here's your squad. March 'em down."

"Forward," said the corporal, placing himself with the front file.

Passing a row of small A tents presently, the corporal looked at his book.

"Tent fifteen; think there's four men in it. Let's see." He thrust his head into the low opening. "How many in here?"

" 'Bout a million, countin' lice and all!" responded a voice, whose tone blent in itself sorrow, anger, hunger, and the sardonic fearlessness of desperation.

"Guess *they* want another man in, if *you* don't," said the corporal, with a pleasant smile. "You, Number Four, what's your name?"

"Philip Sterling."

"Bunk here. Rest, forward,"—and the corporal passed on with his squad, writing, as he went, the name in his book.

A long, cadaverous man sat outside the door of Philip's tent, sunning himself. He was bare to the middle, but held a ragged shirt on his knees, toward which he occasionally made gestures very like those of a compositor setting type.

" 'Fords me a leetle amusement," said he, looking up with a sickly smile toward Philip. "Jest gittin' well o' the feever: cain't git about much yet!"

Sick at heart, Sterling made no reply, but entered the tent. Just inside the entrance stood a low bench, which held a rat-tail file, a beef-bone, a half-dozen gutta-percha buttons, a piece of iron barrel hoop, two oyster shells, and a pocket-knife. Cross-legged on the ground before it, sat a huge individual, who was engaged in polishing, with a rag and the grease of bacon, a gutta-percha ring which he held with difficulty on the tip of his little finger.

For this man's clothes, those three thieves, grease, dirt, and smoke, had drawn lots; but not content with the allotment, all three were evidently contending which should have the whole suit. It appeared likely that dirt would be the happy theif.

"Wash 'em!" said this man one day when the Federal corporal had the impudence to refer to the sacred soil on his clothes—"wash 'em? corp'ral! I'm bound to say 'at you're a dam fool! That mud's what holds 'em together; sticks 'em fast,—like! Ef you was to put them clo's in water they'd go to nothin' jest like a piece o' salt!"

As inside of these clay-clothes a stalwart frame of a man lived and worked, so, inside this stalwart clay-frame lived and worked a fearless soul, which had met death and laughed at it, from the Seven-days to Gettysburg, but which was now engaged in superintending a small manufactory of bone trinkets and gutta-percha rings, the sale of which brought wherewithal to eke out the meagre sustenance of the prison ration.

Sterling threw down his blanket.

"This corner occupied?"

"Wa'al—yes, a leetle, you may say. I should judge thar was about some sebben or eight thousand livin' thar now. You needn't mind *them* tho'; they won't keer ef you sleep thar," observed the huge ringmaker.

"They are very kind, indeed."

"Sorry I cain't offer you a cheer; jest now loaned out all the cheers."

Sterling squatted tailor-wise upon his blanket, placed his chin in his hand, and prepared to go into a terrible sentimental review of the utter loneliness of his position. Suddenly, however, the ludicrous phase of the situation came over him. He smiled, then chuckled, and at last burst into a long, uproarious laugh.

The eye of the ring maker twinkled. His lip quivered. He thrust his head through the opening of the tent and ejected from his mouth a surprising quantity of tobacco-juice. It was his manner of laughing. Beyond this he made no sign.

"Hello, Sterling, where are you?" shouted a cheery voice outside.

Philip showed a merry face through the door, and recognized an old "Ours."

"By the poker, but you are merry for a man that's just come to Point Lookout! As a general thing we may say here,

'My cue is villainous melancholy.'

And of all men in the world *you*, who were always a sort of melancholy Jacques! Have you, like him, heard a fool moralling on the times?" he continued, shaking Philip's hand, and directing their walk toward the head of the division.

"Aye, that have I," replied Sterling.

"We must get you out o' that hole in the 11th div. some way. Let's see; I think I saw an advertisement yesterday on the bulletin-board yonder, of a fellow in the 3d that wanted to sell out. Let's walk up and see."

The bulletin-board was surrounded by a thick crowd, to whom a lucky man on the inside was reading, in a loud voice, a long list of names from a paper tacked to the plank.

"Letters from Dixie," said Sterling's friend.

They placed themselves on the outer edge of the circle, and gradually moved in toward the centre.

"Do you notice a man over on the other side of the crowd yonder, pushing and struggling this way, with his gaze fixed on you?" said Sterling, to his friend. "His eye has a snaky glare in it. He hasn't lost sight of you for ten minutes. Got something against you, hasn't he?"

"He is my Nemesis. Every morning at nine o'clock, I come to the bulletin-board. Every morning at nine o'clock he meets me here, and demands of me a"—

"What?"

"A chew of tobacco! He commenced it two months ago. He has not missed a morning since. One day I attempted to dodge him. I sought cover behind every tent successively in the encampment. My meanderings must have been between five and ten miles in length. I thought I had succeeded. Breathless, but with a proud smile of triumph on my countenance, I walked slowly down the street, when he emerged dignifiedly from behind the next tent, and with disdainful composure inquired if I had ary chaw of terbacker about my clo'es. Since then I have resigned myself. He is a fate!"

"The Fates, then, have learned to chew tobacco, also! *eheu!* what would Pius Æneas have said to see them using spittoons in Hades?"

They were now at the board. It was covered with a thousand strips of paper, bearing in all manner of chirographies a thousand items of information. Mr. A. had changed his residence from No. 3, 4th division, to no. 7, 10th division; Mr. B. had a corner to let in his shop, "splendid stand for the unwanted bean-soup trade"; J. Shankins had a blanket "which he would swop it fur a par of britches, pleese caul at," &c.; the negro minstrels, in big red letters, announced "an entire change of programme, at 5 o'clock, G. M. Admission ten cents. No Confederate money received at the door"; L. Crabbe advertised to meet the eye of his brother, M. Crabbe, who, if in the prison, would call at, &c.; Jaines Haxley inquired "ef any gentleman in the 64th regiment seed his son with his own eyes killed at the Sharpsburg fite"; a facetious individual, blushing to reveal his name, and therefore writing over Anonymous, perpetrated the enormous joke of "Help wanted to assist me in eating my rations. None need apply except with the most unexceptionable reference"; to which was appended the replies of a hundred different applicants for the situation; a sardonic gentleman inquired "if Dixie and the Yanks was still a-havin' high words. Let dogs delight," &c., &c.; J. Shelpole had drawd a par of shues, but one of thum was number six an' wun was No. 10, and "wished to know ef enny gentleman had a shue, size number 10, pleese call at," &c., &c.

"Here it is at last!" said Sterling. The legend ran, *"Fur* privit reesons," (—"to wit," interposed Phil's companion, "a plug of tobacco, or the equivalent thereof in bread, bean-soup, cash, or other commodities,") "the undersined will swop places, fur a little boot, with eny gentleman in the 11th division. Pleese call at, &c., 3d division. Call soon and git a bargin.

"Sined   J. THREEPITS."

"He's your man, Phil. Let's go right up and see him."

"But how do you do it? when my corporal calls the roll"—

"All you've got to do is to answer to the euphonious appelation of Threepits, while Mr. T. will respond to the call for Sterling. The corporal won't know the difference. I can't deny but Mr. Threepits, in the matter of names, will slightly get the advantage in the swap. But it's a very good thing here to have two names; inasmuch as you stand two chances, when the exchange-lists are read out, to go back to Dixie. You must take care, however, that both of you don't answer to the same name,—a circumstance which has several times occurred, and caused no little pleasure to the sharp-witted authorities, as affording a pretext to remand the disappointed prisoner back to his hole."

Joel Chandler Harris

When he was a boy of thirteen, Joel Chandler Harris went to live on the plantation of Joseph Addison Turner, a few miles distant from Eatonton, Georgia, where Harris was born in 1848. At Turnwold he worked on the plantation newspaper, but he spent his spare time listening to the Negro folk tales told him by two of Turner's slaves, Old Harbert and Uncle George Terrell.

In 1866 Turner's The Countryman, *reputed to have been the only newspaper ever published on a plantation, came to an end. For several years thereafter Harris held various newspaper jobs, in Macon, in New Orleans, and in Savannah. In 1876 he moved to Atlanta, where he soon became one of the leading writers on the* Constitution, *which Evan P. Howell and Henry W. Grady were bringing to the forefront of American newspapers. From 1886 until his retirement in 1906, Harris was the* Constitution's *chief editorial writer.*

Harris also contributed to the paper sketches, stories, poems, news notes, and commentary. By 1878 he was using Uncle Remus as one of the masks through which he might speak his mind. But the Uncle Remus of the folk tales evolved slowly. Late in 1877 Harris had read an article on "Folk-lore of Southern Negroes" in Lippincott's *Magazine. In reviewing this article for the* Constitution *Harris commented on the author's ignorance of the derivation of the word "Buh." "The real Southern negro," wrote Harris, "pronounces the word as though it were written 'brer,' and he confines its use to the animals themselves. . . . It is unquestionably a contraction of the word, 'brother.' "*

But the Lippincott *article had given Harris his cue. He tried his hand at setting down, in Negro dialect of course, the tales with which Turner's slaves had entertained him years before. The first Uncle Remus folk tale—"The Story of Mr. Rabbit and Mr. Fox"—appeared in the* Constitution *on July 20, 1879. The famous Tar Baby story was the second in the series that Harris labeled "Uncle Remus Folklore." Others followed rapidly, and in the next year he had accumulated enough to make the first of the Uncle Remus books—Uncle Remus, His Songs and His Sayings. Nine more Uncle Remus collections were to follow.*

At the start Harris relied on his memory for his Uncle Remus lore. When that well ran dry, he persuaded Negroes to tell him more folk tales. He declared that the reluctance he sometimes encountered when he asked for stories disappeared when he led off by telling an Uncle Remus tale himself.

The folklorists were immediately excited by Harris's animal tales, and for a time he was proudly interested in their speculations about the possible African origins of some of his stories and the European and Oriental parallels that could be pointed out in others. He insisted that no matter what analogues the folklorists might find, they could rely on the genuineness of the Uncle Remus stories. In his words: "Not one of them is cooked, and not one nor any part of one is an invention of mine."

Harris was shrewd enough to realize that behind the tricks of Brer Rabbit and the defeats of Brer Fox were concealed the Negro's desire to triumph over the white man—in fiction at least. But he would certainly have been shocked at recent speculations (Commentary, *July 1949) about the particular ways in which the Negro animus against the white man is projected through the stories that Harris—in this view—so innocently took down as amanuensis.*

The story that follows is taken from Uncle Remus: His Songs and Sayings *(New York: D. Appleton & Co.; 1895).*

MR. RABBIT NIBBLES UP THE BUTTER

"De animils en de creeturs," said Uncle Remus, shaking his coffee around in the bottom of his tin-cup, in order to gather up all the sugar, "dey kep' on gittin' mo' en mo' familious wid wunner nudder, twel bimeby, 'twan't long 'fo' Brer Rabbit, en Brer Fox, en Brer Possum

675

got ter sorter bunchin' der perwishuns tergedder in de same shanty. Atter w'ile de roof sorter 'gun ter leak, en one day Brer Rabbit, en Brer Fox, en Brer Possum, 'semble fer ter see ef dey can't kinder patch her up. Dey had a big day's work in front un um, en dey fotch der dinner wid um. Dey lump de vittles up in one pile, en de butter w'at Brer Fox brung, dey goes en puts in de spring-'ouse fer ter keep cool, en den dey went ter wuk, en 'twan't long 'fo' Brer Rabbit stummuck 'gun ter sorter growl en pester 'im. Dat butter er Brer Fox sot heavy on his mine, en his mouf water eve'y time he 'member 'bout it. Present'y he say ter hisse'f dat he bleedzd ter have a nip at dat butter, en den he lay his plans, he did. Fus' news you know, w'ile dey wuz all wukkin' 'long, Brer Rabbit raise his head quick en fling his years forrerd en holler out:

" 'Here I is. W'at you want wid me?' en off he put like sump'n wuz atter 'im.

"He sallied 'roun', ole Brer Rabbit did, en atter he make sho dat nobody ain't foller'n un 'im, inter de spring-'ouse he bounces, en dar he stays twel he git a bait er butter. Den he santer on back en go to wuk.

" 'Whar you bin?' sez Brer Fox, sezee.

" 'I hear my chilluns callin' me,' sez Brer Rabbit, sezee, 'en I hatter go see w'at dey want. My ole 'oman done gone en tuck mighty sick,' sezee.

"Dey wuk on twel bimeby de butter tas'e so good dat ole Brer Rabbit want some mo'. Den he raise up his head, he did, en holler out:

" 'Heyo! Hole on! I'm a comin'! en off he put.

"Dis time he stay right smart w'ile, en w'en he git back Brer Fox ax him whar he bin.

" 'I been ter see my ole 'oman, en she's a sinkin',' sezee.

"Dreckly Brer Rabbit hear um callin' 'im ag'in en off he goes en dis time, bless yo' soul, he gits de butter out so clean dat he kin see hisse'f in de bottom er de bucket. He scrape it clean en lick it dry, en den he go back ter wuk lookin' mo' samer dan a nigger w'at de patter-rollers bin had holt un.

" 'How's yo' ole 'oman dis time?' sez Brer Fox, sezee.

" 'I'm oblije ter you, Brer Fox,' sez Brer Rabbit, sezee, 'but I'm fear'd she's done gone by now,' en dat sorter make Brer Fox en Brer Possum feel in moanin' wid Brer Rabbit.

"Bimeby, w'en dinner-time come, dey all got out der vittles, but Brer Rabbit keep on lookin' lonesome, en Brer Fox en Brer Possum dey sorter rustle roun' fer ter see ef dey can't make Brer Rabbit feel sorter splimmy."

"What is that, Uncle Remus?" asked the little boy.

"Sorter splimmy-splammy, honey—sorter like he in a crowd—sorter like his ole 'oman aint dead ez she mout be. You know how fokes duz w'en dey gits whar people's a moanin'."

The little boy didn't know, fortunately for him, and Uncle Remus went on:

"Brer Fox en Brer Possum rustle roun', dey did, gittin out de vittles, en bimeby Brer Fox, he say, sezee:

" 'Brer Possum, you run down ter de spring en fetch de butter, en I'll sail 'roun' yer en set de table,' sezee.

"Brer Possum, he lope off atter de butter, en dreckly here he come lopin' back wid his years a trimblin' en his tongue a hangin' out. Brer Fox, he holler out:

" 'W'at de matter now, Brer Possum?' sezee.

" 'Yo all better run yer, fokes,' sez Brer Possum, sezee. 'De las' drap er dat butter done gone!'

" 'Whar she gone?' sez Brer Fox, sezee.

" 'Look like she dry up,' sez Brer Possum, sezee.

"Den Brer Rabbit, he look sorter sollum, he did, en he up'n say, sezee:

" 'I speck dat butter melt in somebody mouf,' sezee.

"Den dey went down ter de spring wid Brer Possum, en sho nuff de butter done gone. W'iles dey wuz sputin' over der wunderment, Brer Rabbit say he see tracks all 'roun' dar, en he p'int out dat ef dey'll all go ter sleep, he kin ketch de chap w'at stole de butter. Den dey all lie down en Brer Fox en Brer Possum dey soon drapt off ter sleep, but Brer Rabbit he stay 'wake, en w'en de time come he raise up easy en smear Brer Possum mouf wid de butter on his paws, en den he run off en nibble up de bes' er de dinner w'at dey lef' layin' out, en den he come back en wake up Brer Fox, en show 'im de butter on Brer Possum mouf. Den dey wake up Brer Possum, en tell 'im 'bout it, but c'ose Brer Possum 'ny it ter de las'. Brer Fox, dough, he's a kinder lawyer, en he argafy dis way—dat Brer Possum wuz de fus one at de butter, en de fus one fer ter miss it, en mo'n dat, der hang de signs on his mouf. Brer Possum see dat dey got 'im jammed up in a cornder, en den he up en say dat de way fer ter ketch de man w'at stole de butter is ter b'il' a big bresh-heap en set her afier, en all han's try ter jump over, en de one w'at fall in, den he de chap w'at stole de butter. Brer Rabbit en Brer Fox dey bofe 'gree, dey did, en dey whirl in en b'il' de bresh-heap, en dey b'il' her high en dey b'il' her wide, en den dey totch her off. W'en she got ter blazin' up good, Brer Rabbit, he tuck de fus turn. He sorter step back, en look 'roun' en giggle, en over he went mo' samer dan a bird flyin'. Den come Brer Fox. He got back little fudder, en spit on his han's, en lit out en made de jump, en he come so nigh gittin' in dat de een' er his tail kotch afier. Ain't you never see no fox,

677

honey?" inquired Uncle Remus, in a tone that implied both concilia-
tion and information.

The little boy thought probably he had, but he wouldn't commit
himself.

"Well, den," continued the old man, "nex' time you see one un um,
you look right close en see ef de een' er his tail ain't w'ite. Hit's des like
I tell you. Dey b'ars de skyar er dat bresh-heap down ter dis day. Dey
er marked—dat's w'at dey is—dey er marked."

"And what about Brother Possum?" asked the little boy.

"Ole Brer Possum, he tuck a runnin' start he did, en he come lum-
berin' 'long, en he lit—kerblam!—right in de middle er de fier, en dat
wuz de las' er ole Brer Possum."

"But, Uncle Remus, Brother Possum didn't steal the butter after all,"
said the little boy, who was not at all satisfied with such summary injustice.

"Dat w'at make I say w'at I duz, honey. In dis worril, lots er fokes
is gotter suffer fer udder fokes sins. Look like hit's mighty onwrong;
but hit's des dat away. Tribbalashun seem like she's a waitin' roun' de
cornder fer ter ketch one en all un us, honey."

George Washington Cable

It is one of the ironies of American literary history that George Wash-
ington Cable was fated to introduce the Creoles of New Orleans to
American readers. Though he was born in New Orleans in 1844, had
begun to earn his living there at the age of fourteen, and had served in
the Fourth Mississippi Cavalry during the Civil War, he was an un-
yielding Puritan in the gayest of American cities. As Edward Larocque
Tinker says of the New Orleans of Cable's boyhood: "The city then
was as unbridled a port as any on the continent. Bull-baiting, cock-
fighting, and gambling in every form were rampant. Slavery was con-
sidered sanctioned by Holy Writ, and pretty, cream-colored quad-
roons, tricked out in ribbons, were exposed for sale as 'fancy girls' in
the windows of slave marts. . . . The Creoles, enriched by slave labor
and nourished by French culture, had developed a life of great luxury,
their houses filled with tapestries and fine French furniture. Pride of

possession added to pride of race had made of them a haugthy, high-strung tribe." [1]

In spite of his strict bringing-up by a mother who was determined that the boy should not be as feckless as his father, young Cable was fascinated by this life which he could not admire. By *1873*, when his first story, " *'Sieur George,"* was published, he had listened to many tales about the past of New Orleans and had uncovered many others while studying the history of the city.

Cable learned something about writing during a brief experience as a columnist for the New Orleans Picayune (*1870–1*). His newspaper career ended abruptly when he resigned on being asked to review a theatrical performance. Meanwhile he had begun writing sketches and tales of Creole life. These he showed to Edward King, who was in New Orleans collecting material for his series of articles on "The Great South." King sent some of the stories to his editor, Dr. J. G. Holland of Scribner's Monthly. In a short time Cable's fame was made by these sketches of Creole life, which were eagerly accepted by several Northern magazines. In *1879* seven of them were collected and published by Scribner's as Old Creole Days.

Northern readers took to these stories of proud, quixotic Creoles, finding the settings and characters novel and charming. But the Creoles themselves were outraged. Cable told his readers about the quadroon balls and implied that Creole family lines were occasionally sullied by miscegenation. He also represented the Creole's attempts to speak English in such a way that it could be supposed that he was making fun of their mispronunciations and mistranslations of idiom. When his first novel, The Grandissimes, appeared in *1880*, he made matters worse by building his plot around the relations between a white family and its illegitimate colored relatives.

Actually Cable was by nature more of a champion of causes than he was a creative writer. Propaganda gained over art in his later novels. The local fury against him mounted higher when three of his polemical essays were collected into a volume, The Silent South, in *1885* (see p. *386*). The following year he removed to Northampton, Massachusetts, where he lived until his death, in *1925*.

In spite of the resentment that Cable stirred up in New Orleans, his stories are notable for two achievements: he informed his readers about a little-known subculture of their country and he was the first American writer to treat the Negroes with the understanding necessary to make them real persons instead of stereotypes.

[1] Edward Larocque Tinker: "Cable and the Creoles," *American Literature*, January 1934, p. 313.

'SIEUR GEORGE

IN the heart of New Orleans stands a large four-story brick building, that has so stood for about three-quarters of a century. Its rooms are rented to a class of persons occupying them simply for lack of activity to find better and cheaper quarters elsewhere. With its gray stucco peeling off in broad patches, it has a solemn look of gentility in rags, and stands, or, as it were, hangs, about the corner of two ancient streets, like a faded fop who pretends to be looking for employment.

Under its main archway is a dingy apothecary-shop. On one street is the bazaar of a *modiste en robes et chapeaux* and other humble shops; on the other, the immense batten doors with gratings over the lintels, barred and bolted with masses of cobwebbed iron, like the door of a donjon, are overhung by a creaking sign (left by the sheriff), on which is faintly discernible the mention of wines and liquors. A peep through one of the shops reveals a square court within, hung with many lines of wet clothes, its sides hugged by rotten staircases that seem vainly trying to clamber out of the rubbish.

The neighborhood is one long since given up to fifth-rate shops, whose masters and mistresses display such enticing mottoes as "*Au gagne petit!*" Innumerable children swarm about, and, by some charm of the place, are not run over, but obstruct the sidewalks playing their clamorous games.

The building is a thing of many windows, where passably good-looking women appear and disappear, clad in cotton gowns, watering little outside shelves of flowers and cacti, or hanging canaries' cages. Their husbands are keepers in wine-warehouses, rent-collectors for the agents of old Frenchmen who have been laid up to dry in Paris, custom-house supernumeraries and court-clerks' deputies (for your second-rate Creole is a great seeker for little offices). A decaying cornice hangs over, dropping bits of mortar on passers below, like a boy at a boarding-house.

The landlord is one Kookoo, an ancient Creole of doubtful purity of blood, who in his landlordly old age takes all suggestions of repairs as personal insults. He was but a stripling when his father left him this inheritance, and has grown old and wrinkled and brown, a sort of periodically animate mummy, in the business. He smokes cascarilla, wears velveteen, and is as punctual as an executioner.

To Kookoo's venerable property a certain old man used for many years to come every evening, stumbling through the groups of prat-tling children who frolicked about in the early moonlight—whose name no one knew, but whom all the neighbors designated by the title of 'Sieur George. It was his wont to be seen taking a straight—too straight—course toward his home, never careening to right or left, but

680

now forcing himself slowly forward, as though there were a high gale in front, and now scudding briskly ahead at a ridiculous little dog-trot, as if there were a tornado behind. He would go up the main staircase very carefully, sometimes stopping half-way up for thirty or forty minutes' doze, but getting to the landing eventually, and tramping into his room in the second story, with no little elation to find it still there. Were it not for these slight symptoms of potations, he was such a one as you would pick out of a thousand for a miser. A year or two ago he suddenly disappeared.

A great many years ago, when the old house was still new, a young man with no baggage save a small hair-trunk, came and took the room I have mentioned and another adjoining. He supposed he might stay fifty days—and he staid fifty years and over. This was a very fashionable neighborhood, and he kept the rooms on that account month after month.

But when he had been here about a year something happened to him, so it was rumored, that greatly changed the tenor of his life; and from that time on there began to appear in him and to accumulate upon each other in a manner which became the profound study of Kookoo, the symptoms of a decay, whose cause baffled the landlord's limited powers of conjecture for well-nigh half a century. Hints of a duel, of a reason warped, of disinheritance, and many other unauthorized rumors, fluttered up and floated off, while he became recluse, and, some say, began incidentally to betray the unmanly habit which we have already noticed. His neighbors would have continued neighborly had he allowed them, but he never let himself be understood, and *les Américains* are very droll anyhow; so, as they could do nothing else, they cut him.

So exclusive he became that (though it may have been for economy) he never admitted even a housemaid, but kept his apartments himself. Only the merry serenaders, who in those times used to sing under the balconies, would now and then give him a crumb of their feast for pure fun's sake; and after a while, because they could not find out his full name, called him, at hazard, George—but always prefixing Monsieur. Afterward, when he began to be careless in his dress, and the fashion of serenading had passed away, the commoner people dared to shorten the title to " 'Sieur George."

Many seasons came and went. The city changed like a growing boy; gentility and fashion went uptown, but 'Sieur George still retained his rooms. Every one knew him slightly, and bowed, but no one seemed to know him well, unless it were a brace or so of those convivial fellows in regulation-blue at little Fort St. Charles. He often came home late, with one of these on either arm, all singing different tunes and stopping at every twenty steps to tell secrets. But by and by the fort was demolished, church and government property melted down under the warm demand for building-lots, the city spread like a ringworm,—and one day 'Sieur George steps out of the old house in full regimentals!

The Creole neighbors rush bareheaded into the middle of the street, as though there were an earthquake or a chimney on fire. What to do or say or think they do not know; they are at their wits' ends, therefore well-nigh happy. However, there is a German blacksmith's shop near by, and they watch to see what *Jacob* will do. Jacob steps into the street with every eye upon him; he approaches Monsieur—he addresses to him a few remarks—they shake hands—they engage in some conversation—Monsieur places his hand on his sword!—now Monsieur passes.

The populace crowd around the blacksmith, children clap their hands softly and jump up and down on tiptoes of expectation—'Sieur George is going to the war in Mexico!

"Ah!" says a little girl in the throng, "'Sieur George's two rooms will be empty; I find that very droll."

The landlord,—this same Kookoo,—is in the group. He hurls himself into the house and up the stairs. "Fifteen years pass since he have been in those room!" He arrives at the door—it is shut—"It is lock!"

In short, further investigation revealed that a youngish lady in black, who had been seen by several neighbors to enter the house, but had not, of course, been suspected of such remarkable intentions, had, in company with a middle-aged slave-woman, taken these two rooms, and now, at the slightly-opened door, proffered a month's rent in advance. What could a landlord do but smile? Yet there was a pretext left; "the rooms must need repairs?"—"No, sir; he could look in and see." Joy! he looked in. All was neatness. The floor unbroken, the walls cracked but a little, and the cracks closed with new plaster, no doubt by the jealous hand of 'Sieur George himself. Kookoo's eyes swept sharply round the two apartments. The furniture was all there. Moreover, there was Monsieur's little hair-trunk. He should not soon forget that trunk. One day, fifteen years or more before, he had taken hold of that trunk to assist Monsieur to arrange his apartment, and Monsieur had drawn his fist back and cried to him to "drop it!" *Mais!* there it was, looking very suspicious in Kookoo's eyes, and the lady's domestic, as tidy as a yellow-bird, went and sat on it. Could that trunk contain treasure? It might, for Madame wanted to shut the door, and, in fact, did so.

The lady was quite handsome—had been more so, but was still young—spoke the beautiful language, and kept, in the inner room, her discreet and taciturn mulattress, a tall, straight woman, with a fierce eye, but called by the young Creoles of the neighborhood "confound' good lookin'."

Among *les Américaines*, where the new neighbor always expects to be called upon by the older residents, this lady might have made friends in spite of being as reserved as 'Sieur George; but the reverse being the Creole custom, and she being well pleased to keep her own company, chose mystery rather than society.

The poor landlord was sorely troubled; it must not that any thing *de trop* take place in his house. He watched the two rooms narrowly, but without result, save to find that Madame plied her needle for pay, spent her money for little else besides harpstrings, and took good care of the little trunk of Monsieur. This espionage was a good turn to the mistress and maid, for when Kookoo announced that all was proper, no more was said by outsiders. Their landlord never got but one question answered by the middle-aged maid:

"Madame, he feared, was a litt' bit embarrass' *pour* money, eh?"

"*Non;* Mademoiselle [Mademoiselle, you notice!] had some property, but did not want to eat it up."

Sometimes lady-friends came, in very elegant private carriages, to see her, and one or two seemed to beg her—but in vain—to go away with them; but these gradually dropped off, until lady and servant were alone in the world. And so years, and the Mexican war, went by.

The volunteers came home; peace reigned, and the city went on spreading up and down the land; but 'Sieur George did not return. It overran the country like cocoa-grass. Fields, roads, woodlands, that were once 'Sieur George's places of retreat from mankind, were covered all over with little one-story houses in the "Old Third," and fine residences and gardens up in "Lafayette." Streets went slicing like a butcher's knife, through old colonial estates, whose first masters never dreamed of the city reaching them,—and 'Sieur George was still away. The four-story brick got old and ugly, and the surroundings dim and dreamy. Theatres, processions, dry-goods stores, government establishments, banks, hotels, and all spirit of enterprise were gone to Canal Street and beyond, and the very beggars were gone with them. The little trunk got very old and bald, and still its owner lingered; still the lady, somewhat the worse for lapse of time, looked from the balcony-window in the brief southern twilights, and the maid every morning shook a worn rug or two over the dangerous-looking railing; and yet neither had made friends or enemies.

The two rooms, from having been stingily kept at first, were needing repairs half the time, and the occupants were often moving, now into one, now back into the other; yet the hair-trunk was seen only by glimpses, the landlord, to his infinite chagrin, always being a little too late in offering his services, the women, whether it was light or heavy, having already moved it. He thought it significant.

Late one day of a most bitter winter,—that season when, to the ecstatic amazement of a whole city-full of children, snow covered the streets ankle-deep,—there came a soft tap on the corridor-door of this pair of rooms. The lady opened it, and beheld a tall, lank, iron-gray man, a total stranger, standing behind—Monsieur George! Both men were weather-beaten, scarred, and tattered. Across 'Sieur George's crown, leaving a long, bare streak through his white hair, was the souvenir of a Mexican sabre.

The landlord had accompanied them to the door: it was a magnificent opportunity. Mademoiselle asked them all in, and tried to furnish a seat to each; but failing, 'Sieur George went straight across the room and *sat on the hair-trunk.* The action was so conspicuous, the landlord laid it up in his penetrative mind.

'Sieur George was quiet, or, as it appeared, quieted. The mulattress stood near him, and to her he addressed, in an undertone, most of the little he said, leaving Mademoiselle to his companion. The stranger was a warm talker, and seemed to please the lady from the first; but if he pleased, nothing else did. Kookoo, intensely curious, sought some pre-text for staying, but found none. They were, altogether, an uncongenial company. The lady seemed to think Kookoo had no business there; 'Sieur George seemed to think the same concerning his companion; and the few words between Mademoiselle and 'Sieur George were cool enough. The maid appeared nearly satisfied, but could not avoid casting an anxious eye at times upon her mistress. Naturally the visit was short.

The next day but one the two gentlemen came again in better attire. 'Sieur George evidently disliked his companion, yet would not rid himself of him. The stranger was a gesticulating, stagy fellow, much Monsieur's junior, an incessant talker in Creole-French, always excited on small matters and unable to appreciate a great one. Once, as they were leaving, Kookoo,—accidents will happen,—was under the stairs. As they began to descend the tall man was speaking: "—better to bury it,"—the startled landlord heard him say, and held his breath, thinking of the trunk; but no more was uttered.

A week later they came again.

A week later they came again.

A week later they came yet again!

The landlord's eyes began to open. There must be a courtship in progress. It was very plain now why 'Sieur George had wished not to be accompanied by the tall gentleman; but since his visits had become regular and frequent, it was equally plain why he did not get rid of him;—because it would not look well to be going and coming too often alone. Maybe it was only this tender passion that the tall man had thought "better to bury." Lately there often came sounds of gay conversation from the first of the two rooms, which had been turned into a parlor; and as, week after week, the friends came down-stairs, the tall man was always in high spirits and anxious to embrace 'Sieur George, who,—"sly dog," thought the landlord,—would try to look grave, and only smiled in an embarrassed way. "Ah! Monsieur, you tink to be varry conning; *mais* you not so conning as Kookoo, no;" and the inquisitive little man would shake his head and smile, and shake his head again, as a man has a perfect right to do under the conviction that he has been for twenty years baffled by a riddle and is learning to read it at last; he had guessed what was in 'Sieur George's head, he would by and by guess what was in the trunk.

A few months passed quickly away, and it became apparent to every eye in or about the ancient mansion that the landlord's guess was not so bad; in fact, that Mademoiselle was to be married.

On a certain rainy spring afternoon, a single hired hack drove up to the main entrance of the old house, and after some little bustle and the gathering of a crowd of damp children about the big doorway, 'Sieur George, muffled in a newly-repaired overcoat, jumped out and went up-stairs. A moment later he re-appeared, leading Mademoiselle, wreathed and veiled, down the stairway. Very fair was Mademoiselle still. Her beauty was mature,—fully ripe,—maybe a little too much so, but only a little; and as she came down with the ravishing odor of bridal flowers floating about her, she seemed the garlanded victim of a pagan sacrifice. The mulattress in holiday gear followed behind.

The landlord owed a duty to the community. He arrested the maid on the last step: "Your mistress, she goin' *pour marier* 'Sieur George? It make me glad, glad, glad!"

"Marry 'Sieur George? Non, Monsieur."

"Non? Not marrie 'Sieur George? *Mais comment?*"

"She's going to marry the tall gentleman."

"*Diable!* ze long gentyman!"—With his hands upon his forehead, he watched the carriage trundle away. It passed out of sight through the rain; he turned to enter the house, and all at once tottered under the weight of a tremendous thought—they had left the trunk! He hurled himself up-stairs as he had done seven years before, but again—"Ah, bah!!"—the door was locked, and not a picayune of rent due.

Late that night a small square man, in a wet overcoat, fumbled his way into the damp entrance of the house, stumbled up the cracking stairs, unlocked, after many languid efforts, the door of the two rooms, and falling over the hair-trunk, slept until the morning sunbeams climbed over the balcony and in at the window, and shone full on the back of his head. Old Kookoo, passing the door just then, was surprised to find it slightly ajar—pushed it open silently, and saw, within, 'Sieur George in the act of rising from his knees beside the mysterious trunk! He had come back to be once more the tenant of the two rooms.

'Sieur George, for the second time, was a changed man—changed from bad to worse; from being retired and reticent, he had come, by reason of advancing years, or mayhap that which had left the terrible scar on his face, to be garrulous. When, once in a while, employment sought him (for he never sought employment), whatever remuneration he received went its way for something that left him dingy and threadbare. He now made a lively acquaintance with his landlord, as, indeed, with every soul in the neighborhood, and told all his adventures in Mexican prisons and Cuban cities; including full details of the hardships and perils experienced jointly with the "long gentleman" who had married Mademoiselle, and who was no Mexican or Cuban, but a genuine Louisianian.

"It was he that fancied me," he said, "not I him; but once he had fallen in love with me I hadn't the force to cast him off. How Madame ever should have liked him was one of those woman's freaks that a man mustn't expect to understand. He was no more fit for her than rags are fit for a queen; and I could have choked his head off the night he hugged me round the neck and told me what a suicide she had committed. But other fine women are committing that same folly every day, only they don't wait until they're thirty-four or five to do it.— 'Why don't I like him?' Well, for one reason, he's a drunkard!" Here Kookoo, whose imperfect knowledge of English prevented his intelligent reception of the story, would laugh as if the joke came in just at this point.

However, with all Monsieur's prattle, he never dropped a word about the man he had been before he went away; and the great hair-trunk puzzle was still the same puzzle, growing greater every day.

Thus the two rooms had been the scene of some events quite queer, if not really strange; but the queerest that ever they presented, I guess, was 'Sieur George coming in there one day, crying like a little child, and bearing in his arms an infant—a girl—the lovely offspring of the drunkard whom he so detested, and poor, robbed, spirit-broken and now dead Madame. He took good care of the orphan, for orphan she was very soon. The long gentleman was pulled out of the Old Basin one morning, and 'Sieur George identified the body at the Trémé station. He never hired a nurse—the father had sold the lady's maid quite out of sight; so he brought her through all the little ills and around all the sharp corners of baby-life and childhood, without a human hand to help him, until one evening, having persistently shut his eyes to it for weeks and months, like one trying to sleep in the sunshine, he awoke to the realization that she was a woman. It was a smoky one in November, the first cool day of autumn. The sunset was dimmed by the smoke of burning prairies, the air was full of the ashes of grass and reeds, ragged urchins were lugging home sticks of cordwood, and when a bit of coal fell from a cart in front of Kookoo's old house, a

686

child was boxed half across the street and robbed of the booty by a *blanchisseuse de fin* from over the way.

The old man came home quite steady. He mounted the stairs smartly without stopping to rest, went with a step unusually light and quiet to his chamber and sat by the window opening upon the rusty balcony.

It was a small room, sadly changed from what it had been in old times; but then so was 'Sieur George. Close and dark it was, the walls stained with dampness and the ceiling full of bald places that showed the lathing. The furniture was cheap and meagre, including conspicuously the small, curious-looking hair-trunk. The floor was of wide slabs fastened down with spikes, and sloping up and down in one or two broad undulations, as if they had drifted far enough down the current of time to feel the tide-swell.

However, the floor was clean, the bed well made, the cypress table in place, and the musty smell of the walls partly neutralized by a geranium on the window-sill.

He so coming in and sitting down, an unseen person called from the room adjoining (of which, also, he was still the rentee), to know if he were he, and being answered in the affirmative, said, "Papa George, guess who was here to-day?"

"Kookoo, for the rent?"

"Yes, but he will not come back."

"No? why not?"

"Because you will not pay him."

"No? and why not?"

"Because I have paid him."

"Impossible! where did you get the money?"

"Cannot guess?—Mother Nativity."

"What, not for embroidery?"

"No? and why not? *Mais oui!*"—saying which, and with a pleasant laugh, the speaker entered the room. She was a girl of sixteen or thereabout, very beautiful, with very black hair and eyes. A face and form more entirely out of place you could not have found in the whole city. She sat herself at his feet, and, with her interlocked hands upon his knee, and her face, full of childish innocence mingled with womanly wisdom, turned to his, appeared for a time to take principal part in a conversation which, of course, could not be overheard in the corridor outside.

Whatever was said, she presently rose, he opened his arms, and she sat on his knee and kissed him. This done, there was a silence, both smiling pensively and gazing out over the rotten balcony into the street. After a while she started up, saying something about the change of weather, and, slipping away, thrust a match between the bars of the grate. The old man turned about to the fire, and she from her little room brought a low sewing-chair and sat beside him, laying her head on his knee, and he stroking her brow with his brown palm.

And then, in an altered—a low, sad tone—he began a monotonous recital.

Thus they sat, he talking very steadily and she listening, until all the neighborhood was wrapped in slumber,—all the neighbors, but not Kookoo.

Kookoo in his old age had become a great eavesdropper; his ear and eye took turns at the keyhole that night, for he tells things that were not intended for outside hearers. He heard the girl sobbing, and the old man saying, "But you must go now. You cannot stay with me safely or decently, much as I wish it. The Lord only knows how I'm to bear it, or where you're to go; but He's your Lord, child, and He'll make a place for you. I was your grandfather's death; I frittered your poor, dead mother's fortune away: let that be the last damage I do.

"I have always meant every thing for the best," he added half in soliloquy.

From all Kookoo could gather, he must have been telling her the very story just recounted. She had dropped quite to the floor, hiding her face in her hands, and was saying between her sobs, "I cannot go, Papa George; oh, Papa George, I cannot go!"

Just then 'Sieur George, having kept a good resolution all day, was encouraged by the orphan's pitiful tones to contemplate the most senseless act he ever attempted to commit. He said to the sobbing girl that she was not of his blood; that she was nothing to him by natural ties; that his covenant was with her grandsire to care for his offspring; and though it had been poorly kept, it might be breaking it worse than ever to turn her out upon ever so kind a world.

"I have tried to be good to you all these years. When I took you, a wee little baby, I took you for better or worse. I intended to do well by you all your childhood-days, and to do best at last. I thought surely we should be living well by this time, and you could choose from a world full of homes and a world full of friends.

"I don't see how I missed it!" Here he paused a moment in meditation, and presently resumed with some suddenness:

"I thought that education, far better than Mother Nativity has given you, should have afforded your sweet charms a noble setting; that good mothers and sisters would be wanting to count you into their families, and that the blossom of a happy womanhood would open perfect and full of sweetness.

"I would have given my life for it. I did give it, such as it was; but it was a very poor concern, I know—my life—and not enough to buy any good thing.

"I have had a thought of something, but I'm afraid to tell it. It didn't

688

come to me to-day or yesterday; it has beset me a long time—for months."

The girl gazed into the embers, listening intensely.

"And oh! dearie, if I could only get you to think the same way, you might stay with me then."

"How long?" she asked, without stirring.

"Oh, as long as heaven should let us. But there is only one chance," he said, as it were feeling his way, "only one way for us to stay together. Do you understand me?"

She looked up at the old man with a glance of painful inquiry.

"If you could be—my wife, dearie?"

She uttered a low, distressful cry, and, gliding swiftly into her room, for the first time in her young life turned the key between them.

And the old man sat and wept.

Then Kookoo, peering through the keyhole, saw that they had been looking into the little trunk. The lid was up, but the back was toward the door, and he could see no more than if it had been closed.

He stooped and stared into the aperture until his dry old knees were ready to crack. It seemed as if 'Sieur George was stone, only stone couldn't weep like that.

Every separate bone in his neck was hot with pain. He would have given ten dollars—ten sweet dollars!—to have seen 'Sieur George get up and turn that trunk around.

There! 'Sieur George rose up—what a face!

He started toward the bed, and as he came to the trunk he paused, looked at it, muttered something about "ruin," and something about "fortune," kicked the lid down and threw himself across the bed.

Small profit to old Kookoo that he went to his own couch; sleep was not for the little landlord. For well-nigh half a century he had suspected his tenant of having a treasure hidden in his house, and to-night he had heard his own admission that in the little trunk was a fortune. Kookoo had never felt so poor in all his days before. He felt a Creole's anger, too, that a tenant should be the holder of wealth while his landlord suffered poverty.

And he knew very well, too, did Kookoo, what the tenant would do. If he did not know what he kept in the trunk, he knew what he kept behind it, and he knew he would take enough of it to-night to make him sleep soundly.

No one would ever have supposed Kookoo capable of a crime. He was too fearfully impressed with the extra-hazardous risks of dishonesty; he was old, too, and weak, and, besides all, intensely a coward. Nevertheless, while it was yet two or three hours before daybreak, the sleep-forsaken little man arose, shuffled into his garments, and in his stocking-feet sought the corridor leading to 'Sieur George's apartment.

The November night, as it often does in that region, had grown warm and clear; the stars were sparkling like diamonds pendent in the deep blue heavens, and at every window and lattice and cranny the broad, bright moon poured down its glittering beams upon the hoary-headed thief, as he crept along the mouldering galleries and down the ancient corridor that led to 'Sieur George's chamber.

'Sieur George's door, though ever so slowly opened, protested with a loud creak. The landlord, wet with cold sweat from head to foot, and shaking till the floor trembled, paused for several minutes, and then entered the moon-lit apartment. The tenant, lying as if he had not moved, was sleeping heavily. And now the poor coward trembled so, that to kneel before the trunk, without falling, he did not know how. Twice, thrice, he was near tumbling headlong. He became as cold as ice. But the sleeper stirred, and the thought of losing his opportunity strung his nerves up in an instant. He went softly down upon his knees, laid his hands upon the lid, lifted it, and let in the intense moonlight. The trunk was full, full, crowded down and running over full, of the tickets of the Havana Lottery!

A little after daybreak, Kookoo from his window saw the orphan, pausing on the corner. She stood for a moment, and then dove into the dense fog which had floated in from the river, and disappeared. He never saw her again.

But her Lord is taking care of her. Once only she has seen 'Sieur George. She had been in the belvedere of the house which she now calls home, looking down upon the outspread city. Far away southward and westward the great river glistened in the sunset. Along its sweeping bends the chimneys of a smoking commerce, the magazines of surplus wealth, the gardens of the opulent, the steeples of a hundred sanctuaries and thousands on thousands of mansions and hovels covered the fertile birthright arpents which 'Sieur George, in his fifty years' stay, had seen tricked away from dull colonial Esaus by their blue-eyed brethren of the North. Nearer by she looked upon the forlornly silent region of lowly dwellings, neglected by legislation and shunned by all lovers of comfort, that once had been the smiling fields of her own grandsire's broad plantation; and but a little way off, trudging across the marshy commons, her eye caught sight of 'Sieur George following the sunset out upon the prairies to find a night's rest in the high grass.

She turned at once, gathered the skirt of her pink calico uniform, and, watching her steps through her tears, descended the steep winding-stair to her frequent kneeling-place under the fragrant candles of the chapel-altar in Mother Nativity's asylum.

'Sieur George is houseless. He cannot find the orphan. Mother Nativity seems to know nothing of her. If he could find her now, and could get from her the use of ten dollars for but three days, he knows a combination which would repair all the past; it could not fail, he—thinks. But he cannot find her, and the letters he writes—all containing the one scheme—disappear in the mail-box, and there's an end.

Elizabeth Madox Roberts

The novels and short stories of Elizabeth Madox Roberts (1886–1941) are rich with the essence of her native Kentucky, but she is no mere regional realist. The oblique, symbolic story-telling technique, the artfully artless dialogue, the strong emotions deeply and truly compre·hended, are the work of a poet who taught herself to think in prose. Miss Roberts published her first novel, The Time of Man, *when she was forty. Long before that, even while she was a student at the University of Chicago, she had earned distinction by her verse. Her whole prose work—seven novels and two volumes of short stories—was done within fifteen years. Each of her books was an experiment, in theme or technique, and only one experiment—an attempt at satiric fantasy— failed. All the others are full of interest;* The Time of Man *and the historical novel,* The Great Meadow, *may claim to be Southern, and American, classics.*

The Kentucky country she knew so well Miss Roberts seldom describes directly, but she gives her reader a powerful impression of its quality through the thoughts and dreams of her characters, particularly the deeply conceived single character who dominates each novel or story. These people speak a language that rings true though it is not a literal transcript of the talk the novelist heard among her neighbors in Springfield, Kentucky; rather it is a mingling of the voices she listened to daily with the cadences of old regional ballads and her own subtle symbols and rhythms. Miss Roberts's plots are not important. What matters is the impress conditions and events make upon the minds of the people with whom she is concerned: poverty and disappointment in love, and the cares of marriage, for instance, upon a young girl growing to womanhood in The Time of Man; *the discovery that her father has three Negro bastards upon the heroine of* My Heart and My Flesh; *pioneer hardship and adventure upon Virginia-born Diony in* The Great Meadow. *There is always more in these stories than meets the eye. The reader must read closely and look beneath the lines.*

691

❀

ON THE MOUNTAINSIDE

THERE was a play-party at the schoolhouse at the bottom of the cove. Newt Reddix waited outside the house, listening to the noises as Lester Hunter, the teacher, had listened to them—a new way for Newt. Sound at the bottom of a cove was different from sound at the top, he noticed, for at the top voices spread into a wide thinness. Before Lester came, Newt had let his ears have their own way of listening. Sounds had then been for but one purpose—to tell him what was happening or what was being said. Now the what of happenings and sayings was wrapped about with some unrelated feeling or prettiness, or it stood back beyond some heightened qualities.

"Listen!" Lester had said to him one evening, standing outside a house where a party was going forward. "Listen!" And there were footsteps and outcries of men and women, happy cries, shrill notes of surprise and pretended anger, footsteps on rough wood, unequal intervals, a flare of fiddle playing and a tramp of dancing feet. Down in the cove the sounds from a party were different from those that came from a house on the side of a hill, the cries of men bent and disturbed, distorted by the place, by the sink and rise of land. While he listened, the knowledge that Lester Hunter would soon go out of the country, the school term being over, brought a loneliness to his thought.

He went inside the schoolhouse and flung his hat on the floor beside the door; he would take his part now in the playing. His hat was pinned up in front with a thorn and was as pert a hat as any of those beside the door, and no one would give it dishonor. The schoolteacher was stepping about in the dance, turning Corie Yancey, and the fiddle was scraping the top of a tune. For him the entire party was filled with the teacher's impending departure.

"Ladies change and gents the same," the fiddler called, his voice unblended with the tune he played. Newt fell into place when an older man withdrew in his favor and gave him Ollie Mack for his partner. The teacher danced easily, bent to the curve of the music, neglectful and willing, giving the music the flowing lightness of his limp body.

Newt wanted to dance as the teacher did, but he denied himself and kept the old harsh gesture, pounding the floor more roughly now and then with a deeply accented step. He wanted to tread the music lightly, meeting it halfway, but he would not openly imitate anybody. While he danced he was always, moment by moment, aware of the teacher, aware of him standing to wait his turn, pulling his collar straight, pushing his hands into the pockets of his coat, looking at Ollie Mack when she laughed, looking full into her face with pleasure, unafraid. The teacher had given an air to the dance, and had made it, for him, more bold in form, more like itself or more true to its kind, more gentle in courtesy. Lester had come from one of the low counties of the rolling plain where the curving creeks of the Pigeon River spread slowly, winding broadly to gather up many little rills. Newt had learned somewhere, in his own blood, to hate the lower country for its pleasantness. There the fields rolled out smoothly and the soil was deep. The grass of any roadside was bluegrass mingled, perhaps, with rich weeds. Fat cattle, fine beasts, ate in the mythical pastures. Smooth roads ran between the farms. Dancing, shaking his body stiffly with the beat of the fiddle, Newt saw that Lester took his partner's hand lightly, that he gave equal courtesy to all the women, calling them ladies. He wanted to be as the teacher was, but he could not. The dance drawing to an end, he realized again that in two days more the teacher would go, for he had set his head upon some place far away, down in the settlements, among the lower counties from which he had come six months earlier.

There was pie for a treat, baked by Marthy Anne Sands and brought to the schoolhouse in a great hickory basket. Standing about eating the pie, all were quiet, regretting the teacher's going. Newt wove a vagrant path in and out among them, hearing the talk of the older men and women.

"My little tad, the least one, Becky, is plumb bereft over 'im," one said, a woman speaking.

"Last year at the school there wasn't hardly anybody would go, and look at this. I had to whop Joel to make him stay on the place one day to feed and water the property whilst I had to go. Hit appears like Joel loves book-sense since Les Hunter come up the mountain."

"What makes you in such a swivet to go nohow?" one asked.

"Did you come up the gorge to borrow fire you're in such a swivet to get on?"

"There's a big meeten over to Kitty's branch next light moon. Why don't you stay? No harm in you to be broguen about a small spell."

"You could loafer around a spell and wait for the meeten."

"Big meeten. And nohow the meeten needs youens to help sing."

"What's he in such a swivet to go off for?"

"I got to go. I got to see the other end of the world yet."

"What's he a-sayen?"

"I got to go to the other end of the world."

"That's too far a piece."

"That surely undoubtedly is a right smart piece to go."

"He could stay a spell at my place and welcome. I'd be real proud to have him stay with my folks a spell. And Nate, he'd keep youens a week, that I right well know. Youens could loafer around awhile as well as not."

"He always earns his way and more, ever since he kem up the mountain, always earns his keep, anyhow."

"I've got to go. I'm bound for the other end of this old globe. I'm obliged all the same, but I got a heap to see yet. I'm bound to go."

Newt plowed the corn in the rocky field above the house where he lived, one horse to the plow, or he hoed where the field lay steepest. The teacher was gone now. On Sunday Newt would put on his clean shirt his mother had washed on Friday, and climb up the gorge to the head of the rise and meet there Tige English and Jonathan Evans. Then they would go to see Lum Baker's girls. He would contrive to kiss each girl before the night fell and Lum would cry out: "Come on, you gals now, and milk the cow brutes." Or sometimes they would go down the way to see Corie Yancey and Ollie Mack. To Newt all the place seemed still since the teacher had left, idle, as if it had lost its uses and its future. Going to the well for water he would stare at the winch, at the soft rot of the bucket, at the stones inside the well curb, or he would listen intently to the sounds as the vessel struck the water or beat against the stones.

The noises gave him more than the mere report of a bucket falling into a well to get water; they gave him some comprehension of all things that were yet unknown. The sounds, rich with tonality, as the bucket struck the water, rang with some strange sonority and throbbed with a beat that was like something he could not define, some other, unlike fiddle playing but related to it in its unlikeness. A report had come to him from an outside world and a suspicion of more than he could know in his present state haunted him. He cried out inwardly for the answer, or he looked about him and listened, remembering all that he could of what Lester Hunter had taught—capitals of countries, seaports, buying and selling, nouns, verbs, numbers multiplied together to make other numbers. Now he looked intently and listened. He detected a throb in sound, but again there was a beat in the hot sun over a moist field. One day he thought that he had divined a throb in numbers as he counted, a beat in the recurrences of kinds, but this evaded him. He listened and looked at the well happenings, at the house wall, at the rail fence, at the barn, at the hills going upward toward the top of the gorge.

On every side were evasions. These sights and sounds could not give him enough; they lay flat against the air; they were imbedded within his own flesh and were sunk into his own sense of them. He would stare at the green and brown moss on the broken frame of the well box and stare again at the floating images in the dark of the well water. The rope would twine over the axle as he turned the wooden handle, and the rounds of the rope would fall into orderly place, side by side, as he knew too casually and too well. Since the teacher had gone the place had flattened to an intolerable staleness that gave out meager tokens of withheld qualites and beings—his mother leaning from the door to call him to dinner, his sister dragging his chair to the table and setting his cup beside his place, the old dog running out to bark at some varmint above in the brush. He could hardly separate the fall of his own bare foot from the rock door-step over which he had walked since he could first walk at all. His thirst and his water to drink were one now. His loneliness, as he sat to rest at noon beside the fence, merged and was identified with the still country from brush-grown slope to brush-grown slope.

His father began to clear a new patch below the house; they grubbed at the roots all day when the corn was laid by. One morning in September, when the sun, moving south, was just getting free of Rattlesnake Hill, it came to him that he would go down to the settlements, that he would go to Merryman. All summer he had known that there was a school at Merryman, but he had not thought to go there, for he had no money. It came to him as a settled fact that he would go there and look about at the place. Three high ridges with numberless breaks and gorges intervened; he had heard this said by men who knew or had heard of what lay beyond. The determination to set forth and the wish to go came to him at one instant. "My aim, hit's to go there," he said. "I lay off to do that-there, like I say."

He remembered the teacher more clearly at this moment, saw him in a more sharply detailed picture; his own breath jerked deeply inward as he was himself related, through his intended departure, to the picture. Hunter was remembered cutting wood for the schoolhouse fire, sweethearting the girls and turning them lightly in the dance, or sitting by the fire at night, reading his book, holding the page low to the blaze. He was remembered hallooing back up the mountain the day he left, his voice calling back as he went down the ridge and he himself answering until there was not even a faint hollow whoopee to come up the slope. By the fire Newt had often taken Hunter's book into his hands, but he could never read the strange words nor in any way know what they meant when they were read, for they had stood four-square and hostile against his understanding. His father's voice would fall dully over the slow clearing: "You could work on this-here enduren the while that I cut the corn patch."

He knew that he would go. His determination rejected the clearing, knowing that he would be gone before the corn was ready to cut. It rejected the monotonous passing of the days, the clutter of feet on the stones by the door, the dull, inconspicuous corn patch above. He would walk, taking the short cut over the mountains. Two ridges to go and then there would be a road for his feet, some one had said. He announced his plan to his father one day while they leaned over their grub hoes. There was no willingness offered, but his mind was set, and three days later he had established his plan. His mother had washed his shirts clean and had rolled them into a bundle with his spare socks, and she had baked him bread and a joint of ham. She and his sister stood by the doorway weeping after he had driven back the dog and had shouted his goodbye.

It was a mid-afternoon and the sun beat down into the cove where he traveled. He worked his way through the thick-set laurel, struggling to keep his bundle tied to his shoulders where the brush stood most dense.

The dry clatter of the higher boughs came to his ears, but it was so mingled with the pricking snarls of the twigs on his face that the one sense was not divided from the other. "This durned ivy," he said when the laurel held him back. He matched his strength against boughs or he flashed his wits against snarls and rebounds, hot and weary, tingling with sweat and with the pricking twigs. Pushed back at one place where he tried to find an opening, he assailed another and then another, throwing all his strength angrily against the brush and tearing himself through the mesh with *god-damns* of relief. A large shaded stone that bulged angrily out of the mountainside gave him a space of rest. He stretched himself on the slanting rock, his face away from the sun, and lay for an hour, thinking nothing, feeling the weariness as it beat heavily upon his limbs.

"I'm bodaciously tired," he said, after a long period of torpor. "Could I come by a spring branch, I'd drink me a whole durned quart of it."

Another tree-grown mountain arose across the cove, misty now in the afternoon and in the first haze of autumn, and beyond lay other blue mountains, sinking farther and farther into the air. Back of him it was the same; he had been on the way two weeks now. Before him he knew each one would be dense with laurel until he came to the wagon road. He took to the pathless way after his hour of rest, going forward. When the sun was setting behind Bee Gum Mountain, he saw a house down in the cove, not far as the crow would fly but the distance of two hours' going for him. When he saw the cabin he began to sing, chanting:

> Right hands across and howdy-do,
> Left and back and how are you.

ELIZABETH MADOX ROBERTS: *On the Mountainside*

> Oh, call up yo' dog, oh, call up yo' dog,
> Rink twang a-whoddle lanky day.

The sight of the house quickened his desire for Merryman and the cities and counties in the settlements, and this desire had become more definite in his act of going. His wish was for sure, quick gestures and easy sayings that would come from the mouth as easily as breath. There were for him other things, as yet unrelated to any one place—men playing ball with a great crowd to watch, all the crowd breaking into a laugh at one time; men racing fine horses on a hard, smooth track; music playing; men having things done by machinery; lovely girls not yet imagined; and things to know beyond anything he could recall, and not one of them too fine or too good for him. He sang as he went down the slope, his song leaping out of him. He had heard it said that the lights of Merryman could be seen from Coster Ridge on a clear night, and Coster was now visible standing up in the pale air, for a man had pointed him the way that morning. Singing, he set himself toward the house at the bottom of the cove.

Night was falling when he called "Hello" at the foot of Bee Gum Mountain. The man of the house asked his name and told his own, making him welcome. Supper was over, but the host, whose name was Tom Bland, ordered Nance, his woman, to give the stranger a snack of biscuit bread and bacon, and this Newt ate sitting beside the fire. Another stranger was sitting in the cabin, an old man who kept very still while Nance worked with the utensils, his dim eyes looking into the fire or eyeing Newt, who stared back and searched the looks of the stranger. Then Tom told Nance how they would sleep that night, telling her to give the old man her place in the bed beside himself.

"You could get in bed along with the young ones," he said to her. "The boy here, he could sleep on a shakedown alongside the fireplace."

From gazing into the fire the old stranger would fall asleep, but after a moment he would awake, opening dim, ashamed eyes that glanced feebly at Newt, faintly defying him. Then Nance put some children to bed, her own perhaps, and sat quietly in the corner of the hearth, her hands in her lap. Newt had looked at the host, acquainting himself with him. He was a strong man, far past youth, large-boned and broad-muscled. His heavy feet scraped on the floor when he moved from his chair to the water bucket on the window sill. Newt saw that he on his side had been silently searching out the old stranger. After a while the host and the old man began to talk, Tom speaking first.

"There's a sight of travel now."

"Hit's a moven age."

Between each speech there was a slow pause as each saying was carefully probed before the reply was offered.

697

Tom said: "Two in one night, and last week there was one come by." And then after a while he asked: "Where might youens be bound for, stranger?"

"I'm on my way back," the man said.

There was a long season of quiet. The ideas were richly interspersed with action, for Nance softly jolted back and forth in her chair, her bare feet tapping lightly on the boards of the floor.

"You been far?" Tom asked.

"I been a right far piece. I been to the settlements in Froman county, and then I been to the mines around Tateville and Beemen."

Newt bit nervously at his knuckles and looked at the man, taking from him these signs of the world. The fire burned low, and breaking the long silence Tom said once or twice: "There's a sight of travel now." Newt looked at the old man's feet in their patched shoes, feet that had walked the streets in towns. Indefinite wonders touched the man's feet, his crumpled knees, and his crooked hands that were spread on his lap.

Then Tom said: "Froman, I reckon that's a prime good place to be now."

"Hit may be so, but I wouldn't be-nasty my feet with the dust of hit no longer. Nor any other place down there. I'm on my way back."

The old man's voice quavered over his words toward the close of this speech, and after a little while he added, his voice lifted: "Hit's a far piece back, but a man has a rather about where he'd like to be." Finally he spoke in great anger, his arm raised and his hand threatening: "I've swat my last drop of sweat in that-there country and eat my last meal's victuals. A man has a rather as to the place he likes to be."

This thought lay heavily over the fireplace, shared by all but uncomprehended by Nance, whose skin was rich with blood and life. She sat complacently rocking back and forth in her small chair.

After the long quiet which surrounded this thought the old man began to speak softly, having spent his passion: "I'm on my way back. I been in a study a long time about goen back but seems like I couldn't make hit to go. Work was terrible pressen. But now I'm on my way back where I was borned and my mammy and pappy before me. I was a plumb traitor to my God when I left the mountains and come to the settlements. Many is the day I'd study about that-there and many is the night I lay awake to study about the way back over Coster Ridge, on past Bear Mountain, past Hog Run, past Little Pine Tree, up and on past Louse Run, up, then on over Long Ridge and up into Laurel, into Grady Creek and on up the branch, past the Flat Rock, past the sawmill, past the grove of he-balsams, and then the smoke a-comen outen the chimney and the door open and old Nomie's pup a-comen down the road to meet me. I'd climb the whole way whilst I was a-layen there, in my own mind I would, and I'd see the ivy as plain as you'd see your hand afore your face, and the coves and the he-balsams. In my own mind I'd go back, a step at a time, Coster, Bear Mountain and the Bee Gum, Little Pine Tree, Louse Run, Grady, and I'd see the rocks in the way to go, and a log stretched out in my way maybe. I wouldn't make hit too easy to go. Past Bear Mountain, past Hog Run and the cove, scratchen my way through ivy brush. Then I'd come to myself and there I'd be, a month's travel from as much as a sight of the Flat Rock, and I'd groan and shake and turn over again. I was a traitor to my God."

Nance laid a little stick on the fire, with a glance at Tom, he allowing it without protest. Then she sat back in her stiff chair with a quick movement, her bare feet light on the boards. The old man was talking again.

"Where my mammy was borned before me and her mammy and daddy before again. And no water in all Froman or Tateville but dead pump waters, no freestone like you'd want. How could a man expect to live? Many's the night I've said, could I be on the shady side of the Flat Rock, up past the saw-mill, up past the grove of he-balsams, where the spring branch runs out over the horseshoe rock, and could I get me one drink of that-there cold crystal water I'd ask ne'er thing more of God Almighty in life."

"I know that-there very spring branch," Newt now said. He was eager to enter the drama of the world, and his time now had come. "I know that-there very place. You come to a rock set on end and a hemlock bush set off to the right, she-balsams all off to the left like."

"Mankind, that's just how hit's set. I believe you been right there!"

"A mountain goes straight up afore you as you stand, say this-here is the spring, and the water comes out and runs off over a horse-shoe rock."

"Mankind, that's just how hit's set. I do believe you know that-there very place. You say hit's there just the same?"

"I got me a drink at that-there very spring branch Tuesday 'twas a week ago."

"You drank them waters!" And then he said after a period of wonder: "To think you been to that very spring branch! You been there!"

"We can burn another stick," Tom said, as if in honor of the strange event, and Nance mended the fire again. Outside Newt heard dogs howling far up the slope and some small beast cried.

"To think you been there! You are a-setten right now in hearen of my voice and yet a Tuesday 'twas a week ago you was in the spot I call home. Hit's hard to study over. You come down the mountain fast. That country is powerful hard goen."

"Yes, I come right fast."

"I couldn't make hit back in twice the time and more. Hard goen it was. What made you travel so hard, young man?"

"I'm a-maken hit toward the settlements."

"And what you think to find in the settle-ments, God knows! What you think to see, young man?"

"Learnen. I look to find learnen in the settle-ments."

In the pause that followed the old man gazed at the hearth as if he were looking into time, into all qualities, and he fell momentarily asleep under the impact of his gaze. But presently he looked at Newt and said: "And to think you tasted them waters Tuesday 'twas a week ago!"

"You come to a rock set on end, and here's the hemlock off to the right like, and here to the left goes the gorge."

The old man was asleep, his eyes falling away before the fire. But he waked suddenly and said with kindling eyes, his hand uplifted: "You come from there at a master pace, young man, come from the place I hope to see if God Almighty sees fitten to bless me afore I lay me down and die. You walked, I reckon, right over the spot I pined to see a many is the year, God knows, and it was nothing to you, but take care. The places you knowed when you was a little shirt-tail boy won't go outen your head or outen your recollections."

Then he said, another outbreak after a long pause, his hand again up-lifted: "I reckon you relish learnen, young man, and take a delight in hit, and set a heap of store by the settle-ments. But the places you knowed when you was a little tad, they won't go outen your remem-brance. Your insides is made that way, and made outen what you did when you was a shirt-tail boy, and you'll find it's so. Your dreams of a night and all you pine to see will go back. You won't get shed so easy of hit. You won't get shed."

Newt looked into the fire and a terror grew into his thought. He saw minutely the moss on the well curb and the shapes in which it grew, and saw the three stones that lay beside the well, that lifted his feet out of the mud. The sound made by the bucket in the well as it rocked from wall to wall, as it finally struck the water, rolled acutely back-ward into his inner hearing. He saw the rope twine over the beam as he turned the wooden handle, drawing the full bucket to the top. Three long steps then to the door of the house, the feel of the filled bucket drawing at his arm. Up the loft ladder to his room, his hands drawing up his body, the simple act of climbing, of emerging from some lower place to a higher, and he was buried in the act, submerged in a deep sense of it.

"You may go far and see a heap in life," the old stranger said, slowly, defiantly prophetic, "you may go far, but mark me as I say it, the places you knowed when you was a little tad will be the strongest in your remembrance. It's true, whoever you are and whatever land you come from. Your whole insides is made outen what you done first."

Newt saw in terror what he saw as he gazed into the sinking embers. His mother calling him from the house door, calling him to come to his dinner, her hand uplifted to the door frame. His sister, a little girl, dragging his chair in place and pushing his cup up against the plate. His tears for them dimmed the fire to a vague, red, quivering glow. The floating images in the dark of the well water, the bright light of the sky in the middle as a picture in a frame, and his own head looking into the heart of the picture—these were between him and the fire, moving more inwardly and dragging himself with them as they went. He was bereft, divided, emptied of his every wish, and he gazed at the fire, scarcely seeing it.

There was moving in the room, figures making a dim passage of shadows behind him. Presently he knew that the old man had gone to his sleeping place and that Nance was spreading quilts on the floor to the side of the fireplace. Her strong body was pleasant to sense as she flung out the covers and pulled them into line, and a delight in the strange room, the strange bed, welled over him. His breath was then set to a fluted rhythm as he drew suddenly inward a rich flood of air, a rhythm flowing deeply until it touched the core of his desire for the settlements, laid an amorous pulse on his determination to go there. Learning was the word he cherished and kept identified with his quickened breath. He remembered that the lights of Merryman and the settlements would be brightly dusted over the low valley when he reached Coster.

By the end of the week he would, his eager breath told him, be looking down on to the farther valleys.

Thomas Wolfe

In 1935, the year of Thomas Wolfe's second novel, Of Time and the River, *he also published his only collection of short stories:* From Death to Morning. *Most of these stories—some of them are sketches rather than stories—were episodes salvaged from the gigantic manuscripts of his novels when they were edited down to book size. The stories vary in quality as they do in length. Of the longest of them, a novelette in*

the form of a monologue which permits Eliza Gant to tell her son the story of her life, one critic has said: "It is perhaps Wolfe's most expert technical performance, for he achieves form through the method of apparent formlessness." But even the less successful of these stories show Wolfe as an experimenter in fiction, trying one mode after another. One can look at them more objectively than is possible with the novels where the tumult of experience and the volume of rhetoric overwhelm the reader who is at all sympathetic with Wolfe's themes and style.

The sketch reprinted here is the third of the four impressionistic studies that make up the story called "The Face of the War." These sketches of "heat-brutal August the year the war ended" are apparently autobiographical, as so much of Wolfe's fiction is. The year the First World War ended, Wolfe, at the age of eighteen, worked at the flying field at Hampton, Virginia, as a time-checker. The locale of "The Face of the War" is the Hampton Roads area, and the observer in the four sketches is a young man of Tom Wolfe's age in 1918. In each of the sketches Wolfe tried to capture in words the loneliness of youth and the attraction and revulsion that a young man feels when he experiences for the first time naked brutality or hatred or lust. Particularly remarkable in this third sketch is the skill with which Wolfe makes an often-told story new.

The critics were not kind to From Death to Morning *when it appeared. Wolfe's self-judgment was sounder. He wrote in a presentation copy of the book: "I have a hunch the well known 'reaction' has set in against me, and that I will take a pounding in this book.—Well, I am writing you this because I believe that as good writing as I have ever done is in this book—and because my faith has always been that a good thing is indestructible."*

This sketch is reprinted from From Death to Morning *by Thomas Wolfe; copyright 1932, 1935 by Charles Scribner's Sons; used by permission of the publishers.*

THE FACE OF THE WAR

AGAIN, an image of man's naked desire, brutal and imperative, stripped down to his raw need, savage and incurious as the harsh pang of a starved hunger which takes and rends whatever food it finds—as here: Over the bridge, across the railway track, down in the Negro settlement of Newport News—among the dives and stews and rusty tenements of that grimy, dreary and abominable section, a rude shack of unpainted pine boards, thrown together with the savage haste which war engenders, to pander to a need as savage and insatiate as hunger, as old as life, the need of friendless, unhoused men the world over.

The front part of this rawly new, yet squalid place, has been partitioned off by rude pine boards to form the semblance of a lunch room and soft drink parlor. Within are several tables, furnished with a few fly-specked menu cards, on which half a dozen items are recorded, and at which none of the patrons ever look, and a wooden counter, with its dreary stage property of luke-warm soda pop, a few packages of cigarettes and a box of cheap cigars beneath a dingy little glass case; and beneath a greasy glass humidor, a few stale ham and cheese sandwiches, which have been there since the place was opened, which will be there till the war is done.

Meanwhile, all through the room, the whores, in their thin and meager mummers, act as waitresses, move patiently about among the crowded tables and ply their trade. The men, who are seated at the tables, belong for the most part to that great group of unclassed creatures who drift and float, work, drift, and starve, are now in jail, now out again, now foul, filthy, wretched, hungry, out of luck, riding the rods, the rusty box cars of a freight, snatching their food at night from the boiling slum of hoboes' jungle, now swaggering with funds and brief prosperity—the floaters, drifters, and half-bums, that huge nameless, houseless, rootless and anomalous class that swarm across the nation.

They are the human cinders of the earth. Hard, shabby, scarred and lined of face, common, dull and meager of visage as they are, they have the look of having crawled that morning from the box car in the train yard of another city or of having dropped off a day coach in the morning, looking casually and indifferently about them, carrying a cardboard suitcase with a shirt, two collars and a tie. Yet a legend of great distances is written on them—a kind of atomic desolation. Each is a human spot of moving rust naked before the desolation of the skies that bend above him, unsheltered on the huge and savage wilderness of the earth, across which he is hurled—a spot of grimy gray and dingy brown, clinging to the brake-rods of a loaded freight.

He is a kind of human cinder hurled through space, naked, rootless, nameless, with all that was personal and unique in its one life almost emptied out into that huge vacancy of rust and iron and waste, and lonely and incommunicable distances, in which it lives, through which it has so often been bombarded.

And this atom finds its end at length, perhaps, at some unknown place upon the savage visage of the continent, exploded, a smear of blood on the rock ballast, a scream lost in the roar of pounding wheels, a winding of entrails round the axle rods, a brief indecipherable bobbing of blood and bone and brains upon the wooden ties, or just a shapeless bundle of old soiled brown and gray slumped down at morning in a shabby doorway, on a city street, beneath the elevated structure, a bundle of rags and bone, now cold and lifeless, to be carted out of sight by the police, nameless and forgotten in its death as in its life.

Such, for the most part, were the men who now sat at the tables in this rude house of pleasure, looking about them furtively, warily, with an air of waiting calculation, or indecision, and sometimes glancing at one another with sly, furtive, rather sheepish smiles.

As for the women who attended them, they were prostitutes recruited, for the most part, from the great cities of the North and Middle-West, brutally greedy, rapacious, weary of eye, hard of visage, over-driven, harried and exhausted in their mechanical performance of a profession from which their only hope was to grasp and clutch as much as they could in as short a time as possible. They had the harsh, rasping and strident voices, the almost deliberately exaggerated and inept extravagance of profanity and obscenity, the calculated and over-emphasized style of toughness which one often finds among poor people in the tenement sections of great cities—which one observes even in small children—the constant oath, curse, jeer, threat, menace, and truculent abuse, which really comes from the terrible fear in which they live, as if, in that world of savage aggression and brute rapacity, from which they have somehow to wrest their bitter living, they are afraid that any betrayal of themselves into a gentler, warmer and more tolerant kind of speech and gesture, will make them suspect to their fellows, and lay them open to the assaults, threats, tyrannies, and dominations they fear.

So was it with these women now: one could hear their rasping voices everywhere throughout the smoke-filled room, their harsh jeering laughter, and the extravagant exaggeration and profusion with which they constantly interlarded their strident speech with a few oaths and cries repeated with a brutal monotony—such phrases as "Christ!"—"Jesus!"—"What t' God-damn hell do I care?"—"Come on! Whatcha goin' t' do now! I got no time t' — around wit' yuh! If ya want t' — come on an' pay me—if ya don't, get t' God-damn hell outa here"—being among the expressions one heard most frequently.

Yet, even among these poor, brutally exhausted and fear-ridden women, there was really left, like something pitiably living and indestructible out of life, a kind of buried tenderness, a fearful, almost timid desire to find some friendship, gentleness, even love among the rabble-rout of lost and ruined men to whom they ministered.

And this timid, yet inherent desire for some warmer and more tender relation even in the practice of their profession, was sometimes almost ludicrously apparent as they moved warily about among the tables soliciting patronage from the men they served. Thus, if a man addressed them harshly, brutally, savagely, with an oath—which was a customary form of greeting—they would answer him in kind. But if he spoke to them more quietly, or regarded them with a more kindly smiling look, they might respond to him with a pathetic and ridiculous attempt at coquetry, subduing their rasping voices to a kind of husky, tinny whisper, pressing against him intimately, bending their bedaubed and painted faces close to his, and cajoling him with a pitiable pretense at seductiveness, somewhat in this manner:

"Hello there, big boy! . . . Yuh look lonesome sittin' there all by yourself. . . . Whatcha doin' all alone? . . . Yuh want some company? Huh?"—whispered hoarsely, with a ghastly leer of the smeared lips, and pressing closer—"Wanta have some fun, darling? . . . Come on!"—coaxingly, imperatively, taking the patron by the hand—"I'll show yuh a big time."

It was in response to some such blandishment as this that the boy had got up from his table, left the smoke-filled room accompanied by the woman, and gone out through a door at one side into the corridor that led back to the little partitioned board compartments of the brothel.

Here, it was at once evident that there was nothing to do but wait. A long line of men and women that stretched from one end of the hallway to another stood waiting for their brief occupancies of the little compartments at the other end, all of which were now obviously and audibly occupied.

As they came out into the hall, the woman with the boy called out to another woman at the front end of the line: "Hello, May! . . . Have ya seen Grace?"

"Aah!" said the woman thus addressed, letting cigarette smoke coil from her nostrils as she spoke, and speaking with the rasping, exaggerated and brutal toughness that has been described: "I t'ink she's in number Seven here havin' a ——."

And having conveyed the information in this delicate manner, she then turned to her companion, a brawny, grinning seaman in the uniform of the United States Navy, and with a brisk, yet rather bantering humor, demanded:

"Well, whatcha say, big boy? . . . Gettin' tired of waitin'? . . . Well, it won't be long now . . . Dey'll be troo in dere in a minute an' we're next."

"Dey better had be!" the sailor replied with a kind of jocular savagery. "If dey ain't, I'll tear down duh —— joint! . . . Christ!" he cried in an astounded tone, after listening attentively for a moment. "Holy Jeez!" he said with a dumbfounded laugh. "What t' hell are dey doin' in deh all dis time? Who is dat guy, anyway?—A whole regiment of duh Marines, duh way it sounds t' me! Holy *Je-sus!*" he cried with an astounded laugh, listening again—"Christ!"

"Ah, c'mon, Jack!" the woman said with a kind of brutal, husky tenderness, snuggling close to his brawny arm meanwhile, and lewdly proposing her heavy body against his. "Yuh ain't gonna get impatient on me now, are yuh? . . . Just hold on a minute moeh an' I'll give ya somet'ing ya neveh had befoeh!—"

"If yuh do," the gallant tar said tenderly, drawing his mighty fist back now in a gesture of savage endearment that somehow seemed to please her, "I'll come back here and smack yuh right in duh puss, yuh son-of-a-bitch!" he amorously whispered, and pulled her to him.

Similar conversations and actions were to be observed all up and down the line: there were lewd jests, ribald laughter, and impatiently shouted demands on the noisy occupants of the little compartments to "come on out an' give some of duh rest of us a chanct, f'r Chris' sake!" and other expressions of a similar nature.

It was a brutally hot night in the middle of August: in the hallway the air was stifling, weary, greasily humid. The place was thick, dense, stale and foul with tobacco smoke, the stench of the men, the powder and cheap perfume of the women and over all, unforgettable, over-powering, pungent, resinous, rude and raw as savage nature and man's naked lust, was the odor of the new, unpainted, white-pine lumber of which the whole shambling and haphazard place had been constructed.

Finally, after a long and weary wait in that stifling place, during which time the door of the compartments had opened many times, and many men and women had come out, and many more gone in, the boy and the woman with him had advanced to the head of the line, and were next in the succession of that unending and vociferous column.

Presently, the door of the room for which they waited opened, a man came out, shut the door behind him, and then went quickly down the hall. Then for a moment there was silence, impatient mutters in the line behind them, and at length the woman with the boy, muttering:

"I wondeh what t' hell she's doin' all dis time!—Hey!" she cried harshly, and hammered on the door, "Who's in dere? . . . Come on out, f'r Chris' sake! . . . Yuh're holding up duh line!"

In a moment, a woman's voice answered wearily:

"All right, Fay! . . . Just a moment, dear. . . . I'll be there."

"Oh," the woman with the boy said, in a suddenly quiet, strangely tender kind of voice. "It's Margaret. . . . I guess she's worn out, poor kid." And knocking at the door again, but this time gently, almost timidly, she said in a quiet voice:

"How are yuh, kid? . . . D'ya need any help?"

"No, it's all right, Fay," the girl inside said in the same tired and ut-

706

terly exhausted tone. "I'll be out in a moment. . . . Come on in, honey."

The woman opened the door softly and entered the room. The only furnishings of the hot, raw, and hideous little place, besides a chair, an untidy and rumpled looking bed, and a table, was a cheap dresser on which was a doll girdled with a soiled ribbon of pink silk, tied in a big bow, a photograph of a young sailor inscribed with the words, "To Margaret, the best pal I ever had—Ed"—and a package of cigarettes. An electric fan, revolving slowly from left to right, droned incessantly, and fanned the close stale air with a kind of sporadic and sweltering breeze.

And from moment to moment, as it swung in its half-orbit, the fan would play full upon the face and head of the girl, who was lying on the bed in an attitude of utter pitiable weariness. When this happened, a single strand of her shining hair, which was straight, lank, fine-spun as silk, and of a lovely red-bronze texture, would be disturbed by the movement of the fan and would be blown gently back and forth across her temple.

The girl, who was tall, slender, and very lovely was, save for her shoes and stockings, naked, and she lay extended at full length on the untidy bed, with one arm thrust out in a gesture of complete exhaustion, the other folded underneath her shining hair, and her face, which had a fragile, transparent, almost starved delicacy, turned to one side and resting on her arm, the eyelids closed. And the eyelids also had this delicacy of texture, were violet with weariness, and so transparent that the fine net-work of the veins was plainly visible.

The other woman went softly over to the bed, sat down beside her, and began to speak to her in a low and tender tone. In a moment the girl turned her head towards the woman, opened her eyes, and smiled, in a faint and distant way, as of some one who is just emerging from the drugged spell of an opiate:

"What? . . . What did you say, darling? . . . No, I'm all right," she said faintly, and sitting up, with the other woman's help, she swiftly pulled on over her head the cheap one-piece garment she was wearing, which had been flung back over the chair beside the bed. Then smiling, she stood up, took a cigarette out of the package on the dresser, lighted it, and turning to the boy, who was standing in the door, said ironically, with something of the rasping accent which the other women used, beneath which, however, her pleasant rather husky tone was plainly evident.

"All right, 'Georgia'! Come on in!"

He went in slowly, still looking at her with an astounded stare. He had known her the first moment he had looked at her. She was a girl from the little town where the state university, at which he was a student, was situated, a member of a family of humble decent people, well known in the town: she had disappeared almost two years before, there had been rumor at the time that one of the students had "got her in trouble," and since that time he had neither seen nor heard of her.

"How are all the folks down home?" she said. "How's every one in Hopewell?"

Her luminous smoke-gray eyes were hard and bright as she spoke, her mouth, in her thin young face, was hard and bitter as a blade, and her voice was almost deliberately hard and mocking. And yet, beneath this defiant scornfulness, the strange, husky tenderness of the girl's tone persisted, and as she spoke, she put her slender hand lightly on his arm, with the swift, unconscious tenderness of people in a world of strangers who suddenly meet some one they know from home.

"They're all right," he stammered in a confused and bewildered tone, his face beginning to smoulder with embarrassment as he spoke.

"Well, if you see any one I know," she said in the same ironic tone, "say hello for me. . . . Tell 'em that I sent my love."

"All right," he blurted out stupidly. "I—I—certainly will."

"And I'm mad at you, 'Georgia,' " she said with a kind of mocking reproachfulness, "I'm mad at you for not telling me you were here. . . . The next time you come here you'd better ask for me—or I'll be mad! . . . We homefolks have got to stick together. . . . So you ask for Margaret—or I'll be mad at you—do you hear?"

"All right!" he stammered confusedly again, "I certainly will."

She looked at him a moment longer with her hard bright stare, her bitter, strangely tender smile. Then thrusting her fingers swiftly through his hair, she turned to the other woman and said:

"Be nice to him, Fay. . . . He's one of the folks from down my way. . . . Good-bye, 'Georgia.' . . . When you come back again you ask for Margaret."

"Good-bye," he said, and she was gone, out the door and down that stifling little hall of brutal, crowding, and imperative desire, into the market-place again, where for the thousandth time she would offer the sale of her young slender body to whoever would be there to buy; to solicit, take, accept the patronage of any of the thousand nameless and unknown men that the huge cylinder of chance and of the night might bring to her.

He never saw her after that. She was engulfed into the great vortex of the war, the huge dark abyss and thronging chaos of America, the immense, the cruel, the indifferent and the magic land, where all of us have lived and walked as strangers, where all of us have been so small, so lonely, and forsaken, which has engulfed us all at length, and in whose dark and lonely breast so many lost and nameless men are buried and forgotten.

This, then, was the third visage of calamity, the image of desire, the face of war.

John Crowe Ransom

Few American men of letters have combined the professions of teaching and writing so well as John Crowe Ransom (born in 1888) has done. After graduating from Vanderbilt and studying as a Rhodes scholar at Oxford, Ransom returned to his alma mater, where he taught English for twenty-three years. Since 1937 he has been Carnegie Professor of Poetry at Kenyon College and editor of the Kenyon Review, *which became immediately, under his guidance, one of the best critical journals published in England or America.*

Ransom's poetical talent was stimulated by his contact with the young poets of the Fugitive group at Vanderbilt, several of whom were his students. Aside from his Selected Poems (*1945*), *he has published only three volumes of verse:* Poems about God (*1919*), Chills and Fever (*1924*), *and* Two Gentlemen in Bonds (*1927*). *Though his poems are few in number, their quality is distinguished. They are related, certainly, to the metaphysical poems of Donne and his followers, but they are not in the least derivative in style. They possess a gravity that is never solemn and an elegance which is not decorative but substantial. A Ransom poem is likely to be a revealing verse-epitaph or a verse-portrait in a small frame. As F. O. Matthiessen noted, Ransom's favorite theme is "that of the divided sensibility, torn between reason and imagination, between science and faith."*

These three poems are reprinted from Selected Poems *by John Crowe Ransom, by permission of Alfred A. Knopf, Inc.*

DEAD BOY

THE little cousin is dead, by foul subtraction,
A green bough from Virginia's aged tree,
And none of the county kin like the transaction,
Nor some of the world of outer dark, like me.

A boy not beautiful, nor good, nor clever,
A black cloud full of storms too hot for keeping,
A sword beneath his mother's heart—yet never
Woman bewept her babe as this is weeping.

A pig with a pasty face, so I had said,
Squealing for cookies, kinned by poor pretense
With a noble house. But the little man quite dead,
I see the forebears' antique lineaments.

The elder men have strode by the box of death
To the wide flag porch, and muttering low send round
The bruit of the day. O friendly waste of breath!
Their hearts are hurt with a deep dynastic wound.

He was pale and little, the foolish neighbors say;
The first-fruits, saith the Preacher, the Lord hath taken;
But this was the old tree's late branch wrenched away,
Grieving the sapless limbs, the shorn and shaken.

JUDITH OF BETHULIA

Beautiful as the flying legend of some leopard
She had not yet chosen her great captain or prince
Depositary to her flesh, and our defense;
And a wandering beauty is a blade out of its scabbard.
You know how dangerous, gentlemen of threescore?
May you know it yet ten more.

Nor by process of veiling she grew the less fabulous.
Grey or blue veils, we were desperate to study
The invincible emanations of her white body,
And the winds at her ordered raiment were ominous.
Might she walk in the market, sit in the council of soldiers?
Only of the extreme elders.

But a rare chance was the girl's then, when the Invader
Trumpeted from the south, and rumbled from the north,
Beleaguered the city from four quarters of the earth,
Our soldiery too craven and sick to aid her—
Where were the arms could countervail this horde?
Her beauty was the sword.

She sat with the elders, and proved on their blear visage
How bright was the weapon unrusted in her keeping,
While he lay surfeiting on their harvest heaping,
Wasting the husbandry of their rarest vintage—
And dreaming of the broad-breasted dames for concubine?
These floated on his wine.

He was lapped with bay-leaves, and grass and fumiter weed,
And from under the wine-film encountered his mortal vision,
For even within his tent she accomplished his derision;
She loosed one veil and another, standing unafraid;
And he perished. Nor brushed her with even so much as a daisy?
She found his destruction easy.

The heathen are all perished. The victory was furnished,
We smote them hiding in our vineyards, barns, annexes,
And now their white bones clutter the holes of foxes,
And the chieftain's head, with grinning sockets, and varnished—
Is it hung on the sky with a hideous epitaphy?
No, the woman keeps the trophy.

May God send unto our virtuous lady her prince.
It is stated she went reluctant to that orgy,
Yet a madness fevers our young men, and not the clergy
Nor the elders have turned them unto modesty since.
Inflamed by the thought of her naked beauty with desire?
Yes, and chilled with fear and despair.

TWO IN AUGUST

Two that could not have lived their single lives
As can some husbands and wives
Did something strange: they tensed their vocal cords
And attacked each other with silences and words
Like catapulted stones and arrowed knives.

Dawn was not yet; night is for loving or sleeping,
Sweet dreams or safekeeping;
Yet he of the wide brows that were used to laurel
And she, the famed for gentleness, must quarrel,
Furious both of them, and scared, and weeping.

How sleepers groan, twitch, wake to such a mood
Is not well understood,
Nor why two entities grown almost one
Should rend and murder trying to get undone,
With individual tigers in their blood.

She in terror fled from the marriage chamber
Circuiting the dark rooms like a string of amber
Round and round and back,
And would not light one lamp against the black,
And heard the clock that clanged: Remember, Remember.

And he must tread barefooted the dim lawn,
Soon he was up and gone;
High in the trees the night-mastered birds were crying
With fear upon their tongues, no singing or flying
Which are their lovely attitudes by dawn.

Whether those bird-cries were of heaven or hell
There is no way to tell;
In the long ditch of darkness the man walked
Under the hackberry trees where the birds talked
With words too sad and strange to syllable.

Katherine Anne Porter

*Katherine Anne Porter is one of the most cosmopolitan of Southern
writers. Though she remembers vividly her aristocratic black-gowned
grandmother, who was a bride in Kentucky in 1850, and can trace her
ancestry in an old family of solid wealth in Kentucky, Louisiana, and
Virginia, she was born near San Antonio and early came to know and
love the German colonists in Texas and the Mexicans of her county. As
a girl she also knew the French-Spanish people of New Orleans and
the Cajuns in small Louisiana towns. Later she taught school in Mexico
and wrote of it with an intimate knowledge. She has also lived in
Colorado and in New York City.*

In consequence the America Miss Porter has known is, as she says, "a borderland of strange tongues and commingled races." The people living in this borderland led strange lives—so most other Americans would think—and thus her stories about them have an exotic flavor which some have wrongly called foreign.

To define the quality of a story by Katherine Anne Porter is not easy. Yet her method and style are unique. Some of her stories which seem at first to be mere fragments of experience end in a quiet explosion that has been carefully prepared for along the way. Quite terrible things happen in these stories but we see the conclusive horror at a distance, because Miss Porter has deliberately prevented us from emotional involvement. This detachment comes close to irony. But in holding the reader off in this fashion, she forces him to define the situation and to judge it. Robert Penn Warren finds in her irony "a refusal to accept the code, the formula, the ready-made solution, the hand-me-down morality, the word for the spirit."

Although she is undoubtedly one of the most distinguished of modern American writers, Miss Porter has written comparatively little. Her reputation rests largely on the three collections of stories and nouvelles: Flowering Judas and Other Stories *(1930; expanded in 1935 to include four additional stories);* Pale Horse, Pale Rider *(1939); and* The Leaning Tower and Other Stories *(1944). A volume of reminiscences and critical essays,* The Days Before, *was issued in 1952.*

"The Grave" is from The Leaning Tower and Other Stories, *copyright, 1944, by Katherine Anne Porter. Reprinted by permission of Harcourt, Brace & Company, Inc.*

THE GRAVE

THE grandfather, dead for more than thirty years, had been twice disturbed in his long repose by the constancy and possessiveness of his widow. She removed his bones first to Louisiana and then to Texas as if she had set out to find her own burial place, knowing well she would never return to the places she had left. In Texas she set up a small cemetery in a corner of her first farm, and as the family connection grew, and oddments of relations came over from Kentucky to settle, it contained at last about twenty graves. After the grandmother's death, part of her land was to be sold for the benefit of certain of her children, and the cemetery happened to lie in the part set aside for sale. It was necessary to take up the bodies and bury them again in the family plot in the big new public cemetery, where the grandmother had been buried. At last her husband was to lie beside her for eternity, as she had planned.

The family cemetery had been a pleasant small neglected garden of tangled rose bushes and ragged cedar trees and cypress, the simple flat stones rising out of uncropped sweet-smelling wild grass. The graves were lying open and empty one burning day when Miranda and her brother Paul, who often went together to hunt rabbits and doves, propped their twenty-two Winchester rifles carefully against the rail fence, climbed over and explored among the graves. She was nine years old and he was twelve.

They peered into the pits all shaped alike with such purposeful accuracy, and looking at each other with pleased adventurous eyes, they said in solemn tones: "These were graves!" trying by words to shape a special, suitable emotion in their minds, but they felt nothing except an agreeable thrill of wonder: they were seeing a new sight, doing something they had not done before. In them both there was also a small disappointment at the entire commonplaceness of the actual spectacle. Even if it had once contained a coffin for years upon years, when the coffin was gone a grave was just a hole in the ground. Miranda leaped into the pit that had held her grandfather's bones. Scratching around aimlessly and pleasurably as any young animal, she scooped up a lump of earth and weighed it in her palm. It had a pleasantly sweet, corrupt smell, being mixed with cedar needles and small leaves, and as the crumbs fell apart, she saw a silver dove no larger than a hazel nut, with spread wings and a neat fan-shaped tail. The breast had a deep round hollow in it. Turning it up to the fierce sunlight, she saw that the inside of the hollow was cut in little whorls. She scrambled out, over the pile of loose earth that had fallen back into one end of the grave, calling to Paul that she had found something, he must guess what . . . His head appeared smiling over the rim of another grave. He waved a closed hand at her. "I've got something too!" They ran to compare treasures, making a game of it, so many guesses each, all wrong, and a final showdown with opened palms. Paul had found a thin wide gold ring carved with intricate flowers and leaves. Miranda was smitten at sight of the ring and wished to have it. Paul seemed more impressed by the dove. They made a trade, with some little bickering. After he had got the dove in his hand, Paul said, "Don't you know what this is? This is a screw head for a *coffin!* . . . I'll bet nobody else in the world has one like this!"

Miranda glanced at it without covetousness. She had the gold ring on her thumb; it fitted perfectly. "Maybe we ought to go now," she said, "maybe one of the niggers 'll see us and tell somebody." They knew the land had been sold, the cemetery was no longer theirs, and they felt like trespassers. They climbed back over the fence, slung their rifles loosely under their arms—they had been shooting at targets with various kinds of firearms since they were seven years old—and set out to look for the rabbits and doves or whatever small game might happen along. On these expeditions Miranda always followed at Paul's heels along the path, obeying instructions about handling her gun when going through fences; learning how to stand it up properly so it would not slip and fire unexpectedly; how to wait her time for a shot and not just bang away in the air without looking, spoiling shots for Paul, who really could hit things if given a chance. Now and then, in her excitement at seeing birds whizz up suddenly before her face, or a rabbit leap across her very toes, she lost her head, and almost without sighting she flung her rifle up and pulled the trigger. She hardly ever hit any sort of mark. She had no proper sense of hunting at all. Her brother would be often completely disgusted with her. "You don't care whether you get your bird or not," he said. "That's no way to hunt." Miranda could not understand his indignation. She had seen him smash his hat and yell with fury when he had missed his aim. "What I like about shooting," said Miranda, with exasperating inconsequence, "is pulling the trigger and hearing the noise."

"Then, by golly," said Paul, "whyn't you go back to the range and shoot at bulls-eyes?"

"I'd just as soon," said Miranda, "only like this, we walk around more."

"Well, you just stay behind and stop spoiling my shots," said Paul, who, when he made a kill, wanted to be certain he had made it. Miranda, who alone brought down a bird once in twenty rounds, always claimed as her own any game they got when they fired at the same moment. It was tiresome and unfair and her brother was sick of it.

"Now, the first dove we see, or the first rabbit, is mine," he told her. "And the next will be yours. Remember that and don't get smarty."

"What about snakes?" asked Miranda idly. "Can I have the first snake?"

Waving her thumb gently and watching her gold ring glitter, Miranda lost interest in shooting. She was wearing her summer roughing outfit: dark blue overalls, a light blue shirt, a hired-man's straw hat, and thick brown sandals. Her brother had the same outfit except his was a sober hickory-nut color. Ordinarily Miranda preferred her overalls to any other dress, though it was making rather a scandal in the countryside, for the year was 1903, and in the back country the law of female decorum had teeth in it. Her father had been criticized for letting his girls dress like boys and go careering around astride barebacked horses. Big sister Maria, the really independent and fearless one, in spite of her rather affected ways, rode at a dead run with only a rope knotted around her horse's nose. It was said the motherless family was running down, with the Grandmother no longer there to hold it together. It was known that she had discriminated against her son Harry in her will, and that he was in straits about money. Some of his old neighbors reflected with vicious satisfaction that now he would probably not be so stiffnecked, nor have any more high-stepping horses either. Miranda knew this, though she could not say how. She had met along the road old women of the kind who smoked corn-cob pipes, who had treated her grandmother with most sincere respect. They slanted their gummy old eyes side-ways at the granddaughter and said, "Ain't you ashamed of yoself, Missy? It's aginst the Scriptures to dress like that. Whut yo Pappy thinkin about?" Miranda, with her powerful social sense, which was like a fine set of antennae radiating from every pore of her skin, would feel ashamed because she knew well it was rude and ill-bred to shock anybody, even bad-tempered old crones, though she had faith in her father's judgment and was perfectly comfortable in the clothes. Her father had said, "They're just what you need, and they'll save your dresses for school . . ." This sounded quite simple and natural to her. She had been brought up in rigorous economy. Wastefulness was vulgar. It was also a sin. These were truths; she had heard them repeated many times and never once disputed.

Now the ring, shining with the serene purity of fine gold on her rather grubby thumb, turned her feelings against her overalls and sockless feet, toes sticking through the thick brown leather straps. She wanted to go back to the farmhouse, take a good cold bath, dust herself with plenty of Maria's violet talcum powder—provided Maria was not present to object, of course—put on the thinnest, most becoming dress she owned, with a big sash, and sit in a wicker chair under the trees . . . These things were not all she wanted, of course; she had vague stirrings of desire for luxury and a grand way of living which could not take precise form in her imagination but were founded on family legend of past wealth and leisure. These immediate comforts were what she could have, and she wanted them at once. She lagged rather far behind Paul, and once she thought of just turning back without a word and going home. She stopped, thinking that Paul would never do that to her, and so she would have to tell him. When a rabbit leaped, she let Paul have it without dispute. He killed it with one shot.

When she came up with him, he was already kneeling, examining the wound, the rabbit trailing from his hands. "Right through the head," he said complacently, as if he had aimed for it. He took out his sharp, competent bowie knife and started to skin the body. He did it very cleanly and quickly. Uncle Jimbilly knew how to prepare the skins so that Miranda always had fur coats for her dolls, for though she never cared much for her dolls she liked seeing them in fur coats. The children knelt facing each other over the dead animal. Miranda watched admiringly while her brother stripped the skin away as if he were taking off a glove. The flayed flesh emerged dark scarlet, sleek, firm; Miranda with thumb and finger felt the long fine muscles with the silvery flat strips binding them to the joints. Brother lifted the oddly bloated belly. "Look," he said, in a low amazed voice. "It was going to have young ones."

Very carefully he slit the thin flesh from the center ribs to the flanks, and a scarlet bag appeared. He slit again and pulled the bag open, and there lay a bundle of tiny rabbits, each wrapped in a thin scarlet veil. The brother pulled these off and there they were, dark gray, their sleek wet down lying in minute even ripples, like a baby's head just washed, their unbelievably small delicate ears folded close, their little blind faces almost featureless.

Miranda said, "Oh, I want to *see*," under her breath. She looked and looked—excited but not frightened, for she was accustomed to the sight of animals killed in hunting—filled with pity and astonishment and a kind of shocked delight in the wonderful little creatures for their own sakes, they were so pretty. She touched one of them ever so carefully, "Ah, there's blood running over them," she said and began to tremble without knowing why. Yet she wanted most deeply to see and to know. Having seen, she felt at once as if she had known all along. The very memory of her former ignorance faded, she had always known just this. No one had ever told her anything outright, she had been rather unobservant of the animal life around her because she was so accustomed to animals. They seemed simply disorderly and unaccountably rude in their habits, but altogether natural and not very interesting. Her brother had spoken as if he had known about everything all along. He may have seen all this before. He had never said a word to her, but she knew now a part at least of what he knew. She understood a little of the secret, formless intuitions in her own mind and body, which had been clearing up, taking form, so gradually and so steadily she had not realized that she was learning what she had to know. Paul said cautiously, as if he were talking about something forbidden: "They were just about ready to be born." His voice dropped on the last word. "I know," said Miranda, "like kittens. I know, like babies." She was quietly and terribly agitated, standing again with her rifle under her arm, looking down at the bloody heap. "I don't want the skin," she said, "I won't have it." Paul buried the young rabbits again in their mother's body, wrapped the skin around her, carried her to a clump of sage bushes, and hid her away. He came out again at once and said to Miranda, with an eager friendliness, a confidential tone quite unusual in him, as if he were taking her into an important secret on equal terms: "Listen now. Now you listen to me, and don't ever forget. Don't you ever tell a living soul that you saw this. Don't tell a soul. Don't tell Dad because I'll get into trouble. He'll say I'm leading you into things you ought not to do. He's always saying that. So now don't you go and forget and blab out sometime the way you're always doing . . . Now, that's a secret. Don't you tell."

Miranda never told, she did not even wish to tell anybody. She thought about the whole worrisome affair with confused unhappiness for a few days. Then it sank quietly into her mind and was heaped over by accumulated thousands of impressions, for nearly twenty years. One day she was picking her path among the puddles and crushed refuse of a market street in a strange city of a strange country, when without warning, plain and clear in its true colors as if she looked through a frame upon a scene that had not stirred nor changed since the moment it happened, the episode of that far-off day leaped from its burial place before her mind's eye. She was so reasonlessly horrified she halted suddenly staring, the scene before her eyes dimmed by the vision back of them. An Indian vendor had held up before her a tray of dyed sugar sweets, in the shapes of all kinds of small creatures: birds, baby chicks, baby rabbits, lambs, baby pigs. They were in gay colors and smelled of vanilla, maybe. . . . It was a very hot day and the smell in the market, with its piles of raw flesh and wilting flowers, was like the mingled sweetness and corruption she had smelled that other day in the empty cemetery at home: the day she had remembered always until now vaguely as the time she and her brother had found treasure in the opened graves. Instantly upon this thought the dreadful vision faded, and she saw clearly her brother, whose childhood face she had forgotten, standing again in the blazing sunshine, again twelve years old, a pleased sober smile in his eyes, turning the silver dove over and over in his hands.

Allen Tate

Since the mid-twenties Allen Tate (born in 1899) has been one of the leaders in the Southern literary renaissance. While he was a student at Vanderbilt he helped to organize the group of sixteen writers who called themselves "the Fugitives" and issued the important "little magazine," The Fugitive, of which Tate was one of the editors from 1922 to 1925. Three of the other members of the group, John Crowe Ransom, Donald Davidson, and Robert Penn Warren, were destined, like Tate, to exercise a pervasive influence on American letters.

In 1930 Tate, Ransom, Davidson, and Warren joined eight other

ALLEN TATE: *Ode to the Confederate Dead*

Southerners in the writing of I'll Take My Stand: The South and the Agrarian Tradition. *This volume, which supported a Southern way of life against "what may be called the American or prevailing way," stirred up one of the most interesting controversies of our time. The contributors were accused of being escapists, neo-Confederates, poets and scholars who were meddling with economic and social matters of which they could not be supposed to know much. Their defenders, on the contrary, asserted that the Agrarians were offering the only solution to the problems of the South which could save it from the mediocrity of standardized American life, the Leviathan state, and the evils of industrialization.*

Meanwhile Tate had made a name for himself as one of the best of America's younger poets and critics. The dominant theme of his early verse is the dehumanization of life in our time. Contrary to the assertions of the opponents of the Agrarians, Tate was not then (nor was he later) a romantic traditionalist. Much as he loved the South of his ancestors, its ancient piety and its reverence for classical culture, he has fought the scientism and positivism of the modern world with the modern poet's weapons of irony and wit. Since his conversion to Catholicism he has added to these the resources of his faith.

The body of Tate's poetry is not large. He has not hesitated to suppress poems that he considers inferior or to rework others which he felt he could improve. The latest collection of his verse is Poems, 1922–1947 (*1948*). *Tate has also published biographies of Stonewall Jackson and Jefferson Davis, four volumes of collected critical essays, and one novel,* The Fathers (*1938*), *which is outstanding among fictional treatments of the Civil War period.*

The selections given here are reprinted from Poems, 1922–1947 *by Allen Tate; copyright 1932, 1937, 1948 by Charles Scribner's Sons; used by permission of the publishers.*

ODE TO THE CONFEDERATE DEAD

Row after row with strict impunity
The headstones yield their names to the element,
The wind whirrs without recollection;
In the riven troughs the splayed leaves
Pile up, of nature the casual sacrament
To the seasonal eternity of death;
Then driven by the fierce scrutiny
Of heaven to their election in the vast breath,
They sough the rumor of mortality.

719

Autumn is desolation in the plot
Of a thousand acres where these memories grow
From the inexhaustible bodies that are not
Dead, but feed the grass row after rich row.
Think of the autumns that have come and gone!—
Ambitious November with the humors of the year,
With a particular zeal for every slab,
Staining the uncomfortable angels that rot
On the slabs, a wing chipped here, an arm there:
The brute curiosity of an angel's stare
Turns you, like them, to stone,
Transforms the heaving air
Till plunged to a heavier world below
You shift your sea-space blindly
Heaving, turning like the blind crab.

    Dazed by the wind, only the wind
    The leaves flying, plunge

You know who have waited by the wall
The twilight certainty of an animal,
Those midnight restitutions of the blood
You know—the immitigable pines, the smoky frieze
Of the sky, the sudden call: you know the rage,
The cold pool left by the mounting flood,
Of muted Zeno and Parmenides.
You who have waited for the angry resolution
Of those desires that should be yours tomorrow,
You know the unimportant shrift of death
And praise the vision
And praise the arrogant circumstance
Of those who fall
Rank upon rank, hurried beyond decision—
Here by the sagging gate, stopped by the wall.

    Seeing, seeing only the leaves
    Flying, plunge and expire

Turn your eyes to the immoderate past,
Turn to the inscrutable infantry rising
Demons out of the earth—they will not last.
Stonewall, Stonewall, and the sunken fields of hemp,
Shiloh, Antietam, Malvern Hill, Bull Run.

ALLEN TATE: *Ode to the Confederate Dead*

Lost in that orient of the thick-and-fast
You will curse the setting sun.

    Cursing only the leaves crying
    Like an old man in a storm

You hear the shout, the crazy hemlocks point
With troubled fingers to the silence which
Smothers you, a mummy, in time.

                The hound bitch
Toothless and dying, in a musty cellar
Hears the wind only.

           Now that the salt of their blood
Stiffens the saltier oblivion of the sea,
Seals the malignant purity of the flood,
What shall we who count our days and bow
Our heads with a commemorial woe
In the ribboned coats of grim felicity,
What shall we say of the bones, unclean,
Whose verdurous anonymity will grow?
The ragged arms, the ragged heads and eyes
Lost in these acres of the insane green?
The gray lean spiders come, they come and go;
In a tangle of willows without light
The singular screech-owl's tight
Invisible lyric seeds the mind
With the furious murmur of their chivalry.

    We shall say only the leaves
    Flying, plunge and expire

We shall say only the leaves whispering
In the improbable mist of nightfall
That flies on multiple wing:
Night is the beginning and the end
And in between the ends of distraction
Waits mute speculation, the patient curse
That stones the eyes, or like the jaguar leaps
For his own image in a jungle pool, his victim.

What shall we say who have knowledge
Carried to the heart? Shall we take the act

To the grave? Shall we, more hopeful, set up the grave
In the house? The ravenous grave?

Leave now
The shut gate and the decomposing wall:
The gentle serpent, green in the mulberry bush,
Riots with his tongue through the hush—
Sentinel of the grave who counts us all!

THE MEDITERRANEAN

Quem das finem, rex magne, dolorum?

Where we went in the boat was a long bay
A slingshot wide, walled in by towering stone—
Peaked margin of antiquity's delay,
And we went there out of time's monotone:

Where we went in the black hull no light moved
But a gull white-winged along the feckless wave,
The breeze, unseen but fierce as a body loved,
That boat drove onward like a willing slave:

Where we went in the small ship the seaweed
Parted and gave to us the murmuring shore,
And we made feast and in our secret need
Devoured the very plates Aeneas bore:

Where derelict you see through the low twilight
The green coast that you, thunder-tossed, would win
Drop sail, and hastening to drink all night
Eat dish and bowl to take that sweet land in!

Where we feasted and caroused on the sandless
Pebbles, affecting our day of piracy,
What prophecy of eaten plates could landless
Wanderers fulfil by the ancient sea?

We for that time might taste the famous age
Eternal here yet hidden from our eyes
When lust of power undid its stuffless rage;
They, in a wineskin, bore earth's paradise.

Let us lie down once more by the breathing side
Of Ocean, where our live forefathers sleep
As if the Known Sea still were a month wide—
Atlantis howls but is no longer steep!

What country shall we conquer, what fair land
Unman our conquest and locate our blood?
We've cracked the hemispheres with careless hand!
Now, from the Gates of Hercules we flood

Westward, westward till the barbous brine
Whelms us to the tired land where tasseling corn,
Fat beans, grapes sweeter than muscadine
Rot on the vine: in that land were we born.

ÆNEAS AT WASHINGTON

I myself saw furious with blood
Neoptolemus, at his side the black Atridæ,
Hecuba and the hundred daughters, Priam
Cut down, his filth drenching the holy fires.
In that extremity I bore me well,
A true gentleman, valorous in arms,
Disinterested and honourable. Then fled:
That was a time when civilization
Run by the few fell to the many, and
Crashed to the shout of men, the clang of arms:
Cold victualing I seized, I hoisted up
The old man my father upon my back,
In the smoke made by sea for a new world
Saving little—a mind imperishable
If time is, a love of past things tenuous
As the hesitation of receding love.

(To the reduction of uncitied littorals
We brought chiefly the vigor of prophecy,
Our hunger breeding calculation
And fixed triumphs)

                 I saw the thirsty dove
In the glowing fields of Troy, hemp ripening
And tawny corn, the thickening Blue Grass

All lying rich forever in the green sun.
I see all things apart, the towers that men
Contrive I too contrived long, long ago.
Now I demand little. The singular passion
Abides its object and consumes desire
In the circling shadow of its appetite.
There was a time when the young eyes were slow,
Their flame steady beyond the firstling fire,
I stood in the rain, far from home at nightfall
By the Potomac, the great Dome lit the water,
The city my blood had built I knew no more
While the screech-owl whistled his new delight
Consecutively dark.

        Stuck in the wet mire
Four thousand leagues from the ninth buried city
I thought of Troy, what we had built her for.

Caroline Gordon

In Caroline Gordon's Green Centuries *(1941) two brothers from North Carolina make their way into the new lands in Kentucky and Tennessee which were being opened to settlement in 1769. One of the brothers is captured by the Cherokee Indians and finds the ordered ritual of their life so congenial after the disorganization of the frontier that he refuses to return to the white man's world. This episode puts in striking form the dominant themes of Miss Gordon's fiction: the importance to the individual life of form and status and tradition, and the necessity for roots. All her characters develop or decay with the tightening or loosening of the bonds with family and land.*

In telling her stories Miss Gordon has the same high regard for form. She has studied carefully—though she does not imitate—the techniques of the great novelists, in particular Tolstoy, Flaubert, and Henry James. Her own work shows a steadily increasing mastery of her medium. She can wield the sharp weapon of irony; she knows the dangerous art of basing a novel on a myth; she employs with ingenious originality James's "central intelligence."

Caroline Gordon was born in 1895 on the border between Kentucky

CAROLINE GORDON: *The Brilliant Leaves*

and Tennessee. She married a Kentuckian, the poet and critic Allen Tate. For many years they owned a house on the Cumberland River near Clarksville, and it is of that region that she chiefly writes. Her knowledge of it is astonishingly wide. She is as familiar with the speech and manners of the Holy Roller Cumberland Ridge "covite" as she is with those of the tobacco-planter of the "Black Patch." She knows not only their present but their past, through listening to the tales of elderly relatives and through painstaking research. And as deeply as the people she knows the land. She has looked at it since childhood with fascinated and remembering eyes. Not many novelists have so rich a knowledge of their terrain or a technique so well tempered for writing about it.

"The Brilliant Leaves" is reprinted from The Forest of the South *by Caroline Gordon; copyright 1945 by Caroline Gordon; used by permission of the publishers, Charles Scribner's Sons.*

❁

THE BRILLIANT LEAVES

AT three o'clock he came out on the gallery. His mother and his aunt were at the far end, knitting. He had half an hour to kill and he stood, leaning against a post and listening to their talk. They liked to sit there in the afternoons and gossip about all the people who had come to this summer resort in the last thirty years. The Holloways—he was the grandson of a South Carolina bishop and she allowed her children to go barefooted and never attended vesper services; that Mrs. Paty who had had a fit one day in the post office; the mysterious boarder who came every summer to the Robinsons. They knew them all. They were talking now about something that had happened a long time ago. A girl named Sally Mainwaring had climbed down a rope ladder to meet her sweetheart while her father stood at another window, shotgun in hand. When she got to the ground the lover had scuttled off into the bushes, "and so," his aunt concluded dramatically, "she came back into the house through the front door and was an old maid the rest of her life."

"Those Mainwaring girls were all fast," his mother said reflectively.

"Not fast, Jenny, wild."

"High-spirited," his mother conceded. "Come to think of it, Sally Mainwaring was the first woman I ever saw ride astride. I remember. I was about ten years old and she came by the house on a big black horse. I thought about Queen Elizabeth reviewing the troops at Banbury."

"Tilbury, Jenny. You always get things wrong."

"Tilbury or Banbury," his mother said. "It's all one. Kate, do you throw over a stitch here or just keep on purling?"

He had his watch open in his hand and now he snapped it shut and stepped off the gallery onto the ground. His mother looked up quickly. "Aren't you going to play tennis this afternoon, Jimmy?"

"No," he said. "I thought I'd just take a turn in the woods," and he was gone up the path before she could speak again.

The path took him quickly into the woods. The mountain arched up its western brow here and it was all wooded, but the cottage—the cottage to which his family had come every summer since he was born —was on an open slope facing north. When you stood on the gallery and looked out, you had the roofs of all those little white houses spread below you. He halted once imperceptibly and glanced back. They always looked just alike, those houses. He wondered how his mother and his aunt could sit there every afternoon talking about the people who lived in them.

He took his watch out again. "Meet me at half past three," Evelyn had said. It was only ten minutes past now. He didn't want to get there first and just stand waiting. He slowed his pace. This part of the woods he was in now was full of black gums. The ground under his feet was red with the brilliant, fallen leaves. "Spectacular," his aunt called it. He had come here yesterday on a duty walk with her and with his mother. His aunt kept commenting on the colors of the leaves, and every now and then she would make him pick one up for her. "The entrance to the woods is positively spectacular," she told everybody when she got home.

All the time he had been wondering when Evelyn would get there. And then this morning her letter had come. ". . . We're leaving Friday morning. I've got to get up in a minute and start packing. . . ."

He said over to himself the part about the train. "I'm telling you which one it is, but don't come to meet it. Don't even come to the house—first. I'll meet you at our tree. I can be there by half past . . ."

He came to a log and, standing flat-footed, jumped over it. When he landed on the other side he broke into a run, hands held chest high, feet beating the ground in a heavy rhythm, the kind of stride you used in track. He ran four or five hundred yards then stopped, grinning and looking about him as if there might have been somebody there to see.

Another five hundred yards carried him to the tree. Evelyn was already there, walking up and down, her hands in the pockets of her brown sweater. She heard him, turned and came running, so fast that they bumped into each other. She recoiled but he caught her to him and held her awkwardly until he had pressed his mouth on hers. Her lips, parting beneath his, felt firm and cool, not warm and soft as they had been when they kissed good-by in June under this same tree.

His arm was still about her, but she was pulling away to look up into his face. "Dimmy!" she said.

They both laughed because that was what his aunt called him sometimes and it made him mad. Then they drew apart and started walking down the road. Her brown hair was long, now, and done up in a knot, and she had on Girl Scout shoes and bright red socks and she kept scuffling the leaves up as she went. He walked beside her, his hands in his pockets. Now that he didn't have his arms around her he felt awkward. That was because she was silent, like the picture he had at home on his dresser, not laughing and talking or turning her head the way she really did.

She looked up at him, sidewise. "It's different, isn't it," she said.

His impulse was to stop short but he made himself walk on. He spoke and was surprised to find his voice so deep. "Why is it different, Evelyn?"

Color burned in her smooth cheek. She fixed bright, shy eyes on his. "*Silly!*" she said.

He thought that he must have sounded silly. Still she didn't have any business to say what she had. His face hardened. "Why is it different?" he persisted in the same controlled voice.

She jumped up, high enough to snatch a wine-colored leaf from the bough over her head. "Everything was green, then," she said. "Last time we were here the woods were just turning green."

He remembered the June woods. His face, which some people thought too heavy, lightened. "I know a place where it's still green," he said. "I was there the other day. There's some yellow leaves but it's mostly green. Like summer."

"Come on," she said and caught his extended hand. They raced down the road, scattering the brilliant leaves from under their feet. After a little they came out on the brow of the mountain. There was no red carpet there. What trees could be seen, stunted hackberries mostly, grew in crevices of the rock. They went forward and stood on the great ledge that was called Sunset Point. Below them the valley shimmered in autumn haze. They could see the Murfreesboro road cutting its way through fields of russet sedge, or suddenly white against a patch of winter oats. They watched a black car spin along past the field and disappear into the tunnel of woods that marked the base of the mountain. Suddenly she stretched her arms out and tilted her head back so that she was looking straight into the sky. "The sky's on fire," she cried and laughed out loud like a child.

He touched her arm. "Let's go down there," he said and pointed to the road which wound along the side of the ledge.

They stepped over the drift of dead leaves which choked the entrance and started down. The road slanted steeply along the mountainside. The boughs of the trees met over it in some places. Frail grass grew in the ruts and there were ferns along the edge. What sun got through lay in bright coins on the frail grass and the ferns. The air was cool, not with autumn chill but with the coolness of the deep shade.

The rock they sat down on was tufted with moss. She laid her hand on it, fingers outspread and curving downward. "Look," she said, "every one's like a little pine tree."

"Sometimes they have little flowers on them," he said.

He watched the slim, tanned fingers sink deeper among the little green sprays. "I thought you might not come today," he said. "I heard the train and I thought maybe you didn't come."

"We almost didn't," she said. "Mother got a telegram at the last minute."

"Who from?"

"Aunt Sally Mainwaring. She's always coming to see us."

"Is that the old lady that stays at the Porters'?"

She nodded indifferently. "She's awful crabby."

"I heard mother and my aunt talking about her. They said she climbed out of a window to elope."

She nodded again. "But he was gone when she got down there, so she was an old maid. That's what makes her so crabby."

They both laughed. Off in the woods a bird called, an unbearably sweet note that seemed to belong to summer rather than autumn. She was looking at the road where it disappeared around a great boulder whose base was thick with ferns. "Where does it go?"

"To Cowan. They call it the old Confederate road. My grandfather came along here once."

"What for?"

"I don't know," he answered vaguely. "He said it was a night attack."

She had got up and was moving over to the place where the ferns grew most luxuriantly. She stood and looked down at them. "Just like summer," she said. "It's just like summer in here, isn't it, Jimmy?"

"Yes, it is," he said.

She walked on. He followed her around the corner of the great boulder. "Have you been playing much tennis?" she asked.

"There wasn't anything else to do," he said.

"How's your backhand?"

"Pretty good. There was a new fellow here this summer could beat me two out of three."

"That Jerrold boy from Atlanta?"

"How'd you know about him?"

"Pinky Thomas wrote me."

He was silent. He had not known that she corresponded with Pinky Thomas. "I don't reckon I'll be playing so much tennis from now on," he said at length.

She made no comment. He leaned down and pulled some beggar's lice from his trouser leg. "I don't reckon I'll be up here much next summer. Not more'n two weeks anyhow. You lay off all summer and it shows on you all right. But I don't reckon that makes much difference."

"Why won't you be up here next summer?" she asked in a low voice.

"Dad wants me to go in his office," he said. "I reckon I better start. I suppose—I suppose if you're ever going to make a living you better get started at it."

She did not answer, then suddenly she stepped up on the edge of the rock. He jumped up beside her. "Evelyn," he said, "would you marry me?"

She was looking off through the woods. "They wouldn't let us," she said; "we're too young."

"I know," he said, "but if I go in dad's office. I mean . . . pretty soon I'd get a raise. I mean . . . you would, wouldn't you?"

She turned her head. Their eyes met. Hers were a light, clear brown like the leaves that lie sometimes in the bed of a brook. "I'm perfectly *crazy* about you," she said.

He lifted her in his arms and jumped from the rock. They sank down in the bed of ferns. When he kissed her she kissed him back. She put her arms around his neck and laid her cheek against his, but when he slipped his hand inside the V of her sweater to curve it into the soft hollow under her arm she drew away. "Don't," she said, "please, Jimmy."

"I won't," he said.

She let him kiss her again, then she got to her knees. He sat up straight beside her and caught her hand and held it tight. Her hand fluttered in his then broke away. "It's still in here," she said. "No, it isn't, either. I hear running water."

"It's the falls," he said. "Bridal Veil Falls is round the corner of that big ledge."

"I never have seen it," she said.

"It's not very pretty around there," he said.

She was laughing and her eyes had more than ever that look of leaves in a running brook. "I bet it's prettier than it is here," she said.

He stood up, straightened his tie and passed a hand over his hair then stretched a hand out to her. She jumped up beside him lightly. "It's this way," he said and struck off on a path through the ferns. She

729

followed close. Sometimes they could walk side by side. Sometimes when he had to go in front he put his hand back and she held on to it.

He stopped abruptly beside a big sycamore. She was walking fast and ran into him. He embraced her and kissed her, hard. "You're so sweet," he whispered.

She said again, "I'm *crazy* about you," and then she pulled away to look up at him. "Don't you—don't you like doing things together, Jimmy?"

"Some things," he said and they laughed and after that stepped side by side for a while.

They came out of the hollow and were on the brow of the mountain again. In front of them was a series of limestone ledges that came down one after another like steps. Gushing out from one of them, filling the whole air with the sound of its rushing, was the white waterfall they called the Bridal Veil.

She drew her breath in sharply. "I never was here before," she cried.

He led her past one of the great boulders which were all about them. They set their feet on the ledge from which the water sprang.

"Look," he said, "you can see where it comes out." She leaned forward in the curve of his arm. The water came down out of a fissure in the highest ledge. It was pure and colorless at first, but it whitened as it struck the first rock step. She leaned farther forward, still with his arm curving about her. Far below were a few pools of still water, fringed with ferns, but most of the water kept white with its dashing from ledge to ledge. She turned quickly, and he felt the cold drops of moisture as her cheek brushed his. "It's like a bridal veil," she said.

He was eyeing the great shelf that made the first falls. "There's a place in there where you can stand and be dry as a bone," he said.

"Have you been there?"

He nodded. "Bill Thompson and I climbed through once. Long time ago. We must have been about ten years old."

She was still turned away from the water, facing him. Her eyes brightened. "Would you do it again?" she asked.

He hesitated, conscious of his body that seemed now to belong more to the ground than it had eight years ago. "I reckon I could if I had to," he said.

Her fingers closed on his arm. "Let's do it now."

He stared at her. "Are you crazy?" he asked.

She did not answer. Her face was bent down. He could see that her eyes were traveling along the main ledge. "How did you go?" she asked.

He pointed to a round rock that rose in the middle of the shelf. "We climbed up over that and then when you get back in there it's like a little path."

Her fingers were softly opening and closing on his arm. She reached up suddenly and gave his cheek a feather-light touch. "I *like* doing things together," she said.

He was looking at her steadily. The color had risen in his cheeks. Suddenly he bent and began untying her shoe-laces. "You'll have to take these off if you're going along there," he said.

She stood on one foot and drew off, one after another, shoes and socks. He took his own shoes off and tied them around his neck, then slung hers around, too. "You're the doctor," he said. "Come on."

They climbed to the top of the round rock. He jumped down, then stood braced while she jumped beside him. They stood there and looked down the great black staircase. She squeezed his arm and then she leaned out a little way over the ledge. "Look how the ferns follow the water all the way down," she said.

"Don't try to see too much," he told her and made her straighten up. They stepped carefully along the ledge over the place that he had said was like a little path. The falls were not three feet away, now. He could feel the cold spray on his cheek, could see the place under the water where you could stand and be dry. "Come on," he said. "One more rock to get around."

The second rock did not jut out as far as the other, but the rock under their feet was wet and a little slippery in places. He thought he would go first and then he decided he could help her better from his side. "Go easy," he said.

She stepped lightly past him. He saw her foot go out and her body swing around the rock and then—he never knew. She might have slipped or she might have got scared, but her foot went down, sickeningly, and she was falling backward from the rock. He clutched at her and touched only the smooth top of her head. Her face was before him, thrown sharply backward, white, with staring eyes—and then he had to lean out to see, lying far below among the ferns—the brown heap.

He got down there—he never could tell them afterward what way he took—but he got down there, slipping, sliding, over the wet rocks. She was lying by one of those little pools on her back, her brown hair tangled in the ferns. He knelt beside her. "Evelyn," he said, "are you hurt? Are you hurt very bad?" Her eyes were open but she did not answer except for a moan. He bent over farther, put his hand on her shoulder. "Could you stand up?" he asked. "Oh, darling, couldn't you just stand up?" The moaning sound went on and now he knew that she did not see him and he started up, his hands swinging at his sides.

73¹

Then he knelt down again and tried to lift her up. She screamed twice horribly. He laid her back. The screaming had stopped. He could hear the water rushing down onto the rocks. He passed his hand over his trembling lips. "I got to get some help," he said.

He said that but he took another step toward her before he turned away. His hands, still hanging at his sides, danced as though he were controlling invisible marionettes. He stared at the gray mountain ledge. "I reckon this is the way," he said and started upward, stumbling over the wet rocks.

Fifteen minutes later he came up over the top of the ledge onto the western brow. One of his trouser legs was torn off and blood showed through the fluttering rags of his shirt. He stood on the ledge and put his hand up and wiped the sweat from his forehead and shut his eyes for a second. Then he plunged into the underbrush. A few more minutes and he came out onto the woods road. He ran slower now, lurching sometimes from side to side, but he ran on. He ran and the brilliant, the wine-colored leaves crackled and broke under his feet. His mouth, a taut square, drew in, released whining breaths. His starting eyes fixed the ground, but he did not see the leaves that he ran over. He saw only the white houses that no matter how fast he ran kept always just ahead of him. If he did not hurry they would slide off the hill, slide off and leave him running forever through these woods, over these dead leaves.

Eudora Welty

Since Miss Welty's first story appeared in Manuscript *in 1936, she has published two novels and three collections of short stories. Each of these possesses special characteristics of its own, though Miss Welty chooses to confine her fiction almost exclusively to her own region, the Delta country of Mississippi, and to people who are neither very rich nor very poor. In her first volume,* The Curtain of Green *(1941), the stories range from the hilariously vulgar "The Petrified Man" (a series of conversations in a beauty parlor) to the superbly told "Death of a Traveling Salesman," which is brushed with just the right amount of pathos.*

In 1942 Miss Welty tried her hand at a novelette, The Robber Bridegroom, *which is an uneasy combination of rogue novel, fairy tale, and prose fantasia on a folk-theme. One new effect which Miss Welty sought to achieve here she subsequently mastered in two stories that appeared in her next collection,* The Wide Net (*1943*). *She introduces a historical figure so casually that the reader sees him at first as one might notice any stranger, but by the story's end a kind of magical life has been woven around him. In "First Love" Miss Welty effects this transformation with Aaron Burr. In "A Still Moment" she brings together Audubon, Lorenzo Dow, the preacher, and Murrell, the highwayman, and fuses their lives in a single moment of experience.*

Miss Welty's first full-length novel, Delta Wedding (*1946*), *is bursting with Fairchild kin who have come to help Dabney marry Troy Flavin. Northern readers who may think that there are too many relatives, bringing with them too many things, and telling too many stories, will have to take the word of Southerners that all this talking and eating and family teasing at Shellmound is an authentic picture of plantation life along the Yazoo River.*

Miss Welty's book The Golden Apples (*1949*) *has been called a "Mississippi* Cranford," *an epithet that does not do justice to the strength and admirable intricacy of these related stories about the "main families in Morgana, Mississippi." In this work she has evolved for herself a most congenial medium. For the first time in* Delta Wedding *she attempted to encompass imaginatively a whole community, somewhat as Faulkner does. By linking these stories about the Mac-Lains and the Raineys and the Morrisons she satisfies her desire for this larger scope while at the same time she continues to work in the short-story form, of which she is an undoubted master.*

"Lily Daw and the Three Ladies" is from A Curtain of Green and Other Stories, *copyright, 1941, by Eudora Welty. Reprinted by permission of Harcourt, Brace & Company, Inc.*

LILY DAW AND THE THREE LADIES

Mrs Watts and Mrs Carson were both in the post office in Victory when the letter came from the Ellisville Institute for the Feeble Minded of Mississippi. Aimee Slocum, with her hand still full of mail, ran out in front and handed it straight to Mrs Watts, and they all three read it together. Mrs Watts held it taut between her pink hands, and Mrs Carson underscored each line slowly with her thimbled finger. Everybody else in the post office wondered what was up now.

"What will Lily say," beamed Mrs Carson at last, "when we tell her we're sending her to Ellisville!"

"She'll be tickled to death," said Mrs Watts, and added in a guttural voice to a deaf lady, "Lily Daw's getting in at Ellisville!"

"Don't you all dare go off and tell Lily without me!" called Aimee Slocum, trotting back to finish putting up the mail.

"Do you suppose they'll look after her down there?" Mrs Carson began to carry on a conversation with a group of Baptist ladies waiting in the post office. She was the Baptist preacher's wife.

"I've always heard it was lovely down there, but crowded," said one.

"Lily lets people walk over her so," said another.

"Last night at the tent show—" said another, and then popped her hand over her mouth.

"Don't mind me, I know there are such things in the world," said Mrs Carson, looking down and fingering the tape measure which hung over her bosom.

"Oh, Mrs Carson. Well, anyway, last night at the tent show, why, the man was just before making Lily buy a ticket to get in."

"A ticket!"

"Till my husband went up and explained she wasn't bright, and so did everybody else."

The ladies all clucked their tongues.

"Oh, it was a very nice show," said the lady who had gone. "And Lily acted so nice. She was a perfect lady—just set in her seat and stared."

"Oh, she can be a lady—she can be," said Mrs Carson, shaking her head and turning her eyes up. "That's just what breaks your heart."

"Yes'm, she kept her eyes on—what's that thing makes all the commotion?—the xylophone," said the lady. "Didn't turn her head to the right or to the left the whole time. Set in front of me."

"The point is, what did she do after the show?" asked Mrs Watts practically. "Lily has gotten so she is very mature for her age."

"Oh, Etta!" protested Mrs Carson, looking at her wildly for a moment.

"And that's how come we are sending her to Ellisville," finished Mrs Watts.

"I'm ready, you all," said Aimee Slocum, running out with white powder all over her face. "Mail's up. I don't know how good it's up."

"Well, of course, I do hope it's for the best," said several of the other ladies. They did not go at once to take their mail out of their boxes; they felt a little left out.

The three women stood at the foot of the water tank.

"To find Lily is a different thing," said Aimee Slocum.

"Where in the wide world do you suppose she'd be?" It was Mrs Watts who was carrying the letter.

"I don't see a sign of her either on this side of the street or on the other side," Mrs Carson declared as they walked along.

Ed Newton was stringing Redbird school tablets on the wire across the store.

"If you're after Lily, she come in here while ago and tole me she was fixin' to git married," he said.

"Ed Newton!" cried the ladies all together, clutching one another. Mrs Watts began to fan herself at once with the letter from Ellisville. She wore widow's black, and the least thing made her hot.

"Why she is not. She's going to Ellisville, Ed," said Mrs Carson gently. "Mrs Watts and I and Aimee Slocum are paying her way out of our own pockets. Besides, the boys of Victory are on their honor. Lily's not going to get married, that's just an idea she's got in her head."

"More power to you, ladies," said Ed Newton, spanking himself with a tablet.

When they came to the bridge over the railroad tracks, there was Estelle Mabers, sitting on a rail. She was slowly drinking an orange Ne-Hi.

"Have you seen Lily?" they asked her.

"I'm supposed to be out here watching for her now," said the Mabers girl, as though she weren't there yet. "But for Jewel—Jewel says Lily come in the store while ago and picked out a two-ninety-eight hat and wore it off. Jewel wants to swap her something else for it."

"Oh, Estelle, Lily says she's going to get married!" cried Aimee Slocum.

"Well I declare," said Estelle; she never understood anything.

Loralee Adkins came riding by in her Willys-Knight, tooting the horn to find out what they were talking about.

Aimee threw up her hands and ran out into the street. "Loralee, Loralee, you got to ride us up to Lily Daw's. She's up yonder fixing to get married!"

"Hop in, my land!"

"Well, that just goes to show you right now," said Mrs Watts, groaning as she was helped into the back seat. "What we've got to do is persuade Lily it will be nicer to go to Ellisville."

"Just to think!"

While they rode around the corner Mrs Carson was going on in her sad voice, sad as the soft noises in the hen house at twilight. "We buried Lily's poor defenseless mother. We gave Lily all her food and kindling and every stitch she had on. Sent her to Sunday school to learn the Lord's teachings, had her baptized a Baptist. And when her old father commenced beating her and tried to cut her head off with the butcher knife, why, we went and took her away from him and gave her a place to stay."

The paintless frame house with all the weather vanes was three stories high in places and had yellow and violet stained-glass windows in front and gingerbread around the porch. It leaned steeply to one side, toward the railroad, and the front steps were gone. The car full of ladies drew up under the cedar tree.

"Now Lily's almost grown up," Mrs Carson continued. "In fact, she's grown," she concluded, getting out.

"Talking about getting married," said Mrs Watts disgustedly. "Thanks, Loralee, you run on home."

They climbed over the dusty zinnias onto the porch and walked through the open door without knocking.

"There certainly is always a funny smell in this house. I say it every time I come," said Aimee Slocum.

Lily was there, in the dark of the hall, kneeling on the floor by a small open trunk.

When she saw them she put a zinnia in her mouth, and held still.

"Hello, Lily," said Mrs Carson reproachfully.

"Hello," said Lily. In a minute she gave a suck on the zinnia stem that sounded exactly like a jay bird. There she sat, wearing a petticoat for a dress, one of the things Mrs Carson kept after her about. Her milky-yellow hair streamed freely down from under a new hat. You could see the wavy scar on her throat if you knew it was there.

Mrs Carson and Mrs Watts, the two fattest, sat in the double rocker. Aimee Slocum sat on the wire chair donated from the drugstore that burned.

"Well, what are you doing, Lily?" asked Mrs Watts, who led the rocking.

Lily smiled.

The trunk was old and lined with yellow and brown paper, with an asterisk pattern showing in darker circles and rings. Mutely the ladies indicated to each other that they did not know where in the world it had come from. It was empty except for two bars of soap and a green washcloth, which Lily was now trying to arrange in the bottom.

"Go on and tell us what you're doing, Lily," said Aimee Slocum.

"Packing, silly," said Lily.

"Where are you going?"

"Going to get married, and I bet you wish you was me now," said Lily. But shyness overcame her suddenly, and she popped the zinnia back into her mouth.

"Talk to me, dear," said Mrs Carson. "Tell old Mrs Carson why you want to get married."

736

"No," said Lily, after a moment's hesitation.

"Well, we've thought of something that will be so much nicer," said Mrs Carson. "Why don't you go to Ellisville!"

"Won't that be lovely?" said Mrs Watts. "Goodness, yes."

"It's a lovely place," said Aimee Slocum uncertainly.

"You've got bumps on your face," said Lily.

"Aimee, dear, you stay out of this, if you don't mind," said Mrs Carson anxiously. "I don't know what it is comes over Lily when you come around her."

Lily stared at Aimee Slocum meditatively.

"There! Wouldn't you like to go to Ellisville now?" asked Mrs Carson.

"No'm," said Lily.

"Why not?" All the ladies leaned down toward her in impressive astonishment.

" 'Cause I'm goin' to get married," said Lily.

"Well, and who are you going to marry, dear?" asked Mrs. Watts. She knew how to pin people down and make them deny what they'd already said.

Lily bit her lip and began to smile. She reached into the trunk and held up both cakes of soap and wagged them.

"Tell us," challenged Mrs Watts. "Who you're going to marry, now."

"A man last night."

There was a gasp from each lady. The possible reality of a lover descended suddenly like a summer hail over their heads. Mrs Watts stood up and balanced herself.

"One of those show fellows! A musician!" she cried.

Lily looked up in admiration.

"Did he—did he do anything to you?" In the long run, it was still only Mrs Watts who could take charge.

"Oh, yes'm," said Lily. She patted the cakes of soap fastidiously with the tips of her small fingers and tucked them in with the washcloth.

"What?" demanded Aimee Slocum, rising up and tottering before her scream. "What?" she called out in the hall.

"Don't ask her what," said Mrs Carson, coming up behind. "Tell me, Lily—just yes or no—are you the same as you were?"

"He had a red coat," said Lily graciously. "He took little sticks and went *ping-pong! ding-dong!*"

"Oh, I think I'm going to faint," said Aimee Slocum, but they said, "No, you're not."

"The xylophone!" cried Mrs Watts. "The xylophone player! Why, the coward, he ought to be run out of town on a rail!"

737

"Out of town? He is out of town, by now," cried Aimee. "Can't you read?—the sign in the café—Victory on the ninth, Como on the tenth? He's in Como. Como!"

"All right! We'll bring him back!" cried Mrs Watts. "He can't get away from me!"

"Hush," said Mrs Carson. "I don't think it's any use following that line of reasoning at all. It's better in the long run for him to be gone out of our lives for good and all. That kind of a man. He was after Lily's body alone and he wouldn't ever in this world make the poor little thing happy, even if we went out and forced him to marry her like he ought—at the point of a gun."

"Still—" began Aimee, her eyes widening.

"Shut up," said Mrs Watts. "Mrs Carson, you're right, I expect."

"This is my hope chest—see?" said Lily politely in the pause that followed. "You haven't even looked at it. I've already got soap and a washrag. And I have my hat—on. What are you all going to give me?"

"Lily," said Mrs Watts, starting over, "we'll give you lots of gorgeous things if you'll only go to Ellisville instead of getting married."

"What will you give me?" asked Lily.

"I'll give you a pair of hemstitched pillowcases," said Mrs Carson.

"I'll give you a big caramel cake," said Mrs Watts.

"I'll give you a souvenir from Jackson—a little toy bank," said Aimee Slocum. "Now will you go?"

"No," said Lily.

"I'll give you a pretty little Bible with your name on it in real gold," said Mrs Carson.

"What if I was to give you a pink crêpe de chine brassière with adjustable shoulder straps?" asked Mrs Watts grimly.

"Oh, Etta."

"Well, she needs it," said Mrs Watts. "What would they think if she ran all over Ellisville in a petticoat looking like a Fiji?"

"I wish *I* could go to Ellisville," said Aimee Slocum luringly.

"What will they have for me down there?" asked Lily softly.

"Oh! lots of things. You'll have baskets to weave, I expect. . . ." Mrs Carson looked vaguely at the others.

"Oh, yes indeed, they will let you make all sorts of baskets," said Mrs Watts; then her voice too trailed off.

"No'm, I'd rather get married," said Lily.

"Lily Daw! Now that's just plain stubbornness!" cried Mrs Watts. "You almost said you'd go and then you took it back!"

"We've all asked God, Lily," said Mrs Carson finally, "and God seemed to tell us—Mr Carson, too—that the place where you ought to be, so as to be happy, was Ellisville."

Lily looked reverent, but still stubborn.

"We've really just got to get her there—now!" screamed Aimee Slocum all at once. "Suppose—! She can't stay here!"

"Oh no, no, no," said Mrs Carson hurriedly. "We mustn't think that."

They sat sunken in despair.

"Could I take my hope chest—to go to Ellisville?" asked Lily shyly, looking at them sidewise.

"Why, yes," said Mrs Carson blankly.

Silently they rose once more to their feet.

"Oh, if I could just take my hope chest!"

"All the time it was just her hope chest," Aimee whispered.

Mrs Watts struck her palms together. "It's settled!"

"Praise the fathers," murmured Mrs Carson.

Lily looked up at them, and her eyes gleamed. She cocked her head and spoke out in a proud imitation of someone—someone utterly unknown.

"O.K.—Toots!"

The ladies had been nodding and smiling and backing away toward the door.

"I think I'd better stay," said Mrs Carson, stopping in her tracks. "Where—where could she have learned that terrible expression?"

"Pack up," said Mrs Watts. "Lily Daw is leaving for Ellisville on Number One."

In the station the train was puffing. Nearly everyone in Victory was hanging around waiting for it to leave. The Victory Civic Band had assembled without any orders and was scattered through the crowd. Ed Newton gave false signals to start on his bass horn. A crate full of baby chickens got loose on the platform. Everybody wanted to see Lily all dressed up, but Mrs Carson and Mrs Watts had sneaked her into the train from the other side of the tracks.

The two ladies were going to travel as far as Jackson to help Lily change trains and be sure she went in the right direction.

Lily sat between them on the plush seat with her hair combed and pinned up into a knot under a small blue hat which was Jewel's exchange for the pretty one. She wore a traveling dress made out of part of Mrs Watts's last summer's mourning. Pink straps glowed through. She had a purse and a Bible and a warm cake in a box, all in her lap.

Aimee Slocum had been getting the outgoing mail stamped and bundled. She stood in the aisle of the coach now, tears shaking from her eyes.

"Good-by, Lily," she said. She was the one who felt things.

"Good-by, silly," said Lily.

"Oh, dear, I hope they get our telegram to meet her in Ellisville!"

Aimee cried sorrowfully, as she thought how far away it was. "And it was so hard to get it all in ten words, too."

"Get off, Aimee, before the train starts and you break your neck," said Mrs Watts, all settled and waving her dressy fan gaily. "I declare, it's so hot, as soon as we get a few miles out of town I'm going to slip my corset down."

"Oh, Lily, don't cry down there. Just be good, and do what they tell you—it's all because they love you." Aimee drew her mouth down. She was backing away, down the aisle.

Lily laughed. She pointed across Mrs Carson's bosom out the window toward a man. He had stepped off the train and just stood there, by himself. He was a stranger and wore a cap.

"Look," she said, laughing softly through her fingers.

"Don't—look," said Mrs Carson very distinctly, as if, out of all she had ever spoken, she would impress these two solemn words upon Lily's soft little brain. She added, "Don't look at anything till you get to Ellisville."

Outside, Aimee Slocum was crying so hard she almost ran into the stranger. He wore a cap and was short and seemed to have on perfume, if such a thing could be.

"Could you tell me, madam," he said, "where a little lady lives in this burg name of Miss Lily Daw?" He lifted his cap—and he had red hair.

"What do you want to know for?" Aimee asked before she knew it.

"Talk louder," said the stranger. He almost whispered, himself.

"She's gone away—she's gone to Ellisville!"

"Gone?"

"Gone to Ellisville!"

"Well, I like that!" The man stuck out his bottom lip and puffed till his hair jumped.

"What business did you have with Lily?" cried Aimee suddenly.

"We was only going to get married, that's all," said the man.

Aimee Slocum started to scream in front of all those people. She almost pointed to the long black box she saw lying on the ground at the man's feet. Then she jumped back in fright.

"The xylophone! The xylophone!" she cried, looking back and forth from the man to the hissing train. Which was more terrible? The bell began to ring hollowly, and the man was talking.

"Did you say Ellisville? That in the state of Mississippi?" Like lightning he had pulled out a red notebook entitled, "Permanent Facts & Data." He wrote down something. "I don't hear well."

Aimee nodded her head up and down, and circled around him.

Under "Ellis-Ville Miss" he was drawing a line; now he was flicking it with two little marks. "Maybe she didn't say she would. Maybe she said she wouldn't." He suddenly laughed very loudly, after the way he had whispered. Aimee jumped back. "Women!—Well, if we play anywheres near Ellisville, Miss., in the future I may look her up and I may not," he said.

The bass horn sounded the true signal for the band to begin. White steam rushed out of the engine. Usually the train stopped for only a minute in Victory, but the engineer knew Lily from waving at her, and he knew this was her big day.

"Wait!" Aimee Slocum did scream. "Wait, mister! I can get her for you. Wait, Mister Engineer! Don't go!"

Then there she was back on the train, screaming in Mrs Carson's and Mrs Watts's faces.

"The xylophone player! The xylophone player to marry her! Yonder he is!"

"Nonsense," murmured Mrs Watts, peering over the others to look where Aimee pointed. "If he's there I don't see him. Where is he? You're looking at One-Eye Beasley."

"The little man with the cap—no, with the red hair! Hurry!"

"Is that really him?" Mrs Carson asked Mrs Watts in wonder. "Mercy! He's small, isn't he?"

"Never saw him before in my life!" cried Mrs Watts. But suddenly she shut up her fan.

"Come on! This is a train we're on!" cried Aimee Slocum. Her nerves were all unstrung.

"All right, don't have a conniption fit, girl," said Mrs Watts. "Come on," she said thickly to Mrs Carson.

"Where are we going now?" asked Lily as they struggled down the aisle.

"We're taking you to get married," said Mrs. Watts. "Mrs Carson, you'd better phone up your husband right there in the station."

"But I don't want to git married," said Lily, beginning to whimper. "I'm going to Ellisville."

"Hush, and we'll all have some ice-cream cones later," whispered Mrs Carson.

Just as they climbed down the steps at the back end of the train, the band went into "Independence March."

The xylophone player was still there, patting his foot. He came up and said, "Hello, Toots. What's up—tricks?" and kissed Lily with a smack, after which she hung her head.

"So you're the young man we've heard so much about," said Mrs Watts. Her smile was brilliant. "Here's your little Lily."

"What say?" asked the xylophone player.

"My husband happens to be the Baptist preacher of Victory," said

Mrs Carson in a loud, clear voice. "Isn't that lucky? I can get him here in five minutes: I know exactly where he is."

They were in a circle around the xylophone player, all going into the white waiting room.

"Oh, I feel just like crying, at a time like this," said Aimee Slocum. She looked back and saw the train moving slowly away, going under the bridge at Main Street. Then it disappeared around the curve.

"Oh, the hope chest!" Aimee cried in a stricken voice.

"And whom have we the pleasure of addressing?" Mrs Watts was shouting, while Mrs Carson was ringing up the telephone.

The band went on playing. Some of the people thought Lily was on the train, and some swore she wasn't. Everybody cheered, though, and a straw hat was thrown into the telephone wires.

William Faulkner

When Faulkner received the Nobel Prize in 1950 he was the champion who had come up from the rear to win. Several writers of his generation, notably F. Scott Fitzgerald, Dos Passos, and Hemingway, had already found an appreciative public by the early 1930's when a few perceptive critics were just beginning to discover Faulkner. In spite of the success of Sanctuary *(1931), a succès de scandale, the reading public paid little attention to these vanguard critics. As late as 1940, by which time Faulkner had published several of his major novels—*The Sound and the Fury *(1929),* As I Lay Dying *(1930),* Light in August *(1932),* Absalom! Absalom! *(1936), and* The Hamlet *(1940)—he was known to the general reader, if he was known at all, as a novelist who specialized in violence and wrote page-long sentences through which one stumbled from parenthesis to parenthesis. In 1945 not one of his seventeen books was in print.*

This neglect of a novelist who is now considered the leading American writer of our time can be ascribed in part to his uncertain and fumbling beginnings, but more particularly to the newness of his themes and style. His Saturday Evening Post *stories, mostly concerned with aviators (Faulkner had served with the British Royal Air Force), were competent but commonplace. His first novel,* Soldier's Pay *(1926), the story of a veteran who returns to his Georgia home to die, was overshadowed by Hemingway's influential* The Sun Also Rises, *which came out the same year. In 1927 Faulkner tried still another tack with* Mosquitoes, *a satirical novel in the modish style of the mid-twenties. Meanwhile he had left New Orleans and returned to his native town of Oxford, Mississippi.*

At last, in Sartoris (*1929*), *he began to make use of the legends of his family and region, and the Faulknerian "mythical kingdom," Yoknapatawpha County, was mapped for the first time. But* Sartoris, *though it pictures in detail a Southern family through four generations and two wars, contained so many romantic clichés that reviewers could not distinguish it in the crowd of new novels. In 1929* The Sound and the Fury, *the opening section of which accomplishes the impossible by presenting the stream of consciousness of an idiot, baffled most readers. And* As I Lay Dying, *the next year, and* Sanctuary, *in 1931, confirmed the growing belief that Faulkner was interested only in idiots, perverts, decay, and death.*

Neglected as he was, Faulkner made no concessions to his readers. For many years he held, as Malcolm Cowley remarked in 1946, a "curious attitude toward the public that appears to be lofty indifference (as in the one preface he wrote, for the Modern Library edition of Sanctuary), *but really comes closer to being a mixture of skittery distrust and pure unconsciousness that the public exists." When readers finally caught up with him, after the Second World War, they began to perceive that his brooding sense of the doom resting on the South, his compassion for the Negro, his hatred of all those who are mean in spirit—traits which were explicit in the popular* Intruder in the Dust (*1948*)—*were discernible in his earlier writing as well. What Faulkner said to the young writer of the day, in his Stockholm Address, delivered at the time he received the Nobel Prize, came from a long way back in his experience as a novelist.*

He must teach himself that the basest of all things is to be afraid; and, teaching himself that, forget it forever, leaving no room in his workshop for anything but the old verities and truths of the heart, the old universal truths lacking which any story is ephemeral and doomed—love and honor and pity and pride and compassion and sacrifice.

Whatever new directions Faulkner may yet take—his latest novel, A Fable (*1954*), *is as experimental as any work he has produced—his fame will rest on the extraordinary group of novels and stories which brought into being a whole section of the South—"William Faulkner, sole owner and proprietor," as he wrote on one of the maps he drew of Yoknapatawpha County. Year by year, story by story, he has peopled this county with Sartorises and Compsons (of a decayed house) and the prolific, poor-white Snopeses of Frenchman's Bend, the "invaders"*

743

who may yet destroy what is left of the world of the aristocratic Sartorises. The life that has been lived there, at Sutpen's Hundred, at Varner's Crossroads, in the courthouse town of Jefferson, all the events of all the days, from the moment when the first white men arrive to dispossess the Chickasaws to the moment when Nancy, the Negro woman, out of a strange compassion, strangles Temple Drake's baby, Faulkner has recorded and made vivid for his readers. No other American writer, except Hawthorne, has brought a whole region to life, generation by generation.

In creating his vast saga, Faulkner did not devote a single novel to one of his families and then move on to the next dynasty. Although Sartoris *is the novel which deals most completely and coherently with that family, closest in actuality to his own, nine years later Faulkner had ready* The Unvanquished (*1938*), *a volume of interrelated stories about the Sartoris clan during the period of the Civil War and Reconstruction. A character will move from story to story, appearing now at the center of the action, now on the fringes of it, sometimes as the narrator, elsewhere as the protagonist.*

Often around a novel several preliminary stories are grouped, some of which Faulkner has left as they first appeared, others of which he eventually incorporated in the novel. The story printed here, "Barn Burning," is of this second kind. Portions of it were appropriated for use in the opening pages of The Hamlet (*1940*), *the novel about the obnoxious but undefeatable Snopeses—Ab, Flem, Eck, Ike, I. O., Lump, and Mink. But Ab's other son, the boy in the story who flees from his father and the glare of the fire he has set, disappears in the last paragraph—"on down the hill, toward the dark woods within which the liquid silver voices of the birds called unceasing." He has not been seen again. But Faulkner said years ago that he planned to devote two or three volumes to the Snopes tribe. If there is a sequel to* The Hamlet *and a sequel to the sequel, this lost boy may yet be found.*

"Barn Burning" is the first story in Collected Stories of William Faulkner. *It is reprinted by permission of Random House, Inc. Copyright 1939 by William Faulkner.*

Mr. Faulkner's Nobel Prize Award Speech is also reprinted with the kind permission of Random House, Inc.

BARN BURNING

THE store in which the Justice of the Peace's court was sitting smelled of cheese. The boy, crouched on his nail keg at the back of the crowded room, knew he smelled cheese, and more: from where he sat he could see the ranked shelves close-packed with the solid, squat, dynamic shapes of tin cans whose labels his stomach read, not from the lettering which meant nothing to his mind but from the scarlet devils and the silver curve of fish—this, the cheese which he knew he smelled and the hermetic meat which his intestines believed he smelled coming in intermittent gusts momentary and brief between the other constant one, the smell and sense just a little of fear because mostly of despair and grief, the old fierce pull of blood. He could not see the table where the Justice sat and before which his father and his father's enemy (*our enemy* he thought in that despair; *ourn! mine and hisn both! He's my father!*) stood, but he could hear them, the two of them that is, because his father had said no word yet:

"But what proof have you, Mr. Harris?"

"I told you. The hog got into my corn. I caught it up and sent it back to him. He had no fence that would hold it. I told him so, warned him. The next time I put the hog in my pen. When he came to get it I gave him enough wire to patch up his pen. The next time I put the hog up and kept it. I rode down to his house and saw the wire I gave him still rolled on to the spool in his yard. I told him he could have the hog when he paid me a dollar pound fee. That evening a nigger came with the dollar and got the hog. He was a strange nigger. He said, 'He say to tell you wood and hay kin burn.' I said, 'What?' 'That whut he say to tell you,' the nigger said. 'Wood and hay kin burn.' That night my barn burned. I got the stock out but I lost the barn."

"Where is the nigger? Have you got him?"

"He was a strange nigger, I tell you. I don't know what became of him."

"But that's not proof. Don't you see that's not proof?"

"Get that boy up here. He knows." For a moment the boy thought too that the man meant his older brother until Harris said, "Not him. The little one. The boy," and, crouching, small for his age, small and wiry like his father, in patched and faded jeans even too small for him, with straight, uncombed, brown hair and eyes gray and wild as storm scud, he saw the men between himself and the table part and become a lane of grim faces, at the end of which he saw the Justice, a shabby, collarless, graying man in spectacles, beckoning him. He felt no floor under his bare feet; he seemed to walk beneath the palpable weight of the grim turning faces. His father, stiff in his black Sunday coat donned not for the trial but for the moving, did not even look at him. *He aims for me to lie*, he thought, again with that frantic grief and despair. *And I will have to do hit.*

"What's your name, boy?" the Justice said.

"Colonel Sartoris Snopes," the boy whispered.

"Hey?" the Justice said. "Talk louder. Colonel Sartoris? I reckon anybody named for Colonel Sartoris in this country can't help but tell the truth, can they?" The boy said nothing. *Enemy! Enemy!* he thought; for a moment he could not even see, could not see that the Justice's face was kindly nor discern that his voice was troubled when he spoke to the man named Harris: "Do you want me to question this boy?" But he could hear, and during those subsequent long seconds while there was absolutely no sound in the crowded little room save that of quiet and intent breathing it was as if he had swung outward at the end of a grape vine, over a ravine, and at the top of the swing had been caught in a prolonged instant of mesmerized gravity, weightless in time.

"No!" Harris said violently, explosively. "Damnation! Send him out of here!" Now time, the fluid world, rushed beneath him again, the voices coming to him again through the smell of cheese and sealed meat, the fear and despair and the old grief of blood:

"This case is closed. I can't find against you, Snopes, but I can give you advice. Leave this country and don't come back to it."

His father spoke for the first time, his voice cold and harsh, level, without emphasis: "I aim to. I don't figure to stay in a country among people who . . ." he said something unprintable and vile, addressed to no one.

"That'll do," the Justice said. "Take your wagon and get out of this country before dark. Case dismissed."

His father turned, and he followed the stiff black coat, the wiry figure walking a little stiffly from where a Confederate provost's man's musket ball had taken him in the heel on a stolen horse thirty years ago, followed the two backs now, since his older brother had appeared from somewhere in the crowd, no taller than the father but thicker, chewing tobacco steadily, between the two lines of grim-faced men and out of the store and across the worn gallery and down the sagging steps and among the dogs and half-grown boys in the mild May dust, where as he passed a voice hissed:

"Barn burner!"

Again he could not see, whirling; there was a face in a red haze, moonlike, bigger than the full moon, the owner of it half again his size, he leaping in the red haze toward the face, feeling no blow, feeling no shock when his head struck the earth, scrabbling up and leaping again, feeling no blow this time either and tasting no blood, scrabbling up to see the other boy in full flight and himself already leaping into pursuit as his father's hand jerked him back, the harsh, cold voice speaking above him: "Go get in the wagon."

It stood in a grove of locusts and mulberries across the road. His two hulking sisters in their Sunday dresses and his mother and her sister in calico and sunbonnets were already in it, sitting on and among the sorry residue of the dozen and more movings which even the boy could remember—the battered stove, the broken beds and chairs, the clock inlaid with mother-of-pearl, which would not run, stopped at some fourteen minutes past two o'clock of a dead and forgotten day and time, which had been his mother's dowry. She was crying, though when she saw him she drew her sleeve across her face and began to descend from the wagon. "Get back," the father said.

"He's hurt. I got to get some water and wash his . . ."

"Get back in the wagon," his father said. He got in too, over the tailgate. His father mounted to the seat where the older brother already sat and struck the gaunt mules two savage blows with the peeled willow, but without heat. It was not even sadistic; it was exactly that same quality which in later years would cause his descendants to over-run the engine before putting a motor car into motion, striking and reining back in the same movement. The wagon went on, the store with its quiet crowd of grimly watching men dropped behind; a curve in the road hid it. *Forever* he thought. *Maybe he's done satisfied now, now that he has* . . . stopping himself, not to say it aloud even to himself. His mother's hand touched his shoulder.

"Does hit hurt?" she said.

"Naw," he said. "Hit don't hurt. Lemme be."

"Can't you wipe some of the blood off before hit dries?"

"I'll wash to-night," he said. "Lemme be, I tell you."

The wagon went on. He did not know where they were going. None of them ever did or ever asked, because it was always somewhere, always a house of sorts waiting for them a day or two days or even three days away. Likely his father had already arranged to make a crop on another farm before he . . . Again he had to stop himself. He (the father) always did. There was something about his wolflike independence and even courage when the advantage was at least neutral which impressed strangers, as if they got from his latent ravening ferocity not so much a sense of dependability as a feeling that his ferocious conviction in the rightness of his own actions would be of advantage to all whose interest lay with his.

That night they camped, in a grove of oaks and beeches where a spring ran. The nights were still cool and they had a fire against it, of a rail lifted from a nearby fence and cut into lengths—a small fire, neat, niggard almost, a shrewd fire; such fires were his father's habit and custom always, even in freezing weather. Older, the boy might have remarked this and wondered why not a big one; why should not a man who had not only seen the waste and extravagance of war, but who had in his blood an inherent voracious prodigality with material not his own, have burned everything in sight? Then he might have gone a step farther and thought that that was the reason: that niggard blaze was the living fruit of nights passed during those four years in the woods hiding from all men, blue or gray, with his strings of horses (captured horses, he called them). And older still, he might have divined the true reason: that the element of fire spoke to some deep mainspring of his father's being, as the element of steel or of powder spoke to other men, as the one weapon for the preservation of integrity, else breath were not worth the breathing, and hence to be regarded with respect and used with discretion.

But he did not think this now and he had seen those same niggard blazes all his life. He merely ate his supper beside it and was already half asleep over his iron plate when his father called him, and once more he followed the stiff back, the stiff and ruthless limp, up the slope and on to the starlit road where, turning, he could see his father against the stars but without face or depth—a shape black, flat, and bloodless as though cut from tin in the iron folds of the frockcoat which had not been made for him, the voice harsh like tin and without heat like tin:

"You were fixing to tell them. You would have told him." He didn't answer. His father struck him with the flat of his hand on the side of the head, hard but without heat, exactly as he had struck the two mules at the store, exactly as he would strike either of them with any stick in order to kill a horse fly, his voice still without heat or anger: "You're getting to be a man. You got to learn. You got to learn to stick to your own blood or you ain't going to have any blood to stick to you. Do you think either of them, any man there this morning, would? Don't you know all they wanted was a chance to get at me because they knew I had them beat? Eh?" Later, twenty years later, he was to tell himself, "If I had said they wanted only truth, justice, he would have hit me again." But now he said nothing. He was not crying. He just stood there. "Answer me," his father said.

"Yes," he whispered. His father turned.

"Get on to bed. We'll be there tomorrow."

To-morrow they were there. In the early afternoon the wagon stopped before a paintless two-room house identical almost with the dozen others it had stopped before even in the boy's ten years, and again, as on the other dozen occasions, his mother and aunt got down and began to unload the wagon, although his two sisters and his father and brother had not moved.

"Likely hit ain't fitten for hawgs," one of the sisters said.

"Nevertheless, fit it will and you'll hog it and like it," his father said. "Get out of them chairs and help your Ma unload."

The two sisters got down, big, bovine, in a flutter of cheap ribbons; one of them drew from the jumbled wagon bed a battered lantern, the other a worn broom. His father handed the reins to the older son and began to climb stiffly over the wheel. "When they get unloaded, take the team to the barn and feed them." Then he said, and at first the boy thought he was still speaking to his brother: "Come with me."

"Me?" he said.

"Yes," his father said. "You."

"Abner," his mother said. His father paused and looked back—the harsh level stare beneath the shaggy, graying, irascible brows.

"I reckon I'll have a word with the man that aims to begin to-morrow owning me body and soul for the next eight months."

They went back up the road. A week ago—or before last night, that is—he would have asked where they were going, but not now. His father had struck him before last night but never before had he paused afterward to explain why; it was as if the blow and the following calm, outrageous voice still rang, repercussed, divulging nothing to him save the terrible handicap of being young, the light weight of his few years, just heavy enough to prevent his soaring free of the world as it seemed to be ordered but not heavy enough to keep him footed solid in it, to resist it and try to change the course of its events.

Presently he could see the grove of oaks and cedars and the other flowering trees and shrubs where the house would be, though not the house yet. They walked beside a fence massed with honeysuckle and Cherokee roses and came to a gate swinging open between two brick pillars, and now, beyond a sweep of drive, he saw the house for the first time and at that instant he forgot his father and the terror and despair both, and even when he remembered his father again (who had not stopped) the terror and despair did not return. Because, for all the twelve movings, they had sojourned until now in a poor country, a land of small farms and fields and houses, and he had never seen a house like this before. *Hit's big as a courthouse* he thought quietly, with a surge of peace and joy whose reason he could not have thought into words, being too young for that: *They are safe from him. People whose lives are a part of this peace and dignity are beyond his touch, he no more to them than a buzzing wasp: capable of stinging for a little moment but that's all; the spell of this peace and dignity rendering even the barns and stable and cribs which belong to it impervious to the puny flames he might contrive* . . . this, the peace and joy, ebbing for an instant as he looked again at the stiff black back, the stiff and implacable limp of the figure which was not dwarfed by the house, for the reason that it had never looked big anywhere and which now, against the serene columned backdrop, had more than ever that impervious quality of something cut ruthlessly from tin, depthless, as though, sidewise to the sun, it would cast no shadow. Watching him, the boy remarked the absolutely undeviating course which his father held and saw the stiff foot come squarely down in a pile of fresh droppings where a horse had stood in the drive and which his father could have avoided by a simple change of stride. But it ebbed only for a moment, though he could not have thought this into words either, walking on in the spell of the house, which he could even want but without envy, without sorrow, certainly never with that ravening and jealous rage which unknown to him walked in the ironlike black coat before him: *Maybe he will feel it too. Maybe it will even change him now from what maybe he couldn't help but be.*

They crossed the portico. Now he could hear his father's stiff foot as it came down on the boards with clocklike finality, a sound out of all proportion to the displacement of the body it bore and which was not dwarfed either by the white door before it, as though it had attained to a sort of vicious and ravening minimum not to be dwarfed by anything—the flat, wide, black hat, the formal coat of broadcloth which had once been black but which had now that friction-glazed greenish cast of the bodies of old house flies, the lifted sleeve which was too large, the lifted hand like a curled claw. The door opened so promptly that the boy knew the Negro must have been watching them all the time, an old man with neat grizzled hair, in a linen jacket, who stood barring the door with his body, saying, "Wipe yo foots, white man, fo you come in here. Major ain't home nohow."

"Get out of my way, nigger," his father said, without heat too, flinging the door back and the Negro also and entering, his hat still on his head. And now the boy saw the prints of the stiff foot on the doorjamb and saw them appear on the pale rug behind the machinelike deliberation of the foot which seemed to bear (or transmit) twice the weight which the body compassed. The Negro was shouting "Miss Lula! Miss Lula!" somewhere behind them, then the boy, deluged as though by a warm wave by a suave turn of carpeted stair and a pendant glitter of chandeliers and a mute gleam of gold frames, heard the swift feet and saw her too, a lady—perhaps he had never seen her like before either—in a gray, smooth gown with lace at the throat and an apron tied at the waist and the sleeves turned back, wiping cake or biscuit dough from her hands with a towel as she came up the hall, looking not at his father at all but at the tracks on the blond rug with an expression of incredulous amazement.

"I tried," the Negro cried. "I tole him to . . ."

"Will you please go away?" she said in a shaking voice. "Major de Spain is not at home. Will you please go away?"

His father had not spoken again. He did not speak again. He did not even look at her. He just stood stiff in the center of the rug, in his hat, the shaggy iron-gray brows twitching slightly above the pebble-colored eyes as he appeared to examine the house with brief deliberation. Then with the same deliberation he turned; the boy watched him pivot on the good leg and saw the stiff foot drag round the arc of the turning, leaving a final long and fading smear. His father never looked at it, he never once looked down at the rug. The Negro held the door. It closed behind them, upon the hysteric and indistinguishable woman-wail. His father stopped at the top of the steps and scraped his boot clean on the edge of it. At the gate he stopped again. He stood for a moment, planted stiffly on the stiff foot, looking back at the house. "Pretty and white, ain't it?" he said. "That's sweat. Nigger sweat. Maybe it ain't white enough yet to suit him. Maybe he wants to mix some white sweat with it."

Two hours later the boy was chopping wood behind the house within which his mother and aunt and the two sisters (the mother and aunt, not the two girls, he knew that; even at this distance and muffled by walls the flat loud voices of the two girls emanated an incorrigible idle inertia) were setting up the stove to prepare a meal, when he heard the hooves and saw the linen-clad man on a fine sorrel mare, whom he recognized even before he saw the rolled rug in front of the Negro youth following on a fat bay carriage horse—a suffused, angry face vanishing, still at full gallop, beyond the corner of the house where his father and brother were sitting in the two tilted chairs; and a moment later, almost before he could have put the axe down, he heard the hooves again and watched the sorrel mare go back out of the yard, already galloping again. Then his father began to shout one of the sisters' names, who presently emerged backward from the kitchen door dragging the rolled rug along the ground by one end while the other sister walked behind it.

"If you ain't going to tote, go on and set up the wash pot," the first said.

"You, Sarty!" the second shouted. "Set up the wash pot!" His father appeared at the door, framed against that shabbiness, as he had been against that other bland perfection, impervious to either, the mother's anxious face at his shoulder.

"Go on," the father said. "Pick it up." The two sisters stooped, broad, lethargic; stooping, they presented an incredible expanse of pale cloth and a flutter of tawdry ribbons.

"If I thought enough of a rug to have to git hit all the way from France I wouldn't keep hit where folks coming in would have to tromp on hit," the first said. They raised the rug.

"Abner," the mother said. "Let me do it."

"You go back and git dinner," his father said. "I'll tend to this."

From the woodpile through the rest of the afternoon the boy watched them, the rug spread flat in the dust beside the bubbling wash-pot, the two sisters stooping over it with that profound and lethargic reluctance, while the father stood over them in turn, implacable and grim, driving them though never raising his voice again. He could smell the harsh homemade lye they were using; he saw his mother come to the door once and look toward them with an expression not anxious now but very like despair; he saw his father turn, and he fell to with the axe and saw from the corner of his eye his father raise from the ground a flattish fragment of field stone and examine it and return to the pot, and this time his mother actually spoke: "Abner. Abner. Please don't. Please, Abner."

Then he was done too. It was dusk; the whippoorwills had already begun. He could smell coffee from the room where they would presently eat the cold food remaining from the mid-afternoon meal, though when he entered the house he realized they were having coffee again probably because there was a fire on the hearth, before which the rug now lay spread over the backs of the two chairs. The tracks of his father's foot were gone. Where they had been were now long, water-cloudy scoriations resembling the sporadic course of a lilliputian mowing machine.

It still hung there while they ate the cold food and then went to bed, scattered without order or claim up and down the two rooms, his mother in one bed, where his father would later lie, the older brother in the other, himself, the aunt, and the two sisters on pallets on the floor. But his father was not in bed yet. The last thing the boy remembered was the depthless, harsh silhouette of the hat and coat bending over the rug and it seemed to him that he had not even closed his eyes when the silhouette was standing over him, the fire almost dead behind it, the stiff foot prodding him awake. "Catch up the mule," his father said.

When he returned with the mule his father was standing in the black door, the rolled rug over his shoulder. "Ain't you going to ride?" he said.

"No. Give me your foot."

He bent his knee into his father's hand, the wiry, surprising power flowed smoothly, rising, he rising with it, on to the mule's bare back (they had owned a saddle once; the boy could remember it though not when or where) and with the same effortlessness his father swung the rug up in front of him. Now in the starlight they retraced the afternoon's path, up the dusty road rife with honeysuckle, through the gate and up the black tunnel of the drive to the lightless house, where he sat on the mule and felt the rough warp of the rug drag across his thighs and vanish.

"Don't you want me to help?" he whispered. His father did not answer and now he heard again that stiff foot striking the hollow portico with that wooden and clocklike deliberation, that outrageous overstatement of the weight it carried. The rug, hunched, not flung (the boy could tell that even in the darkness) from his father's shoulder struck the angle of wall and floor with a sound unbelievably loud, thunderous, then the foot again, unhurried and enormous; a light came on in the house and the boy sat, tense, breathing steadily and quietly and just a little fast, though the foot itself did not increase its beat at all, descending the steps now; now the boy could see him.

"Don't you want to ride now?" he whispered. "We kin both ride now," the light within the house altering now, flaring up and sinking. *He's coming down the stairs now,* he thought. He had already ridden the mule up beside the horse block; presently his father was up behind him and he doubled the reins over and slashed the mule across the neck, but before the animal could begin to trot the hard, thin arm came round him, the hard, knotted hand jerking the mule back to a walk.

In the first red rays of the sun they were in the lot, putting plow gear on the mules. This time the sorrel mare was in the lot before he heard it at all, the rider collarless and even bareheaded, trembling, speaking in a shaking voice as the woman in the house had done, his father merely looking up once before stooping again to the hame he was buckling, so that the man on the mare spoke to his stooping back:

"You must realize you have ruined that rug. Wasn't there anybody here, any of your women . . ." he ceased, shaking, the boy watching him, the older brother leaning now in the stable door, chewing, blinking slowly and steadily at nothing apparently. "It cost a hundred dollars. But you never had a hundred dollars. You never will. So I'm going to charge you twenty bushels of corn against your crop. I'll add it in your contract and when you come to the commissary you can sign it. That won't keep Mrs. de Spain quiet but maybe it will teach you to wipe your feet off before you enter her house again."

Then he was gone. The boy looked at his father, who still had not spoken or even looked up again, who was now adjusting the loggerhead in the hame.

"Pap," he said. His father looked at him—the inscrutable face, the shaggy brows beneath which the gray eyes glinted coldly. Suddenly the boy went toward him, fast, stopping as suddenly. "You done the best you could!" he cried. "If he wanted hit done different why didn't he wait and tell you how? He won't git no twenty bushels! He won't git none! We'll gether hit and hide hit! I kin watch . . ."

"Did you put the cutter back in that straight stock like I told you?"

"No, sir," he said.

"Then go do it."

That was Wednesday. During the rest of that week he worked steadily, at what was within his scope and some which was beyond it, with an industry that did not need to be driven nor even commanded twice;

he had this from his mother, with the difference that some at least of what he did he liked to do, such as splitting wood with the half-size axe which his mother and aunt had earned, or saved money somehow, to present him with at Christmas. In company with the two older women (and on one afternoon, even one of the sisters), he built pens for the shoat and the cow which were a part of his father's contract with the landlord, and one afternoon, his father being absent, gone somewhere on one of the mules, he went to the field.

They were running a middle buster now, his brother holding the plow straight while he handled the reins, and walking beside the straining mule, the rich black soil shearing cool and damp against his bare ankles, he thought *Maybe this is the end of it. Maybe even that twenty bushels that seems hard to have to pay for just a rug will be a cheap price for him to stop forever and always from being what he used to be;* thinking, dreaming now, so that his brother had to speak sharply to him to mind the mule: *Maybe he even won't collect the twenty bushels. Maybe it will all add up and balance and vanish—corn, rug, fire; the terror and grief, the being pulled two ways like between two teams of horses—gone, done with for ever and ever.*

Then it was Saturday; he looked up from beneath the mule he was harnessing and saw his father in the black coat and hat. "Not that," his father said. "The wagon gear." And then, two hours later, sitting in the wagon bed behind his father and brother on the seat, the wagon accomplished a final curve, and he saw the weathered paintless store with its tattered tobacco- and patent-medicine posters and the tethered wagons and saddle animals below the gallery. He mounted the gnawed steps behind his father and brother, and there again was the lane of quiet, watching faces for the three of them to walk through. He saw the man in spectacles sitting at the plank table and he did not need to be told this was a Justice of the Peace; he sent one glare of fierce, exultant, partisan defiance at the man in collar and cravat now, whom he had seen but twice before in his life, and that on a galloping horse, who now wore on his face an expression not of rage but of amazed unbelief which the boy could not have known was at the incredible circumstance of being sued by one of his own tenants, and came and stood against his father and cried at the Justice: "He ain't done it! He ain't burnt . . ."

"Go back to the wagon," his father said.

"Burnt?" the Justice said. "Do I understand this rug was burned too?"

"Does anybody here claim it was?" his father said. "Go back to the wagon." But he did not, he merely retreated to the rear of the room, crowded as that other had been, but not to sit down this time, instead, to stand pressing among the motionless bodies, listening to the voices:

"And you claim twenty bushels of corn is too high for the damage you did to the rug?"

"He brought the rug to me and said he wanted the tracks washed out of it. I washed the tracks out and took the rug back to him."

"But you didn't carry the rug back to him in the same condition it was in before you made the tracks on it."

His father did not answer, and now for perhaps half a minute there was no sound at all save that of breathing, the faint, steady suspiration of complete and intent listening.

"You decline to answer that, Mr. Snopes?" Again his father did not answer. "I'm going to find against you, Mr. Snopes. I'm going to find that you were responsible for the injury to Major de Spain's rug and hold you liable for it. But twenty bushels of corn seems a little high for a man in your circumstances to have to pay. Major de Spain claims it cost a hundred dollars. October corn will be worth about fifty cents. I figure that if Major de Spain can stand a ninety-five dollar loss on something he paid cash for, you can stand a five-dollar loss you haven't earned yet. I hold you in damages to Major de Spain to the amount of ten bushels of corn over and above your contract with him, to be paid to him out of your crop at gathering time. Court adjourned."

It had taken no time hardly, the morning was but half begun. He thought they would return home and perhaps back to the field, since they were late, far behind all other farmers. But instead his father passed on behind the wagon, merely indicating with his hand for the older brother to follow with it, and crossed the road toward the blacksmith shop opposite, pressing on after his father, overtaking him, speaking, whispering up at the harsh, calm face beneath the weathered hat: "He won't git no ten bushels neither. He won't git one. We'll . . ." until his father glanced for an instant down at him, the face absolutely calm, the grizzled eyebrows tangled above the cold eyes, the voice almost pleasant, almost gentle:

"You think so? Well, we'll wait till October anyway."

The matter of the wagon—the setting of a spoke or two and the tightening of the tires—did not take long either, the business of the tires accomplished by driving the wagon into the spring branch behind the shop and letting it stand there, the mules nuzzling into the water from time to time, and the boy on the seat with the idle reins, looking up the slope and through the sooty tunnel of the shed where the slow hammer rang and where his father sat on an upended cypress bolt, easily, either talking or listening, still sitting there when the boy brought the dripping wagon up out of the branch and halted it before the door.

"Take them on to the shade and hitch," his father said. He did so and returned. His father and the smith and a third man squatting on his heels inside the door were talking, about crops and animals; the boy, squatting too in the ammoniac dust and hoof-parings and scales of rust, heard his father tell a long and unhurried story out of the time before the birth of the older brother even when he had been a professional horsetrader. And then his father came up beside him where he stood before a tattered last year's circus poster on the other side of the store, gazing rapt and quiet at the scarlet horses, the incredible poisings and convolutions of tulle and tights and the painted leers of comedians, and said, "It's time to eat."

But not at home. Squatting beside his brother against the front wall, he watched his father emerge from the store and produce from a paper sack a segment of cheese and divide it carefully and deliberately into three with his pocket knife and produce crackers from the same sack. They all three squatted on the gallery and ate, slowly, without talking; then in the store again, they drank from a tin dipper tepid water smelling of the cedar bucket and of living beech trees. And still they did not go home. It was a horse lot this time, a tall rail fence upon and along which men stood and sat and out of which one by one horses were led, to be walked and trotted and then cantered back and forth along the road while the slow swapping and buying went on and the sun began to slant westward, they—the three of them—watching and listening, the older brother with his muddy eyes and his steady, inevitable tobacco, the father commenting now and then on certain of the animals, to no one in particular.

It was after sundown when they reached home. They ate supper by lamplight, then, sitting on the doorstep, the boy watched the night fully accomplish, listening to the whippoorwills and the frogs, when he heard his mother's voice: "Abner! No! No! Oh, God. Oh, God. Abner!" and he rose, whirled, and saw the altered light through the door where a candle stub now burned in a bottle neck on the table and his father, still in the hat and coat, at once formal and burlesque as though dressed carefully for some shabby and ceremonial violence, emptying the reservoir of the lamp back into the five-gallon kerosene can from which it had been filled, while the mother tugged at his arm until he shifted the lamp to the other hand and flung her back, not savagely or viciously, just hard, into the wall, her hands flung out against the wall for balance, her mouth open and in her face the same quality of hopeless despair as had been in her voice. Then his father saw him standing in the door.

"Go to the barn and get that can of oil we were oiling the wagon with," he said. The boy did not move. Then he could speak.

"What . . ." he cried. "What are you . . ."

"Go get that oil," his father said. "Go."

Then he was moving, running, outside the house, toward the stable:

this the old habit, the old blood which he had not been permitted to choose for himself, which had been bequeathed him willy nilly and which had run for so long (and who knew where, battening on what of outrage and savagery and lust) before it came to him. *I could keep on,* he thought. *I could run on and on and never look back, never need to see his face again. Only I can't. I can't,* the rusted can in his hand now, the liquid sploshing in it as he ran back to the house and into it, into the sound of his mother's weeping in the next room, and handed the can to his father.

"Ain't you going to even send a nigger?" he cried. "At least you sent a nigger before!"

This time his father didn't strike him. The hand came even faster than the blow had, the same hand which had set the can on the table with almost excruciating care flashing from the can toward him too quick for him to follow it, gripping him by the back of his shirt and on to tiptoe before he had seen it quit the can, the face stooping at him in breathless and frozen ferocity, the cold, dead voice speaking over him to the older brother who leaned against the table, chewing with that steady, curious, sidewise motion of cows:

"Empty the can into the big one and go on. I'll catch up with you."

"Better tie him up to the bedpost," the brother said.

"Do like I told you," the father said. Then the boy was moving, his bunched shirt and the hard, bony hand between his shoulder-blades, his toes just touching the floor, across the room and into the other one, past the sisters sitting with spread heavy thighs in the two chairs over the cold hearth, and to where his mother and aunt sat side by side on the bed, the aunt's arms about his mother's shoulders.

"Hold him," the father said. The aunt made a startled movement. "Not you," the father said. "Lennie. Take hold of him. I want to see you do it." His mother took him by the wrist. "You'll hold him better than that. If he gets loose don't you know what he is going to do? He will go up yonder." He jerked his head toward the road. "Maybe I'd better tie him."

"I'll hold him," his mother whispered.

"See you do then." Then his father was gone, the stiff foot heavy and measured upon the boards, ceasing at last.

Then he began to struggle. His mother caught him in both arms, he jerking and wrenching at them. He would be stronger in the end, he knew that. But he had no time to wait for it. "Lemme go!" he cried. "I don't want to have to hit you!"

"Let him go!" the aunt said. "If he don't go, before God, I am going up there myself!"

"Don't you see I can't?" his mother cried. "Sarty! Sarty! No! No! Help me, Lizzie!"

Then he was free. His aunt grasped at him but it was too late. He whirled, running, his mother stumbled forward on to her knees behind him, crying to the nearer sister: "Catch him, Net! Catch him!" But that was too late too, the sister (the sisters were twins, born at the same time, yet either of them now gave the impression of being, encompassing as much living meat and volume and weight as any other two of the family) not yet having begun to rise from the chair, her head, face, alone merely turned, presenting to him in the flying instant an astonishing expanse of young female features untroubled by any surprise even, wearing only an expression of bovine interest. Then he was out of the room, out of the house, in the mild dust of the starlit road and the heavy rifeness of honeysuckle, the pale ribbon unspooling with terrific slowness under his running feet, reaching the gate at last and turning in, running, his heart and lungs drumming, on up the drive toward the lighted house, the lighted door. He did not knock, he burst in, sobbing for breath, incapable for the moment of speech; he saw the astonished face of the Negro in the linen jacket without knowing when the Negro had appeared.

"De Spain!" he cried, panted. "Where's . . ." then he saw the white man too emerging from a white door down the hall. "Barn!" he cried. "Barn!"

"What?" the white man said. "Barn?"

"Yes!" the boy cried. "Barn!"

"Catch him!" the white man shouted.

But it was too late this time too. The Negro grasped his shirt, but the entire sleeve, rotten with washing, carried away, and he was out that door too and in the drive again, and had actually never ceased to run even while he was screaming into the white man's face.

Behind him the white man was shouting, "My horse! Fetch my horse!" and he thought for an instant of cutting across the park and climbing the fence into the road, but he did not know the park nor how high the vine-massed fence might be and he dared not risk it. So he ran on down the drive, blood and breath roaring; presently he was in the road again though he could not see it. He could not hear either: the galloping mare was almost upon him before he heard her, and even then he held his course, as if the very urgency of his wild grief and need must in a moment more find him wings, waiting until the ultimate instant to hurl himself aside and into the weed-choked roadside ditch as the horse thundered past and on, for an instant in furious silhouette against the stars, the tranquil early summer night sky which, even before the shape of the horse and rider vanished, stained abruptly and violently upward: a long, swirling roar incredible and soundless, blotting the stars, and he springing up and into the road again, running again, knowing it was too late yet still running even after he heard the shot and, an instant later, two shots, pausing now without knowing he had ceased to run, crying "Pap! Pap!", running again before he knew he had begun to run, stumbling, tripping over something and scrabbling up again without ceasing to run, looking backward over his shoulder at the glare as he got up, running on among the invisible trees, panting, sobbing, "Father! Father!"

At midnight he was sitting on the crest of a hill. He did not know it was midnight and he did not know how far he had come. But there was no glare behind him now and he sat now, his back toward what he had called home for four days anyhow, his face toward the dark woods which he would enter when breath was strong again, small, shaking steadily in the chill darkness, hugging himself into the remainder of his thin, rotten shirt, the grief and despair now no longer terror and fear but just grief and despair. *Father. My father,* he thought. "He was brave!" he cried suddenly, aloud but not loud, no more than a whisper: "He was! He was in the war! He was in Colonel Sartoris' cav'ry!" not knowing that his father had gone to that war a private in the fine old European sense, wearing no uniform, admitting the authority of and giving fidelity to no man or army or flag, going to war as Malbrouck himself did: for booty—it meant nothing and less than nothing to him if it were enemy booty or his own.

The slow constellations wheeled on. It would be dawn and then sun-up after a while and he would be hungry. But that would be to-morrow and now he was only cold, and walking would cure that. His breathing was easier now and he decided to get up and go on, and then he found that he had been asleep because he knew it was almost dawn, the night almost over. He could tell that from the whippoorwills. They were everywhere now among the dark trees below him, constant and inflectioned and ceaseless, so that, as the instant for giving over to the day birds drew nearer and nearer, there was no interval at all between them. He got up. He was a little stiff, but walking would cure that too as it would the cold, and soon there would be the sun. He went on down the hill, toward the dark woods within which the liquid silver voices of the birds called unceasing—the rapid and urgent beating of the urgent and quiring heart of the late spring night. He did not look back.

NOBEL PRIZE AWARD SPEECH

Stockholm, Sweden, Dec. 10, 1950

I feel that this award was not made to me as a man, but to my work —a life's work in the agony and sweat of the human spirit, not for glory and least of all for profit, but to create out of the materials of the

759

human spirit something which did not exist before. So this award is only mine in trust. It will not be difficult to find a dedication for the money part of it commensurate with the purpose and significance of its origin. But I would like to do the same with the acclaim too, by using this moment as a pinnacle from which I might be listened to by the young men and women already dedicated to the same anguish and travail, among whom is already that one who will some day stand here where I am standing.

Our tragedy today is a general and universal physical fear so long sustained by now that we can even bear it. There are no longer problems of the spirit. There is only the question: when will I be blown up? Because of this, the young man or woman writing today has forgotten the problems of the human heart in conflict with itself which alone can make good writing because only that is worth writing about, worth the agony and the sweat.

He must learn them again. He must teach himself that the basest of all things is to be afraid; and, teaching himself that, forget it forever, leaving no room in his workshop for anything but the old verities and truths of the heart, the old universal truths lacking which any story is ephemeral and doomed—love and honor and pity and pride and compassion and sacrifice. Until he does so, he labors under a curse. He writes not of love but of lust, of defeats in which nobody loses anything of value, of victories without hope and, worst of all without pity or compassion. His griefs grieve on no universal bones, leaving no scars. He writes not of the heart but of the glands.

Until he relearns these things, he will write as though he stood among and watched the end of man. I decline to accept the end of man. It is easy enough to say that man is immortal simply because he will endure: that when the last ding-dong of doom has clanged and faded from the last worthless rock hanging tideless in the last red and dying evening, that even then there will still be one more sound: that of his puny inexhaustible voice, still talking. I refuse to accept this. I believe that man will not merely endure: he will prevail. He is immortal, not because he alone among creatures has an inexhaustible voice, but because he has a soul, a spirit capable of compassion and sacrifice and endurance. The poet's, the writer's, duty is to write about these things. It is his privilege to help man endure by lifting his heart, by reminding him of the courage and honor and hope and pride and compassion and pity and sacrifice which have been the glory of his past. The poet's voice need not merely be the record of man, it can be one of the props, the pillars to help him endure and prevail.

INDEX OF AUTHORS

i

Index

A NOTE ON THE TYPE

The text of this book was set on the Linotype in JANSON, a recutting made direct from the type cast from matrices made by Anton Janson. Whether or not Janson was of Dutch ancestry is not known, but it is known that he purchased a foundry and was a practicing type-founder in Leipzig during the years 1600 to 1687. Janson's first specimen sheet was issued in 1675. His successor issued a specimen sheet showing all of the Janson types in 1689.

His type is an excellent example of the influential and sturdy Dutch types that prevailed in England prior to the development by William Caslon of his own incomparable designs, which he evolved from these Dutch faces. The Dutch in their turn had been influenced by Garamond in France. The general tone of Janson, however, is darker than Garamond and has a sturdiness and substance quite different from its predecessors. It is a highly legible type, and its individual letters have a pleasing variety of design. Its heavy and light strokes make it sharp and clear, and the full-page effect is characterful and harmonious.

This book was composed, printed, and bound by KINGSPORT PRESS, INC., Kingsport, Tennessee. Paper manufactured by P. H. GLATFELTER CO., Spring Grove, Pennsylvania. Binding design by CHARLES E. SKAGGS.